A Grammar of Mursi

Grammars and Sketches of the World's Languages

Africa

Editor

Gerrit J. Dimmendaal
(*University of Cologne*)

The titles published in this series are listed at *brill.com/gswl*

A Grammar of Mursi

A Nilo-Saharan Language of Ethiopia

By

Firew Girma Worku

BRILL

LEIDEN | BOSTON

This book is based on my doctoral dissertation defended at James Cook University. The research presented and reported in this book was conducted in accordance with the National Health and Medical Research Council (NHMRC) National Statement on Ethical Conduct in Human Research, 2007. The research study proposal received human research ethics approval from the JCU Human Research Ethics Committee on 29 November 2016, Application ID H6785.

The Library of Congress Cataloging-in-Publication Data is available online at http://catalog.loc.gov
LC record available at http://lccn.loc.gov/2020058126

Typeface for the Latin, Greek, and Cyrillic scripts: "Brill". See and download: brill.com/brill-typeface.

ISSN 2352-9342
ISBN 978-90-04-44989-3 (hardback)
ISBN 978-90-04-44991-6 (e-book)

Copyright 2021 by Firew Girma Worku. Published by Koninklijke Brill NV, Leiden, The Netherlands. Koninklijke Brill NV incorporates the imprints Brill, Brill Hes & De Graaf, Brill Nijhoff, Brill Rodopi, Brill Sense, Hotei Publishing, mentis Verlag, Verlag Ferdinand Schöningh and Wilhelm Fink Verlag. Koninklijke Brill NV reserves the right to protect this publication against unauthorized use. Requests for re-use and/or translations must be addressed to Koninklijke Brill NV via brill.com or copyright.com.

This book is printed on acid-free paper and produced in a sustainable manner.

Contents

Acknowledgements IX
List of Tables, Maps, Diagrams, and Figures XI
Abbreviations and Conventions XVI

1 **Introduction** 1
  1.1　The Mursi People: Historical Background　1
  1.2　Linguistic Profile of Mursi　6
  1.3　Geography and Mursi Neighbours　18
  1.4　Economy and Subsistence　20
  1.5　Traditional Leadership　22
  1.6　Local Groups, Clans, Kinship System and Age Sets　24
  1.7　Major Traditional Practices　29
  1.8　Cattle, Color Terms and Naming　33
  1.9　Linguistic Affiliation　36
  1.10　Sociolinguistic Situation　37
  1.11　Previous Studies; Ethnographic Exploration in the Lower Omo Valley　38
  1.12　Fieldwork Methodology and Language Data　40

2 **Phonology**　42
  2.1　Introduction　42
  2.2　Notes on Orthography and Phonetic Transcriptions　42
  2.3　Inventory of Phonemes　45
  2.4　Syllable Structure　64
  2.5　Phonological Processes　65
  2.6　Tone　86
  2.7　Wordhood　91
  2.8　Clitics　97
  2.9　Special Phonology　99
  2.10　Female Register　100

3 **Word Classes**　101
  3.1　Introduction　101
  3.2　Open Word Classes　102
  3.3　Closed Word Classes　132

4 Noun Phrase Structure 174
- 4.1 Introduction 174
- 4.2 Non-clausal Modifiers of NP 174
- 4.3 Clausal Modifiers 193
- 4.4 Nominalizers 201
- 4.5 Complex Modification 203
- 4.6 Summary of Head-Modifier Dependency Relation 206

5 Possession 209
- 5.1 Introduction 209
- 5.2 Juxtaposed System 210
- 5.3 Possessive Construction with A and B Possessors 212
- 5.4 Possessive Construction with C-type (Possessive Pronouns) 215
- 5.5 Pertensive 217
- 5.6 Noun Modification Constructions 222
- 5.7 Predicative Possessive Construction 225
- 5.8 Summary 229

6 Number 232
- 6.1 Introduction 232
- 6.2 The Realization of Number 235
- 6.3 Suffixation 236
- 6.4 Suppletion 254
- 6.5 Number Marking by Tone 254
- 6.6 n/g Alternation 255
- 6.7 The Bound Number/Aspect Marking Forms -t/-ɗ 258
- 6.8 Additional Suffixes 260
- 6.9 Number-Determined Suppletive Verb Forms 262
- 6.10 Reduplication 263
- 6.11 Number Words 263
- 6.12 Number and Agreement 271

7 The Verb and Predicate Structure 274
- 7.1 Introduction 274
- 7.2 Phonological Properties of Verb Roots 274
- 7.3 Morphological Properties 286

8 Adjectives 366
  8.1   Introduction 366
  8.2   Phonological Properties of Adjectives 367
  8.3   Morphological Properties of Adjectives 373
  8.4   Syntactic Properties 386
  8.5   Semantic Properties 397
  8.6   Summary 401

9 Valency Changing Operations 405
  9.1   Introduction 405
  9.2   Valency Decreasing Derivations 407
  9.3   Valency-Increasing Derivations 420

10 Grammatical Relations 435
  10.1 Introduction 435
  10.2 Constituent Order 436
  10.3 Case Markers 463
  10.4 Adpositions 467
  10.5 Verb-Final Suffix 472

11 Comparative Constructions 476
  11.1 Introduction 476
  11.2 Mono-clausal Comparative Construction 476
  11.3 Phrasal plus Mono-clausal Construction 480
  11.4 Bi-clausal Construction Type I 482
  11.5 Bi-clausal Construction Type II 483
  11.6 ɓá Construction 484
  11.7 Other Types of Comparative Constructions 487
  11.8 Equality Construction 488

12 Questions 489
  12.1 Introduction 489
  12.2 Content Questions 490
  12.3 Non-interrogative Particles 508
  12.4 Tag Questions 510
  12.5 Polar Questions 511
  12.6 Other Question Strategies 513

13 **Negation** 516
    13.1 Introduction 516
    13.2 Bound Negators 517
    13.3 Negating a Copula Clause 531
    13.4 Negative Existential Verb níŋɛ 'Not Present' 533
    13.5 Inherently Negative Verb ímág 536
    13.6 Indefinite-Like Words 537
    13.7 Interjection ɪmm ɪmm 'no' 539
    13.8 Tracing and Linking Negators 540

14 **Clause Types, Clause Combining and Coordination** 542
    14.1 Introduction 542
    14.2 Clause Types 542
    14.3 Clause Coordination 589

Appendix: Transcribed Texts 605
Bibliography 649
Subject Index 654

Acknowledgements

I am very grateful to the following people and institutions for giving me their advice, knowledge, trust, encouragement, time, material, and money. Without their support, I would not have been able to finish this grammar.

First and foremost, I would like to thank the Mursi society who taught me their language and culture.

Most of all, I would like to thank my supervisors at the Language and Culture Research Centre (LCRC) of James Cook University, Alexandra Y. Aikhenvald and R.M.W. Dixon, who have been my mentors and constant sources of linguistic knowledge during my time in Cairns. I have learned a lot from your abundant knowledge that made me re-check my data, re-think the data and the analysis, including many of the views presented in this grammar.

Second, I thank my fieldwork Mursi consultants, Barihuny Girinomeri Araro Toko (primary consultant), Barkadhe Kulumedere (secondary consultant), Olirege Regge, Òlítùlà Olibùì, Ngarugo, Olelu Nyamanikiwo, Olikoro Runebisala Dumalo, Olikoro Takui, Barmoy, Olikoro Moges†, Oliregge Bikirinto, Ngarori Kashai, Arsiregge Gomonyokawulo, Bargolony, Olelu Olibui, Bartui Bergere, Olisorali Olibu, and Milisha. Without you, I wouldn't have learnt Mursi.

I owe a huge debt of gratitude to Bettina Mütze who sent me a copy of her MA thesis from Germany at her own expense. Your material on the language was very helpful, so, thank you again.

Bandirachin Mulugeta, an exceptional friend, one of the most genuine people I have ever met, has contributed a lot to this grammar work in great many ways from the very beginning until the last days of the publication process of the book.

Special thanks go to my Jinka/Mursi families, Netsanet Endris (Netsa), Zinabuwa (Zine), Tesfalem Gadisa, Reta Belay, Mesay Seyoum, Esrael Adane, Yalew Ayele, Israel Bekele, Amare-Ayelech (Romos), Samson Ayele, Astewul Bati, Yared Gizachew, Anteneh Yirdaw, Alemneh Tasew, Demirew Yirga, Abinet Ashebir, Alula, Birhanu Tasew, Buche Tasew, Eniyew, Natnael, Mechenew, Mikael, Minyahel Manyazwal, Gude Are, Amede Ali, Dange Jemane (SORC), Berhanu Admasu (SORC), Yodit (SORC), and Mengistu Duncho (Wycliffe Ethiopia).

Next, many thanks to my family (Girma Worku, Biruk Mengesha, Muluken, Alemayehu, Woynishet, Zelalem, Yitagesu, Kidist, Rahel) and dearest friends at home and abroad, Ephrem Belete, Leulseged Kassa, Yemane Gebrekirstos, Henok Adam, Sadik, Kasaman, Bereket Tumay, Girum Shifetaw, Desalegn Woldeyohannes, Gebeyaw Getnet, Mengistu Endris, Adunya Yitna, Adisu, Befikadu

Getachew, Eyob Muse, Jhonny Habte, Belay Bekele, and Mekuanint Mengistu, Beka Mekonin, Yared (Yaya), and Biniam Wubishet.

I thank the following friends and colleagues at JCU who have contributed opinions to my analysis through a number of weekly roundtable meetings of the LCRC: Simon Overall, Kasia Wojtylak, Nick Piper, Grant Aiton, Elena Mihas, Nathan White, Luca Ciucci, Neil (Alex) Walker, Pema Wangdi, Junwei Bai, Carola Emkow, Christoph Holz, Rob Bradshaw, and David Guerrero. Thank you again for your insightful questions and words of encouragement.

My special thanks goes to Brigitta Flick and Betsy Bradshaw who corrected grammatical, technical and stylistic errors of this grammar. For various administrative issues, David Ellis, Amanda Parsonage and Jolene Overall, thanks a lot for your generous support and time.

I am also very grateful to Azeb Amha, Christopher Eales, Daniel Aberra, Felix Ameka, Gerrit Dimmendaal, Maarten Mous, Moges Yigezu, and Rosita Henry for their advice, encouragement, and time.

"Leaders come and go but great leaders always stay in people's heart". Even if I am a hard worker person, I never had as joyful and hopeful times as Abiy's times. Dear Prime Minister Dr. Abiy Ahmed, thank you for the good times you brought to me and citizens of this great nation.

I am immensely grateful to Monika Feinen for her generosity in producing the beautiful maps which we find in the book.

This book would have never been brought to reality without the kindness and various supports from staffs of Brill Publisher.

Finally, I would like to thank the Australian Research Council grant "How gender shapes the world" granted to Distinguished Professor and Australian Laureate Fellow Alexandra Aikhenvald. At James Cook University, I thank the College of Art, Society and Education (CASE) for MRF Competitive Funding Project Grant (2018), and the Graduate Research School for the Scholarship for my research period between July 2019 and January 2020.

Tables, Maps, Diagrams, and Figures

Tables

1.1	The Mursi's subsistence-based seasonal activities	22
1.2	The Mursi clans	26
1.3	Mursi kinship terms and kin relations (Kinship terminologies)	28
1.4	Colours and patterns	35
2.1	Latin-based orthography of Mursi	43
2.2	Ge'ez/Ethiopic-based orthography of Mursi	44
2.3	Consonant phonemes of Mursi	46
2.4	The phonotactic restrictions on the occurrence of consonant	54
2.5	The occurrence of consonant sequences in Mursi	59
2.6	Vowel phonemes of Mursi	59
2.7	Vowel phonemes and the environment in which they occur	62
2.8	Vowel sequences	65
2.9	Intervocalic consonant deletion, Mursi vs. Tirmaga-Chai and Me'en	69
2.10	Syllable shapes of Mursi clitics	98
2.11	Phonological properties of clitics and affixes	98
2.12	Phonology of interjections, ideophones and expressives	99
3.1	Word classes and their functional slots	102
3.2	The structure of a Mursi noun	103
3.3	Mursi kinship nouns	110
3.4	Noun subclasses and their syntactic functions	128
3.5	Demonstrative pronouns	135
3.6	Possessive pronouns	137
3.7	Indefinite pronouns	139
3.8	Manner adverbs	144
3.9	Frequency and degree adverbs	147
3.10	Emphatic/intensifiers, epistemic adverbs	148
3.11	Location, directional, distance adverbs	149
3.12	Number words	156
3.13	Quantifiers	159
3.14	Connectors	162
3.15	Discourse particles	164
3.16	Discourse particles	168
3.17	Ideophones	169
3.18	Expressives	172
3.19	Summary: closed word classes	172

4.1	Bound nominal demonstrative constructions	206
4.2	Non-clausal head modifiers (restrictive modifiers)	207
4.3	Non-clausal head-modifiers (non-restrictive modifiers)	207
4.4	Clausal modifiers	208
5.1	Pertensive markers	218
5.2	Pertensive taking kinship terms	219
5.3	NP-internal possessive construction	230
6.1	The meanings of number and markedness	233
6.2	The realization of number	236
6.3	The plural marker -ɲá on borrowed nouns	245
6.4	Mursi number words	264
6.5	Indefinite pronouns from *kón* and *dŏnéj*	266
6.6	Comparison: *dŏnéj* versu *kón*	266
7.1	A summary of major segmental structures of verb roots	275
7.2	*CVC* verb roots with H tone	276
7.3	*CVC* verb roots with L tone	276
7.4	*k*-initial verb roots	277
7.5	*CVVC* verb roots	278
7.6	*CVCVC* verb roots	278
7.7	*CVCVC* verb roots lacking a V₁=V₂ symmetry	279
7.8	*VC* verb roots	280
7.9	Labile verb root *éʤ* 'shoot'	280
7.10	Labile verb root *iw* 'take'	281
7.11	VCVC (V₁=V₂) verb roots	282
7.12	*VCVC* (V₁≠V₂) and VCVVC verb roots	283
7.13	*VVC, VCV(V)C* verb roots	283
7.14	*VCV* verb roots	284
7.15	The suffix *-d́* in a VCV verb root	284
7.16	*CV(V)* verb roots	285
7.17	*CVCV* verb roots	285
7.18	Trisyllabic verb roots	286
7.19	Polysyllabic roots	286
7.20	The structure of a Mursi verb and suffix-clitic ordering	288
7.21	Bound pronominal S/A suffixes in the imperfective aspect	290
7.22	Bound pronominal S/A suffixes in the perfective aspect realis	290
7.23	S/A suffixes in temporal perfective—*bik* 'break'	290
7.24	S/A suffixes in temporal perfective—*èlèhèn* 'measure'	291
7.25	S/A suffixes in simple perfective—*bik* 'break'	291
7.26	S/A suffixes in simple perfective—*èlèhèn* 'measure'	292
7.27	Bound pronominal S/A suffixes in the perfective aspect irrealis	292

7.28	First/third person syncretism	293
7.29	Object pronominal suffixes	293
7.30	Copula verbs	306
7.31	Auxiliary verb	308
7.32	Imperative construction template	310
7.33	Hortative construction—positive	323
7.34	Hortative construction—negative	324
7.35	Jussive construction	328
7.36	Imperatives and declaratives vis-à-vis negation	330
7.37	Durative past tense markers	336
7.38	Durative future time words	345
7.39	Specific time span words of Mursi	352
7.40	Mursi temporal shifters	354
7.41	Subsecutive construction types	364
8.1	Categories adjectives share with nouns	377
8.2	Categories adjectives share with stative verbs	378
8.3	Different derivation markers to derive nouns of state	380
8.4	Dimension	398
8.5	Value	398
8.6	Colour adjectives	398
8.7	Physical property	399
8.8	Human propensity	402
8.9	Quantification	402
8.10	A comparative summary of adjectives vs verbs/nouns	402
8.11	A comparative syntactic summary of adjectives vs stative verbs/nouns	403
8.12	A summary of the syntactic functions of adjectives	403
9.1	Valency-changing derivational affixes in Mursi	406
9.2	Antipassive suffixes	411
9.3	Benefactive-applicative suffixes	421
9.4	Applicative/comitative suffixes	425
9.5	Causative suffixes	429
9.6	Directional/motion suffixes	432
10.1	Free and nominative pronoun forms of Mursi	452
10.2	A list of Mursi case markers	456
10.3	Nouns that take nominative case (a selection)	458
10.4	Adpositions	468
10.5	Verb-final suffixes	473
12.1	Question (interrogative) words	490
12.2	Non-interrogative particles	509
13.1	Imperfective verb negators	518

13.2	Perfective verb negators 526
13.3	Negative imperfective copula forms 532
13.4	Negative existential verb—imperfective aspect 534
13.5	Negative existential verb—perfective aspect 534
14.1	Speech (reporting) verbs 569
14.2	The coordinative conjunction *nà* 592
14.3	Disjunctive coordinative particles 598
14.4	A summary of major clause types, clause combining and coordination strategies 602

Maps

1	Approximate territory of the Mursi people (the left and right areas are the Omo and Mago National Parks, and Omo and Mago Rivers) (copyright Monika Feinen, reproduced with permission) 2
2	The name 'Murutu', used by Cavendish (1898) (copyright Monika Feinen, reproduced with permission) 4
3	Topography of the Mursi area (copyright Monika Feinen, reproduced with permission) 5
4	The Mursi and their neighbours (copyright Monika Feinen, reproduced with permission) 19
5	The Mursi's local groups (*bùránɲɔ́gá*) (copyright Monika Feinen, reproduced with permission) 25

Diagrams

1.1	Mursi kinship system (adopted from Jørgensen 2011: 52) 27
1.2	Surmic group classification (Dimmendaal 1998: 13) 37
6.1	Tripartite system (6.3A) 234
6.2	Tripartite system (6.3B) 234
7.1	Mursi aspect system vis-à-vis bound pronominal S/A marking 296

Figures

1 Ngatini Elmo planting her Omo garden in October 2010 after the flood had retreated (mursi.org, David Turton 2010)   21
2 Cleaning the Omo River of disease (Source: mursi.org)   24

Abbreviations and Conventions

1	first person
2	second person
3	third person
A	subject of transitive verb
ADJ	adjective
AP	antipassive
ANA:REF	anaphoric reference (see REF:DEM)
APPL	applicative
ATTU	attenuative
AUG	augumentative
AUX	auxiliary
BEN	benefactive
C	consonant
CAUS	causative
C.PRED	copula predicate
CC	copula complement
CCN	clause coordinator
CL	clause
COM	comitative
COMPL	complement
COP	copula
COND	conditional
CONT	continuative
CRD:PART	cordinative.partitive
CS	copula subject
D/PSD	possessed
DO	direct object
DAT	dative
DEF	definite
DEM	demonstrative
DIM	diminutive
DIS.CRD	disjunctive coordinator
DUR	durative
EXC	exclusive
FOC	focus
GEN	genitive
HORT	hortative

ABBREVIATIONS AND CONVENTIONS

EMPH	emphatic
EPENT	epenthetic
IMP	imperative
IMPERV	imperfective
INC	inclusive
INCEPT	inceptive
INDEF	indefinite
INTENS	intensifier
INTERJ	interjection
INTR.PRED	intransitve predicate
IO	indirect object
IRR	irrealis
LOC	locative
MOD	modification marker
MA	motion away
MN	manner
MT	motion towards
NP	noun phrase
N.S	nouns of state
NEG	negative
NOM	nominative
NOMZ	nominalizer
NRSTR	non-restrictive modification marker
O	object of transitive verb
Ø	zero
OBJ	object
OBL	oblique
ORD	ordinal number
PASS	passive
PERT	pertensive
PERV	perfective
pl,PL	plural
PN	pronoun
PNC	phrase coordinator
QUOT	quotative
R/PSR	possessor
RC	relative clause
RS	resolution marker
REC	recent
RECIP	reciprocal

REDUP	reduplication
REF	referential
REFL	reflexive
RSTR	restrictive modification marker
S	subject of intransitive verb
SEQ	sequential
sg, SG	singular
RSTR	restrictive
SBJV	subjunctive
SP	specific
STV	stative
SU	subject
SUBORD	subordinate
TEMP	temporal
tr	transitive
TR.PRED	transitive predicate
V	vowel
VFS	verb-final suffix
/ /	phonemic
=	clitics
[ ]	phonetic
⟨ ⟩	grapheme/orthography
#	word boundary
*	hypothetical reconstruction/ungrammatical

CHAPTER 1

Introduction

1.1 The Mursi People: Historical Background

The Mursi (autodenomination *Mùn* plural or *Mùnì* singular) are a small group of people numbering around 7,500 (Population Census Commission, 2007), who live in the Lower Omo Valley (5° 20′ N and 6° 14′ N), Southern Nations, Nationalities and Peoples Regional State (SNNPRS), Ethiopia. The Mursi are called by alternative names: *Murzi, Murzu, Murutu* (see Map 2), *Meritu, Dama,* and *Mùnèn*. The Amhara (the so-called highlanders or *kúchúmbáj* by the Mursi) call them Mursi and their language *mursiɲa*. Their southern neighbors (the Nyangatom) call them *ɲikalabɔŋ*[1] and their nearest neighbours the Bodi (Me'en) call them *Dama*. However, the Mursi[2] call themselves *mùn* and their language *mùnèn*. They speak Mursi (Ethnologue code ISO 639-3 muz), a Surmic language which belongs to the Nilo-Saharan language family. Their territory has a size of 2,000 km2—and is located in the South Omo Zone of Southwestern Ethiopia. They live in four villages, namely: *Mákkí* (also known by the Mursi as *Mákó*[3]), *Móyzó, Bóngózó,* and *Rómós* (Hayl-Wuha) (see Map 3). These villages lie between two rivers, namely: the Omo (known to the Mursi *Wárr*) to the west and the Mago to the east—and are surrounded by two National Parks named after these two rivers (Omo and Mago)—see Map 1.

There is not much known about their present day's territory. Yet they still claim that their territory was once vast and used to start at *Mákkí* (the Mursi's main village, until now) and stretched right across the Maji plateau (marked by a dot on the left top part of Map 1) in the west to the Bako range in the east.

However, their territorial claim is a historical narration of migration that comes from the Mursi's ancestors and is apparently a story to be told for generations to come, a story very similar to 'Crossing the Red Sea' or 'the Exodus', led by Moses. At the center of all their stories, there was a strong man called,

---

1 The name *ɲikalabɔŋ* probably originates from the Turkana name for the Mursi *ŋalibɔŋ* (a range of hills which lies on a north-eastern and south-western axis and which forms a continuation of the Omo-Mako watershed) (cf. Turton 1973: 3).
2 The name Mursi originates from Murzu (a term used by the Kwegu) and adopted by some of the early travellers (cf. Bender and Turton 1976: 535; Smith 1900: 603; Vannutelli 1899 [2005]: 320). Similar names were mentioned in different literatures by different explorers, for example Murutu by Cavandish (1898: 385).
3 *Mákó* is the Mursi name of the Mago and it refers to the River and the Park.

© FIREW GIRMA WORKU, 2021 | DOI:10.1163/9789004449916_002

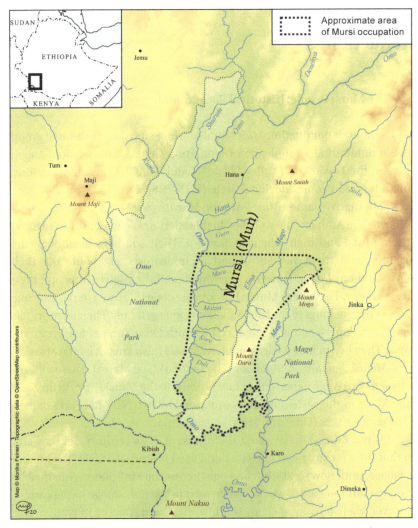

MAP 1   Approximate territory of the Mursi people (the left and right areas are the Omo and Mago National Parks, and Omo and Mago Rivers)
MONIKA FEINEN ©

Káwúlókòrò, who enabled them (the Mursi people) to cross the Omo River and settle at their present area. We will find this story later in this section; see also Appendix, Text IV.

The Mursi became part of the Ethiopian state in the late 19th century following King Menelik II's control of the southern part of the country as his major ambition to establish the modern-day Ethiopia's geopolitical shape (Turton 1988). The late 19th century's territorial expansion led by Menelik II to the Southwestern part of the country was not only for the sake of keeping the geographical and political shape of modern-day Ethiopia, but it was also of economic importance. By the late 1890s, those who were at the top in the Menelik II's Imperial hierarchy already had engaged in collecting tribute and tax from the Mursi and the surrounding areas. At the time, collecting tax and tribute from Mursi as well as from other such societies was not an easy and a smooth process as we may think of today; the process usually involved cattle raids by the highlanders, whom the Mursi call 'kúchúmbáj'. In fact, in regard to the scenario of that time, Smith (1900: 609) wrote, 'The Mursu, whom we found on the banks of the Omo, had escaped the raids of the Abyssinians, and were in a most flourishing condition.' Around the same period, Cavendish (1898: 385) wrote, "After crossing the river, I explored up the right bank, which is densely populated by a strong, rich tribe called the 'Murutu'", (see the map by Cavendish; Map 2).

Turton (1988: 261) who wrote much on the organization of the Mursi society, including their socioeconomic, and traditional political structure, has also written on the Mursi's population movement from 1890s to 1980s. According to Turton, the Mursi themselves describe the migrations they made during this period as 'Looking for a cool place'.

Today's Mursi people are the outcome of three separate population movements that started around two centuries ago and continued until the late 1970s.

Their first migration was around the mid-nineteenth century, as they say from the Ethiopian southwestern lowlands (around the border and juncture of Ethiopia-Sudan) to possibly the area now called southern Mursiland or Kúrúm (Map 3). According to literature and Mursi traditional history and stories, they moved from the Dirka mountain range (see Map 3) to the Omo and the River Mago. This first migration movement had been led by their ancestors and is known to have taken place between 100 and 200 years ago. Of all their three migrations, this one has no written evidence to substantiate it, but is believed to have lasted up to the 1920s. This was a historic moment for the ancestors as well as for the current generation of Mursi as it was a time when they created a legendary story very similar to the story of the parting of the Red Sea by Moses. At the time, there was a strong man called *Káwúlókòrò* who took part in this movement across the Omo. He is still considered by most as a legend who enabled the Mursi to cross the Omo River (see Appendix IV, 'About the Mursi'). According to Turton (1973), the crossing of the Omo and the new settlement in the vicinity of Kúrúm (See Map 3) is regarded by the Mursi as not only the start of a new life but also as a new birth of their current political identity. The major historical reason for the first Mursi population movement was ecological change. Turton (citing Karl Butzer 1971) wrote that after 1896, certain ecological

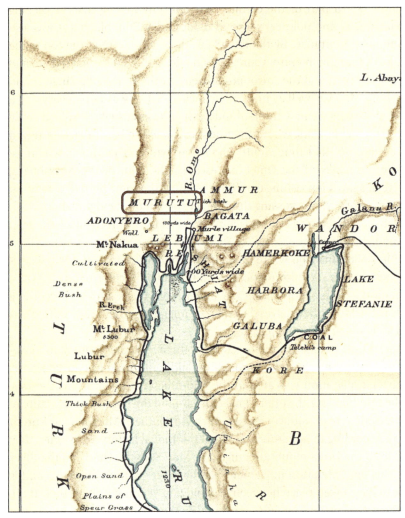

MAP 2   The name 'Murutu', used by Cavendish (1898)
MONIKA FEINEN ©

changes had taken place in the Lower Omo basin (mainly due to reduced rainfall) which resulted in a reduced water discharge from the Omo River to Lake Turkana. This ecological change is still regarded as a major reason for their first territorial expansion towards the Eastern bank of the Omo River. By the late 1890 the Mursi were living on the east side of the Omo River.

The second movement took place in the early 1900s (around 1920s and 1930s). During this period, the Mursi were able to move northwards and expand their territory up to today's northern border River Mara (See Map 3).

INTRODUCTION 5

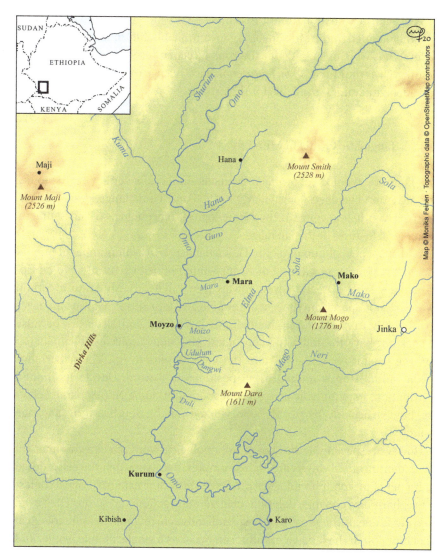

MAP 3   Topography of the Mursi area
MONIKA FEINEN ©

Once more, the Mursi having the intention of expand into the plains of the Lower Omo, started their third and last migration movement at the end of the 1970s. Interestingly, the last movement took them into the arable areas of the Lower Omo but brought them not only into regular contact with their agriculturalist neighbours Aari, but also to the place where once their long-time rivals used to live, i.e. the Bodi (in the upper Mago Valley border).

The main reasons for these three movements are ecological. The former areas abandoned by the Mursi people were uninhabitable, mountainous, rocky valleys; thus were unsuitable for their major economic subsistence, i.e. cattle herding. Or as the Mursi say *bá lálíní* 'cool place' is a place where grazing ground and adequate water is available for their cattle.

1.2 Linguistic Profile of Mursi

The linguistic typological profile of Mursi is similar to a certain degree to the Surmic group languages, particularly to Chai and Tirma languages. The summaries given below concern the phonological, morphological and syntactic typological features of the language.

With respect to phonology, Mursi is a language with a fair number of phonemic distinctions; it has a total of twenty-nine phonemes: twenty-two consonants (see Table 2.3) and seven vowels (see Table 2.6). Mursi, to a certain extent, stands apart from the rest of the Southeastern Surmic Group languages (particularly from its closely related languages Chai and Tirmaga), because it does not have the following consonant phonemes: voiceless bilabial stop /p/, the palatal implosive /ʄ/, and the velar implosive /ɠ/. The occurrence of the glottal stop is limited in all positions in a word. Due to its limited distribution, its phonemic status is questioned by some Nilo-Saharan scholars, but particularly by people who worked on the Southeastern language groups.

However, especially at the level of a phonological word versus a grammatical word identification, vowels are highly complex, because Mursi vowels undergo a number of morphophonological processes; including extensive vowel coalescence, harmony, copying, deletion, change, subtraction and so on. The vowel copying is one of the most widely spread and recurring morphophonological phenomenon in the language, and it can occur as a single, double, triple, and quadruple vowel copying term (see Chapter 2; § 2.5.6.5). Vowel height harmony and vowel fronting harmony may also create a high degree of complexity in the analysis of the properties of vowels. One similarity between consonants and vowels is that both could have lengthened segments, but length in both is phonetically triggered by certain prosodic and phonological processes such as: lengthened consonants at syllable boundaries and historical intervocalic consonant deletion.

The maximal syllable template is CVC. A great majority of Mursi verb roots have monosyllabic CVC shapes. Mursi has also two register tones: High and Low. Both are contrastive and play significant roles both at the lexical and

INTRODUCTION 7

grammatical levels. It is worth to note that grammatical tone plays a significant contrastive role in certain morphological categories such as number, person, and mood.

In terms of morphology, Mursi has three open word classes—verbs, nouns and adjectives; and twelve closed word classes: pronouns, adverbs, adpositions (postpositions and prepositions), question words, number words, quantifiers, connectors, discourse particles, interjections, ideophones, and expressives (discussed in detail in Chapter 3).

Mursi is an agglutinating language with some degree of fusion; it is highly synthetic (up to seven morphemes per word). Mursi is a predominantly suffixing language. Verbs have up to fourteen slots for verbal grammatical categories. Only a maximum of three pre-root slots can be available for both inflectional and derivational markers to be added to the verbal roots at a time (usually a negation marker proclitic followed by suffixes marking subject, causative, aspect, mood and so on). Generally, as in most members of the Surmic group languages, Mursi has few slots for prefixes. A Mursi post-verbal root slot can host a maximum of five suffixes or a combination of both suffixes and an enclitic. For example, verbal affixes appear roughly in the following order:

(1.1)   ŋà=kó-jóg-ón-óŋ-∅=ó-ɔ̀
        NEG.IMPERV=1SU-tell-MT-2PL.OBJ-1PL.INC.SU.IMPERV=NEG-VFS
        'We (inc.) will not tell (it) to you (pl.).'

Except tense, which is marked by two relative time referring particles (*wa* 'recent past'; *be* 'distant past') and by other separate time words, bound pronominals S/A and O arguments, aspect, mood, motion, and most valency and voice changing devices are marked on the verb by inflection and derivation.

Morphologically, nouns can be defined as words that obligatorily inflect for number, case, definiteness, and can occur with deictic categories. Nouns could have up to ten affixal slots for nominal grammatical categories. There is only one pre-root slot for deictic category and nine other post-root slots, of which four are shown by enclitics. Number on nouns can be shown in a number of ways and by two types of morphological forms: suffixes and clitics.

As many Nilo-Saharan languages, Mursi has a complex number marking system. Thus, nouns are divided into four sets based on how they mark number: 'replacive', 'marked plural', 'singulative', and 'suppletive'. Some nouns utilize a tripartite number marking system; 'river' *kídó* (singular), *kídói* (singulative) and *kídén* (plural). A few other nouns may utilize more than one plural suffix: 'silver bracelet' *érésí* (singular), *érésió* (plural) and/or *érésiná* (plural). Interestingly, close kinship nouns stand apart from the rest of noun types in that they can be marked by a special plural number marking suffix -čo. A total of about 70 portmanteau number markers are found in the language, and all are suffixes (see Chapter 6). Nominal morphological categories usually display the following affix-clitic orderings.

(1.2) [hùll-á   ór-é-à
       when-RSTR see.IMPERV-3PL.SU.IMPERV-RSTR
       [ŋà=múɲíɲ-í=tùnù=ŋà]ₙₚ]ᵣ𝒸/𝒮𝒰ᴮ𝒪ᴿᴰ:𝒞ℒ
       DEM=star-SG=FAR=DEF
       'When/while they saw that star ...'

(1.3) [ŋà=ɓég-á-ɲá=ìnù]ₙₚ
       DEM=watch-NOMZ-PL=FAR
       'Those (field) watchings (vigils)'

There are four morphological categories that can be encoded through double marking: two on verbal words and two on nominal words. Of the four, two are encoded through circumclitics (negation on verbs in the imperfective aspect and demonstrative system on nouns). The third grammatical category, which is shown by double marking is causative. Thus, causative derivation in Mursi can be shown by morphological markers circumfixed directly to the verb root. The fourth grammatical category to be shown through double marking is genitive case. It is a very rare feature in that it is the only grammatical category in the language to be indicated by an identical marker in a successive manner, as in (1.4)

(1.4) [zùw-á   bíbí-ó]ₙₚ   bá-ɲ-ɲ]ₙₚ
       people-RSTR big.PL-RSTR local-GEN-GEN
       'Village elders'
       (Lit. 'big (pl) people of the local area')

Mursi utilizes a complex aspect marking system, and aspect falls broadly into two categories: imperfective and perfective. Roughly, aspect can be shown on verbs in the following ways: by bound pronominal subject marking suffixes and by a number of different verb root alternations and a morphological phenomenon. The verb root alternation is quite complex and roughly one-third of Mursi verbs have different root forms for imperfective and perfective aspects. This includes full suppletion, partial suppletion, final consonant reduction/deletion, final syllable reduction, and multiple alternation. There is also one morphological phenomenon, i.e. prefixing t(V)- onto verb roots in the imperfective aspect (see Chapter 7; §7.3.1.2).

Mursi is a nominative-accusative language and has a canonical constituent order AVO (for a transitive clause) and/or SV (for an intransitive clause). Core-arguments in this constituent order are functionally-unmarked. In addition to this, depending on clause types and pragmatic context, two other constituent orders are also utilized: an AOV order (in negated clauses) (as in (1.5b)), and an OVA in a transitive clause and VS in an intransitive clause where post-verbal subjects (S and A) are marked for nominative case (as in (1.6)).

(1.5) a. [nɔ̀ŋ]_A hín-Ø [sátí]_O
 3SG want.IMPERV-3SG.SU.IMPERV watch
 'S/he/it wants the watch.'

 b. [nɔ̀ŋ]_A [sátí]_O ŋà=hín-Ø=ó
 3SG watch NEG.IMPERV=want.IMPERV-3SG.SU.IMPERV=NEG
 'S/He does not want the watch.'

(1.6) a. [lúsì]_O dág-Ø [hírí-ó]_A
 boy hit-3SG.SU.IMPERV man-NOM
 'The man beats the boy.'

 b. [hírí dág-Ø [lúsì-ó]_A
 man hit-3SG.SU.IMPERV boy-NOM
 'The boy beats the man.'

As is shown in (1.5b), in an AOV order, due to strict orders of constituents, negated verbs need to be moved to a clause final positions, and arguments in A/S function are often forced to appear at clause-initial position. In (1.6a–b), the nominative case system of Mursi operates based on an OVA/VS constituent order. Thus, post-verbal subjects in this constituent order are morphologically and formally marked by marked-nominative case suffix -o, for a transitive post-verbal subject argument marker (A) (as in (1.6a–b)).

Mursi marks both the head noun and the dependent form. There are morphological markers for the head noun and for the dependent (modifier) called 'restrictive and non-restrictive modification' form. As a head and dependent marking language, all dependents or modifiers, except number words and quantifiers are required to indicate their dependency relation with the head nouns they modify always by an overt morphological inflection: -a (for restrictive) and -i [-ti] (for non-restrictive). This dependency phenomenon between head nouns and dependents is widely known as 'Construct-Form' (CF) by some Semitists. In Semitic languages this phenomenon is also known by a different term—'construct state'. In fact, other terms are also used: 'status constructs' (Tucker and Bryan 1966), 'modified noun form' (Reh 1996), and 'construct form' (Creissels 2006). In Mursi, both the head noun and the dependent can be marked by the same dependency modification markers: HEAD.NOUN-*a* DEPENDENT (MODIFIER)-*a* (restrictive) or HEAD.NOUN-*i* [-ti] DEPENDENT (MODIFIER) (-*i* [-ti]) (nonrestrictive).

In Mursi, within NPs, head nouns are obligatorily marked by restrictive (as in (1.7)) and nonrestrictive (as in (1.8–1.9)) forms because head nouns are required to fulfill the role of head nouns on the basis of internal structure of NPs.

(1.7) [rúm-á hɔ̀l-à]_NP
cloth-RSTR white.STV-RSTR
'The white dress'

When the head noun is followed/modified by the number word *dɔ́néj* 'one' or a quantifier, then the head noun is obligatorily marked by a non-restrictive modification marker.

(1.8) [érmì-tí dɔ̀nèj]_NP áɨw-ó
child-NRSTR one come.PERV.SG-MT.3SG.SU.PERV
'One child came.'

(1.9) a. [kèn-í mèrì]_NP
tree.PL-NRSTR many
'Many trees'

b. [zùg-tí bù mèrì]_NP
people-NRSTR big many
'Very many people'

The underived adjective *bú* functions as an intensifier, not as a modifier. Thus, the relationship of the head is directly with the quantifier, i.e. *mèrì*. However, within a similar NP construction, if *bu* functions as quantifier, any other modifier following it may not be marked by a nonrestrictive modification marker, as in (1.10).

(1.10) [lɔ̀g-tí bú dáldál-í]_NP
issue-NRSTR big difficult.STV-ADJ
'Many (very) difficult issues'

INTRODUCTION   11

In this grammar, as far as this marking is concerned, instead of the term construct-form, I prefer to call it 'modification marker' (see details of it in Chapter 4).

The same noun modification markers apply in possessive constructions when indicating possession/ownership in light of the head and/or possessed (D) and the dependent and/or possessor (R) dependency relationship within the syntactic frame of 'NP-internal possessive construction'. Accordingly, Mursi has five NP-internal possessive construction types: one structure where R (the possessor) and D (the possessed) human/animate/inanimate item/object are simply juxtaposed within NP—and four other distinct structures where D is followed by R. A possessive relationship that can be expressed by a juxtaposed possessor and possessed is very different from all other possessive relationship construction types. Morphologically, both possessor and possessed nouns do not take any markers. This means that, the possessed item is not marked by 'restrictive/nonrestrictive modification' or 'relator suffix -*a*'. The same is true for the possessor, which does not take any marker including the genitive case, for example, *hírí*$_R$ *sárà*$_D$ ⟨man.SG name.PL⟩ 'The man's name'. There is no marking on either the possessor or the possessed. The noun *sárá* 'name' is an inherently plural noun in Mursi and has no singular counterpart, but the meaning hasn't been affected and still has a singular interpretation. The remaining four types of possessive constructions within an NP involve POSSESSED(D)-*a* R{where the R is a POSSESSOR-GEN (as in (1.11) or a POSSESSIVE PRONOUN (1.12) or a PERTENSIVE MARKER (1.13)).

(1.11) [*érmì-á   hírí-ɲ*]$_{NP}$
        child-RSTR man-GEN
        'Child (son) of man'

(1.12) [*sárá-á   g=àɲù*]$_{NP}$
        name-RSTR PL.PSD=1SG.PSR
        'My name'

(1.13) [*ʤɔ̀ɔ̀gé*]$_{NP}$
        mother.PERT.PL.3.PSR
        'His/her mothers'

As we can see in the examples shown above, the modification marker or the relator suffix attached to D should always be identical. The fifth type of 'NP-internal possessive construction' in Mursi is called 'Noun modification construction' (NMC). It is normally the same as with the three NP construction types mentioned earlier, i.e. a structure where D is followed by R. Yet it stands apart from all previously mentioned possessive construction types because it may involve a series of intermediate possessors (Rs)/modifiers. Therefore the D and the intermediate R's are marked by restrictive modification marker/relator marker -*a* while the real possessor is marked by the genitive case marker. The restrictive modification marker/relator marker -*a* is marked on both NP constituents (the possessed/head noun and on the intermediate possessors/modifiers) (see more in Chapter 4). Welmers (1973) used the term 'associative construction' in reference to nouns which express a wide range of semantic relationships with other nouns occurring as modifiers within the same NP. See the following examples.

(1.14)   [[*zùw-á   ṅàgàs-á*]$_{NP}$ *ɔ́r-ùɲ*]$_{NP}$ *mèzì-d-ó*
         people-RSTR old.STV-RSTR village-GEN discuss-PERV.PL-3PL.IRR
         'The village's elders held a council.'

In addition to genitive case, the last modifier/possessor could be marked by restrictive modification marker/relator marker –*a*, as in (1.15).

(1.15)   *á*   [*lɔ̀g-á*   [*bì-á   gɔ̀lɔ̀ɲ-á*]$_{NP}$]$_{NP}$]
         COP.3.IMPERV issue/matter-RSTR cow-RSTR red.STV-RSTR
         'This (it) is the matter of the red cow.'

For further possessive expression and construction types see Chapter 5.

How aspect is shown in Mursi has been mentioned earlier, so here I focus on mood category. The mood category of Mursi includes imperative, hortative, jussive, reality, and subjunctive. All are expressed by inflectional markings on the verbs. Only the hortative and the jussive moods can be marked by an optional morphological particle *aj/aɲ*. In Mursi, the imperative mood refers to a command given to an addressee (the second person). The verb utilized in the positive imperative construction must always occur in the perfective aspect. The negative imperative construction utilizes a verb in the imperfective aspect. However, in both constructions number can be marked on the verb. The plural suffix -*V* is marked on the verb to denote plural addressee while the bare perfective verb root in its own indicates singular addressee. Person of the subject is unmarked. Verb-final suffixes -*a* (for singular), -*ɛ* (for plural) and a variant of both, -*o* can be added to a clause-finally occurring verbs of the imperative constructions.

(1.16) ʃíg-á
listen.PERV:IMP-VFS
'Listen (2sg.)!'

(1.17) bág-á-ɛ́
eat.PERV:IMP-PL-VFS
'Eat (pl.)!'

(1.18) ʃíg-í-ɛ́
listen.PERV:IMP-PL-VFS
'Listen (pl.)!'

Unlike the positive imperative, the negative imperative utilizes an imperfective verb root and different number suffixes—despite both being commands used to deliver a speaker's intent that a certain course of action must be carried out within a specified period of time. The negative imperative utilizes the imperfective negative proclitic ŋà=, imperfective verb root, and two invariable number suffixes -i (for singular addressee) and -o (for plural addressee). See the examples below.

(1.19) ŋà=zámí-í
NEG.IMPERV=swim.IMPERV-SG
'Don't (sg.) swim!'

(1.20) ŋà=édʒ-ó
NEG.IMPERV=drink.IMPERV-PL
'Don't (pl.) shoot/kill!'

The hortative and the jussive in Mursi are non-canonical imperative moods directed to first and third persons and can be used to denote a mild command. Like the canonical imperative, positive hortative and jussive moods utilize a verb in the perfective aspect for positive whereas negative hortative and jussive moods utilize a verb in the imperfective aspect. An interesting prosodic feature here is that a grammatical tone will be used to distinguish between the hortative and the jussive form. The hortative mood takes a low-toned prefix hortative k(V̀)- *and* a low-toned verb root. It may optionally be preceded by a free form high-toned hortative particle áj [áɲ] (as in (1.22)).

(1.21) kà-màg
1.HORT-catch.PERV
'Let me catch!'

(1.22) áj   k-idô-ò
HORT.PART 1.HORT-mix.PERV-VFS
'Let me mix/combine!'

(1.23) kà-màg-à-ɛ̀
1.HORT-catch.PERV-1PL.INC-VFS
'Let us (inc.) catch!'

(1.24) ŋà=k-èj-t-ò
NEG=1.HORT-shoot.IMPERV-PL-1PL.EXC
'Let us (exc.) not kill!'

The jussive mood refers to a command directed at the third person. The jussive mood marker prefix *k(V)-* and the verb always carry a low-toned melody. Besides, the jussive marker prefix (*k(V)-*) will not be marked when the negated form is used (as in (1.25c)).

(1.25) a. kɔ́-ɲɔ́g-ɔ́
3.JUSS-close.PERV-VFS
'Let him close!'

b. àj   kɔ́-ɲɔ́g-ɔ́-ɛ́
JUSS.PART 3.JUSS-close.PERV-PL-VFS
'Let them close!'

c. ŋà=báns-án-ó
NEG=get.up-MT-SG
'Let him not wake up!'

Subjunctive is one of the three moods in Mursi which are expressed by the irrealis morphological marker within the perfective aspect. Subjunctive, like the other two irrealis moods (hortative and jussive), utilizes a prefix *k(V)-* and a perfective verb root. (The details await us in Chapter 7.)

Adjectives are one of the three open word classes of Mursi. Adjectives are open classes by derivation. Based on the morphological properties they display, Mursi adjectives can be divided into two major categories: underived (*túíní* 'small' and *bùi* 'big') and derived (Type I—mainly from stative verbs; Type II—derived from stative verbs and from other word classes through productive and unproductive morphological derivations). The two underived adjectives display sound iconicity. This phenomenon is an association between sound and meaning. Dixon (2010:69) pointed out that a high front vowel *i* is often naturally associated with a little/small object and a high back vowel *u* with a big/large one. Adjectives always bear the general adjectiviser suffix -*i*, regardless of each adjective's morphological property. Syntactically, adjectives can modify the head of an NP, fill the head of an intransitive predicate slot (as in (1.26)), fill copula complement slots, denote degree of the compared quality in comparative constructions, and function as manner modifiers. The adjective class of Mursi covers all semantic types that can be conveyed by adjectives.

(1.26) [nòŋ]$_S$ [ŋà=ídĭbèn-Ø=nó]$_{INTR.PRED}$
   3SG NEG.IMPERV=fat-3SG.SU.IMPERV=NEG
   'S/he is not fat.'

Reduplication is the only way of marking number on underived adjectives (as in (1.27 and 1.28)). Only the underived adjective can take degree of magnitude markers: free form *gòdĕ* (gèdé) (diminutive 'very small') and the suffix -*sís* (augmentative 'very big').

(1.27) [ùrgùsá-í tííti]$_{NP}$
   fish.PL-NRSTR small:REDUP.PL+NRTSR
   'small/little (pl) fishes'

(1.28) [zùw-á bíbí-ó   bá-ɲ-ɲ]$_{NP}$
   people-RSTR big:REDUP.PL-RSTR local-GEN-GEN
   'Village elders'
   (Lit. 'big (pl) people of the local area')

As Mursi is a free-constituent order language, the order among adjectives within NPs and in sentences is relatively free. As to the ordering of adjectives within NPs, throughout the adjective chapter and this grammar, no more than two adjectival modifiers are available. The details of adjectives are the topic of Chapter 8.

 Mursi has four valency decreasing and four valency increasing derivations. The valency decreasing derivations are passive, antipassive, reciprocal, and reflexive. Benefactive, applicative/comitative, causative, and directional/

motion increase the number of core arguments. Each valency changing derivations may employ more than one strategies, for example, the reciprocal derivation has four different possibilities while reflexive derivation has at least two possibilities (these are topics that have been discussed in detail in Chapter 9).

Grammatical relations in Mursi are marked by constituent order and case. However, case-marking is often employed depending on constituent order system of the language. Mursi is a nominative-accusative language. Although Mursi utilizes case-marking, it is also a head-marking language that has cross-referencing bound pronominal forms to indicate grammatical relations. As a head-marking language, it has participant reference markings on the verb which predominantly indicate grammatical relations. This operates by indexing bound pronominal A and O argument affixes on the verb. In ditransitive clause constructions, argument indexing on the verb often operates according to referential prominence scale hierarchy and verb-adjacency constraint principles (see more on grammatical relations in Chapter 10).

Mursi has sophisticated and elaborate comparative construction techniques.

Comparative constructions explicitly indicate participants being compared and parameter of comparison (often adjectives). Index of comparison may be indicated by attaching a benefactive/dative marker suffix to the element of the parameter of comparison, i.e. 'comparative-benefactive'. Mursi has a total of seven types of comparative constructions: mono-clausal, phrasal plus mono-clausal, bi-clausal (are of two type TYPE I and TYPE II), connector *bá* 'place', *hékó ... tèb* 'same ... as'/*hétó ... tèb* 'be.same ... as' ('as ... as'), and one additional strategy. (Chapter 11 offers more interesting details on comparative constructions.)

Mursi has both question types: content questions and polar questions. Content question words (mostly pronominals) usually occupy clause final argument slots. As a language with an AVO canonical order of constituents, all Mursi question words occur immediately following the verb, i.e. a syntactic position available for grammatical objects. Moreover, sentence-final positions, syntactic slots for core and non-core arguments, may typically function as focus-bearing positions when filled by question words. On the other hand, a polar question in Mursi can be formed either by raising the intonation of the lexical constituents that occur at end of a clause or by placing non-interrogative particles at the end of a declarative statement (see details in Chapter 12).

Typologically, negation constructions in Mursi show various striking features. In Mursi, a number of different negation strategies may be employed to negate verbal constituents. The strategies vary depending on grammatical systems or categories such as aspect, mood, and person-subject. For instance, a verb in the imperfective aspect can be negated by bound circumclitics whereas a verb in the perfective aspect is negated by independent perfective negative particle ŋàni ⟨NEG.PERV⟩ 'not, not yet, still' plus by negative enclitic =ó attached to the perfective verb root. Interestingly, negative declarative clauses have an obligatory SV/AOV, constituent order, for which negated verbs always occupy clause-final positions. This is a syntactic phenomenon that works only for order of negated predicates in negative clauses, which is different from the affirmative clauses in a canonical constituent order SV/AVO and from clauses having a marked-nominative and case marked S/A subjects OVA (in a transitive clause) VS (in an intransitive clause). Many more interesting features of the negation system are discussed in Chapter 13.

Mursi has the following main clause types: conditional, temporal, speech report clause, complement clause, copular clause, and obligation/deontic clause. Each clause type may utilizes one or more varieties of clause combining/linking strategies. In Mursi, clauses can be combined or linked by the following four major clause combining techniques: subordination, complementization, relativisation, and coordination. For instance, a speech report clause in Mursi is introduced by the quotative marker ké ⟨QUOT⟩ 'that'. It always precedes the speech verbs such as élí 'call' and sé 'say'; but it may precede or follow the speech report. ké also functions as complementizer, so the term 'quotative-complementizer' would best explains it.

In some circumstances, it is important to take into account that certain clause types may follow strict subordination rules. Thus, for instance, a conditional clause construction must contain the conditional particle hùllì 'if, when', which almost always occurs at the beginning of the subordinate clause; whereas a constituent that occurs at the subordinate clause-final position is being marked by the subordinate clause marker enclitic =jè [=è] (as in (1.29)).

(1.29) [hùllì bíró él-έ=jè]$_{SUBORD:CL}$
if money exist.IMPERV:PL-3PL.SU.IMPERV=SUBORD
[k-ádʒ-ín húŋ]$_{MAIN:CL}$
1SU-give.IMPERV-2SG.OBJ simply
'If I have money, I will give you (some).'

See Chapter 14 regarding clause types and the ways in which different clause types could combined together.

1.3 Geography and Mursi Neighbours

1.3.1 *Geography*

The South Omo Zone was established in 8 Woredas[4] and 1 city administration, with 16 nationalities living in the Lower Omo Valley. Thus, the zone is a showcase of the nations' lifestyles, dresses, symbolic gestures, dances, and so on. It is a magnificent tourist destination with many beautiful cultural exhibits, stunning landscapes, pleasant climate and other attractive conditions.

One of the eight Woredas in South Omo Zone is the Salamago District, with the capital Hana. Hana is located at 110 km south of the South Omo Zone's capital (Jinka), 635 km from the SNNPRS's capital city (Hawassa), and 860 km away from the Capital of Ethiopia (Addis Ababa). Salamago is home of five different ethnic groups: Mursi, Bodi (Chai/Me'en), Dime and Bacha. The Salamago Woreda is comprised of three climate zones: 5% cool zone, 35% subtropical, 60% tropical, and is covered by three major landscape forms: 13% valley, 25% mountainous, 62% flat land. The Salamago Woreda, area is 45, 1120 ha, has a population of 33, 621, an average temperature of 35 °C, and an annual average rainfall of 625 millimeters.

1.3.2 *Mursi Neighbours*

Among other closely neighbouring linguistic groups, the Mursi share a high degree of linguistic and cultural similarities with the 'Suri' (known as *Chai* to the Mursi). Until recently, the terms 'Suri' and 'Surma' were the main source of confusion among ethnographers and linguistic scholars who have worked on the cultures and languages of Surmic speech communities for many years. At one point, Abbink (1991: 8) wrote, "'Surma', there are distinct territorial groups, including some hardly known ones (like the Bale and the Suri). It [Surma tribe or Surmic speech community] is thus certainly not a homogenous 'tribe', though all these Surma-speakers all share the [same] … mode of existence". Therefore, Abbink suggested one must be careful to use these two terms as ethnic labels and language labels do not always coincide. Following this, in 1998, in a volume published 'Surmic Languages and Cultures', Yigezu and Dimmendaal were able to avoid the misleading nature of these two terms.

---

4 Woreda (also known as Wereda) is the third-level administrative division in the political administrative division system of Ethiopia, following two first-level (Region) and second-level (Zone).

INTRODUCTION

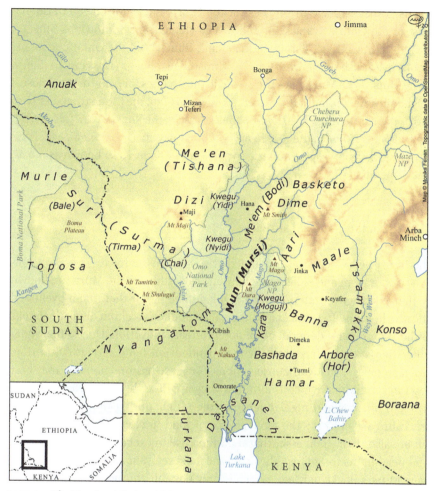

MAP 4   The Mursi and their neighbours
MONIKA FEINEN ©

Dimmendaal (1998: 5) wrote, "Suri and Surma[5] are primarily ethnonyms covering three Surmic speech communities speaking partly different languages namely Chai, Tirma, and Baale. Suri is an ethnonym which refers a people rather than a language".

The Mursi are surrounded by both small and large groups whose speech are from three major African language families: 1) Nilo-Saharan (Chai, Tirma (both

---

5   As an additional justification to these two labels, Dimmendaal (1998: 5) wrote, "neighboring Dizi and Amhara communities refer to these three groups [Chai, Tirma, and Baale] collectively as Surma ...". Suri communities themselves still use the label Surma as selfname.

language speakers live to the west of the Omo), Baale, Me'en (Bod-Tishena) (east of the Omo), Nyangatom and Kwegu (Koegu) (also known as Muguji); 2) Omotic (Aari, Kara, Banna, Bashada and Hamar) (all the Omotic speaking groups live South of the Omo); and 3) a Cushitic language (Dassanech) (South of the Mursi). The Mursi have their own distinct names for some of their closest neighbours. Accordingly, the 'Suri' are known as *Chai*, the Me'en (together with two of their sub-groups) as *Túmúrá*, the Aari as *Su*, the Kara as *Kérà* (also *kéràj*), the Hamar as *Hámárí*, the Kwegu as *Nyídíní* (singular; also *ŋídíní*)/ *Nyídí* (plural), Dassanech as *Geleba*, and the Nyangatom as *Bume* (also known as *Bíméj*) (see Appendix IV).

1.4 Economy and Subsistence

The Mursi people engage in two activities for a living for their major economy: pastoralism and small-scale farming. Nevertheless, the Mursi are known by the central government and by highland people for their main livelihood of cattle herding. To some extent, they also produce sorghum along the banks of the Omo River—dependent on flood retreat cultivation. Due to their hoe-cultivation system, they are heavily dependent on flood retreat cultivation. Based on my two fieldwork observations, I suggest 'pastoral nomads' may best describes the Mursi which is also how they are described by the central government officials and highlanders. For the Mursi, during times of crop failure, cattle are not only the main source of food (including milk and blood) but are also their main asset that the Mursi use to exchange with their highland neighbours for grains. Above all, the most relevant social relationship in every Mursi's life is marriage, which is only possible through cattle exchange. A marriage process that requires the groom's family to pay bridewealth to the family of bride's father (see §1.7.1). It is not possible to think of the Mursi people separately from their pastoralist life. At one point, Turton (1973: 19) described their relationship with cattle as follows: 'For a Mursi, to have no cattle, and to be forced therefore to live "like a monkey" in the Omo forest and bush, to eat fish "like a wading bird" and never to leave the banks of the Omo'. Rarely, apart from exchanging cattle for grains, the Mursi directly sell their cattle in the Jinka market (South Omo Zone's capital city) to buy consumable products they need such as coffee, tobacco, cloth, and ammunitions. Honey and tourism are also additional income sources. In the spring season particularly in October, they often earn some money from tourists, for their dances and by posing for foreign tourists in the villages of *Mákkí* and *Gowa*.

INTRODUCTION

FIGURE 1   Ngatini Elmo planting her Omo garden in October 2010 after the flood had retreated
MURSI.ORG, DAVID TURTON 2010

Their main crop is sorghum, but they also grow maize, beans and chick-peas. The Mursi harvest twice a year. The first planting is done on the banks of the Omo and Mago Rivers, on the fertile soil brought and deposited by the annual flood. After the annual flood retreat, they plant their crops (mainly sorghum) in October and November, and harvest in January and February.

The second planting takes place at a little bit away from the two rivers in forested areas which are suitable for a rain-fed based shifting cultivation. This time the planting takes place between March and April, and the harvest in June and July. In Mursi, a season (a year) can be divided into months on the basis of these two subsistence activities (See Table 1.1 below). Nowadays, due to the local weather condition's unpredictability of factors such as unseasonal and inconsistence rain patterns, it has become difficult for Mursi to feed themselves based on the two life subsistence ways.

Accordingly, the Mursi do not bother about the Ethiopian calendar, which itself is a different calendar from the Western. The Mursi seasonal calendar system is based on their understanding of the nature of the phase of one cycle of the moon. By integrating this knowledge of simple astronomy with other knowledges and skills (related to reading the stomach lining of a goat), they make their own season-based calendar that suits the cattle herding and farming process.

TABLE 1.1 The Mursi's subsistence-based seasonal activities

Names of months	In European calendar	Subsistence events and activities
bérgú dɔ́néj	August–September	The Omo reaches its maximum level; storage of rain-fed harvest
bérgú ràmàn	September–October	The Omo recedes and leaves fertile soil; firing of grass, preparation of plots for flood retreat cultivation
bérgú sízzì	October–November	planting of the flood crops; cattle move to Elma Valley
bérgú wùʃ	November–December	flood crops weeding period
bérgú hááńán	December–January	The Omo reaches its minimum level; flowering of sorghum; protection (bird-scaring); eating of unripe sorghum (tiʃu); burning of other bushbelt cultivation areas
bérgú ìllèj	January–February	flood crop harvesting period
bérgú ìssàbàj	February–March	The Omo water level begins to rise; threshing and storage of crops harvested; bushbelt cultivation
bérgú issej	March–April	the season's main rains begin, planting of rain-fed crops starts; the cattle which were in Elma since October will be moved to headstreams of the Omo's westward-flowing tributaries
bérgú sàkkàl	April–May	rain-fed crops weeding period
bérgú tɔ̀mɔ̀n	May–June	flowering of rain-fed crops; protection (bird-scaring)
bérgú tɔ̀mɔ̀n kó dɔ́néj	June–July	rain-fed crops harvesting period
bérgú tɔ̀mɔ̀n kó ràmàn	July–August	drying, threshing and storing of rain-fed harvest

1.5 Traditional Leadership

The Mursi have their own customary administrative system, thus are governed by their own traditional power structure and hierarchy they have been practicing for the last two centuries. They are governed mainly by four levels of power structure: *Kómórú, Koysi, Hírásábáj* (lit. person/man-of-head), and *Kamisi*. The *Kómórú* (priest king) is the administrator and spiritual leader. He is said to be chosen from the three clans: *Kómórté, Bumai*, and *Gárákúlí*. According to Turton (1973: 253), the first two are among the largest Mursi clans. However, most of the *kómórènà* (priests) are chosen from the *Kómórté* clan. In accordance with their leadership hierarchy, each power structure has its own role and its power is more or less limited by the people. The *Koysi*, *Hírásábáj* and *Kamisi* are also accountable for the *Kómórú*.

Regarding the Kómórú's leadership role, Jørgensen (2011: 8) wrote: 'The only formally defined leadership role in the society is that of Kômoru, or Priest'. The *Kómórú* administers the people, keeps the well-being of the community as a whole, and acts as a mediator between the people and 'Tumu' (God). When the elders file public complaints, the first thing he always does is making a sacrifice of an Ox or a goat. Then, by reading the intestines he pleads with his creator *Tùmù* 'God' to let him destroy different diseases and plagues. He also pleads for the well-being of the cattle, the fertility of the land, and for abundance of water and rain. When the priest gets older or dies, he is succeeded by his oldest son or 'the first born son'. However, his assumed successor has to get approval from the people.

The *Koysi* (*Lúsìakubu*) serves as the *Kómórú*'s counselor. Among his major duties is the following: he prepares a mud from a selected and special type of soil; then he anoints the patient's body. In this traditional ritual system, the *Koysi* treats his people's illnesses and curing their sicknesses by spitting on the patient's head and body. In addition, when there is new arable-land, he blesses the land to make it bring a good harvest; he discharges his traditional ritual duties by slaughtering a goat and pouring the blood of the goat on the new farmland.

The *Hírásábáj* (Lit. 'man of head') or *Híráhátá*—is a dreamer and a prophecy teller. He is the man in charge of making prophecies about the life situation of the community,—about prosperity, peace, and wellbeing in the future. He is an able man who can predict the future sufferings or prosperity the people might face. He not only accepts dreams that come from his own people for interpretations but also dreams and ideas that come from those under his authority, the 'Kamisi'. To interpret the dreams, he gives orders for a traditional ceremony to take place. The purpose of this ceremony is only for dream interpretation; thus, all dreams will be presented to him and will be given cultural and spiritual interpretations. Then the intestine of a cow is read and the interpretations will be made ready to be carried out by members of various leadership organs in accordance with situations in his community. Thus, according to the prophecy that results from the ceremony, the *Hírásábáj* will deliver instructions to be implemented and will monitor the entire prophesy process.

The *Kamisi*'s role is to prepare coffee and execute a spiritual ceremony. When he performs a spiritual ministry, he is responsible for ointing members of the

FIGURE 2   Cleaning the Omo River of disease
SOURCE: MURSI.ORG

community with a white mud and blessing them in accordance with their spiritual beliefs. In this, it is believed that the *Kamisi* will intercede for his community with the creator. In addition to his spiritual roles, he connects his community with their superiors/leaders.

1.6   Local Groups, Clans, Kinship System and Age Sets

The population of Mursi is divided into five *bùránɲɔ́gá* (literally, 'local groups') namely: *Baruba*, *Mugʤo*, *Biogolokare*, *Ariholi*, and *Gangulobíbí*. In Mursi, the *bùránɲɔ́gá* are non-physical boundaries as there are no clan territories these five clans share with one another.

These five *bùránɲɔ́gá* refer to groups of co-residents who share the same territory such as same sites for flood and rain cultivations, cattle herding and so on. There is no clear cut spatial boundaries among the five local groups. Until 1980s, the *Dola* group used to refer to just one local group, the *Biogolokare* (see Map 5). Following the Mursi's occupation of new areas, the *Baruba* and *Mugʤo* were included in the *Dola* local group as separate sub-units. Within the five local groups, there are 18 *kàbičó* (clans), who descended in the male line from the same man's side, but it could be from different co-wives.

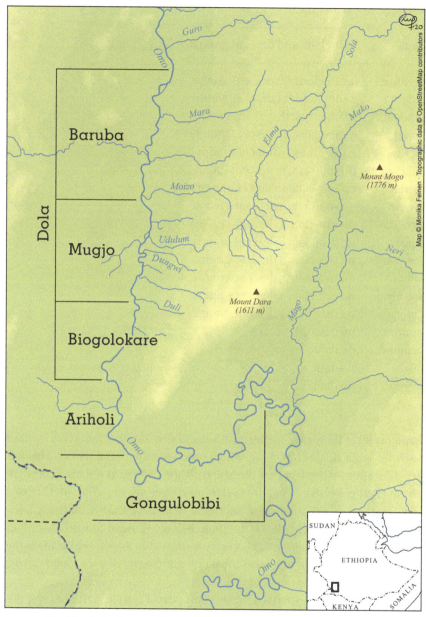

MAP 5 The Mursi's local groups (bùránɲɔ́gá)
MONIKA FEINEN ©

TABLE 1.2   The Mursi clans

Clans	Sub-clans and descent groups
Komorte	4 sub-clans; 32 descent-groups
Juhaj	2 sub-clans; 23 descent-groups
Garakuli	2 sub-clans; 18 descent-groups
Bumai	5 sub-clans; 28 descent-groups
Kagisi	2 sub-clans; 9 descent-groups
Mangwi	no sub-clan; 17 descent-groups
Ngeriaj	no sub-clan; 10 descent-groups
Gongwi	no sub-clan; 4 descent-groups
Berneshe	no sub-clan; 3 descent-groups
Bongosi	no sub-clan; 6 descent-groups
Chermani	no sub-clan; 4 descent-groups
Galnai	no sub-clan; 5 descent-groups
Maiyaiyai	no sub-clan; 3 descent-groups
Changuli	no sub-clan; 7 descent-groups
Gumnai	no data
Gushumi	no data
Isai	no data
Kulgisai	no data

Almost all of these clan names have a singulative number marker -*i*, in order to signify just a single clan name, which otherwise are plural names. This further substantiates the fact that the Mursi always believe in a shared common value, called collective living. Intra-clan marriages are not allowed. Due to a strict marriage rule that limits affinal ties to three generations, marrying a fellow clan member is regarded as a taboo. Before we head toward looking at the Mursi kinship system, it is necessary to note that *kábí* (sing., clan) is the only none-kinship noun that takes the plural number marker -*čo* (⟨kábí-čó⟩ pl., clan).

The Mursi kinship system is a highly complicated system, particularly influenced by a strong patrilineal kinship system principle. I will not go deeper into explaining the connection between the societal structure or the fundamental institutions of the Mursi society and marriage arrangements between clans. But I would argue the two are necessary as they are key to our understanding how the Mursi kinship system works. For instance, in addition to the rule that prohibits inter-clan marriages, there is a general rule that applies to the Mursi as

INTRODUCTION

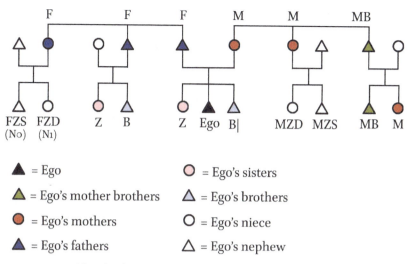

DIAGRAM 1.1   Mursi kinship system
ADOPTED FROM JØRGENSEN 2011: 52

one social group—a rule that allows one to distinguish the boundary between kinship and affinity. As Turton (1973: 181) suggested, this rule prevents new marriages from repeating existing affinal ties for a period of three generations. Thus, the rule effectively turns affines into kinsmen. Jørgensen (2011: 43) noted that the Mursi's social organization is based more or less on kinship, on the basis of complex clan systems. A clan can be a descendent of unilineal groups united through a series of lineages, who are believed to be descended from the same common ancestor. For instance, the rules that govern bridewealth distribution always have to maintain the privilege of the groups linked by marriage. The rule being put in place for marriage, is founded on a general kinship-based system and concentrates around the arrangement of the kinship relations on the mother's side and the father's side. The Diagram 1.1 below illustrates the structure of the Mursi kinship system, as the basis for kin terms associated with both sides (of father's and mother's).

The kinship terms *dàdà* (*fúúné*) and *dʒɔ̀ɔ̀né* refer to 'male parent' and 'female parent' respectively. In other words, rather than just referring to 'father' and 'mother'; both general reference terms can be used to describe those who are believed to have given birth to ego. Jørgensen (2011: 53) who wrote his ethnographic reflections on the Mursi marriage system has noted that *dàdà* (*fúúné*) means all the men and women in ego's parental generations. This includes all parental generations belonging to ego's patriliny by descent. The *dʒɔ̀ɔ̀né* (mother's) side refers to a female member of a descend group to which the ego's descent group is linked by marriage (Jørgensen 2011: 53). It is through this com-

TABLE 1.3 Mursi kinship terms and kin relations (Kinship terminologies)

Kinship terms	Meaning	Kin relations
ʃúúnɛ́	'father'	F, FB, FZ
dʒɔ̀ɔ̀nɛ̀	'mother'	M, MZ, MBD, FBW, MFBD
gòdónà	'brother'	B, FBS
ŋɔ̀nà	'sister'	Z, FBD
ŋà	'wife'	W, BW
máinɛ	'husband'	H, HB
hòjnè	'son, daughter'	S, D, BD, BS, FBDS, FBDD, FBSS, FBSD, WZS, WZD
gàlnè	'brother's wife'	HZ, HB
kɔ̀nén	'sister's husband; wife's brother'	SWF, ZH
kògínɛ́	'grandfather'	FF, FFB, MFB, FMBS, MMB, MMBS
kàkà/Óhíné	'grandmother'	FM, FMZ, FMBD, FMBW, MM, MMZ, MMBD, MBW
óóná	'uncle'	MB, MBS, MBSS
jànèn	'cousin'	HM, WM, WMZ, SWM, DHM
mɛ̀rɛ̀	'daughter-in-law'	SW, ZSW
ŋɔ̀sɔ̀sì	'sister's child'	ZS, ZD, FZB, FZD, FBDS, FBDD
kòkòjè	'great grandfather'	FFBS, MF
ŋàŋnún	'mother's sister's children'	MZS, MZD
áʃàì	'grandchild'	DS, DD, SS, SD, BDS, BDD, BSS, BSD, ZDS, ZDD, ZSS, ZSD, FZSS, FZDS, FZDD
lɔ̀mùgèn	'co-wives'	HBW, 2nd-wife
kóbànèn	'mother-in-law'; ('father-in-law' or 'brother-in-law')	WZH

F=Father, M=Mother, B=Brother, Z=Sister, W=Wife, H=Husband, S=Son, D=Daughter

plex kinship system that the rules governing the distribution of bridewealth operate. In the Mursi kinship relationships, it is the affinal rather than those of descent, which defines genealogical reckoning, the network of interpersonal kinship ties, the compositional one particular to cattle settlement, and so on. In preventing new marriages from repeating existing affinal ties, the dispersal and retention of various affinal groups always keeps mutual exclusive ties between kinship and affinity (Turton 1973: 181). In Mursi, almost everything can be shared or can be possessed alienably (optional), but only kinship nouns cannot be possessed inalienabily (obligatory). Thus, only kinship nouns can be marked with pertensive suffix, which is a marker of inalienability.

With regard to age and age sets, all Mursi men should pass through each of the following seven age grades: *Rúmuɲoj* (0–7), *čáŋálá* (7–10), *dòɲà* (10–16), *Tèrò* (16–20), *Rórá* (20–40), *Bárá* (40–60), and *Kárú* (> 60). There is a ceremony called *nita* 'age set initiation ceremony'. This initiation ceremony takes place in different Mursi villages just once in many many years. The most recent one is known as *Geleba* in 1991 and the previous was known as *Bèná* 'stones' in 1961. From this, we know that the age set initiation ceremony happens once every thirty years. For instance, those who were at the *Rórá* age grade when the last age set formation ceremony took place, now can become *Bárá*.

1.7   Major Traditional Practices

The Mursi are famous for their three major traditional practices: marriage and bridewealth distribution system, duelling (of both sexes, male and female), and body decoration by wearing clay plates in their lower lips. In the sections below, I have described each traditional practice in brief.

1.7.3 *Marriage*
There are five different types of marriages in the Mursi, and each has its own divorce and dowry rates. In order for any one of these five marriage arrangements to take place, families of both (groom's and bride's) must first prove that the groom's claim to the bridewealth of his patrilineal kinswomen is in accordance with the rule that limit the kin reckoning.

Levirate (inheriting the wife of the deceased brother).—Marriage based on inheritance—when the older brother dies, the younger brother marries his older brother's wife. If a younger brother is not alive, then a marriage ceremony can be between the wife of the deceased and the person who is believed to lead or administer the property of the deceased and the whole family. All children born out of wedlock after this marriage will be called on behalf of the deceased.

Marriage based on mutual consent from both sides.—This marriage type involves parents' and relatives' of the boy and the girl, and the marriage is often arranged based on the goodwill of the parties involved. The rate of the bridewealth is determined by the length of time the male is required to pay within a certain period of time The girl's families could ask the boy to help their economy in various ways including working for her family, giving tobacco to her mother and so on. During this marriage process, when both parties are ready for marriage, the cow collection process begins—from his father, from his older brothers, from his cousins, and from all previous acquaintances.

Marriage based on Guma.—This is a marriage arrangement in which the girl's family is guilty of killing a person and needs to compensate the family of the deceased to avoid retribution. In addition to a girl, the compensation to be given to the family of the deceased may include any property, but cattle are usually included in the compensation. Roughly, 60 cattle shall be paid to the dead man's family. The main purpose of this marriage type is that only the girl who represents the compensation can stop the bloodshed between the families. If this girl gives birth to a child and once she pays all the damages to the deceased family, she can reclaim the cattle that was given as compensation. After the girl is married to the deceased's elder or younger brother, and she gaves birth to a son during her marriage, the mother has to give the child up to be adopted by the family of the deceased. Meanwhile, the deceased's family deduct seven cattle from the 60 and return the rest of cattle and the son's mother back to her family. Therefore, the child becomes the child of the deceased person's elder or younger brother, and grows up in the deceased person's family. Once she returns to her family, she stays at her father's house. Whenever a man wants to marry her, she can accept and be married again but this time she can only earn between 20 and 25 cattle; the minimum bridewealth.

However, if her first child is a girl, there is one additional rule that takes place in the *Guma* marriage arrangement. That is, if she gives birth to a girl during this marriage, the baby girl will be given to her family and the marriage will be extended until a son is born. This means, only a compensation of 'male person' can satisfy the deceased's family real demand.

Likewise, if the person killed by her family is woman, this girl will be treated as one of the deceased's family member until she gives birth to a daughter. In other word, the newborn daughter will be given to the deceased family in exchange for the woman killed by her family.

Forced marriage (ídáɲ, literally, 'control by force').—If a young female is found to be pregnant while her father is alive, it is considered a shame to her family. Therefore, first, she will be beaten until she tells the truth. Once the person who impregnated her is known, then the same is forced to marry her unconditionally. If this man does not agree to the new marriage proposal, he will have no choice but is compelled to allow his property to be plundered by her own people. In addition to this, if her family has had a good relationship with his family and friends in the past, the penalty will be high, because he is considered as the one who hurt not only the impregnated girl but also the relationship between the two families.

Marriage based on the consent between the two families—This type of marriage proposal takes place without the knowledge of the two young people. It is based on the two families' consent and needs. The boy's family is usually the one who visits the girl's family. To notify her family of the purpose of their visit. This notification is often started by the expression: 'We have come to your home to drink water'. Following this, there is a second expression used to start the negotiation: 'We are also here to ask your daughter for our boy'.

After the marriage deal is made with massive hospitality from the bride's side, the groom's family will return to the place where they came from. After this, whenever there is any social problem, it is attended to by the groom's family, at any time as long as the bride's family's request for help is in accordance with the existing marriage arrangement. Such requests for support from the bride's family often happens at times of difficulties at her family's home.

According to Mursi's tradition, there are mediators for all kinds of marriages who can implement the bridewealth distribution rules accurately; and the bridewealth is inevitable. The girl's voluntary expressions for her willingness to engage in the process can be shown at various occasions such as in market places, during *Doŋa* dancing, in the workplace, and so on. Once the girl agrees, it means that she is expressing her willingness to make a commitment. She expresses this in two steps: first by giving her own bracelet to the man she likes; second, by giving him her own neckless, and tying it on his hand.

1.7.4 Duelling

There are duelling matches for both sexes: the boys' is called *Dóŋà* 'pole fighting' whereas the girls' is called *Úlá* 'bracelet fighting'. *Donga* is a stick fighting contest that only happens once a year in different villages of the Mursi. *Úlá* on the other hand is a contest of Mursi girls' using 'strike iron bracelets'. The *Úlá* contest allows Mursi women to measure their own strength. The girls' *Úlá* fighting is also known as *dóŋàá dóólùŋ* 'girls' Donga'. Not much is known about the *Úlá* contest type. Therefore, I have focused on the pole or stick contest type.

The Mursi are well known for their traditional stick fighting contest known as 'Donga'. *Donga* has two meanings in Mursi: first it denotes a stick that all young, adult Mursi males carry for protection wherever they go about their daily routine. The second meaning is for a fighting contest between two young men from various Mursi villages.

This stick fighting contest is held on a yearly basis. Usually, it lasts for six days to a couple of weeks in a good harvest season, or in some seasons for less than a week if the harvest is not good. The *Donga* fights will be held around the second week of June lasting until the end of the month. Unmarried young men between 16 and 32 years will take part in the *Donga* contest. The contestants prepare themselves for the contest. By consuming cows' blood and milk a couple months ahead of the contest start. Young Mursi boys do not often eat the meat of their own cattle. Instead, they drink blood collected with a calabash after puncturing the neck artery of their favorite cow with an arrow. Making sure the blood loss will not cause harm to their most valued asset (the cattle). Both (blood and milk) can be consumed in three different forms: raw blood (their favorite one), cooked blood, and/or mixtures of blood and milk.

The wood used for the *Donga* fighting stick comes from a tree called *kàlóchí*, genus Grewia, and is cut from the mature and strong branches of this tree. The length of a *Donga* fighting stick is roughly between 2.60 and 3 meters, equivalent to the height of an adult man with outreached arms above the head. Although the *Donga* stick fighting is a dangerous contest that can cause injury or death, it is one of their most loved traditional ceremonies that the Mursi have kept for many generations as part of their unique traditional social gathering ceremonies. During my first fieldwork stays in the Mursi villages, I was able to attend one *Donga* ceremony.

1.7.5 *Lip Plate*

The Mursi women have probably become the last people in Africa to still wear large pottery or wooden discs or 'lip-plates' (*débìá tùgɔ̀ɲ*) in their lower lips. Another type of traditional decoration is the so-called 'ear-plugs' *débìá ɲàwàɲ*. Clay or wood plates are still worn by many unmarried girls as well as by child-bearing women. In contrast, the ear-plug/plate is also worn by boys. The lip-plate (*débìá tùgɔ̀ɲ*) is a prime symbol of their uniqueness and a major marker of Mursi identity that distinguishes them from other ethnic groups (their neighbours). For the *débìá tùgɔ̀ɲ*, the girl's lip is pierced when she reaches puberty. First, they stretch the size of the pierced lower lip by inserting wooden discs, later they wear a clay-plate once their lip is stretched. Women's lower lip should be stretched enough to be able to hold a clay-plate with a diameter of 12 cm or 14 cm. When a girl's 15 or 16 years old, her lower lip will be cut by her mother, or by another woman from the same village as her mother. The cut lip is held open by a wooden plug until it heals, this can take up to 3 months. It appears that it is up to the individual girl to decide how far the lip should be stretched, by inserting progressively larger plugs over a period of several months. Only a few girls follow up the processes of enlarging their lips seriously; that means, they make sure that their lips must take plates with a diameter of 12 centimeters or more.

The Mursi are an egalitarian community in many ways, this means that girls or womens have the right to decide for themselves to take part or not in the 'lip-piercing traditional culture'. Turton (mursi.org) described their lip-piercing

INTRODUCTION 33

tradition as 'untouched' and 'tribal'; yet it is actually done by on the basis of choice by the young girls. This old tradition of the Mursi is not something that some Mursi old women or men can impose on their girls by force. Many Mursi girls marry happily without their lips pierced. There is also a choice for Mursi women to decide to take up this tradition after they have had one or two children. The motivations are many but the main one is as a marker of an embodied morality. Lip-plate wearing is a unique tradition of Mursi in which the Mursi teach their children to be social, moral and healthy persons. There is quite an extraordinary connection between lip-plate wearing and female speech register. It was first noted by Yigezu (2001) who observed the articulatory and acoustic effects of lip-plates in the speech of Chai women (see § 2.10).

1.8 Cattle, Color Terms and Naming

The Mursi have a special appreciation of their cattle and the skin-colours of their cattle. The two, animate and the physical attribute of the animate, are intertwined. In many ways, in the Mursi community, life develops around activities that are related to cattle and cattle-oriented activities. Cattle and colour terms are the two most significant pastoralist as well as aesthetic values reflected everywhere in their day to day life. Their unique aesthetic value of cattle and colour patterns is what makes the Mursi distinct from other non-pastoralist ethnic groups in the region.

One can find cattle colours and patterns everywhere—from being the mark of wealth to religion. Cattle skin-colour is regarded by some Mursi elders as a cultural symbol of fertility. Cattle skin-colours can be reflected in a number of Mursi material cultures, which are decorations of cattle skin-colours and patterns. Anyone can hear or see an astonishing number of cattle skin-colour terms in the Mursi's day-to-day life; also in many life domains. This includes the recurrent use of terms for cattle skin-colour patterns in their names, clothes, home utensils, and so on. For the Mursi, mainly cattle skin-colour can provide colour pattern for dresses. Mursi colour patterns and terms refer to the skin-colour of their cattle and include green or blue. Only cattle can provide their full-fledged choices of colour palette.

The Mursi person naming system depends on the individual's cattle skin-colour choices. That is, Mursi men's names are indeed compound personal reference terms which usually consist of cattle skin-colours or patterns and other words. On a daily basis, I have observed that a few Mursi men wear collars that exactly match the coat-color of their favorite ox. Aside from cattle herding and some small scale seasonal farming activities, Mursi boys and girls (even adults) spend most of their time on colour experiments such as, painting various colours on their body (they call it 'body arts') and decorating cattle with various colour patterns which predominantly come from their cattle. When their favorite colour choice is not available from their favorite ox, they may pick up certain colours or colour-patterns from other animals or from any available sources. For example, the colour-pattern *tùlài* could be used to refer to "striped" or "tiger" or a similar pattern and represents a colour-pattern for 'streaked, or brindled, streaks, or reddish-brown'.

The shadow of trees on the floor may be described as *tùlài*, without reference to any specific colour-pattern. In order to get the best possible color patterns, they use various means in addition to the colours their cattle have. The practice of ox-modification or beautification and breeding the favorite ox are the two most valued skills that all Mursi men are expected to be equipped with as pastoralists.

The Mursi have nine established colour types, which are entirely derived from the skins of their cattle. They are: *kɔ̀rɔ̀i* 'black, black with blue-purple patches'; *hólí* 'white'; *gólóɲi* 'red, red-purple in high saturation, reddish'; *čài* ⟨*čàgì*⟩ 'green or blue (slate grey, green and blue bluish-grey; ash-coloured)'; *gidàɲi* 'grey, dirty white, red, orange and yellow in low saturation and gray'; *bilèj* ⟨*bilèi*⟩ 'yellow, (or brown with preponderance of yellow, yellowish-brown; tan)'; *čakɔ̀rɔ̀i* 'blue green, greenblack', *čahólí* 'blue, sky, green-white blue', and *régéj* 'pink; flesh-coloured; devil colour (a mental imagery)'.

In addition to aforementioned colour types which also display their own (formal) grammatical structure, there are thirteen colour patterns (see Table 8.6 for complete list of colour terms). Major patterns are *lúlúmí* 'dark brown, brownish colour'; *lùi* 'spotted (white with black head and rump, multi-spotted)'; *sórálí* 'reddish-brown with white belly'; *bálái* 'spots on back only, white back'; *biséní* 'black and white, black patches or spots on white'; *tùlài* 'streaked or brindled, typically, reddish-brown'; and *sírwài* 'dark brown colour, pattern blackish with cream undercoat'.

Mursi men's first names always have a compound word form "ox/bull+colour", based on 'ox/bull and the person's favorite ox/bull coat colour'. Another interesting point is that there are personal names with colour spectrum variations whose ranges could include two or more colours or colour patterns. For instance, a person called 'Òlítùlà' can find his favorite colour from various sources such as 'shades', 'tiger', 'mountain' (by association). Turton (1980: 329) wrote that there is a mountain in Mursiland called *kútúlátúlá* [kútúla+tùlà] ⟨mountain+tula⟩. So, the colour pattern *tùlài* is a derived notion from the mountain's 'streaky' appearance produced by the sun shining on its steep western slopes.

TABLE 1.4   Colours and patterns

Personal names	Colour/ pattern	Similes/association	Associated animals or concrete objects
òlígɔ́lɔ́ɲ	gɔ́lɔ́ɲi	lòmákáwúló, gɔ́lɔ́ɲmèrì	lòmáj 'Ximenia Americana'; a small yellow-orange succulent fruits are edible; káwúló 'ear of cattle'; mèrì 'many'
òlíkɔ̀rɔ̀	kɔ̀rɔ̀i	nèjmèdèrè, rúgámèdèrè	nèj ⟨nèbì⟩ 'buffalo'; mèdèrè 'sheep'; rúgá 'horn'
òlígìɗàɲí	gìɗàɲí	káwúlòlíŋɔ́, gírlèmútíláj	káwúló 'ear of cattle' múlèn 'rhinoceros'
òlélùì	lùì	sámèkáwúló, sámèlù	sámé 'white waist belt'; káwúló 'ear of cattle'
òlísóráĺí	sóráĺí	lugɔ́lɔ́ɲ báná, lugɔ́lɔ́ɲ sènɔ̀	lùì 'back head and buttocks' sènɔ̀ 'hands, front legs'
òlíkíwó	kìwó	sámèkíwó, sámètáwáj	sámè 'white waist belt'; táwáj 'kidney, wing'
òlíɓálá	ɓáláí	čárdónímèdèrè, dóntórí	čár 'leopard'; dɔ̀wùn 'zebra'; tórí 'north'

So in accordance with the compound word form 'ox/bull+colour', a total of ten major Mursi men's names exist: *òlígɔ́lɔ́ɲ* ⟨ox/bull+red⟩ (Oligolony) *òlíkɔ̀rɔ̀* ⟨ox/bull+black⟩ (Olikoro), *òlíɓàlà* ⟨ox/bull+leaf (sg.)⟩ (Olibhala), and so on. An individual man can be called by one of these first names on the basis of his family's wide range colour preferences. The colour preferences are similes of animals or objects. Although these similes refer to default names of animals or objects, they can directly reflect colours or colour pattern of objects by way of cognitive semantic association. They may occur in hetero-compound forms, which means that animals, trees or concrete other objects could combine and produce the colour spectrum of a given family. Table 1.4 below, illustrates the way in which Mursi personal names are produced from various coat-colours of cattle, colour patterns of cattle, and some similes of animals or concrete objects.

For example, when we see the personal name *òlígɔ́lɔ́ɲ*, it is a compound word composed of *òlí* 'ox/bull' and *gɔ́lɔ́ɲi* 'red'. It has two similes: one composed of two concrete objects *lòmáj* and *kawulo* while the other is composed of *gɔ́lɔ́ɲi* and *mèrì*. Thus, a person called by the name *òlígɔ́lɔ́ɲ* can also be recognized by the two similes *lòmákáwúló* and *gɔ́lɔ́ɲmèrì*. Names of individuals can also be composed of similes that consist of one or more than one name of animals or objects that are associated the color pattern of the bull. For example, a person called *òlíɓálá* can be named after the bull that has *ɓáláí* colour pattern, but the word *ɓáláí* does not designate colour in its own. Thus the word *ɓáláí* requires similes associating the person's name and his favorite Ox colour with the colour of other animals or objects that have similar colours or colour patterns. Therefore, two animal names exist as similes: čár, because the colour of the person's favorite ox/bull resembles a 'leopard'; and has a stripe like dɔ̀wùn 'zebra' stretched horizontally on the back. The strip on the back of the ox/bull resembles a horn of a sheep (a straight-shaped horn of a sheep). The word tórí 'North' refers to the stripe on the ox that starts from the head of the ox (North; left) and reaches to its tail South (right).

Outside of the 'ox/bull+colour' form, there are men's names that have 'bàr+' forms. The term bàr (lit. 'night') is a socio-spatial oriented reference name which may be given to men based on the entities, spatial conditions, or celestial bodies, available in the surrounding environment at the time of their birth. However, when bàr is used in naming, it can mean 'man of', for example, bárkámán 'man+war' (lit. 'one who is born at the time of war'). Accordingly, these sorts of names may include: bárgɔ̀lɔ̀ɲ 'man+red', bártáj 'man+moon/month (sg.)', bárkámán 'man+war', bárdórí 'man+house (sg.)', etc.

Women's personal names can be formed by combining ŋa+colour or any other nouns. Women's personal names differ from that of men's in that they must contain the inherently gendered noun ŋàhà 'woman' or adjective ŋàhì 'female'. Some of Mursi women names include: ŋàbìò (Ngabìò) 'woman+cow (pl.)/cattle', ŋàkídó (Ngakidho) ⟨woman+river⟩, ŋàkútúl (Ngakútúl) ⟨woman+mountain⟩, ŋàdóólé (Ngadhole) ⟨woman+girl⟩, ŋàlúsá (Ngalúsà) ⟨woman+boy (pl.)⟩, etc.

1.9 Linguistic Affiliation

In terms of linguistic affiliation, Mursi is one of the Southeast Surmic group language within the Eastern Sudanic Branch of the Nilo-Saharan family. From the Surmic languages, Mursi, Chai, Tirma, Bodi, Me'en, and Kwegu (aslo Koegu)/Muguji are spoken in Ethiopia. The other languages, Didinga, Narim, Tenet, Murle, and Baale are spoken in Sudan (see more on Diagram 1.2).

It was Fleming (in 1983) who proposed using the term Surmic instead of Surma as a family label (Dimmendaal 1998: 9). Among the various issues, the most important point to mention with regard to the classification of the Nilo-Saharan 'Super family' sub-branches and smaller groups is that there are certain inconsistencies until now. To mention just a few, Cerulli in 1942, proposed that various languages classified under Surmic (Tirma, Me'en (also Mekan), etc.) should be included in the Nilotic sub-branch. But, at that time, the 'Nilotic' which Cerulli refers to includes languages which belong to other language families such as Dime. Dime is an Omotic language within the Afro-asiatic

INTRODUCTION 37

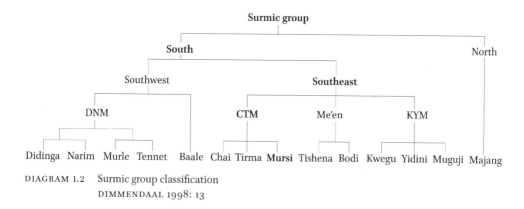

DIAGRAM 1.2 Surmic group classification
DIMMENDAAL 1998: 13

'Super Family' (cf. Dimmendaal 1998: 4). Since then, a number of group names have been proposed for the current Surmic group languages. To list some: 'Murle group' for Didinga-Murle and 'Suri Group' for the Southeastern branch of Surmic (Bryant 1945), 'Beir-Didinga Group', (including Murle (also Beir) Murzu, Longarim, Didinga, Suri, Mekan, Surma) (Greenberg 1955); Didinga-Murle Group (Tucker and Bryan 1956), Surma (Bender 1971), and so on. As a result of this, it is Fleming's (1983) proposal that has got a wider acceptance by many Nilo-Saharan linguistic experts. Fleming classified the so-called Surmic group languages into three clusters: Southwestern group (includes Murle, Didinga, Baale, and so on), Southeastern group (includes Suri, Tirma, Mursi, Me'en. Kwegu, and so on), and North(ern). However, as the latest genetic classification of Surmic languages, Dimmendaal (1998: 13) proposed a new idea for classifying Surmic group languages, and new abbreviations, CTM (Chai, Tirma, Mursi), YKM (Yidinit, Kwegu, Muguji) (both are Southeastern group languages), and DNM (Didinga, Narim, Murle, Tennet) Southwestern group languages. Following Abbink's (1992) clustering of the CTM group, Mursi's linguistic affiliation is within this cluster. These classifications and sub-groupings, however, doesn't include Nyaalam, an endangered Nilo-Saharan language, which is identified and described a couple of years ago by Yigezu (2018).

1.10 Sociolinguistic Situation

Despite the fact that they have a higher level of understanding of the languages spoken by their neighbors, the Mursi can be described as a monolingual society. There is a high degree of mutual intelligibility between the speakers of Mursi and Me'en (Chai) languages. Both languages can form a dialectal continuum of the Southeastern Surmic group. When we consider the nature of the

Mursi speaker language skills, it is very rare to find bilingual or multilingual speakers who are able to communicate or effectively use different languages spoken in the neighboring areas. This means, the Mursi people can be regarded as 'monolinguals' despite the fact that they live in close contact with its neighbours who are alike linguistically as well as culturally. The 2007 National census of Ethiopia reported that the total population of the Mursi ethnic group is approximately 7,500, of which more than 98% were identified as monolinguals in Mursi whereas the rest 2% were bilinguals/multilinguals they speak their native language and at least one more language of their neighbours. This is due to the fact that the Mursi see themselves as well as their languages as very distinct—even from their close neighbours who speak related languages such as Chai and Tirma. Only a few younger people have some competence in Amharic.

Until recently, young Mursi who attend formal schooling in public schools have constituted less than 1% of the total population Literacy rate in second language. As far as I know, there is one primary school (grade 1–4) in Mákkí village where Mursi children attend some subjects in their native language. Until 1989, Mursi had no orthography, consequently it was not a written language. Then, in 1989, a missionary organization called SIM developed an Amharic-based orthography (based on Ethiopic scripts/alphabets). Following this, in 2005, Yigezu has developed a Latin-based orthography for the language. However, as to the vitality level of the *munɛn* language itself, one can say that it is increasing, especially in the last ten years. Currently, a trilingual Mursi-English-Amharic Dictionary is available compiled by David Turton, Moges Yigezu and Olisorali Olibùì (published in 2008).

1.11 Previous Studies; Ethnographic Exploration in the Lower Omo Valley

An ethnographic research exploration into the Lower Omo Valley in general and the Mursi territory in particular was started in the late 19th century. The first exploration attempt in the Mursi area was in 1888 by Count S. Teleki and L.von Hohnel, who were able to reach the northern shore of Lake Rudolf (Turkana). At the time, they saw the Omo River in a huge flood. In 1895, an American medical doctor and explorer called Arthur Donaldson Smith arrived at the Northern end of Lake Rudolf from the east, and attempted to advance further northwards to the river of Omo and to reach the Mako [Mago] river. In 1896, a British explorer, soldier, hunter and travel writer Artur H. Neumann made an expedition to Lake Rudolf and travelled north along the Omo as far as its junction with the Mago. Unfortunately attempts by these explorers were unsuccessful, because none of these explorers reached the area currently called South Omo Zone (often referred to as Lower Omo Valley), and they never encountered an ethnic group called the Mursi.

It was only after 1896 that explorations became successful in many ways. In 1896, an Italian Geographical Society expedition led by a man called Vittorio Bottego travelled southwards through Mursi territory, following the left bank of the Omo River as far as Lake Rudolf. According to Turton (1973: 416), Bottego was the first explorer who reached Mursi country.

The following year, in 1897, H.S. Canendish followed the Omo River northwards from Lake Rudolf as far as the Mako. For the first time, in 1897, the ethnonym 'Murutu' which refers to the then Mursi people was mentioned in the work of Canendish. He also described them (the Mursi) as numerous, strong and rich people. Another man who had the opportunity to visit the Mursi area was A.D. Smith. In 1900, Smith made a journey to the North of Lake Rudolf. Consequently, he reported that the Dassanech had almost ceased to exist. The 'Mursu' (Mursi) on the other hand had escaped the raiders and were in a flourishing condition.

Between 1900 and 1950, several European explorers had the chance to visit the Turkana, the Lower Omo Valley areas and the people who live in these areas. To mention some: J.J. Harrisson in (1900) (reached north-eastern corner of the Omo River), R. de Bourg de Bozas in (1902) (reached the junction of the Omo and Mako), and C.W. Gwynn in 1909 (reached up to the right bank of the Omo River). He later published his journey in 1911.

In 1952, E. Haberland made an expedition to the Bodi (Tishena) area and spent a few days until he was forced to return northwards due to lack of supplies and the deaths of his mules. In 1966, he published an article entitled 'Zur Sprache der Bodi, Mursi and Yidenic in Süd-West-Äthiopien' on *New Afrikanistische Studien*.

David Turton is the first person who studied the social organization of the Mursi people and wrote much on the anthropological side of this group. Since his first fieldwork in the Mursi society in 1968, he wrote on a number of topics regarding Mursi social structure, economy, migration movements, cultural and traditional practices, and so on. In years following 1968 (1968–1970), Turton carried out two anthropological field studies and was able to learn the Mursi language as well. By combining his Mursi knowledge and the information he obtained from the two field studies, in 1976, he and Bender were able to publish the first grammatical sketch of the Mursi language (less than 30 pages). He later published this grammar in French in 1981, under the title 'Le Mùn' ('The Mùn (Mursi))'. In his PhD dissertation ('A Comparative Study of the Phonetics and Phonology of Surmic Languages'), Yigezu (2001: 92–99) revised the phonological system of the language. The latest publication, but one that has made a huge contribution to the language is that of Mütze (2014) titled 'A sketch of the Mursi language'. In her description, Mütze pointed out a number of important features of the language such as Noun Modification Constructions (NMC), aspect, mood, valency changing derivations, and so on. On related languages, Abbink (1991, 2013), Arensen (1998), and Dimmendaal (1998, 2001, 2010, 2011) are among a few scholars who published various scholarly works of linguistic and anthropological studies.

1.12 Fieldwork Methodology and Language Data

This grammar is the first detailed description of the Mursi language written through an immersion fieldwork approach following my two field trips to the villages of the Mursi community in 2017 and in 2019. Based on immersion fieldwork methods (cf. Aikhenvald 2015, Dixon 2010a), which is a suitable fieldwork approach to learn the language, the researcher stays in the villages of the communities who speak the language under study. My first field trip duration in the Mursi community villages was from November 2016 to October 2017 (for about 11 months), and the second was from October 2018 to January 2019 (three months).

The data collected during my two field trips include mainly an extensive corpus of texts of different genres, from different speakers, and from different locations.

Following these field trips, I have been able to record more than 40 hours of audio recordings of stories from different genres (history, stories, sociocultural, and day-to-day life activities, songs, and other). Of this, a four hour audio recording has been transcribed and annotated (yielding over 1000 pages). A four-hour video footage is also available (because participant observation is very important). In addition, the corpus includes hundreds of pages of handwritten field notes, 26 stories (texts), 2 songs, 3 bible chapters, and more. Of the 26 texts, four are attached as appendices.

The bulk of my time in the fieldwork was spent on recording, transcribing, and interlinearizing these texts. All the texts used in this grammar were collected from 16 native speakers of Mursi (language consultants), of whom 14 were males and two were females. The name of my Mursi consultants are as follows: Bàrihuny Girinomeri Araro Toko (30+, Male) (primary consultant; grade 10 student), Bàrkadhe Kulumedere (28+, Male) (secondary consultant; he is currently studying for his Bachelor of Arts in Translation in Kenya), Olirege

Regge (29, Male), Òlítùlà Olibùì (26, Male), Ngarugo (24, Female), Olelu Nyamanikiwo (17, Male), Olikoro Runèbìsala Dumalo (34, Male), Olikoro Takui (28, Male), Bàrmoy (32, Male), Olikoro Moges (26, Male†), Oliregge Bikirinto (23, Male), Ngarori Kashai (19, Female), Arsiregge Gomonyokawulo (40+, Male), Bàrgolony (22+, Male; grade 12 student), Olelu Olibùì (30+, Male; works at SIM, a missionary organization on bible translation), and Bàrtui Bergere (30+, Male; Mago Park Guard/militia). All the data were recorded in three particular places: Romos (Hayl wuha) (one of the Mursi villages about 80 km from Jinka Town), Salamago (Hana Mursi; the main Woreda for Mursi, Bodi and Dime), and Jinka Town (specifically at South Omo Research (SORC) and surrounding areas).

The data have been analyzed within a theoretical framework called Basic Linguistic Theory (BLT) (Dixon 2010a, 2010b and 2012). This is a theory which offers a number of appropriate options to describe what is happening in the language under study. In light of BLT, the all-round text analysis has produced fourteen chapters covering the phonology, morphology and syntax of the language.

CHAPTER 2

Phonology

2.1 Introduction

Mursi is a language with a medium number of phonemes. However, for a large portion of the phonological analysis presented in different sections of this chapter, I believe that the following expression best describes the phonemic inventories of Mursi: 'a language with a complex phonological system'. Especially, at the level of phonological word and grammatical word identification, vowels tend to be highly complex as the language also undergoes an extensive vowel coalescence, harmony, copying, deletion, change, subtraction, and so on. Mursi also has two tone registers: High and Low, and both are contrastive and play significant roles both at the lexical and grammatical levels. In addition, as an agglutinating and highly synthetic language that takes up to ten morphemes per word, morpheme boundaries are another issue that poses complexity in the morphophonological analysis.

Therefore, in sections of the chapter, notes on orthographic and phonetic transcriptions (§ 2.2), inventory of phonemes (§ 2.3), syllable structures (§ 2.4), phonological processes which governs the morphophonological rules (§ 2.5), tone (§ 2.6), and phonological and grammatical words (§ 2.7) are discussed in detail.

2.2 Notes on Orthography and Phonetic Transcriptions

As Mursi is a hitherto unwritten language, it has no fixed orthographic system designed for literacy and other official communication domains. However, there were few attempts made to introduce one of the two common orthographic systems often used in many Ethiopian languages—the Ge'ez (Ethiopic) script and the Latin script. In fact, the Mursi still use the Ge'ez script on a daily basis for some formal and informal purposes such as writing letters at the lower government and administrative levels, courts, informal literacy workbooks and textbooks, and so on. Side by side, the Latin-based script was designed by Yigezu (2005: 246) as he puts it, 'for the transliteration of Mursi texts in order to enable the reader to reproduce the sounds of Mursi speech with reasonable accuracy' (see also Turton et al., 2008: 11–13). Table 2.1 below is a Latin-based orthography suggested for Mursi consonant and vowel inventories by Yigezu.

PHONOLOGY

TABLE 2.1   Latin-based orthography of Mursi

Phoneme in (IPA)	Grapheme	Phoneme in (IPA)	Grapheme	Phoneme in (IPA)	Grapheme
/t/	⟨t⟩	/m/	⟨m⟩	/i/	⟨i⟩
/b/	⟨b⟩	/n/	⟨n⟩	/e/	⟨e⟩
/d/	⟨d⟩	/ɲ/	⟨ny⟩	/ɛ/	⟨ɛ⟩
/k/	⟨k⟩	/ŋ/	⟨ng⟩	/a/	⟨a⟩
/g/	⟨g⟩	/l/	⟨l⟩	/ɔ/	⟨ɔ⟩
/s/	⟨s⟩	/r/	⟨r⟩	/o/	⟨o⟩
/z/	⟨z⟩	/w/	⟨w⟩	/u/	⟨u⟩
/ʃ/	⟨sh⟩	/j/	⟨y⟩		
/h/	⟨h⟩	/ʔ/	⟨'⟩		
/č/	⟨ch⟩	/ɓ/	⟨bh⟩		
/dʒ/	⟨j⟩	/ɗ/	⟨dh⟩		

Table 2.2 below presents the Ge'ez (Ethiopic) script based on orthographic representation of Mursi phonemes.

Therefore, the orthographic representation of Mursi sounds with Ge'ez[1] graphemes treats both consonant and vowel phonemes as one grapheme or one alphabetical letter rather than as two separate graphemes or letters (as a syllabic script). Note that neither of them mark tone.

With respect to sound representation, throughout this grammar, the phonemic inventories were represented by the standard symbols of the International Phonetic Alphabet (IPA) transcriptions. Likewise, throughout all the sections of this grammar, standard transcription notations were used whenever deemed necessary. These include: phonemic is shown by slash notation / /, phonetic by square bracket [ ], and grapheme by angle bracket ⟨ ⟩. For example, the palatal voiceless affricate will be represented as phonemic /č/, phonetic [č], and grapheme ⟨ch⟩.

---

1   Note that the Ge'ez (Ethiopic) scripts (also known as Ge'ez abugida) are always written in a syllabary system, i.e. consonants and vowels are represented by a single grapheme.

TABLE 2.2 Ge'ez/Ethiopic-based orthography of Mursi

Phonemes			Vowels				
Consonants	[ɛ]	[u]	[i]	[a]	[e]	[o]	[ɔ]
[l] ለ	ለ	ሉ	ሊ	ላ	ሌ	ሎ	ሎ
	[lɛ]	[lu]	[li]	[la]	[le]	[lo]	[lɔ]
[m] ም	መ	ሙ	ሚ	ማ	ሜ	ም	ም
	[mɛ]	[mu]	[mi]	[ma]	[me]	[mo]	[mɔ]
[r] ር	ረ	ሩ	ሪ	ራ	ሬ	ር	ር
	[rɛ]	[ru]	[ri]	[ra]	[re]	[ro]	[rɔ]
[s] ስ	ሰ	ሱ	ሲ	ሳ	ሴ	ሶ	ሶ
	[sɛ]	[su]	[si]	[sa]	[se]	[so]	[sɔ]
[ʃ] ሽ	ሸ	ሹ	ሺ	ሻ	ሼ	ሾ	ሾ
	[ʃɛ]	[ʃu]	[ʃi]	[ʃa]	[ʃe]	[ʃo]	[ʃɔ]
[b] ብ	በ	ቡ	ቢ	ባ	ቤ	ቦ	ቦ
	[bɛ]	[bu]	[bi]	[ba]	[be]	[bo]	[bɔ]
[t] ት	ተ	ቱ	ቲ	ታ	ቴ	ቶ	ቶ
	[tɛ]	[tu]	[ti]	[ta]	[te]	[to]	[tɔ]
[č] ች	ቸ	ቹ	ቺ	ቻ	ቼ	ቾ	ቾ
	[čɛ]	[ču]	[či]	[ča]	[če]	[čo]	[čɔ]
[ŋ] ኝ	ኘ	ኙ	ኚ	ኛ	ኜ	ኞ	ኞ
	[ŋɛ]	[ŋu]	[ŋi]	[ŋa]	[ŋe]	[ŋo]	[ŋɔ]
[n] ን	ነ	ኑ	ኒ	ና	ኔ	ኖ	ኖ
	[nɛ]	[nu]	[ni]	[na]	[ne]	[no]	[nɔ]
[ɲ] ኝ	ኘ	ኙ	ኚ	ኛ	ኜ	ኞ	ኞ
	[ɲɛ]	[ɲu]	[ɲi]	[ɲa]	[ɲe]	[ɲo]	[ɲɔ]
[ʔ] ⟨ዐ⟩/⟨አ⟩	አ	ኡ	ኢ	አ	ኤ	አ	ኦ
	[ʔɛ]	[ʔu]	[ʔi]	[ʔa]	[ʔe]	[ʔo]	[ʔɔ]
[k] ክ	ከ	ኩ	ኪ	ካ	ኬ	ኮ	ኮ
	[kɛ]	[ku]	[ki]	[ka]	[ke]	[ko]	[kɔ]
[h] ኽ	ኸ	ኹ	ኺ	ኻ	ኼ	ኾ	-ኽ
	[hɛ]	[hu]	[hi]	[ha]	[he]	[ho]	[hɔ]
[w] ው	ወ	ዉ	ዊ	ዋ	ዌ	ዎ	ዎ
	[wɛ]	[wu]	[wi]	[wa]	[we]	[wo]	[wɔ]
[z] ዝ	ዘ	ዙ	ዚ	ዛ	ዜ	ዞ	-ዝ
	[zɛ]	[zu]	[zi]	[za]	[ze]	[zo]	[zɔ]
[j] ይ	የ	ዩ	ዪ	ያ	ዬ	ዮ	ዮ
	[jɛ]	[ju]	[ji]	[ja]	[je]	[jo]	[jɔ]

TABLE 2.2 Ge'ez/Ethiopic-based orthography of Mursi (cont.)

Phonemes			Vowels				
Consonants	[ɛ]	[u]	[i]	[a]	[e]	[o]	[ɔ]
[d] ደ	ደ	ዱ	ዲ	ዳ	ዴ	ዶ	ዷ
	[dɛ]	[du]	[di]	[da]	[de]	[do]	[dɔ]
[dʒ] ጀ	ጀ	ጁ	ጂ	ጃ	ጄ	ጆ	ጇ
	[dʒɛ]	[dʒu]	[dʒi]	[dʒa]	[dʒe]	[dʒo]	[dʒɔ]
[g] ገ	ገ	ጉ	ጊ	ጋ	ጌ	ጎ	ጏ
	[gɛ]	[gu]	[gi]	[ga]	[ge]	[go]	[gɔ]
[ɓ] ɓ	ɓ	ɓ	ɓ	ɓ	ɓ	ɓ	
	[ɓɛ]	[ɓu]	[ɓi]	[ɓa]	[ɓe]	[ɓo]	[ɓɔ]
[ɗ] ɗ	ɗ	ɗ	ɗ	ɗ	ɗ	ɗ	ɗ
	[ɗɛ]	[ɗu]	[ɗi]	[ɗa]	[ɗe]	[ɗo]	[ɗɔ]

2.3 Inventory of Phonemes

Mursi has a total of 29 phonemes. With respect to certain consonant phonemes, Mursi seems to be to some extent unique compared to the rest Southeastern Surmic group languages in that it lacks the voiceless labial fricative /f/, the voiceless bilabial stop /p/, and ejectives (§ 2.3.1). Nevertheless, like all other languages of the group, it has retained a seven-vowel system (§ 2.3.2).

2.3.1 *Consonant Phonemes*

Mursi has 22 consonant phonemes: six voiceless and voiced stops, two implosives, four voiceless and voiced fricatives, two voiceless and voiced affricates, four nasals, two glides, and two liquids (a lateral /l/ and a trill /r/). Other languages of the Southeastern Surmic group also have an almost comparable number of consonant phonemes. Table 2.3 below displays the full list of the inventory of consonant phonemes.

2.3.1.1 Stops

This category of stops is comprised of six phonemes—three voiceless and three voiced. The voiceless stops are /t/, /k/ and /ʔ/. The voiced stops are /b/, /d/ and /g/. Except for the voiceless glottal stop /ʔ/, all the other members of the group can occur at almost all positions in nominal and verbal roots. The occurrence of the glottal stop is limited in all positions in a word. Mütze (2014: 27) points out that it is used to separate like vowels across word morpheme bound-

TABLE 2.3 Consonant phonemes of Mursi

	Bilabial (labio-labial)	Alveolar			Palatal	Velar	Glottal
		Apico-dental	Apico-alveolar	Post-alveolar	Lamino-palatal	Dorso-velar	
Voiceless stop		t [t]				k [k]	ʔ [ʔ]
Voiced stop	b [b]	d [d]				g [g]	
Implosive	ɓ [ɓ] ⟨bh⟩			ɗ [ɗ] ⟨dh⟩			
Voiceless fricative			s [s]		ʃ [ʃ] ⟨sh⟩		h [h]
Voiced fricative			z [z]				
Voiceless affricate					č [č] ⟨ch⟩		
Voiced affricate					ʤ [ʤ] ⟨dz⟩		
Nasal	m [m]		n [n]		ɲ [ɲ] ⟨ny⟩	ŋ [ŋ] ⟨ng⟩	
Lateral (Liquid)			l [l]				
Trill (Liquid)			r [r]				
Glide	w [w]				j [j] ⟨y⟩		

aries. That is, /ʔ/ is being inserted between proclitics that end with vowels and phonological or grammatical words that begin with the same vowels, as in (2.1a–b).

(2.1) a. /ŋà=àhà=à/ > [ŋàʔàhàà]
DEM=thing.PL=NEAR
'These things'

b. /ŋà=án=ó/ > [ŋàʔánó]
NEG.IMPERV=COP3.IMPERV=NEG
'It is not; are not'

However, the word that is to be combined with the proclitic may sometimes begin with a different vowel from that of the proclitic. An instance of this type is found between the negative imperfective proclitic ŋà= and words containing vowel length as a result of intervocalic consonant deletion. The verb óól 'beg, pray, plead' is one example of a word-initial vowel length, which is a disyllabic verb root in three other Southeastern Surmic group languages closest to Mursi—ógól (Tirmaga and Chai) and oʔol (Me'en):

(2.2) /ŋà=óól-í=ó/ > [ŋàʔóólíó]
NEG.IMPERV=beg-2SG.SU.IMPERV=NEG
'You (sg.) beg'

PHONOLOGY 47

However, the effect of the glottal stop may not be audible in fast speech. At word-final positions, it occurs in a few words such as *hóhúʔ* 'a rope made of cow skin' (contrasted with *hóhú* 'lung') *beleʔ* 'bald' and *bánáʔ* 'fly'. The status of the glottal stop requires additional investigations.

Regarding the occurrence of stops in affixes and clitics, they can be divided into three groups—those that occur in affixes and clitics, those that occur only in affixes and those that do not occur in either. Those that occur in affixes and clitics are /t/ and /g/, as in (2.3a–c) and (2.4a–c).

(2.3) a. /té-hén-ú/
       PERV-want.PERV-2SG.SU.PER
       'You (sg.) wanted'

       b. /bàbì-tín/
          fool-N.STATE
          'Foolishness'

       c. /ŋà=zùg=tùnù/
          DEM=people=FAR
          'Those people'

(2.4) a. /bí-ɲóg-i/ > [bi⟨g/k⟩-ɲógi]
          break-AGT.NOMZ-SG
          '(a) breaker'

       b. /sààn-ɲògà/
          news/story-PL
          'news/stories'

       c. [[gòdón=g-à]ₙₚ-à   g=àɲù]ₙₚ
          brother=PERT:PL-1.PSR-RSTR PL.PSD=1SG.PSR
          'My brothers'

The voiceless velar stop /k/ appears in one predictable position, i.e. in the *k(V)*- prefix, but carrying most important grammatical information of the language—or it is a polyfunctional prefix shape in the following morphological markers: first person singular and plural subjects (S/A), agentless passive, subjunctive and hortative/jussive moods.

(2.5) /kí-hín-í/
       1SU-want.IMPERV-1SG.SU.IMPERV
       'I want'

The two velar stops /k/ and /g/ may be neutralized to the glottal stop /ʔ/ syllable as well as word-finally (see further discussion under §2.5.3). The remaining three stops—/b/, /d/ and /ʔ/ do not occur in affixes and clitics (see Table 2.5). With regard to the occurrence of stops in affixes, it is possible to generalize that with the exception of /b/, /d/ and /ʔ/, all can occur in various positions within affixes—whether in nominal or verbal words.

2.3.1.2 Implosives

Mursi has retained only the bilabial and post-alveolar implosives /ɓ/ and /ɗ/ from Proto-Surmic. In this regard, Mursi aligns with the other two of the Southeastern Surmic group languages—Me'en and koegu. But Chai, another member of the group has retained full range of implosives including velar implosive /ʄ/ (cf. Yigezu (2001: 93–115)). For instance, in terms of pronouncing of the following words, a notable difference can be observed between Mursi and Chai-Tirmaga (also subsumed under a single ethnonym, Suri) speakers.

(2.6) | | Mursi | Chai-Tirmaga | Meaning |
       |---|------------|--------------|------------|
       | a.| [régéi⟨j⟩] | [reʄɛ] | 'pink' |
       | b.| [gìgà] | [ʄiʄa] | 'bone (pl.)' |
       | c.| [gín] | [ʄin] | 'ask' |

On the other hand, all languages of the Southwestern Surmic group have retained a full range of implosives. Majang, another Surmic language which constitutes a single North Surmic group in its own, does not have this phoneme.

Except in the word-final position, the bilabial implosive /ɓ/ occurs in all nominal and verbal word positions: *bàrá* 'rope made from grass (pl.)', *tólóɓέ* 'lizard', *dòrɓìn* 'a kind of tree' (Desert Rose Adenium obesum), *ɓésí* 'hatch', and *ɓág* 'eat'. Despite its occurrence in verb root medial position being unquestionable, it is very limited. This seems due to the fact that a great majority of Mursi verb roots are monosyllabic, and whenever it occurs at initial position of a monosyllabic verb root but is absent from the medial position of a verb root, it means that it is within polysyllabic verbs. Accordingly, there are a few polysyllabic verbs containing this phoneme whose roots appear to be related to ideophones or syllables with inherently reduplicated shapes such as *ɓáɓárí* 'tremble', *ɓíɓíʃí* 'to get goose bumps', and *ɓóɓódέ* 'completely upset'.

However, I have found one polysyllabic verb in my data with /ɓ/, i.e. /tàɓúlé/ and /tàmúlé/ 'dash', with /ɓ/ being in free variation with the bilabial nasal /m/. The bilabial implosive /ɓ/ does not occur in affixes and clitics. Despite this, an instance of grammaticalization was found which appears to be on the way of evolving into a proclitic. That is, the polysemous word [ɓá] 'place, land, country, world' seems to be losing its independence and is bonding/fusing with the near distance marker enclitic =ùnù,—in ŋàɓùnù 'there', as in (2.7).

(2.7) /ŋà=ɓá=ùnù/ > [ŋà=ɓ=ùnù] > [ŋàɓùnù]
DEM=place=FAR
'That place' > 'There'

Borrowed words from Amharic containing the bilabial ejective /p'/ are always readjusted to the bilabial implosive /ɓ/. Such words include: *t'äräp'p'eza* > [*taraɓeza*] 'table', *p'et'ros* > [*ɓitirosi*] 'Peter', and *f(p)'ilip'p'os* > [*ɓilaɓosi*] 'Philip'. Personal names listed here appear to be pronounced in the context of the bible translation which otherwise would have different pronunciations when pronounced in English. For example, 'Paul' would be [bɔ́ɔ̀l] (cf. Mütze 2014).

The velar implosive /ɗ/ appears at all positions in verbal roots, and at word-initial and word-final positions in nominal roots—*dúgúm* 'curve, (bend)', *éséɗ* 'think, calculate', *máɗ* 'teach, advise', *ɗɔ̀è* 'hump', *kéɗɛ́m* 'traditional drinking bowl' and so on. Like the bilabial implosive, the velar implosive /ɗ/ appears in inherently reduplicated verb roots such as *ɓéɗɛ́ɗɛ́g* 'flash (lightening)' (+CV:REDUP) and *kéɗɛ́kéɗɛ́* 'whisper (sense-speech)' (CVCV:REDUP). Implosives are highly unlikely to occur in affixes and clitics. However, there is one instance found in which the velar implosive -*ɗ* functions as a marker of plural number on vowel-final verb roots in the perfective aspect.

(2.8) a. /k-íɗí-ɗ-á/
1SU-add/combine-PL.PERV-1PL.INC.SU.PERV
'We (inc.) combined (it)'

b. /lámí-ɗ-á/
search/find-PL.PERV-3PL.SU.PERV
'They searched'

There is also one interesting scenario where voiced geminate stops develop into implosives. This has also been noted in some Southwestern Surmic group languages such Baale (Yigezu 2001: 203–204; Dimmendaal 2011: 28). That is /bb/ > [ɓ], /dd/ > [ɗ], and /gg/ > [ɠ]. No such development or phonological change has been attested in the Southeastern Surmic group languages. This suggests that they could be an innovation in Southwestern Surmic group languages.

(2.9) òlíbíséní ádísáwá-jè ŋànì kɔ́ɔ́y-∅=ó
Olebhiseni addis.ababa-OBL NEG.PERV 3.SBJV.go-3.IRR=NEG
'Olebhiseni did not go to Addis Ababa.'

As it is shown in (2.9), the geminate voiced alveolar stop /dd/ (in Amharic) has triggered the velar implosive /ɗ/. With respect to the changes from voiced geminate stops to implosives, Yigezu (pp. 204) noted that Southwest Surmic languages result from earlier voiced geminated stops, a phonological change which further fed into the existing pattern of implosive consonants, probably by development.

Outside SWS languages, Mursi seems be an exception in that this development applies to Mursi. Moreover, Mursi may even further distinguish itself from both SES and SWS group languages because unlike in languages of these groups, the velar implosive /ɗ/ can be triggered by stress on the second syllable of the word containing the voiced alveolar stop /d/. See the examples given below.

(2.10) a. [bá-á [tán-á sú'dán-ùŋ]_{NP}]_{NP} nà nɔ̀ŋ té
country-RSTR side-RSTR Sudan-GEN CCN 3SG COP.3.PERV
hírí ódénéí-ni
man strong.ADJ-RS
'... on the other side of Sudan, he is a strong man there.' (MH 6:53:2)

b. [zùw-á so'dok-awu-jan-i]²
people-RSTR Sadducees-ADJ.PL:M-GEN
'People of the Sadducees'

2.3.1.3 Fricatives

Mursi has four fricatives: /s/, /z/, /ʃ/ and /h/. All occur word-initially and word-medially in both nominal as well as verbal words. However, except for the voiceless alveolar fricative /s/ they do not occur at word-final positions—áús 'rest, alight', érés 'cross', úŋús 'sleep'. Their absence from word-final position is due to the fact that either they are deleted or weakened. Two fricative phonemes; the

---

2 Note that the source of the stress in these two names is Amharic—the second noun, which is a modifier the head *zuwa*, contains the Amharic nominalizer -*awi* used to form adjectives expressing a quality or a characteristic, or name of a people. When it is -*awajan*, it refers to plural masculine (Leslau 1995: 240).

PHONOLOGY   51

alveolar /s/ and the glottal /h/, are deleted word-finally. The palatal fricative /ʃ/ is weakened word-finally to the palatal glide /j/. Word-finally, the palatal fricative /ʃ/ is weakened to the post-alveolar glide /j/. For example, *gàʃ* becomes *gàj* 'bush'. There is no good justification to explain why the alveolar fricative phoneme /s/ still stayed untouched at the root-final positions in verbs. It may not be just one but it seems highly convincing that there is generally one dominant phonotactic restriction which governs the roughly 90 percent of Mursi verb roots ending in consonants. That is, if the verb has a consonant-final ending, then it must be retained except in free variation scenarios such as the occurrence of /s/ in free variation with /h/. However, there is one exception in which this does not apply, i.e. when free variation exists.

For example, /s/ and /h/ can occur as free variants, as in *bús ~ búh* 'curse'. Or even between /s/ and /ʃ/ and /h/ and /ʃ/—*rès ~ rèʃ* 'die', *íh ~ íʃ* 'exist' > (it is *i* in underlying form). In fact the palatal fricative /ʃ/ may be weakened in word-final positions of nominal and verbal roots but not in ideophones. Since ideophones have a different phonology, they cannot be easily affected by any regular phonological rules as nouns and verbs (cf. Chapter 3). All, except the voiced alveolar fricative /z/ can occur in affixes: *nèbì-só(sí)* 'buffalo-PL', *áʃá-ʃá* (*áʃá-ì* (singular)) 'grandchildren', *hè-hì* 'body-PL', *dè-hɨ́ɲá* 'compound-PL', and so on. Although /s/ separately appears as a floating emphatic marker clitic (=*so*), they do not occur in clitics.

2.3.1.4   Affricates

Mursi has two affricates: the voiceless palatal affricate /č/ and its counterpart /ʤ/. Both appear in all word positions—*čɔ̀ré* 'hair', *čáč* 'exchange, translate, barter (of goods)', *húč* 'pay, avenge', *gúŋkàčùj* 'pumpkin', *múčúgí* 'half, few', *múʤùsì* 'roten' and so on. They also appear in inherently reduplicated words such as *ʤàmʤamì* 'mistaken' and *kúčúkúčú* 'silence, saying nothing'—by being a disyllabic word in σ₁=σ₂ symmetry or a polysyllabic word in CVCV=CVCV symmetry. Word-finally, both will be neutralized after they are being weakened to the post-alveolar glide /j/. (see §2.5.3 of this chapter). Only the voiceless palatal affricate /č/ is attested in affixes—such as *sìrò ~ síró-ča* 'eland/Nyala-PL', *kàbì ~ kàbì-čó* 'clan-PL', *kì-bìg-án-čo* (1.SBJV-break.PERV-MT-COM) 'I may/might break' and so on. Whereas both are not attested in clitics.

2.3.1.5   Nasals

Mursi has four consonantal nasal phonemes: the bilabial /m/, the alveolar /n/, the post-alveolar /ɲ/, and the velar /ŋ/. All the four nasal phonemes appear in all positions of a word. The bilabial nasal /m/: *mà* 'water', *tɔ̀mɔ̀n* 'ten', *ʤìm* 'lead'; the alveolar nasal /n/: *nani* 'expert', *múnúɗ* 'itch', *kún* 'come'; the post-alveolar nasal /ɲ/: *ɲɔ̀g* 'close, shut', *ɲàbì* 'ear', *tírɨ́ɲí* 'gum', *lɛ̀kɛ̀ɲ* 'knee', *gùɲ* 'see'; and the velar nasal /ŋ/: *ŋér* 'divide', *téŋér* 'frighten', and *nɔ̀ŋ* 's/he, it, (pro.)'. At syllable boundaries, the velar nasal /ŋ/ is most frequently followed by its homorganic counterparts /k/ and /g/—*bàŋkà* 'machete' and *gúŋgàčì* 'pumpkin' (see also § 2.5.6.1). Full or partially inherently reduplicated words may trigger such homorganic sequences, for example *kúŋkúŋ* 'one another' and *góŋgóɲ* 'murmur'.

All nasal phenomes appear in affixes: *kómórú-mò* ⟨priest-N.ST⟩ 'priesthood', *čúr-néj* ⟨wash-NOMZ⟩ 'washed (n.)', *táísí-ɲá* ⟨month-PL⟩ 'months, moons', *kɔ́ɔ́d-ɨ́ɲógí* ⟨kill-AGT.NOMZ⟩ 'a killer', *kò-jòg-ùŋ* ⟨PASS-tell.PERV-2pl.OBJ⟩ 'You (pl.) were not told', and so on. However, only the /n/ and /ŋ/ occur as both clitics—as a proclitic or as an enclitic, as in (2.11a–c).

(2.11) a. [rè-á   n=ùnù]_NP
           body-RSTR SG.PSD=2SG.PSR
           'Your (sg.) body'

       b. ŋànì   ké-dʒèm=nó
           NEG.PERV 1SU-lead.PERV=NEG
           'I have not yet gone.'

       c. [bá-á   [ŋà=lɔ́gt=á   kàmàn-ùɲ=ŋà]_NP]_NP ɨɲè
           place-RSTR DEM=issue=NEAR war-GEN=DEF   2SG
           sén-í   ɛ̀nɛ̀ŋ?
           say-2SG.SU.IMPERV how
           'What is your attitude toward war?'

2.3.1.6 Liquids

The set of this category has two consonant phonemes—the alveolar lateral /l/ and the alveolar trill /r/. Both can occur in all positions of a word, as in *lámí* 'find', *kúli* 'drive, paddle', *óól* 'beg, pray, intercede', *rúí* 'cry', *tìráŋ* 'play', *ɔ́gɔ́r* 'roast', and so on. There is a strict phonotactic restriction with respect to the co-occurrence of these two. That is, the alveolar lateral /l/ can be followed by the alveolar trill /r/ but reverse is not possible. Mütze (2014) noted that as the onset of a cross-syllable consonant cluster, /l/ can only be followed by itself /l/ and by the trill /r/. In this case, in di-or-polysyllabic words, /l/ would function as the coda of the first syllable and as an onset of the next syllable, for example *ɔ̀llàj* [ɔ̀l.làj] 'problem'. But /r/ can never be a coda and an onset of a syllable in a single word at the same time. For example, *búrléléj* [búr.lé.léj] 'kind of tree'. Liquids do not appear in any affixes or clitics.

2.3.1.7 Glides

The two Mursi glides are—the bilabial /w/ and the palatal /j/ occur word-initially and word-medially, as in *wárr* 'River Omo', *wój* 'walk', *áúwús* 'rest, alight', *jàg* 'take back', *áhúj* 'suckle (the breast)', and *gáj* 'know'. They also occur word-finally but to a certain extent they are hard to distinguish from the high vowels /i/ and /u/. The phonemic status of glides at word-final position may be ascertained in three ways. First, unless due to intervocalic consonant deletion or morpheme boundaries or in some words (see §2.3.8), Mursi does not allow sequence of vowels of any type at any position in a word. For example, the first person plural inclusive possessive pronoun for singular possessed object is *nàj* (*n=àj* ~ ⟨SG.PSD=1PL.INC.PSR⟩) 'our (inc.)' but it sounds like a vowel-final morpheme *nài. Therefore, *nàj* should be analyzed as a palatal glide-final morpheme. The same is true for the exclusive possessive pronoun counterpart that has bilabial glide /w/ *nàw* (*n=àw* ~ ⟨SG.PSD=1PL.EXC.PSR⟩) 'our (exc.)'.

Second, word-finally, palatal fricatives and affricates /ʃ/, /č/ and /dʒ/ tend to assimilate to sounds that are alike to their natural classes, i.e. the palatal glide /j/. This evidence suggests that glides indeed are proper consonant phonemes and are permitted in word-final positions as any other consonant phonemes. The third justification would be that they have proper representation in the orthography both in Latin-based and Ge'ez (Ethiopic)-based by graphemes (see Table 1 and 2).

Regarding the occurrence of glides in affixes and clitics, only the palatal glide /j/ can do so—in a suffix or an enclitic, as in (2.12a–d).

(2.12) a. [*jói*]   'wild dog'
        [*jói-já*]   'wild dogs'

    b. [*dòlè-tèj*]   'tortoise-SG'
        [*dòlè-čá*]   'tortoise-PL'

    c. *óg-ú*   *òg-tí*   *bú-sís-i-j*
       cry-3SG.SU.PERV voice-NRSTR big-AUG-ADJ-NRSTR+OBL
       'He cried with a loud voice.'

    d. [*hùlli ók-ú=jè*]_{SUBORD:CL}   [*àɲè*
       if   go-3SG.SU.PERV=SUBORD 1SG
       k-í=ŋà]_{MAIN:CL}
       1SU-exist.IMPERV.SG+1SG.SU.IMPERV=DEF
       'If S/he goes, I will stay here.'

TABLE 2.4 The phonotactic restrictions on the occurrence of consonant phonemes of Mursi

Phoneme	Word positions			Affixal positions		Clitic positions	
	Word-initial	Word-medial	Word-final	Prefix	Suffix	Proclitic	Enclitic
/b/	×	×	×	–	–	–	–
/t/	×	×	×	×	×	–	×
/d/	×	×	×	–	–	–	–
/k/	×	×	×	×	–	–	–
/g/	×	×	×	–	–	×	×
/ʔ/	×	(rare)	(rare)	–	–	–	–
/ɓ/	×	×	–	–	–	–	–
/ɗ/	×	×	×	–	×	–	–
/s/	×	×	×	–	×	–	×
/z/	×	×	–	–	–	–	–
/ʃ/	×	×	(rare)	–	×	–	–
/h/	×	×	(rare)	–	×	–	–
/č/	×	×	×	–	×	–	–
/dʒ/	×	×	×	–	–	–	–
/m/	×	×	×	–	×	–	–
/n/	×	×	×	–	×	×	×
/ɲ/	×	×	×	–	×	–	–
/ŋ/	×	×	×	–	×	×	×
/l/	×	×	×	–	–	–	–
/r/	×	×	×	–	–	–	–
/w/	×	×	×	–	–	–	–
/j/	×	×	×	–	×	–	×

Generally, with respect to the phonotactic restrictions on the occurrence of Mursi consonant phonemes in various positions in a word and in grammatical elements such as in affixes and clitics is summarized in Table 2.4 above.

2.3.2   *Minimal and Near Minimal Pairs*

A further account of the phonetic realization of consonant phonemes is the minimal pair system that enable us to understand if the phonemes of the language may be used to contrast in various phonological environments. Accordingly, minimal and near-minimal pairs are presented below on the basis of each

PHONOLOGY   55

phoneme's natural class or randomly, and each were represented with a single example just to illustrate their occurrence in different phonological environments.

(2.13) *Stops*

[b] vs. [d]	[bè]	'recent past'	[dɛ̀]	'compound'
[b] vs. [ɓ]	[bág]	'show off'	[ɓág]	'eat, bite'
[t] vs. [d]	[màtí]	'You (sg.) drink.'	[màdì]	'breast'
	[tòrbìn]	'type of tree'	[dòrbìn]	'bladder'
[t] vs. [ɗ]	[tɔ́rɔ́k]	'pass gass, fart'	[ɗɔ́rɔ́k]	'dry'
[t] vs. [č]	[tìrì]	'fast'	[čírì]	'early morning'
[g] vs. [h]	[àgà]	'cook (2pl.IMP)!'	[àhà]	'thing (PL.)'
[k] vs. [g]	[kàbì]	'clan'	[gàbì]	'kind of tree'
vs. [h]	[kàhì]	'skirt made of cow skin'		
	[kámá]	'leather bag used to carry flour'	[gàmà]	'marriage'

(2.14) *Implosives*

[ɓ] vs. [ɗ]	[ɓág]	'eat, bite'	[ɗág]	'hit'
	[ɓòì]	'wide'	[ɗòj]	'bone marrow'
[ɗ] vs. [d]	[ɗɔ́ŋà]	'boy (pl.), age set'	[dɔ́ŋà]	'rod'

(2.15) *Fricatives*

[s] vs. [z]	[sèl]	'gap in upper teeth'	[zèl]	'stick'
	[mèsí]	'You (sg.) do'	[mèzì]	'meeting'
[s] vs. [t]	[sààn]	'news, history'	[tààn]	'flood'
[h] vs. [g]	[čàhì]	'shoes'	[čàgì]	'green'

(2.16) *Affricates*

[č] vs. [dʒ]	[čálàj]	'necklace'	[dʒàlàj]	'flower of corn'
[č] vs. [k]	[čàllì]	'good'	[kállí]	'little stick'
[dʒ] vs. [g]	[dʒò]	'human faeces (pl.)'	[gò]	'fire'
[ʃ] vs. [č]	[ʃúr]	'be offended'	[čúr]	'wash'
[ʃ] vs. [z]	[déʃí]	'to sneeze'	[dézí]	'to belch'

(2.17) *Nasals*

[n] vs. [m]	[*kún*]	'come'	[*kúm*]	'feel of, touch'
[n] vs. [ɲ]	[*nèbì*]	'buffalo'	[*ɲàbì*]	'ear'
[m vs. [ŋ]	[*dìmílí*]	'kind of tree'	[*dìŋìlì*]	'walking slowly'
[ɲ] vs. [ŋ]	[*ɲúgí*]	'You (sg.) close'	[*ŋúgí*]	'You (sg.) pull'

(2.18) *Liquids*

[l] vs. [r]	[*kúl*]	'drive, paddle'	[*kúr*]	'dig'
	[*tálá*]	'buy/sell (2sg.IMP)!'	[*tárá*]	'taste (2sg.IMP)!'
	[*bál*]	'place for adult men'	[*bàr*]	'night'
[r] vs. [n]	[*hírí*]	'man'	[*híní*]	'You (sg.) want'

(2.19) *Glides*

[w] vs. [j]	[*nàw*]	'Our (exc.) singular possessed'	[*nàj*]	'Our (inc.) singular possessed'
	[*éwó*]	'debt'	[*ójó*]	'rainy season, year'
[w] vs. [ʔ]	[*wùhù*]	'salty water'	[*ʔúhú*]	'to anoint'

2.3.3 *Consonant Length [Gemination]*

Consonant length is not phonemic in Mursi, but it can occur as contrastive phonetic feature that happens usually as a result of certain geminated consonants at the syllable-medial position. Therefore, I have analyzed consonant length as gemination. Only two words containing geminate palatal liquid /l/ were found as being contrastive, as shown in below:

(2.20) a. /*kállí*/ [kal.li] 'stick, switch' /*kàlì*/ 'day'
       b. /*èllà*/ [ɛl.la] 'cud' /*élà*/ 'stream'

Liquids are among the most frequently occurring geminates at syllable boundaries of a word. The alveolar fricatives /s/ and /z/, bilabial nasal /m/, and the alveolar nasal /n/ also occur as geminated consonants. The examples illustrated below clearly suggest that.

(2.21) a. /*hùllì*/ [hul.li] 'when/if'
        /*čàllì*/ [čal.li] 'good'
        /*kàllà*/ [kal.la] 'epilepsy'
        /*éró*/ [er.ro] 'children'

    b. /ìssèj/   [is.sej]   'eight'
       /ìssàbàj/ [is.sa.baj] 'seven'
       /sízzì/   [siz.zi]   'three'
    c. /ràmàn/   [ram.man]   'two'
       /hínná/   [hin.na]   'type of tree (pl.)'

The voiceless velar stop /k/ and its voiced counterpart tend to occur as geminate although they are extremely rare—the former in *sàkkàl* 'nine' and the latter mostly in pronouns *àggè* 'we' and *ìggè* 'you (pl.)'. As it can be shown in examples above, geminate consonants appear to be properties of disyllabic words. Consequently, they form the coda of the first syllable and the onset of the second. Interestingly, six out of the ten number words have geminate consonants. This seems to be due to the fact that certain lexical items of closed classes, more or less in one semantic category tend to become phonetically similar to each other. Number words of lower values can be good examples. At morpheme boundaries, geminates do not occur. However, one gemination case has been found which appears to be frequent across morpheme boundaries of the language, and it happens under one condition, that is, if a stem or a root that ends in the nasal alveolar /n/ and a morpheme that starts in the same consonant co-occur, as in (2.22a–b).

(2.22) a. [bérgú-ɲá tɔ̀mɔ̀n-nò]$_{NP}$
       year-PL   ten-MOD
       'Ten years'

      b. ŋàméá k-èlì+ì   ké   mùn-ni
         now   PASS-call.PERV-1PL.OBJ QUOT Mursi.PL-RS
         'Now called (by the name of) Mursi.' (MH 1:03:0)

As is illustrated in (2.22), geminates are simply sequences of nasal $C_1.C_1$. Grammatical information carrying morphemes such as antipassives/reciprocals, nominalizer, resolution, and locative markers tend to trigger gemination when being combined with stems/roots that end in the alveolar nasal consonant. At morpheme boundaries, nasals may trigger phonetic gemination when followed by any vowel, for example—*dòrèn-è* ~ [dòrèn-nè] ⟨house.PL-OBL⟩ 'from/to the houses'. The palatal liquid /l/ may also do the same when followed by the high front vowel /i/—*zèl-ì* ~ [zèl-l-ì] ⟨short.stick-NTRSR/CS⟩.

Except for the gemination instances in aforementioned examples at morpheme boundaries, all other C_1+C_2 sequences across morpheme boundaries may epenthetisize segments—/i/, /ɛ/, /n/, and /t/. Since the majority of Mursi verbs end in consonants, these four segments will be epenthesised between the derivational morphemes and the root. A less ambiguous phonological rule is that of the rule that applies to ideophones. Especially, in terms of consonant sequences, ideophones deviate from the canonical shape of words of the language because they allow word-final consonant sequences. Three ideophones bearing a sequence of the alveolar liquid /r/ have been found in my corpus (C_1VCC_2)—the spatial *sórr* 'very far away, far place', the discourse particle *čírr* 'really (mirative marker)' and the temporal particle *dírr* 'always' (see also § 2.9, for special phonology of ideophones, interjections, and expressives).

2.3.4 Consonants Clusters

In Mursi, except in word-medial positions, no two sequence of consonants (C_1C_2) can occur in a word. Even in word-medial position, consonant clusters come from two specific natural classes: nasals and liquids. The only four word-final consonant clusters are also sequences of nasal-liquid /rs/ and /ns/—*gèrs* 'bad', *éŋérs* 'afraid', *gúrt* 'pull', and *báns* 'fly, stand, up'. Regarding consonant clusters of Mursi, the following two generalizations can be made: (i) consonant clusters made up of LC (where L stands for liquids) are the most recurring sequences in the language; (ii) this is followed by NC (where N stands for nasals), the second most recurring consonant sequences. The latter sequence, however, the reverse *CL (where other consonants precede the liquids) hardly ever occurs in the language, except in some inherently reduplicated and borrowed word. Although they are rare, *CN clusters (where consonants precede the nasals) have been found. Table 2.5 below illustrates possible and restricted consonant sequences in Mursi. Thus, boxes with different shading contain consonants, which are connected to one another by different phonological processes.

2.3.5 Vowel Phonemes

Mursi has seven vowels. They are: two high (close) vowels /i/ and /u/, two close-mid vowels /e/ and /o/, two open-mid vowels /ɛ/ and /ɔ/, and an open (low) vowel /a/. The seven-vowel system is the basic configuration for almost all Southeastern Surmic languages (Yigezu 2001: 102). Vowel phonemes are displayed in Table 2.6 below.

Regarding the number of the vowel phonemes of Mursi, the current study aligns with that of the proposal by Yigezu (2001) and Mütze (2014) who claim that Mursi has a seven-vowel system. This is, however, far from the proposal made by Turton and Bender (1976) some four decades ago. In what is believed to be the first piece of work on the language, Turton and Bender came across

PHONOLOGY

TABLE 2.5 The occurrence of consonant sequences in Mursi

	b	t	d	k	g	ʔ	ɓ	ɗ	s	z	ʃ	h	č	dʒ	m	n	ɲ	ŋ	l	r	w	j
b	–	+M	B	±R	–	–	–	–	–	–	–	–	–	–	+	–	–	+	–	U	±R	–	–	±
t	–	+	–	–	–	–	–	–	–	–	–	–	–	–	–	–	–	–	–	–	–	–
d	–	–	_a	–	–	–	–	–	–	–	–	–	–	–	–	–	–	–	–	–	–	–
k	–	+	–	M	–	–	–	–	±B	–	–	+	–	–	–	+	+	–	–	–	–	–
g	–	+	–	C	M	–	–	–	–	–	C	+	–	–	–	+	+	–	–	–	U	–
ʔ	–	–	–	C	–	–	–	–	–	–	C	–	–	–	–	–	–	–	–	–	–	–
ɓ	–	–	–	–	–	–	–	–	–	–	–	–	–	–	–	–	–	–	–	–	–	–
ɗ	–	–	–	–	–	–	–	–	R	–	–	–	–	–	–	–	–	–	–	–	–	–
s	–	±B	–	±B	–	–	–	–	M	–	–	–	–	–	–	±+	–	±+	–	B	–	–
z	–	–	–	–	–	–	–	–	–	M	–	–	–	–	–	–	–	–	–	B	–	–
ʃ	–	–	–	–	–	–	–	–	–	–	–	–	–	–	–	+	–	U	U	–
h	–	–	–	–	–	–	–	–	–	–	–	–	–	–	–	–	–	–	–	–	–	–
č	–	–	–	–	–	–	–	–	–	–	–	–	–	M	–	–	–	–	–	–	–	–
dʒ	–	–	–	–	–	–	–	–	–	–	–	–	–	–	–	–	–	–	–	–	–	–
m	MB	+	–	R	Uᵇ	–	–	–	M+	–	–	–	+	±R	M	M+	–	±+	–	–	–	–
n	B	B	–	RCBM	+MB	–	–	–	MF	–	±F	–	M+	–	–	+	+	+	–	–	–	–
ɲ	–	–	–	–	–	–	–	–	–	–	–	+	–	–	+	M	+	–	–	–	–	–
ŋ	–	+	–	M	M	–	–	–	+	–	±R	–	+	–	–	+	+	–	–	–	–	–
l	±	±	B	±MCR	±RB	–	MRB	MR	M	B	M	R	+	–	±	+	–	+	M+	–	–	–
r	MCR	FM+	M	MC	M	–	M	M+	MF+	–	M	–	M±	±ᶜ	M	M+	+	–	+	M	–	±
w	–	–	–	–	–	–	–	–	–	R	IU	–	±+	–	–	–	–	+	L	–	B	–
j	–	+	B	–	–	–	–	+	±	–	–	+	–	+M	+M	+	+	–	–	U	–

I ~ word-initial, M ~ word-medial, F ~ word-final, + ~ morpheme boundary, B ~ borrowed, ± ~ extremely rare, C ~ compounds, R ~ inherently reduplicated—(hyphen) does not exist, and U ~ unknown.

a The voiced alveolar stop /dd/ sequences are considered as geminate consonants, and they only occur in a few borrowed words of Mursi. They are geminates which usually trigger the post-alveolar implosive /ɗ/.
b Only one word—*ŋɔmgɔri* 'easily broken tree' has been found (Turton et al 2008: 131). It appears to be a compound word as the word *gɔri* has a separate meaning in its own, i.e. 'cloud'.
c Only one word—*mardʒogi* 'wall of poles fastened in the ground; horizontal pieces of wood holding the uprights of a wall together' has been found (Turton et al 2008: 120).

TABLE 2.6 Vowel phonemes of Mursi

	Front	Back
High (close)	/i/ [i]	/u/ [u]
Close-mid	/e/ [e]	/o/ [o]
Open-mid	/ɛ/ [ɛ]	/ɔ/ [ɔ]
Low (open)	/a/ [a]	

with a five-vowel system by excluding two vowel phonemes—/ɛ/ and /ɔ/. They also suggested that four of the five vowels phonemes have allophones—/i/ [ɪ], /u/ [ʊ], /e/ [ɛ], and /o/ [ɔ]. However, the only allophones discovered in this study are [ɪ] and [ʊ]. The phonetic features of the basic phonemes is discussed below in § 2.3.5.1–§ 2.3.5.4.

2.3.5.1 High Vowels /i/ and /u/
The high (close) vowels /i/ and /u/ occur in all positions in a word, and in few closed syllables both may appear in their allophones [ɪ] and [ʊ] respectively, as in (2.23a–e).

(2.23) a. /tírtír/[3]   → [tɪ́rtɪ́r]   'fingernail'
       b. /hírrhírr/   → [hɪ́rrhɪ́rr] 'touch, feel (active)'
       c. /rìŋàj/   → [rɪ̀ŋàj]   'wasp'
       d. /murmuri/   → [mʊrmʊri]   'straight'
       e. /búrbúr/   → [bʊ́rbʊ́r]   'helicopter'

As it can be shown in (2.23a–e), except in one, in all cases allophones tend to occur in close CVC syllables. Besides, as it is shown in the examples above, it appears that the two allophones often occur in inherently reduplicated words. Nevertheless, at this stage, there is no clear reason to point out why this is the case. These allophones may have just occurred randomly because some of the reduplicated words appear as ideophones. The high front vowel /i/ is the only vowel that occurs as prefix on its own, i.e. a causative prefix *í-*. It is also the only vowel which can stand as a complete utterance on its own, i.e. *í-Ø ~ í* ⟨exist.IMPERV-3SG.SU.IMPERV⟩ 's/he, it exists'. The high front vowel does not occur in clitics whereas the high back vowel can occur as enclitic =*ùnù* (distal marker). Other vowels may appear with consonantal prefixes such as *k-* and *t-*. In addition, /i/ may function as an epenthetic vowel, thus it is being inserted between morpheme boundaries to break up impermissible consonant clusters. We may find it even in the enclitic =*ìnù* (an allomorph of the distal distal marker =*ùnù*), but it will be inserted only as epenthetic vowel before nouns that end in any vowel, except /i/. At morpheme boundaries, when /i/ follows the open-mid front vowel /ɛ/, it assimilates to /ɛ/ (see § 2.5.6.3 of this chapter).

---

3 It does not have fixed pronunciation. During my fieldwork stays with the Mursi community, I used to hear when young people pronounce it either way—/tértér/ or /tírtír/.

2.3.5.2 Close-mid Vowels /e/ and /o/

Like the high vowels, the close-mid vowels /e/ and /o/ occur in all environments. Both can occur in clitics, with or without a consonant—but both occur in one particular type of morpheme, i.e. an enclitic. For example, in subordinate marker enclitic =jè [=è], the negator enclitic =ó and the floating emphatic enclitic =so. Vowel assimilation related to the close-mid back vowel /o/ is frequent, and thus it assimilates to the open-mid back vowel /ɔ/ (see § 2.5.6.3 of this chapter).

2.3.5.3 Open-mid Vowels /ɛ/ and /ɔ/

These two open-mid vowels occur in all positions in a word. Both occur in affixes but only the open-mid front vowel /ɛ/ can occur in clitics—as in gòdín=gè (brother=PERT.PL.3.PSR) 'their brother'. Both vowels may involve in certain type of phonological assimilations for specific harmonic features such as fronting and height. For example, in some instances, the open-mid back vowel /ɔ/ can spread to the left and triggers vowel lowering of the preceding vowel. By doing this, it harmonizes with the preceding vowel in tongue height (also known as vowel height harmony), as in (2.24).

(2.24) /kà-ɓág-í-ɔ̀/ → [kàɓágɛ́ɔ]
1SU-eat-1SG.SU.IMPERV-VFS
'I eat.'

Here, the verb-final suffix -ɔ̀ has harmonized in height with the first person singular subject suffix -i.

2.3.5.4 The Low (Open) Vowel /a/

The low-(open) vowel /a/ is the only vowel phoneme that can occur in almost all environments including in proclitics and enclitics, for example, the bound deictic circumclitics ŋà= ... =á and the negative imperfective proclitic ŋà=. Across morpheme boundaries, left to right, the open vowel /a/ usually harmonizes in height with non-high (close) vowels (see section under vowel assimilation, § 2.5.6.4).

The summary below in Table 2.7 illustrates the environments in which Mursi vowel phonemes occur in words and morphemes.

2.3.6　*Minimal Pairs*

TABLE 2.7　Vowel phonemes and the environment in which they occur

Vowel occurrence environments	/i/	/u/	/e/	/o/	/ɛ/	/ɔ/	/a/
Word-initial/medial/final	√	√	√	√	√	√	√
Affixes	√	√	√	√	√	√	√
Proclitics	×	×	×	×	×	×	√
Enclitics	√×	√	√	√	×	×	√

A minimal pair system could be among many other effective systems to verify the phonemic status in some of the vowels in different environments. Therefore, as it is shown below, the minimal pair system is being used in order to identify contrastive vowel phonemes.

(2.25)

/i/ vs. /e/	[élí]	'call'	[éré]	'drop'
/i/ vs. /ɛ/	[ɓíg]	'break'	[ɓég]	'watch; protect'
	[jìrì]	'biceps (pl.)'	[jèrì]	'a kind of bird'
/e/ vs. /ɛ/	[bè]	'distant past'	[bè]	'rock'
/e/ vs. /a/	[élí]	'call'	[álí]	'talk, speak'
/e/ vs. /ɔ/	[és]	'sit'	[ɔ́s]	'roast (on fire)'
/a/ vs. /o/	[jàg]	'return (intr.)'	[jóg]	'tell, explain'
/a/ vs. /ɔ/	[hàlì]	'later'	[hɔ̀lì]	'white'
/u/ vs. /ɔ/	[rúm]	'cloth'	[rɔm]	'ostrich'
/u/ vs. /o/	[dʒù]	'big clay pot'	[dʒò]	'human faeces (pl.)'
/ɔ/ vs. /o/	[ɔ́gór]	'roast'	[ógór]	'steal'
	[sììrɔ̀]	'elk, eland'	[sìrò]	'mule'
/ɔ/ vs. /e/	[kɔ́ɗ]	'kill'	[kéɗ]	'subtract'
vs. /a/			[káɗ]	'remember'

Note that the minimal pairs listed above are a selective list, and they include neither the full list of all possible phonemic contrasts nor do they cover all phonetic environments.

2.3.7 Vowel Length

Vowel length in Mursi is phonetic, not phonemic. Vowel length is the outcome of a historical intervocalic consonant deletion. Despite it being undoubtedly a prototypical member of the Southeastern Surmic Group language, Mursi deviates from the other languages of the group in one aspect, i.e. its trisyllabic words frequently undergo extensive intervocalic consonant deletion (see § 2.5.1.2). For example, in Mursi *kààrì* 'eye' is a disyllabic word in a V.V sequence. However, the same word in other Southeastern Surmic group languages is trisyllabic—*kaβari* (Chai/Tirmaga), *kābārèc* (Me'en), and *kárbo* (Koegu/Muguji). In addition to these, there are also a handful of vowel length instances that are randomly found in some monosyllabic words and ideophones. Inasmuch as vowel length in words whose trisyllabic root forms contracted to disyllabic forms is phonetic, the vowel length that occurs in these words and ideophones is also phonetic. Words with phonetic vowel length include *fèè* 'well', *tíí* 'always', *èè* 'yes', and *óó* 'or' and so on. Interestingly, they are all monosyllabic.

2.3.8 Vowel Sequences

The ongoing consonant deletion in § 2.3.7 almost exclusively happens between homorganic vowels that can underlyingly be seen as $V_1.V_2$ sequences. This would make vowel length instances in the language to be regarded as $V_1.V_2$ sequences underlyingly but they would have $V_1.V_1$ sequences in surface form. Diphthongs do not exist in the language. Nonetheless, there are dozens of heterogeneous vowel sequences, which are of two types: deletion-based and inherent. Heterogeneous vowel sequences that are deletion-based come through the same phonological deletion process that triggers long vowels. Consequently, the voiced velar stop /g/ is among the most frequently deleted consonants. See the examples given below.

(2.26) a. /tùgɔ̀/ > [tùɣɔ̀] > [tùɔ̀] 'mouth'
b. /mùgà/ > [mùɣà] > [mùà] 'woman (pl.)'

Note that it is imperative to see the phonology of other Southeastern Surmic languages before making a conclusive statement about deletion based-vowel sequences. A plausible reason for this is that Mursi words tend to undergo an extensive intervocalic consonant deletion process more often than we expect. In comparison to Suri (of the Baale, Kacipo-Balesi), the alveolar nasal /n/ in Mursi is deleted when it occurs between heterogeneous vowels. In the examples provided below, compare Mursi possessive pronouns and those of Baale.

(2.27)   Mursi   Baale (Kacipo-Balesi)
    a. /nàw/   [nau]   >   /nánájo/   'our (exc.) singular possessed'
    b. /nùj/   [nui]   >   /nánnu/   'yours (singular possessed)'
    c. /nèj/   [nèi]   >   /nánnɛ/   'theirs'

See (§ 2.5.1.3) for a detailed description of phonological processes related to consonant and word-medial syllable deletion (reduction). While such V1.V1 and V1.V2 sequences triggered by intervocalic consonant deletion are common, inherent V1.V2 sequences are also found, mostly in nouns.

(2.28) a. i+a   /dĭá/   [di.a]   'go with'
                 /dian⟨ɲ⟩/   [di.an⟨ɲ⟩]   'evening'
        b. i+ɔ   /mìɔ̀/   [mì.ɔ̀]   'goat kid (pl.)'
                 /kìɔ̀/   [kì.ɔ̀]   'tree (sg.)'
                 /sìɔ̀/   [sì.ɔ̀]   'hand (sg.)'
        c. u+a   /čùànéŋ/   [ču.a.nɛŋ]   'again'
        d. u+i   /tùì/   [tu.i]   'cattle enclosure'
                 /rúí/   [ru.i]   'cry'
        e. ɛ+a   /ŋàméá/   [ŋà.mé.á]   'now, today'
                 /nèàj/   [nɛ.aj]   'S/he, post-verbal subject pronoun'
        f. e+o   /lèó/   [le.o]   'thatch'
        g. ɔ+ɛ   /dɔ̀è/   [dɔ̀.ɛ̀]   'hump'
        h. o+i   /rímwòì/   [rim.wo.i]   'tooth stick, toothbrush'
                 /bìlbìlòì/   [bil.bil.o.i]   'moth'
        i. a+i   /áíw/   [a.iw]   'come.PERV:SG'
        j. a+u   /áú/   [á.ú]   'eldest children'
                 /áús/   [a.us]   'rest, alight'

Table 2.8 below is a summary of $V_1.V_2$ vowel sequences that are either triggered by intervocallic consonant deletion or inherently occur in different environments.

2.4   Syllable Structure

The maximal syllable template is CVC. A great majority of Mursi verb roots have monosyllabic CVC shapes. Just very few monosyllabic verbs may optionally contain $CVC_1(C_2)$, where C_1 stands for the liquids and nasals—*gèrs* 'bad' and *báns* 'fly, stand up'. Apart from these two, four other basic syllable shapes have been identified: V, VC, CV, and CVV. Of these, the CV is the most frequently

TABLE 2.8 Vowel sequences

	/i/	/u/	/e/	/o/	/ɛ/	/ɔ/	/a/
/i/	D,O,+	+	+	+	+	I,+	I,+
/u/	I,D,+	D	??	+	+	+	I,+
/e/	+	+	D,+,O	I,+	+	+	+
/o/	I,+	+	??	D,+	+	+	+
/ɛ/	D,+	+	??	+	D	+	I,+
/ɔ/	+	??	??	??	I	D	??
/a/	I,+,O	I,D	+	+	+	+	D,I,+,O

D = deletion-based, I = inherent, + = morpheme boundary, O = others[a]

a The category 'others' includes borrowed words and ideophones.

occurring syllable shape in the language. The distribution of CVV syllable shape is very much limited, only confined to few words containing phonetic vowel length (see §2.3.7). Some discourse particles, interjections, and ideophones may contain syllable shape which are quite different from those of regular word classes, for example *ɪmm* 'no (disagreement marker)' and *ŋɲ* 'yes (disagreement marker)' (see also §2.3.3). This is, however, the norm with discourse markers and ideophones. Deviation in the syllable shapes of small and closed word classes is often triggered when liquid and nasal consonants occurring at the coda position.

2.5 Phonological Processes

Mursi has most complex sound processes which touch on almost every aspect of the grammar. Although some sound changes may be irregular as they pass through a number of phonological processes, the majority of the sound changes often have rules by which they are governed. Some may seem common and areal. For example, many of the word-final consonant deletion rules typically apply to both Southeastern as well as Southwestern Surmic languages. Quite a few of the common phonological processes are specific to the individual language thus only apply to Mursi. Therefore, the subsequent sections provide detailed account of the phonological processes which occur in simple words as well as in morphologically-complex forms.

2.5.1 *Deletion*

There are five types of deletion in Mursi: two consonant deletion types (word-final intervocalic (word-medial)) and three syllable deletion types, namely,—word-initial, word-medial, and word-final. The first two deletion types (consonant-deletions) have the tendency to trigger vowel lengthening in all three environments of a word—see §2.5.1.1 and §2.5.1.2. The syllable deletion types do not trigger any sort of segment length, yet they could disrupt the sequence of segments in words—see §2.5.1.3–§2.5.1.5.

2.5.1.1 Word-Final Consonant Deletion (Apocope)

The alveolar stops /d/ and /t/, the post-alveolar implosive /ɗ/, and the voiceless fricatives /s/ and /h/ are deleted when occurring word-finally. The deletion of word-final consonants has also been noted in Mütze (2014: 27). Consequently, the rule will be: {/d/, /t/, /ɗ/, /s/ and /h/} → Ø/__#.

(2.29) a. /áɲ   k-àɲìd/   → [áɲ kàŋì]
         HORT/JUSS.PART 1.HORT-bite.PERV
         'Let me bite'

      b. /àj   k-íɗógíɗó/   → [àj kíɗój]
         HORT/JUSS.PART 3.JUSS-raise/feed.PERV
         'Let him raise/feed'

As it is shown in (2.29a–b), the voiced alveolar stop /d/ has been deleted at word-final position. This is due to the fact that there is no grammatical element suffixed to the perfective verb root. Singular hortatory/jussive mood construction forms do not indicate person-number information but rather require only perfective verb roots. Therefore, consonants of consonant-final verb roots can easily be exposed for deletion. In fact, in (2.29), it was not a single phonological process which took place but two—deletion and assimilation (devoicing). Following the deletion of /d/, the voiced velar stop /g/ and the high vowel /i/ have assimilated to the palatal glide /j/. In the same environment, the voiceless counterpart /t/ will also be deleted, as in (2.30).

(2.30) /nɔ̀ŋ dɔ̌t-Ø   ŋà=lɔ̀g=tá/   → [nɔ̀ŋ dɔ́ ŋàlɔ̀ʔtá]
         3SG leave-3SG.SU.IMPERV DEM=issue=NEAR
         'S/he leaves (stops doing) the issue.'

Nevertheless, in the same environment, the post-alveolar implosive /ɗ/ may either be deleted or changed into alveolar nasal /n/. This requires further investigation. Thus, either rules apply: /ɗ/ → Ø/__# or /ɗ/→ [n]/__#.

(2.31) a. /àj   kɔ́-mɔ́d/   → [àj kɔ́m]
         HORT/JUSS.PART 3.JUSS-be.tired.PERV
         'Let him/her be tired'

   b. /nɔ̀ŋ čɔ́d-Ø   lìwá/   → [nɔ̀ŋ čɔ́ lìwá]
      3SG load-3SG.SU.IMPERV sorghum
      'S/he loads sorghum.'

(2.32) /kɔ́d-Ø/   → [kɔ́n]
       kill.IMPERV-3SG.SU.IMPERV
       'S/he kills'

The other two consonants that will be deleted at the same environment are the voiceless fricatives /s/ and /h/ (see example 2.33 and 2.34). As mentioned earlier, consonant deletion is a key source of phonetic vowel length in the language as length doesn't exist in any of its major lexical classes. Word-final consonant deletion can also be classified among many other deletion types which trigger vowel length. In the example illustrated below, two distinct phonological changes have taken place sequentially—haplology (it follow the loss of a whole syllable before a phonetically identical syllable) and deletion.

(2.33) a. /áɲ   kɔ̀-kɔ̀h   bà/ → [áɲ kɔ̀ɔ̀ bà]
         HORT/JUSS.PART 1.HORT-clear.PERV land
         'Let me clear (land).'

Haplology is quite a common phonological process in the language, and frequently occurs when the k(V)- prefix (that always copies the first vowel of the verb root) and k-initial verb roots co-occur side by side. As the result of the co-occurrence of identical syllables, one of them will be deleted and the vowel is what remains and undergoes compensatory lengthening. This does not, however, apply to verbs that have non-k-initial roots, as in (2.33b).

   b. /kú-túh/   → [kútú]
      3.JUSS-spit/bless.PERV
      'Let him spit/bless'

(2.34) a. /kè-ŋès/   → [kè-ŋè] + /o/ (VFS) → [kè-ŋèò]
         1.HORT-run.PERV
         'Let me run!'

b. /kè-ŋès-V/ → [kè-ŋè] + V (PL.INC.) → [kèŋèe]
1.HORT-run.PERV-1PL.INC
'Let us (inc.) run!'

c. /ŋès-V/ → [ŋè] + V (PL.) → [ŋèè]
run.PERV-PL
'Run (pl.)!'

In (2.34a–c), there are two phonotactic constraint rules to be taken into account—a sequence of three vowels is absolutely not permitted, and verb-final suffixes can be attached to verbs after all phonological processes are applied. As it can be shown in all, the verb has an invariable root form for both imperfective and perfective aspects. In (2.34a), the hortative form for first person singular does not require a separate singular number marker. Thus, it does take a verb-final suffix because two heterogeneous vowel sequences are permitted in the language. In (2.34b–c), the first person plural inclusive and the plural imperative forms do take a plural number marker suffix -V. Accordingly, the -V is being suffixed to both forms once the deletion process has taken place. On the verb-final suffixes, further information is found in chapter 7 & 10.

Furthermore, even though consonants [h] and [s] can occur as free variants, and as a result of this they can freely alternate with one another at a word-final position, they cannot be exempted from deletion. Some examples are given below.

(2.35) a. [ɓúh] ~ [ɓús] 'to curse'
b. [kɔ́h] ~ [kɔ́s] 'to clear (farmland)'

At word-final position, the glottal fricative /h/ can occur in free variation with the palatal fricative /ʃ/, but /ʃ/ cannot be deleted at word-final environment instead it will be made to weaken to the palatal glide /j/.

(2.36) a. [íh] ~ [íʃ] 'S/he exists (is present)'
b. [wúʃ] → [wúj] 'four'

2.5.1.2 Intervocalic-Final Consonant Deletion (Syncope)

Almost all of the information regarding intervocalic consonant deletions comes from synchronic analysis. As a result of this, any sort of word-medial consonant elision process can only be justifiable by providing plausible evidence from other closely related Southeastern Surmic group languages, and

TABLE 2.9   Intervocalic consonant deletion, Mursi vs. Tirmaga-Chai and Me'en

Meaning	Mursi	Tirmaga~Chai	Me'en	Remark
'tooth'	[ɲíídàj]	/nigidaj/	/ɲiʔidač/	*g/*ʔ
'foot'	[dʒààrì]	/dʒagari/	/dʒàrēč/	*g
'udder'	[kòòrì]	/dʒogori/		*g
'eye'	[kààrì]	/kaβari/~/kāāri/	/kābārèč/	*β/*b/
'father'	[ʃúúnέ]	/ʃɔgɔnɛ/~/čɔgɔnɛ/	/ʃuɓūnɛ⟨b⟩/	*g/*β/*b
'tomorrow'	[ròònɔ̀]	/rogono/	/daamo/	*g
'squat'	[líínɔ́]	/ligin(nd)ɔ/		*g
'beg/pray'	[óól]	/ogol/	/ōʔō/	*g/*ʔ
'to be sick'	[íláás]	/ilagas/	/ilaʔas/	*g/*ʔ
'donkey'	[sììrɔ̀]	/sigirɔ/		*g
'clay'	[dììr]	/digir/		*g

all comparisons presented below are synchronically generated ones. Therefore synchronic evidence shows that {/b/ ~*β, /g/~ *ʔ/*ɓ} are deleted when occurring between identical vowels. Hence, the phonological rule to be applied here is: {/g/[ʔ], /ɓ/[β,b]} → Ø/ V__V.

As it is illustrated in Table 2.9 above, with the exception of a few words, the deletion is totally confined to specific type of words, i.e. those whose second syllable involve the velar stop /g/. What we see here is also a complete deletion historical scenario. In the best case scenario, we would have had one more stage before this deletion happening, that is the velar stop /g/ weakens and becomes [ɣ] (see § 2.5.3 on consonant weakening). At morpheme boundaries, whenever we see phonetic vowel length in disyllabic nominal and verbal words, at least in the majority of cases, that does mean that they have passed through word-medial deletion process.

2.5.1.3   Word-Initial Syllable Deletion (Haplology)

There is strong synchronic evidence which substantiates that at least some of the possessive pronouns of Mursi have had originated from a $CV_1.CV_1.CV_2$ syllable shape. This can, however, only be attested by comparing its possessive pronouns with those of other closely related languages of the SES and SWS. Thus, the examples below show the word-initial deletion process that has taken place in Mursi possessive pronouns (vis-à-vis Baale possessive pronouns).

(2.37)   Mursi   Baale
   a. /nànù/   < /nánànú/   'Mine, singular possessed'
   b. /gàɲù/   < /gágàɲu/   'Mine, plural possessed'
   c. /nùnù/   < /nánùnu/   'Yours, singular possessed'
   d. /gùɲù/   < /gágùɲu/   'yours, plural possessed'
   e. /nènè/   < /nánaènè/   'His/hers, singular possessed'
   f. /gèɲè/   < /gágèɲè/   'His/hers, plural possessed'

As it is shown in (2.37a–f), the cognate forms of Baale are similar to Mursi except Mursi possessive pronoun forms undergo syllable deletion at word-initial position. In addition to possessive pronouns, such deletion has been attested in one of the Southeastern variety of the Suri (i.e. Tirmaga). For example, the instrumental interrogative word in Mursi is *ɔ́nɔ́ŋɔ́* 'with.what?' (Lit. 'by what means') whereas in Tirmaga it is—*ɔ́nɔ́nɔ́ŋɔ́* (cf. Bryant 2013: 62). So, in Mursi these identical syllables are deleted when occurring in the same environment. This particular type of deletion is also known as haplology.

2.5.1.4   Word-Medial Syllable Deletion

On the other hand, in a rather rare word formation process in the language, compounding, adjective-adjective compound sequences may undergo a syllable deletion process. So there is a special morphological operation associated with compounding; particularly associated to deletion word-medial syllable. Accordingly, the last syllable of the first compound element will be deleted in the compounding process. This is being carried out in line with the consonant co-occurrence restriction rule of the language. Two typical examples illustrating this specific deletion process are given below:

3(2.38)   Adjective-adjective
   a. /čàkɔ̀rɔ̀i/ < [čàgì-kɔ̀rɔ̀i]   (green-black)   'green'
   b. /čàhɔ́lí/ < [čàgì-hɔ́lí]   (green-white)   'blue'

Both examples in (2.38a–b), could trigger suspicion because both look like instances of a morpheme-boundary consonant deletion rather than as containing a string of segments. Plausible evidence for this would be that the adjective suffix *-i* cannot be marked twice on a single compound adjective word thus it is omitted from the first element. Therefore, the next step will be deletion of the voiced velar stop /g/. In principle, a homorganic sequence of [*gk] may be allowed between compound-driven morpheme boundaries, but at this stage it seems very difficult to make assertions because both may be neutralized to the glottal stop /ʔ/ or can coalesce as a single segment *g/*k. My Mursi lan-

PHONOLOGY   71

guage consultants when they worked with me during my two separate fieldwork period often used to prefer to insert the glottal stop /ʔ/ between these two compound adjective boundaries. The glottal stop /ʔ/ is, however, absent while they utter them in fast speech. Above all, a sequence of [*ʔg] does not exist or at least is not attested so far in the language. Therefore, based on these factors, a word-medial syllable deletion would best describe the morphophonological scenario in (2.38).

2.5.1.5   Word-Final Syllable Deletion

Word-final syllable deletion differs in the type depicted in §2.5.1.4 in that it may be treated as part of the morphophonologic process of the language. The word-final syllable deletion is basically one that is peculiar in its type but rarely applied in a word-final environment according to the aspectual system of the language. Examples depicting the former type are given below in (2.39a–c).

(2.39)   Imperfective   Perfective
       a. /ɔ́ŋɔ́n/   /t-ɔ́ŋ/   'smell/stink (unpleasant smell)'
       b. /ɔ́ŋón/   /t-óŋ/   'throw, lanch (a boat)'
       c. /úŋús/   /t-úŋ/   'sleep'

Here, the perfective aspect marker prefix *t(V)-* which applied only to a few of verb root types can in no way alone indicate the perfective aspect. Instead, the final syllable of each imperfective verb roots has to be deleted before taking up the perfective prefix *t(V)-*.

2.5.2   *Devoicing*

Mursi does not have the voiceless bilabial plosive /p/ but it may appear in only extremely rare environments as an allophone of the voiced counterpart /b/. For example, certain environments in which [p] appears include: only a few lexical items containing the voiced bilabial stop /b/ at morpheme boundary, word-finally, reduplicated forms and interjections/ideophones. With respect to devoicing of /b/ at word-final environment, the phonological rule that applies is the following: /b/ → [p]/__ # (see 2.40a–c).

(2.40)   a. /ké-čébt-à/   → [kéčéptà]
              1SU-tie.up.PERV-1PL.INC.SU.PERV
              'We (inc.) have tied (up).'

          b. /sáb/   → [sáp]   'leather decoration on cattle'

c. /kɔ̀b.kɔ̀b/ → [kɔ̀p.kɔ̀p] 'quickly (Lit. follow.follow)'

d. *paf wà   áɨ́w-ó*
   INTERJ REC.PAST come.PERV.SG-MT.3SG.SU.PERV
   '(The boy) has come! (able to surprised suddenly)'

2.5.3 Lenition

Based on what we saw in § 2.5.2 and the data which follows under this section, three allophones of /b/ have been identified: [p], [β] and [w]. In fact, /w/ is a full-fledged phoneme. Intervocalically, the voiced bilabial stop /b/ lenites to the voiced labial fricative [β] and the bilabial glide [w]. The general morphological process which describes the lenition of /b/ is the intervocalic spirantization, and has the following general rule: /b/ → [β/w]/ V__V. More specifically, the /b/ undergoes the lenition process before [-back] or [+back] vowel. Therefore, to obtain the two allophones, the following specific rules must be put in place:

i. /b/ → [β]/ __ [-back]
ii. /b/ → [w]/ __ [+back]

(2.41) a. /nèbì/   → [nèβì]   'buffalo'
       b. /ɲàbì/   → [ɲàβì]   'ear (sg.)'
       c. /čòbàj/ → [čòwàj] 'pig'

Not all lexical items containing /b/ undergo the lenition process. From this point of view there are a number of lexical items exempted from this process. While this is the case, the reverse process (voicing) may also apply to the bilabial glide /w/. Accordingly, /w/ becomes [β/b] with the same phonological rule /w/ → [β/b]/ V__V.

(2.42) a. /àj   k-áɨ́w-έ/   → [káíβέ]/ [káíbέ]
       HORT/JUSS.PART 3.JUSS-go.PERV:PL-VFS
       'Let them go!'

b. /ɨ́w-á/ → [íβá]/ [íbá]
   take-MT:3SG.SU.PERV
   'S/he took (it)'

The third person plural perfective form of 'go' is *áítá* ⟨áí-t-á⟩ (go.PERV-PL-3.SU), and it takes the third person plural irrealis marker suffix -*o*. This produces a vowel sequence that does not exist in the language, i.e. **aio*. Later in the process, the irrealis marker becomes bilabial glide /w/—**aio > aiw*. The velar plosives /g/ and /k/ lenite (weaken) to the glottal stop [ʔ] word-finally and rarely at morpheme boundaries: /g, k/→[ʔ]/{__# or __#__}.

(2.43) a. /hólóg/ → [hólóʔ] 'dance'

b. /tùtùg/ → [tùtùʔ] 'door, enterance (sg.)'

c. /jɔ̀g múgt-á/ → [jɔ̀g múʔtá]
3PL gather.PERV-3PL.SU.PERV
'They gathered (it).'

d. /ʃíg ŋà=lɔ̀g=tá/ → [ʃíʔ ŋàlɔ̀ʔtá]
listen.PERV:IMP DEM=issue=NEAR
'Listen (sg.) to this issue!'

The voiced velar stop /g/ can also lenite (weakens) to [ɣ] intervocalically, as in (2.44).

(2.44) a. /ɓùgùj/ → [ɓùɣùj] 'back'
b. /mùgà/ → [mùɣà] 'women'
c. /tùgɔ̀/ → [tùɣɔ̀] 'mouth'

Similarly, the palatal affricates /ʤ/ and /č/ and the palatal fricative /ʃ/ lenite to the palatal glide [j] word-finally: /ʤ, č, ʃ/ →[j]/__#.

(2.45) a. /àj kéʤ/[4] → [àj kéj]
HORT/JUSS.PART 3.JUSS-shoot.PERV
'Let him/her shoot!'

b. /nɔ̀ŋ óʤ-Ø hólóg/ → [nɔ̀ŋ ój hólóʔ]
3SG sing-3SG:SU:IMPERV song
'S/he sings a song.'

---

4 We might see a number of hortative-jussive mood related constructions in the discussions of certain phonological processes, especially, in those that are related to consonantal changes at word-final positions. This is due to the fact that hortative-jussive forms often occur in root forms because there is little affixation or almost no morphological operation that takes place on the hortative-jussive verb forms. Therefore, as it is a language whose majority verb roots end in consonants, there are a great deal of changes which take place at word-final environments.

c. /čáč/ → [čáj]   'translate; exchange'

d. /húč/ → [húj]   'avenge, pay'

e. /wúʃ/ → [wúj]   'four'

f. /gàʃ/ → [gàj]   'bush'

2.5.4 Fricative Simplification

The alveolar fricatives /s/ and /z/ can undergo a simplification process to their dental allophone counterparts [θ] and [ð]. While their allophonic status is indisputable, Yigezu (2001: 100) and Mütze (2014) reported that both [θ] and [ð] occur in free variation. The voiceless alveolar fricative /s/ becomes [θ] word-initially and intervocalically whereas its voiced counterpart /z/ becomes [ð] intervocalically:

/s/ → [θ] / { #__ , V__V }   and /z/ → [ð] / V__V

(2.46) a. /sízzì/   → [θízzì]   'three'
b. /kásáj/   → [káθáj]   'sand'
c. /lásá/   → [láθá]   'bread (sg.)'
d. /mèzì/   → [mèðì]   'meeting'
e. /mèzèzèj/ → [mèðèðèj] 'poisonous spider (sg.)'.

Fricative simplification, a process that occurs in relation to the speech register of both female and male, and is associated with removal of lower incisors (see § 2.10).

2.5.5 Cluster Reduction

In rapid speech, the liquid /l/ and the nasal /ŋ/ may be reduced from the coda of the first syllables of an inherently reduplicated disyllabic word roots. Only two from a dozen disyllabic adjectival roots containing inherently reduplicated syllables were found to reduce their clusters.

(2.47) a. /dáldáŋ-í/ → [dá.dáŋ.í]   'hard, difficult, expensive'
b. /dĭŋdĭŋ-í/ → [dĭ.dĭŋ.í]   'heavy'

Therefore, the first syllables in both adjectives were underlying closed CVC forms, but now have open CV surface forms. Note that the suffix -i is a general adjectivizer so not part of the roots.

2.5.6 *Assimilation*

2.5.6.1 Velarization

The alveolar nasal /n/ is velarized to velar nasal [ŋ] when followed by velar stops /k/ and /g/: /n/→[ŋ]/ __ [k/g].

(2.48) a. /čángáláj/ → [čáŋgáláj] 'an age grade of young boys'
b. /áʃángárá/ → [áʃáŋgárá] 'servant, slave'
c. /bànkà/ →[bàŋkà] 'machete'

Velarization is among the rarest phonological processes one can find in the language. Yet, related to the velar nasal /ŋ/, one peculiar process has been detected called velar strengthening. This happens when the velar nasal /ŋ/ is followed by a palatal glide /j/, i.e. /ŋj/ > [ŋŋ].

(2.49) /kíɲáŋ/ 'crocodile (sg.)'
/kíɲáŋ-já/ →[kíɲáŋŋá] 'crocodile (pl.)'

2.5.6.2 Loan Adaptation; Phonetic Mapping

In the context of Mursi, phonetic mapping may be regarded as a phonetic approximation of segments which mainly applies to borrowed lexical items containing sounds that do not exist in the language. In Mursi, the majority of lexical items that are borrowed from other languages (usually from Amharic) can be adapted on the basis of a process called, phonetic mapping. To a large extent, the term 'monolingual' may best describe the Mursi. This is due to the fact that they speak mainly Mursi. They also speak Amharic but only in few situations of contact with other highlanders for issues such as trade, tourism and governmental activities. Therefore, they have little access to the actual pronunciation of Amharic. Consequently, phonetic mapping is a very frequent phonological process which is found in Mursi; especially, while speakers try to replace certain borrowed words by other words phonetically closest to their own.

Most importantly, phonetic mapping can only be applied to segments that are absent from the sound inventory of the language. These include consonants [p], [f], [č'], [k'], [p'] and vowels [ä/ə] and [ɨ]. These Amharic segments will be adapted to Mursi phonology.

(2.50) Amharic Mursi
a. [papaja] > /bábáj/ 'papaya' [p] > /b/
b. [polis] > /bólísí/ 'police' [p] > /b/
c. [foto] > /bòtò/ 'photograph' [f] > /b/
d. [färändʒ] > /háránčí/ 'white man' [h] > /h/

e. [bɨrč'č'ik'o]   > /búrčúkú/   'water glass'   [č'] > /č/,
                                                    [k'] > /k/,
                                                    [ɨ] > /u/
f. ['t'äräp'p'eza] > /tárábéizá/ 'table'   [p'] > /ɓ/
g. [fättäna]   > /bètèná/   'examination'   [ä] > /ɛ/
h. [bärbbäre]   > /bàràbàràj/ 'pepper'   [ä] > /a/
i. [däbtär]   > /dóbtèrì/   'exercise book' [ä] > /o/
j. [dɨst]   > /dískí/   'aluminum pot'   [ɨ] > /i/

Many of the phonetic mapping cases involving the vowels would be good examples of vowel decentralization. That is, central vowels in the source language will be made decentralized because of the influence of the none-central Mursi vowels (as in (2.50d–j)).

2.5.6.3   Vowel Assimilation

Vowel assimilation happens when sequences of vowels with different voice qualities occur at post-verbal root positions. As it is a highly suffixing language, vowel assimilation is a recurring phenomenon between morpheme boundaries. The two most common vowel assimilation types are the close-mid back vowel /o/ assimilates to an open-mid back vowel [ɔ] when followed by the [ɔ], and the high front vowel /i/ assimilates to open-mid front vowel [ɛ] when followed by {[a], [ɛ], [ɔ]}.

i.   /o/ → [ɔ]/__ɔ
ii. /i/ → [ɛ]/__{a, ɛ, ɔ}

(2.51) a. /k-ítím-ò-ɔ̀/   → [kítímɔ̀ɔ̀]
        1SU-burn-1PL.EXC.SU.IMPERV-VFS
        'We (inc.) burn (it).'

The third person plural jussive form is also found to trigger a leftward assimilation of /o/ to [ɔ] resulting in full assimilation, as in (2.51b)

       b. /àj   kɔ́-mɔ́ɗ-ɔ́-ó/   → [àj kɔ́mɔ́ɗɔ́ɔ́]
          HORT-JUSS:PART 3.JUSS-be.tired.PERV-PL-VFS
          'Let them be tired!'

The justification is that the three non-high vowels [a, ɛ, ɔ] may cause the high vowel /i/ to be changed into non-high vowel [ɛ] and this is directly associated to vowel height assimilation. (see also vowel height assimilation/harmony, § 2.5.6.4).

(2.52) a. /kì-á   n=ànù/   → [kèá nànù]
          tree-RSTR SG.PSD=1SG.PSR
          'My tree'

      b. /kì-ʃìl-ì-έ/   → [kìʃìlὲέ]
          1SU-stand.PERV-PL.INC-VFS
          'Let us (inc.) stand (rise.up).' (cf. Mütze 2014).

      c. /se-á   ké   ànè ká-már-ì-ɔ̀/   → [kámárὲɔ̀]
          say-3SG.SU.PERV QUOT 1SG 1SU-dislike-1SG.SU.IMPERV-VFS
          'He said, 'I won't'.'

      d. /lúsì dág-Ø   hírí-ɔ́/   → [lúsì dág híréɔ́]
          boy hit-3SG.SU.IMPERV man-NOM
          'The man hit the boy.'

An assimilation scenario was found in which the high front vowel /i/ becomes a palatal glide [j] when followed by [ɛ]; following this all front vowels in a word are changed into back vowels, as in the following example.

(2.53) /rúí-ὲ-ɔ̀/   → [rújɔ̀ɔ̀]
        cry.IMPERV-3PL.SU.IMPERV-VFS
        'They cry'

2.5.6.4   Vowel Height Assimilation (Harmony)

Mursi vowels can undergo a height harmony process that constitutes another form of assimilation on its own. There are two types of vowel height harmonies—(i) height harmony of two or more vowels within verbal and nominal roots, and (ii) height harmony between vowels of the roots of these two word classes and the vowels in suffix boundaries. The first type is very strict, straightforward and more common in the verbal roots than in nominal roots. Accordingly, close-mid vowels /e/ and /o/ do not co-occur in the same verbal root with open-mid vowels /ɛ/ and /ɔ/. However, the high vowels /i/ and /u/ and the open /a/ can cooccur in the same root with both close-mid and open-mid vowels. See vowel harmony restrictions in nominal (2.54) and verbal (2.55) roots in the following examples.

(2.54) a. /tóbèj/   'bright star'
       b. /rìʤὲn/   'shade (pl.)'
       c. /dóóléj/   'girl'

d. /ʃébél/ 'sheath (for a knife)'
e. /mùdĕn/ 'mouse (pl.)'
f. /àbén/ 'antelope'
g. /bènèni/ 'relative'
h. /tɔ́lɔ́bɛ́/ 'lizard'

(2.55) a. /ɓésí/ 'hatch'
b. /dĕzí/ 'burp'
c. /mósí/ 'wish'
d. /ʃúmó/ 'flap'
e. /érés/ 'cross'
f. /ébég/ 'blow, expose, reveal'
g. /ógór/ 'steal'
h. /ɔ́gɔ́r/ 'roast'

The low (open) vowel /a/ is neutral or opaque as it does not trigger height harmony with any particular vowel classes. This means that, in the same verbal root, the vowel /a/ can co-occur with all other vowels including itself. Some examples were presented as follows.

(2.56) a. /ítáb/ 'deceive'
b. /áhúj/ 'to suck'
c. /ɲɔ̀màj/ 'razor'
d. /lɛ̀ɛ́dà/ 'jute mallow (a shrub)'
e. /élà/ 'water hole'
f. /àɲè/ 'I (pro.)'

Nevertheless, in the height harmony between the vowels of word roots and their affixes, the vowel /a/ can harmonize with /ɛ/, /ɔ/, N+/i/ and itself /a/. The vowel height harmony in Mursi is always determined by the root vowels. Moreover, the Mursi vowel height harmony system does not apply to all levels of the morphological interactions between verb root vowels roots and their suffixes. It only applies between verb roots and two suffixes namely—first person singular object suffix -áɲ/-óɲ [-high/+high] and motion towards (ventive) marker suffix [-án(a)/-ón(o)] [-high/+high]. So, it is determined partly by morphological context. Verb roots containing high vowels /i/, /e/, /o/ harmonize with first person object suffix [-óɲ] and motion marker suffix [-ón(o)]. On the other hand, verb roots containing non-high vowels /ɛ/, /a/, /ɔ/ harmonize with first person object suffix [-áɲ] and motion marker suffix [-án(a)].

	Root vowels	First person object suffix
i.	{/i/, /e/, /o/}	~ /o/
ii.	{/ɛ/, /a/, /ɔ/}	~ /a/
iii.	{/i, e, u+CC(N)}	~ /a/

(2.57) Vowel height harmony between high-vowel verb roots and [-óɲ]

Root	1st person object suffix	Subject suffix	Verb-final suffix	Meaning
íɓ	-óɲ	-Ø	-ɔ̀	'S/he grabs me'
édʒ	-óɲ	-ɛ́	-ɔ̀	'They shoot me'
ór	-óɲ	-ɛ́	-ɔ̀	'They see me'
ítón	-óɲ	-ɛ́	-ɔ̀	'They send me'

(2.58) Vowel height harmony between non-high-vowel verb roots and [-áɲ]

Root	1st person object suffix	Subject suffix	Verb-final suffix	Meaning
bɔ́n	-áɲ	-Ø	-ɔ̀	'S/he arrived for/to me'
dág	-áɲ	-ɛ́	-ɔ̀	'They beat me'
ádʒ	-áɲ	-ɛ́	-ɔ̀	'They give me'
jɛ́w	-áɲ	-í	-ɔ̀	'You (sg.) believe me'

As it is shown in (2.57 and 2.58), the vowels in the verb roots determine the vowel-height of the object suffixes that follow their roots. In (2.57), the entire vowel height harmony process between the high vowels in the roots and the suffix [-óɲ] can be explained either by lowering the vowel of the suffix one step or making it equivalent. With the exception of the lowering of the vowel of the suffix after the [-high] vowels, the same process applies to those in (2.58). The subject and the verb-final final suffixes are outside the domain of vowel height harmony. This appears to be due to the fact that they are not subject to vowel harmony as they are not immediately adjacent to the root.

There are however three exceptional cases detected which go against vowel height harmony process. The first is that at coda position consonant clusters are not allowed in Mursi. But, the morpheme /t/ which often epenthesised to indicate perfective aspect on verbs that do not alter their root shape for aspect will create CC sequences and block the harmony (2.59).

(2.59) ŋànì   kú-čúgt-áɲ=ó
        NEG.PERV 1SU-suck.PERV-1SG.OBJ=NEG
        'I haven't sucked (it).'
        (Lit. 'I haven't sucked to me.')

The second exception is the fact that the nasals /n/ and /m/ and alveolar fricative /s/ have the tendency of blocking the vowel height harmony between roots vowels and suffix vowel. Although this would require further study, it could also be a natural exception to the language at the same time. See the examples below.

(2.60) a. núŋ-n-áɲ-ɔ̀
          exist.NEG-SG-1SG.OBJ-VSF
          'I am not present'
          (Lit. 'Me not exist/present')

      b. sén-áɲ-Ø   ké
          say.IMPERV-1SG.OBJ-3SG.SU.IMPERV QUOT
          'S/he says to me, …'

      c. dúm-áɲ-έ   kὲnɔ̀   àɲὲ
          collect-1SG.OBJ-3PL.SU.IMPERV wood.PL 1SG
          'They collect (fetch) wood for me.'

      d. kù-tùs-áɲ-ɔ̀
          PASS-bless-1SG.OBJ-VFS
          'I am blessed'

Except (2.60a), that could perhaps be regarded as similar to that of (2.59), a CC cluster blocking the harmony, the rest are peculiar cases which need to be addressed in future investigations.

The third exception is very interesting. That is, it is a special instance where we would see the verb root and the two suffixes that harmonize with it co-occur in a single harmony process.

(2.61) ìggè ŋànì   ŋà=íw-án-áɲ=ó
2PL NEG.PERV NEG.IMPERV-take-MT-1SG.OBJ=2PL.SU.IMPERV+NEG
'You (pl.) still haven't accepted me.'

The height harmony process between the vowels of verb roots and the vowels of motion suffixes applies in exactly the same way as the above. The examples given below strengthen this fact, particularly (2.62a1–a2) with different verb roots containing vowels which harmonize with [+/-high] vowels of the motion suffixes.

(2.62) a1. ŋà=kì=tùnù   égís-ónó   kààrì
           DEM=tree.SG=FAR ripe.IMPERV-MT.3SG.SU.IMPERV seed
           mèrì
           many

OR a2. ŋà=kì=tùnù   dɔ́ŋ-áná   bùràj mèrì
       DEM=tree.SG=FAR pick/lift-MT.3SG.SU.IMPERV fruit many
       'That tree bears much fruit.'

   b. éd-oń-ɛ́
      pick-MT-3PL.SU.IMPERV
      'They pick up.' (motion towards)

   c. kɔ́-ŋɔ́w-án-ɔ́
      1SU-steep.down-MT.1SG.SU.IMPERV-VFS
      'I will fall.' (motion towards)

   d. jàg-án   bé
      return-MT.2SG.SU.IMPERV axe
      'You (sg.) return the axe.'

Above all, it is to be noted that it is the vowel of the first syllable of a verb, which is crucial and triggers a vowel height harmony. As is shown in (2.62a–d), the verb roots have contained both [-high] and [+high] vowels, however, it is only the vowel of the first syllable which directly harmonizes with the vowel of the motion suffix (see also 2.62e).

   e. kó [hùllì ŋànì   ká-čáhúr-án=ó=jè]_{SUBORD:CL}
      PCN if/when NEG.PERV 1SU-strew-MT=NEG=SUBORD
      '... and if I haven't strewn (it).'

In this regard, the vowel height harmony and the vowel copying process are proofs which indicate the point at which phonology and morphosyntax interact with one another. Particularly, vowel copying which we see in § 2.5.6.6, couldn't be considered as a phonological process that exists to satisfy purely a phonological requirement.

2.5.6.5   *i*-Initial Verb Roots as a Special Class
Another striking feature of Mursi phonology is the distinction between verb roots that start in high front vowel /i/ and roots that start with non-high front vowels. In í-initial verb roots, vowels that can occur in their second syllables are /a/ and /o/, and /i/ itself. Mursi has few verb roots that start with the high front vowel and most of these verbs behave like lexicalized causative verbs. There is diachronic evidence which substantiates the fact that the prefix í- had a causative function, probably at an earlier stage of the language. See the following examples:

(2.63) a. /ígóm/   'permit, allow, admit, obey, consent'
       b. /ílál/   'console, encourage'
       c. /ídóg/   'feed/raise, enlarge'
       d. /ílób/   'try, attempt'
       e. /ítáb/   'deceive/lie'
       f. /íláás/   'be sick'
       g. /ítím/   'ignite'
       h. /írít/   'give birth, bear'

All of them have one feature in common, i.e. they all are disyllabic roots and their second syllables end in a consonant-final CVC shape. Therefore, I called this set of verb roots 'í-vowel' types. The second set of verb roots can be distinguished from the 'í-harmony' types in that they lack the high front vowel in neither of their syllables. They are primarily known for repeating the vowels of their first syllables in their post-initial syllables (second and third syllables)—or $V_1 = V_2$ ($\sigma_1 = \sigma_2$). Examples are shown in (2.64).

(2.64) a. /érés/   'cross'
       b. /úgún/   'push'
       c. /ógór/   'steal'
       d. /márág/   'walk around, wander'
       e. /dɔ́rɔ́k/   'dry'
       f. /čɔ́bɔ́s/   'suck, kiss'
       g. /čólós/   'wish'

PHONOLOGY 83

    h. /lɔ̀tɔ̀g/   'wet'
    i. /tɔ́rɔ́k/   'pass gas, fart'
    j. /túkúr/   'stir'
    k. /ɛ́dɛ́mɛ́s/   'learn'

As we can see in (2.64), vowels of the first syllables of each roots are always crucial because they are the one that determine and initiate vowel harmony (left-to-right). Therefore, we may divide the words listed above into different vowel harmony types according to their patterns or vowel quality sequences they display, for example fronting or rounding harmony. But they can also generally be referred to as displaying transparent progressive harmony.

2.5.6.6   Vowel Copying

Typologically, Mursi is one the few languages of the world that have a rare morphophonological feature called vowel copying. At least, the other languages that have this feature and that I know of, are Surmic languages. In the context of Mursi, vowel copying is a morphophonological process of copying the vowel of a verb root and putting it in prefix or suffix slots for certain morphosyntactic functions. A number of linguists have referred this type of segmental spreading phenomenon in terms such as melodic copying (Marantz 1982) and correspondence-based copying (McCarthy and Prince 1995). There are also a few linguists who treat the copying phenomenon in the same way as spreading. I, however, prefer to stick to the term 'vowel copying' because copying is quite different from spreading. First of all, Mursi has two types of vowel copying—right-to-left (prefixal) and left-to-right (suffixal). The latter doesn't show any sign of spreading but rather it undergoes a vowel copying process. Nevertheless, the phonological motivation for the former one (prefixal) may be the phonotactic constraint of the language which triggers the copying, for example the prohibition of consonant clusters at word-initial position. This would probably be equivalent with another phonotactic constraint-based process term called copy-vowel epenthesis or echo epenthesis. Main characteristics of the vowel-copying process include:
– Vowel-initial verb roots cannot undergo a vowel copying process,
– Only the vowel of the first syllable of a verb root is copied,
– Phonetic long vowels cannot be copied (resulting from historical intervocalic consonant deletion-based verb roots) (see aslo § 2.5.1.2), and
– Some *k*-initial verb roots could trigger compensatory vowel lengthening (see rule iii below).

Accordingly, three distinctive phonological rules can be devised as can be seen below:

- /kV-/ → [kV₁-] / __+C₁V₁(C₂) (for consonant-initial verb roots)
- /k-/ → [k-] / __+V₁(V₂)C₁ (for vowel-initial verb roots)
- /kV-/ → [kV₁V₁-]/ __+kV₁C₁ (for *k*-initial verb roots)

The morphological markings which utilize the prefix k- and the respective vowel copied from the verb root-initial syllable into its V slot are: first person S/A argument markers, third person subjunctive, agentless passive, and hortative-jussive moods. Some examples are presented as follow:

(2.65) a1. /ták-á/
know.PERV-3SG.SU.PERV
'S/he knew.'

a2. [ká-ták-á]
1SU-know.PERV-1SG.SU.PERV
'I have known.'

b1. /ár-á/
see.PERV-3SG.SU.PERV
'He/she saw.'

b2. [k-ár-á]
1SU-see.PERV-1SG.SU.PERV
'I saw (it).'

c1. /kú-kún-í/   →[Ø-kún-í] ~ [kúúní]
1SU-come.IMPERV-1SG.SU.IMPERV
'I came.'

c2. /kú-kúnásíd-à/
1SU-dream.PERV-1PL.INC.SU.PERV
→[Ø-kúnásídà] ~ [kúúnásídà]

'We (inc.) dreamed.'

As is shown in (2.65c1–c2), *k*-initial verb roots usually trigger compensatory vowel lengthening. One of the redundant *kV*- shapes will be deleted, but the vowel along its tone will be retained in the root. This demonstrates the fact that vowel copying phenomenon may also appear in one more identical phonological process but with a different prefix, i.e. perfective aspect marker prefix *t(V)-*.

(2.66) a. /lɔ̀m/ 'have (IMPERV.)'   /tɔ̀-lɔ̀m/ 'have (PERV.)'
b. /már/ 'refuse/dislike (IMPERV.)'   /tá-már/ 'refuse, dislike (PERV.)'
c. /óɲ/ 'wash (IMPERV.)'   /t-óɲ/ 'wash (PERV.)'

Therefore, Mursi displays single, double, triple, and quadruple vowel copying morphophonological phenomena, all of which are determined by morphological context.

(2.67) *Single vowel copying*
/kí-hín-í/
1SU-want.IMPERV-1SG.SU.IMPERV
'I want'

(2.68) *Double vowel copying*
a. /kɛ́-tɛ́+hɛ́n-à/
1SU-PERV+want-1SG.SU.PERV
'I wanted'

b. /kà-ɓàg-à/
PASS-eat.PERV-PASS.3SU
'(It) was eaten.'

The suffix -*a* is the third person passive subject form copied directly from the vowel of the verb root.

(2.69) *Triple vowel copying*
/kìɔ̀   kɛ̀-tɛ̀-ŋɛ̀d-ɛ̀   ɓé-ɔ̀/
tree.SG PASS-PERV-cut-PASS.3SU axe.SG-OBL
'The tree was cut with an axe.'

(2.69) requires obligatory oblique argument, otherwise it must be the verb marked by a verb-final suffix (cf. Mütze 2014). The verb-final suffix is a vowel, which is identical with the vowel of the verb root, as can be shown in the quadruple vowel copying example given below.

(2.70) *Quaduple vowel copying*
/kìɔ̀   kɛ̀-tɛ̀-ŋɛ̀d-ɛ́-ɛ̀/
tree.SG PASS-PERV-cut-PASS.3SU-VFS
'The tree was cut.'

2.6 Tone

Mursi has two tone levels—High (H) and Low (L). This contradicts what Turton and Bender suggested more than four decades ago. Turton and Bender (1976: 559) suggested that Mursi has four registered tones: high, mid, low, and falling. However, in this study, mid and falling tones are not attested. Besides, Yigezu (2001) in his study of the comparative phonetics and phonology of Surmic languages, suggested three tone levels for Mursi—high, mid and low. The latest study on the language has showed only two tone levels—high and low (Mütze 2014). Therefore, as far as tone levels of Mursi is concerned, at this stage, the current study is in line with Mütze's discovery—Low and High.

In Mursi, tone is important both lexically and grammatically. The syllable is the main tone-bearing unit in the language. A phonological word, whether it has a nominal root or verbal root must have at least one syllable as a tone-bearing unit. Thus, it is the number of syllables carrying distinct tone levels which create different tonal melodies on nouns and verbs. That means that different tonal melodies will automatically generate tonal patterns depending on number of syllables in a word. Tonal patterns, however, may not come in a straightforward way even if two simple register tones exist.

Most importantly, as any other morphosyntactic criteria, tone may be used as a phonological level criterion to distinguish between two word classes—nouns and verbs.

Accordingly, depending on the number of syllables in a phonological word, nominal words display six tone melodies whereas verbal words display three tonal melodies.

(2.71) Monosyllabic nouns—two tone melodies
    a. /bà/   L   'place, land, country'
    b. /bè/   L   'stone'
    c. /ɔ́r/   H   'settlement, homestead, village'
    d. /sáj/   H   'leather dress (women's clothing)'

(2.72) Disyllabic nouns—four tone melodies
    a. /àɲè/   LL   'I (Pro.)'
    b. /lògó/   LH   'word, issue (sg.)'
    c. /lúsì/   HL   'boy (sg.)'
    d. /hírí/   HH   'man (sg.)'

According to observations in this study and in Mütze's sketch work, the L surface tone melodies may display two properties. First, there are nouns with

PHONOLOGY   87

an invariably L surface tone melody regardless of the environments in which they occur in clauses. I have quoted examples from Mütze (2014) in 2.73a–c.

(2.73) An invariable (stable) L surface tone melody carrying nouns
    a. *kònù*   *ʤìm-Ø*   *sáb-ɔ̀*
       snake.SG lead-3SG.SU.IMPERV first/head-OBL
       'The snake leads first'

    b. *kònù*   *dák-ú*   *bà*
       snake.SG fall-3SG.SU.PERV ground
       'The snake fell down.'

    c. *ŋà=ìn=à*   *á*   *kònù*
       DEM=3SG.PN.SP=NEAR COP.3.IMPERV snake.SG
       'This is a snake.'

As is shown in (2.73a–c), *kònù* 'snake' shows a stable L surface tone melody on its final syllable, it cannot influence change its melody, and it can in no way change its melody by the influence of the tone melodies on the preceding or following verbs.

Second, there are nouns with dynamic tone melodies that display L tone melodies underlyingly but they may change into H surface tone melodies when followed by verbs with L surface tone melodies.

(2.74) A dynamic (unstable) L surface tone melody carrying nouns
    a. *dàdà*   *dák-ú*   *bà*
       father.PERT:1SG.PSR fall-3SG.SU.PERV ground
       'My father fell down.'

    b. *dàdá*   *ʤìm-Ø*   *sáb-ɔ̀*
       father.PERT:1SG.PSR lead-3SG.SU.IMPERV first/head-OBL
       'My father leads first.'

    c. *ŋà=ìn=à*   *á*   *dàdà*
       DEM=3SG.PN.SP=NEAR COP.3SG.IMPERV father.PERT:1SG.PSR
       'This is (my) father'

The noun *dàdà* '(my) father' is a LL surface melody carrying noun (as in (2.74a)). However, the L surface tone melody on its second syllable becomes H surface tone when followed by a low-toned verb (as in (2.74b)). As can be shown in both (2.73c) and (2.74c), in clause final environments, the tone melodies of nouns are not being affected as there is no element that follows them.

The six tone melodies of monosyllabic and disyllabic nouns listed earlier and including other tone melodies of polysyllabic nouns not listed here make Mursi nouns have very diverse tone patterns. On the contrary, tonal melodies of verbs are built upon only three inherent lexical tones: H, HL and LH. Roughly more than 90 percent of Mursi monosyllabic verb roots are inherently H-toned. Tone spreading and/or tone association is always leftward. In accordance with the lexical tone patterns observed on verb roots, the following basic rules may partially govern the tone assignment system on verb roots.

– H-toned verb roots always surface with a level H tone under any environment.

(2.75) a. čúr-ó rúm-ína
wash.IMPERV-2PL.SU.IMPERV cloth-PL
'You (pl.) wash clothes.'

This rule remains constant even when a zero suffix bound pronominal suffix accompanies a H-toned verb root, as in (2.75b).

b. lúsì dág-Ø hírí-ó
boy hit-3SG.SU.IMPERV man-NOM
'The man beats the boy.'

– In H-toned verb root of HL melody, L is deleted and becomes H. A similar rule is suggested by Mütze (2014) but needs further study. See the following examples.

(2.76) a. édʒ-ì bì
shoot.IMPERV-2SG.SU.IMPERV cow
'You (sg.) shoot the cow.'

b. édʒ-Ø bì
shoot.IMPERV-3SG.SU.IMPERV cow
'He shoots the cow.'

In (2.76a), the H-tone associates with the HL verb root itself, not with something else that follows the verb. Tone association other than the lexical verb itself appears to be the property of a polar tone associated with LH verb roots.

The reason is that tone polarity on verb roots usually happens when the H tone associates with toneless suffixes. Thus, the tone polarity on LH verbs can be interpreted in terms of the following two rules:
- The L tone of the verb root associates with a polar tone (H) of the suffix (as in (2.77a–b)).
- If the suffix attached to the verb root has zero morpheme realization, then the L tone of the verb root associates with a polar tone (H) of the following word (as in (2.77c)).

(2.77) a. *hàlí kì-dìr-í   dórí*
later 1SU-sweep-1SG.SU.IMPERV house
'I shall sweep the room later.'

b. *gùɲ-í   bì*
see/watch-2SG.SU.IMPERV COW.SG
'You (sg.) see the cow.' (Mütze 2014)

c. *gúɲ-Ø   bì*
see/watch-3SG.SU.IMPERV COW.SG
'He sees the cow.' (Mütze 2014)

In (2.77a–b), the tonal polarity operates on the verb itself whereas in (2.77c) the tone polarity operates between the tone of the verb root and the following word. Moreover, Mursi shows a two-way lexical tonal contrast. Lexical tonal contrasts are presented as follows.

(2.78) a. /mùnì/ LL 'Mursi person' /múnì/ HL 'muscle'
b. /ɲàwà/ LL 'ear (pl.)' /ɲáwà/ HL 'blood'
c. /kàkà/ LL 'grandmother' /kàká/ LH 'molar (pl.)'
d. /kòrù/ LL 'lowland' /kòrú/ LH 'chisel'
e. /làlàŋ/ LL 'bracelet' /láláŋ/ HH 'a kind of tree'

As we can see, all lexical tonal contrasts come in disyllabic forms. Only two monosyllabic examples were found to be lexically contrastive—one nominal is mentioned by Mütze (2014) *mór* 'abdominal fat' vs. *mòr* 'calf' and the other one is verbal *ɓág* 'to eat' vs. *ɓàg* 'to live'.

In addition, despite it being functionally limited to certain grammatical categories such as number and person, Mursi also exhibits grammatical tone. Some examples are presented as follows.

(2.79) a. /bùgùj/ LL 'back (sg.)' /búgúj/ HH 'back (pl.)'
b. /kìlòj/ LL 'heron (sg.)' /kílój/ HH 'heron (pl.)'
c. /hùnnàj/ LL 'small stream (sg.)' /húnnáj/ HH 'small stream (pl.)'

Apart from the examples illustrated in (2.79) depicting the function of tone as a grammatical number marker, grammatical tone can also be used to distinguish between first person and third person subjects in hortative-jussive constructions. In other words, grammatical tone distinguishes between hortative and jussive moods.

(2.80) a. *kà-màg*
1.HORT-catch.PERV
'Let me catch!'

b. *k-èlèhèn*
1.HORT-measure.PERV
'Let me measure!'

c. *k-éléhén-é*
3.JUSS-measure.PERV-VFS
'Let him measure!'

As can be shown in (2.80a–b), the hortative form takes a L-toned verb root or on the prefix *k(V̀)*- because the *V* is direct copy of the verb root's vowel plus tone. On the other hand, the jussive form always carry a H-toned verb root. Both constructions can optionally be preceded by a free form hortative-jussive particle *aj* [aɲ]. This particle always carries an opposite tone of the verb root, for which the two tones form a tone polarity. Compare examples (2.81a) and (2.81b–c).

(2.81) a. *áj   kè-sèrè   kàrì*
HORT.PART 1.HORT-inherit.PERV.1PL.INC together
'Let us (inc.) inherit'

b. *àj   ké-séré-ó*
JUSSI.PART 3.JUSS-inherit.PERV-VFS
'Let him inherit'

c. *àj   ké-séré-t-ó*
JUSSI.PART 3.JUSS-inherit.PERV-PL-VFS
'Let them inherit'

In (2.81a), there is a vowel coalescence—the root's final vowel and the morpheme -V of the first person plural inclusive markers are identical, i.e. *e+e > e*.

2.7 Wordhood

In sections following, the phonological and grammatical status of a 'word' or 'wordhood' is discussed briefly by utilizing phonological and grammatical criteria. Thus, a phonological word (§ 2.7.1) and a grammatical word (§ 2.7.2), and mismatches and coincidences between the two (§ 2.7.1) were addressed.

2.7.1   *A Phonological Word*

A phonological word is a phonological unit larger than the syllable (Dixon and Aikhenvald 2003: 13). A phonological word in Mursi has the following major phonological properties: segmental features (internal syllabic structure), prosodic features (tone assignment and vowel height harmony), and word boundary-related phonological processes. Accordingly, the following properties define a phonological word in Musi:

- A phonological word does not contain cluster of consonants at word-initial and word-final positions (§ 2.3.4).
- Unless historical intervocalic consonant deletion is involved, a phonological word does not contain vowel length. There may be a requirement that a monosyllabic phonological word should undergo compulsory lengthening (§ 2.3.7).
- Due to a segmental restriction on the co-occurrence of long vowels between morpheme boundaries, the glottal stop /ʔ/ may be inserted to mark the beginning of a phonological word (§ 2.3.1.1).
- Lack of occurrence of the bilabial implosive in word-final position (§ 2.3.1.2)
- Lack of occurrence of fricatives in word-final positions (§ 2.3.1.3).
- Neutralisation of affricates word-finally (§ 2.3.1.4).

These points (i–vi) indicate that there are fewer distinctions made in word-final position than in any other position within a word (a statement supported by cross-linguistic studies, e.g. Dixon 2010, also Dixon and Aikhenvald 2003). For the phonotactic restrictions on the occurrence of consonants in Mursi, see Table 2.4.

- Syllable is the tone-bearing unit and a phonological word must consists of one syllable carrying its own tone melody (§ 2.6).
- A phonological word mostly consists of lexical tone melodies, which is different from mainly a grammatical word that may be accompanied by one or more than one grammatical morphemes (§ 2.6).

- Mursi vowels can undergo a height harmony process that constitutes another form of assimilation on its own. Vowel height harmony can clearly distinguish a phonological word from a grammatical word. Accordingly, close-mid vowels /e/ and /o/ do not co-occur in the same phonological word with open-mid vowels /ɛ/ and /ɔ/ (§ 2.5.6.4).
- Certain phonological rules can designate a phonological word status, namely lenition, deletion, and velarization.
- At a phonological word-final position, consonants {/d/, /t/, /ɗ/, /s/ and /h/} are deleted (§ 2.5.1.1). For example, The alveolar stops /d/ and /t/, the post-alveolar implosive /ɗ/, and the voiceless fricatives /s/ and /h/ are deleted when occurring word-finally (§ 2.5.1.1.)
- Synchronic evidence shows that {/b/ ~*β, /g/~ *ʔ/*ɓ} are deleted when occurring between identical vowels of a phonological word (see § 2.5.1.2).
- In Mursi, there is a word-medial syllable deletion in which the last syllable of the first compound element gets deleted in the compounding process (§ 2.5.1.4).
- Intervocalically, the voiced bilabial stop /b/ lenites to the voiced labial fricative [β] and the bilabial glide [w] (§ 2.5.3). While this is the case, the reverse process (voicing) may also apply on the bilabial glide /w/. Accordingly, /w/ becomes [β/b] with the same phonological rule /w/ → [β/b]/ V__V. The velar plosives /g/ and /k/ lenite (weaken) to the glottal stop [ʔ] word-finally and rarely at morpheme boundaries: /g, k/→[ʔ]/ __{__# or __#__}. The voiced velar stop /g/ can also lenite (weaken) to [ɣ] intervocalically. Similarly, the palatal affricates /ʤ/ and /č/ and the palatal fricative /ʃ/ lenite to the palatal glide [j] word-finally: /ʤ, č, ʃ/ →[j]/__#.
- The velar plosives /g/ and /k/ lenite (weaken) to the glottal stop [ʔ] word-finally and rarely at morpheme boundaries. This could mark the final boundary of a phonological word (§ 2.5.3). Similarly, the palatal affricates /ʤ/ and /č/ and the palatal fricative /ʃ/ lenite to the palatal glide [j] word-finally (§ 2.5.3).
- The alveolar fricatives /s/ and /z/ can undergo a simplification process to their dental allophone counterparts [θ] and [ð]. The voiceless alveolar fricative /s/ becomes [θ] word-initially and intervocalically whereas its voiced counterpart /z/ becomes [ð] intervocalically: /s/→ [θ] / {#__ or V__V} and /z/ → [ð]/ V__V (§ 2.5.4).
- In rapid speech, the liquid /l/ and the nasal /ŋ/ may be reduced from the coda of the first syllables of an inherently reduplicated disyllabic word root (§ 2.5.5).
- At syllable-medial position, the alveolar nasal /n/ is velarized to velar nasal [ŋ] when followed by velar stops /k/ and /g/: /n/→[ŋ]/ __ [k/g] (assimilation, particularly velarization, see § 2.5.6.1).

PHONOLOGY   93

– A phonological word mostly consists of lexical tone melodies, which is different from mainly a grammatical word that may be accompanied by one or more than one grammatical morphemes. A phonological word whether it is a nominal root or verbal root must have at least one syllable as a tone-bearing unit. Thus it is the number of syllables carrying distinct tone levels which creates different tonal melodies on nouns and verbs (§ 2.6).

However, we may find a notable sound pattern difference between a phonological word and ideophones (plus interjections/expressives). For instance, consonant clusters such as: *bs, *mk, *mɗ, *sɗ, gj, and *ŋt are found in ideophones while such clusters do not exist in a phonological word. In Mursi, non-phonemic consonants or vowels may be found in ideophones and in interjections—*p (voiceless bilabial stop) *ɨ (close central vowel). Mursi expressives can a C₁VC₂ shapes (where C₂ stands for voiceless postalveolar fricative [ʃ]). There is no such syllable shape pattern in a phonological word (§ 2.9).

2.7.2 A Grammatical Word

A grammatical word may contain a number of grammatical elements, mainly three are crucial: (i) they always occur together (cohesiveness), (ii) they occur in a fixed order, and (iii) they have a conventionalized coherence and meaning (Dixon and Aikhenvald 2003: 19). Even though few exceptional conditions exist, almost all grammatical words of Mursi can be governed by these three criteria. Thus, a grammatical word in Mursi must consist of a root (nominal or verbal) and a minimum of one morpheme. A grammatical word therefore can consist of from two up to seven grammatical elements (morphemes) that occur together. See the examples given below:

(2.82)   a. *bág-Ø*
             eat.IMPERV-3SG.SU.IMPERV
             'S/he eats.'

         b. [*hùll-á   ór-ɛ́-á*
             when-RSTR   see.IMPERV-3PL.SU.IMPERV-RSTR
             [*ŋà=múɲɨ́ɲ-í=tùnù=ŋà*]ₙₚ]ᵣc/SUBORD:CL
             DEM=star-SG=FAR=DEF
             'When/while they saw that star ...'

         c. *ŋà=kó-jóg-ón-óŋ-Ø=ó-ɔ̀*
             NEG.IMPERV=1SU-tell.IMPERV-MT-2PL.OBJ-1PL.INC.SU.IMPERV=NEG-VFS
             'We (inc.) will not tell (it) to you (pl).'

In (2.82a), we see a minimal verbal word consisting of a root (the citation form) marked by a zero morpheme third person singular subject marker on the imperfective aspect. In (2.82b) is a maximal nominal word consisting of four grammatical elements—a suffix and three clitics. A minimal nominal word can be extracted out of (2.82b), i.e. *múɲíɲ-í* 'star (sg.)'. Of these, the demonstrative system shown by the circumclitics (*ŋà= ... =tùnù*), is a good indication of grammatical elements cohesiveness in a grammatical word. The order of these grammatical elements in no way changes. In (2.82c), we find a typical example that shows the morphological nature of a word in Mursi, i.e. agglutinating and predominantly suffixing. Like the circumclitics indicating the demonstrative system on nominals (2.82b), negation on verbs is mainly indicated by circumclitics (*ŋà= ... =ó*). Both the circumclitics could then be taken as a perfect proof that grammatical elements occur in a fixed order. As shown clearly, all the grammatical words in (2.82a–c) have a conventionalized coherence and full-fledged meaning.

2.7.3 *Mismatches and Coincidences Between the Two Word Types*

There are two major instances of word formations which cause coincidences and mismatches between a phonological word and a grammatical word—compounds (§ 2.7.3.1) and reduplication (§ 2.7.3.2).

2.7.3.1 Compounds

Mursi has a few compounds—mainly noun-noun and noun-quantifier. A compound word is one grammatical word consisting of two phonological words. Compounds can easily be recognized as having two forms either from the same word class or from two different word classes, and by bearing no dependency markers (relators). For example, the restrictive and non-restrictive relators *-a* and *-i/-ti* on the head of an NP. Mursi has five types of compounds—noun-noun, noun-verb, noun numeral/quantifier, adjective-adjective, and adverb-adverb.

(2.83) noun-noun
    a. /sábáwànné/   [sábá-wànné]   (head-pain)   'headache'
    b. /dóríkɛ́ŋɔ́/   [dórí-kɛ́ŋɔ́]   (house-belly)   'floor'
    c. /dórítàrár/   [dórí-tàrár]   (house-roof)   'thatch'

(2.84) noun-verb
    a. /bámágà/   [bá-mág-à]   (place-hold-NOMZ) 'hidden (place)'
    b. /kàarèčáktín/   [kàarè-čák-tín]   (eye:pl-sew-NOMZ) 'blind (person)'

(2.85) *noun-numeral/quantifier*
  a. /hírkón/   [hírí-kón]   (man-one)   'someone; twenty'
  b. /zùdákákán/   [zùgò-dákákán]   (people-all)   'everybody'
  c. /àhádákákán/   [àh-á-dákákán]   (thing-PL-all) 'everything'

(2.86) *adjective-adjective*
  a. /čàkɔ̀rɔ̀ì/   [čágí-kɔ̀rɔ̀ì]   (green-black) 'green'
  b. /čáhɔ̀lí/   [čágí-hɔ̀lí]   (green-white) 'blue'

(2.87) *adverb-adverb*
  a. /kàlìkèŋɔ̀/   [kàlì-kèŋɔ̀]   (day-center)   'noon; mid-day'
  b. /hàlíɓèlè/   [hàlí-ɓèlè]   (later-morning) 'tomorrow'

In compounds, as they are typically composed of more than one phonological word, word boundary associated phonological rules may apply to the last syllable of the first compound word. For example, in (2.85b), the noun *zùgò* 'people', the final vowel may be elided at any time. So, the root *zùg* undergoes a lenition process /g/→[ʔ] followed by deletion of /g/ because */ʔd/ clusters cannot be permitted in any environment (recall deletion and lenition rule in §2.5.3). Finally, we will get the truncated form *zù*.

Compounds are the only one which raise mismatches between the two word types. In Mursi, two clitics can make up one grammatical word, however, they do not form a separate phonological word on their own. Only the two circumclitics (of demonstratives and negations) seem to be eligible for coming together and form a full-fledged utterance.

(2.88) a. /ŋà=∅=á/   → [ŋáà]
           DEM=∅=NEAR
           'Here'

        b. /ŋà=án=ó/   → [ŋà=∅=ó] ~ [ŋà=ʔ=ó] ~ [ŋájò]
           NEG=COP.3.IMPERV=NEG
           'It is not'

In (2.88a), there will be no nominal form which intervenes between the demonstrative proclitic *ŋà=* and the distal marker enclitic *=á*, whereas in (2.88b), a copula verb root in the imperfective aspect has intervened between the negation circumclictics. The glottal stop /ʔ/ is inserted between the boundary of the two clitics, nonetheless it is pronounced as a lamino-palatal glide ⟨j⟩ in fast speech. In addition, tone assignment to a floating clitic is another issue for further study.

2.7.3.2   Reduplication

Reduplication is not productive in Mursi. However, there a few reduplicated words, mainly occurring in two types—those that are composed of two phonological words but form one grammatical word, and those that constitute one phonological word and one grammatical word.

(2.89) a. /kɔ́b/ 'follow'   /kɔ́bkɔ́b/   [kɔ́b.kɔ́b]   'quickly'

b. /dàrì/ 'to move secretly'   /dàrdàr/   [dàr.dàr]   'to steep downhill'

c. /kɛ́ɗ/ 'cut'   /kɛ́ɗúkɛ́ɗú/   [kɛ́ɗú.kɛ́ɗú]   'cut into pieces'

d. /jàg/ 'return (tr.)'   /jágájágá/   [jágá.jágá]   'go back and forth'

e. /búí/ 'big (sg.)'   /bíbí/   [bí.bí]   'big (pl.)'

f. /tííní/ 'small (sg.)'   /tííti/   [tííti]   'small (pl.)'

g. zùwò   [dɔ́nɛ́.dɔ́nɛ́]
people   one:REDUP
'Everyone'
(Lit. people one-one.)

As it is shown in the examples above, reduplication can be full (as in (2.89a–b)), where a full and unreduced phonological word form is copied. Or it could be partial (2.89c–d) which involves segment reductions from the coda of the first phonological word. In the case of full reduplication, monosyllabic verb roots are reduplicated whereas. in partial reduplication vowel alternation and even deletion may take place. In (2.89a), the high back vowel /u/ is deleted and instead replaced by the general adjectivizer suffix -*i*, i.e. *búí* > *bí*. Since the reduplicated form *bíbí+í* > *bíbí* constitutes one grammatical word instead of two, therefore, it takes only one adjectivizer suffix at a time. Likewise, without a change in functional meaning, the numeral *dɔ́nɛ́j* 'one' (2.89e) is used as a numeral. Note that *dɔ́nɛ́j*—may sometimes appears in its full form, but drops the approximant /j/, depending on the speech speed of speakers.

The second types are those with inherent reduplication consisting of one phonological word and one grammatical word. They cannot be decomposed into two distinct phonological words. Hence, phonological and grammatical words coincide.

(2.90) a. sé [mɛ́dú.mɛ́dú]   'blink' (lit. say-blink.blink)
b. dógí [čɔ́b.čɔ́b]   'squat' (lit. to tread on (and) kiss.kiss)
c. /ɓíbíʃí/   [ɓi.ɓi.ʃi]   'to get goose bumps'
d. /ɓédɛ́dɛ́g/   [ɓɛ.dɛ.dɛg]   'flash (lightening)'
e. /ɓárɓárí/   [ɓar.ɓari]   'tremble'
f. /kédɛ́kédɛ́/   [kédɛ́.kédɛ́]   'whisper (sense-speech)'
g. /kúčúkúčú/   [kúčú.kúčú]   'silence, saying nothing'
h. /hélɛ́ŋhélɛ́ŋ/   [hélɛ́ŋ.hélɛ́ŋ]   'become loose'

As we can see in both examples (2.90), they are morphologically deficient in that they do not take grammatical markers. Therefore, inherently reduplicated verbs may require an auxiliary verb sé 'to say' (2.90a) or some other support verbs. Not all of these inherently reduplicated words clearly indicate boundaries of the reduplicants. For example, ɓíbíʃí and ɓédɛ́dɛ́g could have had *ɓiʃɓiʃi /*ɓedɛgdɛg, but co-occurrence of consonant cluster restrictions are to be taken into account. Accordingly, neither *ʃɓ nor *dg cluster is allowed in any environment. Some of the semantics that the reduplicated grammatical words could carry are repetition, plurality, and distribution.

2.8 Clitics

Clitics are morphological elements which do not have the full set of properties of an independent (phonological) word, and may form a phonological unit with the word that precedes it or follows it (Matthews 1997: 56 cited in Aikhenvald 2003:42). Above all, Aikhenvald (ff. 42) points out, 'clitics are prosaically deficient or unusual in certain ways'. Mursi has seven clitics and each has its own syllable (including C 'consonant') and morphosyntactic function: demonstrative, definite, negative, number, subordinate, emphatic, and discourse particle. Of the seven morphosyntactic functions, demonstrative and negation are shown by circumclitics. In Mursi, circumclitics (proclitics combined with enclitics) can form independent phonological words. This means, both the demonstrative and negation circumclitics can form independent phonological words having the same semantic category as the one they form when attached to their hosts (see example 2.88). Table 2.10 below illustrates syllabic shapes of Mursi clitics.

One indication that clitics are prosodically deficient is that the phonological properties which apply to enclitics may not apply to proclitics. For example, vowel height and rounding harmony rules apply to enclitics, however, they do in no way influence proclitics. No Mursi affixes exist that I know of which are

TABLE 2.10 Syllable shapes of Mursi clitics

Morphosyntactic function	Clitics		Syllable shapes
	Proclitics	Enclitic	
Demonstrative	ŋà=	=á [=tá/=ná], =nù [=unu/=ìnù/=tùnù/=nùnù]	V, CV
Definite	none	=ŋà	CV
Negation	ŋà=	=ó [=no/=to/	V
Number	n= and g=	=n and =g	C
Subordinate	none	=jè [=è]	CV
Emphatic	none	=so (also so)	CV
Discourse particle	none	=čii (also čii)	CVV

TABLE 2.11 Phonological properties of clitics and affixes

	Clitics	Affixes
Vowel height and rounding harmony rules	do not apply on proclitics; they may be applied to enclitics	can be governed by these rules
Consonant cluster/ sequence restriction rules	do not apply to proclitics and their host; the rules do apply only between enclitics and their host;	consonant cluster or sequence restriction rules apply to affixes and roots/affixes
Tone change	fixed tonal melody (proclitics)	rarely have tonal melody
Form independent phonological **words**	yes (circmclitics)	no

exempted from these two vowel harmony rules. Table 2.11 is a comparative summary between clitics and affixes on the basis of phonological properties they display.

2.9 Special Phonology

Interjections, ideophones and expressives may have forms that are quite different from the regular internal phonological properties of words, especially with regard to syllabic structure. As we recall from §2.3.3 and §2.3.7, Mursi has neither consonant length nor vowel length. However, phonetic length of both types exist in the language. The former type is trigged by gemination whereas the latter is due to an intervocalic consonant deletion. Contrary to this, we may find that the consonant and vowel lengths interjections, ideophones and expressives are not phonetic neither. Table 2.12 demonstrates the peculiar sound and sound patterns displayed in interjections, ideophones and expressives.

TABLE 2.12 Phonology of interjections, ideophones and expressives

Phonological properties	Interjections	Ideophones	Expressives
Consonant length	CC (NN)	none	none
Vowel length	VV	none	none
Consonant cluster/ sequence	none	*bs/*mk/*md/*sd/*gj/*ŋt	none
Non-phonemic vowel or consonant	*ɪ (close central vowel)	*p (voiceless bilabial stop)	none
Syllable shapes	VV, VCC, CVV	$(C_1V_1C_2).(C_1V_1C_2)$ $(C_1V_1C_2).(C_1V_1C_2).(C_1V_1C_2)$ $(C_1V_1).(C_1V_1).(C_1V_1)$ ... etc.	CVʃ
Tone	unpredictable	unpredictable	fixed (high)
Sound-symbolic or onomatopoeic	no	yes	yes

For example, in Table 2.11 above, expressives can easily be recognized by having simple monosyllabic patterns composed of C_1VC_2 (CVʃ) shapes (where C_2 stands for voiceless postalveolar fricative [ʃ]). There are no such phonological restrictions on any other types of word classes as to what a word must include or exclude at the word-final positions.

2.10 Female Register

There are quite rare and peculiar differences between female and male speech registers in Mursi. The speech registers in Mursi happen mainly due to physiological effects in speech production. It is a peculiar instance in which Mursi's female or male speech production physiological organs are partially affected by their traditional practices such as body beautification, body scarification, and body ornamentation. Yigezu (2001:203) has noted two traditional practices in the Chai people: (i) the lip-plate piercing tradition, which was imperative for any girl attending puberty, but currently is optional tradition being practiced by girls of the same age; (ii) the cultural practice of removing the lower incisors in both—female and male. Like the Chai society, the Mursi have similar traditions traditional practiced by both sex groups. In terms of typological similarities, there is no language closer to Mursi than Chai.

In Chai, as Yigezu (2001: 208) noted, three possible strategies are employed in compensating for the loss of the lower lip: (i) place of articulation is maintained if the manner changes, (ii) manner of articulation is maintained if the point of articulation changes, and (iii) both the place and the manner of articulation change. Yigezu has also mentioned three consonant changes happen based on the three ways of compensating for the loss of the lower lip: (i) Strategy I—[b] > {β}, [ɓ] > {w} and [β] > {ɸ, (ii) Strategy II—[b] > [d], [ɓ] > [ɗ], [s] > {θ}, [p] > [t] and [m] > [ŋ], and (iii) Strategy III—[b] > [ð].

In Mursi, as shown in these Categories, the alveolar fricatives /s/ and /z/ can undergo a simplification process to their dental allophone counterparts [θ] and [ð]. The voiceless alveolar fricative /s/ becomes [θ] word-initially and intervocalically (Strategy I) whereas its voiced counterpart /z/ becomes [ð] intervocalically (Strategy III): /s/→ [θ] / {#__ or V__V} (/sízzì/→[θízzì]) 'three', /kásáj/→[káθáj] 'sand'; and /z/ → [ð]/ V__V (§ 2.5.4). Strategy I is directly associated to Mursi's lenition rule, in which, intervocalically, the voiced bilabial stop /b/ lenites to the voiced labial fricative [β] and the bilabial glide [w]. The general morphological process that explains lenition of /b/ intervocallically is called intervocalic spirantization; and has a rule: /b/ → [β/w]/ V__V (see § 2.5.3). The rule that governs Strategy III is available in § 2.5.4. Similar to Chai, in Mursi the production of the following consonant sounds are partially affected by the lower lip piercing tradition (cf. Yigezu 2001: 203–221; 2005: 241–257; Lüpke 2010: 6 ff.); see also § 1.7.3.

CHAPTER 3

Word classes

3.1 Introduction

Mursi has three open word classes and twelve closed word classes. The open word classes are: nouns (§3.2.1), verbs (§3.2.2) and adjectives (§3.2.3). The set of closed word classes include pronouns (§3.3.1), adverbs (§3.3.2), adpositions (§3.3.3) (prepositions and postpositions), question words (3.3.4), number words and quantifiers (§3.3.5), connectors and discourse particles (§3.3.6), interjections (§3.3.7), ideophones (§3.3.8), and expressives (§3.3.9). Although each word class displays their own distinct morphological, syntactic and semantic properties, establishing a straightforward distinctions between word classes may not be always easy. For example, some members of the adjective class share certain morphological categories with nouns—such as number, demonstrative and definite. Likewise, adjectives can also share morphological categories with verbs—such as person, mood, valency changing derivations and negation.

As these morphological categories do not exclusively apply to each and every members of a particular word class, extensive morphological and syntactic criteria must be applied in order to distinguish one from the other before making either a characterization statement or establishing exceptions. Moreover, as suggested in Aikhenvald (2015: 81), morphological structure and categories on one hand, and syntactic functional slots in a clause on the other hand are among the essential criteria for distinguishing between word classes. Apart from the two productive criteria, one phonological criterion has been found to be a salient segmental property of verb roots for distinguishing verbs from the rest word classes, i.e. roughly 90 percent of Mursi verb roots end in consonants. This will be discussed in §7.2, Chapter 7. In addition, interjections and expressives have also a peculiar phonology quite different from other word classes (see the last two subsequent sections of chapter 2). Therefore, this chapter presents a detailed account of morphological and syntactic features of word classes based on the language's internal structure. Before embarking onto the details of each word classes. Table 3.1 below shows a summary of word classes vis-à-vis their syntactic functions and functional slots.

The syntactic functions and functional slots of the word classes listed in Table 3.1 above may be possible properties of a particular word class as a whole and only represent general syntactic features of that particular class. However,

TABLE 3.1   Word classes and their functional slots

Syntactic function	Noun	Verb	Adjective	Pronoun	Adverb
Head of transitive predicate	×	√	√ (very rare, only derived)	×	×
Head of intransitive predicate	×	√	√ (derived)	×	×
Core or oblique argument	√	×	×	√	×
Copula subject (CS)	√	×	×	×	×
Copula complement (CC)	√	×	√	??	×
Head of NP	√	×	×	√	×
Possessum in NP	√	×	×	??	×
Possessor in NP	√	×	×	??	×
Modifier within an NP	√	×	√	√	×
Modifier of a verb	×	×	some	×	√

some word classes may have sub-classes with their own specific syntactic functions, for example, the noun class has about five members, and each sub-classes may show some degree of peculiarities of morphology and syntax in line with general feature of the class.

3.2   Open Word Classes

In the following sections, the morphological, syntactic and semantic properties of the three open word classes of the language, nouns (§ 3.2.1), verbs (§ 3.2.2) and adjectives (§ 3.2.3) are discussed.

3.2.1   *Nouns*

A noun class generally includes simple nouns, relator nouns, place names, kinship nouns, proper names, and compound nouns. Apart from these, all other nouns can be members of this class through various derivations mainly from verbs and adjectives. The morphological categories that these noun types in general take (§ 3.2.1.1) and the syntactic functional slots they fill in a clause (§ 3.2.1.2) will be discussed. Following this, descriptions have been provided for each noun type (see § 3.2.1.3). Mursi has no grammatical gender, but a brief overview of natural gendered nouns is presented in (§ 3.2.4).

3.2.1.1 Morphological Categories of Nouns

Morphologically, nouns can be defined as words that obligatorily inflect for number, case, demonstrative, and definiteness. Number on nouns can be shown in a number of ways and by two morphological forms: suffixes and clitics. There is only one pre-root slot for deictic function and nine other post-root slots of which four are shown by enclitics. Table 3.2 below is a schematic representation of the structure of a Mursi noun and suffix-clitic ordering.

TABLE 3.2   The structure of a Mursi noun

Slot	Morphological category	Morphological form
SLOT 1	demonstrative	proclitic
SLOT 2	root	root
SLOT 3	number	suffix
SLOT 4	case	suffix
SLOT 5	nominalizer	suffix
SLOT 6	pertensive	enclitic
SLOT 7	modification/relator	suffix
SLOT 8	proximal/distal	enclitic
SLOT 9	emphatic marker	enclitic
SLOT 10	definiteness	enclitic
SLOT 11	subordinate	enclitic

Note that not all these morphological categories of nouns can be added to noun roots at a time. At the same time, noun roots cannot have the same capacity in taking these categories at once. For example, de-verbal nouns or nouns derived from verbs by the nominalizer -*a* can take nominative and other case morphologies. This is not the case for other de-verbal nouns.

Based on the morphological slots shown in Table 3.2, the morphological category indicating the demonstrative function takes SLOT 1. The demonstrative system of Mursi is always shown by circumclitics. That is, the demonstrative marker proclitic (SLOT 1) always co-occurs with a two-way deictic contrast marker enclitic (SLOT 8) (see Chapter 4, §4.2.1). SLOT 2 is a noun root itself. The noun root refers to simple nouns and relator nouns. Aside from these, the term de-verbal noun can be appropriate for all other morphological form of nouns which co-occur with SLOT 5. On nouns that are derived from verbs, number marking is applied after the nominalizer, as in (3.1).

(3.1)   [ŋà=bég-á-ɲá-ìnù]_NP
        DEM=watch-NOMZ-PL=FAR
        'Those (field) watchings (vigils)'

SLOT 3 is generally a slot for overt tripartite coding of number—replacive, plural, and singulative. About 70 portmanteau number marking suffixes fill this nominal slot (see number system, Chapter 5). Apart from the noun class, some members of the adjective class namely dimension and colour adjectives may take overt number marking (see § 3.4 of this chapter, and Chapter 8). The case system which marks both core and non-core constituents fills SLOT 4. The case marking system depends highly on constituent order. In general, nouns can be marked for case suffixes of any type when occurring post-verbally (see Chapter 10). SLOT 6 can be filled by the pertensive morphology. Only kinship nouns take pertensive morphology.

(3.2)   a. *gòdóná*   'brother (my)'

        b. *gòdón=gà* 'brothers (my)'

        c. *gòdón=gà-čó*
           brother=PERT.1PL.PSR-PL
           'Our brothers'

        d. *gòdón=gà-čó-à*
           brother=PERT.1PL.PSR-PL
           g=àw/g=àj
           PL.PSD=1PL.EXC.PRS/PL.PSD=1PL.INC.PRS
           'Our (exc./inc.) brothers'

Pertensive morphology on the kinship nouns indicates number of possessed, possessor and person (as in (3.2b–c)). The possessive pronouns can follow kinship nouns marked by pertensive morphology usually when further grammatical information (first person inclusive/exclusive distinction) is required, as in (3.2d). This may also show kinship nouns that may be marked for the same category twice—or literally on the basis of a recursive system (see Chapter 4). Furthermore, the suffix -*čo* is a plural number marker that can occur only with few kinship nouns (see Chapter 6 for a full list of -*čo* taking kinship nouns). As can be seen in (3.2d), whenever a modifier follows the head within an NP, the head noun will then be marked for modification/relator marker suffix: -*a* (restrictive) and -*ti*/-*i* (non-restrictive). Therefore SLOT 7 will be filled by a modification/relator marker. SLOTS 8–11 are clitics which will be marked on nouns occurring in NPs and clauses. The following examples clearly indicate the three slots—definite and subordinate (3.3a) and emphatic (3.3b).

(3.3) a. ŋà=zùg=tà=ŋà=jè   [hínísí-á   g=èj]_NP
         DEM=people=NEAR=DEF=SUBORD heart-RSTR   PL.SPD=3PL.PSR
         'For these people's heart ...'

     b. [hír-á   màd-ì]_NP   bág   tílá=só
         man-RSTR   teach-NOMZ eat.PERV:IMP   food=EMPH
         'Master, eat!'
         (Lit. Teacher, please eat (sg.) food!)

The emphatic marker =so in (3.3b) is a floating enclitic as it can also occur in free form.

3.2.1.2 Syntactic Function and Functional Slots of Nouns

Syntactically, nouns can head NPs, can be possessum and possessor in NPs, modifier within an NP, copula subjects and complements in a clause, and can fill core or oblique argument slots. The first four functional slots of nouns are indicated below within a single example (3.4a).

(3.4) [čɔ̌r-á   [ŋà=mɔ̀r=à]_NP]_NP
       hair-RSTR   DEM=calf=NEAR
       'The hair of this calf'

In (3.4), čɔ̌rà 'hair' is head of NP in noun modification construction form and ŋàmɔ̀rà 'this calf' is a modifier noun, which is an NP itself. At the same time, čɔ̌rà can be a possessum thus ŋàmɔ̀rà becomes a possessor. The whole NP is (3.4) can be a copula subject as we can see in (3.5) below.

(3.5) [čɔ̌r-á   [ŋà=mɔ̀r=á]_NP]_NP:CS   á   [čàll-ì]_CC
       hair-RSTR   DEM=calf=NEAR   COP.3.IMPERV   good.STV-ADJ
       'The hair of this calf is cold.'

(3.6) [jɔ̀g]_CS   á   [sú]¹_CC
       3PL   COP.3.IMPERV   Aari
       'They are the Aari.' (MH 4: 6:8)

In (3.6), sú 'the Aari people' is a complement clause.

---

1 Sú is an ethnonym which the Mursi use to call their agriculturalist neighbors, the Aari people.

3.2.1.3   Noun Subclasses

Within its open class of nouns, Mursi has about six subclasses: simple nouns, relator nouns, place names, kinship nouns, proper names, and compound nouns. These subclasses of noun may differ from one another in terms of inflecting for some grammatical features, for example for number and case. The semantics that each subclass show could also be another basis for sub-classifying them into such different types. Therefore, each subclass show the following grammatical and sematic features.

3.2.1.3.1   *Simple Nouns*

Simple nouns include: body parts, animals, plants, utensils and ornaments and so on. These could indicate grammatical number in two ways: either by morphological forms or they may inherently occur in plural forms.

(3.7) a. *ŋò*   'neck (sg.)'   *ŋòčín*   'neck (pl.)'
       b. *rɔ̀sɔ̀*   'dog (sg.)'   *rɔ̀sí*   'dog (pl.)'
       c. *bíríní*   'thorn (sg.)'   *bírínɔ́*   'thorn (pl.)'
       d. *bɛ̀*   'stone (sg.)'   *bɛ̀ná*   'stone (pl.)'

Nouns that are inherently plural are mass nouns—mostly nouns referring to liquids such as *mà* 'water', *ɓrà* 'urine', *ɲáwà* 'blood', etc. The only non-liquid noun member that occurs in plural form is *sárá* 'name'. Some members of the simple noun subclass may take more than one plural number marking such as 'silver bracelet' *érésí* (sg.) vs. *érésíó /érésíɲá* (pl.). Based on the grammatical number markers they take, simple nouns may be further sub-divided into small classes or categories (see Chapter 6). Simple nouns are in no way possessed obligatorily. But all simple nouns can potentially be possessed optionally.

3.2.1.3.2   *Relator Nouns*

Relator nouns are nouns that are mostly derived from body parts so as to denote spatial relations. The fact that relator nouns are the results of a slow process of grammaticalization, with a clear transition from prototypical membership of fully inflected noun subclass or category to a less prototypical category (relator category). Their new subclass or category most likely limits their grammatical distributions and inflectional potentials. For example, when they are being used to specify spatial relations, they sometimes drop the final segment of their roots, instead they take oblique case markers. Some example are presented as follows.

(3.8) a. *sábá*   'head (sg.)'   ~ *sáb-ɔ̀*   'in front of, first, ahead of'
       b. *mùmɔ̀*   'forehead (sg.)'   ~ *mùm-ɔ̀*   'in front of'
       c. *rɔ̀ɲòj*   'side of body (sg.)' ~ *rɔ̀ɲ-ɔ̀*   'side, next to (smth.)'
       d. *kèŋɔ̀*   'belly (sg.)'   ~ *kèŋ-ɔ̀*   'center, middle'
       e. *ɓùgùj*   'back (sg.)'   ~ *ɓùgùj-ɔ̀*   'behind'

Not only do they drop their final segments, once they undergo a sematic shift, they do not take number markers. Most importantly, relator nouns in Mursi can be characterized as those that are semantically specialized nouns for referring spatial information, but syntactically they may not be distinguished from other simple noun subclasses. Syntactically, relator nouns mostly take the final slot of a clause. Although clause-final slots are primarily filled by relator nouns carrying oblique case, medial slots can also host relators. In clause medial slot, a relator noun does not take an oblique case if it heads NP. Compare the following examples (3.9) and (3.10).

(3.9) *bì*   *í-Ø*   [*ɓùgùj-á*   *ɲákàr-ùɲ*]$_{NP}$
       cow.SG   exist.IMPERV-3SG.SU.IMPERV   back-RSTR   Nyakarin-GEN
       'The cow is behind Nyakarin.'
       (Lit. behind Nyakarin's back) (Mütze 2014)

(3.10) *wà*   *nɔ̀ŋ*   *kì-čìb-ò*   *sènɔ̀*   *ɓùgùj-ɔ̀*
       REC.PAST   3SG   PASS-tie.PERV-PASS.3SU   hand.PL   back-OBL
       'His hands were tied behind his back.'

As we can see in (3.9), relator nouns can function as head of NPs as any other nouns. Unless by its morphology and syntactic slot, the relator noun *ɓùgùjɔ̀* in (3.10) has identical meaning for both categories (body part and locative). For a full list of relator nouns, see §10.4 of Chapter 10.

3.2.1.3.3 Place Names

Inherently place names differ from other subclasses mainly by the grammatical categories they take. Inherently place names have two key features: (i) they do not take number marking, and (ii) may take oblique case marker when referring to stative locations. Below are place names not marked for oblique and locative cases (3.11). In (3.12), the same nouns are marked for oblique and locative cases.

(3.11) ŋàméá tó-jé   bá-á   [∅ k-èlè-ò   ké
       now   in-OBL place-RSTR [∅ PASS-call.PERV-PASS.3.PL QUOT
       mùn   màkó kó mì kó bóŋósó kó márà]_RC dákákán
       Mursi.PL Mákkí PNC Mis PNC Bongoso PNC Mara] all
       kàrì
       together ...
       'Now, in places called of the Mursi's: Mákkí, Mis, Bongoso, and Mara all together ...' (ME 8:47:9)[2]

Four place names are listed in (3.11) without being marked for oblique case—one which appears to be in vocative form *Màkó* 'Mákkí, the main village where the majority of Mursi people live', *Mì* 'a place where ancestors of the current day Mursi people used to live; grazing land', *Bongoso*, and *Márà*. Recall the deletion rule that applies to the alveolar fricative /s/ word-finally (see § 2.5.1.1 of Chapter 2).

(3.12) ŋàméá zùwò   màkó-jé   ŋɲ   mìs-ɔ́   ŋɲ   bóŋósó
       now   people Mákkí-OBL INTERJ Mis-OBL INTERJ Bongoso.OBL
       ŋɲ   ɔ́r-í   dákákán dakan márà-jé
       INTERJ village-LOC all   all   Mara-OBL
       '... now the people in Mákkí, in Mis, in Bongoso, in all villages, in Mara ...' (ME 18:52:8)

As it can be shown in (3.12), at least two of four allomorphs of the oblique case markers have been attached to place names: *-je* (following all vowel final nouns) and *-ɔ* (consonant-final nouns). The final vowel of *bóŋósó* and the oblique case allomorph *-ɔ* have coalesced.

The fact is that the oblique case covers various case functions including the locative case. But when it is used on place names, this case suffix alone would not be enough to convey the appropriate semantics. It is primarily the motion verb which provides the full-fledge semantics. Thus, the motion verb would make the distinction between 'motion away from the speaker' and 'motion towards the speaker' from the specific location.

(3.13) bàrì   kùùn-í   ʤínkà-jé
       yesterday 1SU.come.IMPERV-1SG.SU.IMPERV Jinka-OBL
       'Yesterday I came from Jinka.'

---

2 Texts coded in ME (stands for 'Mursi Economy') are not included in the Appendix.

WORD CLASSES 109

Place names can be modifiers of head nouns within an NP, thus can take a genitive case like any other nouns, as in (3.14).

(3.14) [zùw-à mìs-òɲ]_NP
people-RSTR grassland-GEN
'of the grassland people (Mis people)'

Nouns referring to certain geographical features such as the generic place term *bá* 'place, land/ground, country, world', *mà* 'water/river', *kídó* 'river', *wárr* 'Omo River' take a locative marker that is different from the oblique case marker----*i* (following vowel-final nouns) and -*ni* (following liquids and the alveolar nasal /n/).

(3.15) kó-hód-á   k-óí-tó
1SU-put.PERV-1PL.INC.SU.PERV 1SU-put.PERV-1PL.EXC.SU.PERV
óɟɟ-ó   **bá-ì-nì**
stalk-PL **place-LOC-RS**
'... then we (inc.) come and we (exc.) put sorghum stalks on the ground.'
(KW 1:38:5)

(3.16) kóód-ónó   bá-ì   ké   **dírká**
1SU.take.out-MT.1PL.INC.SU.IMPERV place-LOC QUOT **Dirka**
'... we (inc.) were heading to a place called Dirka (name of a town).'
(MH 0:31:2)

(3.17) káwúlókɔrɔ kéd-ú   **wárr-nì**
Kawulokoro cut-3SG.SU.PERV **Omo.river-LOC**
'Kawulokoro cut the Omo River.' (MH 0:38:2)

The noun *ɔr* 'village' in (3.12) could be a sole place name being marked for locative case. The reason is that *ɔr* has other meanings referring to habitation: 'homestead, settlement'.

3.2.1.3.4 *Kinship Nouns*
Kinship nouns of Mursi display two unique features: number and pertensive markers. These two grammatical categories are confined to kinship nouns that other subclasses of nouns cannot simply display. The special number marker suffix which applies to a few kinship nouns is -*čo*.

TABLE 3.3   Mursi kinship nouns

Number		Meaning	Pertensive
Singular	**Plural**		
dàdà	dàdàčó	'father'	~ a+a > a
màmà	màmàčó	'mother'	~ a+a > a
kàkà	kàkàčó	'grandmother'	~ a+a > a
dòŋò	dòŋòčó	'the co-wives mothers'	no
mèrè	mèrèčó	'daughter-in-law'	no
ʃúúnɛ́	ʃúúgɛ́	'father'	+a,u,ɛ
dʒɔ̀ɔ̀nɛ́	dʒɔ̀ɔ̀gɛ́	'mother'	+a,u,ɛ
gòdóná	gòdóngá	'brother'	+a,u,ɛ
ŋɔ̀nà	ŋɔ̀nìgèn	'sister'	+a,u,ɛ
kògóná	–	'grandfather'	+a,u,ɛ
óóná	–	'uncle'	+a,u,ɛ
jànèn	jànìgèn	'cousin'	+a,u,ɛ
áú	áúɲá	'firstborn child, eldest'	+a,u,ɛ
bóʃù	bóʃúɲá	'youngest child'	+a,u,ɛ
ŋɔ̀sɔ̀sì	ŋɔ̀sɔ̀ná	'sister's child'	+a,u,ɛ

As it is illustrated in Table 3.3 above, as far as my data suggest at this stage, just a few kinship nouns can be possessed inalienably. Mursi's inalienably kinship nouns include: *dàdà* and *màmà* (can only be possessed by first persons), and *ʃúúnɛ́, dʒɔ̀ɔ̀nɛ́, gòdóná, ŋɔ̀nà, kògóná, kàkà,* and *óóná* (can be possessed by all persons). Inalienably possessed kinship nouns can easily be distinguished from the alienable possessed ones in that they can occur without the possessive pronouns. In this case, they only require pertensive markers: +*a* (first person), +*u* (second person) and +*ɛ* (third person) for possessors.

(3.18)   a1.   [dàdà]ₙₚ
               father.PERT.1.PSR
               'My father'

The noun's final vowel and the first person pertensive vowel were fused, i.e. *a+a > a*. In (3.18a2) below, following the pertensive form, the plural possessor marker *-ɲo* is attached to the noun.

a2. [dàdá-ɲó]_NP
     father.PERT.1.PSR-PL
     'Our father'

On the other hand, as can be shown in the following examples, the kinship-based plural marker is attached to *dàdà*, indicating plural number of both the possessor and possessed. The possessive pronoun in (3.18a4) has just one function, i.e. it distinguishes between first person plural inclusive and exclusive possessors.

a3. [dàdá-čó]_NP
     father.PERT.1.PSR-PL
     'Our fathers'

a4. [dàdá-čó-á   g=àw]_NP
     father.PERT.1.PSR-PL-RSTR PL.PSD=1PL.EXC.PSR
     'Our (exc.) fathers'

An interesting example is as follows, where the kinship noun *dàdà* is being marked for plural number and genitive case suffix. Nevertheless, no information about the possessor is mentioned explicitly.

(3.19) dàdà-čó-ŋ
       father-PL-GEN
       'of the fathers'

The other interesting phenomenon may be that of the kinship nouns which the Mursi use to refer to their sisters' and brothers' children. For instance, my sister's children are addressed as *ŋɔ̀sɔ̀ná* 'sister's children', but my brother's children are just called *éróà gànù* 'my children'. This is due to the fact that the Mursi marriage system allows a *Levirate* (marriage based on inheritance).

Marriage based on inheritance is only allowed when the older brother dies, the younger brother marries his older brother's wife. Therefore, one need not necessarily be obligated to use a possessive construction when addressing his sister's children.

Kinship nouns may take a state derivational marker *-mò*, a morpheme usually used to derive a noun from another noun. But what is more interesting is that this noun-state formation marker morpheme is being attached to an inalienably possessed kinship noun or an NP. As is shown in the following example, *jànìgèn* 'cousin (pl.)' is an NP on its own.

(3.20) ká-dág-ènè-Ø   zèrí-mò zèrí-mò-j
        1SU-hit-RECIP-1PL.INC.SU.IMPERV race-N.S race-N.S-GEN
        jànù=gè-mò   jànù=gè-mò-j
        cousin=PERT.PL.2.PSR-N.S   cousin=PERT.PL.2.PSR-N.S-GEN
        'We (inc.) beat each other, race by race, by cousinhood by cousinhood ...' (KW 2:26:4)
        (Lit. 'by your cousinhood by your cousinhood')

For more discussion on kinship terms, see the section dealing with the kinship system of Mursi in Chapter 1; and possession and kinship nouns in Chapter 5.

3.2.1.3.5 Proper Names

From a morphological point of view, one-third of Mursi proper names are compounds. Both men and women names may be formed from two separate subclasses of nouns mainly, by combining cattle names and their coat-colors, time words and geographic features/cultural artifacts, two inherently gendered nouns and so on. The first proper name type is composed from the noun òlí 'ox/bull' and the coat-colour on it.

(3.21) a. òlígòlòɲ   òlì+gòlòɲ-i   ⟨ox/bull+red⟩
        b. òlíkòrò   òlí+kòrò-i   ⟨ox/bull+black⟩
        c. òlíbàlà   òlí+bàlógi   ⟨ox/bull+leaf (sg.)⟩

The general adjectivizer suffix -i will be deleted since it has no function on nouns. In (3.21c), the singular marker -i is deleted because proper names do no take number markers, and the rest of the second element of the compound is reduced for reasons unknown at this stage. This is the most common personal name of Mursi men followed by bárá 'man, age grade of senior person' plus other nouns (colour terms/geographic features/place names/events, and so on).

(3.22) a. bárgòlòɲ   bár+gòlòɲ-i   ⟨man+red⟩
        b. bártáj   bár+tágí   ⟨man+moon/month (sg.)⟩
        c. bárkámán   bár+kámán   ⟨man+war⟩
        d. bárdórí   bár+dórí   ⟨man+house (sg.)⟩

As can be shown in (3.22), the final vowel, from the first element of the compound (/a/) will be deleted. This indirectly avoids the similarities that may arise between compounds and noun phrases,—for example between bárgòlòɲ 'Bàrgolony' and *bárá-á gɔ̀lɔ̀ɲi ⟨man-RSTR red⟩ *'red man'. In (3.22b), tágí becomes tái~táj due to the intervocalic consonant deletion which applies to the velar stop /g/ (see §2.5.1.2 of Chapter 2). Those listed in (3.21) and (3.22) above are men's personal names. Those of women's personal names can also be formed in the same way. However, women's personal names differ from that of men's in that they must contain the inherently gendered noun ŋàhà 'woman' or adjective ŋàhì 'female'. In the formation of compound nouns, the first element of the compound must always constitute a noun.

(3.23) a. ŋàbìò   ŋàhà+bìò   ⟨woman+cow (pl.)/cattle⟩
b. ŋàlúsá   ŋàhà+lùsà   ⟨woman+boy (pl.)⟩
c. ŋàdőólé   ŋàhà+dőólé   ⟨woman+girl⟩
d. ŋàkídő   ŋàhà+kídő   ⟨woman+river⟩
e. ŋàkútúl   ŋàhà+kútúl   ⟨woman+mountain⟩

The vowel (/a/) will be deleted for the same reason explained above in (3.22). As the result of this, noun form ŋàh appears, and finally we see a more reduced form ŋà. As we recall from the deletion rule in 2.5.1.1 of Chapter 2, the alveolar fricative /s/ is deleted when occurring word-finally.

Morphologically, proper names can take genitive case when they are possessors in NPs. Proper nouns also differ from other subclasses of nouns in that they use zero morpheme as genitive case marker. That is, Ø following proper nouns ending in post-alveolar nasal /ɲ/ and palatal glide /j/. Proper nouns that end in other consonants take -i whereas those which end in vowels take –j (except for i-final proper nouns). See the examples given below:

(3.24) a. [kààrì-à   bárhúɲ-Ø]$_{NP}$
     eye-RSTR Bàrihuny-GEN
     'Barihuny's eye'

b. [érmì-à   ŋàkútúl-i]$_{NP}$
   child-RSTR Ngakútúl-GEN
   'Ngakútúl's child'

c. [érmì-à   òlíkɔ̀rɔ̀-j]$_{NP}$
   child-RSTR Olikoro-GEN
   'Olikoro's child'

A detailed discussion on the colour terms and naming system of Mursi has been provided in Chapter 1.

3.2.1.3.6 *Compound Nouns*

Mursi has a limited set of real compound nouns. However, phrasal nouns are highly productive. In terms of the morphological way that compound nouns are formed, they are not different from other compound words. But compound nouns composed of noun-noun elements differ from all other types of compounds in the way they take plural number marking.

(3.25) a. [màdì tùwɔ́]
      breast mouth.SG
      'nipple'

   b. [màdì-ó tùgì]
      breast-PL mouth.PL
      'nipples'

As it is shown in (3.25a–b), the way number is marked on both nouns of the compounds is similar to some extent to some NPs with noun modifiers. In NPs with noun modifiers, number agreement between the head noun and the noun modifiers is mostly obligatory. But, these are simple compound nouns as they have no modification marker that may indicate syntactic dependency as NPs do. Interestingly, the number marking system utilized on the first noun of the compound differs from that on the second noun. The first noun utilizes regular plural number marker while the second noun utilizes replacive number marking system. Additional examples are given in (3.26a1–c) below.

(3.26) a1. [bì[3] ʤɔ̀ɔ̀nɛ̀]
       cow.SG mother.SG
       'cow'

   a2. [bì-ó ʤɔ̀ɔ̀gɛ̀]
       cow-PL mother.PL
       'cows'

   b1. [kààrì èrì]
       eye.SG skin.SG
       'eyelid'

---

3 *bì* 'cattle' is also a collective noun. However, it occasionally may also be used interchangeably with 'cow'.

b1. [kààrè èrɔ́]
eye.PL skin.PL
'eyelids'

c. [rè   èrì]
body.SG skin.SG
'skin (of human)'

d. [sìò   tárá[r]]
hand.SG roof
'palm of hand'

e. [dórí tárár]_NP dér-Ø-ɔ̀
house roof   leak-3SG.SU.IMPERV-VFS
'The roof (of the house) is leaking.'

Syntactically, compound nouns can occur in limited slots in clauses compared to other type of compounds. They can appear in only three syntactic functional slots: S, CS and CC. Many of Mursi compound nouns are body part nouns and nouns that require natural gender. As we can see from the examples given above, Mursi compound nouns can be referred to as endocentric because they always carry the semantics of one of their parts. Only one of the compound element can determine their grammatical categories, i.e. always the first noun of the compound. Compound nouns can function as any other non-compound nouns, but they can neither be possessor nor possessed.

Phrasal nouns on the other hand are the same as NPs. They have similar morphosyntactic properties to NPs. In addition, phrasal nouns should not necessarily be composed of two separate nouns. Like modifiers of the head of NPs, any element in a modifier slot can constitute the second element of the phrasal nouns. But, like canonical NPs, the noun that must appear at the head slot must be an underived noun, as in (2.27).

(3.27) [hír-á   ŋɔ́l-à]_NP
man-RSTR kneel-NOMZ
'crippled (person)'

The phonological properties of compounds in general has been discussed in § 2.7.3.1 Chapter 2.

3.2.1.3.7 *Inherently Gendered Nouns*

Mursi has no grammatical gender. There are, however, certain kinship nouns and animal nouns that are inherently gendered. Only a few inherently gendered nouns exist outside these two such as *búsój* 'witch craft, evil eye (F.)'

(3.28)

Male		Female	
lúsì	'boy'	dóóléj	'girl'
kògónà	'grandfather'	kàkà	'grandmother'
hírí	'man'	múwáj	'woman'
–	–	sùrò	'mule'
òlè	'bull/ox'	bì	'cow'
kòlà	'he-goat'	–	–

hírí (of human) and *bì* (of animal) can be used as default gendered male and female nouns respectively. 'he-goat' has an opposite term being shown by modification construction (as in (3.29c)). Moreover, gender specification on human and animate nouns which have no grammatical gender may be indicated by two adjectival gender specifiers—*màgì* 'male' and *ŋàhì* 'female'. Therefore, noun modification construction will be mandatory in order to indicate the gender of the head noun in NPs.

(3.29) a. [hír-á   mà]ₙₚ
           person-RSTR male.RSTR
           'man'
           (Lit. 'male person')

        b. [hír-á   ŋàh-à]ₙₚ
           person-RSTR female-RSTR
           'woman'
           (Lit. 'female person')

        c. [tòŋ-à   ŋàh-à]ₙₚ
           goat-RTSR   female-RSTR
           'she-goat'

In noun modification construction, the general adjectivizer suffix -*i* of the adjectives has been replaced by restrictive modification marker -*a*. In (3.29), a vowel coalescence process has taken place following intervocalic deletion of the velar stop /g/.

3.2.1.3.8 De-verbal Nouns

Nouns can be derived from verbs by applying various nominalizers on the verb roots. About eight nominalizers have been found in my data. Many of de-verbal nouns have monosyllabic root shapes in their primary class. De-verbal nouns may take nominal categories—number, case and deictic markers. They differ from one another in terms of their syntactic functions and the functional slots they may take in phrases and clauses. De-verbal nouns can function as S, A and O arguments, copula subject and copula complements, possessed, and modifier within NPs.

3.2.1.3.8.1   Nominalization with -*i*

The nominalizer suffix -*i* in Mursi can be added mostly to stative verb roots to form nouns. This nominalizer is almost identical with the general adjective suffix -*i* and it only is applied on stative verbs. Whether the suffix -*i* is a nominalizer or an adjectivizer seems to depend on the syntactic function and functional slots of grammatical items in which the suffix -*i* occupy in clauses or phrases.

(3.30) a. *á*   [*lòg-á*   *ràmà-í-ùɲ*]$_{NP}$
COM.3.IMPERV word/issue-RSTR be.tall.STV-NOMZ-GEN
'This is the issue of tallness'

b. [*àɲè*]$_{CS}$ [*k-án-í*]$_{C.PRED}$ [*kòrò-í*]$_{CC}$
1SG   1SU-COP.IMPERV-1SG.SU.IMPERV be.black.STV-ADJ
'I am black.'

In (3.30a), *ràmàga* 'tall', which is in underlying free form *ràmàga* becomes *ràmà* following deletion of the velar stop, is in a noun modification construction. Syntactically, it is a verbless clause complement, therefore it is not the same as a derived adjective from a stative verb functioning as a copula complement (as in (3.30b)). The semantics in (3.30a) is that of an abstract noun describing a state of affairs. This is as opposed to its attributive meaning when functioning as real adjective, as in (3.30c).

c. [[*kútúl-í*   *ràmà-í*]$_{NP}$ *tún-ó*]$_{AD.P}$
mountain-NRSTR be.tall.STV-ADJ top-OBL
'On a high mountain'

The genitive case in (3.30) appear to have a phrasal scope, but it needs additional investigation to find out whether it is indeed phrasal or limited to modifiers within NPs.

3.2.1.3.8.2   Nominalization with -tin

De-verbal nouns can also be derived from stative verbs by suffixing the nominalizer -tin on stative roots. All de-verbal nouns derived from stative verbs denote state of affairs or are nouns of state.

(3.31) a. gùrgùrì   'be wise, skilled' gùrgùr-tín   'wisdom, knowledge'
       b. lɔ́tɔ́gí   'be wet'   lɔ́tɔ́k-tín   'liquid'
       c. dáldálí   'be hard'   dáldál-ín   'hardness'
       d. dĭŋdĭŋí   'be heavy'   dĭŋdĭŋ-ín   'weight'
       e. gèrsí   'be bad'   gèrès-ín   'sin'
       f. dɔ́rɔ́sí   'be dry'   dɔ́sɔ́s-ín   'drought'

The segmental form of this nominalizer is phonologically conditioned: -tin mostly following stative verbs that have liquid or alveolar-final roots, and rarely following those that have high front vowel /i/ final roots. Its allomorph -in occurs usually following roots which end in nasals and fricatives.

These de-verbal nouns can act as subject of an intransitive verb (3.32), as modifiers within NPs (3.33) and as the possessed (3.34–3.35).

(3.32) ràmà-tín   kún-Ø   tílà-jé
       be.tall.STV-NOMZ come.IMPERV-3SG.SU.IMPERV   food-OBL
       'Tallness comes from food.'

(3.33) nɔ̀ŋ á   [[hír-á   gùrgùr-tín-ó]_NP
       3SG COP.3.IMPERV   man-RSTR   skilled.STV-NOMZ-MOD
       dádál-á]_NP   háŋ
       be.difficult.STV-RTSR.MOD   INTENS
       'S/he is a man of great abilities.'
       (Lit. 'very heavy skilled man')

(3.34) nɔ̀ŋ á   [[hír-á   lɔ́m-à   gùrgùr-tín-á]_NP
       3SG COP.3.IMPERV   man-RSTR   have-NOMZ   skilled.STV-NOMZ-RSTR
       álí-ɲ]_NP
       voice/talk-GEN
       'S/he is an able speaker.'
       (Lit. 'S/he is a man having knowledge of speaking.')

(3.35) ŋàní iggè sábɔ̀ lámí-ò   [hɔ́l-ín-á
yet   2PL first find-2PL.SU.IMPERV be.white-NOMZ-RSTR
kòmòrù-mó tùm-óɲ]ₙₚ
king-N.S   sky-GEN
'But seek you (pl.) first the kingdom of God, and his righteousness.'
(Lit. 'the righteousness of the kingdom of God')

3.2.1.3.8.3   Nominalization with -mò

Interestingly, de-verbal nouns describing state of affairs can be derived from stative verbs as well as from other nouns by a single derivational marker suffix -mò. The fact that those stative verbs from which de-verbal nouns of state derive are in their adjectival forms.

(3.36) a. gèrèsímó   'criminal'   < gèrsì   'be bad'
       b. karkarimo 'laziness'   < karkari 'be lazy'
       c. čàllìmó   'peaceful'   < čàllì   'be good'

(3.37) a. érímó   'childhood' < érmì   'child'
       b. hírímó   'manhood'   < hírí   'man'
       c. súmó   'sunny'   < sú   'sun'
       d. kásámó   'sandy'   < kásáj   'sand'

In (3.36a–c), when we say stative verbs we mean the roots from which de-verbal nouns of state are derived. Otherwise, in their current forms, they all are derived adjectives carrying the adjectivizer suffix -i. In (3.37a–d), all nouns of state are derived from the same class, i.e. noun. Morphologically, they are defective in that they do not take any nominal morphology.

De-verbal nouns denoting state can function as possessed nouns within NPs (as in (3.34)), but as far as my field notes reveal, they do not function as S/A argument. See the examples given below.

(3.38) a. áʃáŋgárá-mò dɔ́t-ú
          slave-N.S   leave-3SG.SU.IMPERV
          'He abolished slavery.'
          (Lit. 'slavery, he abandoned')

       b. zìní-mò nɔ̀ŋ á   gèrs-ì
          thief-N.S 3SG COP.3.IMPERV bad.STV-ADJ
          'Stealing is bad.'
          (Lit. 'stealing/theft, it is bad')

In (3.38a), the S argument has been indicated by bound pronominal suffix -*u* not by the de-verbal noun. The de-verbal noun *zìnímo* in (3.38b) is not a copula complement on its own, but rather it acts as a topical adjunct when it precedes the copula subject *nɔ̀ŋ*. Further investigation is needed to know whether any other syntactic functional slots these de-verbal nouns may possess in clauses.

3.2.1.3.8.4   Nominalization with –*a*

The nominalizer -*a* is a primary nominalizer of Mursi which usually be used to derive nouns from dynamic monosyllabic verb roots. Derived nouns by this nominalizer can take nominal inflections—number, case and demonstratives.

They take nominative and oblique cases like underived nouns. The nominative case will be attached to these nouns when they occur at post-verbal positions (as in (3.39a; 3.42d)), whereas the oblique case will be attached to those occurring as peripheral arguments. Examples are presented as follows.

(3.39) a. *lófán   hín-Ø   ɓég-á-j*
slingshot want.IMPERV-3SG.SU.IMPERV watch-NOMZ-NOM
'Field-watching wants/requires a slingshot.'

   b. [*gòdón=gà-čó-à   g=àw*]ₙₚ
brother=PERT.1PL.PSR-PL-RSTR PL.PSD=1PL.EXC.PRS
hóɲ   ɓég-á-jé
come.3PL.SU.IMPERV watch-NOMZ-OBL
'Our (exc.) brothers come from the field-watching.'

   c. *kí-hín-í   [lófán-à*
1SU-want.IMPERV-1SG.SU.IMPERV slingshot-RTSR
[*ɓég-á-ɲ*]ₙₚ
watch-NOMZ-GEN
'I want/require for field-watching slingshot.'

The examples in (3.39a and 3.39c) were cited from Mütze (2014). Syntactically, these de-verbal nouns can be modifier within NPs (as in (3.39c)) and modified by bound demonstratives (3.40).

(3.40) [[*ŋà=ɓég-á-ɲá=ínù*]ₙₚ   [*ɓá-á   mùn-ùɲ*]ₙₚ]ₙₚ
DEM=keep/watch-NOMZ-PL=FAR place-RSTR Mursi-GEN
'The field-watching/field-keeping of Mursiland'
(Lit. 'The field-watching place of Mursi')

They can also be modified or possessed by other modifiers/possessors (3.41).

(3.41) **daʃi-á**[4]   [n=ènè]_NP   ádʒ-∅-è
work-NOMZ+RSTR SG.PSD=3SG.PSR give-3SG.SU.IMPERV-COM
zùwò   àlèj
people chair
'His job was to show the people to their seats.'

In clauses, they can function as core arguments: A, O, copula subject, and copula complement, as in (3.42a–e).

(3.42) a. [dórí **dìr-à**]_CS   á   [dáldál-í]_CC
house **sweep**-NOMZ COP.3.IMPERV hard.STV-ADJ
'House sweeping is hard.'

b. [ànè]_A [édʒ-á]_O   ŋà=kí-hín-ì=ó
1SG **shoot**-NOMZ NEG=1SU-want.IMPERV-1SG.SU.IMPERV=NEG
'I don't want shooting.'

c. kì-gìn-ín-o   ànè **gín-à**?
1.SBJV-ask-1SG.OBJ-IRR 1SG **ask**-NOMZ
'May I ask a question?'

d. àggè ké-ɓégt-o   ɓá-á   kó
1PL 1SU-keep.PERV-1PL.EXC.SU.PERV cause/place-RSTR PNC
ɓon-á-j   sààn
arrive-NOMZ-NOM news
'We waited for the arrival of news.'

e. àggè ké-ɓég-o   málsí-tí   [ké
1PL 1SU-keep-1PL.EXC.SU.IMPERV answer-NRSTR COMPL
jag-á   kɔ́b]_COMPL:CL
return-NOMZ quick
'We expect an early reply.'

Nevertheless, monosyllabic dynamic verbs are not the only ones which can be nominalized by the -a, non-monosyllabic stative verbs can also be deverbalized in the same way. See also the following examples.

---

4   Note that the nominalizer -a and the restrictive marker -a on the head noun have coalesced—

(3.43) a. [mɔ̀dɔ̀s-á   bàrì   n=ɛ̀nɛ̀]ₙₚ
tired.STV-NOMZ+RSTR yesterday SG.PSD=3SG.PSR
mɔ̀dɔ̀f-á   wà   á   hólólój hún̄
be.tired.STV-NOMZ REC.PAST COP.3.IMPERV empty simply/just
'All his (yesterday's) efforts were in vain.'

b. [[zùw-á   ɲàgàs-á]ₙₚ   ɔ́r-ùɲ]ₙₚ
people-RTSR old.STV-NOMZ+RSTR village-GEN
mèzìd-ò
discuss.PERV.PL-3PL.IRR
'The village elders held a council.'

3.2.1.3.8.5   Nominalization with –sɛ/-ɛsɛ[5]
The other nominalizer is -sɛ, which is used to derive deverbal nouns from both dynamic and stative monosyllabic intransitive verb roots. This nominalizer has two allomorphs: -ɛ following verbs that are composed of non-high vowels, -e following monosyllabic roots that contain high vowels or the neutral vowel /a/.

(3.44) a. [hír-á   kɔ́d-ɛ̀sɛ̀-n-à]ₙₚ
man-RTSR write-NOMZ-SG-RSTR
'correspondent'

b. tél-í   hùl(l)-á   [zùw-á
exist.PERV.PL-3PL.IRR when-RSTR people-RSTR
rès-ɛ̀-à]ₙₚ
die.IMPERV-NOMZ-RSTR
'They became like dead ones.'
(Lit. 'At the time they became as dead people.')

c. ɲànìjè [lɔ̀g-á   mès-è-á]   jɔ̀kíù   ɲà=més-í-ó
but   issue-RSTR do-NOMZ-RTSR 3PL.NOM NEG=do-PL.IMP-VFS
'But don't do (pl.) according to their works.'

---

a+a > a. This vowel coalescing process is very recurrent as these two morphemes co-occur on such type of de-verbal nouns heading NPs.

5 Note that the nominilizer form -ɛsɛ is distinguished from the otherwise identical benefactive marker -ɛsɛ (on perfective and positive imperative verb roots). The initial vowel -ɛ of the nominalizer -ɛsɛ is an epenthetic vowel being inserted between some consonant-final verb roots and -sɛ.

d. úrɔ́ ìr-ì   wáŋ! úrɔ́ á
   milk drink.PERV.IMP-PL INTENS milk COP.3.IMPERV
   čàll-ì   [bá-á   bás-é-ɲ]
   good.STV-ADJ place-RTSR live.IMPERV-NOMZ-GEN
   'Drink (pl.) much milk! Milk is good for (the) health.'

Note that the nominative case whether on independent nouns by suffixes or fused forms on personal pronouns (as in (3.44c)) can only occur post-verbally. This, however, will be changed when a negated verb appears in the clause because the negated verb always occurs preceding the nominative case carrying noun or pronoun. As it is shown from the examples illustrated above, such deverbal nouns can take number and case. They also function as modifiers within NPs and can be possessed or possessors. The semantics associated with these deverbal nouns may include—result or object of an action.

3.2.1.3.8.6   Nominalization with -nèj

This nominalizer derives deverbal nouns whose syntactic function is confined to copula complement slots. The majority of these nouns are derived from transitive verb roots. They do not take any nominal morphology. As an allomorph, the derivational suffix -ínéj will be attached to the verbal roots following obstruents. Descriptive examples are presented as follows.

(3.45) a. [nɔ̀ŋ]_CS á   [túh-ìnèj]_CC
          3SG   COP.3.IMPERV bless-NOMZ
          'He is blessed'

      b. na ŋà=b=ùnù   lɔ́ hírí sìɔ̀ úwás-ìnèj
         CCN DEM=place=FAR have man hand currupt-NOMZ
         '(and/then) there was a man who had his hand withered'

      c. [íggé-á]_CS   [Ø ŋà=bá=á   číb-ìnèn-á]_RC
         3PL.PN.SP-RTSR [Ø DEM=place=NEAR [tie.IMPERV-NOMZ-RSTR
         [tùmù tùn-ɔ̀]_OBL á   [číb-ìnèj]_CC
         sky   on.top-OBL COP.3.IMPERV tie.IMPERV-NOMZ
         'Those who are tied on earth, are tied in heaven.'

      d. [rúmí-ɲá]_CS á   [čúr-néj]_CC
         cloth-PL   COP.3.IMPERV wash-NOMZ
         'The cloth are washed.'

Since they occupy a few syntactic slots available to nominals in phrases and clauses, they behave as less nominal compared with other deverbal nouns. They also behave like adjectives in that they may denote attributes (as in (3.45a)). Interestingly, some of these verb roots can be deverbalized by two separated nominalizers, *číb-ìnèn* 'tied' and *číb-ìnèj* 'tied' as can be shown in (3.45c). The only difference between these deverbal nouns is their syntax. The former deverbal noun types, can among other functions, be modifiers within NPs, whereas the latter ones can only be copula complements in copular constructions.

3.2.1.3.8.7   Nominalization with *-nèn*

The nominalizer *-nèn* is the second most productive nominalizer after the *-a*. It primarily nominalizes S/A participants. This de-verbalizer morpheme resembles the de-transitivizer antipassive (of first and second persons) and the reciprocal morpheme *-nèn*. As far as my field notes show, there is no synchronic relationship between the two homophonous derivational suffixes. This is a rather rare instance of morphological form coincidence. Most deverbal nouns derived by this nominalizer are agent nouns.

(3.46)   a.   [*hír-á   kóh-ìnèn-á*]$_{NP}$
              man-RTSR farm.IMPERV-NOMZ-RSTR
              'farmer'

         b.   *àggè*]$_{CS}$ *k-án-ó*   [*zùw-á*
              1PL   1SU-COP.IMPERV-1SG.EXC.SU.IMPERV people-RSTR
              kóh-ìnèn-o]$_{NP:CC}$
              farm.IMPERV-NOMZ-RTSR:PL
              'We (exc.) are farmers.'

In the NP in (3.46b), I am not sure what the role of the suffix *-o* is. Therefore, until substantiated with further morphological investigation, I have preferred to analyze it as a plural modification marker. In fact, plural number suffixes, which are applied to these types of deverbal nouns are complex and lack consistency. Compare the plural number marker in (3.46b) with that of (3.47b).

(3.47)   a.   [*nòŋ*]$_{CS}$ *án-á*   [*hír-á   óól-nèn-á*]$_{NP:CC}$
              3SG   COP.IMPERV-TEMP man-RTSR beg-NOMZ-RSTR
              'It is the beggar's.'

b. [zùw-á   óól-nèn-è-á]
   people-RSTR beg.IMPERV-NOMZ-PL-RTSR
   '(the) beggars'

The restrictive marker suffix -a (on the head noun and on the modifier) is obligatory unless otherwise absent due to the following two conditions: when the bound demonstrative circumclitics are attached to the head noun and when the definite marker enclitic =ŋà is attached to the modifier.

(3.48) [[ŋà=hír=inù]_NP óól-nè̀[6]=ŋà]_NP
       DEM=man=FAR beg.IMPERV-NONZ=DEF
       'the beggar; that beggar'

Such deverbal nouns can functions as core arguments in a clause, for example as S argument in the example below.

(3.49) [hír-á   kóh-inèn-á]_NP:S   kɔ̀j-Ø
       man-RSTR farm.IMPERV-NOMZ-RSTR go-3SG.SU.IMPERV
       gáwá-je
       marker-OBL
       'The farmer goes to the market.'

Within phrases, they can be possessors in NPs, modifier within NPs,

(3.50) [[múwá-á   [hír-á   kóh-inèn-á]_NP]_NP
       woman-RSTR man-RTSR farm.IMPERV-NOMZ-RSTR
       'the wife of the farmer'

Additional examples of agent nominals include: hír-á dáf-inèn-á ⟨man-RTSR work.IMPERV-NOMZ-RSTR⟩ 'servant, worker'; hír-á mád-inèn-á ⟨man-RTSR teach.IMPERV-NOMZ-RSTR⟩ 'teacher', hír-á ɓég-inèn-á ⟨man-RTSR watch.IMPERV-NOMZ-RSTR⟩ 'watchman' and so on. As we have seen from the examples presented so far, the fact is that many of such nouns are those the Mursi lacked in their language. Young people still prefer to use the Amharic version of these nouns.

Aside from these agent referring nominalized nouns, the nominalizer -nèn can also be used to derive non-agent nouns or non-subject nouns, as in (3.51).

---

[6] The two nasals in óól-nèn=ŋà were merged into a single segmet [ŋ], i.e. n+ŋ > ŋ.

(3.51) [àh-á　　　bárár-á　　　màt-inèn-ùɲ]_NP
　　　　thing-RSTR powerful-RSTR drink-NOMZ-GEN
　　　　'Alcoholic drink'
　　　　(Lit. 'a powerful drinking thing')

barara is a modification form of the adjective *bárárí* 'powerful'. In this case it functions as an intermediate modifier, otherwise the nominalization above could refer to any sort of drink—*aha màt-ínèn-ùɲ* 'drinking thing'. Above all, it is not common to see derived nouns by the nominalizer *-nèn* being marked for genitive case as are real possessors.

(3.52) a. *ám-inèn*
　　　　　　eat.IMPERV-NOMZ
　　　　　　'eating'

　　　　b. *túh-inèn-à*
　　　　　　bless.IMPERV-NOMZ-ATT
　　　　　　'one who blessed'

The verb 'to bless' has identical verb roots for both transitivity values (intransitive and transitive)—*túh*. But when the nominalizer suffix *-nèn* is added to it, it tells us that the verb had an intransitive sense. And this may generate just another nominalization: 'blessing'. It is the suffix *-a*, with an attributive function, that helps the nominalizer provide a full-fledged meaning. Note that there is a distinction between (3.52b) and (3.45a), even if both may convey a comparable semantics. In principle, the one in (3.52b) can be changed into agent noun by a noun modification construction—*hírá túhìnènà* 'blessed man'.

3.2.1.3.8.8　　Zero-Marked Nominalization

The final de-verbal nominalization type involves zero derivation. In other words, the verb root itself can be a de-verbal noun. Typical syntactic slots available for such deverbal nouns include modifier within NPs and complements in clauses.

(3.53) a. *wà　　　kí-ʃĭgt-o　　　　　　　　　　　[ɔ̀g-á*
　　　　　REC.PAST 1SU-hear.PERV-1PL.EXC.SU.PERV shout-NOMZ+RSTR
　　　　　tìráŋ-Ø-ùɲ]
　　　　　lay-NOMZ-GEN
　　　　　'We heard shouts of joy.'

b. dɔ̀nɛ̀-nɛ̀n   ók-ú   kútúl-ɔ̀   tùmù óól-Ø
   one-NOMZ go-3SG.SU.PERV mountain-OBL god pray-NOMZ
   'He went to the mountain by himself (alone) to pray.'

It is interesting to see the number word *dɔ̃nέj* 'one' have additional functions: (i) one as an adjective without taking any additional derivational marker, (ii) as indefinite referential marker, (iii) as modifier within an NP taking the nouns of state marker suffix *-in* ⟨-ɛn⟩ (dɔnɛn '(be) alone'), and (iv) as an adverb 'alone' with the derivational suffix *-nɛ̀n* (as in (3.53b)). See Chapter 6 for further discussion on the number word 'one'. Some verbal roots are morphologically productive in accepting different nominalizer suffixes, as in (3.54a–c). Examine the examples given below.

(3.54) a. ógór-Ø
           steal-NOMZ
           'theft'

       b. [hír-á   ógór-nɛ̀n-á]
          man-RSTR steal-NOMZ-RSTR
          'robber'

       c. zìní-mɔ̀
          thief-NOMZ
          'thieving, stealing'

Examples (3.54a) and (3.54c) have identical meanings. They, however, differ in their morphological make ups and syntactic functional slots.

3.2.1.3.9 *Summarizing the Noun Class*

In a summary, three grammatical properties have been employed to define the various subclasses of nouns: morphological, syntactic and semantic.

To sum up the discussion of the largest open word class in the language, it is also important to rewind the three grammatical properties employed to define the class. As can be shown in the summary Table 3.4 below, Mursi nouns were divided into eight subclasses based on the semantic properties they display. In addition, although there are up to twelve nominal morphological slots in general, the majority of them can take three major morphological categories: number, case and demonstrative deictics. Not all of them have the same morphological capacity with regard to taking certain inflectional elements. For example, the subclass of compound nouns do not take any morphologi-

TABLE 3.4 Noun subclasses and their syntactic functions

Noun subclasses	Syntactic functions					
	Core arguments (A, S, O)	Peripheral/ obliques	CS	CC	Head of an NP	Possessor/ possessee	Modifier within an NP
Simple nouns	√	√	√	√	√	√	√
Relator nouns	×	√	×	×	√	possessee	×
Place names	O	√	√	√	×	possessee	√
Kinship nouns	√	√	√	√	no data	√	√
Proper names	√	×	√	√	×	possessor	√
Compound nouns	S	no data	√	√	×	×	×
Inherently gendered nouns	√	√	√	√	√	√	√
De-verbal nouns	some	√	√	√	×	√	√

cal inflection except number. But on the other hand simple nouns can take up to four inflections at a time. Similarly, the syntactic functions they may possess and the functional slots they occupy within phrases and clauses vary according to their subclasses. The noun subclasses and its syntactic functions and functional slots are summarized in Table 3.4 above.

3.2.2 *Verbs*

A verb in Mursi can make up a full-fledged complete sentence. Such a sentence can have two objects when a ditransitive verb is being used. Verbs have up to fourteen slots for verbal grammatical categories. Of these, three are prefixal slots while the rest are suffixal. Mursi verbs obligatorily are inflected for bound pronominal S/A and O arguments (participant reference), aspect, mood, motion/direction, valency-changing derivations, and negation (see §7.3.1 of Chapter 7).

Valence and negation are discussed in Chapter 9 and Chapter 12 respectively. Except for tense and reflexive action that are expressed by separate grammatical words, all the other components of non-spatial and spatial setting in Mursi are expressed in the inflectional system. Moreover, two verbal grammatical categories—causative and negation have double markings. The former may be shown by circumfixes while the latter by circumclitics.

Interestingly, there are a few instances in which the size of the morphological categories which a single verb root can take, and the syllable shape of the verb root itself correlate. For example, monosyllabic verb roots usually take as many inflectional categories as they can. Disyllabic verb roots take less inflections compared to monosyllabic verb roots. There are a dozen trisyllabic verb roots which take fewer morphological categories. Ideophone-like verbs may take just one, or sometimes may not take any verbal morphological categories at all. They rather use auxiliary verbs in order to indicate grammatical information they carry.

However, as exceptions, there are a few monosyllabic and disyllabic verb roots which take a prefix and just one or two suffixes at a maximum. Verbs such as *élí* 'call', the auxiliary verb *sé* 'say', an existential verb *íh* 'exist, present', the verb *lɔ̀m* 'have' and polysyllabic ideophone-like verbs are among those that take few inflectional and derivational categories (see §7.2 and §7.3 of Chapter 7). Although phonological features cannot serve as criteria to distinguish the verb class from other word classes, certain phonological features are confined to only verbals. For example, the majority of Mursi verbs have monosyllabic CVC consonant-final roots. In addition, full suppletion of roots for a particular grammatical category is a sole feature of the verb class (see §7.3.1.2.2).

Mursi has also five inherently number-determined verb roots: *ádʒ* 'give', *kún* 'come, bring', *ɔ́k* 'go', *íh* 'exist/present', and *ésé* 'sit'. Plural arguments involved in these verbs are: O arguments for first verb while S arguments for the rest four verbs. All five of these verbs distinguish aspect by multiple root alternations. That means that each of these verbs undergo three to four root alternations (§7.3.1.2.7).

The syntactic criteria are the primary ones which clearly distinguish the verb class from other open and closed word classes. Syntactically, all Mursi verbs are categorized into the following four transitivity classes: intransitive, transitive, ditransitive, and ambitransitive (also known as 'labile'). The first two transitivity classes will account for nearly all of the verb classes. Only three ditransitive verbs have been found in my corpus: *ádʒ* 'give', *jóg* 'tell' and *dól* 'show, announce' (see Chapter 10). Mursi has quite a few labile verbs. Verbs such as *táb* 'deceive/lie' has 'labile' (A-S) nature of its own. Interestingly, verbs with a VC syllable shape are associated with labile nature (S=O and A=S) (see §7.2.2.1). Verbs can function as head of a transitive as well as intransitive predicates. The only other word class which functions as head of a predicate is an adjective. But adjectives which do so belong to one particular subclass of adjectives, i.e. only those that are derived from stative verbs can function as head of an intransitive predicate.

Based on semantic criteria, Mursi verbs can mainly be divided into two subclasses: active and stative. Aikhenvald (2015: 91) noted that active verbs are those that primarily denote a process or a volitional activity. They include motion and posture verbs. These types of verbs form the largest subclass of verbs in the language. On the other hand, stative verbs are those that mainly denote states—*mɔ́dɔ́s* 'be tired' *múɲús* 'be angry', *lɔ́tɔ́g* 'be wet', *dɔ̃rɔ́s* 'dry' and so on. Mursi stative verbs are the major source for more than one-third of derived adjectives (see Chapter 8). Moreover, stative verbs are usually associated with heads of intransitive predicates—as a verb subclass and as an adjective subclass (derived adjectives).

Other small closed subclasses of verbs are copula verbs (§ 7.3.1.2.9 and § 14.2.5) and auxiliary verbs (§ 7.3.1.2.10). Both these two subclasses are morphologically deficient in that they only inflect a few verbal categories. Copula verbs may be inflected for S arguments, negation, and mood (only subjunctive), as in (3.55).

(3.55) àɲè ŋà=k-án-í=ó
 1SG NEG=1SU-COP.IMPERV-1SG.SU.IMPERV=NEG
 'I am not'

Therefore, a copular clause consists of a predicate (semi inflected copula verb for these three categories), and two core arguments—copula subject (CS) and copula complement (CC). As pointed out by Dixon (2012: 159), copula constructions primarily indicate five major semantic relations: (i) identity, (ii) attribution, (iii) possession, (iv) benefaction, and (v) location.

In Mursi, the first four relations can be shown by copula verbs. Like copula verbs, auxiliary verbs can be inflected for bound pronominal S/A and O arguments. In addition to these, an auxiliary verb may be inflected for mood (passive and hortative-jussive).

(3.56) àj kè-sèd-à-íɲ-ò
 POL PASS-say.PERV-PASS-2SG.OBJ-VFS
 'May you be said/told!'

Hortative (for first person) and jussive (for third person) is shown by a prefix *k(V)-*. However, the particle *aj/aɲ* which I called *hortative-jussive particle* (⟨HORT-JUSS.PART⟩) in this grammar may be used for second person as an expression of politeness. Therefore, ⟨POL⟩ could be an appropriate label for this particular purpose (second person polite marker).

3.2.3 *Adjectives*
Adjectives comprise the third largest open word class in Mursi. Adjectives comprise an open class just by derivation. Without their derived members, adjec-

tives would have formed a closed class consisting of just two members—*tííní* 'small' and *búí* 'big'. Due to their phonological and morphosyntactic properties they display, I have labeled these two adjectives as 'underived'. Thus, the two form one of the smallest subclasses of words in the language (see § 8.2.1 & § 8.3.1).

Adjectives share a number of grammatical properties with nouns and verbs. For example, adjectives may be marked for number in the same way as nouns. When modifying the head of an NP, they may take nominal grammatical categories such as case and definite markers, as in (3.57).

(3.57) [ŋà=hír=á   gèrs-í-ɲ=ŋà]ₙₚ
        DEM=man=NEAR bad.STV-ADJ-GEN=DEF
        'of the bad man'

However, adjectives share quite a substantially larger number of morphological and grammatical properties with verbs than nouns. Both adjectives and verbs share the following categories: bound pronominal S/O arguments, passive-nominalizer, comparative-benefactive (own term), negation and verb-final suffix. The following examples clearly show the grammatical categories that both adjectives and verbs have in common (repeated from § 8.4.2)

(3.58) [nɔ̀ŋ]ₛ [ŋà=ídíbèn-∅=no]_INTR.PRED
        3SG   NEG.IMPERV=fat-3SG.SU.IMPERV=NEG
        'He is not fat.'

(3.59) [k-íláás-í-ɔ̀]_S:INTR.PRED
        1SU-sick-1SG.SU.IMPERV-VFS
        'I am sick.'

In order to be considered an adjectives, all adjectives (underived and derived) must bear the general adjectiviser suffix -*i*.

Syntactically, adjectives can modify the head of an NP, fill the head of an intransitive predicate slot, fill copula complement slots, denote degree of the compared quality in comparative constructions, and function as manner modifiers.

The adjective class of Mursi covers all semantic types that can be conveyed by adjectives. A total of about 160 adjectives have been identified in this study (see Chapter 8).

3.3 Closed Word Classes

As mentioned earlier in the introductory section, pronouns, adverbs, adpositions, question words, number words and quantifiers, connectors, interjections, ideophones, expressives, and discourse particles comprise the closed word class of the language.

3.3.1 *Pronouns*

Pronouns constitute a small closed class. Pronouns in Mursi are of six types and each forms their own closed subclasses: personal pronouns, specific pronouns, demonstrative pronouns, possessive pronouns, indefinite pronouns, and relative pronouns.

3.3.1.1 Personal Pronouns

Mursi has a total of thirteen personal pronouns—six as pre-verbal subjects and seven post-verbal subjects. Those which occur post-verbally are marked as nominative personal pronouns forms. The post-verbal pronoun of the third person plural has two forms—*jòkù* and *jòkíù* '3pl (NOM.)', of the same meaning and function. A full list of personal pronouns is found in Table 10.1 of §10.2.2.1.

Dixon (2010a: 207) pointed out that pronouns have more restricted possibilities than nouns at syntactic level. Mursi personal pronouns adhere to this fact. They may function as S, A, O, and E arguments in clauses. Like nouns they can be copula subjects in copular clauses, but they cannot be copula complements. Moreover, they cannot function as NP heads, modifiers within NPs, possessed or possessors. To see how grammatical number is indicated on personal pronouns, refer to Chapter 6. Note that Mursi utilizes both free pronouns and bound pronouns systems.

In languages such as Mursi, there are clear contrastive properties being employed to distinguish between the free and bound pronoun systems (cf. Dixon 2010a: 212).

3.3.1.2 Specific Pronouns

Mursi has two specific pronouns that share some properties with the personal and demonstrative pronouns—*ìn* (⟨3sg.PN.SP⟩) and *ìgg* (⟨3pl.PN.SP⟩). These two may function as nouns or as anaphoric pronouns. Most importantly, they two can be referred to by the term 'third person specific pronouns'. Specific pronouns share two properties with free pronouns. First, both can be used as third person pronouns, and the plural specific pronoun form *ìgg* can also be used to refer to second person plural.

(3.60) iggè-á   [Ø héj-á   mìs-ɔ̀]_RC   úrɔ́
2PL.PN.SP-RSTR [Ø go.2PL-RSTR grazing.land-OBL] milk
ŋà=lɔ̀n-ó
NEG.IMPERV=have/take.IMPERV-IMP.PL
'You (pl.) who go to the grazing land, don't take milk with you!'

As it is shown in (3.60), the third person plural specific pronoun form *igg* functioning as second person plural free pronouns. But undeniably it is specific pronoun as it is modified by a relative clause and has already been marked for restrictive modification marker *-a*.

Generally, unlike free personal pronouns, specific pronouns can be modified directly by other constituents as well as by relative clause modifiers. This means, like any other nouns in noun modification constructions, specific pronouns can be marked by restrictive/non-restrictive modification suffix *-a/-ti* (*-i*), depicting a dependency relation between them as head and their modifiers (see the examples given in 3.62)

Second, like free pronouns, it cannot function as copula complement, as in (3.61a).

(3.61) a. á   gìój   ìgg=inù?
          COP.3.IMPERV who/which.PL 3PL.PN.SP=FAR
          'Who were they?'

      *b. gioj a igginu?

As it is shown in (3.61a), like personal pronouns specific pronouns cannot occur in copula complement slots. Thus, the interrogative pronoun *gìój* is set to co-occur side by side with specific pronoun *ìgg*. If *ìgg* were a nominal or an NP, it would have been questioned like a copula complement and will have the structure of *(3.61b). They are also demonstrative-like because they may take proximal/distal marker enclitics (as in (3.61a)).

Other than the two similarities mentioned above, special pronouns are just like the English dummy 'one'. When they function as third person special pronoun or dummy, they can be modified by either restrictive or nonrestrictive modifiers. Some examples are given below.

(3.62) a. á   ígg-í   nój?
           COP.3.IMPERV 3PL.PN.SP-NRSTR who.NOM
           'Which ones?'

    b.   *ɨɲè hín-í*   [*írsásí-ɲá-í*   *mèrì*]_{NP}?
        2SG want.IMPERV-2SG.SU.IMPERV pencil-PL.NRSTR many
        'Do you want many pencils?'

    b1. *àɲè* [*ígg-í*   *mèrì*]_{NP}
         1SG 3PL.PN.SP-NRSTR many
        ŋà=kí-hín-i=ó
        NEG.IMPERV=1SU-want.IMPERV-1SG.SU.IMPERV=NEG
        'I don't want many.'

    b2. *àɲè kí-hín-í*   [*ín-í*
        1SG 1SU-want.IMPERV-1SG.SU.IMPERV 3SG.PN.SP-NRSTR
        dɔ̃néj]_{NP} *sɔ̀ŋ*   (*írsásí*)
        one   only pencil
        'I want only one (pencil).'

They behave like nominals as shown in the examples above—all are in noun modification constructions. Note that some interrogative pronouns in Mursi are pro-phrasal in that they may come in modification forms, as in (3.62a). Besides, specific pronouns are usually modified exactly the same way as nominals. As it is illustrated in (3.62), they are marked for non-restrictive modification marker because interrogatives, quantifiers and numerals are non-restrictive modifiers in Mursi. In (3.62b1), *írsásí* is optional because it has already been mentioned in (3.62b).

Within NPs, when specific pronouns are modified by what are considered to be restrictive modifiers (usually possessive pronouns and adjectives), they are being marked for restrictive modification marker *-a*, as in the following examples.

(3.63) a. [*ín-á*   *n=ànù*]_{NP}   *ŋànó*
           3SG.PN.SP-RSTR SG.PSD=1SG.PSR not
        'It is not mine.'

        b. [*ín-á*   *gólɔ́ɲ-ná*]_{NP} *á*   *ŋàrúgo*
           3SG.PN.SP-RSTR red-SG-RSTR COP.3.IMPERV Nyarugo
        'The red one is Abebech's.'

TABLE 3.5 Demonstrative pronouns

Demonstrative (proclitic)	Specific pronoun	sg/pl	Distance (enclitics)	
			Near	Far
ŋà=	ìn	sg.	=á	
ŋà=	ìn	sg.		=ùnù
ŋà=	ìggè	pl.	=à	
ŋà=	ìggè	pl.		=nù

    c. [ín-á   bú-sèn-á]$_{NP}$ ŋà=ìggè=à
       3SG.PN.SP-RSTR big-COMP.BEN-RSTR DEM=3PL.PN.SP=NEAR
       á   jél-á
       COP.3.IMPERV love-NOMZ
       'The greatest of these is love.'

In (3.63c), ŋàìggèà is a nominal demonstrative pronoun composed of deictic circumclitics and the third person plural specific pronoun (see § 4.2.1.2 and the discussion under demonstrative pronouns § 3.2.1.3 below).

3.3.1.3 Demonstrative Pronouns

The demonstrative modifiers are of two types—those that co-occur with nouns (Type I), and those that co-occur with specific pronouns (Type II). In this section, only Type II are discussed. Type I are discussed in detail in § 4.2.1.1 as part of the noun modification construction of the language.

Demonstrative pronouns are formed from the bound demonstrative circumclitics and the two specific pronouns we have seen in the section discussed above. There are four nominal demonstrative pronouns: ŋàìnà 'this', ŋàìnùnù 'that', ŋàìggèà 'these', and ŋàìggènù 'those'.

Diessel (1999: 30) suggested two stages of grammaticalization processes with regard to the development of pronominal demonstratives. The first is that at some point, at the initial stage of the grammaticalization process, demonstratives and third person pronouns may co-occur as two independent forms. This partially asserts that Mursi demonstrative proclitic ŋà= and third person specific pronouns had been functioning side by side until their second stage. Distance marking enclitics[7] may have developed at later stages because there

---

7 Both enclitics (the proximal =a and the distal =ùnù) have phonologically conditioned allo-

is still some evidence that distance marking enclitics can be used independent of the demonstrative system. The occurrence of the distal marker enclitic =nù/=ùnù in the examples shown below suggests that it still can function alone without the need for the demonstrative proclitic ŋà=.

(3.64) a. hùll-á   bè   ɓ=ùnù
          when-RSTR DIST.PAST place=FAR
          'at that time'

   b. ɓ=ùnù   lɔ̀g-ti=nù
      place=FAR issue-NRSTR=FAR
      ká-gáj-Ø
      1SU-know.IMPERV-1PL.INC.SU.IMPERV
      'That the thing (issue) we (inc.) know.'

   c. ŋà=kɔ́-í   gɔ̀rɔ̀   ɓ=ùnù
      NEG.IMPERV=go.IMPERV-SG.IMP road.SG place=FAR
      ɓòì=ŋà
      wide.ADJ=DEF
      'Don't (sg.) go on the wide road!'

The second stage of grammaticalization involves coalescence of the demonstrative circumclitics and third person specific pronouns. This stage reflects the current morphological composition of the demonstrative pronouns.

Syntactically, Type II demonstratives have two functions, modifiers within NPs and copula subjects in copular clauses, as in the following examples (3.65a–b are repeated from § 4.2.1.2)

(3.65) a. [lúsì ŋàìnà]_NP
          boy this
          'this boy'

---

morphs. The proximal =a can be manifested as =a following nouns ending in [a] and following inherently plural nouns ending in alveolar (mostly); =ta following nouns ending in high front vowel [i] or following nouns ending in stops/plosives; and =na following nouns ending in the bilabial nasal [m]. The distal =ùnù can occur in =ùnù following nouns ending in consonant, =tùnù following nouns ending in high front vowel [i], =nùnù nouns ending in bilabial nasal [m], and =ìnù following nouns ending in all other vowels.

TABLE 3.6 Possessive pronouns

	Singular possessed		Plural possessed	
	Singular possessor	Plural possessor	Singular possessor	Plural possessor
1	nànù	nàj (inc.) nàw (exc.)	gà̰ɲù	gà̰j (inc.) gàw (exc.)
2	nùnù	nùj	gṵ̀ɲù	gṵ̀j
3	nὲnὲ	nὲj	gὲ̰ɲὲ	gὲ̰j

    b. [lúsì ŋàinùnù]_NP
       boy that
       'That boy'

(3.66) [ŋàinà]_CS á   [àlèj]_CC
       this   COP.3.IMPERV chair.SG
       'This is a chair.'

Note that Type I demonstratives have identical morphological components as Type II, but they differ from Type II in two aspects. Type I demonstratives can occur in an NP with a noun and they can make up an NP on their own, as in (3.67).

(3.67) [ŋà=hír=ùnù]_NP
       DEM=man.SG=FAR
       'that man'

Both types, however, have deictic functions. For further discussions on the two demonstrative types and their syntactic functions, see § 4.2.1.1.

3.3.1.4   Possessive Pronouns

Mursi has fourteen free possessive pronouns, as shown in Table 3.6 above. Possessive pronouns come carrying three grammatical information markers about the items to be possessed. These are: person of the possessor, number of the possessor and number of the possessed item

    As can be shown in Table 3.6, the first person plural possessive pronouns make a distinction between inclusive and exclusive possessors. Syntactic functions of the possessive pronouns include: possessors or modifiers within an NP (3.68), reflexive pronoun (3.69), and auto-reflexive (3.70).

(3.68) [[*írsásí-á*   *n=ènè*]_NP   *gólóɲ-á*]_NP
pencil-RSTR SG.PSD=3SG.PRS red.STV-RSTR:MOD
'His/her red pencil'

(3.69) *nòŋ hàlí óɲ-Ø*   [*sábá-à*   *n=ènè*]_NP:REFL
3SG later wash.IMPERV-3sg.SU.IMPERV head-RSTR SG.PSD=3SG.PRS
'S/he will wash herself/himself.'

(3.70) [[*nòŋ té*   *íláás-ì*   [*hínís-á*   *n=ènè*]_NP   *tó-jé*
3SG COP.3.PERV sick.STV-ADJ heart-rstr SG.PSD=3SG.PRS in-OBL
'He/she become ill in her heart.'

Further details on possessive pronouns are also available in Chapter 5 (possession) and Chapter 9 (reflexive constructions).

3.3.1.5   Indefinite Pronouns

Mursi has two types of indefinite pronouns—compound-type and NP-type. Compounds in Mursi can easily be distinguished from NPs for bearing no dependency markers (*-a/-i/-ti*) in contrast to those which occur on heads of noun phrases. Besides, they may also undergo some phonological processes, for example, they may delete the coda of their first element. Table 3.7 below presents a list of Mursi indefinite pronouns. The fact is that three of the indefinite pronouns have a word status; *kón, gén* and *àhìtì*.

The first two—*kón* and *gen* function both as pronouns (3.71) and as modifiers within NPs (3.72).

(3.71) ***kón-á***   *dúgt-ò*   *nà*   ***kón-á***   *ɲáj-ò*
one-RSTR plant.PERV-3.IRR CNN one-RSTR cut-3.IRR
á   *lògó*   *ʃééʃéé*
COP.3.IMPERV word true.REDUP
'One sows and another harvests, this is a word of truth.'

(3.72) *ká-lám-í*   [[*kè-á*   *kód-á-ɲ*]_NP   ***kón***]_NP
1SU-look.for-1SG.SU.IMPERV thing.SG-RSTR write-NOMZ-GEN one
'I want another pencil.'

TABLE 3.7 Indefinite pronouns

Indefinite pronouns	Meaning	Type	Possible source
kón/kóná	'one, another, other, certain'	word	kón 'one' + -a (restrictive modification)
gén/géná	'others, some'	word	g= is plural marker clitic + -a (restrictive modification)
húbdákákán	'all, whole'	compound	húb 'all/whole' +dákákán 'all'
zùwò dákákán	'everybody'	NP	zùwò 'people' + dákákán 'all'
àhà dákákán	'everything'	NP	àhà 'thing.PL' + dákákán 'all'
àhìtì	'nothing'	word	àhì 'thing.SG' + -ti (non-restrictive modification)
àhìtì dɔ́néj	'nobody'	NP	àhì 'thing.SG' + -ti (non-restrictive modification) + dɔ́néj 'one'
hírkóná	'anybody, someone'	compound	hírí 'man' + kón 'one' + -á (restrictive modification)
tánkóno	'anyone'	word+ compound	(side-side-one)

(3.73)   [gín-á   **kón-á**]   húŋ   lɔ̀m-í-ɔ̀
         ask-NOMZ **another-RSTR** simply have-2SG.SU.IMPERV-VF
         'Have you any other question?'

Both *kón* and *gén* agree in number with the head nouns they modify, but head nouns modified by the two cannot be marked with the restrictive marker suffix -a. However, the indefinite pronouns themselves can optionally be marked with the restrictive marker. Moreover, head nouns modified by indefinite pronoun can function as S or O arguments.

(3.74)   ŋànìjè   [zùwò gén-á]_NP:S   í-báj-sí-ò
         however people others-RSTR CAUS-heal-CAUS-3SG.IRR
         'He saved others, however ...'

(3.75)   [ùrgùsá gén-á]_NP:S   k-ám-n-ɔ̀
         fish.PL other-RSTR   PASS-eat.PERV-PL.3.PASS-VFS
         'Some fish are edible.'

In (3.76) below, *gén* is in O function, whether it be with quantifier *bòi* or on its own. In both ways the verb following it (*fílé*) will be a complement clause.

(3.76) [nɔ̀ŋ]_S ár-ú   [gén]_O   bòi fíl-έ
       3SG see.PERV-3PL.SU.PERV other.PL all stand-3PL.SU.IMPERV
       'He saw others standing idle'

In narrations, indefinite pronouns can have anaphoric functions, as in (3.77).

(3.77) [zùw-á   g=àw]_NP   [Ø bè   gén   bè
       people-RSTR PL.PSD=1PL.EXC.PSR [Ø DIST.PAST other DIST.PAST
       kɔ́-dɔ́t-ó   mà   tùnò]_RC
       1SU-leave-1PL.EXC.SU.IMPERV water on.top
       'Our (exc.) other people (who) we (exc.) left at the top of the waters (river) ...' (MH 1:10:7)

In Suri (a much closer language to Mursi, Southeastern Surmic group), indefinite pronouns are often used in presentational sentences to introduce new participant or ideas to the listener (Bryant 2013: 52). The distinction between *kón* and *dɔ́néj* 'one' rests on the morphosyntactic properties they display (3.78) (see also Chapter 6).

(3.78) màmà   kóno   kó ʤɔ̀ɔ̀nè
       mother.PERT.SG.1.PSR one.INDEF PNC mother.PERT.3.PSR
       á   dɔ́néj
       COP.3.IMPERV   one
       'My mother and his mother are one (the same).' (KW 2:34:4)

As it is the case in many other languages of the world, the development of *kón/kóná* from a number word to an indefinite pronoun is a simple grammaticalization process. This was be substantiated by Givón (1981) who noted that the development of the numeral 'one' as a marker for singular-indefinite nouns or indefinite marker is a universal process.

In this study, *kón/kóná* has been analyzed as indefinite pronouns rather than as indefinite article or determiner. In other words, the function of *kón/kóna* may not be confined to indefinite pronouns.

The other indefinite pronouns are those whose morphological forms split between compounds and NPs: *húbdákákán*, *zùwò dákákán* and *àhà dákákán*. They function only as S argument, as shown in the following examples.

(3.79) [zùwò dákákán]_NP:S wà áít-á
people all REC.PAST go.PERV-3PL.SU.PERV
'Everybody else has gone.'

(3.80) [múgá-á n=ɛ̀nɛ̀] kó [éró-á g=ɛ̀ɲɛ̀]
wife-RSTR SG.PSD=3SG.PSR PNC children-RSTR PL.PSD=3SG.PSR
kó [àh-á dákákán]
PNC thing-PL all
'... his wife, his children, and everything (he owned).'

The three indefinite pronouns shown above need to be studied further. The indefinite noun *àhì* '(a) thing' or a combination of indefinite noun and numeral *àhì+dɔ́néj* ⟨thing+one⟩ can be the basis for indefinite pronouns. The grammaticalization process which generates these indefinite pronouns is more or less the same as that which generated those mentioned earlier. In addition, Aikhenvald (2015: 195) noted that indefinites can be the basis for negatives. Likewise, *àhìtì* 'nothing' and *àhìtì dɔ́néj* ⟨[thing.SG-RSTR one]_NP⟩ 'nobody' are among those indefinites whose meaning may also denote negation (see also §13.6). In the following examples, both are in S function.

(3.81) a. ŋà=kàlì=tá áhí-tí [Ø ká-dáfí]_RC
DEM=day=NEAR thing.SG-NRSTR [Ø 1SU-do.1SG.SU.IMPERV]
níŋɛ̀
not.present/exist.3.IMPERV
'I have nothing else to do today.'
(Lit. 'Today, one thing that I do there is not.')

b. múgt-á íggé-à [Ø
gather.PERV.IMP-PL 3PL.PN.SP-RSTR [Ø
dɔ́gt-ìnɛ̀n-ɛ-á]_RC [àhì-tí dɔ́néj]
remain:PL-AP-3PL.SU.IMPERVRTSR] thing.SG-NRTSR one
kɔ̀-dɔ̀t-ɛ́
PASS-leave.PERV.3-VFS
'Gather up (pl.) (the fragments) that remain, that nothing be lost!'

The last two indefinite pronoun in Table 3.7 are compounds—*hírkóná* 'anybody, someone' and *tán tánkóno* 'anyone'. Like many of the indefinite pronouns we saw above, both occur in limited syntactic functional slots in that they function only as S arguments.

(3.82) hírkón-á   ŋà=bá=á   íʃé?
        one.man-RSTR DEM=place=NEAR   present/exist.IMPERV
        'Is anybody (someone) else here?'

(3.83) hírkón-á   húŋ   dáʃì-ò   ŋà=dàmì=tùnù
        one.man-RSTR simply work-3.IRR   DEM=rule/way=FAR
        'Anybody can do that'
        (Lit. 'Anybody simply do that way/accordingly.')

(3.84) tánkónó ín-í   bè   ór-Ø   tùmù
        side.one REL-RSTR DIST.PAST   see.IMPERV-3SG.SU.IMPERV   god
        nìŋè
        not.present/exist.3.IMPERV
        'Not that anyone has seen God.'
        (Lit. 'No man has seen the God/Anyone that has seen God there is not.')

In (3.85), *iní* is a relative pronoun (see the next section).

3.3.1.6   Relative Pronoun

Mursi has two relative pronouns that are derived from specific pronouns in §3.3.1.2. They are *iní* 'who/that/which (sg.)', and *iggì* 'who/which (pl.)'. Even though both can function pronominally, they are not prototypical relative pronouns. Both can be head/common argument of a relative clause. As a derived subclass of pronouns, they are morphologically deficient thus they must always occur with the non-restrictive marker suffix *-i*. Carrying the non-restrictive marker suffix may enable them to accept a wide range of modifiers from various word classes to modify the head. In other words, with the help of these relative pronouns, any clause having a relative clause structure can modify the head, as illustrated below.

(3.85) àŋè   [ín-í   tííní]$_{RC}$
        1SG   REL.PN-RSTR   small.SG
        ŋà=kí-hín-í=ó
        NEG=1SU-want.IMPERV-1SG.SU.IMPERV=NEG
        'I don't want the one which is small.'

(3.86) ín-í   [Ø hín-Ø-í]$_{RC}$
        REL.PN.SG-NRSTR   [Ø want.IMPERV-3SG.SU.IMPERV-NRSTR]
        ká-bág-á   ín-á
        3.JUSS-eat.PERV-VFS   3SG.PN.SP-RSTR

WORD CLASSES   143

        [ŋà=hín-∅=ó]_RC   kí-tíráŋ
        NEG=want.IMPERV-3SG.SU.IMPERV=NEG   3.JUSS-play.PERV
        'He who wants (to eat) let him eat, and he who doesn't want (to eat) let
        him play.'

(3.87) ʃíg-é-è   ígg-í   [lɔ̀m-ò   ɲàwà]_RC
        hear-3PL.SU.IMPERV-COM REL.PN.PL-NRSTR   [have-3.IRR ear.PL]
        gá   ʃijt-ò
        ATTU   hear.PERV-3PL.IRR
        'They who have ears to hear, let them hear.'

To see further functions of these two pronouns, as modifiers, refer to Chapter 5.

3.3.2 Adverbs

Adverbs in Mursi are members of a small closed word class and whose main syntactic function is modifying verbs. Five subclasses of adverbs have been found in Mursi: manner (§3.3.2.1), time (§3.3.2.2), frequency and degree (§3.3.2.3), emphatic/intensifiers (§3.3.2.4), and locative (position and direction) (§3.3.2.5). Not all adverbs occur simply in natural adverbial forms. Some can be formed from adjectives with the help of the general adverbializer suffix -o[-no]. Some have identical forms with adjectives. They can only be distinguished from adjectives by their syntactic functions or by the syntactic slots they occupy in a clause.

3.3.2.1 Manner Adverbs

The subclass which consists of manner adverbs have members of derived and non-derived forms. Forms such as čùmùnò and čàllìnò are adjectives derived from verbs. For this specific subclass of adverbs, the process of deriving adverbs from adjectives as well as from other word classes varies.

(3.88) Adverb   Adjective (stative)   Verb   Meaning
     a. čùmùnò   čùmùn   čùmùn   'cheerfully, happily'
     b. čàllìnò   čàllì   čàll   'well'
     c. kɔ́bkɔ́b   –   kɔ́b   'quickly'

In (3.88), čùmùnò is derived from the adjectival form čùmùn. The adjectival form itself is a stative verb like many other derived adjectives. Morphologically, adjectives are much closer to adverbs than any other word class. So in the above case it is quite appropriate and plausible to say that (3.88a) is derived from the adjective form rather than from the stative one. In addition, example

TABLE 3.8   Manner adverbs

Manner adverbs	Meaning
ʃàù	'quickly, fast, soon'
hàlὲ hàlὲ	'slowly'
ʃὲὲ	'carefully, truly, well'
dɨ́g	'firmly, well'
dàmìsì	'clearly, properly, accordingly'
díŋísí	'slowly'
čùmùnò	'cheerfully, happily, gladly'
čàllìnò	'well'
kɔ́bkɔ́b	'quickly'

(3.88b) also strengthens this statement, that *čàllìno* is not directly derived from the stative verb root, rather it is from the adjectival stem. There are instances where adverbs are derived from active verb roots through reduplication (as in (3.88c))—*kɔ́bkɔ́b* ⟨follow.follow⟩ 'quickly' > *kɔ́b* 'follow'. Table 3.8 above shows a list of manner adverbs.

Manner adverbs mostly occur at clause-final positions following verbs, as in (3.89a–d).

(3.89) a. nɔ̀ŋ   ók-ú   čàll-ì-nò
           3SG go-3SG.SU.PERV good.STV-ADJ-ADV
           'S/he went well.'

       b. nɔ̀ŋ   bɔ̀rɔ̀t-ú   čùmùn-ò
           3SG jump-3SG.SU.PERV happy.STV-ADV
           'S/he jumped cheerfully.'
           (Lit. happily)

       c. nɔ̀ŋ   áɨ́w-ó   ʃàù
           3SG come.PERV.SG-MT.3SG.SU.PERV quickly
           'S/he came quickly.'

       d. àɲè   kú-čúg-í   ʃàù
           1SG 1SU-chase-1SG.SU.IMPERV fast
           'I drive fast.'

Interestingly, adverbs which share identical meaning with adjectives may distinguish themselves by form. For example, the adverb *fàù* (3.89d) has semantically equivalent adjectival form, i.e. *tìrì* (3.90).

(3.90) [čár]_CS á   [tìr-ì]_CC
        leopard COP.3.IMPERV fast-ADJ
        'A leopard is fast.'

Sometimes setting the distinction between adverbs and adjective can be problematic, semantically as well as syntactically. One instance in which such problem arises is when an adjectival form carrying the adverbializer suffix is used in the comparative construction.

(3.91) [túrúmél-á ràmàg-á]_NP   tìr-tìn-ò   hékɔ́   báwúrú téb
        car-RSTR long.STV-RSTR fast-N.S-ADV   same/like plane   as
        'A train is as fast as a plane.'

As we recall from §3.2.1.3.8, the suffix *-tìn* is a nominalizer, which is used to derive deverbal nouns from stative verb roots that denote state of affairs (nouns of state). In (3.91), it is more of an adverb than an adjective because the adverbializer marker *-o* is attached to it. On the other hand, it is an adjective because it denotes the manner of how the comparee and the standard are fast. However, such specific case is confined to only one type of comparative construction— '*as ... as*' or '*the same ... as*'. Literally, (3.91) can also mean '(a/the) long car is fast like as plane.' (see also Chapter 12).

3.3.2.2   Time Adverbs

Time adverbs in Mursi are tense markers. Since tense in Mursi is typically expressed by separate lexical time words, time word are used as temporal adverbs. Time referring adverbs constitute the largest of all subclasses of adverbs. A few of them share one morphological aspect with some locative adverbs and demonstratives pronouns, i.e. they take bound deictic demonstrative circumclitics (*ŋà= ... =á/=ùnù*). As in the following examples, the adverbs in (3.92) and (3.93) are comprised of *méá* 'now' and *méáré* 'immediately, right now' on one hand and the bound demonstrative circumclitics on the other hand.

(3.92) ŋàméárè   ŋà=kà-dàfi-ɛ́
        now   NEG=1.HORT-do.PERV-VFS
        'Let me not do (it) now.'

(3.93) ŋàméá ŋɔ́jɔ̀ úhán-Ø   [tán-á
today wind blow-3SG.SU.IMPERV other.side-RSTR
ŋɔ́-čá   sús-ɔ̀]$_{NP}$
descend-APPL+RSTR sun-OBL
'An easterly wind is blowing today.'

Despite a few of them also appearing at clause-final or medial slots, a great majority of time adverbs occur at the beginning of a clause.

(3.94) jóg-óɲ   àɲè ŋàhùllùnù
tell-1SG.OBJ 1SG at.that.time
'Tell (sg.) me at once!'
(Lit. 'Tell (sg.) me at a time (at the same time)!')

(3.95) bè   ŋàhùllùnù nɔ̀ŋ ŋànì   k-ìrìčà=ó
DIST.PAST at.that.time 3SG not.yet 3.SBJV-born.APPL=NEG
'At the time he was not yet born.'

Time adverbs/temporal adverbs are elaborated in depth in §7.3.1.4.

3.3.2.3 Frequency and Degree Adverbs

In Mursi, adverbs of frequency are one that indicate how often something/an action happens. Some of frequency and degree referring adverbs are at least semantically subclass-crossing ones. This means, they are partly temporal adverbs because the frequency happenings or actions cannot be specified outside a temporal reference (see also §7.3.1.4.3).

(3.96) àɲè tíítíí   k-éján-Ø   [[màmà]$_{NP}$
1SG always 1SU-help.IMPERV-1.IRR mother.PERT.1.SG.PSR+RSTR
n=ànù]$_{NP}$
SG.PSD=1SG.PSR
'I was always helping my mother.'

(3.97) àggè ŋàbá dáfí-ò   ŋàŋà
1PL here work-NOMZ like.this/this.way
ŋà=ká-gán-Ø-έ=ó   dóg
NEG=1SU-know.IMPERV-1PL.INC.SU.IMPERV-APPL=NEG at.all
'We (inc.) are not able to do this at all.'

A list of frequency and degree adverbs is given in Table 3.9 below.

TABLE 3.9 Frequency and degree adverbs

Frequency & degree	Meaning
ríb	'all the day, all day long'
dóg	'at all, never, forever'
dírr	'for a long time'
tíítíí	'often, always' < tíí 'all the time'
kàlì kàlì	'everyday, daily'
čùànéŋ	'again'
бókóno бókóno	'sometimes'

As shown in the table above, *tíítíí* is a reduplicated form of the continuous or durative marker *tíí*. Two other adverbs have repeated forms: one repeats the noun *kàlì* 'day' and while repeats a compound indefinite location word *бókónó* ⟨place+one⟩ 'somewhere'.

3.3.2.4 Emphatic, Intensifiers, Epistemic Adverbs

Mursi emphatic and intensification inferring adverbs may also be used in adjectival function. They usually occur clause-finally. The first five adverbs in Table 3.10 have emphatic or intensifying functions. The same emphatic and intensifiers can also be used in modification of adjectives. They either describe/modify the quality of the action or emphasise or amplify the action referred to by the verb. Unlike the two, epistemic inferring adverbs can occur clause-initially and clause-finally. They may be used when an information is believed to contain some hidden facts, possibilities, or information that creates an exclamative or dubious situation. They also commonly occur in information questions that require verification (see § 12.3).

Some examples are presented as follows.

(3.98)   бág   [áčúg-á   čàll-á]$_{NP}$ sɔ̀ŋ!
         eat.PERV.IMP meat-RSTR good.STV-RSTR only
         'Eat (sg.) only good meat!'

(3.99)   tá   ŋà=hír=á   sé   kɔ́ɔ́n
         maybe DEM=people=NEAR   COMPL   3.SBJV.kill.PERV
         rèè   ká?
         body+PERT.SG.3.PSR   perhaps
         'Will he kill himself?'
         (Lit. 'Maybe the man want to kill himself perhaps?')

TABLE 3.10 Emphatic/intensifiers, epistemic adverbs

Emphatic/intensifier	Meaning	Type
húŋ	'simply, just, already'	emph./intens.
háŋ	'very much'	emph./intens.
wáŋ	'very much'	emph./intens.
gòrí	'powerfully'	emph./intens.
tíítí gòrí	'a little bit'	emph./intens.
ɓòìtííní	'a little bit'	emph./intens.
sòŋ	'only'	emph./intens.
kákó	'perhaps'	epistemic
máníkó	'perhaps'	epistemic
ká	'perhaps'	epistemic
tá	'maybe'	epistemic

The distinction among *húŋ*, *háŋ* and *wáŋ* is not always clear. In order to check if there any significant differences exist among these three, there is one productive way to find out. The emphatic *húŋ* is the only one that can modify the existential verb *íh* 'exist, present', as in (3.100a).

(3.100) a. í-Ø   húŋ
            exist.3SG.SU.IMPERV simply/just
            'He simply exists.'
            (Lit. 'He just exists.')

       b. *í-Ø   háŋ(wáŋ)/sòŋ
           exist.3SG.SU.IMPERV much/only

Bryan (1999: 65) has also employed the same technique for Tirmaga to distinguish the difference between such emphatic adverbs. In fact, the emphatic *wáŋ* can acquire additional contextual meanings—'well, properly'. As we can see in the examples below, it has no fixed position in clauses. In (3.101a), it somehow follows the verb but which intervening between the NP head-like noun *dórí* and modifier-like numeral *dɔ́néj*. In (3.101b), it follows the verb directly.

(3.101) a. rɔ̀sɔ̀   ɓék-ú   dórí   wáŋ   dɔ́néj
            dog.SG keep-3SG.SU.PERV house.SG EMPH one
            'The dog watches our house well.'

WORD CLASSES 149

TABLE 3.11 Location, directional, distance adverbs

Locative	Meaning
ŋáà	'here'
ŋàɓá	'here'
ŋàɓùnù	'there'
ʤá	'near'
rènà	'far'
sórr	'very far away'
dìb	'straight ahead'
sìtèn	'right'
kàŋìtèn	'left'
ŋàŋà	'like this, this way'

  b. *rúm-íɲá čúr-ú wáŋ dɔ́néj*
   cloth-PL wash.PERV.IMP-PL EMPH one
   'Wash your (pl.) clothes properly!'

In both of these examples, numeral *dɔ́néj* functions as special possessive reflexive marker 'one's own'. Number agreement for the first example is contextual as it requires further background information; otherwise it will be ungrammatical. For the second example, at least the imperative verb form has a plural number. *ɓòitííní* serves as degree referring adverb.

(3.102) *kàl-á rònɔ́ wùréɔ́ áw-ó   ɓòitííní*
   day/time-RSTR in.the.future after come.PERV.IMP-MT a.little.bit
   ʃàù!
   fast
   'Next time come a little (bit) earlier!'

3.3.2.5 Locative, Directional and Distance Adverbs
Locative adverbs are extensions of the morphological configurations of the demonstrative circumclitics. *ŋáà* 'here', *ŋàɓá* 'here' and *ŋàɓùnù* 'there' are local adverbial demonstratives derived from the noun *bá/ɓá* 'place' and the demonstrative circumclitics *ŋà=* ... *=á* (near)/*=ùnù* (far). In fact, *ŋáà* is made by combining of circumclitics without a noun denoting a location (*bá/ɓá*). Recall that circumclitics can form a phonological word (see Chapter 2).

(3.103) a. ŋáà   < ŋà=+=á   ⟨DEM+NEAR⟩   'here'
       b. ŋàbá   < ŋà=bá=á   ⟨DEM+place+NEAR⟩   'here'
       c. ŋàbùnù   < ŋà=bá=ùnù   ⟨DEM+place+FAR⟩   'there'

Although (3.103b–c) allow a place word to intervene between the circumclitics, they form one phonological word. In addition, (3.103c) may also occur with a locative marker suffix -i, as in ŋà=bá-(í)=ùnù ⟨DEM=place-(LOC)=FAR⟩.

Local adverbial demonstratives usually occur at clause final positions following the verbs they modify, but exceptions also exist, as in (3.104e).

(3.104) a. nòŋ   í-Ø   ŋáà
          3SG   exist.IMPERV-3SG.SU.IMPERV   here
          'It is here'

       b. áíw-ó   ŋáà
          come.PERV.IMP-MT here
          'Come (sg.) here!'

       c. kà-dàʃi   ŋàbá
          1.HORT-do.PERV   here
          'Let me do (it) here!'

       d. o   dáʃi   ŋà=b=ùnù
          POL do.PERV.IMP   DEM=place=FAR
          'Do (sg.) it there!'

       e. ŋàméá   ŋà=b=ùnù   dáʃiØ   òŋ?
          today/now DEM=place=FAR work.NOMZ   what
          'What work is there now?'

(3.105) nòŋ [bá-á   bág-á]_NP   í-Ø   rènà
       3sg place-RSTR   live-NOMZ.RSTR exist.IMPERV-3SG.SU.IMPERV   far
       'His abode is far away.'

The adverb ŋàŋà has two functions—manner and locative. It can take some morphology such as the subordinate enclitic (3.106) and definite enclitic (3.107).

(3.106) [hùllì sédá-í⁸   ŋàŋà=jè]ₛᵤʙₒʀᴅ:ᴄʟ   àggè
[when say.PERV.PL-1PL.OBJ+3PL.IRR like.this=SUBORD] 1PL
k-áí-tó   hóló-te
1SU-go.PERV-1PL.EXC.SU dance-OBL
'When they talk to us like that, we go to the dancing ...' (KW 2:48:0)

(3.107) àŋè ŋà=kí-hín-í=ó   ŋà=wàrkátì=tá
1SG NEG=1SU-want.IMPERV-1SG.SU.IMPERV=NEG DEM=book=NEAR
hékɔ́ ŋàŋà=ŋà   ád-áɲ-ò
same like.this=DEF give.PERV-1SG.OBJ-3SG.IRR
'I don't like this book; give me (another).'

3.3.3 Adpositions

The adposition class is divided in two subclasses: postpositions and prepositions. Mursi can be referred as a postpositional language as it has just two prepositions. Postpositions can further be divided into two types: underived and derived. The underived ones have monosyllabic shapes, whereas the derived ones have some monosyllabic but predominantly disyllabic shapes. In addition, many of the derived postpositions come from body part nouns. A table containing the whole list of postpositions is found in §10.4. All postpositions of both types, except the one (níŋè 'without') which is unique, occur with oblique case markers. Therefore, their main function is to mark non-core arguments.

(3.108) mà   tó-jé
water in-OBL
'Water on (the) inside'

(3.109) áɲ   nɔ̀ŋ k-ók   mùm-ɔ̀ nà
JUSS.PART 3SG 3.JUSS-go.PERV.SG face-OBL CCN
kó-dól-èsè   gɔ̀rɔ̀
3.JUSS-show-PERV.BEN road
'Let him go in front and show the way.'

The oblique case can be an optional element due to two reasons: (i) if the postposition itself is able to convey the intended meaning, as in the examples shown below.

---

8 The first person plural object suffix -i and the third person plural irrealis subject suffix -i have coalesced.

(3.110) mà **kèrgèn**
water **middle**
'Water in the middle.'

(3.111) jɔ̀g bàg-ɛ́ kóná **tún**
3PL live-3PL.SU.IMPERV store **above**
'They live above the store.'

(ii) when a postposition is being used in a noun modification construction. In this case, they are subject to taking restrictive modification marker -a (3.112).

(3.112) lúsì bág-Ø [bá-á [mùm-á [ɲɔ̀nì-á
boy.SG show.off-3SG.SU.IMPERV place-RSTR **face-RSTR** sister-RSTR
n=ènè]_NP]_NP]_NP
SG.PSD=3SG.PSR
'The boy was showing off in front of his sister.'

They usually occupy clause-final slots in non-complex clauses and in clauses having a postposition-free noun modification constructions. Or in a clause containing negation (as in (3.113a)). The postposition bái 'under, down' stands apart from the rest in that it also can be used as verbal word 'to sit'. When it is used with an existential or a copula verb of a similar meaning, its verbal function will be neutralized (3.113a–b). Uniquely from the rest, the postposition bái 'under, down' can also occur with the locative case ⟨ground/place-LOC⟩.

(3.113) a. bá-ì ŋà=íf-ón-í
ground-LOC NEG.IMPERV=exsit.IMPERV-MT-SG
'Do not (sg.) sit down!'
(Lit. 'Don't (sg.) exist here/be down.')

b. nɔ̀ŋ ké-té-á bá-ì lài
3SG 3.SBJV-be.PERV-3SG.SU.PERV ground-LOC silently
'S/he silently (Lit. staying quiet) sat down.'

c. kìò bá-ì bá-ì
tree.SG ground-LOC ground-LOC
'Under (down) (of) the tree'

As it is seen in (3.113c), bai has a repeated form but the repetition does not alter its basic meaning.

WORD CLASSES

The three Mursi prepositions are *sábɔ̀* 'front, in front of', *tutuɔ* 'in front of' and *wùréɔ́* 'behind, next, after'. *sábɔ̀* and *tútúɔ̀* are grammaticalized body part nouns—*sáb-ɔ̀* ⟨head-OBL⟩ and *tútúg-ɔ* [tútúyɔ̀] ⟨mouth-OBL⟩. Furthermore, *tútúgɔ̀* 'door, gate' has been made a re-lexicalized body part noun, which itself is the origin for the latter meaning. Thus *tutuɔ* is a derived from *tùgɔ̀* 'mouth' just by reduplicating root and adding the oblique case marker suffix -ɔ to the reduplicated form [tùg.tùg+ɔ].

(3.114) a. *lúkój   í-Ø   bì   sáb-ɔ̀*
chicken exist.IMPERV-3SG.SU.IMPERV cow head-OBL
'The chicken is in front of (Lit. at the head) the cow.'

b. [*hír-á   ɓég-ìnèn-á*]ₙₚ   *ʃíl-Ø   dórí*
man-RTSR keep-NOMZ-RSTR   stand-3SG.IRR house.SG
tútúg-ɔ̀
mouth-OBL
'The guard stood in front of the house.'

c. *hólísó   á   nɔ̀ŋ   wùréɔ́*
police   COP.3.IMPERV   3SG   behind
'The police are after him.'

Moreover, *sábɔ̀* and *wùréɔ́* may also be used as time words, as can be shown in the following sentences.

(3.115) a. *àŋè   ké-té-á   ŋà=ɓ=ùnù   [táís-íɲá*
1SG   1SU-be.PERV-1SG.SU.PERV   DEM=place=FAR   month-PL
ràmàn-ó]ₙₚ   *sáb-ɔ̀*
two-MOD   head-OBL
'I was there two months ago.'
(Lit. 'before two months')

b. *nɔ̀ŋ   hàlì   kɔ́ɔ́j-Ø   [gáwá-ɲá   ràmàn-o*]ₙₚ   *wùréɔ́*
3SG   later   3.SBJV.go-3.IRR   market-PL   two-MOD   after
'He will go after two weeks.'

A rather more interesting aspect of these two prepositions is that they have another function, i.e. they can also be ordinal number words—*sábɔ̀* 'first' and *wùréɔ́* 'last' (see Chapter 6).

3.3.4 Question Words

Question words form a class of their own but can primarily be realized in two subclasses: simple-forms and modification-forms. Simple forms may occur with or without case markers. For example, ɔ́nɔ́ŋ 'what?' is a simple form without a case marker. But when an oblique (instrumental) case marker suffix -ɔ is attached to ɔ́nɔ́ŋ, it forms a different question word, ɔ́nɔ̀ŋɔ́ 'with.what' (Lit. 'by what means'). For a complete list of Mursi question words, see §12.2 (Table 12.1).

(3.116) mèsí   ɔ̀ŋ?   [mèsí] > /mèsí+i/
       work.2SG.SU.IMPERV what.OBJ
       'What are you doing?'

(3.117) hírí ɓág-Ø   ɔ́nɔ́ŋ?   ɓág-Ø
       man bite-3SG.SU.IMPERV what.NOM bite-3SG.SU.IMPERV
       gùʃúr-Ø
       hyena-NOM
       'What bit the man? (It is) the hyena (that) bit.'

(3.118) a. bè   ɓág-Ø   ɔ́nɔ̀ŋɔ́?
          DIST.PAST eat-3SG.SU.IMPERV what.INSTR
          'With what did s/he eat?'

       b. érmì dág-Ø   ɔ́nɔ̀ŋɔ́?
          child beat-3SG.SU.IMPERV what.INSTR
          'With what did s/he beat a child?'

On the other hand, modification forms are those inherently occuring as modifiers within NPs—nì ⟨who.GEN.SG⟩ 'whose (sg.)' and gì ⟨who.GEN.PL⟩ 'whose (pl.)'. Any noun that replaces these two possessive question words is required to occur either in genitive case form or in possessive form, as exemplified below.

(3.119) nà   érmì-á   [nìj?]_NP   jɔ̀g séd-á   ké
       CCN child-RSTR who.GEN.SG   3PL say.PERV-3PL.SU.PERV QUOT
       á   [érmì-á   dawiti-j=so]_NP
       COP.3.IMPERV child-RSTR david-GEN=EMPH
       'Whose son is he?' 'They say to (him), "The son of David."'

(3.120) ŋà=ìggè=á   á   [gáwátí-ɲá-á   gì?]_NP
       DEM=3PL.PN.SP=NEAR COP.3.IMPERV plate-PL-RSTR who.GEN.PL
       'Whose plates are these?'

WORD CLASSES   155

All except one (*ténèŋ* 'why?') occupy the clause final argument slots. As a canonical AVO/SV language, question words occupy the syntactic slots available for object and oblique arguments. By using questions words, one can question the referents of a clause final argument slots (NPs), location, time, quantity, and the like. Despite these facts, *ténèŋ* deviates from the typical sentence-final pattern of interrogatives.

(3.121) *ténèŋ   ìnè   kéŋá-Ø-ò   jɔ̀g   tìráŋ=ŋà?*
         why   2sg   deny-3PL.OBJ-2/3.IRR   3PL   play=DEF
         'Why do you forbid them to play?'

The strict clause-initial slot of *ténèŋ* is not a coincidence but rather has to do with the type of question one wants to ask, for example a rhetorical question. Otherwise one can use the clause-final version *kè ɔ̀ŋ* 'why?', as in (3.122).

(3.122) *"híh!"   nà   ìnè   kíŋáŋ   húŋ   bák-ú   kè ɔ̀ŋ   kó*
         INTERJ!   CCN   2SG   crocodile   simply   eat-3SG.SU.PERV   why?   PNC
         básáj   bák-ú   kè ɔ̀ŋ
         monitor.lizard   eat-3SG.SU.PERV   why?
         '"Hih!" why did you (sg.) eat a crocodile? Also you (sg.) ate a monitor lizard why? Don't say, "Hunger hit me?!" Aj!' (MH 4:30:6)

Or, interestingly, one may use both forms (3.123).

(3.123) *ténèŋ   ʃíl-Ø-ɛ-o   kè ɔ̀ŋ?*
         why   stand-3SG.IRR-APPL-MT.PERV   why
         'Why did he bring an accusation against him?'

Question words and questioning are described in detail in Chapter 12.

3.3.5   *Number Words and Quantifiers*
The commonality between number words and quantifiers is that both can directly modify heads of NPs and can be copula complements. When modifying heads within NPs, they do not take any morphology. But a head modified by number words and quantifiers will be marked with the non-restrictive dependency marking suffix *-i/-ti*. This means that the dependency relation between head nouns on one hand and number words/quantifiers on the other hand is always a non-restrictive one. However, unlike other noun modification constructions (NPs), neither the head nouns they modify nor they themselves take the restrictive modification marker *-a*.

TABLE 3.12 Number words

Number words	Meaning	Remark
dɔ́néj	'one'	also kón 'only one' indefinite pronoun
ràmàn	'two'	it can be changed into ordinal number by -ne and can also take modification form marker -o
sízzí	'three'	it can be changed into ordinal number by -ne and can also take modification form marker -o
wùʃ[a]	'four'	~ wùj weakening /ʃ/→[j]/__#
háánán	'five'	hájíná in Suri (cf. Bryant 1999: 27)
íllé	'six'	lacks
íssábài	'seven'	also ⟨j⟩ ~íssábàj
íssé	'eight'	also ⟨j⟩ ~ isséj
sákkàl	'nine'	may be from Cushitic languages, e.g. sagal (Oromo)
tɔ́mɔ́n	'ten'	It could be a borrowed term.[b]
hírkón	'twenty'	Lit. ⟨man+one⟩ 'man one'
zùwò ràmàn	'forty'	Lit. ⟨people two⟩ 'two people'
ʃítí dɔ́néj ʃíɲà dɔ́néj	'thousand'	ʃíɲá is loan word from Amharic ʃí 'Thousand' -ti is a non-restrictive marker while -ɲá is plural suffix

a The cardinal number 'four' has two varieties: it can be pronounced with either the palatal *wùj* word-finally or metathesis form *ùwì* whose origin is unknown.

b *tɔ́mmɔ́n* 'ten' is a widespread numeral and appears to be an areal form found in the rest of the three language families of Ethiopia—Afroasiatic, Cushitic and Omotic. Outside these families, the number word *ten* has similar forms in some languages of the Nilo-Saharan subfamilies (also common in Nilotic). For instance, *tom* represents 'ten': in Nubian, Nera—*túmum*, in Nyangi, IK—*tɔmin/tomin*, Surmic, Murle—*tomon*.

3.3.5.1   Number Words

Mursi has a ten-based number system, also known as 'decimal system'. All number words except two appear to be a non-borrowed ones (see Table 3.12 above). Unlike some Surmic languages, Mursi does not form numerals from six to nine by combining lower numerals and quinary form. Number words for those higher than ten can be formed by combining *tɔ́mɔ́n* 'ten'/ *hírkón* 'twenty', etc and those from one to nine (see Chapter 6). The number word *hírkón* is derived from the noun *hírí* 'man' and the indefinite pronoun *kón* 'one' (literally 'one man's ten fingers and ten toes'). The number word 'forty' is *zùwò ràmàn* (literally 'two people'). Additional information on how number words are formed for higher numerals is available in Chapter 6.

WORD CLASSES

As mentioned earlier, a noun modified by a number word cannot be marked with restrictive modification. This is due to the fact that the dependency relation between that of head nouns and number word modifiers is always free.

(3.124) [zùwò háánán]_{NP} sɔ̀ŋ
people five only
'only five people'

This relation of the two in NPs will be changed when there is an intermediate modifier intervening between the head noun and the number word modifier (3.125).

(3.125) [[bì-á gìdã̀ŋ-à]_{NP} háánán]_{NP}
cow-RSTR brown.STV-RSTR five
'Five brown cows'

Number agreement between a head noun in singular and a number word 'one' is indicated by a non-restrictive marker -i/-ti.

(3.126) a. érmì-tí [dɔ́néj]_{NP} áìw-ó
child-NTSTR one come.PERV.SG-MT.3SG.SU.PERV
'one child came.'

b. [ʃì-tí dɔ́néj]
thousand-NRSTR one
'(One) thousand'

Number words can function as copula complements like any other modifiers of head nouns within an NP. For a question asked in (3.127a), one could answer a clause containing number word as a copula complement (3.127b). The one in (3.127c) can also be another possible candidate.

(3.127) a. támárí-ɲá-í él-é
student-PL-NRSTR exist.IMPERV.PL-3PL.SU.IMPERV
á ísɔ̀ŋ?
COP.3.IMPERV how.many
'How many students are present?'

b. támárí-ɲá él-é á
student-PL exist.IMPERV.PL-3PL.SU.IMPERV COP.3.IMPERV

>   *háánán*
>   five
>   'Five students are present.'
>   (Lit. 'Students present are five.')
>
> c. *ŋà=ɓ=ùnù*   [*támárí-ɲá háánán*]$_{NP}$
>   DEM=place=FAR student-PL five
>   *él-ɛ́*
>   exist.IMPERV.PL-3PL.SU.IMPERV
>   'There are five students.'

There are three ordinal numbers in Mursi. Further discussion is in §6.11.2 (cf. pp. 290–291). Two of them are derived from the number words 'two' and 'three'—*ràmàn-nè* ⟨two-ORD⟩ 'second' and *sízzì-nè* ⟨three-ORD⟩ 'third' The ordinal number word for 'one' is a grammaticalized body part noun *sábá* 'head'—*sábá* > *sábɔ́* 'front, in front of' (preposition) > *sábɔ̀* 'before' (time word) > *sabu-ne* 'first' (ordinal number).

> (3.128) a. *nà   ín-á   sábú-nè   gàm-ànà   mùgàj*
>   CCN   3SG.PN.SP-RSTR first-ORD marry-MT:3SG.SU.IMPER   woman
>   '… and the first (one) married a wife'
>
> b. *úŋɔ́   sízzì-nè*
>   night.PL third-ORD
>   'the third day'

But only the number word *dɔ́nɛ́j* is used to convey a distributive meaning. This can be done by placing the grammaticalized body part noun *kɛŋɔ* 'belly' before it and by reduplicating its full form (3.129).

> (3.129) *àstàmàrì-ɲà áli-ɛ́   kèŋɔ̀ dɔ́nɛ́dɔ́nɛ́*
>   teacher-PL   talk-3PL.SU.IMPERV belly one:REDUP
>   'The teachers are talking one after the other.'

In addition, when any number word higher than 'two' is used side by side with the plural form *kèŋì* 'bellies' it can yield a multiplicative reading, for example, *kèŋì sízzì* 'three times' (Lit. 'three bellies') (see Chapter 6).

3.3.5.2 Quantifiers

Quantifiers in Mursi form a small-sized class of their own. Some may belong to the class of adjectives while others belong to the class of adverbs; thus this counts them among a few word-class crossing words. For example, *mèrì* 'many' and *múčúgí* 'little, a little' belong to the subclass of adjectives, i.e. derived adjectives. Both take the general adjectivizer suffix *-i*.

TABLE 3.13 Quantifiers

Quantifiers	Meaning
mèrì	'many, abundant'
múčúgí	'little, a few, half'
ɓòìtííni	'a little (bit)'
dínío	'full'
dɔ́nɛ́nɛ́n	'only'
dákákán	'all, total'
dààì	'all'
ɓókón	'some'
sòŋ	'only'

Syntactically, some quantifiers function in the same way as number words—that is, NP heads may take a non-restrictive suffix when modified by quantifiers. Below are examples which demonstrate the syntactic function of quantifiers—modifiers within a noun phrase (3.130–3.132) and copula complements (3.133).

(3.130) [zùg-tí   bù mèrì]ₙₚ
        people-NRSTR big many
        'very many people'

(3.131) [úŋ-ní   múčúg-í]ₙₚ   wùréɔ́
        night.PL-NRSTR few.STV-NRSTR   after
        'after few (some) days'

(3.132) [àhà   dààì]ₙₚ géɲ-ónó   nèàj
        thing.PL all   create.IMPERV-MT:3SG.SU.IMPERV 3SG.PVS
        'All come into being through him.'
        (Lit. 'He created every things through him.')

(3.133) ŋà=bá=á   tó-jé   [àh-á   gàʃ-ùɲ]_NP   á
        DEM=place=NEAR in-OBL thing-PL forest-GEN COP.3.IMPERV
        mèrì   háŋ
        many   INTENS
        'There are many animals in this country.'

Quantifiers which belong to the class of adjectives function adjectivally as well as take the restrictive morphology, as in (3.134).

(3.134) kídó   tó-jé   [ùrgùs-á   dǐní-ò]_NP
        river.SG in-OBL fish-PL.RSTR full-RSTR.MOD
        'The river abounds with fishes.'
        (Lit. 'The river, inside is full of fishes.')

Modification marker seems to be dropped when another grammatical element is attached to the quantifier word, as in the example shown below.

(3.135) [àɲè wà   kí-ʃǐg-í]   [jɔ̀g sén-ɛ́]
        1SG REC.PAST 1SU-hear-1SG.SU.IMPERV 3PL say-3PL.SU.IMPERV
        [ɓ=ùnù   gòl [mà dǐní=jè]_NP]_SUBORD:CL
        place=FAR river water full=SUBORD
        'I have heard (them say) that the river is full of water.'

The quantifier dàài 'all' may function as an adjective (3.132; 3.136a.) or as an adverb (3.136b).

(3.136) a. [hùllì [ɓá-á   zùwò-ɲ]_NP dàài á
           if   place-RSTR people-GEN all   COP.3.IMPERV
           čàll-ì=jè]_SUBORD:CL   kó   [àɲè]_CS á
           good.STV-ADJ=SUBORD PNC/PREP 1SG   COP.3.IMPERV
           [čàll-ì]_CC   húŋ
           good.STV-ADJ simply/just
           'It is all right with me if it is all right with everybody else.'

        b. kó   ìggè lɔ̀gó ɲànì   ŋà=dúl-úɲ=nó   dàài?
           PNC 2PL word NEG.PERV NEG=feel-2PL.OBJ=NEG all
           'Have you (pl.) understood all these things?'

The quantifier ɓòìtíìní 'a little bit' functions only as an adverb, as in the following examples.

(3.137) kàl-á   rònɔ́   wùréɔ́ áw-ó   ɓòitííní
       day/time-RSTR in.the.future after come.PERV.IMP-MT a.little.bit
       ʃàù!
       fast
       'Next time come a little earlier!'

(3.138) a[ɲ]   àggè k-àw-ò   ɔ́r-ɔ́
       HORT:PART 1PL 1.HORT-go.PERV-1PL.INC.SU.PERV settlement-OBL
       nà   k-àùs-ò   ɓòitííní
       CCN 1.HORT-rest.PERV-1PL.INC.SU a.little.bit
       'Let us (inc.) go home and rest a little!'

3.3.6 Connectors and Discourse Particles
From the morphological point of view, there is only one notable difference found between connectors and discourse particles. That is, the two discourse particles can occur as free particles or as morphemes being attached to their hosts. Connectors are always free particles forming a full-fledged phonological word and a grammatical word.

3.3.6.1   Connectors
Mursi has a limited set of connectives which are mainly used to connect two nouns or clauses.

The connectives *kó/ké* 'and, with' are identical syntactically as well as semantically. Both function as coordinative conjunction particle or even as prepositions. Any two nouns or NPs can be conjoined by these two phrasal conjunctions. However, there are two major differences between the two:
- the connector *ké* cannot be used as conjunction in number words that are higher than ten (as in (3.139)), and
- the connector *ké* cannot be used (to conjoin the comparees or the participants) in comparative constructions, as shown in (3.140).

(3.139) bérgú tɔ̀mɔ̀n **kó**   dɔ̃́néj
       year   ten   PNC   one
       'Hamle (November)'
       (Lit. 'year ten with one')

(3.140) PARTICIPANTS   PARAMETER COMPAREE
       [múwáj **kó** hírí], [bú]   hírí-ɔ́
       woman PCN man   big   man-NOM
       'The man is bigger than the woman.'
       (Lit. 'from the woman and the man, the man is the big one.')

TABLE 3.14 Connectors

Connectors	Meaning	Function & source
ké	'and/with'	phrasal conjunction (§ 14.3.1.1)
kó	'and/with'	phrasal conjunction (§ 14.3.1.1)
nà	'and, then, so'	clausal connector, coordinative conjunction simultaneous and successive marker, narration or temporal progression marker and so on (§ 14.2.2.2; § 14.2.2.5)
hùllì	'if, when'	clausal; conditional marker (§ 14.2.1; § 14.2.2)
kó hùllì	'even though'	~ Lit. 'and if'; concessive marker (§ 14.2.2.2)
nà hùllì	'then'	~ Lit. 'and when' (§ 14.3.1.1)
ɓá	'in place of, because'	~ Lit. 'place'; cause, reason, complementizer, mark (in comparative construction), substitutive clause marker (§ 14.2.2.6)
óó	'or'	Disjunctive coordination (§ 14.3.1.3)
kóó	'or'	Disjunctive coordination (§ 14.3.1.3)
ŋànì	'not yet'	
ŋànìjè	'however'	contrastive coordination (§ 14.3.1.2)
kó ɓòì	'until'	future time clause (§ 14.2.2.7)

Other than the two exceptions noted above, *kó* and *ké* function in one and the same way. Both can interchangeably be used when they function as prepositional or comitative markers.

(3.141) té   kó/ké čàll-ì
        COP.PER:IMP with good.stv-adj
        'Good bye!'
        (Lit. 'be (stay) with peace!')

The stative-inchoative reading in (3.141) originated from the perfective imperative copula verb form *té*. There seems to be no limit as to how many phrasal conjunctions can be used when one conjoins with a series of nouns.

(3.142) bàrtùj kó   ŋàtùj kó   ŋàdórá ám-é   músí-ɲá
        Bartuy PNC Ngatuy PNC Ngadora eat-3PL.SU.IMPERV banana-PL
        kàrì
        together
        'Bartuy and Ngatuy and Ngadora are eating a banana each.'

The clausal connector *nà* 'and' has a number of function at the clausal level and beyond. It primarily conjoins two clauses referring to events linked to one another in a temporally simultaneous and successive ways.

(3.143) *nà   ménéɲí   dɔ́t-ú   jesusi nà   ók-ú*
CCN:NARR devil   leave-3SG.SU.PERV   Jesus   CCN go-3SG.SU.PERV
nà   [lúsà-á   túmó-ɲ]_NP   hód-á   nà
CCN   son.PL-RSTR   God-GEN   come.PERV.PL-3PL.SU   CCN
ílál-á   jesusi
confort-3PL.SU.PERV   Jesus
'Then the devil left him (Jesus) and he went (the devil), and angels (Lit. 'Sons of God') came and attended him (Jesus).'

When *nà* occurs at the beginning (clause-initial position) of a story/narration, it functions as a narration or temporal progression marker, or logical continuity marker. Thus, in other words, *nà* may be considered a chronological sequencer of the events taking place in the narration. See the following examples:

(3.144) *nà   k-íw-áná   rò*
CCN:NARR 1SU-take.IMPERV-MT.1PL.INC.SU.IMPERV cloth
[kèj-á   bú   dɔ́ldɔ́l-á]_NP   kó   [[sáj   bú-sísí
thing-RSTR   big   hard.STV-RSTR   PNC   leather_dress   big-AUG
dɔ́rɔ́s-á]_NP   múgá-ɲ]_NP
hard/dry.STV-RSTR   woman-GEN
'Thus, we take a kind of cloth that is a very solid, very dry leather dress of women.' (KW 1:59:4)

(3.145) *nà   áíw-ó   nà*
CCN:NARR come.PERV.SG-MT.3SG.SU.PERV   CCN
téhén-ú   [b[b]ásá-í   bág-ò]_COMPL:CL
want.PERV-3SG.SU.PERV   monitor.lizard-NOM   eat-3SG.IRR
'So, he came and decided to eat the monitor lizard.'

Clausal connectives have been elaborated extensively in Chapter 14.

3.3.6.2   Discourse Particles
Discourse particles form a smaller closed word class in the language. The meaning being conveyed by these discourse particles may cover a wide range of functional areas from polite marker to quotative (in speech report). Except for the quotative marker particle *ké* (see also §14.2.3.1) which always precedes speech

TABLE 3.15 Discourse particles

Discourse particles	Meaning	Function
so (=so)	'behold, please'	emphatic particle, polite marker
-ni	'then, thus, so then'	marker of a resolution of a dilemma or goal or termination of a complicated action/event/conflict
čii (=čii)	'so!, Hmm'	astonishment plus irony;
ké	'that'	quotative, complement marker (§14.2.3)
dá	'really, was it, oh!'	epistemic, mirativity ~'surprisingly' discourse marker (see §12.3)
čírr	'really (?)'	epistemic, confirmation, to elicit acquiescence from the addressee (cf. Aikhenvald 2015: 199) (see §12.3)
tɔ́b	'clearly, openly'	can be an adverb but best fits to the smallish class of discourse particles

verbs (but it may precede or follow a speech report), they have no fixed functional slots in clauses.

Three members of this class are manifested in two morphological forms—*so* and *čii* (also as floating enclitics =*so* and =*čii*), and -*ni* as just a suffix. Many of these particles are optional because they merely add a piece of extra information to the existing meaning of a clause or a story line. For example, the floating emphatic enclitic =*so* can occur on nouns, verbs and adverbs—often attaches to the last elements of a clause or narrative texts.

(3.146) a. ŋà=hír=nù   tá   á   nèŋ
         DEM=man=FAR UNCERT COP.3.IMPERV what
         gín-ò=**sò**
         ask-3SG.IRR=**EMPH**
         'Ask the man whom he is talking about!'

       b. ŋànìjè ìɲè tá   wà   án-í
          but   2SG UNCERT REC.PAST COP.IMPERV-2SG.SU.IMPERV
          kómórú-**ni**=sò
          king/leader-**RES**=EMPH
          'So you are a king?!'

c. [hír-á màɗ-ì] bág tílá=só
man-RSTR teach-NOMZ eat.PERV.IMP food=EMPH
'Master, eat.'
(Lit. 'Teacher, please eat (sg.) food!')

As it is depicted in (3.146a–b), the emphatic enclitic =so attaches to hosts that are being emphasized. Thus, a constituent emphasized by this floating enclitic can be a topic or focused element.

(3.147) a. àggè kɔ̀-lɔ̀m-Ø làsén háánán kó ùrgùs-á
1PL 1SU-have-1SG.INC.SU.IMPERV read five PNC fish-RSTR
ràmàn sɔ́ŋ só
two only EMPH
'We have here but five loaves and two fishes.'

b. me kɔ́bkɔ́b só sátí kɔ́ɔ́j-Ø nà
do.PERV.IMP quickly EMPH time 3.SBJV.go-3.IRR CCN
gár-á=sò
finish-3SG.SU.PERV=EMPH
'Hurry, else you will be late.'
(Lit. 'Please do quickly! The time will go and finished!')

The suffix -ni is a discourse resolution marker but it does not function as an independent particle. This discourse resolution marker suffix is also found in the Tirmaga language and has two functions (Bryant 1993: 41). The two functions of -ni in a narration are: (i) it indicates the resolution of a dilemma or goal, and (ii) it shows the state of equilibrium has been reached at the conclusion of an episode. In Mursi, -ni indicates a result or a solution which has taken place after a serious of complicated actions or events.

In narration, it indicates a settlement or an end of a situation with a positive outcome after a long standing conflict or situation. Examine the following examples.

(3.148) [hùllì nè k-íɲ[9]-ò=jè]_{SUBORD:CL} té
if 3SG 3.SBJV-touch.1PL.OBJ-3SG.IRR=SUBORD COP.3.PERV

---

9 The verb 'to touch' is ɲana, and has a root form ⟨ɲ⟩. In (3.148), there was the first person plural object suffix -i but has been already assimilated into the root.

```
kílí-ni  té              gèrs-ì
kili-RS  COP.3.PERV      bad.STV-ADJ
```
'If he (Teri (sg.)) touches us, it becomes "Kili". It gets bad.' (KW 1:17:8)

(3.149) čùànéŋ ŋà=lɔ́g=tù   hàlì   ájt-ɛ   tèrò-ú-ni
         again   DEM=issue=FAR   later take.PL.PERV-APPL.3   teri.PL-NOM-RS
         té   [lɔ́g-tí   g=èj]_NP
         COP.3.PERV   issue-NRSTR   PL.PSD=3PL.PSR

'Then later the Teru take up this issue (Kili) and thus it becomes their issue.' (KW 1:28:8)

In both (3.148) and (3.149), the resolutions are outcomes or answers to the question "so what finally happened?". The story behind these two examples is that in Mursiland, following the harvest season which takes place twice in a year (December–January and June–July), the *dɔ̀ŋà* (middle aged boys) go in large groups into the cultivation areas and collect the decapitated sorghum stalks (*ólʃó*). The age grade of the boys who collect the sorghum stalks is found in Text I (Appendix I). When the collection of the sorghum stalks is over, the *dɔ̀ŋà*, who collected the stalks, kneel in a compact group at the tree, facing the *rórá* (senior), who accuse them, of failing to carry out the duties of their age grade. This can be very serious if they attack girls while collecting sorghum stalks because this is not showing sufficient respect to their 'fathers', the *rórá*. Therefore, this offence becomes 'Kili' (as in (3.148)) or it becomes the issue of the *tèró* (age grade for young men) who attacked the girls (as in (3.149)).

The particle *čii* is usually used in ironic expressions which indicate astonishment about something very small. It may be used as a diminutive marker particle and can appear between the head noun and the modifier within an NP.

(3.150) a. [[ŋà=àlèj=á]_NP   čii tíí=ŋà]_NP   (~tííŋa < [tíín=ŋà])
           DEM=chair=NEAR   so   small=DEF
           'This so small chair!'

       b. ŋà=bá=á   čii   tííní   gode   ádʒ-áɲ-à
          DEM=place=NEAR   so   small   DEMU   give.IMPERV-1SG.OBJ-2SG.IRR
          mèsí-Ø   sɔ̀ŋ   ènèŋ?
          do-3SG.SU.IMPERV   only how
          'To what avail (Lit. what will it do for me) did you give me so little?'

In (3.50a), the discourse particle *čìi* may function as modifier of the adjective *tíiní* or as a default intensifier.

The discourse particles *dá* and *čírr* have literally the same meaning ('really?') and almost a comparable function. Both may be used in information questions that require verification (see more in §12.3). Some examples were presented as follows.

(3.151) a. nòŋ **dá** bàrì gìrŋàj gár-ú
3SG **really** yesterday nose dissapear-3SG.SU.PERV
'He threw off a cold.'

b. ín-í elijas **dá?**
3SG.PN.SP-NRSTR Elijah **really**
'Is that you, Elijah?'

c. bá bàg-ò gáw[j]-ó **čírr?**
place live-3SG.IRR know.IMPERV-2PL.SU.IMPERV **really**
'Do you (pl.) know the place he lives at?'

From a syntactic perspective, *tób* 'clearly, openly, publicly' should have been in the class of adverbs. However, *tób* always only appears at the end of a few discourse types.

(3.152) a. ké ín-í k-àr-ì **tób**
COMPL 3SG.PN.SP-NRSTR PASS-see.PERV.PASS.3.SU **clearly**
'So that it may be clearly seen.'

b. *jesusi ŋà=lòg=tá jóg-èsè [mùmì-á*
jesus DEM=word=NEAR tell-BEN.3SG.SU.PERV face.PL-RSTR
g=èj]$_{NP}$ **tób**
PL.PSD=3P.PSR **clearly**
'Jesus told them very clearly what he meant.'

(3.153) kàl-á wùréś [zùw-á ajhudaj]$_{NP}$ kèrgèn-ò **tób**
day/time-RSTR after people-RTSR jew.GEN middle-OBL **clearly**
ŋànì ŋà=wój-∅=ó
NEG.PERV NEG.IMPERV=walk-3SG.SU.IMPERV=NEG
'After that time/day, he hasn't walked openly between the Jews.'

TABLE 3.16 Discourse particles

Interjections	Meaning	Function & source
ɪmm!	'no!'	disagreement, disapproval
ɪɲɲ!	'yes!'	agreement, approval
híh!	'huh!'	to express disgust; also used to express discontent/reproach
hee! hee!	'hey! hey!'	to express surprise, to laugh ironically
aj!	'ah!'	to express disgust or revulsion
éé!	'yes!, Ok!, all right'	to express confirmation expresses willingness or agreement

3.3.7 *Interjections*

Mursi has a fair number of interjections which form a small closed class of their own, a heterogeneous class of words. They mainly serve to express human emotions and feelings. Unlike other closed word classes in the language, interjections lack fixed syntactic functions slots. However, a few of them may have clause-initial preferences. Above is Table 3.16 containing a list of Mursi interjections.

As it can be seen in the table above, interjections may contain forms that are quite different from the regular internal phonological structure of words. As we recall, both consonant and vowel length do not exist in Mursi. Phonetic based consonant and vowel length may, however, exist word-medially. Examples depicting the use of interjection are provided below.

(3.154) *"hee   hee   woinanoje   bóʃójè"   sén-é*
       INTERJ INTERJ *woynanoye* boshoye say.IMPERV-3PL.SU.IMPERV
       ŋàŋà
       like.this
       '"hee! hee! woynanoye boshoye", they say like this.' (MH 1:10:7)

(3.155) *híh!   nà   ɪɲè   kíɲáŋ   húŋ   ɓák-ú   kὲ ɔ̀ŋ*
       INTERJ! CCN 2SG crocodile simply eat-3SG.SU.PERV why?
       '"Hih!" (and) why did you (sg.) eat crocodile?' (MH 4:30:6)

The negative interjection *ɪmm* 'no' may also be used for answering a 'yes/no' questions (see §13.7).

TABLE 3.17 Ideophones

Ideophones	Meaning/function
ŋóm	to refer to an action related to the breaking of something completely; breaking/shattering objects into pieces
ɗóm	to refer to an action related to the breaking of something completely
túl	Very reddish!
páf	to appear suddenly; sudden popping up
kóŋ	to refer to an act of dying
réb	to lie down suddenly
sɛ́bsɛ́b	walking very quietly and sneakily (being out of someone's sight)
kɛ́mkɛ́m	breaking something wooden or a breakable thing completely (intensity)
kɛ́lkɛ́l	to refer to a leg broken badly
ɗɛmɗɛm	to refer to a misbehavior
ɗósɗós	to pound something strongly and repeatedly; to beat (hit) someone badly
ɗúsɗús	a feeling one has when touched by insects or some other things frequently
kámčú kámčú	a food or something being eaten completely
jágjágjág	to fall down to the ground very badly (to humans)
ɓóɓóɓóɓɔ́	to fall from a tree very badly (for a snake)
bórčóčó	sound created by water when something steps into water suddenly, asplash
kɔ̀kɔ́ʃ kɔ̀kɔ́ʃ	move about restlessly; wonder about aimlessly; stagger
tíŋtíŋ tíŋtíŋ	sound for stamping
dʒúdʒúdʒú	splash sounds of water

3.3.8 *Ideophones*

Mursi ideophones form a separate class of onomatopoeic words. They primarily denote meanings of actions usually being expressed by action verbs. Aikhenvald (2015: 200) pointed out that ideophones are 'sound-symbolic: their phonological form resembles the sound or impression associated with the action or with the referent'. All Mursi ideophones, at least the ones listed in Table 3.17 above, consist of mono- and disyllabic morphemes. Some may occur in inherently reduplicated patterns. *jágjágjág* seems to be exceptional in that it has a triplicated pattern.

The meanings of Mursi ideophones are diverse and are hard to pinpoint easily as they are not derived from other word classes. Unlike other word classes, ideophones do not seem to have an independent meaning. As can be seen from the above meanings assigned to them in Table 3.17, a good attempt has been made to define them contextually rather than through their direct denotational meanings.

(3.156) hírí bík-ú   [dóɲà-á   lúsì-ɲ]_NP **kɛ́mkɛ́m**
man break-3SG.SU.PERV rod-RSTR boy-GEN IDEO
'The man broke kɛmkɛm the boy's stick.'

(3.157) wà   lìwá   kà-ɓàgt-à   ɓòì
REC.PAST sorghum PASS-eat.PERV-PASS.3.SU completely
kámčúkámčú
IDEO
'The sorghum was eaten completely kamčukamču.'

(3.158) ká-dág-ín-í   dósdós nà
1SU-hit-2SG.OBJ-1SG.SU.IMPERV IDEO CCN
rès-é[í]
die.IMPERV-2SG.SU.IMPERV
'I will hit you dosdos and you die!'

(3.159) [hùllì tùrè rógé-Ø=jè]_SUBORD:CL   túŋ   rɛ́b
when gun shout-3SG.SU.IMPERV=SUBORD] sleep.PERV.IMP IDEO
háŋ
very
'When you hear the sound of gunshot, lie down!'
(Lit. 'when a gun shouts, sleep rɛb (sg.)!')

Ideophones may also offer a vivid representation of an idea in sound (Doke 1935 as cited in Nuckolls 1999: 239). In other words, ideophones may also be able to describe manner (see §3.3.9), colour, smell, action, or intensity. The colour intensifier ideophone *túl* 'really' is among many which are good examples of this statement. *túl* is an ideophone which oftentimes the Mursi use to describe a highly saturated or 'pure' red stimulus. Turton (1980: 327) in his article entitled 'There's No Such Beast: Cattle and Colour Naming Among the Mursi' has described well how the Mursi use *túl* for intensifying a red colour and how they uniquely have acquired the skills of putting idea in sounds. An identical colour intensifying ideophone (*túl*) has been found in the Suri language (Bryant, unpublished sketch grammar).

3.3.9 Expressives

Expressives may appear very similar to those of ideophones but differ in one major aspect. That is, expressives may function as 'sound symbolic adverbs'—typically as manner adverbs. Phonologically, expressives can easily be recognized by having simple monosyllabic patterns composed of C_1VC_2 shapes (where C_2 stands for voiceless postalveolar fricative [ʃ]). Syntactically, like adverbs, expressives occur following the predicate or following the completive or manner adverb particle ɓòì—but they have fixed syntactic slots within a clause, i.e. always appear at clause-final positions. Like ideophones, expressions do not have their own inherent meanings.

(3.160) ʤààrí ɓíč-á   ɓòì   *háʃ*
       leg   break-3SG.SU.PERV completely EXPRESSIVE
       'The leg broke completely *háʃ*.'

(3.161) érmì   dák-ú   bá   *lúʃ*   nà
       boy.SG fall-3SG.SU.PERV ground EXPRESSIVE   CCN
       èr-á   ɓòì
       die.PERV-3SG.SU.PERV   completely
       'The boy fell down (eg. from a tree) *luʃ* and died.'

When expressives occur in repeated forms, they denote iterative actions. Not only do they depict iterative actions, but they also may sometimes describe reciprocal actions. As is shown in the example given below, the fact that the comitative marker attached to the verb may yield reciprocity. But the real reciprocal marker suffix does not simply abandon the verb in such specific case for the sake of a comitative marker whose semantic function is secondary.

(3.162) zùwò   dákt-è   *háʃháʃ*
       people hit.PERV.PL-RECIP.3   EXPRESSIVE
       'The people beat each other very badly.'

At the same time, as we can see in (3.161) and (3.162), expressives would indeed function as adverbs. In fact, both expressives and ideophones require further research for us to be able to understand what their role is in the grammar of the language.

TABLE 3.18 Expressives

Expressives	Meaning
ɓéʃ	'something suddenly happening'
lúʃ	'describes the way of dying'
háʃ	'a sound of something breaking'
ráʃ	'describes the sound of falling'
mɔ́ʃ	'as an intensifier for being tired'

3.3.10 *A Summary of Closed Word Classes*

In Table 3.19 below, a short summary of Mursi closed word classes has been provided. Thus this summary is aimed at showing major syntactic functions of the closed word classes, and shows which are among these closed classes could take certain morphological categories such as case and number. Besides, syntactic functional categories such as modifiers and intensifiers could refers to those categories of the closed word classes whose main function are nominal or verbal modification/intensification.

TABLE 3.19 Summary: closed word classes

Word class	Syntactic functions					Morphology (case/numb.)	
	Head of NP	Modifier	Intensifier	S/A, O, E	CS/CC	Case	Numb.
Personal pronouns	×	×	×	√	CS	√	×
Specific pronouns	√	×	×	×	CS	×	×
Demonstrative pronouns	×	√	×	S	CS	×	×
Possessive pronouns	×	√	×	×	CC	×	×
Indefinite pronouns	SOME	√	×	SOME	?	×	SOME
Relative pronouns	×	×	×	SOME	?	×	×
Adverbs	×	√	SOME	×	×	×	×
Adpositions	×	×	×	E	×	√	×
Question words	×	???	×	SOME	CC	SOME	×

TABLE 3.19 Summary: closed word classes (*cont.*)

Word class	Syntactic functions					Morphology (case/numb.)	
	Head of NP	Modifier	Intensifier	S/A, O, E	CS/CC	Case	Numb.
Number words	×[a]	√	???	×	CC	×	×
Quantifiers	×	√	SOME	×	CC	×	×
Ideophones	×	SOME	SOME	×	×	×	×
Expressives	×	SOME	??	×	×	×	×

a The borrowed number word (from Amharic) *ʃi* 'thoudand' is an exceptional case because it can function as a head within an NP. Interestingly, its modifier is also a number word *d́ńéj* 'one' (see § 3.3.5.1).

CHAPTER 4

Noun phrase structure

4.1 Introduction

A Noun Phrase (NP) is a nominal structure that fills a core or a peripheral argument slot in a clause. Major constituents of a Mursi noun phrase include: simple nouns, pronouns, adjectives, stative verbs, de-verbal nouns, demonstratives, and determiners (numerals and quantifiers). Mursi noun phrases can be headed by personal pronouns, nouns, demonstrative pronouns, proper names, and de-verbal nouns, as in (4.1–4.3).

(4.1) [ànè]$_{NP:A}$ ká-tál-á-ni   [čój kó [bárbárí gáwá-jè]$_{NP}$]$_{NP:O}$
      1SG   1SU-buy-1SG.SU.PERV-RS salt PNC pepper market-OBL
      'I bought salt and pepper from the market.'

(4.2) [hìrì]$_{NP:A}$ bɔ̀rɔ́t-∅-ɔ̀
      man   jump-3SG.SU.IMPERV-VFS
      'The man jumps.'

(4.3) [ɓàllógì]$_{NP:S}$ nɔ́-sèn   bá
      leaf   go.down.PERV-MA ground
      'The leaf fell towards the ground.'

Mursi is a head-initial language. It marks both the head and the dependent. The head noun normally utilizes two head-marking systems: modification markers (also known as Construct Forms (CF)) which marks a noun for being modified, and pertensives which mark the noun possessed in a possessive noun phrase. In Mursi, the noun phrase can occur in two major construction types: one involving non-clausal modification (§4.2), and one involving clausal modification (§4.3).

4.2 Non-clausal Modifiers of NP

The non-clausal modifiers of an NP include: demonstrative determiners (§4.2.1), adjectives (§4.2.2), genitives (§4.2.3), possessive pronouns (§4.2.4) number words (§4.2.5), and specific indefinite pronouns (§4.2.6).

4.2.1 *Demonstratives*

The demonstrative modifiers are of two types: those that occur with nouns (Type I, § 4.2.1.1) and those with pronouns (Type II, § 4.2.1.2). See more on the morphosyntactic nature of demonstrative in § 3.3.1.3.

4.2.1.1   Nominal Demonstrative Pronouns (Type I)

Type I nominal demonstrative pronouns are deictic expressions which indicate the relative distance from the speaker. They can function as a full NP. They are bound forms comprised of circumclitics and can be marked on the noun they modify simultaneously. The proclic ŋà= ⟨DEM⟩ which denotes the demonstrative function is constant while the two enclitics =á ⟨NEAR⟩ and =ùnù ⟨FAR⟩ denote the relative spatial location (proximal and distal) of their referents (cf. Dixon 2012: 234). The templates below illustrate a full NP made from a noun and a modifying bound deictic circumclitic.

i.   DEM=NOUN.ROOT-(NUM)=NEAR/FAR
ii. DEM=VERB.ROOR-NOMZ-(NUM)=NEAR/FAR

(4.4) [ŋà=hír=á]$_{NP}$
DEM=man=NEAR
'this man'

(4.5) [ŋà=ɓég-á-ɲá-ìnù]$_{NP}$
DEM=watch-NOMZ-PL=FAR
'those (field) watchings'

In a bound nominal demonstrative construction, number can be marked on the noun itself.

(4.6) [ŋà=àh-à=á]$_{NP}$
DEM=thing-PL=NEAR
'these things'

Nouns modified by these nominal demonstrative circumclitics cannot take a case suffix marking a core or non-core syntactic function. However, their local adverbial demonstrative form can take a locative case suffix. Exceptional case have been found where the word *bá* 'place' is marked with a locative case, as in (4.7).

(4.7) nà   tél-í   ŋà=bà-ì=nù]$_{NP}$ [tíí   kó   ɓòì
       CCN exist.PERV-3.IRR DEM=place-LOC=FAR   DUR   PNC   COMPLET

> hàlì rès-è herediwosi-j
> later die.IMPERV-NOMZ Herod-GEN
> 'And he was there until the death of Herod.'

They can also occur in subject function (copula subject) and modify other nouns in Noun Modification construction.

(4.8) [čɔ̀r-á [ŋà=mɔ̀r=á]_NP]_NP á   làlìn-ì
       hair-RSTR DEM=calf=NEAR COP.3.IMPERV cold.STV-ADJ
       'The hair of this calf is cold.'

Although (4.8) is a type noun modification construction which requires further marking both on the head and the modifier, only the head is marked with a construct-form suffix. The bound deictic circumclitics have restricted the noun from inflecting for further grammatical roles. In (4.8), the modifier ŋamɔra is in its canonical place, and has a role seemingly modifying the noun in construct-form/relator suffix, but, its role is just to refer to a specific item or what body part of the calf is being referred to.

A head noun inflected for deictic elements can only be modified by a possessive pronoun or by a possessive NP. See the following two examples.

(4.9) ạ̀ŋè [ké ɓá]¹ kómórú [[[ŋà=éró=á]_NP   g=ạ̀ŋù]_NP
       1SG CRD place lord   DEM=children=NEAR PL.PSD=1SG.PRS
       kó   ràmàn=ŋà]_NP ké   kóná   ạ̀j   sìɔ̀   sìtèn
       CRD.PART two=DEF   PNC one.INDEF JUSS.PART hand right
       kóná   ạ̀j   sìɔ̀   kàŋìtèn
       one.INDEF JUSS.PART hand left
       'Grant that these, my two sons may sit, the one on your right hand, and the other on the left.'

In (4.9), the demonstrative construction ŋàéróá 'these children' does not take the construct-form suffix -a, and it has no restrictive role over the modifiers as head nouns do in that particular canonical order. On the other hand, the role of the possessive pronoun gạ̀ŋù is to draw attention to the fact that the children belong to the woman and to provide further information that she has just two sons.

---

1 The ké ɓá is used in a subordinate clause to refer to a subsequent time margin—paralleled by the English 'until' or 'until x in place'.

(4.10) [ŋà=ɓég-á-ɲá=ìnù]_NP [ɓá-á   mùn-ùɲ]_NP]_NP
DEM=watch-NOMZ-PL=FAR place-RSTR Mursi-GEN
'those field-watchings place of the Mursi'

Adjectives, numerals or other sorts of non-clausal modifiers cannot directly modify a head noun inflected for bound deictic elements. For adjectives to modify a head noun with bound demonstratives, they must occur in a copula complement position.

(4.11) [ŋà=hír=ùnù]_NP:CS á   [čàll-i]_CC
DEM=man=FAR COP.3.IMPERV good.STV-ADJ
'that good man'
(Lit. 'that man is good')

In contrast, adjectives can directly modify head nouns that occur with no bound deictic inflections, as in (4.12a–b).

(4.12) a. [hírí čàll-á]_NP
man good.STV-RSTR
'a good man'

b. [rúm-á   hɔ̀l-á]_NP
cloth-RTSR white.RSTR
'the white dress'

In (4.12a) we see a non-restrictive relationship between the head noun and the modifier. In (4.12b), the relationship between the head noun and the modifier is restrictive in which both elements are marked with the construct-form/relator suffix. Only proper nouns and nouns with deictic demonstratives can have an NP construction with unmarked head (as in (4.8, 4.9, 4.12a)). A restrictive and non-restrictive relationship of head nouns and their modifiers is discussed in § 4.3.1.1.

In addition, numerals must follow the partitive conjunction particle kó[2] so as to modify a head noun that inflects for bound deictic elements.

---

2 In his survey 'moveable-k', Greenberg (1981) noted that the ki is assumed to have a demonstrative function. In addition, Dimmendaal (2018) argued that the element *ki is an extremely stable preposition in many Nilo-Saharan languages including Turkana. Its function is to introduce attributive phrases in noun phrases.

(4.13) [[ŋà=lɔ̀g=tá]ₙₚ   kó   ràmàn=ŋà]ₙₚ
       DEM=word=NEAR CRD:PART two=DEF
       'these two commandments'
       (Lit. 'two of the commandments')

(4.14) [[ŋà=zùg=tá]ₙₚ   kó   tɔ̀mɔ̀n kó   ràmàn-ne]ₙₚ
       DEM=people=NEAR CRD:PART ten   CONJ two-ORD
       'these (the) twelfth'
       (Lit. 'these (the) twelfth people')

It is important to note that the bound deictic clitics always function as noun-modifying spatial demonstratives and can make up a full NP with the nouns they modify. When such an NP is modified by another nominal or adjective or even by a proper name, no relator is required but just the definite marker =ŋà on the modifiers. Illustrations are given below:

(4.15) [[ŋà=hír=á]ₙₚ   íláá-á=ŋà]ₙₚ   hín-Ø   bòì
       DEM=man=NEAR sick-NOMZ=DEF want-3SG.SU.IMPERV all
       wà   sán   hádáí-jè
       REC.PAST stay.INF mat-OBL
       'The sick man had to stay in bed.'
       (Lit. The sick man is wanted to stay in the bed.)

(4.16) [[ŋà=zùg=tá]ₙₚ   bíbí=ŋà]ₙₚ
       DEM=people=NEAR big.PL=DEF
       'The elders/rulers'
       (Lit. the big (pl) people)

(4.17) [[ŋà=hòì=tá]ₙₚ   samaria=ŋà]ₙₚ
       DEM=woman=NEAR Samaria=DEF
       'The woman of Samaria'

4.2.1.2   Nominal Demonstrative Pronouns (Type II)
Type II nominal demonstrative pronouns occur with the third person special pronouns—ŋàinà 'this', ŋàinùnù 'that', ŋàiggèà 'these' and ŋàiggènù 'those'. These forms cannot be marked for number or any other inflection. Morphologically, the only distinction between Type I and Type II is that the latter can also occur as bound demonstrative pronouns. Except for the two specific pronouns ìn ⟨3SG.PN.SP⟩ and ìggè ⟨3pl PN.SP⟩, they are morphologically alike with Type I.

However, in Type I any simple noun or a de-verbal noun can be modified by noun-modifying spatial demonstratives circumclitics whereas in Type II only the two specific pronouns can occur in between the circumclitics.

(4.18) [ŋà=ìn=nù]_NP/CS   á   [gótó-á   zùw-á]_NP/CC
        DEM=3SG.PN.SP=FAR COP.3.IMPERV rule-RSTR people-RSTR
        'that is the custom/culture of (the) people ...' (KW 2:57:6)

Unlike Type I (see example 4.8), Type II nominal demonstrative pronouns can modify a head noun which is unmarked for construct-form/relator suffix, as in (4.19).

(4.19) [lúsì ŋàìnà]_NP [lúsì ŋàìnùnù]_NP
        boy this   boy that
        'this boy' 'that boy'

They may also function as local adverbials, as in (4.20).

(4.20) ŋàìnà ŋà=kí-hín-í
        this   NEG=1SU-want.IMPERV-1SG.SU.IMPERV
        'I don't want the one here'

4.2.2 Adjective Modifiers

Mursi has two underived adjectives—*tííní* 'small' and *búí* 'big', and more than one hundred derived adjectives from stative verb roots which often take an adjectiviser suffix *-i*. Both types (underived and derived) can function as modifiers of head nouns.

(4.21) [hír-á   édʒ-ò-á]   éč-ú
        man-RSTR kill.IMPERV-IRR-NOMZ:RSTR   kill.PERV-3SG.SU.PERV
        [ŋàtùn búí]_NP
        lion big.SG
        'The hunter killed the big lion.'

(4.22) [ŋà=ìn=nù   èrmì=tùnù] tííní   gòdé]_NP]_NP
        DEM=3SG.PN.SP=FAR   child=FAR small.SG INTENS:DEMUN
        'that small child'
        (Lit. 'that very little girl')

When the head noun is modified by both types of adjectival modifiers, it must be marked with the construct-form suffixes: -a (restrictive) or -í³ (non-restrictive). See the following examples.

(4.23) [hòì-á   tííno   gòdé]ₙₚ   sé-á   ké
       girl-RTSR small.SG INTENS:DEMUN say-3SG.SU.PERV QUOT
       kí-hín-í   [rúm-ní   gɔ̀lɔ̀ɲ-i]ₙₚ
       1SU-want.IMPERV-1SG.SU.IMPERV cloth-NRSTR red.STV-ADJ
       '"I too want a red dress," said the little girl.'

Underived adjectives do agree in number with their heads whereas derived adjectives do not.

(4.24) [dórén-á   bíbí]ₙₚ
       house.PL-RTSR big.REDUP.PL
       'big houses'

(4.25) sábɔ dĕl-á   [tííti-ó]ₙₚ   múg-íné-ɔ̀
       first girl.PL-RSTR small.REDUP.PL-RSTR.MOD gather-RECIP.3-VFS
       'First, little girls will gather together.' (KW 0:11:4–0:21:6)

(4.26) kíɲáŋ   kó   ɓásáj   kó   [àhà-í
       crocodile PNC monitor.lizard PNC thing.PL-NRSTR
       tííti]ₙₚ
       small:REDUP.PL+NRSTR
       '... a crocodile, monitor lizard, and small things.' (MH 4:47:4)

Although derived adjectives for stative verb roots do not agree in number with the head noun, number can be shown either on the head noun itself (as in (4.26)) or by a number word in (4.27).

(4.27) [[débì-ɲá   gɔ́lɔ̀ɲ-á]ₙₚ   ràmàn]ₙₚ bàrì
       lip.plate-PL+RSTR red.STV-RSTR two   yesterday
       ká-tál-á
       1SU-buy-1SG.SU.PERV
       'Yesterday I bought two red lip-plates.'

---

3 /-i/ has phonological conditioned allomorphs [-ti], [-ni] (see the Chapter 6 on number system).

(4.28) [[bì-á   gìdàɲ-á]_NP   háánán]_NP
       cow.SG-RSTR brown.STV-RSTR five
       'Five brown cows'

(4.29) [[bì-á   gìdàɲ-á]_NP   mèrì]_NP
       cow.SG-RSTR brown.STV-RSTR many
       'Many brown cows'

As illustrated above (in 4.27–4.29), when a head noun is modified by more than one modifier, an adjective referring to a color term becomes the nearest modifier of the head noun.

In addition, within an NP the underived adjective *búí* can serve as a modifier of a derived adjective.

(4.30) [lɔ̀g-tí   bú dáldá-í]_NP
       issue-NRSTR big difficult.STV-ADJ
       'Very (many) difficult issues'

(4.31) [sài   bú-sís-i]   dɔ́rɔ́s-á   múgá-ɲ]_NP]_NP
       leather.dress big-AUG-ADJ hard/dry.STV-RSTR woman.PL-GEN
       '... a much dried women's leather dress.' (KW 1:59:4)

In (4.30), *búí* functions as a modifier of *dáldálí*—as an intensifier or a quantifier. Interestingly, within an NP, it can also take the suffix *–sisi* as augmentative marker or comparative degree marker (as in (4.31)). When the adjective *búí* functions as augmentative marker, it drops the general adjectivizer suffix *–i* and behaves like an intensifier.

4.2.3   Genitive Modifiers

In Mursi, common nouns can be modified by other nouns with a genitive case form. All the modifying nouns must occur in genitive case form while the head noun must be marked with a construct-form/relator suffix. In addition to common and proper nouns, derived adjectives and relator nouns (mostly grammaticalized body part terms) can occur in the modifier slot of genitive construction. The template below indicates a typical genitive NP construction.

[Head-(NUMB)-RSTR MODIFIER-(NUMB)(CASE)-GEN]

(4.32) kú-mug-íné-Ø   bòi dóněj
       1SU-gather-RECIP-1PL.INC.SU.IMPERV all one
       ké-héj-Ø   [bá-á   [ólʃ-ó
       1SU-go.IMPERV-1PL.INC.SU.IMPERV place-RSTR stalk-PL
       bɛra-ɲ]_NP]_NP
       sorghum.type-GEN
       'We (inc.) gather as one and we (inc.) go to a place where sorghum stalks exist.' (KW 0:11:4–0:21:6)

(4.33) ŋà=bá=á   [àh-à-á   gàʃ-ùɲ]_NP   él-ɛ́?
       DEM=place=NEAR thing-PL-RTSR forest-GEN exist.IMPERV.PL-3.SU
       'Are there any wild animals about?'
       (Lit. There things of the forest exist/present?)

(4.34) òlítúlá á   [érmì-á   ŋàkútúl-ì]_NP
       Òlítùlà COP.3.IMPERV child-RSTR Ngakútúl-GEN
       'Olitula is Ngakútúl's child.'

As Mursi is a head and a dependent marking language, it is a must for modifiers to indicate that they are in relation with the head nouns they modify by an overt morphological inflection, for example the genitive case, as in (4.32–4.34). However, not all dependents are modifiers. In (4.32), *ólʃó* is a dependent non-modifier because it doesn't have a direct relation with the head noun. That means *ólʃó* should have been marked for a restrictive modification marker *-a*. In (4.32) and (4.33) we see that genitive case marked common and proper nouns directly modifying their heads.

Oblique-marked relator nouns can modify the head noun in genitive NP constructions. The modifier nouns are often grammaticalized body part nouns which function as relator nouns. They specify the spatial relation and specific location of an object. In the example below, we see double case marking where the genitive case is added to an oblique-marked relator noun.

(4.35) [mà-à   mùm-ɔ̀-ɲ]_NP
       water-RTSR face-OBL-GEN
       'water on the front (side)'

NOUN PHRASE STRUCTURE   183

(4.36) [dórí-á   bò-i-ɲ]_NP
        house-RSTR out-OBL-GEN
        'house on the top'
        (Lit. house of the upper place)

(4.37) jòg   á   sú   á   [sú-á   tán-ò-j]_NP
        3PL COP.3.IMPERV Aari COP.3.IMPERV Aari-RSTR side-OBL-GEN
        'They are the Aari of that side of the river.' (MH 4:6:8)

In addition, in genitive NP construction, a nominalized verb can function as head noun.

(4.38) ŋà=tàn=ùnù   á   [gúɲ-á-à
        DEM=side.of.river=FAR COP.3.IMPERV watch-NOMZ-RSTR
        zùwò-ɲ]_NP
        people-GEN
        'On the other side of the river are people's fields.'

4.2.4 *Possessive Modifiers*
Possessive modifiers are of two types—independent (free) possessive pronouns and pertensive modifiers. Possessive pronouns are obligatory constituents for all types of NPs that have free possessive pronoun modifiers, except in one type, i.e. pertensive-marked kinship terms.

4.2.4.1   Independent Possessive Pronoun
Mursi possessive pronouns are independent pronouns that agree with modified head noun for person and number. They specify person of the possessor, number of the possessor and number of the possessed object. Thus, number agreement between the head noun and the possessive pronoun modifiers is obligatory.

        ([HEAD.N-(NUMB)-RSTR _Possessum POSS.PRO_Possessor])

(4.39) [[írsásí-á   n=ènè]_NP   goloɲ-á]_NP
        pencil-RSTR SG.PSD=3SG.PRS red.STV-RSTR
        'His red pencil'
        (Lit. his pencil red)

(4.40) [[gòdóná-á   n=ànù]_NP   bó]_NP
        brother.PERT.SG.1.PSR-RSTR SG.PSD=1SG.PSR big

> *í-Ø*   *bá-á*   *ítíjóbíjá-ì*
> exist.IMPERV-3SG.SU.IMPERV place-RSTR Ethiopia-GEN
> 'My elder brother is in Ethiopia.'

In (4.39), the head noun *írsásí* can only be modified by free possessive pronouns. In (4.40), the possessive pronoun is optional because the bound pertensive suffix (in bold) can modify the head noun (see §4.2.4.2). The head noun *gòdónà* 'my brother' can stand alone without the need for modifier possessive pronoun.

Free possessive pronouns can modify common nouns, kinship nouns, proper nouns, nouns modified by bound demonstratives, and compound nouns.

4.2.4.2 Pertensive Modifiers

A pertensive modifier occurs in a bound-suffix/enclitic form on certain pertensive-marked kinship nouns. The pertensives in Mursi are inalienable possession markers which always attach to possessed kinship nouns or to the head noun they modify.

$$\begin{bmatrix} [\text{HEAD.N}_{\text{Possessum}}\text{-PERT}_{\text{Possessor}}] \\ [[\text{HEAD.N}_{\text{Possessum}}\text{-PERT}_{\text{Possessor}}] \ (\text{POSS.PRO}_{\text{Possessor}})] \end{bmatrix}$$

(4.41) *ká-bá-Ø*   *dàài kó*   [*dàdá=jè*]$_{NP}$
1SU-eat-1PL.INC.SU.IMPERV all   PNC father.PERT.SG.1.PSR=SUBORD
kó   [*màmà=jè*]$_{NP}$ *kó*   [*éró=jè*]$_{NP}$
PNC mother.PERT.SG.1.PSR=SUBORD PNC children=SUBORD
'We (inc.) all eat it, my father, my mother, the children ...' (MH 8:39:6)

In (4.41) the kinship form *dàdá* 'father' and *màmà* 'mother' is used only for first person. When possessed by second and third person, they may be realized as different forms (also common in some Surmic languages cf. Unseth 1991), as shown in the examples below.

(4.42) [*màmà*]$_{NP}$ *kónó*   *kó*   [*dʒɔ̀ɔ̀nè*]$_{NP}$
mother.PERT.SG.1.PSR one.INDEF PNC mother.PERT.SG.3.PSR
á   *dónéj*
COP.3.IMPERV one
'My mother and his mother are one (the same).' (KW 2:34:4)

(4.43) [*ʃúúnù*]$_{NP}$ *kó*   [*dʒúúnù*]$_{NP}$
father.PERT.SG.2.PSR PCN mother.PERT.SG.2.PSR

NOUN PHRASE STRUCTURE

    dɔ́ŋ-á[4]
    respect.PERV-IMP.VFS
    'Respect you father and you mother!'

It appears that possessive pronouns optionally follow the pertensive construction depending on the number of the possessor. In both examples (4.42 and 4.43) all the kinship nouns have singular number possessors. Thus, in pertensive-marked kinship nouns, possessive pronouns not only have a modifying function but also function as number agreement markers—see examples below.

(4.44) a. [*dàdá-čó-á*   *g=àw*]
           father.PERT.SG.1.PSR-PL-RSTR PL.PSD=1PL.EXC.PSR
           'Our (exc.) fathers'

       b. [*gòdóŋ=gà-čo-à*   *g=ùɲù*]
           brother=PERT:1/2PSR-PL-RSTR PL.PSD=2SG.PSR
           'Your (sg.) brothers'

To get further information on possessive NP types, see a summary of it in § 5.8.

4.2.5 Numerals

Numerals can modify the head noun they follow directly. However, both the head noun and the modifier numeral do not take any marking. When a numeral modifier is greater than 'one', the head noun must occur in plural form as well, as in (4.45a–b).

(4.45) a. [*únɔ́*   *sízzì*]$_{NP}$
           night.PL three
           'Three days'
           (Lit. three nights)

        b. [*gárčɔ́*   *tɔ̀mɔ̀n* *kó*   *ràmàn*]$_{NP}$
           basket.PL ten   PNC two
           'Twelve baskets'

---

4 The clause final suffix -*a* is added to the verb if the imperative verb occurs in clause-final position.

When the numeral 'one' modifies a noun, the modified noun adds a non-restrictive (NRSTR) suffix -*ti*, as in (4.44c).

    c. [érmì-tí   dɔ́néj]_{NP} áíw-ó
       child-NRSTR one   come.PERV.SG-MT.3SG.SU.PERV
       'One child came.'

As can be seen in the example above, the function of the count singular suffix is to indicate a singulative referent. Or it indicates that the head is a countable noun. If the head is a countable noun, it takes the non-restrictive modification suffix so as to indicate that the head noun can be individuated and can come in countable numbers, as in the examples below.

    d. [zùg-tí   ŋàhì   ràmàn]_{NP}
       people-NRSTR female two
       'Two women'

    e. [zùg-tí   kó   ràmàn kààrèčàgì]_{NP}[5]
       people-NRSTR CRD:PART two   blind
       'Two blind men'

If adjectives are used in an intermediate modifying position, number agreement between the head and the numeral modifier is absent, as in (4.46).

(4.46) [[bì-á   gɔ̀lɔ̀ŋ-à]_{NP}   hááná́n]_{NP}
       COW-RSTR red.STV-RSTR:MOD five
       'Five red cows'

4.2.6 *Indefinite* kóná *'Another' and* gena *'Others'*

The specific indefinite pronouns *kóná* (specific singular), which is a derived form of the numeral *kón* 'one' and *gena* (specific plural) can function as modifiers of a head noun. When the specific indefinite pronouns modify the head noun, they may be marked with the construct-form suffixes. In this noun modification construction, head nouns are not marked with construct-suffixes of both types (restrictive and non-restrictive).

---

5 *čagi* 'green/unripe' ~ *kaarɛ+čagi* (Lit. eyes+green) metaphorically 'blind'.

(4.47) [múgáj kóná]ₙₚ tál-ú fùllèj bíró mèrì
woman.SG one.INDEF.MOD buy-3SG.SU.PERV oil money many
háŋ
INTENS
'A certain woman bought a very expensive oil.'

(4.48) ŋànìjè [zùwò géná]ₙₚ í-báj-sí-ò bá
yet people other.INDEF CAUS-heal-CAUS-3.IRR place
sé í-báj-sí-Ø [rèr-á
say.3SG.AUX CAUS-heal-CAUS-3SG.SU.IMPERV body-RSTR
n=ùnù]ₙₚ
SG.PSD=2SG.PSR
'He saved others; himself he cannot save.'
(Lit. He saved other people, not yet he save his own body.)

The specific indefinite modifiers often occur in the head-modifier position following the head noun they modify, as in (4.47) and (4.48). When there is no explicit information about the referent's identity, as in (4.47), the specific indefinite pronoun may function as indefinite article. They can also fill an independent argument slot in a clause functioning as pronouns, or as headless modifiers, as in (4.49).

(4.49) nà dɔ́néj k-àit-è nà [kóná]
CCN one PASS-take.PERV-APPL CCN one.INDEF
dɔ́t-é-Ø
leave-MA-3SG.SU.IMPERV
'... and one shall be taken, and the other left.'

When an NP containing specific indefinite pronoun function as O argument or occurring in a post-verbal slot, it takes a post-verbal form (so marked nominative case is associated with the post-verbal position), as in (4.50).

(4.50) kóná áín-ɛ-Ø bíró [ʃí-tí
one.INDEF give.PERV.SG-APPL.3.IRR money thousand-NRSTR
dɔ́néj]ₙₚ nà nɔ̀ŋ ók-ú bá kónó
one CCN 3SG go-3SG.SU.PERV place one.INDEF.NOM
'He gave to another one thousand, and walked to another (place).'

4.2.7   Quantifiers

Quantifiers can directly modify NPs. Syntactically, quantifiers often behave like the number word *dŏnéj* 'one' and indefinite pronouns, i.e. a head of an NP modified by quantifiers do not take a noun modification marker suffix (construct-form suffix). However, within an NP number agreement between the head noun and quantifier is obligatory.

i.   *dákákán* 'all, whole'

(4.51) a. zùwò   màt-ɛ-a   [ŋà=mà=á
        people drink-3PL.SU.IMPERV-NOMZ DEM=water=NEAR
        dákákán]$_{NP}$
        all
        'All the people drinking this water.'

   b. [ŋà=lɔ̀gí-ɲá=á   dákákán]$_{NP}$ [hùllì   ŋànì[6]
       DEM=issue-PL=NEAR all   when/if NEG.PERV
       kú-búg-ɲèsɛ̀=ó=jè]$_{SUBORD:CL}$ bá
       3.SBJV-achieve-BEN=NEG=SUBORD   place/world
       ŋà=bónnós-ó=ó
       NEG.IMPERV=exit.IMPERV-3.IRR=NEG
       'This world shall not pass, until all these things be fulfilled.'

In (4.51), *má* 'water' is a pluralia tantúm, i.e. an inherently plural mass noun (see §6.1 for further details).

(4.52) [[zùw-á   ór-ùɲ]$_{NP}$ dákákán]$_{NP}$ múg-č+áná
       people-RSTR village-GEN whole   gather-APPL+MT.3PL.SU.PERV
       hóɗ-á
       come.PERV.PL-3PL.SU.PERV
       'The whole city came out.'
       (Lit. All people of the village gathered-up and came.)

(4.53) [sààn-á   ŋà=hòì=tá]$_{NP}$ hàlì   kò-jòg-Ø
       story-RSTR DEM=woman=NEAR   later PASS-tell.PERV-3SG.IRR
       [bá-á   dákákán]$_{NP}$
       place-RSTR whole
       'The story of this woman will be told to the whole world.'

---

6   Note that the negative word *ŋànì* has various functions such as 'not yet, still, until'.

ii. dàài 'Every; All'

The quantifier *dàài* has a similar distribution and function as *dákákán*, but *dàài* has more a distributive quantifier property than *dákákán*. In addition, *dàài* appears to have no fixed position within a clause or an NP, thus it shows some syntactic properties of the floating quantifier.

(4.54) a. [àhà   dàài]_{NP} gén-ónó   nèà
thing.PL all   create.IMPERV-MT.3SG.SU.IMPERV 3SG.NOM
'All come into being through him.'
(Lit. He created all things through him.)

b. nà [zùwò dákákán] dɔ́t-ì   nà
CCN people all   leave-3PL.IRR CCN
áw-ó   ɔ́r-ɔ́
come.PERV.SG-MT.3SG.SU.PERV village-OBL
'And every man went into his own house.'

In (4.54), *dàài* functions as an adverb. With its distributive meaning ('every, all') quantifies not only individuals (father, mother or children) but also quantifies groups from all different sexes and age sets—males and females or adults and children.

(4.55) [ká-bá-Ø   dàài] [kó
1SU-eat-1PL.INC.SU.IMPERV all   PNC
dàdá=jè]   [kó   màmà=jè]
father.PERT.SG.1.PSR=SUBORD PNC mother.PERT.SG.1.PSR=SUBORD
[kó   éró=jè]   [jòg ŋà=ká-bá
PNC children=SUBORD   3PL NEG.IMPERV=3.SBJV-eat.PERV
dákákán] hírí   már-ì   nèŋ
all   person refuse-3.IRR who?
'We (inc.) all eat it, my father, my mother, the children; they all eat it. What man could refuse it?' (MH 8:39:6)

The quantifier *dákákán* can also be used adverbially, as in the example below.

(4.56) àŋè dákákán á   ŋàŋà   hétɔ́
1SG all   COP.3.IMPERV like.this same
'It is all the same to me.'

iii. *mèrì* 'Many'

Unlike other head modifying quantifiers, *mèrì* can be preceded by an adjectival intensifier. In (4.57) below, the adjective *bú* 'big' is a general intensifier which provides a gradable meaning to the degree quantifier *mèrì*. It can also occur with singular and plural heads of NP, as in (4.57) and (4.58).

(4.57) [dóólé bú   mèrì]ₙₚ él   rènà ŋà=b=ùnù
       girl.PL INTENS many   exist.IMPERV.PL far   DEM=place=FAR
       'Many women were there far away.'
       (Lit. very many women)

(4.58) bá   bòrɔ̀ óó   rònɔ̀   kéd-ú   [kèn-ì
       place days.ago DISJ:CRD in.the.future cut-3SG.SU.PERV tree.PL
       mèrì háŋ]ₙₚ
       many INSTENS
       'He cut more wood than usual.'
       (Lit. 'Unlike in place of days ago, later he cut very many trees.')

The adjective *bu*, even with its intensifier function, as in (4.57), never occurs in any post-modifier positions. But other intensifiers such as *háŋ* 'very' always occur after adjectival or quantifier modifiers, as in (4.58).

iv. *múčúgí* 'Few, Some' and *tííní* 'a Few, Little'

Both *múčúgí* and *tííní* are adjectives. The difference between the two is that the former is a derived adjective while the latter is an underived adjective. But both function as quantifiers. Since they were originally adjectives, when they functioned as quantifiers, they must occur in noun modification construction form and must be marked with the construct-form suffix.

As we see in the following example, both the head and the modifiers can be marked for dependency relationship—restrictive in (4.59) and non-restrictive in (4.60 and 4.61).

(4.59) ŋà=b=ùnù   tád-∅-è   [[zùw-á
       DEM=place=FAR   put.on-3SG.SU.IMPERV-APPL people-RSTR
       múčúg-á]   íláás-é-á]   sòŋ   sìɔ̀
       few.STV-RSTR   sick-3PL.SU.IMPERV-NOMZ only hand
       'He laid his hands upon a few people that are sick.'

(4.60) [[úŋ-ní   múčúg-í]ₙₚ wùréɔ́
       night.PL-NRSTR few.STV-ADJ after
       'After a few (some) days.'

(4.61) jɔ̀g séd-á   ké   àggè
        3PL say.PERV-3PL.SU.PERV QUOT 1PL
        kɔ̀-lɔ̀m-ó   tílén   ìssàbàj kó   [ùrgùsá-j
        1SU-have-1PL.EXC.SU.IMPERV bread.PL seven   PNC fish.PL-NRSTR
        títí-j]_NP
        small.PL:REDUP-NRSTR
        'They said, "we have seven loaves and a few little fishes".'

4.2.8 Apposed NP

In Mursi, an apposed NP is a type of possessive construction where the possessed and the possessor are simply apposed. In other words, in apposed NP construction, the modifier precedes the modified head noun. It is often used to indicate whole-part and kinship relation. When the modifiers precede the head noun they modify, no dependency marker is attached to the modifying element and to the head noun.

(4.62) a. [érmì   ʤààrì]_NP lɔ̀-Ø   ŋɔ̀dɔ̀rì
          child.SG leg.SG   has-3SG.SU.IMPERV wound
          'The child's leg has a wound.'

       b. [hírí   kààrì]_NP
          man.SG eye.SG
          'the man's eye'

       c. [ʃòi   rówá]_NP
          bird.SG feather
          'feather of a bird'

       d. [kìɔ̀   ɲàbì]_NP
          tree.SG ear.SG
          'branch of a tree'
          (Lit. 'ear of a tree')

If the head is an inalienably possessed kinship noun, a pertensive marker is always attached to its root.

(4.63) [érmì   ([ʤɔ̀ɔ̀nɛ̀]_NP)]_NP
       child.SG mother.PERT.SG.3.PSR
       'Child's mother'
       (Lit. the child-his mother)

See the Chapter on possession for further discussion of § 4.2.8.

4.2.9 Relative (General) Pronouns[7]

Mursi has two relative (general) pronouns that function as the head of a modified NP. They can also occur in place of modifiers in clauses that have comparative-like constructions. They can be marked with the construct-form suffixes like head nouns and nominal and adjectival modifiers. Their role as general pronouns is restricted—only allowed in non-clausal modification constructions. However, they can also function as relative pronouns in clausal modification constructions. In clausal modification construction, they often serve as relative modifiers of the head noun. The =*n*= 'SG' and =*g*= 'PL' are bound number clitics denoting only number of antecedents: *in-a* 'that, the one who' ⟨3SG.G.PN-RSTR⟩, *ín=í* 'that, which' ⟨3SG.PN-NRSTR⟩, *íggá* 'those; those who' ⟨3PL.PN-RSTR⟩, and *íggí* 'those, those who' ⟨3PL.PN-NRSTR⟩ (see § 3.3.1.6).

(4.64) [hárté-á   dóólé-ɲ]_NP   kó   [ín-á   [ín-á
        donkey-RSTR female-GEN PNC 3SG.PN.SP-RSTR 3SG.PN.SP-RSTR
        màg-á   húŋ-á]_NP   á   dádál-í
        male-RSTR INTENS-RSTR COP.3.IMPERV strong.STV-ADJ
        'Is a female donkey stronger than a male donkey?'
        (Lit. female donkey is really stronger than that that of male?)

(4.65) [bá-á[8]   mèdèrní-á   kó   ràmàn]_NP bér-á
        place-RSTR sheep-RSTR PNC   two   choose-3SG.SU.PERV
        [ín-á   tíín-ó]   nà   kéd-á
        3SG.PN.SP-RSTR small-RSTR.MOD CCN slaughter-3SG.SU.PERV
        ɓòì
        COMPLETIVE
        'He selected the smaller of his two sheep and slaughtered (it).'

(4.66) àɲè_A   [ígg-í   mèrì]_NP:O
        1SG   3PL.PN.SP-NRSTR many
        ŋà=kí-hín-í=ó   àɲè
        NEG=1SU-want-1SG.SU.IMPERV=NEG 1SG

---

7 Since general pronouns have a wide range of functional domain and distribution, I have labelled them by different terms. Thus, it is necessary to note that the following three terms have identical morphological realization: general pronouns, specific pronouns and relative pronouns.

8 In a comparative construction, *ba* 'place, place of' is used as standard marker.

NOUN PHRASE STRUCTURE 193

kí-hín-í [*ín-í* *dɔ́néj sɔ̀ŋ*
1SU-want.IMPERV-1SG.SU.IMPERV 3SG.PN.SP-NRSTR one only
írsásí]_{NP}
pencil
'I don't want many, I want only that one pencil.'
(Lit. I don't want those many, I want only that one pencil.)

As illustrated in the examples above, relative pronouns can plausibly fulfil the noun modification construction requirements. As any other nominal head, they can be marked with the head-modifier dependency marker suffixes of both types: restrictive (RSTR), as in (4.64 and 4.65) and non-restrictive (NRSTR), as in (4.66). Moreover, general pronouns have wide distribution when they function as relative pronouns within clausal NP modifiers (see § 4.2.9).

4.3 Clausal Modifiers

A head noun in construct form can be modified by clausal modifiers, namely by a relative clause and by a nominalized clause. In relative clause modifier construction, the relative clause is often headed by relative pronouns (§ 4.3.2). On the other hand, a nominalized clause modifier may be headed by a fully inflected verb (§ 4.3.3). The heads of both relative and nominalized clause modifiers can be marked with construct form suffixes of both type—restrictive and non-restrictive. However, when the restrictive marker suffix -*a* is added to the head of a nominalized clause modifier, it can only be analysed as underlying form. Both of these clausal modifier constructions utilize the gap strategy (§ 4.3.3).

Therefore, before I start a discussion on the two clausal modifier types of nouns, a short introduction of the Mursi construct form is provided in (§ 4.3.1).

4.3.1 *Introduction to Head and Dependent Modification System*

Cross-linguistically, it is not common to see languages that mark both the head and the dependent with a special morphological marking. It is a rare phenomenon to find languages that have obligatory head-modifier dependency relationship markers. However, Mursi is among the few languages in the world that have an overt morphological marking for head nouns and for the dependents. The term 'dependent' here directly refers to any 'modifier'. However, in order to convey the notion to be discussed in this section, I find the term 'dependent' more appropriate. Thus, this dependency phenomenon of head nouns and dependents is known as Construct-Form (CF). In Semitic languages this phenomenon is known by a different term—construct state.

For years, a number of Semitic linguists have dealt with this topic. Some have also proposed various terms for it. For instance, 'status constructus' (Turker and Bryan 1966), 'antigenitive' (Anderson 1988), 'modified noun form' (Reh 1996), and 'construct form' (Criessels 2006).

The terms given above by various linguists are purely morphological. They are case-oriented terms particularly focusing on the genitive case. In other words, terms such as *genitive* and *antigenitive* are mostly morphological properties of dependents in NPs. For example, in Mursi, case is entirely a property of dependents whereas construct form is a property of head nouns. In Mursi, the construct form (a 'modification marker' from now on) suffix is a kind of relator that indicates the dependency relationship between the head and the dependent. Therefore, the modification marker on head nouns is a syntactic property which provides information about the internal structure of NPs.

In Mursi, construct form is a particular instance of a head marking and a dependent marking system. But there are also a few instances where we can get the modification suffixes on modifiers. For example, when the modifier itself is a noun, or when two or more heads/modifiers co-occur as relative clause modifier, in nominalized clause modifiers, and embedded noun modification constructions. In this case, we get a series of modification forms with embedded modifiers.

First, one has to understand whether the construct form phenomenon is an internal structure of NPs or is controlled by other NP external related syntactic information. It is possible to see what the head-modifier dependency relationship looks like. One finds that there are two head-modifier dependency relationships: restrictive and non-restrictive. As in some Western Nilotic languages which show this form of dependency relationships in their NP internal structure, the choice between the two (restrictive/non-restrictive) depends on the type of modifiers. Both restrictive and non-restrictive markers attached to the head of a relative clause can also entail that the relative clause modifier should appear right-adjoined to the NP.

4.3.1.1   Restrictive Modification Marker *-a*

The construct form suffix /-a/ operates as a restrictive marker in noun modification construction. When it appears on head nouns or on relative pronouns, it restricts the reference of the common argument to occur in particular sets. In Mursi, even if a relative pronoun is obligatory in a relative clause modifying a noun, the relative pronoun itself must be marked with a restrictive form suffix. Aikhenvald (2015: 354) points out that a restrictive relative clause provides

NOUN PHRASE STRUCTURE   195

information about the common argument by specifying, narrowing or restricting its reference.

4.3.1.2 Non-restrictive modification marker –*i* [-ti/-ni]
A non-restrictive relationship between the noun and the modifying relative clause is shown by attaching the non-restrictive marker /-i/ to both heads (noun and relative pronoun). In non-restrictive relationship, it provides additional information about the reference of the common argument.

4.3.2 *Relative Clause Modifiers*
Mursi employs a post nominal relative clause strategy. The same head-modifier pattern of the non-clausal modifiers applies in relative clause constructions. Based on the nature of restrictive (§ 4.3.1.1) and non-restrictive (§ 4.3.1.2) dependency relationships between the head and the relative clause modifier, I further divide the relative clause modifiers into two classes: restrictive relative clause modifier (§ 4.3.2.1) and non-restrictive relative clause modifier (§ 4.3.2.2).

4.3.2.1 Restrictive Relative Clause Modifier
A restrictive relative clause modifier of the head noun can be headed by relative pronouns and by bound pronominals on verbs. The CA in the RC can be in S or A function. In few instances, the CA in the RC can function as an object or oblique argument. The following template illustrates the structure of Mursi restrictive relative clause modifier.

i. Internally headed RC—[Head-*a* (S/A) V (O) (OBL)]$_{RELATIVE\ CLAUSE}$
ii. Topical/Focal—NP [Head-*a* (S/A) V (O) (OBL)]$_{RELATIVE\ CLAUSE}$

(4.67) [*ín-á   jéb-áɲ-ì   àɲè*]$_{RC:A}$ *húɲ*
       3SG.PN.SP-RSTR belive-1SG.OBJ-3.IRR 1SG   thirst
       ŋà=dág-Ø-Ø=ó   dóg
       NEG=hit.IMPERV-3SG.OBJ-3SG.SU.IMPERV=NEG   forever
       'He that (whoever) believes in me shall never thirst.'
       (Lit. He who believe in me, thirst will not hit him forever.)

(4.68) *nɔ̀ŋ* [*ín-á   kɔ́w-án-áɲ-ì   wùréɔ́*]$_{RC}$ *nà*
       3SG 3SG.PN.SP-RSTR 1SU.follow-MT-1SG.OBJ-3SG.IRR after   CCN
       bá   sé   àɲè
       place say.3SG.AUX 1SG
       'He who follows after me, he wants me.'

In (4.67), (A_RC = O_MC) the CA and the head of the RC is the 3sg relative pronoun, thus this construction has an internally headed RC. However, given that Mursi relative clauses are strictly postnominal, the relative clause in (4.67) can be an externally headed one. The same pattern is shown in (4.68) except for the 3sg independent pronoun, which is a topicalized and fronted NP before the relative clause (A_RC = S_MC). In both constructions, the CA argument in the RC is in A function. In (4.69), the CA argument in the RC is in A function, while in the MC is in S function.

(4.69) jɔ̀g íggέ-à [Ø bág-ε-á áčúg nà
3PL 3PL.PN.SP-RSTR [Ø eat-3PL.SU.IMPERV-RSTR flesh CCN
màt-έ-á ɲàwà]_RC jɔ̀g dákákán él
drink-3PL.SU.IMPERV-RSTR blood 3PL all exist.IMPERV.PL
bás-έ-ó tíí
live.IMPERV-NOMZ-NOM DUR
'They, those who eat (my) flesh and drink (my) blood, they all have eternal life.'

In the restrictive relative clause construction, when the RC consists of more than one verb, each verb within the RC is marked with the restrictive suffix –a, as in (4.69). Without the NP, this construction appears to be very similar to which is called corelative (left-adjoined) relative clause.

The relativization strategy other than the possessive pronoun in the examples above is a 'gap strategy'. Mursi utilizes the 'gap strategy' in the absence of a relative pronoun headed CA in the RC, the restrictive suffix -a is attached to the restrictively modified noun and to the following verb, which is the CA in the RC.

(4.70) zùw-á [Ø jéb-έ-á [sárá-á
people-RSTR [Ø believe-3PL.SU.IMPERV-RSTR name.PL-RSTR
g=ὲɲὲ]_NP]_RC
PL.PSD=3SG.PSR
'The people who believe in his name.'

When the restrictive marker suffix –a occurs on the verb, in which case it functions both as a restrictive relative clause head or CA marker and at the same time as a nominalizer. Not all CAs in the RC will occur with the restrictive marker suffix, as in (4.71).

(4.71) án-í   hòj-á   [Ø bàrì
        COP.IMPERV-2SG.SU.IMPERV   female-RSTR [Ø yesterday
        kún-í   bàrì]_RC
        come-2SG.SU.IMPERV   yesterday
        'The one who came yesterday is you (woman).'

There is no mention of the role of the NP within the RC. The only head-modifier relationship between the head and the RC is possessed-possessor where the possessive pronoun *gàw* in the RC serves as a modifier.

(4.72) a. zùw-á   [Ø bè   g=àw
           people-RSTR   [Ø DIST.PAST   PL.SPD=1PL.EXC.PSR
           kɔ́-dɔ́t-ó   tán-ɔ̀]_RC   ŋàméá k-èlì
           1SU-leave-1PL.EXC.SU.PERV   river.side-OBL] now   PASS-call.PERV
           ké   bófú
           QUOT   Boshu
           'The people who were ours (exc.) and abandoned (them) on the other side are now called Boshu.' (MH 0:56:0)

In cases like (4.72), which is a good example of discontinuous NP, it is worth to note the syntactic structure of the language, i.e. AVO. Even if the CA is not overtly stated in the RC, it is in indirect object function. But, the CA in the MC is in direct object function. In the gap strategy, relative pronouns can be placed outside the RC and may function as an NP. When relative pronouns are stated as an NP, they often carry a very specific and narrow identity of the referent, which is to be specified either in the RC or in the MC. Thus, they can be called specific pronouns, as in (4.72b).

       b. íggé-à   [Ø bè
           3PL.PN.SP-RSTR   [Ø DIST.PAST
           kó-hóɲ-ó   ŋà=táná=á]_RC:S
           1SU-come.IMPERV.PL-1PL.EXC.SU.IMPERV   DEM=river.side=NEAR]
           ŋàméá k-èlè   kó   mùn
           now   PASS-call.PERV PREP Mursi.PL
           'Those who we (exc.) (have) come from this side of the river are now called (with/by the name of) Mursi.' (MH 1:03:0)

Yet there is no information provided about the CA in the MC. As shown in (4.72b), the verb in RC is a fully inflected verb in S function but this time it didn't carry none of the CA information. The CA is not in the passive verb *kele* 'called' neither. As Mursi is a bound pronominal language which marks core arguments, one may expect that the CA of (4.72b) would occur in the RC. Rather, the CA in (4.72b) is explicitly stated in peripheral function by instrumental/preposition particle *kó* 'with (by)'.

The CA can be stated in the RC by gap strategy and by copula complement in the MC, which makes the NP modified in copula subject position.

(4.73) *lúsà-á*   [Ø *bàrì*   *ká-dág-í*]_{RC}   *á*
        boy.PL:RSTR [Ø yesterday 1SU-hit-1SG.SU.IMPERV COP.3.IMPERV
        [*gòdón=gà-čó-á*   *g=ànù*]_{NP:CC}
        brother=PERT.PL.1.PSR-PL-RSTR PL.PSD=1SG.PSR
        'The boys who I flogged
        (Lit. who I flogged them) yesterday are my brothers.'

(4.74) *hír-á*   [Ø *bàrì*   *kún-ó*]_{RC}   *á*
        person-RSTR [Ø yesterday come-3SG.SU.PERV] COP.3.IMPERV
        [*támártí*   *čàll-ì*   *háŋ*]_{CC}
        student.SG good.STV-ADJ INTENS
        'The good student who came yesterday'
        (Lit. 'The person who came yesterday is a good student.')

In a restrictive relative clause construction, the CA can be stated in various syntactic slots within RC. The CA can be in core syntactic functions—for example as S, A in (4.75a–b) and as O in (4.75c).

(4.75) a. *zìní-ɲá*   [Ø *wà*   *k-ìlààg-à*   *kó*   *nòŋ*]_{RC}
           thief-PL [Ø REC.PAST PASS-hung.PERV-PAS.3SU PNC 3SG]
           'The thieves who were crucified with him.'

       b. *zùwò-á*   [Ø *lòm-é-á*   *bìò*]_{RC}
           people-RSTR [Ø have-3PL.SU.IMPERV-RSTR COW.PL]
           hóɗ-á
           come.PERV.PL-3PL.SU.PERV
           'Those people who have cows, come!'

       c. *hòj-á*   [Ø *bàrì*   *kún-ú*   *wà*
           female-RSTR [Ø yesterday come-3SG.SU.PERV REC.PAST
           í-Ø   *táná*]_{RC}   *áí-čá*
           to.be-3SG.SU.IMPERV side of river_bed] take-APPL.3PL.SU.PERV

kátámá-jè
town-OBL
'They took the young girl that came yesterday to town.'

It is also possible to get two CAs in two RCs—where one RC is embedded within another, as in (4.76).

(4.76) gá   hód-á   gón-ó   hírí
       ATTU:PL   come.PERV.PL-IMP.PL see.PERV-IMP.PL   man
       [[Ø jóg-óɲ-Ø   [lɔ̀g-a   tá
       [[Ø tell-1SG.OBJ-3SG.IRR issue-RSTR ATTU:SG
       kè-mèsí   dákákán=ɲà]_RC]_RC
       1SU-do+1SG.SU.IMPERV   all=DEF]]
       'Come, see a man who told me all things that ever I did.'

The CA can also occur in oblique, copula subject and copula complement syntactic slots, as in the examples below.

(4.77) a. ɲà=ìggè=á   [Ø él   ór   tó-jé]_RC
          DEM=3PL.PN.SP=NEAR   [Ø exist.IMPERV.PL settlement in-OBL]
          á   [bìò-a   òlítùlà-i]_NP
          COP.3.IMPERV   cow.PL-RSTR Òlítùlà-GEN
          'Those that are in the settlement are Olitula's cows.'

       b. [[ín-á   kí-hín-í]_RC]_CS   á   [na
          3SG.PN.SP-RSTR   1SU-want-1SG.SU.IMPERV COP.3.IMPERV   SG.RSTR
          hɔ̀l-a]_CC
          white.STV-RSTR
          'The kind which I want is white.'
          (Lit. 'The one which I want is white.')

       c. múwáí-tá   [Ø wà   dáfí-Ø   woti]_RC
          woman.SG-RSTR   [Ø REC.PAST   work-3SG.SU.IMPERV   stew
          [ɲà-á]_CS   á   [n=ànù]_CC
          wife-RSTR   COP.3.IMPERV   SG.PSD=1SG.PSR
          'The woman who is preparing the stew is my wife.'

In terms of function, restrictive relative clause modifiers focus on the identity of the referent of the CA. Head noun often supplies a class to which referents must belong and narrow the size of the set to which referents belong. Above all, the head marked with the restrictive suffix may show that referents may further be restricted by the restrictive relative clause.

4.3.2.2   Non-restrictive Relative Clause Modifier

In terms of clausal structure and pattern, non-restrictive relative clause modifiers are almost like those of restrictive ones. In non-restrictive relative clause construction, relative pronouns that indicate the CA are marked with the non-restrictive suffix *–i*. In addition, both the head noun and the verb in the relative clause can be marked with the non-restrictive suffix. The non-restrictive marker suffix has an allomorph [-ti], and it is phonologically conditioned.

(4.78)   *ŋà=hòì=tá*   [*ín-í*
         DEM=female=NEAR 3SG.PN.SP-NRSTR
         dúm-Ø-í   *kènɔ̀=ŋà*]ᴿᶜ
         collect-3SG.SU.IMPERV-NRSTR wood=DEF
         'The woman who is collecting the wood.'

In (4.78), apart from the non-restrictive nature of the relative clause, the noun itself is restricted by the deictic inflection. No further restricting element or specific descriptor can come between the NP and the relative pronoun, but it is possible to add new information after the relative clause. Therefore the modifier that comes after the restrictive clause may serve to add new information or draw attention (*=who is the woman?; then what about her?*).

(4.79)   *nɔ̀ŋ* [*ín-í*   *bè*   *ór-Ø*
         3SG 3SG.PN.SP-NRSTR DIST.PAST see.IMPERV-3SG.SU.IMPERV
         tùmù]ᴿᶜ *níŋè*
         God   not.present
         'He who has seen God is not present.'

As illustrated in (4.79), the NP which is indicated by the 3sg subject refers to anyone who has never seen God in whatsoever. The relative pronoun marked with the non-restrictive suffix doesn't help the relative clause restrict the referent's identity, but it rather indicates that the referent is not specific. For easier distinction between restrictive and non-restrictive relative clauses, compare the following examples—restrictive in (4.80) and non-restrictive (4.81).

(4.80)   *ŋà=ɔ́r=ùnù*   ***érmì-á***   [Ø *ógór-ó*   *rúm-íŋá*]ᴿᶜ
         DEM=village=FAR **boy-RSTR** [Ø steal-3SG.SU.PERV cloth-PL

íʃé
is.present.IMPERV.SG
'The boy who stole the clothes is in the village.'

(4.81) ŋà=ɔ́r=ùnù   **érmì-tí**   [Ø ógór-ó   rúm-íɲá]_RC
        DEM=village=FAR **boy-NRSTR** [Ø steal-3SG.SU.PERV cloth-PL]
        íʃé
        is.present.IMPERV.SG
        'In that village there is a boy who stole clothes.'

As can be seen from the examples above, the major difference between the two depends on the semantic types that they convey. In other words, the semantic difference between the two comes from the relative markers that operate on NPs and on verbs in the RC. In (4.80), the head noun is marked by a restrictive relative suffix -*a* while the head noun in (4.81) is marked by a non-restrictive relative suffix -*ti*. In (4.80), the referent (*érmìa* 'the boy') and his whereabout is known. So the information provided about the referent is not new. Anybody who heard the background information about the stolen clothes now can understand that this boy lives in the village. In contrast, in (4.81) the referent is a certain boy (*érmìti* 'a boy'), and adds new information to an already-known background information (it could be an existing suspicion).

4.4 Nominalizers

Mursi has eight major nominalizer suffixes that are used to derive nouns from other word classes mainly from verbs. Of the eight, the following three: /-a/ and /-i/, and /-nèj/ can be attached to nouns that functions as heads of NPs. The first two nominalizer suffixes can also be attached to head nouns and their dependents, and can function as restrictive and non-restrictive markers at non-clausal as well as clausal level NPs, as discussed throughout this chapter. Further morphosyntactic properties and functions of each nominalizer is discussed in § 3.2.1.3.8. Given that both /-a/ and /-i/ can hold even more elaborate morphosyntactic functions, the function of the nominalizer /-nèj/ is discussed here in brief here.

  Unlike nouns derived by the two nominalizers, nouns derived by the nominalizer /-nèj/ are deficient in taking morphological inflections. Syntactically, they occur often at NP and clause final positions. Their best salient syntactic feature is a copula clause, where they can fill CS and CC slots, as in (4.82a–b).

(4.82) a. hír-á   [∅ kún-í   [sárá-á   kómór-ùɲ]ₙₚ]ᵣc [ɲè]cs
man-RSTR [∅ come-2/3.IRR name-RSTR Lord-GEN   2SG
án-í   [túhú-nèj]cc
COP.IMPERV-2/3SG bless-NOMZ
'Blessed is he that comes in the name of the Lord.'

b. íggé-á   [∅ ŋà=bá=à   číb-ìnèn-á]   [tùmù
3PL.PN.SP-RSTR [∅ DEM=place=NEAR tie-AP-3PL.SU.PERV sky
tún-ɔ̀]cs   á   [číb-ínéj]cc
top-OBL COP.3.IMPERV tie-NOMZ
'Whoever is tied on earth is tied in heaven.'

Or in the same copular complement slot, we can get ɔginɛj 'loosened':

[tùmù tún-ɔ̀]   á   ɔ̀g-ìnèj cc
sky   top-OBL COP.3.IMPERV release-NOMZ
'(they) are loosed in heaven'

In (4.83) below, the derived noun goč̌onɛj can function as modifier of the head kèá 'thing (of)'. The head has a generic instrumental reading and it is not marked for instrumental case, thus it can be substituted by another 'water drawer'.

(4.83) a. ìɲè kè-á   [∅ góč̌-ó-nèj]ʀc   mà
2SG thing-RSTR [∅ draw-EPENT-NOMZ water
níŋè-ní-ɲ-ɔ̀
have.not-2SG.SU-SG-VFS
'You don't have the thing for drawing water.'

b. jɔ̀g [∅ ŋà=zùg=tùnù   [húč̌-a-nèj]   wà
3PL [∅ DEM=people=FAR pay-EPENT-NOMZ] REC.PAST
ʤɔ́d-á   ŋàbùnù
acquire.PERV:PL-3SG.SU.PERV there
'They, those people got their reward/payment right there.'

c. nà   ŋàbùnù lɔ̀   hírí [∅ sìɔ̀   úwás-ínéj]ʀc
CCN there   have man [∅ hand corrupt-NOMZ]
'And there was a man who had a withered hand.'

d. ŋà=zùg=tá=ŋà=jè]   [[hínísí-á   g=èj]_NP
   DEM=people=NEAR=DEF=SUBORD   heart-RSTR PL.SPD=3PL.PSR
   ạṇùj-ù-nèj]_NP
   doum.palm-EPENT-NOMZ
   'For this people's heart is waxed.'
   (Lit. 'For these people's heart waxed')

4.5 Complex Modification

Complex noun modification construction in Mursi may consist of a head modified by more than one modifier. In a complex NP, one or more than one intermediate modifier can occur between the head and the main modifier. Intermediate modifiers can form independent NPs on their own. Except, every other modifier, often the last one in complex modification is invariably assigned the construct form (restrictive) suffix. Depending on their head-modifier configuration, complex NPs can have ambiguous meanings, as in the following examples.

(4.84) nɔ̀ŋ á   hír-á   [Ø lɔ̀m-Ø-á
        3SG COP.3.IMPERV   man-RSTR   [Ø have-3SG.SU.IMPERV-RSTR
        [gùrgùr-tín-á   álí-ɲ]_NP]_RC
        knowledge-N.S-RSTR speaking-GEN
        'S/he is an able speaker.'
        (Lit. 'He is a man of possessing the knowledge of speaking; or having knowledge of speaking.')

From example (4.84), three distinct NP types or configurations can be extracted: (i) an NP headed by *hírá* 'man (of)' modified a noun in genitive case *álíɲ* '(of) speaking' ~ *hírá álíɲ* 'man of speaking', (ii) an NP headed by *gùrgùrtíná* 'knowledge (of)' is directly modified by *álíɲ* ~ *gùrgùrtíná álíɲ* 'knowledge of speaking', and (iii) the NP *hírá* modified by the relative clause, as in (4.85).

(4.85) nɔ̀ŋ á   hír-á   [Ø lɔ̀m-Ø-á
        3SG COP.3.IMPERV   man-RSTR   [Ø have-3SG.SU.IMPERV-RSTR
        [gùrgùr-tín-á   álí-ɲ]_NP]_RC
        knowledge-N.S-RSTR speaking-GEN]]
        'He is a person who has knowledge of speaking.'

Another similar complex NP modification construction is illustrated below.

(4.86) lúsí   bág-Ø   [bá-á   [[mùm-á
        boy.SG show.off-3SG.SU.IMPERV place-RSTR face-RSTR
        [ŋɔ̀nɛ̀-à   n=ɛ̀nɛ̀]ₙₚ]ₙₚ]ₙₚ
        sister.PERT:3SG.PSR-RSTR   SG.PSD=3SG.PSR
        'The boy was showing off in front of his sister.'
        (Lit. 'The boy was showing off in the face of his sister.')

The difference between (4.85) and (4.86) is that the NP in the latter cannot be modified by a relative clause. The NP in (4.86) is the object of the clause, but composed of three distinct NPs and each can stand on their own as full NP. The first NP is *mùmá ŋɔ̀nɛ̀* 'face of his sister' and the restrictive (construct form) suffix is not marked on the modifier *ŋɔ̀nɛ̀*. If the modifier *ŋɔ̀nɛ̀* is marked with a restrictive suffix –*a* (*ŋɔ̀nɛ̀-a*), it cannot be a modifier but it can be an NP head. Thus, when it is marked with the restrictive suffix, it could indicate that its next specific relation is with the constituent placed at the final modifier position, i.e. *nɛ̀nɛ̀*. Thus, *ŋɔ̀nɛ̀à nɛ̀nɛ̀* 'his sister' is the second NP. The last NP is the whole NP structure other than the spatial connector word *ba*, i.e. *mùmá ŋɔ̀nɛ̀à nɛ̀nɛ̀* '(the) face of his sister'. In addition, the kinship noun *ŋɔ̀nɛ̀* 'his sister' is being marked with a pertensive suffix, thus it can be considered as the forth NP. Attempting to modify the head noun *mùmá* directly by the last modifier *nɛ̀nɛ̀* could bring about an ambiguous meaning. This is due to the fact that Mursi has no grammatical gender thus *mùmá nɛ̀nɛ̀* could mean 'face of the body' or 'face of her sister'.

Unlike the head-relative clause modifier relation illustrated in (§ 4.3.3), the head-intermediate modifier relations are not only dedicated only to the expression of specific relation but also to the expression of possession. In (4.85) and (4.86), the complex modification construction is used to indicate linguistic possession.

(4.87) [zùw-á   bìò-ɲ]ₙₚ   jɔ̀g   gáj-ɛ́   [[bì-á
        people-RSTR   cow.PL-GEN 3PL   know-3PL.SU.IMPERV cow-RSTR
        g=ɛ̀j]ₙₚ   míʃíró-á   él   ɲàwà-jè]ₙₚ
        PL.PSD=3PL.PSR earmark-RSTR exist.IMPERV:PL   *ear*-OBL
        'The owners recognize their cattle by means of earmarks.'
        (Lit. 'The owners of the cows know their cattle by the marks existing on their ear.')

In (4.87), the oblique-marked[9] noun *nàwàjè* 'on ear' with the existential verb *él* 'exist/present' forms instrumental NP. Thus, the two can be combined together as one argument *élnàwàjè* 'on (the) ear'. Although it is used to encode a locative source of the *míʃíró* 'earmark', it hasn't lost its primary function as oblique NP.

(4.88) jòg jóg-έ   [[lɔ̀g-á   hírí n=ὲj   ɓòi]
       3PL speak-3PL.SU.IMPERV word-RSTR man SG.PSD=3PL.PSR all
       [hùll-à   góg-òɲ]ₙₚ]ₙₚ
       when-RSTR noise-GEN
       'They echoed every word of their leader.'
       (Lit. 'They spoke every word of their man while making a noise.')

Even if the primary function of *ɓòi* 'all' is adverbial ('completely'), it can also function as quantifier 'every',[10] as in (4.88). Therefore, the whole structure after the verb is just one complex NP containing two distinct uncoordinated NPs. The head of the entire NP is *lɔ̀gá* 'word (of)'. In the first NP, the possessive pronoun and the quantifier are modifier of *lɔ̀gá* while in the second NP the noun in genitive case *gógòɲ* 'noise (of)' modifies the temporal word *hùllá* 'at a time, while'. As one would expect, *hírí* seems the head of this complex NP. But in noun modification construction systems, the head has to fulfil one major syntactic requirement, i.e. the head itself must occur in a construct form to indicate that it is ready to be modified. From the construct form requirement point of view, *hírí* is not in construct form, thus it doesn't qualify to be modified.

In addition to serving as expression of possession, the Mursi complex NP construction allows new modifier words from other grammatical categories—such as the spatial term *hùllá* from temporal/conditional marker *hùllí* 'when/if' in (4.88).

---

9   Recall oblique case in Mursi marks both locative and instrumental functions. The locative function of oblique case can include locative arguments and locative adjuncts.
10 There is another word comparable with *ɓòi*, i.e. *dàài* 'all'. It has similar function to *ɓòi*, but *dàài* has a different syntactic distribution within an NP and has a distributive quantifier meaning (see also § 4.2.7).

4.6 Summary of Head-Modifier Dependency Relation

Under this section, the head-modifier dependency relation of all NP types is summarized. For each NP type, the morphosyntactic properties of the head and their modifiers have been summarized.

i. **Non-clausal and Non-noun Modification Constructions**
Table 4.1 below summarises the non-clausal and non-noun modification construction form, which is expressed by bound nominal demonstrative pronouns, as discussed in (§ 4.2.1.1)—Nominal demonstrative pronouns Type I and Type II.

ii. **Non-clausal Modifiers in Noun Modification Constructions**
At non-clausal dependency level, the head-modifier relation dependency is often expressed in a way that the syntactically dependent constituents (intermediate modifiers) are introduced by construct-form suffixes (restrictive and non-restrictive).

Note that in [Head-*a*(-i) modifier-*a*] dependency relation—if the modifier is a noun, then it denotes a quality but with a possible distributional property of an adjective.

iii. **Clausal Modifiers**
A clausal modifier of the NP is mainly the relative clause which involves finite verbs. The verb in a relative clause modifier usually consists of full verbal inflections, and a construct form suffix for a restrictive and sometimes for a nominalizing function. Given that the canonical constituent order of Mursi is AVO, nominal subjects are always in its preverbal position, preceding the relative clause. Table 4.4 below is a summary of the structure of relative clauses modifying the NP.

TABLE 4.1 Bound nominal demonstrative constructions

	Type I	Type II
can modify nouns	yes	yes
can modify verbs	yes (nominalized verbs)	no
can function as full NP	yes	no
can head NP	yes	yes
can function as adverb	rare (with locative case)	local adverbials

TABLE 4.1　Bound nominal demonstrative constructions (*cont.*)

	Type I	Type II
can be modified by other modifier	by a numeral (with a coordinative partitive *kó* between the two); when occurring in CC position	
can occur as S, O	yes	no
can occur as CS, CC	yes	as CS

TABLE 4.2　Non-clausal head modifiers (restrictive modifiers)

Head	Restrictive suffix	Modifier	Suffix
Noun	-a [-ta]	Adjective (derived)	/-a/ (restrictive attributive)
	-a [-ta]	Adjective (derived)	/-i/ (adjectivizer)
	-a [-ta]	Nouns	/-ɲ/ and /-i/ (genitive case)
	-a [-ta]	Possessive pronouns	no
	-a [-ta]	Numerals	no
	-a [-ta]	Indefinites	/-a/ (restrictive)
	-a [-ta]	Quantifiers	/-a/ and /-i/[a]

a　A few derived adjectives exist that function as quantifiers.

TABLE 4.3　Non-clausal head-modifiers (non-restrictive modifiers)

Head	Restrictive suffix	Modifier	Suffix
Noun	-i [-ti]	Adjective (derived)	/-a/ (restrictive attributive)
	-i [-ti]	Adjective (derived)	/-i/ (adjectivizer)
	-i [-ti]	Nouns	/-ɲ/ and /-i/ (genitive case)
	-i [-ti]	Possessive pronouns	no
	-i [-ti]	Numerals	no
	-i [-ti]	Quantifiers	/-i/ (adjectivizer non-restrictive)

TABLE 4.4 Clausal modifiers

Head/NP	Head suffix (RSTR/NRSTR)	Relative clause	CA of the relative clause
Noun	-a/-i	[Ø v-a (O) (OBL)]	Gap strategy
Nouns	-a/-i	[Ø NON-V v-a(O) (OBL)]	Gap strategy
Noun	Ø	[Ø v-a (O) (OBL)]	Gap strategy
Dem.pron	Ø	[Ø v-a (O) (OBL)]	Gap strategy
Personal pronoun	Ø	[REL.PRO-a/-i v (O) (OBL)]	Relative pronoun
Relative pronoun	Ø	[REL.PRO-a/-i v (O) (OBL)]	Internally headed/CA
Relative pronoun	Ø	[REL.PRO-a/-i v]	Internally headed/CA

CHAPTER 5

Possession

5.1 Introduction

Mursi has a fairly rich syntactic system for the expression of possession or ownership. One plausible reason for acquiring such a rich expression of syntactic construction of possession is that it has both head and dependent marking system. As a head-dependent marking language, both the head and the dependent are marked by appropriate dependency relation marking morphological elements. As we recall from Chapter 4, the head can be marked with two different morphologies—modification markers (restrictive/non-restrictive) and pertensive. When it is converted into possessive construction, the head is always the possessed noun (D) and the dependent/modifier is the possessor (R). In other words, taking the two distinct morphological markings to be used on possessed nouns, and the various possessor types into account, it would be logical to expect very diverse possessive construction types in the language. The various syntactic constructions and possibilities of indicating possession/ownership should follow the syntactic frame of 'NP-internal possessive construction'.

Possession within an NP can be viewed as one of the realizations of a broader concept of association or relationship between two nouns (Aikhenvald 2013:2). Accordingly, five NP-internal possessive construction types have been identified in Mursi: one structure where R and D are simply juxtaposed within an NP, and four other distinct structures where D is followed by R. The five NP-internal possessive construction types are:

i. Juxtaposed (possessor-possessum) (§5.2)
  [NOUN$_{Possessor}$ NOUN$_{Possessed}$]
ii. Possessum-possessor (§5.3)
  A. [HEAD.N-MOD/RELATOR$_{Possessed}$ POSSESSOR-GEN$_{Possessor}$]
  B. [HEAD.N-MOD/RELATOR$_{Possessed}$ PROPER.NAME-GEN$_{Possessor}$]
iii. Possessum-possessor (where the possessor is a possessive pronoun) (§5.4)
  [[HEAD.N-MOD/RELATOR$_{Possessed}$ POSS. PRO$_{Possessor}$]
iv. Pertensive (§5.5)
  A1. [HEAD.N$_{Possessed}$-PERT$_{Possessor}$] (synthetic structure)
  A2. [HEAD.N$_{Possessed}$-PERT$_{Possessor}$ (POSS. PRO$_{Possessor}$)] (analytic structure)
v. Noun Modification Constructions (§5.6)
  [HEAD.N-RSTR/RELATOR$_{Possessed}$ POSSESSOR-RSTR/RELATOR$_{possessor}$]

These possessive constructions (i–v) can be subdivided into core and non-core possessive relations. However, both types almost always can cover the following possessive relationships: ownership, whole-part relationship, kinship relationship, attribution of a person/animal/thing, statement of orientation or location, association, and a nominalization (cf. Dixon 2010a: 262–263). There is one more possessive relationship construction which can be expressed without the need for an NP-internal possessive construction—known as predicative possessive construction (Dixon 2010: 265). In Mursi, there are three verbs which could be used to show possessive relationships through predicative construction: the verb *lɔ̀m* 'have', the existential verb *ih* 'exist/present', and the copula verb *a* < COP.3SG/PL.IMPERV 'be'. This possessive relationship type is discussed in §5.7.

Regarding the semantic nature of possessed nouns (D's), I would prefer to make one strong generalization, that is, almost all Mursi simple nouns can be possessed as long as they take the two modification markers. However, only a few kinship nouns and just one non-kinship noun *rɛ* 'body' can be possessed inalienably or obligatorily. Inalienably possessed nouns can be easily distinguished from alienably possessed ones by their ability to take a pertensive morphology. With regard to the semantic nature of the possessors (R's), four categories have been identified—simple nouns (A), proper names (B), possessive pronouns (C), and modified-modifiers (D). Each of these categories has been elaborated in detail in their respective possessive relation types.

Regardless of their semantic nature, all possessors take the phonologically conditioned genitive case markers that usually occur in different forms. The genitive suffix *-ɲ* is used in an instance when an oblique case (even a nominative case) is attached to the possessor noun and follows a vowel-final nouns. The genitive suffix *-ùɲ* is used following nasal/liquid-final nouns. The genitive suffix *-òɲ* when an oblique case marker (also a nominative case) can be suffixed to the possessor noun in a way that looks inseparable. With a dorso-velar consonant, *-ùŋ*, is used often following vowel-final plural nouns, but it has unpredictable distribution in the majority of cases. Other forms of the same case maker suffix include: *-j* following vowel-final proper names, *-i* (following consonant-final proper names/proper nouns), and *-Ø* following nouns ending with the palatal nasal /ɲ/.

5.2 Juxtaposed System

A possessive relationship that can be expressed by a juxtaposed possessor and possessed is very different from all other possessive relationship construction

POSSESSION

types. Morphologically, both possessor and possessed nouns do not take any marker. Syntactically, the possessor noun (R) always precedes the possessed noun (D). Semantically, the possessive relationships through the juxtaposed system (R-D) are confined to ownership and whole-part relationships. The ownership relationship is used to refer to the young of animals only. The noun *hòjnè* ~ 'the young' is only used to refer to the offspring of animals, as in (5.1a–b).

(5.1)   a.   [*bì*$_R$ *hòjnè*$_D$]
          cow   kid
          'offspring of (the) cow'
          (Lit. 'Calf of (the) cow')

      b.   [*tòŋò*$_R$ *hòjnè*$_D$]
          goat   kid
          'kid of the goat'

If necessary, one way to prove that the possessive relationship constructions in (5.1a–b) are intended to refer to ownership and are not intended for simple noun formations is that there are terms of reference for both of them, *mòr* 'calf' for (5.1a) and *mèèn* '(goat) kid' for (5.1b). These are also quite different from compound nouns (compare with § 3.2.1.3.3).

On the other hand, the whole-part relationship covers body parts of human and animals, plants, and objects.

(5.2)   [*érmì*$_R$ *dʒààrè*$_D$]$_{NP}$ *lò*-Ø   *ŋòdòrì*
       child.SG leg.SG   has-3SG.SU.IMPERV sore
       'The child's leg has a sore.'

(5.3)   [*hírí*$_R$ *kààrì*$_D$]
       man.SG   eye.SG
       'The man's eye'

(5.4)   [*búŋáj*$_R$ *kààrì*$_D$]
       bull.SG   eye.SG
       'Eye of a bull'

(5.5)   [*nèbì*$_R$ *kàjó*$_D$]
       buffalo.SG tongue.SG
       'The buffalo's tongue'

(5.6) [bì$_R$ màdi$_D$]
cow.SG breast.SG
'The cow's breast'

(5.7) [kiò$_R$ ɲàbì$_D$]
tree.SG ear.SG
'The tree's branch'
(Lit. 'The tree's ear')

(5.8) [dórí$_R$ tútúg$_D$]
house.SG door.SG
'The house's door'

In juxtaposed possessive construction system, the absence of number agreement between the possessor and possessed does not affect the meaning of the construction at all. In my corpus, an example of a juxtaposed construction referring to an association possessive relationship type has been found:

(5.9) [hírí$_R$ sárà$_D$]
man.SG name.PL
'The man's name'

As it is shown in (5.9), the noun *sárá* 'name' is an inherently plural noun in Mursi and has no singular counterpart, but the meaning hasn't been affected and still has a singular interpretation.

A single most effective method of distinguishing between an inalienably possessed referent and that of an alienably possessed referent depends on the natural relationship that exists between the possessed item and the possessor. In many languages, whole-part and kinship relations are usually grouped among a few possessive relations being possessed inalienably. This is due to the fact that whole-part and kinship relations could involve a closer link between referents than ownership does (Aikhenvald 2013: 8). In the light of this, I would be inclined to suggest that the whole-part relations which we saw in the examples above could possibly be interpreted as reflecting inalienable possession.

5.3   **Possessive Construction with A and B Possessors**

The second type of possessive construction within an NP involves simple noun possessors (in the A type NP-internal possessive construction) or proper name

POSSESSION

possessors (in the B type NP-internal possessive construction). Possessive constructions involving these two possessors will have almost identical constructions. In this possessive construction, both the possessed and the possessor take nominal morphology. The possessed item is always marked with a relator suffix -a whereas the possessor is marked with the genitive case. Therefore, the possessed (D) is linked to the possessor (R) by this relator suffix and the D precedes the R (D-R).

(5.10) A-type possessors
    a. [érmì-a   hírí-ɲ]
       child-RSTR man-GEN
       'Child (son) of man'

    b. [úr-á   bì-ɲ]
       milk-RSTR cow-GEN
       'Milk of the cow'

    c. [zíwá-á   mùn-ùɲ]
       medicine-RSTR mursi.PL-GEN
       'Medicine of the Mursi'

    d. [mà   kútúl-òɲ]
       water+RSTR mountain-OBL.GEN
       'Mountain water (water of a mountain)'

    e. [zùw-á   mìs-òɲ]
       people-RTSR grassland-OBL.GEN
       'People of the grassland'

    f. [lɔ̀g-á   áú-ɲá-ùŋ]
       word/issue-RSTR eldest.child-PL-GEN
       'Thing/issue of the eldest children'

    g. [bùnà-á   kútúl-i]
       coffee-RSTR mountain-GEN
       'Mountain coffee'

The examples in (5.10a–c) express ownership while the example in (5.10d) expresses source and location. Thus (5.10d) requires an oblique case marker. As it can be shown, its form is changed from the typical oblique case suffix -ɔ to -o due to the effect of vowel-height harmony. The same marking applies to (5.10e) but the meaning expressed is an 'association' type. Both (5.10d) and (5.10e) are instances of a double case marking system. In (5.10f), the genitive case marker *-uɲ* always occurs following plural possessors. (5.10g) is almost an identical construction with (5.10d), except for the absence the oblique case marker in (g). Due to this, (5.10g) seems to illustrate a simple noun modification construction rather than a possessive construction. Nouns ending in liquid take the *-i* genitive suffix.

However, when possessors are proper names, the genitive case markers may apply based on the phonological conditions or even sometimes apply outside the phonological rules/motivations. For example (5.11a–b) are in line with the phonologically-conditioning where the palatal nasal of the /ɲ/-final proper names and the genitive morpheme *-ɲ* simply merge, whereas the genitive suffix *-i* follows liquid-final proper names.

(5.11) B-type possessors
    a. [čɔ̀r-á   báríhúɲ]
       hair-RSTR Barihuny.GEN
       'Hair of Barihuny'

    b. [érmì-á   ŋàkútúl-í]
       child-RSTR Ngakútúl-GEN
       'Ngakutu's child'

    c. [bì-ò-á   tókó-í]
       cow-PL-RSTR toko-GEN
       'Toko's cows'

In (5.11c), the genitive suffix *-i* is used simply because the possessor is a proper name. In other words, it is a morphologically-motivated/conditioned one. Possessive constructions with A-type possessor may also be used to form simple non-compound nouns, as in (5.12a–b).

(5.12) a. [čɔ̀r-à   čàmún-úɲ]
       hair-RSTR chin-GEN
       'Hair of chin ('beard')'

    b. [àlì-a   gùfúr-ùɲ]
       stool-RSTR hyena-GEN
       'Hyena's stool ('mushroom')'

A possessive construction with an A-type possessor also encompasses core relationships such as kinship, ownership, association, orientation/location (5.13), and source or material (5.15).

(5.13) sábɔ̀ kósì   kó sààní tóɲ   [táná-á
first traditional.cup PNC plate wash.PERV.IMP side-RSTR
kèŋ-ùɲ]   ŋànìjè [táná-á bɔ́-ɲ]   ... hàlì
belly/center-GEN but side-RSTR outside-GEN ... later
kɔ́ɔj-Ø   ké hɔ̀l-è[i]=jè
3.SBJV.go-3.IRR COMPL white.STV-ADJ=SUBORD
'Wash first the inside of the cup and dish ... that their outside may also be clean.'
(Lit. 'First wash (sg.) the inside (center) of the cup and dish ... but (their) outside later become white.')

It is possible to indicate a statement of location or source by a body part noun in possessed function, as in (5.14–15).

(5.14) érmì   í-Ø   [bùgùj-á ɲákàr-ùɲ]
child.SG to.be-3SG.SU.IMPERV back-RSTR nyakarin-GEN
'The child is behind (the) Nyakarin's back.'

(5.15) [ŋɔ̀dɔ̀r-èn-á   sígí-ó-ùŋ]
wound-PL-RSTR iron-PL-GEN
'Wounds of irons'

5.4 Possessive Construction with C-type (Possessive Pronouns)

Type-C are possessive pronouns that naturally occur carrying three grammatical information details: person of the possessor, number of the possessor and number of the possessed item (see §3.3.1.4). Number of a possessed item is shown by a proclitic *n*= singular and *g*= plural. It is the number of the possessed items being shown by segmentable proclitics. Morphological information of person and number of the possessor is difficult to segment into small morphemes even though the boundary between them usually can be detectable (see §2.3.8; §2.5.1.3). Nevertheless, markers of the person of the possessors can easy be identified as they have segmental realizations—/-a/ first person /-u/ second person and /-ɛ/ third person. Morphological analysis of the possessive pronouns is presented below for some selected forms.

(5.16)   Number of D=person+number of R
    nànù   ~ [n=à+nù]   'Mine, singular possessed'
    gàɲù   ~ [g=à+ɲù]   'Mine, plural possessed'
    nùnù   ~ [n=ù+nù]   'Yours, singular possessed'
    nɛ̀nɛ̀   ~ [n=ɛ̀+nɛ̀]   'His/hers, singular possessed'
    nàw   ~ [n=àw]   'Our (exc.) singular possessed'
    gàw   ~ [g=àw]   'Our (exc.) plural possessed'
    gàj   ~ [g=àj]   'Our (inc.) plural possessed'

(5.17) a. [zíwá-á   n=ànù]
          medicine-RSTR SG.PSD=1SG.PSR
          'My medicine'

       b. [čɔ̌r-à   g=àɲù]
          hair-RTSR PL.PSD=1SG.PSR
          'My hair'

In order to distinguish whether a specific noun is inherently singular or not; or is mass noun, collective noun, and so on, the best way is to combine them with possessive pronouns. For example, imagine that nothing is known about the number of the noun *čɔ́rá* 'hair' as it is shown in (5.17b); but the possessive pronoun indirectly tells us about the number of the nouns it modifies. This is the only way that we can know that the noun *sárá* 'name' is inherently plural (5.18).

(5.18) [sárá-a   g=àɲù]
       name-RSTR PL.PSD=1SG.PSR
       'My name'

In addition, the first person plural possessive pronouns do distinguish between inclusive and exclusive possessors—(5.19a–b).

(5.19) a. ŋà=éró=à   á   [támárí-ɲá-á
          DEM=children=NEAR COP.3.IMPERV student-PL-RSTR
          g=àw]
          PL.PSD=1PL.EXC.PSR
          'These children are our (exc.) students.'

       b. ŋà=éró=ìnù   á   [éró-á
          DEM=children=FAR COP.3.IMPERV children-RSTR

g=àj]
PL.PSD=1PL.INC.PSR
'These children are ours (inc.).'

In practice, if possessive pronouns are the possessors, almost any noun in Mursi can optionally be possessed. Examples demonstrating this are given as follows:

(5.20) a. [*éséd-á-á*   *n=ànù*]
think-NOMZ-RSTR SG.PSD=1SG.PSR
'My idea'

b. [*gùrgùr-tín-á*   *n=ànù*]
knowledge/skill-N.S.NOMZ-RSTR SG.PSD=1SG.PSR
'My knowledge'

c. [*dáʃi-á*   *n=ànù*]
work.NOMZ-RSTR SG.PSD=1SG.PSR
'My work (job)'

d. *čùmùn-á-á*   *n=ànù*]
happy.STV-NOMZ-RTSR SG.PSD=1SG.PSR
'My happiness (joy)'

e. [*úŋó-á*   *g=àɲù*]
day-RTSR PL.PSD=1SG.PSR
'My day'

f. [*bérgú-ɲá-á*   *g=àɲù*]
year/season-PL-RSTR PL.PSD=1SG.PSR
'My age'

As can be shown in (5.20a–d), all nominalized nouns (from both active and stative verbs) behave alike, i.e. all can be possessed optionally.

5.5   Pertensive

Pertensive marking on D is the single most productive way of showing inalienably possessed nouns within an NP-internal possession construction. A few close kinship terms and a noun *rɛ* 'body' can be marked by pertensive mark-

TABLE 5.1   Pertensive markers

	Pertensive	Number of D + person
1	=nà (sg.)	=n-à ~ PERT.SG-1.PSR
	=gà (pl.)	=g-à ~ PERT.PL-1.PSR
2	=nù (sg.)	=n-ù ~ PERT.SG-2.PSR
	=gù (pl.)	=g-ù ~ PERT.PL-2.PSR
3	=nɛ̀ (sg.)	=n-ɛ̀ ~ PERT.SG-3.PSR
	=gɛ̀ (pl.)	=g-ɛ̀ ~ PERT.PL-3.PSR

ers. The pertensive markers have two functions, (1) they confirm that the noun to which it is attached is in D function, and (2) they specify the number of the R.

The pertensive marker enclitics on singular possessed kinship nouns often merge with the noun roots therefore they cannot easily be segmentable.

Interestingly, in relation to kinship possession, Mursi employs synthetic (direct) and analytic (indirect) possession types. Only kinship relationship by blood (consanguineal) as listed in Table 5.2 can be possessed inalienably or directly. These kinship terms always are possessed inalienably and occur in synthetic constructions. Outside from those listed in Table 5.2, all other kinship relationships of blood and marriage (affinal) can be possessed alienably (indirectly), thus they occur in analytic constructions. As Aikhenvald (2019: 11–12) noted, one reason for the analytic structure/possessive construction originates from the fact that components have to be individuated and made specific rather than genetic. In other words, if there is less proximity between components, then they are labeled to be part of the analytic structure.

The first two kinship nouns (*dàdà* and *màmà*) can only be possessed by first persons.

(5.21)   a. [*dàdà*]
father.PERT.SG.1.PSR
'My father'

b. [*dàdá-ɲó*]
father.PERT.1.PSR-PL
'Our father'

TABLE 5.2   Pertensive taking kinship terms

Singular	Plural	Meaning
dàdà	dàdàčó	'father'
màmà	màmàčó	'mother'
ʃúúné	ʃúúgé	'father'
dʒɔ̀ɔ̀né	dʒɔ̀ɔ̀gé	'mother'
gòdóná	gòdóngá	'brother'
ŋɔ̀nà	ŋɔ̀nìgèn	'sister'
kògónà	–	'grandfather'
óóná	–	'uncle'

    c. [dàdá-čó]
       father.PERT.1.PSR-PL
       'Our fathers'

    d. [dàdá-čó-á   g=àw]$_{NP}$
       father.PERT.1.PSR-PL-RSTR PL.PSD=1PL.EXC.PSR
       'Our (exc.) fathers'

The most peculiar feature of all in the synthetic structure is the number marking on D, which is always added to possessed kinship noun after the pertensive information. Note that inalienably possessed kinship nouns can also occur in analytic construction or indirect possession. This means that inalienably possessed kinship nouns can be used in a direct and in an indirect possessive construction (cf. Aikhenvald 2019: 12). However, when the pertensive marked inalienably possessed kinship nouns occur with optional possessive pronouns, there are two reasons for such co-occurrence. First, the pertensive markers do not show clear information about number of possessor (as in (5.21c)). Second, the pertensive markers do not distinguish between first person plural inclusive and exclusive possessors (as in (5.21d)).

(5.22) [màmà]   á   nèŋ?
        mother.PERT.SG.1.PSR COP.3.IMPERV who
        'Who is my mother?'

Both *dàdà* 'father' and *màmà* 'mother' have different forms for second and third person R's (pertensive forms).

(5.23) Second person R
    a. [ʃúúnù]　　　　　[ʃúúgù]
       father.PERT.SG.2.PSR　father.PERT.PL.2.PSR
       'Your father'　　　　'Your fathers'

    b. [ʃúúnù]　　　　kó　[ʤúúnù]
       father.PERT.SG.2.PSR PNC mother.PERT.SG.2.PSR
       dő̃ŋ-á
       respect.PERV.IMP-VFS
       'Respect your father and (your) mother!'

(5.24) Third person R
    a. [ʃúúnɛ́]　　　　　[ʃúúgɛ́]
       father.PERT.SG.3.PSR　father.PERT.PL.3.PSR
       'His/her father'　　　'His/her fathers'

    b. [ʤɔ̀ɔ̀nɛ́]　　　　　[ʤɔ̀ɔ̀gɛ́]
       mother.PERT.SG.3.PSR mother.PERT.PL.3.PSR
       'His/her mother'　　 'His/her mothers'

The other inalienable possessed kinship nouns always occur in their original forms or do not alter their morphological forms for person of R. See the following examples.

(5.25) a. [gòdóná]
       brother.PERT.SG.1.PSR
       'My brother'

    b. [gòdón=gá]
       brother=PERT.PL.1.PSR
       'My brothers'

    c. [gòdón=gà-čó]
       brother=PERT.PL.1.PSR-PL
       'My brothers'

    d. [ŋɔ̀no=gà-čó]
       sister=PERT.PL.1.PSR-PL
       'My sisters'

When we see the pertensive markers at first glance (5.25c–d), they appear to be attached to D primarily in order to refer to number of D, but they exist mainly to indicate that a plural kinship noun is being possessed. Due to this, inalienably possessed kinship nouns must be marked by plural number marker suffix -čo. The suffix -čo is a kinship-specific number marker, it can only be marked on nouns denoting close kinship relations, as in (5.26a–c).

(5.26) Singular   Plural   Meaning
   a. kàkà   kàkàčó   'grandmother'
   b. dòŋò   dòŋòčó   'the co-wives mothers'
   c. mèrè   mèrèčó   'daughter-in-law'

Although kinship nouns in (5.26a–c) take the suffix -čo, they cannot be inalienably possessed. These and other kinship nouns from both types (consanguineal and affinal) can be possessed alienably. Possessive pronouns are used as R's, and thus possession is expressed by an analytic structure (5.27).

(5.27) [mèrè-čó-à   g=ùŋù]$_{NP}$
        daughter-in-law-PL-RSTR PL.PSD=2PL.PSR
        áʤ-àŋ-è   tílá
        give.IMPERV-1SG.OBJ-3PL.SU.IMPERV food
        'Your (pl.) daughters-in-laws gave me food.'

Two kinship nouns, however, deviate from all other types in terms of the way they take plural number marking and the way they are used in a possessive constructions—jànèn (sg.)/jànìgèn (pl.) 'cousin' and ŋɔ̀nè (sg.) /ŋɔ̀nìgèn (pl.) 'sisters to each other (siblings)'.

(5.28) ká-dág-ènè-Ø   zèrí-mò zèré-mò-j
        1SU-hit-RECIP-1PL.INC.SU.IMPERV   race-NS race-NS-GEN
        [jànùgè-mò   jànùgè-mò-j]   jànùgè-mò'   á
        cousin.PL-NS cousin.PL-NS-GEN   cousin.PL-NS   COP.3.IMPERV
        ɓá   ké   ké[1]
        CAUSE/REASON   PREP QUOT
        'We (inc.) beat each other, race by race, by cousinhood by cousinhood, instead, cousinhood is what is called.' (KW 2:26:4)

---

[1] It is an elliptical construction. In its regular clausal construction, the kinship noun janugemo in the single quotation mark should have come after the quotative marker.

(5.29) [màmà]   kónó   kó   [ɟɔ̀ɔ̀nɛ̀]
       mother.PERT.SG.1.PSR one.INDEF PNC mother.PERT.SG.3.PSR
       á   dɔ́nɛ́j ŋɔ̀nìgɛ̀n
       COP.3.IMPERV   one   sibling.PL
       'My mother and his mother are one (the same), sisters (to each other).'
       (KW 2:34:4)

As we can see in the examples illustrated above, both *jànìgèn* and *ŋɔnigɛn* appear in pertensive forms as possessed plural kinship nouns. Both stand apart from other kinship nouns because they change their original form when they are used in possessive construction. For example, *jànìgèn* is a simple non-possessed plural form, but when used in synthetic structure, it change into *ŋɔ̀nògàčó* (as in (5.25d)). In its pertensive form, it takes the plural number marker suffix *–čo* instead of taking the pertensive marker =*ga* and attaching it to the form *ŋɔ̀nìgɛ̀n*. A series of internal-vowel changes have been also observed in some kinship nouns—*gòdóná* 'my brother' → *gòdìnè* 'His/her brother', *jànìgèn* 'sisters' → *jànùgè* 'sisters' (as in 5.28). These internal-vowel changes, however, are mainly of two types /o/→/i/ or /i/→/u/ or just /o/~/u/~/i/. At this stage, I would say these changes are phonologically-motivated but it is too early to make any generalization.

5.6 Noun Modification Constructions

The noun modification construction (NMC) is normally the same as simple NP construction. Yet it stands apart from the previous four possessive construction types because it may involve a series of intermediate possessors/modifiers. The template below could illustrate NMC well.

[HEAD.N-RSTR/REL$_{Possessum}$ MODIFIER-RSTR/REL$_{possessor}$X] MODIFIER-RSTR/REL$_{possessor}$Y]] ... MODIFIER-GEN$_{possessor}$Z]]]

From NP construction point of view, the head noun may be counted as real or first head whereas the second and third nouns as intermediate modifiers. But from the possessive construction point of view, the head noun would be D whereas the second and third nouns are intermediate possessors (R's). The last modifier within an NP construction becomes the real R in possessive construction. Therefore, the D and the intermediate R's are marked by restrictive/relator marker -*a* while the erstwhile possessor will be marked by the genitive case marker.

The restrictive/relator marker -*a* on the possessed/head noun and on the intermediate possessors/modifiers is called by different names but mainly by Construct Form (CF)[2] (cf. Chapter 4). Welmers (1973) used the term 'associative construction' in reference to nouns which express a wide range of semantic relationships with other nouns and occur as modifiers within the same NP. Different semantic aspects can be covered with this construction such as material, content, place of origin, place of use, time of use, function, and quality (Èjèbá 2016:134).

(5.30)   á   [gúɲá-à   [zùw-à   mìs-ɔ̀ɲ]$_{NP}$]$_{NP}$
        COP.3.IMPERV field.PL-RSTR people-RSTR grassland-OBL.GEN
        'These are the fields of the grassland people' (Mütze 2014)

(5.31)   [[zùw-á   ɲàgàs-á]$_{NP}$ ɔ́r-ùɲ]$_{NP}$ mèzì-á̆-ó
        people-RSTR old.STV-RSTR village-GEN discuss-PERV.PL-3PL.IRR
        'The village's elders held a council.'

In both cases, for example one could say *gúɲáà mìsɔ̀ɲ* 'fields of the grassland' without the intermediate possessor *zùwà* 'people of' (as in (5.30)) and *zùwá ɔ̀rùɲ* 'people of the village' without the intermediate possessor or the attributive *ɲàgàsá* 'old (of)'. As long as one specific possessive construction makes sense, there is no limit on how many intermediate possessors/modifiers may be used within an NP. Besides, the last possessor of a noun modification construction can be a possessive pronoun (as in (5.32), repeated from §3.3.3), or just a simple noun marked by oblique case (5.33–5.34), or an adjective (5.34).

(5.32)   lúsì   bág-Ø   [bá-á   [mùm-á   [ŋɔ̀nì-á
        boy.SG show.off-3SG.SU.IMPERV place-RSTR face-RSTR sister-RSTR
        n=ènè]$_{NP}$]$_{NP}$]$_{NP}$
        SG.PSD=3SG.PSR
        'The boy was showing off in front of his sister.'

(5.33)   [bá-á   [tán-á   [ŋɔ́č-á   sús-ɔ́]$_{NP}$]$_{NP}$]$_{NP}$
        place-RSTR side-RSTR nape.of.neck-RSTR sun-OBL

---

[2] Different terms have been employed for Construct Form: Welmers (1973) 'Associative Construction', Van de Velde (2013) 'Connective Construction', Gregersen (1961) 'Status Construction', Tucker and Bryan (1966) 'Antigenitive', and Andersen (2016) 'Construct-State'.

        ká-gáj-í   ʃéé   hán
        1SU-know.IMPERV-1SG.SU.IMPERV well very
        'I know the eastern part pretty well.'
        (Lit. 'I know the place on the other side of sunrise very well.')

(5.34) [kátámá-á [tán-á   ŋóč̵-a   sús-ɔ̀]_NP]_NP
       town-RSTR side-RSTR nape.of.neck-RSTR sun-OBL
       ɓák-ú   bá-á   ʃɨ̀ŋ-ɔ̀
       eat-3SG.SU.PERV cause/place-RSTR earthquake-OBL/INSTR
       'The east side of the city was destroyed by the earthquake.'

(5.35) á   [lɔ̀g-á   [bì-á   gɔ̀lɔ̀ɲ-á]_NP]_NP]
       COP.3.IMPERV issue/matter-RSTR cow-RSTR red.STV-RSTR
       'This (it) is the matter of the red cow.'

In a noun modification construction, rarely, the possessor/head can also occur on the left-side. Therefore, it doesn't take a genitive case marking. Genitive case is the feature of possessors/modifiers occurring at the right-edge within NPs, as in (5.35).

(5.36) nɔ̀ŋ á   [[hír-á   gùrgùr-tín-a]_NP dádál-á]_NP
       3SG COP.3.IMPERV man-RSTR skill-N.S-RSTR hard.STV-RSTR
       hán
       INTENS
       'S/he is a man of great abilities.'
       (Lit. 'S/he is a man of very strong skills/knowledges.')

Whenever the final element at the right-edge of an NP is a simple noun, the genitive case marker attaches to this simple noun—expressing the R, as in (5.37 repeated from §3.2.1.3.8).

(5.37) nɔ̀ŋ á   [[hír-á   lɔ́m-à   gùrgùr-tín-á]_NP
       3SG COP.3.IMPERV man-RSTR have-NOMZ skilled.STV-NOMZ-RSTR
       álí-ɲ]_NP
       voice/talk-GEN
       'S/he is an able speaker.'
       (Lit. 'S/he is a man having knowledge of speaking.)'

The possessive meanings to be conveyed by these noun modification constructions cover ownership (5.30), association (5.31;5.35), orientation/location (5.32–5.34), and attributes of a person (5.36–5.37).

5.7 Predicative Possessive Construction

A possessive relationship can be established within a clause, in the form of predicative possession (Aikhenvald 2013: 27). Predicative possessive construction in Mursi can be expressed by the verb lɔ̀m 'have/hold/grab' (§ 5.7.1), existential verb íh 'exist' (§ 5.7.2), and an invariable copula verb á ⟨COP.3.IMPERV⟩ (for both singular/plural) (§ 5.7.3).

5.7.1 With the Verb lɔ̀m 'Have'

The verb lɔ̀m 'have' is a transitive verb, has no perfective form and can never be used in command and passive constructions. A possessive construction produced with the help of this verb may be translated as in English—R$_A$ have/hold/grasp D$_O$ (cf. Dixon 2010: 299) (where subject of the transitive verb lɔ̀m (A) is the same as the possessor (R); and the object (O) is the same as the possessed (D)). The possessed noun can be any simple or derived noun or any possessable object in O slot.

(5.38) [abɛbɛ]$_{R:A}$ lɔ̀m-Ø [gòdín=gè sízzì]$_{D:O}$
Abebe has-3SG.SU.IMPERV brother=PERT.PL.3.PSR three
'Abebe has three brothers.'

(5.39) [ŋà=múwáí=tùnù]$_{R:A/NP}$ lɔ̀m-Ø [dórí čàll-ì
DEM=woman.SG=FAR has-3SG.SU.IMPERV house good.STV-ADJ
háŋ]$_{D:O/NP}$
INTENS
'That woman has a nice house.'

(5.40) [érmì ʤààrè]$_{R:A/NP}$ lɔ̀-Ø [ŋɔ̀dɔ̀rì]$_{D:O}$
child leg has-3SG.SU.IMPERV sore
'The child's leg has a sore.'

When the verb lɔ̀m is nominalized, it can occur in a relative clause that modifies a head noun by gap strategy.

(5.41) zùwó-á [Ø lɔ̀m-è-á bì-ò]$_{RC}$
people-RSTR [Ø have-3PL.SU.IMPERV-NOMZ cow-PL]
hòd-á
come.PERV.PL-3PL.SU.PERV
'Those people who have cows came!'
(Lit. 'people having cows')

This verb may still function as an intransitive verb 'exist' (as in (5.42–5.44)) or it may co-occur with the existential verb itself in a single predicative possessive construction (as in (5.42)).

(5.42) sárí tó-jé lɔ̀m-ò [mèdèrní mèrì háŋ]
fence in-OBL have-3.IRR sheep.PL INTENS many
'There are many sheep in the enclosure.'
(Lit. 'Inside the enclosure very many sheep exist.')

(5.43) dórí-á [Ø tó-jé lɔ̀m-à tɔ̀ŋɔ̀]_RC
house-RSTR [Ø in-OBL have-3SG.SU.PERV goat]
'There is a goat in the house.'
(Lit. 'The house that has a goat in it.')

(5.44) hír-á [Ø lɔ̀m-á čàll-in]_RC lɔ̀m-Ø
man-RSTR [Ø has-3SG.SU.PERV good.STV-N.S] have-3SG.SU.IMPERV
[kòmòr-á dónén-á]_NP sóŋ
God-RSTR one/alone-RSTR only
'There is none good but one, that is God.'
(Lit. 'A person who has good, there exists God alone only.')

(5.45) ɲàɲùrè]_R:A/NP [lɔ̀m-Ø [ɲàj]_D:O él
cat have-3SG.SU.IMPERV ear.PL exist.3PL.SU.IMPERV
dìb
straight
'A cat has pointed ears.'
(Lit. 'A cat has ears exist straight.')

In (5.44), the adjective čàllì 'good' (whose origin is a stative verb) is nominalized by nouns of state marker suffix -in; thus it is a noun.

5.7.2   *With the Existential Verb* ih *'Exist/Present'*

The verb of existence has four different roots, each of which comes carrying a grammatical information such as person and aspect. What makes the existential verb different from the verb 'have' is that the verb 'exist' is an intransitive verb used with D in S function, and then the R becomes a peripheral NP often marked by the preposition/comitative particle kó 'with' or oblique case marker -ɔ/-je attached to D. A positive existential possessive predication will have the following schema: D exists with R or D exists for R, as in (5.46–5.49).

(5.46) [dórí]_D í-∅ gòr-ò sìò sìtèn
house exist.IMPERV-3SG.SU.IMPERV path-OBL hand.sg right
'His house is on the right.'

(5.47) [ŋà=àhà=á]_D él úkúrá-jè
DEM=thing.PL=NEAR exist.3SG.SU.IMPERV pocket-OBL
áín-áɲ-ò
give.PERV.SG-1SG.OBJ-VFS
'Give (sg.) me what is in your pocket.'

(5.48) kó ŋà=ʃɔwá=á wòj-è ŋɔ́jɔ́
PNC DEM=bird.PL=NEAR move/walk-3PL.SU.IMPERV wind
tò-jè=ŋà góto íʃé
in-OBL=DEF order exist.3.SU
'... and the birds of the air have nests.'
(Lit. '... and the birds moving in the air there are nests.')

(5.49) àɲè tílá k-ám-í nà ìggè
1SG food 1SU-eat.IMPERV-1SG.SU.IMPERV CCN 2PL
Ímágo íʃé
don't.know.2PL.SU.IMPERV exist.3.SU
'I have food to eat that you (pl.) do not know.'

Note that the existential verb in Mursi has also some irregular variants such *iʃe* (uninflected form) (as in (5.48–5.49)) or (as in (5.50)). The existential possessive predication construction can also be shown by a schema where the R precedes the D.

(5.50) [nɔ̀ŋ]_R [ŋɔ̀nè]_D íhé
3SG sister.PERT.SG.3.PSR exist.IMPERV.SG
'He has a sister'
(Lit. 'he-his sister there is.')

These existential possessive predication constructions shown above can be expressed by the negative counterpart *núŋè* 'there is not; not present/exist'. The negative existential possessive construction is used to express the absence of the D. In Mursi, all negated verbs including the negative existential verb always occur at clause-final positions. This generates another existential predicative possessive schema: R-D NEGATIVE.EXISTANCIAL. Some examples are provided as follows:

(5.51) [ànè]ᴿ [làsàj]_D níŋè-n-àɲ-ó
　　　 1SG　　bread　 not.present/exist-SG-1SG.OBJ-VFS
　　　 'I don't have bread.'
　　　 (Lit. 'I don't have bread to me.')

(5.52) [ànè]ᴿ [làsàj]_D níŋè
　　　 1SG　　bread　 not.present/exist.3.SU
　　　 'I don't have bread.'

(5.53) nà　　　dóóléj jàg-á　　　　　　　nà　　sé-á　　　　　　　ké
　　　 CCN:NARR girl.SG answer-3SG.SU.PERV CCN say-3SG.SU.PERV QUOT
　　　 "[ànè]ᴿ [hírí]_D níŋ-n-áɲ-ò"
　　　 1SG　 man　 not.present/exist-SG-1SG.OBJ-VFS
　　　 'The woman answered and said, "I have no husband".'

5.7.3　Using a Copula Verb

Possessive relationships can be expressed with a copular construction (Dixon 2010: 302; Aikhenvald 2013: 29). The copula verb in Mursi inflects for person and number, and alters its root form for aspect. However, a possessive relationship through a copula construction can only be shown by one specific copula verb form, i.e. the third person imperfective form *á* ⟨COP.3SG/PL.IMPERV⟩. Accordingly, a possessive relationship construction using this copula verb may yield the schema: D (copula subject) COPULA VERB R (copula complement).

(5.54) D copula R
　　　 a. [ín-á　　　　　 gólóɲ-n-á]_D:CS　　　 á　　　　　　　 [ŋàrúgó]_R:CC
　　　　　 3SG.PN.SP-RSTR red.STV-SG-RSTR COP.3.IMPERV Ngarugo
　　　　　 'The red one is Ngarugo's.'

　　　 b. [ín-á　　　　　 gólóɲ-á]_D:CS　　　 án-á　　　　　　　 [ŋàtèrì]_R:CC
　　　　　 3SG.PN.SP-RSTR red.STV-RSTR COP.IMPERV-ANA Ngateri
　　　　　 'The red one is Ngateri's.'

As we can see from the examples illustrated in (5.54a–b), the copular clauses utilize a noun modification construction-based NP as their D (CS) whose real D is in fact the specific pronoun *in*. Note that these two copular constructions referring to a possessive relationship differ from other types which may look alike. For example, copular constructions whose Rs (CCs) are full-fledged possessive constructions on their own—can contain pertensive form (5.55a) or pertensive plus genitive form (5.55b).

(5.55) a. [ŋàìnà]_{D:CS}   á   [ŋɔ̀nà]_{D.R:CC}
       DEM=3SG.PN.SP=NEAR COP.3.IMPERV sister.PERT.SG.1.PSR
       'This is my sister.'

   b. [nɔ̀ŋ]_{D:CS} án-á   [ŋɔ̀nà-j]_{D.R:CC}
      3SG   COP.IMPERV-ANA sister.PERT.SG.1.PSR-GEN
      'It is my sister's.'

However, if the R (CC) is a noun modification construction (simple NP), the possessive relationship is that of the copular construction-driven one, as in (5.56).

(5.56) [nɔ̀ŋ]_{D:CS} án-á   [hír-á   óól-nèn-á]_{R:CC}
       3SG   COP.IMPERV-ANA man-RSTR beg-NOMZ-RSTR
       'It is the beggar's.'

One instance has been found in my corpus where D (CS) functions as a topic (5.57). The fact that D (CC) is a possessive pronoun which must be linked to D.

(5.57) [[sátíní]_D [nɔ̀ŋ]_D]_{CS} á   [n=ànù]_{R:CC}
       box   3SG   COP.3.IMPERV SG.PSD=1SG.PSR
       'The box is mine.'
       (Lit. 'the box—it is mine')

5.8 Summary

Table 5.3 below is a summary of the possessive construction types, and highlights the morphological, syntactic and semantic nature of the possessive relationships of the NP-internal-driven possessive constructions.

TABLE 5.3 NP-internal possessive construction

Possessive construction type		The morphosyntactic and semantic nature of the possessive relationship					
		The nature of D	The nature of R	Marking on D	Marking on R	Semantics	Alienably/ inalienably possessed
Juxtaposed (R-D)		animates, body parts, objects, name	human, animates, plants, objects	NONE	NONE	ownership whole-part association	both ??
Possessum-possessor (D-R)	A TYPE	human, animates, any simple noun	human, animates, kinship, any simple noun	-a	genitive -n [-ųn]/[-uŋ], ∅ genitive+oblique -on	kinship, ownership association orientation/location source or material	alienably possessed
	B TYPE	human, animates, body part, any simple noun	proper names	-a	genitive -i [-j], ∅	ownership	alienably possessed
Possessum-possessor (D-R)		any noun	possessive pronouns	-a	NONE	kinship, ownership whole-part, attribute association	alienably possessed
Pertensive (D=PERT.R)	A TYPE	close kinship nouns (8), rɛ 'body (of human)'	pertensive markers referring human possessors	pertensive enclitics	none or rarely a plural marker - čo following the pertensive	kinship ownership	inalienably possessed

POSSESSION

TABLE 5.3 NP-internal possessive construction (*cont.*)

Possessive construction type		The nature of D	The nature of R	Marking on D	Marking on R	Semantics	Alienably/inalienably possessed
	B TYPE	close kinship nouns (8), *rɛ* 'body (of human)'	possessive pronouns (optional)	pertensive enclitics	none or rarely a plural marker - *čo* following the pertensive	kinship ownership	inalienably possessed[a]
Noun Modification Constructions	(D- (R₁) (R₂) R)	human, animates, body part, kinship, simple nouns	human, animates, any simple noun, possessive pronoun	-*a* (on D and on intermediate Rs)	on the last R: genitive-*ɲ* [-ũɲ]/[-uɲ], Ø genitive+oblique -*oɲ*, oblique -*o*	ownership association orientation/location attribute	alienably possessed
	(R- (D₁) (D₂) D)	human, simple nouns	human, animates,	-*a* (on all Ds)	-*a*	ownership association orientation/location attribute	

The morphosyntactic and semantic nature of the possessive relationship

a Possessive pronouns are entirely optional Rs for pertensive B type possessive constructions. Following the pertensive structures, the existence of possessive pronouns (as optional Rs) does not mean the Ds are 'inalienable possessed'.

CHAPTER 6

Number

6.1 Introduction

Like many other Nilo-Saharan languages, Mursi has a complex number marking system. Mursi nouns can be divided into four sets based on how they mark number: 'replacive', 'marked plural', 'singulative' and 'suppletive'. However, with respect to overtly marking of number on nouns, a 'tripartite' number system could be a convenient label which best specifies grammatical number of referents. The overt tripartite number coding system on nouns includes: replacive marking (both singular and plural are morphologically marked), plural (plural marked, singular unmarked) and singulative (singular marked, plural unmarked). Including morphemes and allomorphs, about 70 different portmanteau suffixes have been discovered within the tripartite system. The suppletive system of coding of number has many unpredictable morphological manifestations and forms. Therefore, it stands apart from the three number codings that constituted the tripartite system.

These four number marking systems can only be used to specify the grammatical number of referents or nominals. In other words, outside the noun class, they can never be used to specify number of other word classes. Rarely do a few derived adjectives take a specific type of plural marker suffix like nouns.

From a point of view of meaning, all functions behave in the same way, that is, denote references number. The meaning of number, as Aikhenvald (2015: 111) wrote, 'distinguishes reference to one individual from reference to more than one'. Accordingly, Mursi number marking suffixes distinguish two type of nominal reference:

i. singular ~ referring to one
ii. plural ~ referring to more than one

The singular system itself is of two types: singular and singulative. Semantically, both are one and the same number marking systems referring to one referent. Broadly speaking, singulative and replacive are the two number marking systems in the language in which singular morphological number marking suffixes can overtly convey singular meanings. This semantic distinction can be extended to the plural system where one may find a distinction between plural and pluralia tantúm. The term 'pluralia tantúm' refers to those nouns that are inherently plural, and mainly those associated with mass nouns or liquids, as in (6.1a–d).

© FIREW GIRMA WORKU, 2021 | DOI:10.1163/9789004449916_007

NUMBER

TABLE 6.1 The meanings of number and markedness

Number marking system	Singular	Plural
replacive	marked	marked
marked plural	unmarked	marked
singulative	marked	unmarked
suppletive	unmarked	unmarked

(6.1) a. mɔ̀dà̰   'saliva'
       b. ɲáwà   'blood'
       c. mà   'water'
       d. sárá   'name'

The only difference between plural and pluralia tantúm is that nouns which inherently occur as the pluralia tantúm do not take any morphological number marking. Besides, they may easily be distinguished by showing complete number agreement with their possessive pronouns modifiers within NPs. This is evident in a possessive relationship construction as shown in the example below.

(6.2) a. [sárá-à   g=àɲù]$_{NP}$
          name-RTSR PL.PSD=1SG.PSR
          'My name'
          (Lit. 'My name (pl.)')

       b. *[sárá-a   n=ànù]
          name-RSTR SG.PSD=1SG.PSR (ungrammatical)

Table 6.1 above is a summary showing meanings of number being referred to by the morphological number markings.

Not all, but oftentimes some nouns belonging to one specific number marking system tend to show some degree of semantic similarities. For example, a tripartite system alone has more than fifty well established and elaborated sets in which individual members/nouns are being coded by a variety of number marking suffixes. From a corpus size of approximately 600 nouns, 20 suffixes of replacive system that fall in 9 categories, 17 suffixes with marked plural systems that form 11 categories, and one singulative suffix have been identified. For collective/mass nouns, singulative is the single most common and frequent

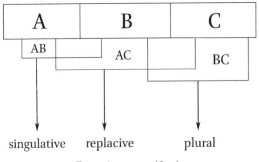

DIAGRAM 6.1   Tripartite system (6.3a)

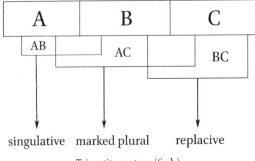

DIAGRAM 6.2   Tripartite system (6.3b)

strategy. For some, if not noun classes, at least noun categories can be established based on their semantic groupings and phonological endings. Establishing semantic/phonological-based noun categories is not always easy and plain. There are nouns which do not simply fall into one specific noun category. This is due to the fact that there are a few nouns that belong to more than one number marking systems. Therefore I have represented the tripartite system by three categorical symbols A, B and C (where A stands for singular, B for singulative and C for plural).

(6.3)   Singular (A)   Singulative (B)   Plural (C)   Meaning
   a. *kídó*   *kídòi* (one river)   *kídén*   'river'
   b. *zèl*   *zèllí* (one short stick) *zèllíɲá*   'short stick'

Here, an important point to be taken into consideration is that we must check number of a referent not only in relation to one of its counterparts but also in relation to other possible counterparts. For example, in (6.3a), A in relation to B forms the singulative system. Similarly, A↔C and B↔C can form replacive and plural making systems respectively. In (6.3b), as it is also shown in Diagram 6.2

below, A↔B forms the singulative system, A↔C forms the marked plural system, and B↔C forms the replacive system.

In fact, there may be a few semantic motivations for some nouns having identical forms and meanings but taking different number marking systems. The semantic motivation is one which defines the internal properties of members of a given category (see §6.3). For instance, the singulative forms *kídòi* 'river' and *zèllí* 'short stick' can only be used within an NP and if their modifier is the number word *dɔ́nɛ́j* 'one'. In this case, the suffix *-i* can be used as a singulative marker as well as a non-restrictive marker (6.4a–b)

(6.4)   a.   [*kídò-i*   *dɔ́nɛ́j*]$_{NP}$
           river-NRSTR one
           'One river'

       b.   [*zèll-í*   *dɔ́nɛ́j*]$_{NP}$
           short.stick-NRSTR one
           'One short stick'

In certain discourse contexts, speakers were being observed using these two nouns without mentioning the modifier *dɔ́nɛ́j*. Two more nouns have been found in my corpus which belong to more than one number marking systems: one replacive—*ʃɔgàj* (singular)/*ʃɔgàčín* (plural) ~ *ʃɔgàɲà* (plural) 'kind of stone being used for sharpening' and the other marked plural—*érésí* (singular)/*érésíó* (marked plural) ~ *érésíɲá* (marked plural) 'silver bracelet'.

6.2   The Realization of Number

In Mursi, number reference can be coded by three major ways: morphological process (affixation), lexical number words and quantifiers. Number can also be indicated on nouns and on a few verbs by internal change (partially suppletive system). Mursi has both overt and covert grammatical number marking systems. Grammatical number can be shown on nouns, pronouns, derived adjectives, and verbs overtly. Number can be shown on verbs covertly where the marking of number of the core arguments (S/A and O) co-occur with the sets of suppletive forms of existential and motion verbs. Tone is one way which can rarely be used to indicate grammatical number on nouns. See Table 6.2 for the realization of number system and where number is shown.

TABLE 6.2 The realization of number

Realization	Morphological system	Where number is marked/shown	Remark
Suffixation	portmanteau morphemes/suffixes	nouns	singulative, marked plural and replacive (see § 6.3)
Suppletion	none	nouns and verbs	it could be complete/partial (see § 6.4)
Tone	tone	nouns and verbs	(see § 6.5)
n/g alternation	clitics and bound form	Nominals	(see § 6.6)
Clitization	n=/g=; =n/=g	nouns, possessive pronouns	(see § 6.6.1)
Fused/bound form	n/g	pronouns (personal, demonstrative, interrogative and relative, indefinite)	(see § 6.6.2)
The bound number/aspect marking forms	-t/-ɗ	verbs	number and/or aspect (see § 6.7, p. 281)
Additional suffixes	-V, -i, -o, -a [-ta, -na]	verbs and adjectives	(see § 6.8)
Number-determined suppletive forms	none	verbs	(see § 6.9)
Reduplication	–	adjectives and number words	(see § 6.10)
Number words	number word	within NPs or CC	(see § 6.11)

6.3 Suffixation

Suffixation is the most productive number-marking morphological process in which the grammatical number of many Mursi nouns can be shown. All the three number marking systems that form the 'tripartite' utilize suffixation. For collective/mass nouns, singulative (unmarked plural) is a common strategy.

A number of explanations can be adopted for the variety of number marking possibilities in Mursi. Nevertheless, the notion of prototype is the best explanation that I found at this stage to understand why speakers prefer one specific number marker for a particular category. A category could have a 'prototype word' (always a noun) containing the semantics or the concept that function as a center to other members in the category. A prototypical noun, therefore, can be regarded as one holding a general meaning that could be 'central' or 'ideal' to members within a category. Each category usually has its own unique prototype that is central to all its members.

Arensen (1998:186) has adopted a similar approach called 'prototype theory' to sort out plural markers of Murle into structured categories. He lived among the cattle-raising Murle people (a Nilotic ethnic group) of the Sudan-side in the southeastern Sudan. Their language is part of the Surmic group of the Nilo-Saharan family. While he attempting to categorize Murle nouns, he realized that 'the prototype-approach' is the best approach to understand Murle pluralization. In his argument about a prototype approach, he wrote,

> There is also chaining within a category. One object is connected to another and that to another until the original connection may not be obvious ... an item belongs to a category not because it shares certain common features, but because there are connections to the central prototype.
>
> pp. 186

It is necessary to take into account that each category differs in terms of semantics as well as membership distribution. For instance, one category may contain more animate referents than others, while another category may be composed of nouns associated only with farming or body parts. In addition, there are number marking suffixes of one specific category that can also provide the same function to two or more categories. Therefore, for some nouns within a tripartite system, a number of categories have been established based on a prototype-based categorization approach.

6.3.1 *Replacive*

Replacive number marking system differs from the other two systems (marked plural and singulative) in that it is rich, complex and has many unpredictable number marking suffix shapes. It consists about 20 different number marking portmanteau suffixes. The distribution and phonetic variation of some suffixes is phonologically conditioned. For example, there may be insertion of an epenthetic vowel [-i] following a consonant-final noun; or there may be a vowel height harmony depending on the phonetic nature of the vowel in the root.

A.   CATEGORY I: -í [-j] (singular) versus {-a/-ɛ/-o [-ɔ]/-ɲá [-íɲá]} (plural)
CATEGORY I is established on the basis of nouns that take the singular marker suffix -i (following consonant-final nouns; [-j] following vowel-final nouns) on one hand and nouns that take all the plural marker suffixes on the other hand.

(6.5)   Singular   Plural
       a. lús-ì   lús-à   'boy'
       b. bár-í   bár-á   'man, senior, age set (group)'
       c. àh-ì   àh-à   'thing, object'
       d. čérédén-ì   čérédén-à   'porcupine'
       e. gúsús-ì   gúsús-à   'big back ant'
       f. kútúsén-ì   kútúsén-à   'kidney'
       g. ɲàb-ì   ɲàw-à   'ear'
       h. lètán-ì   lètán-à   'earlobe'

(6.6)   Singular   Plural
       a. ʤààr-ì   ʤààr-ɛ̀   'leg'
       b. kààr-ì   kààr-ɛ̀   'eye'

Both nouns shown in example (6.6) have undergone an intervocalic consonant deletion [g] that, however, some other Surmic group languages retained.

(6.7)   Singular   Plural
       a. èrí   èr-o   'leather (animal skin)'
       b. úlf-ì   úlf-ó   'sorghum stalk'
       c. tèr-ì   tèr-ó   'young man, age set (group)'
       d. bírín-í   bírín-ɔ́   'thorn'

(6.8)   Singular   Plural
       a. mɔ̀ʤɔ̀là-j   mɔ̀ʤɔ̀là-ɲá̀   'sandflea'
       b. gùnàtè-j   gùnàtè-ɲá̀   'thunder'

CATEGORY I consists of four sets of nouns that can be shown by one singular suffix and five plural suffixes. Many of these nouns are associated with men's age set, animal and plant covers. There is also an interesting semantic correlation between the singular forms and their counterparts—for example, some of them have to do with pain or objects which inflict pain. They may also refer to a part of a human body that is injured because of participating in various activities such as stick fighting. There is no doubt that at the time of land clearing, men's legs are a body part often exposed to an injury caused by a thorn or

NUMBER

sorghum stalks, or bitten by insects that cause pain. It can also be considered as a prototypical category for some human body part nouns (as in (6.5f–h; 6.6)).

B. CATEGORY II: {-i, -ɔ,[-o] -u, -a} (singular) versus -ɛna (plural)
Except for 'lung' and 'priest', this category is composed of nouns that are harmful and those with the ability to bite and cause pain. The closest category to the CATEGORY II is CATEGORY III.

(6.9)   Singular   Plural
    a. màrfàr-ì   màrfàr-èná   'termite'
    b. ŋɔ̀dɔ̀r-ì   ŋɔ̀dɔ̀r-èná   'sore'

(6.10)   Singular   Plural
    a. sùìr-ɔ́   sùìr-èná   'mule'
    b. gùfúr-ɔ́   gùfúr-èná   'hyena'
    c. ŋɔ̀r-ɔ́   ŋɔ̀r-èná   'elephant'

(6.11)   Singular   Plural
    a. hóh-ú   hòh-èná   'lung'
    b. kómór-ú   kómór-èná   'priest, leader'

C. CATEGORY III: {-a, -aj [-ai], -i, -o [-ɔ], -ɛ} (singular) versus -ɛn (plural)
This category is composed of two sets. The first set consists of member nouns that take the suffixes -a, -aj [-ai], and -i as singular marker (6.12–6.14). Members of this set are associated with habitation, things that are basic for dwelling/habitation and some labor-based domains of men and women. The word 'dwelling pole' symbolizes family under one roof or one center point for family gathering; the roof needs a structure that supports it, i.e. the dwelling pole. Food, water and house are the basics for life. Cattle are the most valuable assets to the Mursi—both economically as well as culturally. Labor division may apply—preparation of food, fetching water from waterhole/river, carrying children at home are done by women. Men usually help with some heavy works such as protecting sorghum in the field and herding cattle. The Mursi life usually develops around the social and cultural values that originate as a result of the activities related to members of this set.

(6.12)   Singular   Plural
    a. tíl-á   tìl-én   'food'
    b. dɔ́ŋ-à   dɔ́ŋ-èn   'dwelling pole'
    c. él-à   él-én   'waterhole' ~ [-én]

	d. *múd-à*	*mùd-ɛ́n*	'big metal needle'
	e. *àčùg-à*	*àčùg-ɛ̀ná*	'meat'
	f. *ɓɔ́č-à*	*ɓɔ́č-ɛn*	'thin (N./ADJ.)'
	g. *gás-à*	*gás-ɛn*	'work party'
(6.13)	Singular	Plural	
	a. *búŋ-áj[i]*	*bùŋ-ɛ́n*	'castrated bull/ox'
	b. *mɔ́d-àj*	*mɔ̀d-ɛ́n*	'mouse'
	c. *àms-àj*	*àms-ɛ́n*	'bird-scaring platform'

(6.14)	Singular	Plural	
	a. *dór-í*	*dòr-ɛ̀n*	'house'
	b. *ɓír-ɛ́*	*ɓírɛ́-n*	'walking stick; smoke'
	c. *túr-ɛ́*	*túrɛ́-n*	'gun'

As can be shown below in (6.14), the suffix *-ɛn* will be attached to nouns containing consonant-final roots whereas the suffix *-n* may be attached to nouns having *-e* [-ɛ] final roots/singular forms.

The second set has members that take the singular suffix *-o* [-ɔ] and the plural counterpart *-ɛn*. As can be shown in the examples given below, this set doesn't contain members which have a consistent semantic content and correspondence with one another. But members correspond to mainly two nominal types: animal and natural beings.

(6.15)	Singular	Plural	
	a. *árr-ó*	*árr-ɛ̀n*	'hippopotamus'
	b. *àbb-ò*	*àbb-ɛ̀n*	'antelope'
	c. *kíd-ó*	*kìd-ɛ́n*	'river'
	d. *íd-ó*	*íd-ɛ́n*	'mist' ~ [-én]
	e. *kítt-ɔ́*	*kítt-ɛ̀n*	'scorpion' ~ [-ɔ́]

| (6.16) | Singular | Plural | |
| | *mèdèr-ɛ̀* | *mèdèr-ní* | 'sheep' ~ [-ní] |

In terms of number marking suffix form, the noun *mèdèrɛ̀* stands apart from the rest of the members in (6.16). Yet this is the closest set for it to be a member of.

D. CATEGORY IV: {*-oj*, [-oi], *-ui*, *-u*, *-ej*, *i*, *-o*} (singular) versus {*-ai*, *-a*, *-o*, *-ɔ*} (plural) Despite a number of different number marking portmanteau suffixes, they do not fetch a single semantic based-set for their members.

Nevertheless, on the basis of the natural class of some members of this category, I have established three possible semantic sets. Set A—the two birds mentioned in (6.17c) and (6.20a) share one natural shape with the object mentioned in (6.19b), i.e. both birds have a sickle-shaped beak that resembles the shape of a 'bill-hook'. There is one more possibility to make a semantic extension further than this; the noun 'bone' in (6.21a) can be associated with the mouth of the two birds (via 'strength' or 'the items make-up'). Set B may be regarded as a set which consist of 'spider web', 'white mushroom', 'pumpkin', 'intestine', and 'snake' in that each is linked to one another via a 'circular shape'. Furthermore, camels' fatty deposit called the 'hump' has this circular shape thus may be included to this set.

(6.17)   Singular   Plural
- a. *máɗ-ój*   *máɗ-íá*   'spider web'
- b. *gàlif-òj*   *gàlif-á*   'camel'
- c. *kílíč-ói*   *kílíč-á*   'black kite'
- d. *ɓùkk-òi*   *ɓòkk-á*   'white mushroom'
- e. *gúŋkàč-ùì*   *gúŋkàč-á*   'pumpkin' ~ [-ui]
- f. *čɔ̀ll-òj*   *čɔ̀ll-á*   'intestine'

(6.18)   Singular   Plural
         kòn-ù   *kòn-á*   'snake'

(6.19)   Singular   Plural
- a. *gàrč-ù*   *gàrč-ó*   'basket'
- b. *wèl-ù*   *wèl-ɔ́*   'bill-hook'
- c. *kɔ̀l-ù*   *kɔ̀l-ó*   'charcoal'
- d. *fàl-ù*   *fàl-ó*   'soft porridge'

(6.20)   Singular   Plural
- a. *kòɗ-èj*   *kòɗ-ó*   'buzzard'
- b. *dúrúm-èj*   *dúrúm-ó*   'tree stump'
- c. *gíŋ-ɛ̀*   *gíŋ-ó*   'grave'

(6.21)   Singular   Plural
- a. *gìg-èj*   *gìg-à*   'bone'
- b. *dòl-è*   *dòl-jà*   'small cooking pot'

Set C is another way of associating a few members of this category that are related to cooking utensils such as 'small cooking pot' and 'basket' ('flour container') that have to do with the preparation of 'porridge'. This may also include anything having to do with the 'means of preparation' itself such as 'tree stump' and 'charcoal'. An exceptional example though is the following, which semantically fits in this category and resembles it (6.17c) in terms of the singular number marking suffix it takes.

(6.22)   dȕŋ-wì   dòŋ-á   'vulture'

The suffix /-wi/ could be a phonetically motivated one and it can be interpreted as [-ui] ~ [-i].

E.   CATEGORY V: -j [-i] (singular) versus -čín (plural)
Despite also having its members belonging to the marked singular system, semantically, this category is identical to that of CATEGORY IV of the marked plural system. Many of the members (from both 'replacive' and 'marked plural' systems) are associated with tools commonly used in cultivation and hunting. Generally, its members are often associated with hunting materials and the animals being hunted (see CATEGORY VIII § 6.3.2).

(6.23)   Singular   Plural
   a. ɲɔ̀mà-j   ɲɔ̀mà-čín   'razor'
   b. čòbà-i   čòbà-čín   'pig'
   c. dór-í   dór-čín   'nest'

F.   CATEGORY VI: {-tej [-tei], -toj [-toi], -j [-i], -te} (singular) versus -čá (plural)
This category contains a list of wild animals. None of these animals are considered domestic animals by the Mursi. The Mursi do not even clearly distinguish between donkey and mule (rarely between mule and horse). For example, the same term *hárté* may be used to refer to 'donkey' and 'horse'. Sometimes they use a different term for 'mule', i.e. *sùrɔ̀*.[1]

(6.24)   Singular   Plural
   a. dòlè-tèj   dòlè-čá   'tortoise'
   b. gárá-tèj   gárá-čá   'monkey'

---

[1] 'Mule, Donkey, and Horse' are the three most common domestic animals in many societies in Ethiopia, but they are not be domesticated by the Mursi society. Thus, these animals may have been brought to the Mursi area by the highlanders (usually the Amhara).

(6.25) Singular   Plural
        mùɲá-tòj   mùɲá-čá   'Genet'

(6.26) Singular   Plural
        ɓólóŋó-ì   ɓólóŋó-čá 'corn cob'

(6.27) Singular   Plural
        a. átálá-t(t)é átálá-čá 'guinea fowl'
        b. hár-té   hár-čá   'mule'

Some of these animals are in fact crop ('corn cob') damaging ones.

G. CATEGORY VII: {-a, -ɔ[-o]} (singular) versus -i (plural)
With the exception of two ('tail', 'dog' and 'road'), this is a dedicated category VII for human body part nouns.

(6.28) Singular   Plural
        sáb-á   sáb-í   'head'

(6.29) Singular   Plural
        a. kèŋ-ɔ̀   kèŋ-ì   'belly'
        b. tùg-ɔ̀   tùg-ì   'mouth'
        c. mùm-ɔ̀   mùm-ì   'face, forehead'
        d. kàìj-ó   kàj-ì   'tongue'
        e. jìr-ɔ̀   jìr-ì   'biceps'
        f. kùr-ó   kùr-í   'tail'
        g. gɔ̀r-ɔ̀   gɔ̀r-í   'road, path'
        h. rɔ̀s-ɔ̀   rɔ̀s-í   'dog'

CATEGORY VII can be viewed from another angle in the way it incorporates most of these body part nouns, that is, as relator nouns. When they function as relator nouns, they can take oblique case and singular number marking suffixes (see §10.4).

H. CATEGORY VIII: -e [-ɛ] (singular) versus {-a, -i} (plural)
This category is composed of a small number of human as well as animal body part nouns that have unique or unusual appearances or characteristics. See the following examples.

(6.30)   Singular   Plural
   a. kàlúg-é   kàlúg-á   'arm pit'
   b. kùdùh-é   kùdùh-á   'navel'
   c. dɔ̀-ὲ   dɔ̀-ì   'hump'

CATEGORY IX is composed of nouns which take various portmanteau or miscellaneous suffixes: {-i, oi, -e, -ɔ, -nèj} (singular) versus {-na, -ɲá [-íɲá], -ia} (plural).

(6.31)   Singular   Plural
   a. tíhá-ì   tíhá-nà   'light rain shower'
   b. kéré-j   kéré-nà   'horn'
   c. ʃìr-òi   ʃìr-íɲá   'weed'
   d. hùl-è   hùl-íɲá   'flower'
   e. lɔ̀g-ɔ́   lɔ̀g-ìɲá   'issue'
   f. áfá-ì   áfá-fá   'grandchildren'
   g. ŋɔ̀r-nèj   ŋɔ̀r-íá   'butter'

An important point that we should take into consideration is that these nouns do not have one uniform number marker suffix that can put them together to form one semantic category. However, one may find a semantic association even between some of these nouns, if needed. For example, in some African societies, nouns such as 'weed' and 'flower' may form a semantic opposition, but they normally are categorized in the same taxonomy (see Dimmendaal 2000 and Storch 2005 for a similar approach and similar opaque system).

6.3.2   Marked Plural
A marked plural number marking system in general consist of phonologically unpredictable plural suffixes. Some plural marking suffixes of this system are also markers of plural referents in the replacive system.

A.   CATEGORY I: -ɲá [-íɲá]
The plural marker suffix -ɲá is the most productive number marking suffix that serves in two separate number marking systems. Members of this category lack a proper defining semantic feature or a prototypical manifestation. However, the fact is that the Mursi pay a great deal of emphasis to the social and cultural values related to their cattle. This may be expressed through social groupings at different age sets/levels and the social roles being carried out by the respective age levels such as preparing snares installed in holes, cattle closures and so on. For example, keeping cattle is the responsibility of young children in a family.

NUMBER 245

TABLE 6.3 The plural marker -ɲá on borrowed nouns

Amharic	Mursi	Plural	Meaning
nəgadde	ŋágádí	ɲagadi-ɲá	'merchant'
astämari	àstàmàrì	àstàmàrì-ɲà	'teacher'
ərsas	írsási	irsas-íɲá	'pencil'
dänb	dàmì	dàmí-ɲá	'custom/law'
barti	bátírí	bátírí-ɲá	'flash light, torch'
ʃi	ʃí	ʃí-ɲá	'thousand'
dəha	dáhá	dáhá-ɲá	'poor'
balagara	bàlàgáráj	bàlágárá-ɲá	'enemy'

There was a widespread practice of extracting the upper teeth from children whose upper milk teeth develop before their lower teeth. If the upper teeth sprout first, therefore it is regarded as 'bad luck' or 'evil'; and the children are believed to cause various problems and damages, bring evil spirits and misfortune in the society. It is common in the Hamar and Kara societies (close neighbours to the Mursi). Therefore, the upper teeth of the firstborn child is extracted—see example (6.32c) and (6.32g).

(6.32)   Singular   Plural
  a. kàbì   kàbì-ɲá   'clan'
  b. čár   čár-íɲá   'leopard'
  c. sìl   síl-íɲá   'a single gap in the upper teeth'
  d. tùì   tùì-ɲá   'cattle enclosure'
  e. tólóɓé   tólóɓé-ɲá   'lizard'
  f. bóʃú   bóʃú-ɲá   'youngest child'
  g. áú   áú-ɲá   'eldest, first-born child'
  h. lóg   lóg-íɲá   'hole'
  i. òlí   òlí-ɲá   'bull'

CATEGORY I is also a default category for Mursi borrowed nouns (from Amahric). Thus, borrowed nouns are being marked by the suffix /-ɲá/ in the same way as other nouns are. With the exception of a few, almost all Mursi borrowed nouns fall into this category. Table 6.3 presents the default plural number marker suffix -ɲá attached to some borrowed nouns.

Of course ʃi a number word that functions the same way as nouns when modified by number words. Like nouns, it takes a non-restrictive modification marker -*ti* when modified by the number word *dɔ́néj* 'one'. When it is modified by a number word higher than one, it takes the plural marker suffix -*ɲá*, as in (6.33).

(6.33) [*hírí dɔ́néj*]ₙₚ *áín-ɛ́*   *bíró* [*ʃĭ-ɲá*   *háánán*]ₙₚ
man one   give.PERV.SG-BEN.3 money thousand-PL five
kóná   *áín-ɛ́*   *bíró* [*ʃĭ-ɲá*   *ràmàn*]ₙₚ
another give.PERV.SG-BEN.3 money thousand-PL two
kóná   *áín-ɛ́*   *bíró* [*ʃĭ-tì*   *dɔ́néj*]ₙₚ *nà*
another give.PERV.SG-BEN.3 money thousand-NRSTR one   CCN
nɔ̀ŋ *ók-ú*   *bákónó*
3SG went.PERV-3SG.SBJ.PERV place.one:INDEF
'... to one man he gave five thousand, to another two thousand, and to another one thousand; and he went to another place.'

These borrowed nouns may be of a particular interest to future investigators because borrowed nouns in Mursi display a great deal of difference in regard to the morphology of loan words. There could be some unspecified motivations which need to be investigated as to why only this particular number marking suffix be used.

B. CATEGORY II: -*ja* [-ia]
This suffix also occurs with nouns from CATEGORY IV and CATEGORY IX within the replacive number marking system, i.e. *mád-ój* (sg.)/*mád-íá* (pl.) 'spider web' and *ŋɔr-nèj* (sg.)/*ŋɔr-ia* (pl.) 'butter'. This time, however, it occurs on nouns denoting dangerous wild animals that have strong teeth.

(6.34)   Singular   Plural
    a. *jói*   *jói-já*   'wild dog'
    b. *kíɲáŋ*   *kíɲáŋ-já*   'crocodile'

C. CATEGORY III: -*a* and -*o*
Nouns belonging to this category typically share a common feature—'shape'. Nouns that take the plural suffix /-a/ may refer to items with circular or curved forms. In addition, items belonging to this group may also refer to round objects worn by women such as women's adornments (6.35a–d).

(6.35)   Singular   Plural
    a. *mɔ̀r*   *mɔ̀r-à*   'calf'
    b. *bèr*   *bèr-á*   'spear'

	Singular	Plural	
c.	làlàŋ	làlàŋ-à	'bracelet'
d.	dùmàɲ	dùmàɲ-à	'earring'
e.	kédém	kédém-á	'calabash'
f.	bóhùn	bóhùn-à	'cliff'
g.	tírtír	tírtír-à	'fingernail'

Except for 'spear' and 'cliff', and 'fingernail', the rest of the nouns can qualify for the notion of central or prototypical membership of this group. These three noun exceptions may be associated with objects that have 'sharp' or 'pointy' parts, thus they can be associated with the next set of nouns (-o taking nouns). One may also associate 'spear' with 'calabash' because Mursi men usually carry a water or milk container made from a calabash when going on a hunt.

Nouns which take the plural suffix /-o/ are associated with 'long or sharp' objects (6.36a–e) and with animals that have long necks and legs (6.37a–c). A few body part nouns, particularly those that carry the prototypical property are also members of this category (6.38a–c).

(6.36) Object

	Singular	Plural	
a.	érésí	érésí-o	'silver bracelet'
b.	kállí	kállí-o	'little stick, switch'
c.	gúsí	gúsí-ó	'gourd'
d. ʃèbèl	ʃèbèl-ò	'sheath'
e.	túrúŋ	túrúŋ-ó	'bow and arrow'

(6.37) Animals

	Singular	Plural	
a.	kírín	kírín-ó	'giraffe'
b.	dɔ̀wùn	dɔ̀wùn-ó	'zebra'
c. ʃígín	ʃígín-ó	'hartebeest'
d.	bì	bì-ò	'cow'

(6.38) Body parts

	Singular	Plural	
a.	màdì	màdì-ó	'breast'[2]
b.	gàwùl	gàwùl-ó	'shoulder; shoulder blade'
c.	tórí	tórí-ó	'penis'
d.	sái	sái-ò	'animal skin (women's clothing)'

---

2 Free variation: màddì/màddió versu wàdì/wàdìó 'breast'.

D. CATEGORY IV: -*i* [-j]

From a morphological form point of view, CATEGORY IV can be a counterpart of the singulative number marking system in which many Mursi collective nouns will be marked with the singulative suffix -*i* [-j]. This category may include objects that are linked to human body part nouns through a metaphoric transfer or by semantic extension. For example, the term *tùgɔ̀* 'mouth' in (6.39e) is extended to a part of a house *tútúg* 'door', which is a clear instance of semantic extension.

(6.39)   Singular   Plural
   a. *lùdùm*   *lùdùm-ì*   'chest'
   b. *gìròŋ*   *gìróŋ-í*   'nose'
   c. *čàmùn*   *čàmun-í*   'chin'
   d. *kɔ́rɔ́ŋ*   *kɔ́rɔ́ŋ-í*   'throat'
   e. *tútúg*   *tùtùg-ì*   'door'

E. CATEGORY V: {-*na* [-ɛna, -ena, -jena],[3] -*n* [-ɛn] and -*ɛa* [-ea]}

Plural marking suffix forms of this category are less predictable, yet seem to be ruled by phonological motivations: -*na* following vowel-final CV shape nouns, -*ɛna* [-ena] following consonant-final CVC shape nouns, -*jena* following vowel-final mono-or disyllabic nouns, and -*ɛa* [-ea] following consonant-final disyllabic nouns. CATEGORY V can be closely associated with CATEGORY II and III of the replacive number marking system.

(6.40)   Singular   Plural
   a. *bè*   *bè-ná*   'stone'
   b. *rɔ̀m*   *rɔ̀m-èná*   'ostrich'
   c. *mìs*   *mìs-èná*   'grazing land'
   d. *óhí*   *óh-⟨j⟩èná*   'riverside forest with no undergrowth'
   e. *hój*   *hóh-èná ⟨-jena⟩*   'warthog'

(6.41)   Singular   Plural
   a. *dékè*   *déké-n*   'leather dress'
   b. *túré*   *tùré-n*   'gun'
   c. *sú*   *sùs-èn*   'sun'

---

3 Rarely, some suffixes still show a remnants of an earlier stage of cross-height vowel harmony system.

(6.42) Singular Plural
  a. *lóʃán*   *lòʃàn-èá*   'slingshot'
  b. *báŋár*   *bàŋàr-èá*   'platform to dry grain'
  c. *kárám*   *kárám-èá*   'colobus monkey'
  d. *ʤóróg*   *ʤóróg-èà*   'oryx'
  e. *ŋàtùɲ*   *ŋàtùɲ-ɛa*   'lion'

The category contains a few animals that may cause harm to humans or have the ability to bite and cause pain. It also lists a few places where these respective animals usually live. The two places mentioned are places where the Mursi practice cattle herding and hoe-cultivation. The latter process takes place at the Omo and Mago rivers after the flood has receded and the banks (*ohijena*) have been cleared of vegetation. River-bank land is the area of the main crop cultivation of the Mursi. The Mursi herd their cattle in the wooded grasslands which rise towards the Omo-Mago watershed. They call the area used for this purpose *mìsèná* 'grazing lands'. CATEGORY V also include nouns referring to objects used by the Mursi to protect themselves from some dangerous animals as well as to prevent their crops from wild animals that can cause damage. There is a part that may refer to a series of crop cultivation steps which incorporates some processes starting from planting, protecting the crop from wild animals, drying the crop by exposing it to the sun, to beating the stalks with a stone to free the grain seeds, and so on.

F. CATEGORY VI: *-ɲógá*

CATEGORY VI is associated with local division of the population *búráɲógà* 'local groups', to have priests who attend to the well-being of the local groups and act as a means of communication between them and *tùmù* 'God' who live in *tùmùtùn* 'heaven'. The priest delivers news/issues to their God when the people are threatened by disasters such as flood, disease, and drought and so on.

(6.43) Singular   Plural
  a. *táán*   *tààn-ɲògá*   'flood'
  b. *mùttán*   *mùttán-ɲògá*   'disease'
  c. *tùmùtùn*   *tùmùtùn-ɲògá*   'heaven'
  d. *sààn*   *sààn-ɲògá*   'news'
  e. *búrán*   *búrá-ɲógà*   'local group'

G. CATEGORY VII: -čá

Even though the nouns which occur in this category are small in size, its members are directly associated with CATEGORY X of the replacive number marking system. Animals listed in (6.44a–b) are associated with those that damage the Mursi's crop.

(6.44)   Singular   Plural
       a.   sìrò   sìrò-čá   'eland, Nyala'
       b.   làràŋè   làràŋè-čá   'badger'
       c.   kòrmì   kòrmì-čá   'fish hook'

CATEGORY VII also aligns with CATEGORY VIII, but mainly by its members shown in (6.45c). Before ending this category it is necessary to mention an important secondary source of subsistence, namely fishing.

H. CATEGORY VIII: -čín

Membership of this category can be defined as a one-time full preparation for a series of agricultural activities within one season such as weeding, protection and harvesting. Therefore, nouns referring to tools, utilities and food that are commonly used for cultivation, hunting, cooking, shelter, sleeping and so on are included within this category.

(6.45)   Singular   Plural
       a.   gàhà   gàhà-čín   'shelter in cultivation area'
       b.   gò   gò-čín   'fire'
       c.   ŋò   ŋò-čín   'neck'
       d.   wàrà   wàrà-čín   'knife'
       e.   kòlá   kòlá-čín   'ram'
       f.   súrá   súrá-čín   'duiker'
       g.   lòjà   lòjà-čín   'jackal'
       h.   gàisà   gàisá-čín   'hoe'
       i.   bàŋkà   bàŋkà-čín   'machete, bush knife'
       j.   hádá́   hádá́-čín   'sleeping mat'

I. CATEGORY IX: -čo

This is the only category that contains nouns from one and the same 'natural', 'prototypical' class, i.e. close kinship nouns. The plural marker suffix -čo can be shown on close kinship nouns in two ways—either by attaching it directly to the noun roots (as in (6.46a–e)) or following the pertensive marker within NP-internal possessive constructions (as in (6.47)).

(6.46) Singular   Plural
   a. *kàkà*   *kàkà-čó*   'grandparent'
   b. *dàdá*   *dàdá-čó*   'father'
   c. *màmà*   *màmà-čó*   'mother'
   d. *kàbì*   *kàbì-čó*   'clan'
   e. *mèrè*   *mèrè-čó*   'daughter-in-law'

(6.47) [*gòdón=gà-čo*]
        brother=PERT.PL.1.PSR-PL
        'My brothers'

In NP-internal possessive constructions, it indicates number of the possessed kinship noun. The noun 'clan' *kàbì* appears distantly related to the rest of the members of the category, but in fact it is not. A 'clan' in Mursi is a congregation of people who are believed to be descended in the male line from different co-wives with the same man (Turton 1973: 111). In addition, Jørgensen (2011: 43) wrote, 'the Mursi, like many other societies where social organization is based more or less on kinship, have complex clan systems'. Therefore, clanship can be a prototype or central to this category. When the Mursi want to refer to any other clans other than their own, they use *kàbì-ɲá* 'clans'. This makes me wonder if the Mursi indeed have such distinct forms because these are typical forms/words being used for inclusion and exclusion of a certain group of people.

J.   CATEGORY X: *-hi, -hiɲa*

CATEGORY X has two members: one refers to a human 'body' and the other refers to a 'compound' (an area enclosed by a fence). The two are connected to one another by a semantic knowledge of body known as body schema, a dynamic online representation of the relative location of body parts in space (Majid & van Staden 2015: 572).

(6.48) Singular   Plural
   a. *rè*   *rè-hì*   'body'
   b. *dè*   *dè-híɲá*   'compound'

By the same analogy, body part nouns will be assigned secondary meanings on the basis of some other factors such as cultural and religious practices, for example, the Mursi do not have a word for 'map'. Instead they use an internal body part noun *čɔ̀llɔ̀j* 'intestine, stomach lining' to represent their understanding of the notion of map.

K.   CATEGORY XI: *-so* and *-sí*

This category contains three members that form their plural with the unproductive plural suffixes *-so* and *-sí*. Only two entries have been found with *-so* which are both animals associated with unique physical appearances or colour.

(6.49) Singular   Plural
  a. *nèbì*   *nèbì-só*   'buffalo'
  b. *hólí*   *hólí-só*   'waterbuck'
  c. *híní*   *híní-sí*   'heart'

An interesting point here is that the noun *nèbì* can take both plural suffixes—*nèbì-sì* 'buffalos'. According to my Mursi consultants, the only difference between the two is that one can use the form in (6.50a) if s/he is watching the animal itself in person. At this stage, I can't be sure whether this has to do with evidentiality or not.

6.3.3   *Singulative*

The singulative number marking system functions in reverse from the marked plural number marking system which attaches plural suffixes to nouns. However, the semantics which is usually portrayed by the singulative system is not only confined to referring to singular referents but also to notions such as singleton, individuative, mass opposition, collectiveness and so on. The singulative number marking mainly includes nouns that normally occur in large numbers, mass nouns, uncountable nouns, collective, and so on. Nouns in the singulative system cannot be inflected for plural form but with corresponding inflected singular forms marked by singulative markers *-i* usually following consonant-final nouns and [-j] following vowel-final nouns.

(6.50) Singular   Plural
  a. *bùrá-j*   *bùrá*   'egg, fruit'
  b. *dúgú-j*   *dugu*   'seed'
  c. *dùrùmò-j*   *dùrùmò*   'tree stump'
  d. *bàlóg-ì*   *bàlóg*   'leaf'
  e. *lìwá-j*   *lìwá*   'sorghum'
  f. *hɔ̀gò-ì*   *hɔgo*   'bean'
  g. *tèwá-ì*   *tèwá*   'wing'
  h. *ʃòà-ì*   *ʃòwá*   'bird'
  i. *kírɔ́ŋó-ì*   *kírɔ́ŋɔ́*   'fly'
  j. *sísá-j*   *sísá*   'bee'
  k. *úɲó-j*   *úɲó*   'flea'

l.	bílbíló-j	bílbíló	'moth'
m.	kùrúdó-j	kúrúdó	'worm'
n.	čɔ̀llɔ̀-j	čɔ̀llà	'intestine'
o.	múrdá-j	múrdá	'wrinkle'
p.	čòdúgá-j	čódúgá	'piece of dried meat'
q.	kísíŋó-j	kísíŋó	'cooking stone'

Among nouns which fit into the singulative category include plant parts/products (6.50a–d), grains consumed by humans (6.50e–f), animals and insects which live in large number (those that function as a unit collectively or in congregate) (6.50g–m) uncountable (6.50n–o), and a portion from an item that exists in a large quantity (or as generic ~ àčùgà 'meat') (6.50p). As in many societies, the Mursi also cook their food by using a widely known type of cooking method, that is, by arranging three stones to make a stand for a cooking pot. Unless these three stones exist as one collective entity, each stone as a single unit cannot function on its own. In his study of the social organization of the Mursi people, Turton (1973: 223) noted that the Mursi give special emphasis for the number 'three'. They have a saying about the completeness of the number 'three' in which 'cooking stone' is mentioned (p. 223), 'Indeed, the Mursi recognise that there is a certain completeness about the number three, which they express by means of the aphorism "it takes only three stones to boil a pot".'

(6.51)   Singular   Plural
    a. bènèn-ì   bènèn   'relative'
    b. lùkùrì   lùkùr   'age mate/friend'
    c. múgái   mùgà   'married woman'
    d. mùn-ì   mùn   'Mursi person'

One could connect the nouns in (6.51a–d) together through a more general understanding of parts the social system and societal structure of the Mursi people. The Mursi usually count members of their own clan as their relatives. They sometimes go beyond the ethnic boundary and may also accept new members into their local or ethnic membership. This happen oftentimes by marriage, and Mursi men are the ones who usually marry someone outside from their clan/ethnic group.

There are a few nouns which only occur in the singulative forms but lack plural forms, as in (6.52a–c).

(6.52) a. làɲɔ̀j   'grass'
        b. madoj   'spider'
        c. giwoj   'butterfly'

These nouns are typical members of singulatives and refer to plant and insect types that cannot be made up into numerous smaller distinct units. There are still a few generic nouns which could take the plural marker *-ɲa* to indicate variants or different species of the same seed, as in (6.53a–c).

(6.53) Singular Plural
    a. *lìwá* *lìwá-ɲá* 'sorghum'
    b. *dùgú* *dùgú-ɲá* 'seed'
    c. *kónò* *kónó-ɲá* 'corn'

6.4 Suppletion

The fourth number marking system is suppletion. Suppletions are of two types: partial (weak) and full. Both types, however, involve internal changes and do not pertain to any semantic relationship with one another. A list of nouns having partial and full forms are given below.

(6.54) Singular Plural
    a. *kìɔ̀* *kènɔ̀* 'tree'
    b. *sìɔ̀* *sènɔ̀* 'hand'
    c. *tɔ̀ŋɔ̀* *tènɔ̀* 'goat'
    d. *mèèn* *mìɔ̀* 'goat kid'
    e. *érmì* *éró* 'child'

In the partial suppletion, singular noun forms share at least their initial segment or a syllable with their plural counterparts. In contrast, in full suppletion, the change is a complete one, therefore there will be no form similarity between the singular and plural forms. There are a few nouns which undergo such suppletion as can be shown below.

(6.55) Singular Plural
    a. *hírí* *zùgò* 'man'
    b. *kèj* *gál* 'thing'

6.5 Number Marking by Tone

Cross-linguistically, Mursi can be categorized among a few languages in the world that utilize tone to make a distinction between singular and plural numbers. A few nouns utilize tone to indicate grammatical number, as shown in (6.56a–c). A low tone on nouns usually indicates singular number while a high tone bears plural number.

(6.56) Singular Plural
    a. *ɓùgùj* *ɓúgúj* 'back (of human)'
    b. *hùnnàj* *húnnáj* 'small stream of water'
    c. *gìrŋàj* *gìrŋáj* 'nose'
    d. *kìlòì* *kìlóí* 'heron'
    e. *čèrità* *čérítá* 'sore caused by wearing beads on the neck'

In addition, grammatical tone may also be used on verbs to distinguish between third person singular and third person plural subjects in the imperfective aspect, as shown in the following examples.

(6.57) a. *sé* ⟨say.3SG.AUX⟩ 'He says' H
      b. *sè* ⟨say.3SG.AUX⟩ 'They say' L

6.6 n/g Alternation

The *n/g* alternation (where **n* for singular and **g* for plural) is one of the most widely spread number marking alternations in the Nilo Saharan family. This singular/plural alternation is found in many languages of the family such as Tama, Kadu, Fur, and in several Kordofanian groups. It was Bryan and Tucker who discovered the existence of this number-based alternation (Tucker and Bryan 1966: 22 cited in Bender 2000: 58). With regard to this alternation, they noted that the singular/plural *n/k* and/or *t/k* patterns occur in various morphological categories as a substrata/areal feature.

In Mursi, the *n/g* singular/plural alternation occur in two forms: in clitics and in fused/bound forms. As clitic, they occur on possessive pronouns and on kinship nouns (pertensive forms) which both refer to one specific type of grammatical construction, i.e. possession (§ 6.6.1). As bound forms, they occur only in pronouns (personal, demonstrative, interrogative and relative, indefinite) (§ 6.6.2). The *n/g* alternations do not occur in simple nouns.

6.6.1 *The Clitics* =n= *(Singular) and* =g= *(Plural)*

The *n/g* alternation, as a clitic, can occur in proclitic (n=/g=) and in enclitic forms (=n/=g). The proclitic forms of the *n/g* alternation only occur in the possessive pronouns.

(6.58) Possessive pronoun forms
    a. *n=ànù*
       SG.PSD=1SG.PSR
       'Mine, (singular possessed)'

    b. *n=àj*
       SG.PSD=1PL.INC.PSR
       'Our (inc.), singular possessed'

    c. *g=àɲù*
       PL.PSD=1SG.PSR
       'Mine, (plural possessed)'

    d. *g=àj*
       PL.PSD=1PL.INC.PSR
       'Our (inc.), (plural possessed)'

Therefore, as is illustrated in the possessive pronouns, both *n* and *g* have proclitic form realizations, and primarily marks number of the possessed items (see also § 3.3.1.4; § 5.4). An interesting detail concerning the examples above is that the bound/fused singular form *n* in the singular possessive pronouns could also refer to the singular possessor.

As enclitics, the *n/g* function as pertensive markers on close kinship nouns. As in their proclitic function, they indicate only the number of these inalienably possessed nouns. See the following examples:

(6.59) a. [ʤɔ̀ɔ̀=*nɛ́*]
       mother=PERT.SG.3.PSR
       'His/her mother'

    b. [ʤɔ̀ɔ̀=*gɛ́*]
       mother=PERT.PL.3.PSR
       'His/her mothers'

    c. [gòdó=*ná*]
       brother=PERT.SG.1.PSR
       'My brother'

    d. [gòdón=*gá*]
       brother=PERT.PL.1.PSR
       'My brothers'

6.6.2 Fused/Bound n/g Singular/Plural Alternation

Whether it is a diachronic or synchronic, at various grammatical levels of individual languages, change could happen and change is an inevitability. Therefore, over time, languages may develop bound morphemes from other morphemes possibly from the unbound ones having the same function. At this stage, this is what I came across as the best explanation for the scenario that took place in the Mursi fused/bound *n/g* singular/plural forms. Both of the fused/bound n/g forms may display phonological-conditioned variants: *n ~ ɲ* and *g ~ k*.

In Mursi the *n/g*[4] alternation occurs only in pronominals thus it may be considered as a pronominal category. Some examples are given below for each pronominal types.

(6.60) *Personal pronouns*
   a. *àɲè* '1SG' vs. *àggè* '1PL (INC/EXC)'
   b. *nɔ̀ŋ* '3SG' vs. *jɔ̀k* '3PL'

In the intervocalic environment, the bound singular form *n* can be realized by a palatal variant [ɲ]. Except in the 3rd person pronouns which could display minor phonological-based changes both in form and position, the *n/k* alternation usually have regular and predictable forms in all other personal pronouns.

Demonstrative pronouns in Mursi occur in the 3rd person singular/plural relative pronouns *ìn* ⟨3SG.PN.SP⟩ and *ìggè* ⟨3PL.PN.SP⟩ and bound demonstrative clitics. Therefore, the relative/specific pronouns distinguish between singular and plural number by the *n/g* alternation.

(6.61) Demonstrative pronouns   Relative pronouns
   ŋàinà   'This'   *iní*   'who/that/which (sg.)'
                                        non-specific (-restrictive)
   ŋàinùnù   'That'   *iná*   'the one who (sg.)'
                                        specific (restrictive)
   ŋàiggèà   'These'   *iggí*   'who/which (pl.)'
                                        non-specific (-restrictive)
   ŋàiggèinù   'Those'   *iggèá* 'those who'
                                        specific (restrictive)

---

4 From the *n/g* alternation, the occurrence of singular marker form *n* in personal pronouns of the Surmic group languages is consistent (both in SES and SWS). For example, from the SES languages: Koegu *aan* ⟨1SG⟩ (Hieda 1998: 348) and Me'en *áni* ⟨1SG⟩ (Will 1998: 450). From the SWS languages: Tennet *anét* ⟨1SG⟩ (Randal 1998: 234) and Baale *anda* ⟨1SG⟩ (Yigezu and Dimmendaal 1998: 299).

The *n/g* pattern described for the personal pronouns is seen clearly in the singular and plural demonstrative and specific pronouns illustrated above.

The interrogative word 'who?' can be manifested in modification and pronoun forms. Thus, the bound n/g alternation that occurs with four different forms of this interrogative pronoun indicates singular and plural possession (6.62).

(6.62) Interrogatives
    a. *nì* ⟨who.GEN.SG⟩ 'whose?' modification form, singular possession
    b. *gì* ⟨who.GEN.PL⟩ 'whose?' modification form, plural possession
    c. *nì+nì* ⟨who.PRO.SG⟩ 'whose?' pronoun form, singular possession
    d. *gì+gì* ⟨who.PRO.PL⟩ 'whose?' pronoun form, plural possession

The interrogatives in modification forms reduplicate their forms in order to yield full pronoun forms.

6.7 The Bound Number/Aspect Marking Forms -t/-ɗ

Mursi has two aspects: imperfective and perfective. Aspect is primarily indicated by root changes (about one-third of verbs of the language) and by bound pronominal S/A argument marking suffixes. The bound pronominal suffixes are also used to mark person and number of the S/A arguments on verbs. For example, the verb *óól* 'beg' has identical forms for both aspects, as shown in the example below.

(6.63)

	Imperfective	Perfective	
1SG	*k-óól-í*	*k-óol-à*	'I beg/begged'
2SG	*óól-í*	*óól-ú*	'You (sg.) beg/begged'
3SG	*óól-Ø*	*óól-à*	'S/he begs/begged'
1PL.INC	*k-óól-Ø*	*k-óól-ò*	'We (inc.) beg/begged'
1PL.EXC	*k-óól-ó*	*k-óól-à*	'We (exc.) beg/begged'
2PL	*óól-ó*	*óól-ò*	'You (pl.) beg/begged'
3PL	*óól-ɛ́*	*óól-á*	'They beg/begged'

In this case, the bound pronominal marking suffixes are required to indicate person and number of the S/A arguments. On verb forms such in (6.63), the tone would be the last option to distinguish the difference between imperfective and perfective aspects. As it is illustrated in (6.63), the difference between second person plural imperfective and perfective forms has been indicated by the tone on the bound pronominal S argument marker suffix -ɔ (high tone ~ imperfective and low tone ~ perfective).

However, there are instances where the verb roots tend to have identical forms for both imperfective and perfective aspects. In such instances, a number of the S/A arguments can also be shown by bound forms *t/d* attached to the verbs, as in (6.64–6.67).

(6.64)

		Imperfective	Perfective	
	1SG	ká-ɓák-í-ɔ̀	ká-ɓák-à	'I eat/ate (it)'
	2SG	ɓák-í-ɔ̀	ɓák-ú	'You (sg.) eat/ate (it)'
	3SG	ɓák-t-ɔ̀	ɓák-à	'S/he eats/ate (it)'
	1PL.INC	ká-ɓák-t-Ø-ɔ̀	ká-ɓák-t-à	'We (inc.) eat/ate (it)'
	1PL.EXC	ká-ɓák-t-ó-ɔ̀	ká-ɓák-t-ò	'We (exc.) eat/ate (it)'
	2PL	ɓág-ó-ɔ̀	ɓák-t-ò	'You (sg.) eat/ate (it)'
	3PL	ɓág-ɛ́-ɔ̀	ɓák-t-á	'They eat/ate (it)'

(6.65)

		Imperfective	Perfective	
	1SG	kà-dàsí-í-ɔ́	ká-dásí-à	'I forget/forgot'
	2SG	dàsí-í-ɔ́	dásí-ú	'You (sg.) forget/forgot'
	3SG	dàsí-Ø-ɔ́	dásí-à	'S/he forgets/forgot'
	1PL.INC	ká-dásí-Ø-ɔ́	ká-dásí-d-à	'We (inc.) forget/forgot'
	1PL.EXC	ká-dásí-o-ɔ́	ká-dásí-d-ò	'We (exc.) forget/forgot'
	2PL	dásí-o-ɔ̀	dásí-d-ù	'You (pl.) forget/forgot'
	3PL	dásí-ɛ̀-ɔ̀	dásí-d-á	'They forget/forgot'

The bound forms *t* (following a consonant-final verb root) (6.64) and *d* (following a vowel-final verb root) (6.65) are used as markers of plural persons. Mütze (2014) has noted existence of the /t/ form on verbs in the perfective aspect. She also described it as a form which often precedes the subject suffix in the plural. However, she also mentioned that it can also occasionally occur in the singular. I would agree with one of her analyses that emphasizes that the bound plural number marker form *t* occasionally occurs in the singular forms. This can be shown in the third person singular imperfective form in (6.64) and in (6.66) in the example shown below.

(6.66)

		Imperfective	Perfective	
	1SG	k-óg-í-ɔ̀	k-ák-à	'I cook/cooked (it).'
	2SG	óg-í-ɔ̀	ák-ú	'You (sg.) cook/cooked (it).'
	3SG	óg-t-Ø-ɔ̀	ák-à	'S/he cooks/cooked (it).'
	1PL.INC	k-ók-t-Ø-ɔ̀	k-ák-t-à	'We (inc.) cook/cooked (it).'

1PL.EXC	k-ók-t-ó-ɔ̀	k-ák-t-ò	'We (exc.) cook/cooked (it).'
2PL	óg-ó-ɔ̀	ák-t-ù	'You (pl.) cook/cooked (it).'
3PL	óg-έ-ɔ̀	ák-t-á	'They cook/cooked (it).'

Nevertheless, the *t* in the singular forms is not like the bound form that occur in the plural forms. The *t* in the singular forms (6.64, 6.66) has a function of disambiguating potentially identical forms. For example, in the second person plural form of the imperfective aspect, the second person plural bound pronominal suffix -*o* and the verb final suffix -*ɔ̀* may coalesce. Thus without *t*, second person plural form (*óg-ó-ɔ̀*) will have an almost identical form with the third person singular from (*óg-t-Ø-ɔ̀*).

Mütze (2014) has mentioned *t* as a segment to be inserted between perfective verb roots and plural subject suffixes. But she didn't mention it's variant *ɗ*. The fact is that the bound form t/ɗ may occur with verbs in the imperfective aspect. Thus, both bound plural marking forms *t/ɗ* can occur with a plural subject requiring verb roots/forms in both imperfective and perfective aspects. See the example below.

(6.67)
	Imperfective	Perfective	
1SG	k-íw-án-o	k-íw-á-o	'I take/took (it).'
2SG	íw-án-o	íw-á-ú	'You (sg.) take/took (it).'
3SG	íw-áná	íw-á-à	'S/he takes/took (it).'
1PL.INC	k-íw-áná	k-íb-t-á-à	'We (inc.) take/took (it).'
2PL	íb-t-á-ó	íb-t-á-ù	'You (pl.) take/took (it).'
3PL	íb-t-á-ɛ	íb-t-á-á	'They take/took (it).'

The bound plural *t/ɗ* forms may be blocked when other grammatical marking suffixes are attached to the verb root. As can be shown in (6.67), the full form of 'motion towards' (ventive) marker suffix (-*áná*) will be attached to verb roots of third person singular and first person plural forms.

6.8 Additional Suffixes

Grammatical number can be shown by various suffixes on verbs and adjectives. In the imperative construction, only plural number is shown on perfective verb roots. Person/subject cannot be marked on the imperative forms. Number of addressee can be marked on the verb by a vowel suffix -*V* (vowel-copying) which is usually identical with the vowel of the verb root.

(6.68) a. *fíg-í-è*
 listen.PERV:IMP-PL-VFS
 'Listen (pl.)!'

 b. *bíg-í-è*
 break.PERV:IMP-PL-VFS
 'Break (pl.) (it)!'

 c. *bág-á-è*
 eat.PERV:IMP-PL-VFS
 'Eat (pl.)!'

However, there is a difference between positive and negative imperative constructions.

In the negative imperative construction, singular addressee can also be marked on the verb root but in the imperfective aspect. Unlike in the positive imperatives, vowel copying is not applicable in the negative imperative constructions. The suffix -*i* marks singular addressee whereas -*o* marks plural addressee, as in (6.69a–d).

(6.69) a. *ŋà=édʒ-í*
 NEG.IMPERV=shoot.IMPERV-SG.IMP
 'Don't (sg.) shoot/kill!'

 b. *ŋà=zámí-í*
 NEG.IMPERV=swim.IMPERV-SG.IMP
 'Don't (sg.) swim!'

 c. *ŋà=édʒ-ó*
 NEG.IMPERV=shoot.IMPERV-PL.IMP
 'Don't (pl.) shoot (kill)!'

 d. *ŋà=màt-ó*
 NEG.IMPERV=drink.IMPERV-PL.IMP
 'Don't (2PL) drink!'

A few derived adjectives can be marked for number in the same way as nouns, but by slightly different number-marking suffixes. Two derived adjectives of dimension and two adjectives of colour take an overt plural number marking. These four adjectives take the plural suffix -*a*. This is a plural suffix usually marked on nouns that belong to CATEGORY III in the marked plural system. What is unusual about this plural suffix is that it has allomorphs [-ta] and [-na].

(6.70) Singular   Plural
   a. gólɔ́ɲí   gólɔ́ɲ-á   'red'
   b. ràmàì   ràm⟨a⟩ì-tá   'long'
   c. kɔ̀rrɔ̀ì   kɔ̀rrɔ̀ì-tà   'black'
   d. mɔ̀kɔ̀ɲì   mɔ̀kɔ̀ì-ná   'short'

In addition, there is one adjective that utilizes a replacive number marking system—bɔ́č-á (sg.) and bɔ́č-èn (pl.) 'thin'.

6.9 Number-Determined Suppletive Verb Forms

Including Africa, number-determined suppletive forms of verbs are found in a wide range of languages (Dixon 2012: 63). Baale (a Southwest Surmic language) has similar verb root alternation system to indicate number on verbs (Yigezu and Dimmendaal, 1998: 302). In Mursi, a few verb roots can undergo suppletions three to four times. Number-determined suppletive verb forms usually operate in accordance with the aspectual system of the language. Five verbs with number-determined suppletive forms have been found—four intransitive verbs (one verb of existence, one verb of posture and two verbs of motion) and a ditransitive verb 'give'.

(6.71) Imperfective   Perfective   Argument   Meaning
                                            involved
        Singular/plural   Singular/plural
   a. í⟨h⟩/él   té/tél   S   'exist, present'
   b. ésé/él   té/tél   S   'sit'
   c. ɔ́k⟨g⟩/héj   ɔ́k/áí⟨t⟩   S   'go'
   d. kún/hóɲ   áɨw/hóɗ   S   'come'
   e. ádʒ   áín/áɗ   O   'give'

Verb roots in (6.71a, b, and d) can undergo up to four term suppletions while the verb roots 'go' and 'give' could display three term suppletions. The verb 'go' and 'give' show an invariable root form in one of the two aspect categories.

NUMBER 263

6.10   Reduplication

Reduplication is not a productive morphological way to indicate grammatical number in Mursi. However, reduplication may be a semi-productive way to indicate plural number on the two underived adjectives. As it can be shown in the examples below, plural forms of the two underived adjectives of Mursi is shown by reduplication.

(6.72)   búí   'big (sg.)'   bíbí   'big (pl.)'
         tííní 'small (sg.)'   tútí   'big (pl.)'

(6.73)   [[ŋà=zùg=tà]$_{NP}$ bíbí=ŋà]$_{NP:S}$ gáj-έ
         DEM=people=NEAR   big.PL=DEF   know.IMPERV-3PL.SU.IMPERV
         'The rulers know.'
         (Lit. 'The big (pl.) people know.')

6.11   Number words

The Mursi have a fully inflected verb *toj* 'count' which they often use to count heads of cattle. This is related to decisions usually made by informants pertaining to the distribution of bridewealth of counting at least 37 head of cattle. This will be undertaken with a tally counting—usually using small stones or pebbles.

Mursi has a ten-based number system, also known as 'decimal system'. See § 3.3.1.1 for a full list of Mursi number words. Unlike some Surmic languages, number words one to ten are non-loan ones. In addition, unlike some Surmic languages, Mursi does not form number words six to nine by combining the lower numerals and the quinary form (five as the base). For number words higher than ten, a combining *tómón* 'ten', *hírkón* 'twenty', etc and number words one to nine are used together (see § 3.3.1.1 Table 3.12). The particle *kó* 'and' functions as a conjunction particle to connect two number words and form a number word that is higher than them. The number word for 'twenty' *hírkón* is a compound word derived from two words: the noun *hírí* 'man' and the indefinite number word *kón* 'one' (Lit. 'One man/person'; referring to ten fingers and ten toes of one man). Therefore, the number word 'twenty' and the multiples of 'twenty' do not require the conjunction particle *kó* (see Table 6.4 below). The number word for 'hundred' has two forms—the Mursi form *zùwò háánán* (Lit. 'five people') and the Amharic form *matto* ⟨mäto⟩.

TABLE 6.4 Mursi number words

Number words	Meaning	Remark
hírkón	'twenty'	Lit. ⟨man+one⟩ 'man one'
hírkón kó tɔ́mɔ́n	'thirty'	Lit. ⟨one man and ten⟩
zùwò ràmàn	'forty'	Lit. ⟨people two⟩ 'two people'
zùwò ràmàn kó tɔ́mɔ́n	'fifty'	Lit. ⟨two people and ten⟩
zùwò sízzí	'sixty'	Lit. ⟨three people⟩
zùwò sízzí kó tɔ́mɔ́n	'seventy'	Lit. ⟨three people and ten⟩
zùwò wùʃ	'eighty'	Lit. ⟨four people⟩
zùwò wùʃ kó tɔ́mɔ́n	'nighty'	Lit. ⟨four people and ten⟩
zùwò háánán	'hundred'	Lit. ⟨people five⟩ or *matto* from Amharic

6.11.1 *The Number Word* dɔ́néj *'One' and the Indefinite* kón *'One'*

There is a clear difference between the number word *dɔ́néj* and *kón*—not only in the way they are combined with other number words but also in the way they modify nouns within NPs. As we recall from Chapter 4, when nouns are modified by number words higher than two, they do not take modification or dependency markers (restrictive and/or non-restrictive), as in the following examples.

(6.74) a. [úŋɔ́   sízzì]
           night.PL three
           'Three days'
           (Lit. 'three nights')

   b. [gàrčó   tɔ̀mɔ̀n kó   ràmàn]
      basket.PL ten   and two
      'Twelve baskets'

   c. [[débì-ɲá   gɔ̀lɔ̀ɲ-à]$_{NP}$ ràmàn]$_{NP}$ bàrì   ká-tál-à
      lip.plate-PL red.STV-PL   two   yesterday 1SU-buy-1SG.SU.PERV
      'Yesterday I bought two red lip-plates.'

However, the number word *dɔ́néj* 'one' stands apart from the rest of number words because it triggers the head to be marked with a non-restrictive modification marker. In an NP where *dɔ́néj* is the modifier, regardless of the head's word class status, the non-restrictive modification marker *-i/-ti* must be attached to the singular head (6.75a–c).

(6.75) a. [érmì-ti dɔ̃néj]_NP átw-ó
child-NTSTR one come.PERV-MT.3SG.SU.PERV
'One child came.'

b. [ʃí-tí dɔ̃néj]
thousand-NRSTR one
'(One) thousand'

c. [(jɔ̀g) ŋɔ̀nɛ̀-à n=ɛ̀j]
3PL sister.PERT.SG.3.PSR-RTSR SG.PSD=3PL.PSR
tál-á dʒù [bírój-tí dɔ̃néj]
sell-3SG.SU.PERV clay.pot birr-RSTR one
'Their sister sold her water pot for one dollar.'

Besides the instances shown above, the only place where the non-restrictive modification marker -i/-ti may be attached to the head and be modified by a number word higher than one is in coordinative partitive constructions.

(6.76) zùg-tí kó ràmàn [kààrì+čàgí]
people-NRTSR CRD.PART two eye+blind/green
'Two blind men (two of the blind men)'

From the example in (6.76), one can easily understand that there were some other men, at least more than two. On the other hand, the indefinite marker/word kón 'one' can function alone or be combined with other nouns. When combined with nominals, it usually yields indefinite pronouns (see § 3.3.1.5, Table 3.7). Both dɔ̃néj and kón may function as a modifier within an NP. Interestingly, the head modified by kón does not take any modification marking, however, kón itself as a modifier can take another modification marker (-a or -o). Table 6.5 below illustrates indefinite pronouns which are derived from both words.

In addition, a few morphological differences were observed between dɔ̃néj and kón. For example, dɔ̃néj may occur in a reduplicated form and be used with the plural form of 'belly' kèŋì in order to create a distributive meaning. In contrast, kón cannot be reduplicated but can take other morphology for example the restrictive modification marker. In simple clauses, kón can function as S argument while dɔ̃néj cannot. Nevertheless, dɔ̃néj has at least one role in clauses, a copula complement. In Table 6.6 below, a brief comparison between the number word dɔ̃néj and the indefinite word kón is presented as follows.

TABLE 6.5   Indefinite pronouns from *kón* and *ɖɔ́nɛ́j*

Word class/ morphological status	ɖɔ́nɛ́j Number word	kón Indefinite pronoun/ marker
can stand alone	yes	yes
has an equivalent plural counterpart form	no	yes; *gén(a)* 'some, other'
can be reduplicated	yes (distributive)	no[a]
take modification marker	no	*-a* and *-o*
can form indefinite pronoun	not productive	yes
modifier within NP	yes	yes
can be core argument	no	S
can be a copula subject	no	??
can be a copula complement	yes	no

a   Maybe there is one. I suspect, the verb *kɔnkɔna* 'to turn someone against another person' may have been derived from the indefinite *kon* by reduplication. It literally means (⟨one-one⟩).

TABLE 6.6   Comparison: *ɖɔ́nɛ́j* versu *kón*

Indefinite	Meaning	Type	Possible source
kón/kóná	'one, another, other, certain'	alone	kón 'one' + -a (restrictive modification)
hírkóná	'anybody, someone'	compound	hírí 'man' + kón 'one' + -a (restrictive modification)
tánkónó	'anyone'	word+compound	⟨side-side-one⟩
ɓókónó	'somewhere; anywhere'	compound	ɓó < ɓa 'place' + kón 'one'+ -a (restrictive modification)
àhìtì ɖɔ́nɛ́j	'nobody'	NP	àhì 'thing.SG' + -ti (non-restrictive modification) + ɖɔ́nɛ́j 'one'

The following example is a piece of evidence which best describes the syntactic difference between the two (repeated from example 3.78).

(6.77) màmà   kónó   kó   dʒɔ̀ɔ̀nè
       mother.PERT.SG.1.PSR one.INDEF PNC mother.PERT.SG.3.PSR
       á   dɔ́néj
       COP.3.IMPERV one
       'My mother and his mothers are one (the same).' (KW 2:34:4)

6.11.2 Deriving Ordinal Number Words

With regard to the development of ordinal numbers, Dixon (2012: 74) stated that in many cases they are derived from their cardinal congeners. Mursi has three ordinal numbers. Of these, two of them are derived from lower cardinal *ràmàn* 'two' and *sízzí* 'three'. Thus, the ordinal number 'second' and 'third' are formed by attaching the morphological marker suffix *-nè* to them—*ràmàn-nè* ⟨two-ORD⟩ and *sízzì-nè* ⟨three-ORD⟩. Examples were given in § 3.3.5.1. Additional examples are presented as follows.

(6.78) nà   [úŋɔ́   sízzì-nè]   ká-báns-á
       CCN nigh.PL three-ORD   3.SBJV-get.up-3SG.SU.PERV
       'And on the third day he shall rise.'

In order to create an innovative form of ordinal number higher than ten, one should attach the ordinal number marker suffix *-ne* to the smaller cardinal number on the right edge (cf. p. 179). However, at this stage, it only applies to one ordinal number form higher than ten, i.e. 'twelfth', as in the following examples.

(6.79) a. ìggè tɔ̀mɔ̀n kó ràmàn-nè
          2PL ten   PNC two-ORD
          'You (PL), the twelfth'

       b. ŋà=zùg=tà   kó   tɔ̀mɔ̀n kó ràmàn-nè
          DEM=people= NEAR   CRD.PART ten   PNC twelve-ORD
          'These (the) twelfth people'

In a construction that has partitive reading, the ordinal number marker *-ne* may be omitted. Instead, a genitive case marker will be attached to the cardinal number which shows the partitioning, as in (6.80).

(6.80) tɔ̀mɔ̀n   kó   ràmàn   dɔ́néi(j)-ɲ   hír-á   ké   joɗa
        ten   PNC   two   one-GEN   man-RSTR   QUOT   Judas
        áíw-ó
        come.PERV.SG-MT.3SG.SU.PERV
        'Judas, one of the twelve, came.'

In relation to the ordinal number 'two', there is one more way in which comparable semantics could be conveyed—using the cardinal number 'two' and the body part noun *kèɲì* 'bellies'.

(6.81) kèɲì   ràmàn-o   [zùw-á   ɔ́r]   [dɔ́nén-a]_RC
        belly.PL two-MOD   people-RSTR   village   [be_one-RSTR]
        téjél   hùll-á   [rè-á   n=ùnù]_REFL
        like/love.PERV.IMP   when-NOMZ   body-RSTR   SG.PSD=2SG.PSR
        'The second, which is one, "Love your neighbour as yourself."'
        (Lit. 'second time ...')

This is similar to a multiplicative construction (see § 6.11.3). With the same ordinal number marker -*ne*, the meaning 'twin' can be expressed (6.82).

(6.82) ŋà=ìggè=à   kó   ràmàn-nè
        DEM=3PL.PN.SP=NEAR   PNC   two-ORD
        'These, the twins'

It is not clear but when the second syllable of *ràmàn* is repeated, it may yield interpretations such as 'pair' and 'couple', as in (6.83).

(6.83) a. [ràmàmàn]   óó   [čàll-ì   kàrì]
           two   or   good.STV-ADJ   together
           'Either (one) is correct; Either one or both are good.'
           (Lit. 'both are correct/good.')

        b. nɔ̀ŋ kɔ́n-Ø-nè   [sènɔ̀   ràmàmàn]_NP   nà
           3SG write-3SG.SU.IMPERV-APPL   hand.PL two   CCN
           ɔ́wán-á
           manage-3SG.SU.PERV
           'He can write with either hand.'

The ordinal number 'first' in Mursi is a product of grammaticalization (see § 3.3.51). Like ordinal numbers 'second' and 'third' which take the derivational marker -ne, the ordinal number 'first' also takes this marker. However, the word class from which the ordinal number 'first' derived is a noun rather than a number word (body part noun *saba* 'head'). See the following examples (6.84a repeated from 3.128).

(6.84) a. nà   ín-á   sábú-nè   gàm-ànà
       CCN 3SG.PN.SP-RSTR head-ORD marry-MT:3SG.SU.IMPERV
       mùgàj
       woman
       '... and the first (one) married a wife'

   b. {[ójó-á   sábú-nè]_NP (nɔ̀ŋ) gùjò dág-Ø
      rainy.season-RSTR head-RSTR 3SG   rain hit-3SG.SU.IMPERV
      wáŋ} {méá ŋà=ʔójó=a   nɔ̀ŋ dák-ú
      much now   DEM=rainy.season=NEAR 3SG hit-3SG.SU.PERV
      ké   tíín-í   sɔ̀ŋ}
      COMPL small-ADJ only
      'Last year (Lit. 'first year') it rained much but this year it has only rained a little.'

6.11.3 *Deriving Forms with a Multiplicative Meaning*
Cardinal numbers can be combined with the plural form of a grammaticalized body part noun *kɛŋ-i* <belly-PL in order to produce a multiplicative reading.

(6.85) a. [húllí gòdónà   dɔ̃m-áɲ-ò=jè]_SUBORD:CL
         [if   bother.PERT.SG.1.PSR insult-1SG.OBJ-3SG.IRR=SUBORD]
         aj   kà-gàj   ké-sé-sè   kèŋì   ísɔ̀ŋ?
         HORT-JUSS.PART 1.HORT-know 1SU-say-BEN.3 belly.PL how.may?
         ké-sé-sè   kèŋì   issàbàj?
         1SU-say-BEN.3 belly.PL seven
         '"If my brother commits an offense against me, how many times shall I forgive him? Seven times?"'

   b. ʃúúné dák-ú   lúsì   kèŋì   sízzì
      father hit-3SG.SU.PERV boy.SG belly.PL three
      'The father beat the son three times'

   c. k-ígóm-èsè   kèŋì   mátó
      3.SBJV-allow.PERV-BEN.3 belly.PL hundred
      '... he shall receive hundredfold.'

The multiplicative form may also mean 'many times', as it is shown in (6.85c).

6.11.4 *Deriving Forms with a Distributive Meaning*
In addition to the multiplicative construction, one can convey the notion of distributive number by reduplication of the cardinal number *dɔ́néj* 'one'. To produce a distributive reading, the singular form of the body part noun *kèŋɔ̀* 'belly.sg' will be used together with the reduplicated form *dɔ́nédɔ́né* ⟨one.one⟩.

(6.86) a. àstàmàrì-ɲà áli-ɛ́   kèŋɔ̀   dɔ́nédɔ́né
teacher-PL talk-3PL.SU.IMPERV belly.SG one:REDUP
'The teachers are talking one after the other.'

The fact is that sentences containing distributive meanings can be ambiguous. For example, the above sentence could also mean 'The teachers are talking one by one (taking turn talking)'.

b. nà   ŋà=zùg=tùnù   kò   [zùw-á   ɲàgàs-á]
CCN DEM=people=FAR PNC people-RSTR old.STV-RST
bán-á   dɔ́nédɔ́né
get.up-3PL.SU.PERV one:REDUP
'... and those (who) were with the elders got up one by one.'

In fast speech, the palatal approximant /j/ is dropped—/dɔ́néjdɔ́néj/ ~ [dɔ́nédɔ́né]. However, in order to indicate something separated from the group, collection or unit, the plural form *kɛŋi* may be used.

(6.87) a. bè   [jìrìsì tùg-ɔ̀]   kèŋi   dɔ́nédɔ́né
DIST.PAST sea mouth-OBL   belly.PL one:REDUP
lɔ̀m-á   [dòrèn-á   zùw-á]
have-3SG.SU.PERV house.PL-RSTR people-RSTR
[dág-è-à   ùrgùs-á]_RC
strike/hit-3PL.SU.IMPERV-NOMZ fish-PL
'There were a few stray fishermen's huts along the beach.'
(Lit. 'The beach had one-one (a few stray) houses of the people who strike fish.')

6.12 Number and Agreement

Within NPs, number agreement between heads and modifiers is obligatory. Modifiers within NPs take an obligatory number agreement marker. In addition, obligatory number agreement within NPs depends on the modifier of the head. If the head is modified by bound demonstratives, the number is already an inherent part of the head noun itself, as in (6.88a).

(6.88) a. [ŋà=gàʃà-ɲá̀=à]
 DEM=shield-PL=NEAR
 'These shields'

If the modifier is an independent demonstrative pronoun, the head receives appropriate number marking that make it agree with its modifier (6.88b).

 b. [lúsì   ŋà=ìn=à]
 boy.SG DEM=3SG.PN.SP=NEAR
 'This boy'

In noun modification construction, demonstrative constructions that are already in modification forms/functions, can function as modifiers of other head nouns, which are in the singular forms, as in (6.89).

(6.89) [čɔ̀r-á   ŋà=mɔ̀r=à]
 hair-RSTR DEM=calf=NEAR
 'The hair (fur) (sg.) of this calf'

However, if the head noun in (6.89) is modified by cardinal number *dɔ́néj* 'one', it takes the appropriate number marking suffix and the non-restrictive modification marker -*i* [-ti].

(6.90) [čɔ̀rtòì-tí   dɔ́néj]
 lock.of.hair-SG-NRSTR one
 'A lock of hair'
 (Lit. 'one lock of hair')

This applies to all countable or potentially countable nouns if they are to be modified by the cardinal number word 'one'.

(6.91) [rúm-ní   dɔ́néj]
       cloth-NRSTR one
       'One cloth'

The underived adjectives *tííní* 'small' and *búí* 'big' agree in number with the head nouns they modify. They are the only modifiers that show number agreement with their heads by reduplication.

(6.92) a. [hír-á   bó]
          man-RSTR big.SG
          'Big man'

       b. [zùw-á   bíbí-ó]
          people-RSTR big:REDUP-RSTR.MOD
          'Elders'
          (Lit. 'big (PL) people')

The noun *bì* 'cow' is used to refer to cattle in general of both genders. Thus, it displays two type of agreement. Within NPs, it does not necessarily require a plural number marker to agree with plural modifiers. This fact is evident if a person's intention is to not refer to a specific/particular cow.

(6.93) a. [[bì-á   gìdǎɲ-à]$_{NP}$ háánán]$_{NP}$
          cow-RSTR brown.STV-RSTR.PL five
          'Five brown cows'

       b. [[bì-á   gìdǎɲ-à]$_{NP}$ mèrì]$_{NP}$
          cow-RSTR brown.STV-RSRT.PL many
          'Many brown cows'

Nevertheless, in copular clauses, when functioning as a copula subject, it must take a plural number marker suffix and agree in number with the copula complement.

(6.94) [bì-ò]$_{CS}$ á   [mèrì]$_{CC}$
       cow-PL COP.3.IMPERV many
       'The cows are many'

In a few instances, number agreement between the copula subject and copula complement may appear optional, as in the following copular clause.

(6.95) [ŋà=gɔ̀r=à]_CS   á   [bèná]_CC
DEM=road=NEAR COP.3SG.IMPERV stone.PL
'This road is rocky'

But the plural number marker attached to the copula complement in (6.95) denotes an adjectival meaning rather than a plural referent. Therefore both (CS and CC) have singular number.

CHAPTER 7

The Verb and Predicate Structure

7.1 Introduction

The verb is the second largest open word class in Mursi. The verb is a primary word which functions as head of a predicate. Adjectives that function as heads of intransitive predicates are those that are derived from stative verbs. This chapter offers an overview of the phonological properties of the verb roots, and component grammatical elements associated with the inflectional categories of the verb such as subject and object agreement, aspect, and mood. Verbs and their component grammatical elements constitute one of the most complex parts of Mursi morphology. Some verb roots can undergo up to four time morphological alternations to indicate aspect. Others undergo up to two or more than two-term verb root alternations in order to indicate grammatical number and aspect.

Moreover, a number of most salient phonological and morphological properties of verbs are discussed in this chapter. Based on the phonological properties they display, verb roots have been classified into three major types, and a number of sub-types may exist within each type (§7.2). The subsequent section (§7.3) will illustrate some of the verbal inflections—participant reference (§7.3.1.1), aspect (§7.3.1.2), mood (§7.3.1.3), tense (§7.3.1.4) followed by the multiverbal constructions (§7.3.1.5). Also, in two sub-sections, copula verbs in (§7.3.1.2.9) and auxiliary in (§7.3.1.2.10) are discussed in detail respectively.

7.2 Phonological Properties of Verb Roots

The segmental structure of roots is one of the most salient phonological features of the verbs. Roughly 90 percent of Mursi verb roots start and end in consonants. Of these, about one-third have monosyllabic CVC shapes, thus they form Type I category (§7.2.1). Although very few in number, disyllabic and trisyllabic consonant-final verb roots are also discussed in this category. Type II are vowel-initial verb roots; they differ from those in Type I by having V onsets (§7.2.2). Some members of Type II verb roots co-exist with remnants of old and fossilized causative prefixes. Type III are vowel-final verb roots (§7.2.3). Unlike Type I and II, Type III verbs take a special aspect/number marker suffix -d. For major segmental structures of verb roots, see the summary given in Table 7.1 below.

THE VERB AND PREDICATE STRUCTURE

TABLE 7.1 A summary of major segmental structures of verb roots

	Initial	Final	Shapes
Type I	C	C	CVC, CVVC, and CVCVC
Type II	V	C/V	VC, VCVC, VCVVC, VVC, VCV(V)C, and VCV
Type III	C	V	CV(V) and CVCV

7.2.1 Type I Verb Roots

All Type I verb roots have closed syllables. They mainly include monomorphemic CVC, CVVC, and CVCVC shapes. Unlike the other two types (Type II and III), Type I verb roots have inherent tone melodies—usually H tone. Semantically, a great majority of its members denote action.

7.2.1.1 CVC Verb Roots

The CVC verb roots are action verbs. They usually undergo a partial or full root suppletion processes to indicate aspect distinctions. Table 7.2 below depicts Mursi H-toned CVC verb roots.

Some members of Type I verb roots display a seemingly phonosemantic correspondence. For example, the first three verb roots in Table 7.2 have *bg/dg* consonants that have to do with 'applying or exerting of force'. Likewise, the three verb roots above the last three are verb roots that contain palatal plosive codas (CVč), and they exhibit the semantics of 'take and give'. Only these two verbs of Mursi have /č/ final roots. The last three in Table 7.2 and the following three verb roots *čó l* 'sing' *dŏl* 'warn' and *dól* 'announce' can be grouped into one semantic type—'communication'. Verb roots such as *bm* [lɔn] 'have', *mág* 'grab, hold, catch', *múg* 'gather, collect', and *mès* 'serve, do' may best fit into the semantic category—'possess or pull together'. The tonal counterparts for verbs in Table 7.2 will be L-toned CVC verb roots as shown in Table 7.3 below.

Monomorphemic CVC verbs in Table 7.3 and a dozen others have inherently L-toned roots.

k-initial verb roots differ from all other verb root types in two ways. First, except for *k*-initial verb roots, all verb roots take either a *kV*- or *k*- prefix, where the prefix *k*- encodes first person subject, third person irrealis, passive voice, and hortative and jussive moods. The choice between the *kV*- and *k*- prefixes depends on the onset of the verb roots: *kV*- for consonant-initial for roots and *k*- for vowel-initial verb roots. Second, k-initial verb roots undergo a recurrent compensatory lengthening or haplology processes where this sometimes leads to a confusion in identifying the morphological boundary between the roots of

TABLE 7.2   *CVC* verb roots with H tone

Root	Gloss	Tone
ɓág	'bite, eat'	H
ɓíg	'break'	H
ɗág	'hit'	H
ʃǐg	'hear, listen'	H
ŋér	'divide'	H
čúr	'wash'	H
čɔ́ɗ	'load'	H
ɓɛ́g	'watch, protect'	H
bág	'show off'	H
čáč	'exchange'	H
húč	'avenge, pay'	H
jéb	'believe'	H
jél	'like, love'	H
jóg	'tell, explain'	H

TABLE 7.3   *CVC* verb roots with L tone

Root	Gloss	Tone
ʤìm	'lead'	L
dìr	'sweep'	L
nìs	'kill, slaughter'	L
gùɲ	'see'	L
jàg	'return (intr.)'	L
màt	'drink'	L

k-initial verbs and component grammatical elements (carrying subject, aspect, voice and mood). Example (7.1) illustrates the compensatory lengthening phenomenon that happens upon on the loss of a whole syllable before a phonetically identical syllable:

(7.1)   /kú-kún-í/   →   [Ø-kún-í]   →   [kúúní]   'I came'
        /ká-káɗ-áná/   →   [Ø-káɗ-áná]   →   [kááɗáná]   'I remember'

THE VERB AND PREDICATE STRUCTURE	277

TABLE 7.4 *k*-initial verb roots

Root	Gloss	Tone
kún	'come'	H
kád́	'remember'	H
kɔ́d́	'begin'	H
kɔ́h	'clear land'	H
kɔ́d́	'kill'	H
kéd́	'subtract'	H
kéŋ	'protect'	H
kɔ́b	'follow'	H
kúl	'drive, paddle'	H
kúm	'feel, touch'	H
kúr	'dig'	H

However, not all k-initial verb roots necessarily acquire a VV sequence. In other words, they do not undergo a compensatory lengthening process. The fact is that even if they are few, k-initial roots receive the kV- prefix like any other verb—as can be seen in (7.2).

(7.2) a. *kú-kúm-nèn-ɔ́*
1SU-feel-AP-VFS
'I am feeling (touching).'

b. *ké-kéŋ-í-ɔ̀*
1SU-protect-1SG.SU.IMPERV-VFS
'I am protecting.'

7.2.1.2   CVVC Verb Roots

In terms of a segmental structure, verbs having a CVVC root are different from those created by a compensatory lengthening process. Moreover, segmentally, CVVC verb roots differ from the other verb root types in that the VV sequence is the result of intervocalic consonant deletion. The disyllabic realization of these roots is attested in the genetically closely related language of Chai (a Southeastern Surmic group). For example, the verb *liin* 'squat, intercede' has a disyllabic realization in Chai—as *ligin*.

Similar deletions of an intervocalic consonants between two identical vowels are widely attested in vowel-initial trisyllabic verb roots (see Table 7.13).

TABLE 7.5   *CVVC* verb roots

Root	Gloss	Tone
líín	'squat, intercede'	H/HH
gáán	'know'	H/HH
tɔ́ɔ́ɗ	'build, construct'	H/HH

TABLE 7.6   *CVCVC* verb roots

Root	Gloss	Tone
márág	'go around, wander'	HH
dɔ́rɔ́k	'dry'	HH
čóbós	'suck, kiss'	HH
čólós	'wish'	HH
dúgúm	'curve'	HH
lɔ́tɔ́g	'wet'	HH
múnúd	'itch'	HH
téŋér	'frighten'	HH
tɔ́rɔ́k	'pass gas, fart'	HH
túkúr	'stir'	HH
kútúr	'drag'	HH
kúrúd⟨t⟩	'snore'	HH
bɔrɔd⟨t⟩	'jump, climb'	LL

Most importantly, nominal roots incorporate almost one-third of the newly emerging VV sequences of the language.

7.2.1.3   CVCVC Verb Roots

Verbs which occur in CVCVC shapes are of two types: those that have disyllabic roots where their σ_1 and σ_2 acquire one and the same vowel ($V_1=V_2$) and those that have disyllabic roots with different vowels in their σ_1 and σ_2 ($V_1 \neq V_2$).

As can be shown in Table 7.6, there is syntactic as well as semantic information which can be extracted out of these monomorphemic verb roots, i.e. most of them belong to an intransitive stative verb category.

The verb roots in Table 7.7 differ from those in Table 7.7 only by lacking syllables carrying a $V_1=V_2$ symmetry in their syllables, otherwise, they also form an intransitive stative verb category.

THE VERB AND PREDICATE STRUCTURE

TABLE 7.7 *CVCVC* verb roots lacking a V₁=V₂ symmetry

Root	Gloss	Tone
wésúʔ	'damage'	HH
kárúh	'scratch'	HH
tówúl	'creep'	HH
tógíw	'float'	HH
tìráɲ	'play'	LH

In general, all the verb roots discussed so far under §7.1.1 primarily mark aspect by subject suffixes, *t(V-)* prefix, vowel, and consonant change. In the absence of these aspect marking options, the suffix *-t* and *-d* shall mark the perfective aspect. The choice between the two suffixes depends on the verb root-final segments. Accordingly, the majority of the consonant-final verb roots take the suffix *-t* while the vowel-final verb roots take the suffix *-d*. We shall see the grammatical role of these two suffixes in §7.3.1.2.1.

7.2.2 Type II verb roots

Vowel-initial verb roots differ from consonant-initial verb roots mainly by two phonologically motivated morphological features. They do take the prefix *k-* (of the first person subject, irrealis, passive voice, hortative and jussive mood marker) and the *t-* perfective aspect marker.

7.2.2.1 VC verb roots

Monosyllabic VC shape verb roots carry a H-tone melody and most of them are action verbs. Table 7.8 below depicts Mursi CVC verb roots carrying H and L tones.

In addition, VC verb roots mostly consist of labile verbs (both, S=O and A=S). However, labile verbs can be misleading when they appear in imperfective and perfective aspect. They appear in different verb root forms in the imperfective and perfective aspect. Nevertheless, a great majority of labile verb roots do not alter their roots for aspect. For instance, let us examine some of the labile verb roots from the examples in Table 7.8—édʒ 'shoot, sting' and íw 'take, receive'. These two verb roots have identical base forms. What is makes them different from each other is a morpheme boundary phenomenon. Consider the following three remarks:
– ⟨1pl.INC⟩ and ⟨3sg⟩ subjects are morphologically unmarked or they may be marked by the motion towards suffix (ventive) in the imperfective aspect.

TABLE 7.8   *VC* verb roots

Root	Gloss	Tone
ádʒ	'give'	H
áŋ	'pass'	H
ɔ̀g	'shout, yell'	L
ɔ́g	'untie'	H
ók	'go'	H
édʒ	'shoot, sting'	H
és	'sit'	H
ɔ́s	'roast (on fire)'	H
ódʒ	'put'	H
àg	'cook'	L
ór	'see'	H
ér	'pour'	H
íw	'take, receive'	H

TABLE 7.9   Labile verb root *édʒ* 'shoot'

	Imperfective		Perfective	
1SG	kédʒíɔ̀	'I shoot (it)'	kéčá	'I shot (it).'
2SG	édʒíɔ̀	'You shoot (it)'	éčú	'You shot (it).'
3SG	éjtɔ̀	'S/he shoot (it)'	éčá	'S/he shot (it).'
1PL.INC	kéjtɔ̀	'We shoot (it)'	kéjtá	'We shot (it).'
2PL	édʒɔ́ɔ̀	'You shoot (it)'	éjtó	'You shot (it)'
3PL	édʒéɔ̀	'They shoot (it)'	éjtá	'They shot (it).'

– Motion toward (ventive) markers: -*áná* for ⟨1PL.INC.IMPERV⟩ and 3sg subjects, -*án* for all other persons in the imperfective aspect, ⟨2SG.SU⟩ is omitted in the imperfective aspect, and -*a* for all persons in perfective aspect.
– Palatal affricates weaken to a palatal approximant [j] word-finally—/dʒ, č/ →[j]/_# and intervocalically, the voiced bilabial plosive /b/ lenites to bilabial approximant [w].

Accordingly, in the imperfective aspect, the third person singular form of the root will contain the verb root *édʒ* and Ø (zero morpheme). Thus, the palatal affricate /dʒ/ becomes palatal approximant word-finally which results in [éjtɔ̀].

THE VERB AND PREDICATE STRUCTURE   281

TABLE 7.10 Labile verb root *iw* 'take'

	Imperfective		Perfective	
1SG	kíwánɔ̀	'I take (it)'	kíwáó	'I took (it).'
2SG	íwánɔ̀	'You take (it)'	íwáú	'You took (it).'
3SG	íwáná	'S/he take (it)'	íwá	'S/he took (it).'
1PL.INC	kíwáná	'We take (it)'	kíbtá	'We took (it).'
2PL	íbtáɔ̀	'You take (it)'	íbtáú	'You took (it)'
3PL	íbtá	'They take (it)'	íbtáá	'They took (it).'

The suffix -ɔ̀ is just a verb-final suffix in the imperfective aspect. In the perfective aspect, /t/ always precedes the subject suffix if the verb has a consonant-final root.

The full ventive suffix form /-áná/ is attached to the verb roots in the 3sg. and 1pl.INC. forms because subject suffixes for these two are not marked morphologically. The roots in 2sg. and 3sg. forms behave differently, thus they are exceptional. Like those in the perfective aspect, they take the ventive suffix -*a* instead of -*án*. They also add the suffix -*t* before plural subject suffixes. Both are exceptional because they have also dropped their subject suffixes. As can be seen in Table 7.10, the rest of verbs contain a verb-final approximant /w/. Further relevant points are discussed in (§ 7.9).

7.2.2.2   VCVC verb roots

Like the consonant-initial verb roots in § 7.2.1.3, the verbs in Table 7.11 are disyllabic containing phonologically identical vowels ($V_1 = V_2$) in their σ_1 and σ_2. Vowel fronting and round harmony are major manifestations of the VCVC verb roots.

While comparing the verb roots of Table 7.11 with those in Table 7.12, two phonologically interesting facts have emerged. First, in Table 7.11 there are no *í*-initial verb roots—except the last two on the list. Second, some of the verbs in Table 7.11 have transitive roots, and are verbs usually associated with experiential meanings. Table 7.12 below contains a few list of Mursi *VCVC* ($V_1 \neq V_2$) and *VCVVC* verb roots, whereas Table 7.13 contains *VVC* and *VCV(V)C* verb roots

From *í*-initial verb roots in Table 7.12 and Table 7.13, we can deduce two historical changes, one vanishing morphological feature and the other one an emerging phonological feature. In a number of descriptive works on the Eastern Sudanic languages of the Nilo-Saharan family, the prefix *í*- is widely

TABLE 7.11   VCVC (V₁=V₂) verb roots

Root	Gloss	Tone
óŋón	'smell (intr.)'	HH
óŋóŋ	'lose (tr.)'	HH
úŋús	'sleep'	HH
ógór	'steal'	HH
ógór	'roast'	HH
éséd́	'think, calculate'	HH
úgún	'push, animate'	HH
úgúm	'contempt'	HH
ébég	'blow, expose, reveal'	HH
úhún	'blow (intr.)'	HH
éŋér	'afraid'	HH
érés	'cross'	HH
úllút/urrút	'dash, spill'	HH
účúr	'mix, combine'	HH
írít	'give birth, bear'	HH
ítím	'ignite'	HH

attested, and used to have had a causative function. It has now vanished in some languages or almost is at the stage of vanishing. Yet, including Mursi, remnants of this prefix is still attested in a few Surmic languages. It can occur as a prefix or as circumfix in double causative *í-* ... *-sí* [*-ísí*]. For example, *íbónsí* ⟨CAUS-bon-CAUS⟩ 'make someone leave' and *íbáísí* ⟨CAUS-ba-CAUS⟩ 'cure, make someone recover' are morphologically analyzable while *ídílsí* 'make something smooth' is morphologically unsegmentable or unanalyzable.

Apparently, even within the last four decades, a number of slow changes are taking place in the language, for example some verbs containing the prefix *í-* are now getting lexicalized with *í-* bearing a seemingly transitivizer function (see further the causatives section in Chapter 9).

The other emerging feature, which is also more frequent in nouns than verbs, is the intervocalic deletion of consonants. This is recognizable only by comparing the verb roots contain long vowels with some of the trisyllabic verb roots of Chai (a Southeast Surmic language, also known as Suri). In Table 7.13 above, we have two roots containing long vowels: *ílááś* and *óól* (Mursi)—whereas in Chai these two roots are realized as *ílágás* and *ógól*. The consonant-initial *tóód́* 'kill' ~ *tóyódá* is another example.

TABLE 7.12 *VCVC* (V₁≠V₂) and *VCVVC* verb roots

Root	Gloss	Tone
ígóm	'admit, obey, consent'	HH
ílál	'console, encourage'	HH
ídóg	'feed/raise, enlarge'	HH
ítáb	'deceive'	HH
ílób	'try, attempt'	HH
ítón	'send'	HH
ídán	'lead, direct'	HH
áhúj	'to suck'	HH
áŋíd⟨t⟩	'bite'	HH
íɲán	'touch'	HH
ítíɲán	'meet'	HHH
íbónsí	'make (someone) leave, contribute, cost'	HHH
íbáísí	'to cure, recover'	HHH
ídílsí	'make smooth'	HHH

TABLE 7.13 *VVC, VCV(V)C* verb roots

Root	Gloss	Tone
áús	'rest, alight'	HH
óól	'beg, pray, beseech'	HH
íláás	'(be) sick'	HHH

The VCV types in Table 7.14 are transitional between Type I and Type III verb roots. They accept the features of both types. For example, the prefix *k-* is the feature of Type I verb roots whereas the suffix *-d'* is the feature of Type III verb roots (see §7.1.3). Both these two affixes are reflected on VCV verb roots—for example, the verb root *idó* 'add, combine, mix', as in Table 7.15.

TABLE 7.14 *VCV* verb roots

Root	Gloss	Tone
ídó	'add, combine, mix'	HH
íwó	'breed, guard'	HH
ísá	'greet'	HH
ító	'carry (on head)'	HH
íbá	'warn'	HH
álí	'talk, speak'	HH
élí	'call someone'	HH
éré	'drop'	HH

TABLE 7.15 The suffix -*d́* in a *VCV* verb root

	Perfective	
1SG	kídóá	'I combined (it)'
2SG	ídóú	'You combined (it)'
3SG	ídóá	'S/he combined (it)'
1PL.INC	kídĭdá	'We combined (it)'
1PL.EXC	kídódó	'We combined (it)'
2PL	ídódó	'You combined (it)'
3PL	ídódá	'They combined (it)'

7.2.3   *Type III verb roots*

Type III verbs contain vowel-final roots. They are fewer in number compared from the previous two types. Type III verb roots are mainly of two types: CV(V) (Table 7.16) and CVCV (Table 7.17). The CVCV roots mostly end with the high front vowel, as in Table 7.17.

As can be shown on the list in Table 7.17, most of the CVCV verb roots belong to the intransitive class. As vowel-final type, CVCV verb roots can only be conjugated with the bicategorical function suffix [number+aspect] -*d́*.

THE VERB AND PREDICATE STRUCTURE

TABLE 7.16 *CV(V)* verb roots

Root	Gloss	Tone
rè	'wait for'	H
sé	'say'	H*
dĭ	'fill'	H
rúí	'cry'	HH
dĭá	'go with someone'	HH

TABLE 7.17 *CVCV* verb roots

Root	Gloss	Tone
zámí	'swim'	HH
dézí	'burp'	HH
mèzì	'discuss'	LL
kúlí	'drive, paddle'	HH
lámí	'want, desire, find'	HH
ɓésí	'hatch'	HH
čúrí	'gag'	HH
mósí	'wish'	HH
dásí	'forget'	HH
dúrí	'dance'	HH
múɲí	'pout'	HH
ʃŭmó	'flap'	HH

7.2.4 Trisyllabic Verb Roots

Mursi verbs are predominantly composed of mono and disyllabic roots. Despite this, a small number of trisyllabic verb roots also exist. Some share certain segmental properties with the monosyllabic and trisyllabic verb roots such as: carrying phonetically identical vowels ($V_1=V_2$) in their first and second syllables, carrying inherently reduplicated syllables, and lexicalized causative roots. Yet others appear in compounds and even loan verbs.

There are also a few polysyllabic verbs whose origin appears to be related to ideophones yet have syllable and morpheme like inherently reduplicated shapes, an in Table 7.19.

These polysyllabic verbs stand apart from other verbs in that they are defi-

TABLE 7.18 Trisyllabic Verb Roots

Root	Gloss	Remark
dárdárí	'steep downhill'	> maybe from *dari* 'move sneakily'
úbúbúl	'roll'	> *ububulanu* (tr.) *ubublanɛ* (intr.)
úlúgúɲ	'hide'	> maybe from *ulub* 'cover' and *guɲ* 'see'
úsúrsí	'burn (tr.)'	> a lexicalized causative from *sur* 'burn (intr.)'
dáhóló?	'dance'	> maybe a compound verb > *hóló?* 'song'
ʤámárí	'begin'	> a loan verb (Amharic *ʤämärä* 'begin')

TABLE 7.19 Polysyllabic roots

Root	Gloss	Remark
bíbíʃí	'to get goose bumps'	CV:REDUP+
bábárí	'tremble'	CV:REDUP+
bédédég	'flash (lightening)'	+CV:REDUP
mílmílmíl	'glitter'	CVC:REDUP
kédékédé	'whisper (sense-speech)'	CVCV:REDUP
hóhóhóhó	'whisper (object)'	CVCV:REDUP
kúčúkúčú	'silence, saying nothing'	CVCV:REDUP
héléŋhéléŋ	'become loose'	CVCVC:REDUP
bíríkbírík	'shine brightly (also glitter)'	CVCVC:REDUP

cient in terms of certain grammatical categories. They do not take any verbal morphology, and thus they usually occur with the auxiliary verb *se* 'say'.

7.3 Morphological Properties

The morphological properties generally cover all aspects of Mursi verbs. Mursi verb roots in general can be marked for verbal inflectional categories such as, valence, negation, motion, and for syntactic canonicity (verb-final suffix). These can be subdivided into two major morphological categories: inflection (§ 7.3.1) and derivation (§ 7.3.2). Except for tense and reflexive action that are expressed by separate grammatical words, all the rest of non-spatial and spatial settings in Mursi are expressed in the inflectional system. The derivational morphology normally covers three grammatical categories: causative, nominalization, relativization.

Mursi is an agglutinating language with some degree of fusion; it is highly synthetic (up to seven morphemes per verb root). It also is predominantly a suffixing language and has a few slots for prefixes. Verbal roots have three prefix slots. Given the agglutinating nature of Mursi morphology, there is a correlation between the shape of verb roots and the number of inflectional elements they may take. Monosyllabic verb roots usually take as many inflectional categories as they can. Disyllabic verb roots take just a few inflections and trisyllabic roots take fewer. Verb-like ideophone verb roots may take just one, or may not take an inflection at all. As an exception, there are few monosyllabic and disyllabic verb roots which take a prefix and just one or two suffixes at a maximum. The eroded verb root *élí* 'call', an auxiliary *sé* 'say', an existential verb *íh* 'exist, present', the verb *lɔ̀m* 'have' and polysyllabic ideophone-like verbs are among those that take few inflectional and derivational categories.

Note that not all these verbal categories can be added to verb roots at a time, and not all verb roots have the same capacity in taking of these categories. Some grammatical categories may occupy the same slot, and they may also be adjacent categories in overlapping situations. For example, the majority of *t(V)*-prefixing verb roots are intransitive stative verbs and they never co-occur with the causatives in Mursi. In Mursi, there are four double markings: negation, causative, aspect and hortative/jussive. Tense is primarily marked by separate time words.

The following two examples in (7.3) and (7.4) illustrate the verbal complex—where (7.3a–b) are clause final predicates, thus marked for verb-final suffix while (7.4) is in a non-clause final predicate position and unmarked for verb-final suffix.

(7.3) a. *húllí=ŋà   ìggè [tɔ̀mɔ̀n kó   ràmàn-nè] bè   áɲój*
TEMP/COND 2PL ten   PNC two-ORD DIST.PAST 1SG-PVS
ŋà=kí-bír-ón-úŋ=ó-ɔ̀?
NEG.IMPERV=1SU-choose-MT-2PL.OBJ=NEG-VFS
'Have I not chosen you twelfth?'

The complex predicate in (7.3a) contains six verbal component slots: 1, 2, root, 7, 8, 10, and 14 while (7.4b) contains all the verbal slots of (7.3a) and one additional slot, i.e. slot 9.

TABLE 7.20 The structure of a Mursi verb and suffix-clitic ordering

Slot	Function	Morpheme	Morphological formation		
SLOT 1	Negation (imperfective)	ŋà=	inflection	proclitic	(§ 13.2.1; § 2.8)
	– Negation perfective	k(V)-	inflection	prefix	(§ 13.2.2)
SLOT 2	First person (S, A)	k(V)-	inflection	prefix	(§ 7.3.1.1)
	– Passive	k(V)-	inflection	prefix	(§ 9.2.1)
	– Hortar./Juss./Subjun.	k(V)-	inflection	prefix	(§ 7.3.1.3.2–§ 7.3.1.3.4)
SLOT 3	Aspect (perfective)	t(V)-	inflection	prefix	(§ 7.3.1.2.4)
SLOT 4	Causative	í-	derivation	prefix	(§ 9.3.3)
SLOT 5	ROOT	ROOT	ROOT	ROOT	(§ 7.2–§ 7.2.3)
SLOT 6	Causative	-ísí(-sí)	derivation	suffix	(§ 9.3.3)
SLOT 7	Number/Aspect (S, A)	-t/-d́	inflection	suffix	(§ 6.7)
	– Direction/ Motion (ventive)	-áná/-ónó -a/-o	inflection	suffix	(§ 9.3.4)
	– Direction/ motion (itive)	-sɛn/-sɛ	inflection	suffix	(§ 9.3.4)
	– Imperative (plural)	-V	inflection	suffix	(§ 7.3.1.3.1)
	– Hortative/ Jussive	-V	inflection	suffix	(§ 7.3.1.3.2; § 7.3.1.3.3)
	– Benefactive-applicative	-ɛ̀sɛ̀n(-sɛ̀n)	inflection	suffix	(§ 9.3.1)
	– Reciprocal/antipassive	-nɛ̀n/-nɛ̀	inflection	suffix	(§ 9.2.3; § 9.2.2)
	– Applicative/commitative	-ɛ -čo/-čV -čiŋ	inflection	suffix	(§ 9.3.2) (e.g. 7.113b)
	– Agentive	-ɲógi(-a)	derivation	suffix	(e.g. 2.4; 8.9)
SLOT 8	Participant reference O		inflection	suffix	(§ 7.3.1.1)
SLOT 9	Participant reference S/A		inflection	suffix	(§ 7.3.1.1)
SLOT 10	Negation	=ó	inflection	enclitic	(§ 13.2.1; 13.2.2)
SLOT 11	Relativizer	-a	inflection	suffix	(§ 4.3.3)
SLOT 12	Resolution marker	-ni	inflection	suffix	(§ 3.3.6.2; § 14.2.2.2)
SLOT 13	Subordinate marker	=jè(=è)	inflection	enclitic	(§ 14.2.1)
SLOT 14	Verb-final suffix	-a/-ɛ/-o/-ɔ/nɔ	inflection	suffix	(§ 10.5)

b. ŋà=kó-jóg-ón-óŋ-Ø=ó-ɔ̀
NEG.IMPERV=1SU-tell-MT-2PL:OBJ-1PL:INC:SU:IMPERV=NEG-VFS
'We (inc.) will not tell (it) to you (pl).'

(7.4) àɲè ŋà=lɔ́g=tá   ìggè kàrì ké   d́néj
1SG DEM=word/issue=NEAR 2PL all D.SP one
ŋà=kó-jóg-ó-úŋ=nó   zùw-á   [Ø bè
NEG.IMPERV=1SU-tell-MT-2PL:OBJ=NEG people-RSTR [Ø DIST.PAST

kí-bír-ón-úŋ-ó]rc *ạ̀ɲè ká-gá-úŋ-nɔ́*
1SU-choose-MT-2SG.OBJ-RSTR] 1SG 1SU-know-2PL.OBJ-VFS
'I speak not of you all; I know whom I have chosen.'

As shown in both (7.3) and (7.4), tense is not marked on the verb but indicated by a separate time word *bè* ⟨DISTANT PAST⟩.

7.3.1 Verbal Inflection

Mursi verbs are mainly inflected for bound pronominal S/A and O arguments (participant reference), aspect and mood (AM), motion/direction, valence, and negation. Valence and negation are discussed in chapter 9 and chapter 12 respectively.

7.3.1.1   Participant Reference

Participant referents are cross-referenced on the verb. In SCHEME II and throughout this grammar, the term 'participant reference (markers)' and 'bound pronominal (markers)' have been used interchangeably. Thus, all the bound pronominals: S (subject of an intransitive verb), A (subject of a transitive verb), and O argument markers are cross-referenced on the verb. The bound pronominal markers of the S/A arguments are different for imperfective and perfective aspect. Even within the perfective aspect, they display distinct suffixes on the basis of realis and irrealis moods.

Mursi has inclusive-exclusive distinction in the first person plural. In the imperfective aspect, third person singular is morphologically unmarked. The prefix *k(V)-* marks all first person singular and plural S/A arguments in the imperfective aspect and third person S/A of the irrealis in the perfective.

As illustrated in Table 7.22, the temporal perfective and simple perfective can be viewed within one grammatical reality of an event 'realis' and both are marked by distinct bound pronominal S/A argument suffixes. As Dixon (2012: 22) points out, 'realis refers to something which has happened or is happening'. Thus, within the framework of Dixon's 'realis' as a reality bounded by time of an event, it is possible to link the grammatical meaning of Mursi realis mood into: temporal perfective (as an event happened), and simple perfective (in general has no reference to temporality). Bryant (2013:60) has made similar S/A distinctions for Chai (Suri) language for what he called the temporal perfective (usage in non-narrative) and simple perfective (usage in narrative).

The verb in the temporal perfective form may include a tense marker lexical word *wa* 'recent past' and the verb-final consonant may geminate if the verb-root's final consonant is nasal, as shown in Table 7.24 below.

TABLE 7.21 Bound pronominal S/A suffixes in the imperfective aspect

Imperfective

	Singular	Plural
1	k(V)-ROOT-i	INC. k(V)-ROOT-Ø EXC. k(V)-ROOT-o
2	ROOT-i	ROOT-o
3	ROOT-Ø	ROOT-ɛ

TABLE 7.22 Bound pronominal S/A suffixes in the perfective aspect—realis

	Temporal perfective Singular	Temporal perfective Plural	Simple perfective Singular	Simple perfective Plural
1	k(V)-ROOT-a	INC. k(V)-ROOT-a EXC. k(V)-ROOT-o	k(V)-ROOT-a	INC. k(V)-ROOT-Vɛ EXC. k(V)-ROOT-o
2	ROOT-u	ROOT-o	ROOT-u	ROOT-o
3	ROOT-a	ROOT-a	ROOT-a[V]	ROOT-Vɛ

TABLE 7.23 S/A suffixes in temporal perfective—ɓik 'break'

	S/A suffix	Gloss
1sg	kí-ɓík-á	'I had broken'
2sg	ɓík-ú	'You (SG) had broken'
3sg	ɓík-á	'S/he it has broken'
1pl.inc.	kí-ɓík-t-á	'We have broken'
1pl.exc.	kí-ɓík-t-ó	'We have broken'
2pl	ɓík-t-ó	'You had broken'
3pl	ɓík-t-á	'They had broken'

THE VERB AND PREDICATE STRUCTURE   291

TABLE 7.24 S/A suffixes in temporal perfective—*èlèhèn* 'measure'

	Tense	S/A suffix	Gloss
1sg	wà	k-èlèhèn-á	'I have measured'
2sg	wà	èlèhèn-ú	'You have measured'
3sg	wà	èlèhèn-á	'S/he have measured'
1pl.inc.	wà	k-èlèhèn-ná	'We have measured'
1pl.exc.	wà	k-èlèhèn-nó	'We have measured'
2pl	wà	èlèhèn-nó	'You have measured'
3pl	wà	èlèhèn-ná	'They have measured'

TABLE 7.25 S/A suffixes in simple perfective—*ɓik* 'break'

	S/A suffix	Gloss
1sg	kí-ɓík-à	'I broke'
2sg	ɓík-ù	'You broke'
3sg	ɓíg-ɛ̀	'S/he broke'
1pl.INC.	kí-ɓíg-è	'We broke'
1pl.EXC.	kí-ɓíg-ò	'We broke'
2pl	ɓíg-t-ò	'You broke'
3pl	ɓíg-èɛ̀	'They broke'

Moreover, as can be shown in Table 7.23 and 7.24 above, the major difference between the temporal and simple perfective come from the first person plural inclusive and the third person plural subject bound pronominal S/A argument suffixes. With regard to simple perfective in Chai (Suri) language, Bryant (2013:61) noted that the first person plural inclusive and the third person plural subject suffixes copy the vowel of the preceding verb root. Vowel copying is not the case in Mursi, even if there is some sort of segmental resemblance between the simple perfective subject suffixes and the vowel of the verb roots. The subject suffix –Vɛ ⟨1pl.INC., 3pl.⟩ that occur only on the simple perfective forms of verb seems to have phonologically motivated variants, as shown in Table 7.25 and 7.26 above.

There is an exceptional instance where the third person singular form is marked by the same subject suffix as the first and third person plural forms. In

TABLE 7.26   S/A suffixes in simple perfective—
            èlèhèn 'measure'

	S/A suffix	Gloss
1sg	k-èlèhèn-á	'I measured'
2sg	èlèhèn-ú	'You measured'
3sg	èlèhèn-ú	'S/he measured'
1pl.INC.	k-èlèhèn-ɛ	'We measured'
1pl.EXC.	k-èlèhèn-ó	'We measured'
2pl	èlèhèn-ó	'You measured'
3pl	èlèhèn-ɛ́	'They measured'

TABLE 7.27   Bound pronominal S/A suffixes
            in the perfective aspect—irrealis

Hortative/jussive/subjunctive

	Singular	Plural
1	k(V)-ROOT-Ø	INC. k(V)-ROOT-V
		EXC. k(V)-ROOT-tò
3	k(V)-ROOT-Ø	k(V)-ROOT-V́

Table 7.25 above, the subject suffix of the third person simple perfective form is -ɛ, which is not regular.

In Mursi, the irrealis system includes hortative, jussive and subjunctive moods and utilizes distinct bound pronominal S/A argument suffixes. Dixon (2012: 22) points out that irrealis denotes two situations: 'something which has not (yet) happened' and 'something which did not happen in the past, but might have'. See further discussion in § 7.3.1.3.4.

The fact is that both realis and irrealis operate within the aspect system of the languages, which is independent of a tense system. The main reason I distinctly treated the term subjunctive within the irrealis mood is that it has a separate lexical word in addition to the subject markers that indicate a subjunctive construction.

The first and the third person in the perfective aspect display syncretism where the first person of the perfective-realis and the third person of the perfective-irrealis are syncretic.

TABLE 7.28 First/third person syncretism

	Perfective-realis		Perfective-irrealis	
	Singular	Plural	Singular	Plural
1	k(V)-ROOT-a	k(V)-ROOT-a	k(V)-ROOT-Ø	k(V)-ROOT-V
		k(V)-ROOT-o		k(V)-ROOT-tò
3	ROOT-a	ROOT-a	k(V)-ROOT-Ø	k(V)-ROOT-V́

TABLE 7.29 Object pronominal suffixes

	Singular	Plural
1	-áɲ/-óɲ	-i
2	-íɲ	-ùŋ [-oŋ]
3	Ø	Ø

Mursi has six bound pronominal O argument markers, as can be seen in Table 7.29 below. The two variants of the first person singular object suffix are the result of vowel height harmony. In addition, the third person object suffix -ùŋ has an allomorph [-oŋ]. The third person object argument is morphologically unmarked.

When bound pronominal S/A and O argument markers co-occur on verbs, the O argument always precedes the S/A argument. In rare instances, the co-occurrence order of the S/A and O argument marking may be inconsistent, i.e. the marking of object suffixes appears to result in the omission of some subject suffixes from a suffix position. It should be noted that the omission of subject suffixes is sometimes related to the transitivity of verbs and mood. The following conditions must be fulfilled that would govern the entire co-occurrence relation between S/A and O suffixes:

i. The second and third person subject suffixes can be omitted if they co-occur with the first person object suffix.
ii. The first and third person subject suffixes can be omitted if they co-occur with the second person object suffix (as in (7.5)).

(7.5) k-ór-ɨ́ɲ dórí tó-jé
1SU-see.IMPERV-2SG.OBJ house in-OBL
'I see you (sg.) in the house.'

iii. If a first person subject is stated and is not in a suffix position, it must be stated at least in the prefix position (see example 7.5).
iv. As it is a highly participant reference marking language, the information carried by the omitted subject marking suffixes must be retrievable from adjacent independent arguments or be recoverable from the context. However, due to some unusual narration types in different genres of stories, exceptional cases may exist, as exemplified below in 7.6.

(7.6) híh! ná ɨɲè kɨ́ɲáŋ húŋ ɓák-ú kɛ̀ ɔ̀ŋ kó
INTERJ CCN 2SG crocodile simply eat-3SG.SU.PERV why? PNC
ɓásáj ɓák-ú kɛ̀ ɔ̀ŋ dág-ɑ́ɲ-Ø
monitor.lizard eat-3SG.SU.PERV why? hit-1SG.OBJ-3SG.SU
hózò-j aj!?
hanger-NOM INTERJ
'"Hih!" why did you (sg.) eat a crocodile? Also you (sg.) ate a monitor lizard why? Don't say, "Hunger hit me?!" Aj!' (MH 4:30:6)

Note that the first person object suffix (dág-ɑ́ɲ ⟨hit-1SG.OBJ⟩) in (7.6) is subject-switching. It is switching from where the narrator is describing a situation between his people and the other neighboring people with whom they used to fight a long time ago over cattle looting and grazing land. So, then he suddenly became emotional and started telling the story with an irony by involving himself as first speaker.

Unlike bound pronominal S/A suffixes, bound pronominal object suffixes may undergo a vowel height harmony process, as shown in (7.7a–c; 7.8).

(7.7) a. rɛ̀ ɑ́n-ɑ́ɲ mà
body COP.IMPERV-1SG.OBJ water
'I get wet.'
(Lit. 'body to me is water')

b. rɛ̀hì ɑ́n-í mà
body.PL COP.IMPERV-1PL.OBJ water
'We get wet.'
(Lit. 'bodies to us are water')

c. *nìɲ-n-áɲ-ɔ̀*
exist.NEG-EPENT-1SG.OBJ-VFS
'I am not present'
(Lit. 'Me not exist/present')

(7.8) *ìɲè wà jóg-é-í-ú[o] àggè*
2SG REC.PAST tell-MA-1PL.OBJ-2SG.SU.PERV 1PL
'You (sg.) have told us.'

The use of intransitive verb *irid* '(be) born' as transitive 'give birth' requires the passive form prefix *k-*, the ventive suffix as dative (an extension to the core argument E), and just object suffixes.

(7.9) a. *k-ìrìd-òn-óɲ-nɔ̀*
PASS-born-DAT-1SG.OBJ-VFS
'I gave birth'
(Lit. 'It born to me')

b. *k-ìrìd-òn-Ø-ɔ̀*
PASS-born-DAT-3SG.OBJ-VFS
'He gave birth'
(Lit. 'It born to him')

c. *k-ìrìd-òn-í-t-ɔ̀*
PASS-born-DAT-1PL.OBJ-PERV:PL-VFS
'We gave birth'
(Lit. 'It born to us')

7.3.1.2 Aspect

Mursi utilizes a complex system of aspect marking that can be subsumed within two broad categories: imperfective and perfective. Regarding these two notions, a straightforward definition is as follows. Perfective indicates 'the view of a situation as a single whole, without distinction of the various separate phases that make up that situation; while the imperfective pays essential attention to the internal structure of the situation' (Comrie 1976:16).

In light of the above holistic definition of imperfective and perfective, Mursi sets certain mood and voice categories into one of the two aspectual categories. For instance, an imperfective verb root is used for negative imperative mood while the perfective verb root is used for positive imperative, hortative/jussive and subjunctive moods. The passive voice also utilize the perfective verb root. All categories of mood are discussed in § 7.3.1.2.

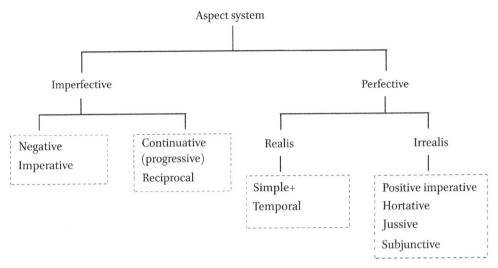

DIAGRAM 7.1   Mursi aspect system vis-à-vis bound pronominal S/A marking
              Note: Note that there are no irrealis distinctions in the imperfective aspect.

Aspect in Mursi is mostly associated with full verb root. Aspect is shown on verbs in the following ways—(i) by bound pronominal subject marking suffixes (§ 7.3.1.2.1) and (ii) a number of different verb root alternations and morphological phenomena (§ 7.3.1.2.2–§ 7.3.1.2.7). Each of these aspect marking categories clearly indicate the imperfective and perfective aspectual distinctions.

7.3.1.2.1   *Subject Pronominal Suffixes*
The bound pronominal subject suffixes are used as the only aspect marking elements on verbs when verb roots have invariable forms for both imperfective and perfective aspect. Thus, each invariable verb root is assigned a subject suffix of its own which enables it to distinguish the two aspectual distinctions overtly. Imperfective and perfective aspect distinction by subject suffixes are illustrated in (7.10) and (7.11). For the purpose of number of the S/A distinction in the perfective aspect, two verbs, having distinct root shapes were selected: *bág* 'eat' (consonant-final root) and *lámí* 'search, find' (vowel-final root).

(7.10)

	Imperfective	Gloss	Perfective	Gloss
1sg.	ká-bág-í	'I eat'	ká-bág-á	'I ate'
2sg.	bág-í	'You eat'	bág-ú	'You are'
3sg.	bág-Ø	'S/he eats'	bág-á	'S/he ate'
1pl.INC.	ká-bág-Ø	'We eat'	ká-bág-t-á	'We ate'
1pl.EXC.	ká-bág-ó	'We eat'	ká-bág-t-ó	'We ate'
2pl.	bág-ó	'You eat'	bág-t-ó	'You ate'
3pl.	bág-é	'They eat'	bág-t-á	'They ate'

(7.11)

	Imperfective	Perfective	Gloss
1sg.	ká-lámí-í	ká-lámí-á	'I search/searched'
2sg.	lámí-í	lámí-ú	'You search/searched'
3sg.	lámí-Ø	lámí-a	'S/he searches/searched'
1pl.INC.	ká-lámí-Ø	ká-lámí-d-á	'We search/searched'
1pl.EXC.	ká-lámí-ó	ká-lámí-d-ó	'We search/searched'
2pl.	lámí-ó	lámí-d-ó	'You search/searched'
3pl.	lámí-ɛ́	lámí-d-á	'They search/searched'

It appears that Mursi is a highly strategic language in the way it keeps back-ups for the various deficiencies that might happen in certain grammatical categories. For instance, in both (7.10) and (7.11), the imperfective form of the 1pl.EXC. and 2pl. are identical to those in the perfective aspect. In fact, without the bicategorical markers -t and -d, it would be impossible to distinguish between imperfective and perfective forms. Here the term bicategorical is used to indicate the function of -t and -d in two grammatical categories—as number and as aspect markers. I tentatively prefer to label these two suffixes as 'completive markers'.

The suffix -t has been noted as a plural suffix for Suri (Chai) (Bryant 2013:62). However, Mütze (2014) pointed out that this suffix occasionally precedes the subject suffix in the plural in perfective aspect. In both works, no mention has been made of the suffix -d. Nevertheless, Mütze was right in pointing out the suffix -t also occurs in the singular. The suffix -t has different functions when it occur before singular subjects in the imperfective aspect and when it occur before plural subjects in the perfective aspect. On the other hand, it has bicategorical morphological functions when it occurs preceding plural subjects in the perfective aspect. In the imperfective aspect, the suffix -t appears only with the third person singular and first person plural inclusive subjects. Morphologically, both subjects are apparently marked by zero suffix. Compare the forms in the examples below.

(7.12) a. dág 'hit'

	Imperfective	Perfective	Gloss
3sg.	dág-t-Ø-ɔ̀	dák-á	'S/he hits/hit'
3pl.	dág-ɛ-ɔ̀	dák-t-á	'They hit'
1pl.INC.	ká-dák-t-Ø-ɔ̀	ká-dák-t-á	'We (inc.) hit'

b. *dug* 'plant'

	Imperfective	Perfective	Gloss
3sg.	dúg-t-Ø-ɔ̀	dúk-á	'S/he plants/planted'
3pl.	dúg-ɛ-ɔ̀	dúk-t-á	'They plant/planted'
1pl.INC.	kú-dúk-t-Ø-ɔ̀	kú-dúk-t-á	'We (inc.) plant/planted'

As can be seen from the form of the third person singular and first person plural in the imperfective aspect, the verb-final suffix -ɔ̀ is the only element next to the roots. This means that the root's final segment (velar plosive) /g/ lenites to the glottal stop [ʔ] word-finally, because in both cases the roots are clause-final words. In other word, we would have **daʔ* and **duʔ* verb root forms, a form that never exist in the language. The glottal stop /ʔ/ is epenthesised often between clitics that end in a vowel and phonological or grammatical words that begin in a vowel. In addition, the verb-final suffix -ɔ̀ is a morphologically marked syntactic element and it never had a morphological role. It appears that the suffix -*t* is occasionally inserted before the verb-final suffix -ɔ̀ perhaps to indicate some sort of distinction between the morphological inflection and syntactic inflection.

7.3.1.2.2 Full Suppletion

A full suppletive forms of verb roots are used to distinguish between the two aspectual meanings, and they in no way have similarities with even a single segment. They are mostly monosyllabic verb roots and belong to different transitivity classes. Some examples are illustrated in (7.13) and (7.14).

(7.13)

	Imperfective	Perfective	Gloss
1sg.	kà-màt-í	k-ìr-á	'I drink/drank'
2sg.	màt-í	ìr-ú	'You drink/drank'
3sg.	màt-Ø	ir-á	'S/he drinks/drank'
1pl.INC.	kà-màt-Ø	k-ìr-t-á	'We drink/drank'
1pl.EXC.	kà-màt-ó	k-ìr-t-ó	'We drink/drank'
2pl.	màt-ó	ìr-t-ó	'You drink/drank'
3pl.	màt-έ	ìr-t-á	'They drink/drank'

(7.14)

	Imperfective	Perfective	Gloss
1sg.	ká-gáj-í	ká-ták-á	'I know/knew'
2sg.	gáj-í	ták-ú	'You know/knew'
3sg.	gáj-Ø	ták-á	'S/he knows/knew'
1pl.INC.	ká-gáj-Ø	ká-ták-t-á	'We know/knew'
1pl.EXC.	ká-gáj-ó	ká-ták-t-ó	'We know/knew'

	2pl.	gáj-ó	ták-t-ó	'You know/knew'
	3pl.	gáj-έ	ták-t-á	'They know/knew'

7.3.1.2.3 Partial Root Suppletion

Verb roots may distingush aspect by a partial root suppletion. A partial verb root suppletion applies to both consonant and vowel initial roots. Verbs such as ŋór 'carry', ór 'see' and og 'cook' undergo a partial root suppletion process.

(7.15)

	Imperfective	Perfective	Gloss
3sg.	ŋór-Ø-ɔ̀	ŋár-á	'S/he carries/carried'
3pl.	ŋór-ɛ-ɔ̀	ŋár-t-á	'They carry/carried'
3sg.	ór-Ø-ɔ̀	ár-á	'S/he sees/saw'
3pl.	ór-ɛ-ɔ̀	ár-t-a	'They see/saw'
3sg.	òg-t-ɔ̀	àk⟨g⟩-á	'S/he cooks/cooked'
3pl.	òg-ɛ-ɔ̀	àk-t-á	'They cook/cooked'

7.3.1.2.4 Prefixing t(V)-

Verb roots which distinguish aspect by a *t(V)*- prefix are regularly associated with one syntactic value, i.e. intransitive. Semantically, t(V)- prefixing roots are state experiential and benefactive verbs denoting affection, desire, sensation, and so on. Like other prefixes (except the causative), this prefix copies the first vowel of the verb root. Thus, the prefix *t*- is attached to a verb root that begins with a vowel while the prefix *tV*- is attached to a verb root that begins with a consonant.

(7.16)

Imperfective	Perfective	Gloss
lɔ̀m	tɔ̀-lɔ̀m	'have'
már	tá-már	'dislike, refuse'
hár	tá-hár	'vomit'
óɲ	t-óɲ	'wash'

The roots in (7.16) do not undergo further root alternation process. On the other hand, the verb roots in (7.17) below undergo a two-step change despite the fact that they are *t(V)*- prefixing type.

(7.17)

	Imperfective	Perfective	Gloss
a.	hín	tè-hén	'want desire'
b. éŋérs	t-éŋér	'afraid'
c. rú[rúj]	tú-r⟨rr⟩	'cry'

As it is shown in (7.17), two-step changes have been displayed, namely, internal vowel change and *tV-* prefixing (7.17a), final consonant reduction followed *t-* prefixing (7.17b), and vowel reduction (7.17c). There is one more verb that can take the *tV-* prefix in the imperfective as well as in the perfective aspects—*jél* 'like, love'. For a perfective aspect, it can be manifested either with its initial consonant altered form or in its regular *tV-* prefixed form.

(7.18)
		Imperfective	Perfective	Gloss
	1sg.	*ké-jél-í*	*ké-té-jél-à*	'I like/liked'
	1pl.INC.	*ké-jél-Ø*	*ké-té-jél-á*	'We like/liked'
	3sg.	*jél-Ø*	*té-jél-á*	'S/he likes/liked'
	3pl.	*jél-ɛ́*	*té-jél-á*	'They like/liked'

(7.19)
		Imperfective	Perfective	Gloss
	1sg.	*ké-jél-í*	*ké-tél-à*	'I like/liked'
	1pl.INC.	*ké-jél-Ø*	*ké-tél-á*	'We like/liked'
	3sg.	*jél-Ø*	*tél-à*	'S/he likes/liked'
	3pl.	*jél-ɛ́*	*tél-á*	'They like/liked'

In (7.18), a *tV-* prefixed form of the root in the perfective aspect distinguishes aspect. The other variety of the same verb root is in a morphologically unsegmentable form where the perfective aspect prefix and the root are fused together as one, as show in (7.19). When this is seen from outside, it appears that the change is root-internal which is being manifested in the form of initial-consonant suppletion. Besides, *t(V)-* prefixing verb roots can be further divided into two—those that take the suffix *-t* (for example *mar, eɲɛrs, ru* [ruj]) and those that do not. The roots that do not take the suffix *-t* tend to have similar forms in their first person singular/plural and third person singular/plural forms in the perfective aspect. Thus they can be distinguished only by the tone marked on their subject suffixes. Interestingly, in (7.18) one may see an instance of double vowel copying process (cf. §2.5.6.5).

7.3.1.2.5 *Final Consonant Reduction/Deletion*

Some of verbs that undergo a root-final consonant deletion (reduction/subtraction) include stative and auxiliary verbs. Alveolars /s/ and /n/ which often occur at the root final position of these verbs are the ones that are most exposed to deletion.

(7.20) a. *bans* 'fly, stand up'

	Imperfective	Perfective	Gloss
1sg.	ká-báns-í-ɔ̀	ká-bán-á	'I fly/flew'
2sg.	báns-í-ɔ̀	bán-ú	'You fly/flew'
3sg.	bánás-Ø-ɔ̀	bán-á	'S/he flies/flew'

b. *mɔ̀dɔ̀s* 'be tired'

	Imperfective	Perfective	Gloss
1sg.	kɔ̀-mɔ̀dɔ̀s-í-ɔ̀	kɔ̀-mɔ̀d-á	'I get/got tired'
2sg.	mɔ̀dɔ̀s-í-ɔ̀	mɔ̀d-ú	'You get/got tired'
3sg.	mɔ̀dɔ̀s-Ø-ɔ̀	mɔ̀d-á	'S/he gets/got tired'

c. *múɲús* 'be angry'

	Imperfective	Perfective	Gloss
1sg.	kú-múɲús-í-ɔ̀	kú-múɲí-á	'I get/got angry'
2sg.	múɲús-í-ɔ̀	múɲí-ú	'You get/got angry'
3sg.	múɲús-Ø-ɔ̀	múɲí-á	'S/he gets/got angry'
1pl.EXC.	kú-múɲús-ó	kú-múɲí-d-ó	'We get/got angry'

In (7.20c), it is not only final consonant deletion that has taken place but also a vowel fronting where the high back vowel is being replaced by the high front vowel. Thus, like a vowel-final verb root, it also takes the suffix -*d* (of a perfective-plural marker). The auxiliary verb *sén* 'to say' has an eroded-like root, undergoes a similar final consonant reduction process and takes the suffix -*d* like ⟨1pl.EXC.⟩ in (7.21).

(7.21)

	Imperfective	Perfective	Gloss
1sg.	ké-sén-í	ké-sé-á	'I say/said'
2pl.	sén-ó	sé-d-ó	'You (pl.) say/said'
3pl.	sén-έ	sé-d-á	'They say/said'

It can occur with a direct speech particle ké in the third person singular imperfective that makes it unique among verbs—*sé ké* ⟨say.imperv quot⟩ 'say that' (cf. §7.3.1.2.10). We must note that alveolars are in general deleted in the syllable-final position but they are deleted only when they occur as the last segments of a word. In the above cases, at least, the alveolars /s/ and /n/ are preceded by the subject suffixes, thus they are certainly not the last segments. In short, the deletion is morphologically-driven, it is not phonological.

7.3.1.2.6 *Final Syllable Reduction*

Despite the fact that they are a few, Mursi verbs can indicate aspectual distinctions by reducing their root final syllables, as in (7.22).

(7.22)   Imperfective   Perfective   Gloss
         ɔ́ŋɔ́n-Ø-ɔ̀   t-ɔ́ŋ-á   'S/he smells (stinks)/smelt'
         ɔ́ŋón-Ø-ɔ̀   t-óŋ-á   'S/he throws/threw; launch (of a boat)'
         úɲús-Ø-ɔ̀   t-úŋ-á   'S/he sleeps/slept'

These verbs not only reduce their syllables but also take the prefix *t(V)-*. They may also be also regarded as a sub-type of verbs that indicate aspectual distinctions by prefixing *t(V)-*.

7.3.1.2.7 *Multiple Alternations*

Aspect can be shown by multiple root alternations which may take place one at a time. Multiple root alternations occur in two ways—the first involves a combination of *t(V)-* prefixing and deletion while the second involves a three or four term root supletion. Typical examples are *géɲ* 'create, repair, fix' and *gúrt* 'pull'.

(7.23)   Imperfective   Perfective   Gloss
    a. 3sg.   géɲ-Ø-t-ɔ̀   téɲ-á   'S/he creates/created'
       3pl.   géɲ-έ-ɔ̀   téɲ-n-á   'They create/created'

The verb *gurt* 'pull' has a /t/ final root, thus it displays a geminate [tt] in the third person singular and first person plural inclusive forms in the imperfective aspect. Thus a vowel which is identical with the vowel of the root is inserted between the root and the suffix *-t* in a way that doesn't violate the consonant co-occurrence restrictions—/gurt-Ø-t-ɔ̀/→ [gurut-Ø-t-ɔ̀].

                Imperfective   Perfective   Gloss
   b. 3sg.   gúrút-Ø-t-ɔ̀   túr-á   'S/he pulls/pulled'
      3pl.   gúrt-έ-ɔ̀   túr-t-á   'They pull/pulled'
      1pl.INC. kúrút-Ø-t-ɔ̀   kútúr-t-á   'We pull/pulled'

Note that the base form is *gurt* not *gúrút*. What is taking place here is that this verb needs one or more morphological reshaping processes to happen at a time—mainly deletion and a *t(V)-* prefixing. Both changes take place in the perfective aspect, i.e. first a perfective aspect marker prefix *t(V)-* will be added to the imperfective root, thus results an underlying form /tugurut/. Then, the most frequently occurring morphonological rule of the language comes next which is the deletion of a consonant between two identical vowels. As always a velar plosive /g/ is deleted—/tugurut/ ~ [turut]. After the two root reshaping processes, root-final syllable deletion may optionally apply to the third person singular perfective root [turut] ~ [túr].

Many Nilo-Saharan linguists (especially those who work on Eastern Sudanic languages) argue that verbs such as *gurt* 'pull' could indicate aspect by metathesis of—/gurt/ > [gurut] > [turug] > [tur]>. However, the correct analysis is a *t(V)*- prefixing rule (morphological rule) that applies on the basis of phonotactic constraint rule (phonological rule) which follows: *t(V)*- prefixing /gurt/ > [t-gurt] >; deletion of /g/ (consonant clusters are not allowed at word-initial positions) > [turt], and finally we get a *CVC* shape > [tur]. However, that is not the case. In order to make such a claim, first one has to properly understand the phonological rules of the language under investigation. In this regard, verb roots with a *t-final* consonant can be tricky.

The second type of verbs that distinguish aspect by multiple root alternations are number-determined suppletive verbs—*ádʒ* 'give', *kún* 'come, bring', *ɔ́k* 'go', *íh* 'exist/present', *ésé* 'sit'. Each of these verbs undergo three to four root alternations. The verb *ádʒ* 'give' has the same root form for all persons in the imperfective aspect while in the perfective aspect it shows two forms—*áín* with singular subject and *ad* with plural subjects.

(7.24)

Imperfective	Gloss	Perfective	Gloss
k-ádʒ-í-ɔ̀		k-áín-ɛ-á	
ádʒ-í-ɔ̀		áín-ɛ-ú	1/2/3(SG) 'gave'
ádʒ-Ø-ɔ̀		áín-ɛ-á	
k-ádʒ-Ø-ɔ̀	1/2/3(SG/PL) 'give'	k-ád-á	
k-ádʒ-ó-ɔ̀		k-ád-ó	
ádʒ-ó-ɔ̀		ád-ó	1/2/3 (PL) 'gave'
ádʒ-ɛ-ɔ̀		ád-á	

The verb *kun* 'come' shows a four-term root suppletion: two terms in the imperfective aspect and two terms in the perfective aspect and each is directly associated with number.

(7.25)

	Imperfective	Perfective	Gloss
1sg.	kúún-í	k-áíw-ó	'I come/came.'
2sg.	kún-í	áíw-ó	'You (sg.) come/came.'
3sg.	kún-Ø	áíw-ò	'S/he comes/came.'

1pl.INC	kó-hóɲ-Ø	kó-hód́-á-á	'We come/came.'
1pl.EXC	kó-hóɲ-nó	kó-hód́-á-ó	'We come/came.'
2pl.	hóɲ-ó	hód́-á-ó	'You (pl.) come/came.'
3pl.	hóɲ-nò	hód́-á-à	'They come/came.'

The long vowel in the first person singular is the result of compensatory lengthening that comes when the first person subject marker prefix *ku-* is fused with the root—*ku-kún* ~ ⟨kúún⟩. The intransitive verb *kún* 'come' can be transitivized and bears the meaning 'bring' when the comitative-applicative suffix -ɛ is added to it. First person plural inclusive and second person plural take an allomorph of -ɛ, i.e. -čo.

(7.26)

	Imperfective	Perfective	Gloss
1sg.	kúún-ɛ-í	kúúj-á-ɛ-ó	'I bring/brought'
2sg.	kún-ɛ-í	kúj-á-ɛ-ó	'You (sg.) bring/brought'
3sg.	kún-ɛ-Ø	kúč-á-á	'S/he brings/brought'
1pl.INC.	kó-hóɲ-čo-Ø	kó-hóč-á-á	'We bring/brought'
1pl.EXC.	kó-hóɲ-ɛ-ó	kó-hóč-á-ó	'We bring/brought'
2pl.	hóɲ-čo-ó	hóč-á-ó	'You (pl.) bring/brought'
3pl.	hóɲɲ-ɛ-ɛ́	hóč-á-á	'They bring/brought'

As can be shown in (7.44), all the forms of the intransitive verb 'come' are marked with the comitative-applicative suffix. The allomorph -čo also marks person (1st INC, 2nd) and number (plural) of the applicative argument.

The third person plural subject suffix -ɛ in the imperfective aspect and the comitative-applicative suffix -ɛ attract gemination /hóɲɛɛ/ ~ [hóɲɲɛ]. On the other hand, all the perfective verb forms are marked with an invariable ventive (motion toward) suffix -*a* in addition to the comitative-applicative derivation suffix. In Mursi, both comitative-applicative and ventive are valency increasing derivational devices (see valency changing derivation Chapter 9).

7.3.1.2.8 *The Suffix* -nèn

In Mursi, the reciprocal suffix *-nèn* is used to expresses reciprocity, antipassive, progressive, and habitual actions. While it is used as progressive/habitual suffix, it can help to distinguish imperfective aspect from the perfective. The suffix –*nɛn* is also the second most productive multi-functional affix next to the prefix *k(V)-*. From a morphological point of view, the suffix *-nèn* can be treated as both inflectional as well as a derivation marker. It can also function as a nominalizer and may be used to derive nouns from verbs. Like most verbal suffixes, the suffix *-nɛn* is also a portmanteau suffix which varies according to aspect of the verb and person and number of the subject. In the imperfective aspect, first and second person take *-nèn* while the third person takes *-nè*, whereas all verb roots and persons in perfective aspect take the suffix *-ɛ*. The high front vowel /i/ is often epenthesised between consonant clusters.

(7.27)   Imperfective   Perfective   Gloss
   1sg.   kɔ́-lɔ̀tɔ̀g-ìnèn-ɔ̀   kɔ́-lɔ̀tɔ̀g-ɛ-á   'I get/got wet'
   2sg.   lɔ̀tɔ̀g-ìnèn-ɔ̀   lɔ̀tɔ̀g-ɛ-ú   'You get/got wet'
   3sg.   lɔ̀tɔ̀g-íné-ɔ̀   lɔ̀tɔ̀g-ɛ-á   'S/he get/got wet.'

Inherently reciprocal verbs such as *fíg* 'agree' and the verb *fɔla* 'suffer' (where the S argument is the sufferer/experiencer and the underlying O argument is the illness) express joint actions or situations and they take the suffix *-nèn*. Moreover, the suffix *-nèn* is often used with intransitive verb roots.

The suffix *-nèn* is a progressive/continuative aspect marker used to refer to an ongoing or dynamic process. This suffix is different from other aspect markers in that it is a polysemous suffix, which is also used as a valency changing marker in antipassive and reciprocal constructions. It can also be used as an action verb nominalizer. The fact is that the progressive marker *-nèn* can be attached to most of Mursi verbs independent of their semantic category, but is often attached to verbs that do not make any distinction between imperfective and perfective aspect.

(7.27-a)   ìnè   hàlì   támárí-nèn-ɔ̀
           2SG   later   learn-1/2.PROG-VFS
           'You will learn later.'

(7.27-b)   [ŋòná-à   n=ànù]ₙₚ   ók-ú   gáwá-jè   ná
           sister-RTSR SG.PSD=1SG.PSR   go-3SG.SU.PERV   markert-OBL   CCN
           ŋànì   àŋè   kɔ́-dɔ́t-inèn   dórí-jè-j
           but   1SG   1SU-leave-1/2.PROG house-OBL-NOM
           'My sister went to the market, but I stayed at home.'
           (Lit. 'My sister went to the marker and, but I am staying at the home.')

As far as the relation between the progressive aspect and antipassive derivation construction is concerned, both have a single aspectual category in common, i.e. in that both utilize imperfective aspect verb roots. See the example given below.

TABLE 7.30 Copula verbs

	Imperfective		Perfective	
	Singular	Plural	Singular	Plural
1	k-án-í	k-án-Ø (INC.)	ké-te(w)-a	ké-téd-ó-Ø (INC.)
		k-án-ó (EXC.)		ké-téd-ó-u (EXC.)
2	án-í	án-ó	té-ú	téd-ó
3	á	á	té	té

(7.27-c) ìggè màt-inèn-ó-ɔ̀
2PL drink.IMPERV-AP-2PL.SU.IMPERV-VFS
'You (pl.) are drinking.'

In few instances, the three (progressive, antipassive and reciprocal) may be shown at a time without causing any syntactic or semantic disambiguation. In the example below, the verb *bír* 'collect' has the same verb root form in both imperfective and perfective aspects, and at the same time indicates a continuous, antipassive and reciprocal actions.

(7.27-d) ŋànèjè kí-bír-nèn-á   húllí
but 1SU-collect-RECIP/PROG-1PL.INC.SU.PERV when
hód-á   nà   hód-á   íbt-á
come.PERV.PL-3SU CCN come.PERV.PL-3SU take-3PL.SU.PERV
óĺf-ó   gál-á   [g=í
stalk-PL thing.PL-RSTR [PL.GPN=NRESTR
n=àj-o=jè]_RC
SG.PSD=1PL.INC.PSR-??=SUBORD]
'But, while we are collecting, and if they come and take the stalk things that are ours ...' (KW 0:48:2)

7.3.1.2.9 *Copula Verbs*
Copula verbs in Mursi share a number of morphosyntactic properties with regular verbs and occupy the verbal position like any other verb in the canonical constituent order CS COP CC. However, when copula verbs function as predicates in a copular clause, they bear a number of special semantics associated to their syntactic position. The morphological property of copula verbs is discussed below. Copular clause is discussed in Chapter 14. Except

for third person, copula verbs are also inflected for person and number like regular verbs.

Copula verbs have distinct root forms for aspect—thus the root *an* 'is, be' is the base form of the imperfective aspect while *te* 'was, became' is the base form of the perfective aspect. We know that the third person singular subject suffix is not marked on verbs in the imperfective aspect. In such cases, there may be a possibility of deletion of the base's final segment (alveolar nasal) word-finally, i.e. /an/ ~ [a]. However, this only makes sense for the third person singular form of the imperfective aspect. Interestingly, when the third person form is negated the real form emerges. Compare the following examples:

(7.28) a1. *k-án-í*   *àɲè*
            1SU-COP.IMPERV-1SG.SU.IMPERV 1SG
            'I am'

       a2. *àɲè ŋà=k-án-í=ó*
            1SG NEG=COP.IMPERV-1SG.SU.IMPERV=NEG
            'I am not'

       b1. *á*   *nɔ̀ŋ*
            COP.3.IMPERV 3SG
            'He (it) is.'

       b2. *nɔ̀ŋ ŋà=án=ó*   →[ŋà=án-∅=ó]
            3SG NEG=COP.IMPERV=NEG
            'He (it) is not'

       c1. *á*   *jɔ̀g*
            COP.3.IMPERV 3PL
            'They are'

       c2. *jɔ̀g ŋà=áj=ó*
            3PL NEG=COP.3.IMPERV=NEG
            'They are not'

As we see (7.28b2), the negated form of the third person copula verb is the real form and it occurs as *ŋàànó* [ŋàʔánó]. The glottal stop /ʔ/ is often epenthesised between a proclitic that ends with a vowel and a root that begins with the same vowel. Whereas in (7.28c2), the copula form *ŋààjó* often occurs in free and lexicalized form and there is a tendency to epenthesise the palatal approximant

TABLE 7.31 Auxiliary verb

	Imperfective		Perfective	
	Singular	Plural	Singular	Plural
1	ké-sen-i	ké-sé-Ø (INC.)	ké-sé-á	ké-séd-á (INC.)
		ké-sén-ó (EXC.)		ké-séd-ó (EXC.)
2	sén-í	sén-ó	sé-ú	séd-ó
3	sé	sén-ɛ́	sé-á	séd-á

/j/ to block a sequence of three vowels when segmenting is required. In fast speech, however, only ŋàjó is recognized and it can be used as independent (free-form) negative copula word/particle denoting a meaning 'not, it is not, are not'

7.3.1.2.10 Auxiliary Verb

In a number of Semitic, Cushitic and Omotic languages of Ethiopia, the verb 'say' has wider functions among which is that it can be used to derive verb idioms and can be conjugated with other verbs as an auxiliary verb. Apparently, similar functions of the verb 'say' are attested in some Nilo-Saharan languages of Ethiopia, at least in the Southeast Surmic group—Mursi and Suri (Chai-Tirmaga-Me'en). The verb *sén* 'to say' appears to be the base form in the imperfective aspect. It is inflected for bound pronominal S/A and O arguments but it doesn't take full verbal inflections. For example, it cannot be negated and used in imperative construction. When an imperative form is needed, there is another verb which substitutes and is used to deliver a command, i.e.—*jog* 'say, speak, tell'.

Or rather, a command can be rendered through a jussive construction format, as in (7.29b). So, this is a like a command strategy.

(7.29) a. *kè-sè-Ø   ŋàŋà*
         PASS-say.PERV-3SG.OBJ like.this
         'It is being said'
         (Lit. 'It is said like this.')

      b. *aj   kè-sèd-á-ín-ó*
         JUSS.PART PASS-say.PERV-MT-2SG.OBJ-VFS
         'Let you (sg.) be told!'

THE VERB AND PREDICATE STRUCTURE

However, only the imperfective forms can fully function as auxiliary verbs. In such cases, they are often marked for person and number of the subject while the main verb that follows can be fully marked for the necessary agreement inflections. The semantics associated with auxiliary verbs include the expression of desire, intent, perception, uncertainty and so on.

(7.30) màmà   bá   sé   ké-té
        mother.PERT.SG.1.PSR place/CAUSE say.3SG.AUX 1SU-COP.PERV
        hír-á   kɔ́h-ìnɛ̀n-a   hín-Ø-ɔ̀
        man-RSTR farm/clear-NOMZ-RSTR   want-3SG.SU.IMPERV-VFS
        'My mother wants me to become a farmer.'
        (Lit. 'My mother in place want I be farmer, she wants.')

(7.31) [àhì-tí   hín-í   sé   ɔ́g-ɛ́=jè]_SUBORD:CL
        thing.SG-RTSR want-2SG.SU.IMPERV say.SG.AUX go-APPL=SUBORD
        kón-á   á   ɔ̀ŋ?
        one.INDEF-RSTR COP.3.IMPERV what?
        'What else do you want to take along?'
        (Lit. 'The thing that you (sg.) want to take, another is what?')

(7.32) bá-á   ŋà=lɔ̀gt=á   kámán-ùŋ=ŋà   ìŋè
        place-RSTR DEM=issue=NEAR   war-GEN=DEF   2SG
        sén-í   ɛ̀nɛ̀ŋ?
        say-2SG.SU.IMPERV how
        'What is your attitude toward war?'

(7.33) ká   sé   á   ʃɔ́l   bíí
        maybe say.3SG.AUX COP.3.IMPERV sharpened.wood AUT.REFL
        bɛ̀   á   ɔ̀ŋ   á   kì-tí
        DISTANT.PAST COP.3.IMPERV what COP.3.IMPERV wood-NRSTR
        [Ø nɔ̀ŋ   dáldá-í   hékɔ́ bɛ̀]_RC
        [Ø 3sg hard.STV-ADJ same stone]
        '... or maybe was it was sharp wood by itself or what was it? It is wood, which is strong like stone.' (MH: 2:03:0–2:12:09)

As it shown in the examples above—desire/intent (7.30 and 7.31), perception (7.32), and uncertainty (7.33).

TABLE 7.32   Imperative construction template

| | Positive imperative | | Negative imperative | |
	Singular	Plural	Singular	Plural
V-final	ROOT.PERV-a/-o	ROOT.PERV-V-ɛ	ŋà=ROOT.IMPERV-i	ŋà=ROOT.IMPERV-o
Non-final	ROOT.PERV	ROOT.PERV-V		

7.3.1.3   Mood

The mood category of Mursi includes imperative (7.3.1.3.1), hortative (7.3.1.3.2), jussive (7.3.1.3.3), reality status (7.3.1.3.4), and subjunctive (7.3.1.3). All are expressed by inflectional markings on the verbs. Only the hortative-jussive mood can be marked by an optional free morphological particle *aj/aɲ*. All utilize affixes with the exception of the negative imperative that utilizes the negative proclitic. All mood constructions utilize the perfective aspect verb roots.

7.3.1.3.1   *Imperative*

As Aikhenvald (2010: 2) puts it, 'imperative mood is the commonest way of expressing commands in the languages of the world'. In Mursi, the imperative mood refers to a command given to an addressee (the second person). The verb utilized in the positive imperative construction must always occur in the perfective aspect. The negative imperative construction utilizes a verb in the imperfective aspect. However, in both constructions number can be marked on the verb. The plural suffix -*V* is marked on the verb to denote plural addressee while the bare perfective verb root on its own indicates singular addressee. Person of the subject is unmarked (always second person). Verb-final suffixes -*a* (for singular), -*ɛ* (for plural) and variants of both -*o* can be added to a clause-finally occurring verbs of the imperative constructions.

In an instance when there is difficulty in making a distinction between imperfective and perfective aspects of the verb roots, one form of the root may be taken and can be glossed as perfective. Table 7.32 above presents the template of imperative on mood in Mursi and the verb forms and inflections utilized in the positive and negative imperative constructions.

(7.34)   a. *ʃíg-à*
             listen.PERV:IMP-VFS
             'Listen (2sg.)!'

b. *túnúg-ò*
   enter.PERV:IMP-VFS
   'Enter (2sg.)!'

However, there are few a verbs of the imperative form that do not take the verb-final suffixes *-a* or *-o*, for example, *áín* 'give' and *ré* 'wait', in (7.34c–d) below.

c. *áín-ɛ́*[1]
   give.PERV:IMP-TR
   'Give (2sg.)!'

d. *ré*
   wait.PERV:IMP
   'Wait (sg.)!'

The plural suffix form *-V* normally comes from the verb root where –V represents any 'V' value of the verb root. The plural suffix *-V* is a copy of the vowel of the verb root.

(7.35) a. *fíg-í-ɛ̀*
   listen.PERV:IMP-PL-VFS
   'Listen (pl.)!'

b. *bíg-í-ɛ̀*
   break.PERV:IMP-PL-VFS
   'Break (pl.)!'

c. *bág-á-ɛ̀*
   eat.PERV:IMP-PL-VFS
   'Eat (pl.)!'

d. *bón-ó-ɛ̀*
   arrive.PERV:IMP-PL-VFS
   'Arrive (pl.)!'

---

[1] In Mursi, it is obligatory for ditransitive verbs to indicate their transitivity by a morphological marker attached to their roots despite their transitivity being semantically known.

e. *túnúg-ú-è*
   enter.PERV:IMP-PL-VFS
   'Enter (pl.)!'

Note that in the imperative as well as in all other constructions, verbs cannot be marked with the verb-final suffix unless they occur clause-finally. However, a few motion verbs occur with the ventive (motion toward) suffix -*a* or -*o*. In such cases, the ventive suffix more likely tends to fuse with the verb-final suffix, as in (7.36a–b).

(7.36) a. *áíw-ó-ò*   [aiwo] < [o] < /o+o/
         come.PERV.SG:IMP-MT.PERV-VFS
         'Come (sg.)!'

   b. *áíw-ó*   *kì-dì-ì*   *kàrì*
      come.PERV.SG-MT.PERV 1.HORT-go.with-1PL.INC together
      [*bá-á*   *hùlè-č-ùŋ*]!
      place-RSTR flower-INSTR-GEN
      'Come (sg.) with me to the flower show!'

   c. *hód-á-á*   [hóda] < [a] < /a+a/
      come.PERV.PL:IMP-MT.PERV-VFS
      'Come (pl.)!'

In (7.36c), if the verb hadn't been a number-determined suppletive, there would be a chance to see a sequence of three vowels—one for number, one for ventive and one for verb-final. The verb itself has reduced unnecessary suffix redundancies. As it is shown above, the verb 'come' shows a bit of deviation when it is used in plural imperative form; in that it takes the verb-final suffix of the singular forms. Regarding number marking on the verb of the imperative form, the following exceptions have to be taken into account:

− For closed CVC and CVCVC ($V_1=V_2$) verb roots, number is marked by copying the vowel of these verbs roots; for vowel-final CVCV ($V_1=V_2$) verb roots, number is morphologically unmarked (=marked by the absence of the vowel of the same value with $V_1=V_2$). See the following examples:

(7.37) a. *té-jél-é*
         PERV-love/like.IMP-PL
         'Love/like (pl.)!'

b. *séré-è*
inherit.PERV.IMP-VFS
'Inherit (pl.)!'

- Number-determined suppletive verb roots do not take plural marking—for example, *ád-è* (give.PERV:PL-VFS) 'Give (pl.)!' and *hódá* 'Come (pl.)!' (7.36c).
- For vowel-final CVCV (V₁≠V₂) verb roots, number is left unmarked—for example, *dáfi-è* (do.PERV:IMP-VFS) 'Do (pl.)!', *sání-è* (stay.PERV:IMP-VFS) 'Stay (pl.)!'.
- For verbs with a sequence of V₁V₁ and V₁V₂ vowels, number may be marked depending on the vowel height harmony of the vowels in the roots—*óól-í-è* (beg.PERV:IMP-PL-VFS) 'Beg (pl.)!', *áíb-é-è* (go.PERV:IMP-PL-VFS) 'Go (pl.)!'. There may be exceptional/irregular cases that may apply to some verbs and thus number can be expressed on their roots by means of vowel height harmony neutralization—*tóón-á-è* (kill.PERV:IMP-PL-VFS) 'Kill (pl.)!'. But for non-vowel sequence carrying verb roots, both vowel height harmony and vowel height harmony neutralization may apply—*ŋèd-ò-è* (run.PERV:IMP-PL-VFS) 'Run (pl.)!', *ɲóg-é-è* (close.PERV:IMP-PL-VFS) 'close (pl.)!' and *tál-í-è* (buy/sell.PERV:IMP-PL-VFS) 'Buy/sell (pl.)!'.

Person cannot be indicated or marked on the verb in the imperative form whatsoever, even when two coordinated imperative forms occur in one construction. Some examples are illustrated below.

(7.38) a. *óg-ó   nà   góɲ   bì-ò*
go.PERV:IMP-MT CCN see.PERV:IMP COW-PL
'Go see the cattle!' or 'Go (sg.) and see (sg.) the cattle!'

b. *áíb-é   nà   góɲ-á   bì-ò*
go.PERV:IMP-PL CCN look.PERV:IMP-PL COW-PL
'Go (pl.) and see the cattle!'

The most interesting point in (7.38b) is that it is not clear why the singular form of root *aib* [w] 'go/come' is used instead of *hód* 'come (pl.)'. Pronominal object suffixes can be cross-referenced on the imperative verb form but is depending on the transitivity nature of the verb. If the verb in the imperative form is transitive, an object pronominal can be marked on the verb directly. If the verb is ditransitive, there is no marking on the verb but just a free personal pronoun follows the imperative verb form.

(7.39) a. *édʒ-ò*
kill.PERV:IMP-VFS
'Kill (sg.) him!'

b. *édʒ-óɲ-ò*
kill.PERV:IMP-1SG.OBJ-VFS
'Kill (sg.) me!'

c. *éj*²   *ŋà=hírí=nù*
kill.PERV:IMP DEM=man=NEAR
'Kill (sg.) the man!'

Third person object marker is not marked on the imperative form of the verb, as can be seen in (7.39a). No mention of third person as direct or indirect object not even by a free pronoun, as shown below.

(7.40) a. *áín-ɛ*³   *àɲè*
give.PERV:IMP-TR 1SG
'Give (sg) it to me!'

b. *áín-ɛ́*
give.PERV:IMP-TR
'Give (sg.) him!' or 'Give (sg.) it to him!'

Second person possessive pronoun is avoided since it gives a reflective meaning to the imperative form, as in (7.40c). In fact, (7.40c) would have a different form for a reflexive or declarative sentence (7.40d).

c. *áín-ɛ́*   *sìɔ̀*
give.PERV:IMP-TR hand
'Surrender (sg.)!'
(Lit. 'Give (sg.) hand!')

---

2 The palatal affricate weakens to a palatal approximant [j] word-finally, /dʒ/ →[j]/__# (see Chapter 2).
3 The plural number marker suffix on the imperative form -ɛ and the transitivizer suffix -ɛ are similar.

d. ádʒ-í   sìɔ̀-á   n=ùnù
   give.IMPERV-2SG.SU.IMPER hand-RSTR SG.PSD=2SG.PSR
   'Give your hand'

In order to make a command to an addressee that also involves a reflexive pronoun, an intransitive verb is preferred over a transitive. The intransitive process verb *ér* 'die' will be used instead of the transitive action-process verb *édʒ* 'kill, shoot'.

(7.41) ér   [rè-á   n=ùnù]
       die.PERV:IMP body-RSTR SG.PSD=2SG.PSR
       'Kill yourself!'
       (Lit. 'Die yourself!')

A non-canonical imperative form can also be used for persons other than the addressee (Aikhenvald 2010: 47). Mursi utilizes a non-canonical imperative constructions by a morphological marking on the verb. The hortative prefix *k(V)-* (where V́ carries a High tone) for first person and the jussive prefix *k(V)-* (where V̀ carries a Low tone) for third person are used to carry out commands other than to the addressee. However, the real non-command forms of the hortative and jussive constructions make use of the free form particle *aj/aɲ* in addition to the *k(V)-* form prefixes.

(7.42) a. kò-jòg-ò
       1.HORT-say.PERV-VFS
       'Let me say!'

       b. kò-jòg-t-ò
       1.HORT-say.PERV-PL-1PL.EXC.SU
       'Let us (exc.) say!'

       c. k-éléhén-ɛ́
       3.JUSS-measure.PERV-VFS
       'Let him measure!'

       d. k-éléhén-ɛ́-ɛ́
       3.JUSS-measure.PERV-PL-VFS
       'Let them measure!'

Moreover, hortative/jussive moods associated with the non-command meanings may have optional free subject pronouns that occur preceding the whole structure of both mood forms. This is however not possible in command forms—maybe in a very rare case for first person singular, where the first person pronoun may follow the imperative-hortative structure, as in (7.43a).

(7.43) a. *k-èlèhèn*   *ànè*
       1.HORT-measure.PERV 1SG
       'Let me measure!'

Or as in (7.43b), the hortative prefix of first person and the jussive of third person may overlap with the second person subjunctive prefix, which is as a mild command or polite marker.

b. *dórí-a   bùrtɔ*[4] *bú čàll-á*
   house-RSTR ANA:REF big good.STV-RTSR
   kà-tàl-á-è
   1/2HORT-buy.PERV-MT-VFS
   'Buy that good house (polite)!'

In fact, in Mursi, the second person singular imperative form shows a similarity in prefix with the first person plural inclusive hortative form.[5] The motion suffix *-a* indicates the direction of the action of the addressee whether buying or selling, in the otherwise unidentifiable verb *tal* 'buy, sell'. This motion suffix can only be used in the perfective aspect.

Like the various number and verb-final marking suffixes which are only used in the imperatives, the benefactive suffix *-esɛ* also functions only for positive imperative. Declarative and other types of sentences utilize the other variety of this suffix, i.e. *-èsèn*.

(7.44) *ódʒ-èsè*   *mèdèrè tùì*   *tó-jé*
       put.PERV-BEN:IMP sheep enclosure in-OBL
       'Keep the ram in the enclosure!'

---

4 *burtɔ* 'many days ago, more than 2–3 days ago' is a time word which also functions as demonstrative manner adverb, i.e. ⟨past mentioned; referential demonstrative⟩.

5 Furthermore, first and second person singular subjunctive forms tend to be identical, for example, *kaiɲo* 'I may giving' *kaiɲo* 'You (sg.) may giving'.

THE VERB AND PREDICATE STRUCTURE

The interaction of imperative and aspect resides in the distinction between positive and negative imperatives. This is due to the nature of negative imperatives which require an action to be acted upon immediately at the time the speaker commands, what to do right at that moment. The reality status which the positive imperative (realis) and the negative imperative (irrealis) is also related to the speaker's intention and rationality,—whether a command is to be carried out, will be performed immediately, or shall be delayed seems to be a key point to be taken into account. Thus from a reality mood point of view, negative imperative expresses the speaker's intention that the action not be carried out immediately.

Unlike the positive imperative, the negative imperative utilizes an imperfective verb root and different number suffixes—despite both being commands used to deliver a speaker's intent that a certain course of action must be carried out within a specified period of time. The negative imperative utilizes the imperfective negative proclitic *ŋà=*, imperfective verb root, and two invariable number suffixes -*i* (for singular addressee) and -*o* (for plural addressee). See the examples below—singular addressee (7.45a–c) and plural addressee (7.46a–c).

(7.45) a. *ŋà=éʤ-í*
NEG.IMPERV=shoot.IMPERV-SG
'Don't (sg.) shoot/kill!'

b. *ŋà=ɔ́g-í*
NEG.IMPERV=shout.IMPERV-SG
'Don't (sg.) shout!'

c. *ŋà=zámí-í*
NEG.IMPERV=swim.IMPERV-SG
'Don't (sg.) swim!'

(7.46) a. *ŋà=éʤ-ó*
NEG.IMPERV=drink.IMPERV-PL
'Don't (pl.) shoot/kill!'

b. *ŋà=čɔ́ll-ó*
NEG.IMPERV=sing.IMPERV-PL
'Don't (pl.) sing!'

c. *ŋà=zámí-ó*
NEG.IMPERV=swim.IMPERV-PL
'Don't (pl.) swim!'

Unlike in declarative sentences in which both subjects of intransitive and transitive verbs are obligatory marked on the verb, imperative sentences always drop markers of both subjects. In addition, in Mursi, both subject and the object of a transitive verb are cross-referenced on the verb. Semantically, object of a transitive verb and the recipient/ beneficiary of a ditransitive verb are regarded as primary object, thus, they are cross-referenced on the verb. In the positive as well as negative imperatives, subject of any transitivity class is not required, only object arguments are obligatorily marked on the verb.

(7.47) a. ŋà=éʤ-óɲ-í
NEG.IMPERV=drink.IMPERV-1SG.OBJ-SG-SG
'Don't (sg.) kill me!'

b. ŋà=éʤ-í-ɛ́
NEG.IMPERV=drink.IMPERV-1PL.OBJ-SG
'Don't (sg.) kill us!'

c. ŋà=áʤ-áɲ-i
NEG.IMPERV=give.IMPERV-1SG.OBJ-SG
'Don't give (it to) me!'

d. ŋà=áʤ-í
NEG.IMPERV=give.IMPERV-1PL.OBJ
'Don't (sg.) give (it to) us!'

There is also an interesting interaction between imperatives and adverbial words (time and locative). Time words (adverbs) often occur at the beginning of a declarative sentence.

(7.48) a. ŋàméré dáʃí
now   do.PERV:IMP
'Do (sg.) now!'

b. ŋàméré dáʃí=ŋà
now   do.PERV:IMP=DEF
'Do now!' or 'Do it (sg.) right now!'

Locative adverbs are demonstrative constructions referring to distance. Distance referring locative adverbs often constitute the last position of a sentence.

c1. *dáʄĭ*   *ŋàbá*⁶
     do.PERV:IMP here
     'Do (sg.) here!'

c2. *dáʄĭ=ŋà*   *ŋàbá*
     do.PERV:IMP=DEF here
     'Do (sg.) here!' or 'Do it (sg.) right here!'

The above forms indicate some degree of urgency that the actions have to happen in bounded time and space 'now and here'. Number and verb-final suffixes are not marked on the verb for reasons not clear at this stage.

d.   *o*   *dáʄĭ*   *ŋàbùnù*⁷
     POL do.PERV:IMP there
     'Do (sg.) there!'

e1. *o*   *dáʄĭ*   *hàlì* *wùréɔ́*
     POL do.PERV:IMP later   last
     'Do later!'

e2. *hàlì hàlì*   *dáʄĭ*
     later later do.PERV:IMP
     'Do (sg.) later!' 'Do (sg.) slowly!'

The example shown in (7.48d–e2) indicate delayed imperatives accompanied by a polite marker particle *o*. Imperatives referring to high degree of urgency may be shorter in form (7.49a) and can contain time and locative words that tend to substitute one another. Some examples are illustrated below.

(7.49) a. *túŋ-ó*   *bá*
           PERV.sleep:IMP-MT place
           'Sleep (sg.)!' (here and now)

       b. *áɨw-ó*   *ŋáà*
           come.PERV:IMP-MT here
           'Come (sg.) here!' (here and now)

---

6 /ŋàbá/ is the contraction form of [ŋà=bá=a] ⟨DEM=place=NEAR⟩ 'this place'.
7 /ŋàbùnù/ is the contraction form of [ŋà=bá=unu] ⟨DEM=place=FAR⟩ 'that place'.

The locative adverb *ŋaa* can also refer to time contextually as it is not a genuine local adverbial word rather it is a composition of the demonstrative proclitc *ŋà=* and the proximal enclitic *=á*. The proclitic *ŋà=* can also operate as a floating clitic, thus it can also be attached to an imperative verb as a definite marker, for example, *fílŋà* (stand:PERV.IMP=DEF) 'Stand (sg.) here!'. Some imperative forms may contain two verbs, one of which is only used with distal imperative. It is also used to indicate that the command must take place away from the place of the speaker (7.49a–b). In fact, the ventive (motion toward) suffix indicates only the point of reference/location the speaker wants the addressee must sit at. The exact place of reference could be made by any demonstrative system including pointing and lip protruding, whereas in (7.50b) for example, at least the activity location and proximity are known, i.e. at the place of the speaker and/or near to the speaker.

(7.50) a. *té-í   ŋàiŋà*
        be.PERV:IMP-SG this:DEF
        'Sit (sg.) here!'

   b. *ɔ́g-ó   té-í   ŋàbùnù*
      go.PERV:IMP-MT sit.PERV:IMP-SG there
      'Sit (sg.) there!'

Some imperative forms may not contain a verb at all, as in (7.51a–b). But, non-verbal imperative constructions may require a context when they are used to order someone to do something. See the following examples:

(7.51) a. *bùnù*
        'Away (sg)!' (Lit. Out there! Out!)

   b. *ŋàméré tíí   ŋàbá*
      now   DUR here
      'Sit (sg.) still!'
      (Lit. 'Until now here!')

An exception is shown below in (7.52) in which the adjective *bííbíí* 'different' combines with the subjunctive and the non-canonical imperative marker particle *aj* 'let' to express a command directed to second persons.

(7.52) a. k-àj   bííbíí
         SBJV-JUSS/HORT.PART different
         'Separate (sg.)!'
         (Lit. 'Let you (sg.) separated!')

      b. àj   bíí   bííbíí
         JUSS/HORT.PART AUT.REFL different
         'Separate (pl.)!'

In (7.52b), the auto-reflexive particle *bíí* shows that the speaker has no control[8] over the activity that he/she commanded to be performed/executed. Rather the command that is given by the speaker will be performed by the will of the addressee. Non-canonical imperative forms of the third and first person plural are even more interesting.

(7.53) a. áj   í⟨í+i⟩   kàrì
         JUSS.PART exist.3PL.IRR together
         'Let them not scatter!'
         (Lit. 'Let them exist together!')

      b. ŋà=kè-hèj   bííbíí
         NEG=1.HORT-go.IMPERV:PL different
         'Let us not disperse!'
         (Lit. 'Let us go not different/separate!')

Mursi has an attenuative particle that to some extent weakens the strong sense of the imperative. The particle *gá* 'let' in (7.54a–b) below is an attenuative marker which softens the harshness of the request.

(7.54) a. [gá   tóŋ   ŋà=bómbí=tá]   nà
         ATTU throw.PERV:IMP DEM=ball=NEAR CCN
         [k-ar-í-to   táá
         1.HORT-see.PERV-1PL.OBJ-1PL.EXC.SU ATTU:UNCERT
         óŋón-í]   nà   k-ój   kó   òrì?
         throw.IMPERV-2SG.SU.IMPERV CCN SBJV-put PNC where
         'Let's see how far you can throw the ball!'
         (Lit 'Throw (sg.) the ball and let us see where you may throw it and will put it to!')

---

8 In addition, the polite particle o can also indicate a command that the speaker lacks control over the action, for example, *o rodo* (POL spill.PERV:IMP-VFS) 'please, be spilled!'.

b. *gá   ítón-óɲ   bómbí*
   ATTU send.PERV:IMP-1SG.OBJ ball
   'Throw the ball over to me!'

Another attenuative particle is *bòitííní* 'a little bit' which appears to have an idiosyncratic form but basically can be morphologically segmentable into *bòi* 'high' and *tini > tííní* 'little'.

(7.55) *kàl-á   [Ø rònɔ́   wùréɔ́]*_{RC} *áw-ó*
       day-RSTR [Ø in.the.future after]   come.PERV:IMP-2/3.IRR
       bòitííní   ʃàù
       a.little.bit fast
       'Next time come a little earlier!'
       (Lit. 'The day that is in future.')

But if a hortative/jussive mood is used to give a command and request at the same time, that requires a hortative/jussive answer, a copula comes at the beginning of a sentence. Just for the purpose of Mursi grammar, I labelled the function of this copula as 'anticipatory request-reply' marker, as in (7.56).

(7.56) *á   àggè k-ai-o   ɔ́r-ɔ́   ná*
       COP.3.IMPERV 1PL 1.HORT-go.PERV-1PL.INC.SU home-OBL CCN
       k-àùs-ò   tííní
       1.HORT-rest.PERV-1PL.INC.SU a.little/few
       'Let us (inc.) go home and rest a little!'

Finally, there are still a few verbs that do not distinguish between singular and plural imperative forms. They neither take verbal inflections nor any other sort of markers that indicate number.

(7.57) a. *čóllò hòlò?*[9] 'Sing (sg.)!'   > (sing song)
          čóllò hóló?   'Sing (pl.)!'
       b. *dáhòlò?*   'Dance (sg.)!'
          dáhóló?   'Dance (pl.)!'

---

9 *hóló?* 'music' refers to song and dance (cultural form of singing and dancing) and it is a noun, while *čóllò* 'sing' only refers the action of singing and dancing (it is a verb).

THE VERB AND PREDICATE STRUCTURE   323

TABLE 7.33 Hortative construction—positive

Singular	Plural
(aj/aɲ) k(V̀)-RÒÒT.PERV	(INC.) (aj/aɲ) k(V̀)-RÒÒT.PERV-V
	(EXC.) (aj/aɲ) k(V̀)-RÒÒT.PERV-t-ò

Commands can be directed at first person ('me', 'us') and third person ('him', 'her', 'them') (Aikhenvald 2010: 47). Commands directed at first person are known as hortative §7.3.1.3.2, while those that are directed at third person are known as jussive §7.3.1.3.3. In Mursi, both constitute the irrealis mood.

7.3.1.3.2 *Hortative*

The hortative in Mursi is a non-canonical imperative mood directed towards first person and can be used to denote a mild command. As seen on Table 7.33, hortative is part of the irrealis mood and only utilizes a perfective verb root. This is due to the fact that the irrealis in general signals some degree of completeness while on the other hand the basic assumption of the imperfective aspect signals incompleteness. The hortative form takes a low-toned prefix $k(V̀)$- and is optionally preceded by a free form high-toned hortative particle *aj* [aɲ]. As in many verbal inflectional prefixes of Mursi, the vowel of the prefix $k(V̀)$- is copied from a consonant-initial perfective verb root's vowel. The hortative template is illustrated above.

(7.58)   a. *kà-màg*
         1.HORT-catch.PERV
         'Let me catch!'

   b. *kà-màg-à-ɛ̀*
      1.HORT-catch.PERV-1PL.INC-VFS
      'Let us (inc.) catch!'

   c. *kò-jòg-t-ò*
      1.HORT-say.PERV-PL-1.EXC
      'Let us (exc.) say!'

As can be shown in (7.58b), the *-V* of the first person plural inclusive is copied from the verb root. whereas the first person plural exclusive is marked by *-o* and also epenthesised *-t*. Verb-final suffixes *-a*, *-o* and *-ɛ* can be suffixed to a perfec-

TABLE 7.34 Hortative construction—negative

Singular	Plural
ŋà=k(V)-ROOT.IMPERV-i	(INC.) ŋà=k(V)-ROOT.IMPERV-Ø
	(EXC.) ŋà=k(V)-ROOT.IMPERV-(t/n)o

tive verb root (for first person) and after inclusive/exclusive markers (for both first person plural). The verb-final suffix -ɛ is often suffixed to plural forms.

(7.59) a. kì-ɓìk-á
1.HORT-catch.PERV-VFS
'Let me break (it)!'

b. kà-làmì-ó
1.HORT-seek.PERV-VFS
'Let me seek!'

c. kè-rè-ó
1.HORT-wait.PERV-VFS
'Let me keep!'

d. kì-ɓìg-ì-ɛ́
1.HORT-break.PERV-1PL.INC-VFS
'Let us (inc.) break (it)!'

e. k-ìr-ì-ɛ́
1.HORT-drink.PERV-1PL.INC-VFS
'Let us (inc.) drink!'

Negation on hortative is marked in the same way as on the canonical imperative forms. The difference is that the verb turns into imperfective aspect when negated, as can be shown by the negative hortative template above.

(7.60) a. ŋà=k-èj-t-ò
NEG=1.HORT-shoot.IMPERV-PL-1PL.EXC
'Let us (exc.) not kill!'

b. ŋà=kùùn-ì
   NEG=1.HORT-come.IMPERV-SG
   'Let me not come!'

c. ŋà=kò-hòɲ-Ø
   NEG=1.HORT-come.IMPERV:PL-1PL.INC
   'Let us (inc.) not come!'

As it is illustrated in (7.60a–c) above, the particle *aj/aɲ* has no function in the negative hortative construction. Thus, it is excluded from all types of non-canonical negative imperative constructions. The distinction between the two hortative particles *aj* and *aɲ* is not clear at this stage (also occurring with jussive forms) but both forms seem to be associated with the idiolect and stylistic preference of speakers.

(7.61) a. áj   k-ìdô-ó
          HORT.PART 1.HORT-mix.PERV-VFS
          'Let me mix/combine.'

       b. áɲ   kì-dìr-ó
          HORT.PART 1.HORT-swipe/wipe.PERV-VFS
          'Let me swipe/wipe.'

However, there is viable evidence that both hortative and jussive forms which take *aj/aɲ* particles tend be used for polite requests other than orders or commands. Besides, in a rare instances, a verb tends be uninflected for person in a hortative form but can be inflected for person when it is in a jussive form. When such instances occur, the person can be shown by a personal pronoun function as in O function or an associative word *kàrì* 'together, with' may be used. Compare the following hortative forms (7.62a–b) and jussive forms in (7.62c–d).

(7.62) a. kè-sèrè   áɲój
          1.HORT-inherit.PERV 1SG-PVS
          'Let me inherit.'

       b. kè-sèrè   kàrì
          1.HORT-inherit.PERV together
          'Let us inherit.'

c. *ké-séré-ò*
3.JUSS-inherit.PERV-VFS
'Let him inherit.'

d. *ké-séré-t-ò*
3.JUSS-inherit.PERV-PL-VFS
'Let them inherit.'

The first person plural hortative form in (7.62b) does not distinguish between inclusive and exclusive. As we have seen in (7.51), imperative use of a morphologically deficient verb or of a verb whose semantic origin is a non-verbal, tend to behave differently when used in imperatives. The reduplicated *kɔ́bkɔ́b* 'quick' is a derived adverb from the verb root *kɔb* 'to follow', has a secondary function as a verb 'hurry'. It doesn't take any verbal inflection in its reduplicated form. Neither indicates aspect or number. As shown below in (7.63b–c), the first person singular and plural hortative forms are indistinguishable.

(7.63) a. *kɔ̀-kɔ̀bkɔ̀b*
1.HORT-hurry
'Let me hurry!' or
(Lit. 'Let me be quick!')

b. *k-àj   kɔ̀bkɔ̀b*
1.HORT-JUSS/HORT.PART hurry
'Let me hurry!'

OR c. *k-áj   kɔ̀bkɔ̀b*
1.HORT-JUSS/HORT.PART hurry
'Let us hurry!'

This verb can be even more interesting when it appears in a canonical imperative form.

(7.64) a. *o   kɔ́bkɔ́b*
POL quick
'Quick (sg.)!'

b. *aj   kɔ́bkɔ́b*
HORT/JUSS.PART quick
'Quick (pl.)!'

A synonymous verbs can be used separately for first person singular and first person plural hortative forms, as in (7.64a–b). The choice between the two is not clear. The verb in the hortative mood form in (7.65a), *keme*, is exactly similar in form to the second person subjunctive forms,—because second person subjective verb forms tend to reduce either their final segment or syllable; *me* is a perfective subjunctive form of a vowel-final verb *mèsí* 'do'.

(7.65) a. kè-mè   koma
          1.HORT-do.PERV weak
          'Let me melt.'

      b. kà-dàfi   koma
          1.HORT-do.PERV weak
          'Let us melt.'

The canonical imperative versions are as follows—*dáfi koma* (do weak) 'Melt (sg.)!' and *dáfi koma kàrì* (do weak together) 'Melt (pl.)!'. Finally, there are still a few irregular positive and negative hortative constructions that do not utilize the two aforementioned templates.

(7.66) a. rè   ŋà=gín-í   [háb-á[10]   [rè-á   n=ùnù]$_{NP}$]$_{NP}$
          body NEG=ask-SG   head-RSTR   body-RSTR SG.PSD=1SG.PSR
          'Let me not think!'
          (Lit. 'Body don't ask head of my body!')

      b. hábí   ŋà=gín-ó   á   bùnù
          head.PL NEG=ask-PL COP.3.IMPERV there
          'Let us not think!'
          (Lit. 'Heads don't (pl.) ask are there/out!')

      c. ŋà=ki-gìn-ì   ŋàbùnù hábí
          NEG=1.HORT-ask-1PL.OBJ there   head.PL
          'Let us not think!'

      d. ŋà=ki-fil=ó   bài
          NEG=1.HORT-stand=NEG sit
          'Let me not sit!'
          (Lit. 'Let me stand not sit!')

---

10   Note that *haba* and *sábá* 'head' are free variations or euphonies. In many instances, the glottal voiceless fricative /h/ is a free variant of alveolar voiceless fricative /s/.

TABLE 7.35 Jussive construction

	Singular	Plural
POSITIVE	(aj/aɲ) k(V́)-RÒÒT.PERV	(aj/aɲ) k(V́)-RÒÒT.PERV-(t/n)V
NEGATIVE	ŋà=ROOT.IMPERV-i/-ɔ	ŋà=ROOT.IMPERV-ɛ

    e. *ŋà=kè-tèl-ì*   *bàì*
        NEG=1.HORT-sit.PERV-1PL.OBJ sit
        'Let us not sit!'
        (Lit. 'Let us not seated sit!')

7.3.1.3.3 Jussive

The jussive mood refers to a command directed at the third person. Jussive and hortative moods of Mursi are similar in many ways except for the following properties of the jussive:

- the jussive mood marker prefix *k(V)-* always carries a low-toned melody,
- the jussive marker prefix (*k(V)-*) will not be marked when the negated for is used,
- number will not be marked on the singular form of the jussive mood while number can be shown on the singular of the negative jussive form, and
- the singular of the negative jussive form may take the verb-final suffix of the non-imperative moods, i.e. *-ɔ*, whereas the plural of the negative jussive form takes the common verb-final suffix of the non-canonical imperative forms, i.e. *-ɛ*.

(7.67) a. *kɔ́-ɲɔ́g-ɔ́*   (=strong)
       3.JUSS-close.PERV-VFS
       'Let him close (it)!'

     b. *àj*   *kɔ́-ɲɔ́g-ɔ́-ɛ́*
       JUSS.PART 3.JUSS-close.PERV-PL-VFS (=mild)
       'Let them close (it)!'

     c. *àj*   *kɔ́-jóg-t-ɔ̀*
       JUSS.PART 3.JUSS-tell-PERV-PL
       'Let them say!'

Rarely both singular and plural forms of the jussive can only be distinguished by the verb-final suffix of the plural form, as in (7.68a–b).

(7.68) a. àj ká-dáʄĩ
   JUSS.PART 3.JUSS-work.PERV
   'Let him work!'

   b. àj ká-dáʄĩ-è̩
   JUSS.PART 3.JUSS-work.PERV-VFS
   'Let them work!'

Negative forms utilize imperfective verb roots and at the same time do not take the jussive marker prefix. Therefore, the singular form of a jussive mood may never marked as are any other imperfective aspect verbs of a declarative mood. See the examples below.

(7.69) a. ŋà=báns-án-ó
   NEG=get.up-MT-SG
   'Let him not wake up!'

   b. ŋà=è̩lè̩hè̩n-í
   NEG=measure-SG
   'Let him not make (something) similar!'

   c. ŋà=báns-é̩-è̩
   NEG=get.up-PL-VFS
   'Let them not wake up (stand up)!'

   d. ŋà=tímírtí-é̩
   NEG=teach-PL
   'Let them not teach!'

Number agreement in negative jussive mood other than number suffixes can be shown on suppletive verb root itself or by other non-number marking inflectional suffixes.

(7.70) a. jɔ̀g tó-jé ŋà=hóɲ-í
   3PL in-OBL NEG=come.IMPERV:PL-PL
   'Let them not come in!'

TABLE 7.36 Imperatives and declaratives vis-à-vis negation

Mood	Imperfective	Perfective
Imperative (canonical)	ŋà=ROOT.IMPERV:IMP	not attested
Imperative (non-canonical)	ŋà=k(V)-ROOT.IMPERV (HORTATIVE) ŋà=ROOT.IMPERV (JUSSIVE)	not attested
Declarative	ŋà=ROOT.IMPERV=ó	ŋànì k-ROOT.PERV=ó

b. *nɔ̀ŋ ŋà=dɔ́ŋ-áná*
3SG NEG=pick.up-IMPERV.3.MT
'Let him (her) not pick up!'

In (7.70a), the suppletive verb root indicates plural while the motion suffix -*áná* in (7.70b) occurs only as the third person singular and first person plural inclusive indicator. Negated verbs always take the sentence-final position, thus the postposition word is now preceding the predicate, as can be seen in (7.70b).

To sum up, the second person singular form of the canonical imperative is one of the shortest formally marked forms in the language—*rɛ* (wait.PERV: IMP) 'wait (sg.)!' and the second person plural form of the canonical imperative is the shortest of all morphologically marked forms. The perfective verb root alone can denote an abrupt command directed to second person addressee. All inflectional morphology of the canonical and non-canonical (hortative/jussive) imperative can be exhaustively marked on the positive as well as on the negative imperative verb from slot 1, 2, 7, and 14.

Moreover, both canonical and non-canonical imperatives can be negated in the same way as declaratives but indeed imperatives differ in one way, that is, imperatives can be negated just by the proclitic marker *ŋà=*. Regarding the marking of negation on imperatives and declaratives, a comparative summary is given in Table 7.36 above.

7.3.1.3.4 *Subjunctive*

Subjunctive is one of the three moods in Mursi which are expressed by the irrealis morphological marker within the perfective aspect. Subjunctive, like the other two irrealis moods (hortative and jussive), utilizes a prefix *k(V)-* and a perfective verb root. However in Mursi, it should be noted that the relation of the subjunctive mood with the perfective aspect can be viewed within the following conditions:

- Subjunctive irrealis operates within the context of completeness of a situation but not within the reality of an event or a situation, thus a complete action/situation is indicated by perfective aspect.
- Mursi lacks a morphological tense system and tense is expressed by separate time word, thus the irrealis subjunctive functions independently of the tense system.
- Subjunctive irrealis is used to express desire, wish, perception, prediction, uncertainty/certainty, possibility, obligation, and ability/potential.
- Subjunctive irrealis utilizes the prefix k(V)- for first and third persons—rarely for second person.
- Subjunctive irrealis often occurs in complement and subordinate clauses.
- The time frame of the subjunctive irrealis mood in the complement or subordinate clause may differ from the time frame of the main clause.

A complement clause containing a subjunctive mood can be introduced by a grammaticalized verb *sé* 'to say', an invariable complementizer form whose origin is an auxiliary. *sé* also functions as direct and indirect speech marker along with another direct speech marker particle *ké* 'this/thing'. In reason and purpose-type clauses, *sé* often preceded by the multi-function word *bá* 'place' ~ ⟨CAUSE, REASON, PURPOSE⟩.

Subjunctive mood template:

    ... (bá) (sé) k(V)-ROOT.PERV-(object/motion/valency, etc.) ...

(7.71) Desire

a. *nɔ̀ŋ   ŋà=hín-Ø=ó*   [*bá*   *sé*
   3SG NEG=want-3SG.SU.IMPERV=NEG   place/CAUSE say.COMPZR
   k-áίw-ɛ́=jè]_{SUBORD:CL}   *òrì   húŋ*]
   3.SBJV-come.PERV-RES=SUBORD] where simply
   'S/he did not want to come anyway.'

b. *ŋà=dáín-à*   [*bá*   *sé*
   DEM=late.afternoon=NEAR   place/CAUSE say.COMPZR
   k-ɔ́g=jè]_{SUBORD:CL}   *bókónó*]
   1.SBJV-go.PERV-SUBORD anywhere
   ŋà=kí-hín-í=ó
   NEG=1SU-want-1SG.SU.IMPERV=NEG
   'I don't want to go anywhere tonight.'

c. *nɔ̀ŋ   hín-Ø*   *sé*
   3SG want.IMPERV-3SG.SU.IMPERV say.COMPZR

k-ɛ́j-à támárí-ɲá
3.SBJV-help.PERV-IRR student-PL
'S/he wants to help the student.'

(7.72) Wish
    a. ténèŋ hùllì lómíɲá k-ígí húŋ?
       why if lemon.PL 3.SBJV-ripe.PERV simply
       'I wish the lemons were ripe.'
       (Lit. 'were the lemons ripe!')

    b. aɲè бà sé ké-té=jè hínènò
       1SG place/CAUSE say.COMPZR 1.SBJV-COP.PERV=SUBORD alive
       hín бòì k-ér húŋ
       want.IMPERV compeletely:DEO 1.SBJV-die.PERV simply
       á čàll-ì
       COM.3.IMPERV good.STV-ADJ
       'Being dead is better for me than being alive.'
       (Lit. 'I instead of being alive, it is better I should die.')

Note that a sequence of *hin* and *бòì* is a typical deontic marking configuration other than the rare lexical deontic markers in the language.

(7.73) Uncertainty+request
    a. ŋà=hòì=tá бá ŋà=zùg=tá
       DEM=woman=NEAR place/CAUSE DEM=people=NEAR
       sé ká-tál-ɛ dórí ŋànì ʃik=ó
       say.COMPL 3.SBJV-buy.PERV-APPL house not.yet hear=NEG
       'Woman, have you (sg.) not heard that they are going to buy that house?'

In a few instances, only person marker may be shown on the subjunctive mood forms. Number agreement may not be shown on the subjunctive mood forms, rather it can be indicated by independent referential means—*ŋàùgtá,* as in (7.73a).

    b. aɲè бá sé k-ídǐd-ó kó
       1SG place/CAUSE say.COMPL 1.SBJV-go.with.PERV-MT PNC
       ŋà=zùg=tùnù ŋànì k-ését=ó
       DEM=people=FAR NEG.PERV 1.SBJV-think.PERV=NEG
       'I did not think of going with them.'

c. *ké-rɛ-ín-ɔ̀*
1.SBJV-wait.PERV-2SG.OBJ-VFS
'May I wait for you?'

The clause in (7.73c) is independent clause and denotes request.

(7.74) Possibility (action nearly averted) (cf. Kuteva 1998)
bá   ŋà=lɔ́g=tá   sé   k-ár-á
place/CAUSE DEM=issue=NEAR say.COMPL 3.SBJV-see.PERV-MT
kɔ́n k-ɛ́j   čírr
one 3.SBJV-spoil.PERV realy
'He nearly lost his sight in the accident.'

(7.75) Obligation—(*hin bòi k(V)*-root.perv)
a. *hín   bòi   ká-lámí   bókónó*
want.IMPERV completely:DEO 1.SBJV-find.PERV somewhere
'We will have to look around elsewhere.'

b. *hín   boj   [[zùw-á   g=àj]ₙₚ*
want.IMPERV completely:DEO PEOPLE-rstr PL.PSD=1PL.INC.PSR
ɲàgàs-a]ₙₚ   kɔ́-dɔŋ-nɔ
old.STV-RSTR 1.SBJV-respect.PERV-VFS
'We (inc.) must respect our elders.'

The verb in the subjunctive mood could also occur outside the complement or subordinate clause (7.75a–b) but it may occur following the negative temporal subordinate marker *ŋàni*[11] 'not yet, still', as in (7.76a).

(7.76) a. *bè   ŋà=hùl=ùnù   nɔ̀ŋ ŋànì k-íríčá=ó*
DIST.PAST DEM=time=FAR 3SG not.yet 3.SBJV-born.PERV=NEG
'At the time, he was not yet born.'

b. *wà   k-ítóón-ó   ɔ́r-ɔ́*
REC.PAST 3.SBJV-send.PERV-MT home-OBL
'S/he showed him/her home.'
(Lit. 'S/he sent (it) to the home.')

---

11 This particle also used as a persistive marker.

Strictly speaking, the occurrence of the subjunctive mood form we have seen in the examples above is more evident in the complement and subordinate clauses. Moreover, regarding the subjunctive mood form and the function and distribution of *sé*, as a complementizer, as an auxiliary verb, as a direct speech marker (along with *ké*) and as a fully inflected verb root 'say', the example below would to some extent illustrate the point briefly. Below is a text from an old oral story of the Mursi titled 'There was no death in Mursi'.

(7.77)   nà   gin-ón-Ø-ì   nà   sé-Ø   ké
         CCN ask-MT-3SG.OBJ-3SG.IRR CCN   say-3SG.SU.IMPERV   QUOT
         heee!! sén-í   k-ér   nój
         heee!!! say-2SG.SU.IMPERV 3.SBJV-die.PERV   who.NOM?
         'He asked him, saying: "Who are you saying will die?"'

   b[ɓ]ásá-ì
   monitor.lizard-SG
   'The monitor lizard'
   (Implied: And the monitor lizard was afraid of being eaten and said this)

   téŋér-á   ɓág-á-è   nà
   afraid.PERV-3SG.SU.PERV   eat.PERV-3SG.SU.PERV-APPL:RES CCN
   sén-á   ké   ah, ah, ah
   say-3SG.SBJ.PERV   QUOT   no no no
   'Was afraid of being eaten and said this, "No! No! No!".' (ND 3.6)

   k-ér   mùnì-o,   k-ér   mùnì-ó
   3.SBJV-die.PERV   Mursi-NOM 3.SBJV-die.PERV   Mursi-NOM
   '"The Mursi will die, the Mursi will die."' (ND 3.6–3.7)

The second person may rarely takes the subjunctive mood marker prefix, and when it takes it aligns with the first person subjunctive form.

(7.78)   Subjunctive form   Meaning
   1sg.   k-àìn-o   'I may be giving'
   2sg.   k-áín-o   'You (sg.) may giving'
   3sg.   k-áín-ɛ   'S/he may giving'

The suffix *-o* of the first and second person subjunctive forms is a verb-final suffix while the suffix *-ɛ* is a applicative marker (see Chapter 9). The verb in

THE VERB AND PREDICATE STRUCTURE

the subjunctive mood may not be often marked for number or subject suffixes but may be marked with other grammatatical categories such as motion and valency changing devices. For example, in (7.79), the verb in the subjunctive irrealis is suffixed with motion and applicative markers.

(7.79) a. *kì-bìg-án-čó*
   1.SBJV-break.PERV-MT-APPL
   'I may/might break'

b. *kí-bíg-án-čó*
   3.SBJV-break.PERV-MT-APPL
   'S/he may/might break'

As can be seen in (7.79a–b), person can only be distinguished by grammatical tone where first person is marked by low tone while third person is marked by high tone. Plural number can be indicated by various internal morphological mechanisms or by suffixation of the *-t/-d́* (aspect-number) alternations. Further discussion on the subjunctive mood vis-à-vis complement and subordinate clauses and negation is addressed in the chapters dealing each of the topics.

7.3.1.4 Tense

Mursi has no inflectional system that marks tense on the verb, thus tense is marked by separate lexical time words. The tense system of Mursi are of two types: primary tense markers (particles *be* 'distant past' and *wa* 'recent past') and secondary tense markers (mainly lexical time adverbs). These two lexical tense marking types fall into five sub-types/classes as noted by Dixon (2012: 20): durative (§7.3.1.4.1–§7.3.1.4.2), frequency (§7.3.1.4.3), specific time spans (§7.3.1.4.4), temporal shifters (§7.3.1.4.5), and expectation related time words (§7.3.1.4.6). Therefore, both primary and secondary tense markers are dealt with together in accordance with the five sub-types, which strictly speaking as is the easiest and ideal way to deal with them.

7.3.1.4.1 *Durative: Past Tense*

The primary tense markers *bè* and *wà* often occur at the beginning of a clause. Also, the verb that follows these two tense particles must be in the perfective aspect form.

TABLE 7.37 Durative past tense markers 4

Durative: past tense

Particles	Meaning	Remark
bè	'distant past'	primary tense marker
wà	'recent past'	primary tense marker
bòrtɔ̀	'mid distant'	'many days ago, before yesterday'
bè kíŋíɲ	'a very long time ago'	⟨kíŋíɲ⟩ 'ancient, antique, long ago'
bè sábɔ̀	'long time ago in the beginning'	⟨sábɔ̀⟩ 'head, first, beginning'
dírr	'for a long time'	indefinite time marker

7.3.1.4.1.1 /be/ 'Distant Past'

The distant past time particle *bè* always occurs at the beginning of declarative and interrogative sentences and may function as a past perfect tense marker.

(7.80) a. *bè   bík-á*
          DIST.PAST break-3SG.SU.PERV
          'He had broken (it).'

      b. *bè   kí-bík-á*
          DIST.PAST 1SU-break-1SG.SU.PERV
          'I had broken (it).'

      c. *bè   túrúmél ʃɔ́lá-j   bóns-èsèn   mìnáŋ?*
          DIST.PAST car   suffer-NOMZ arrive-BEN when
          'When did the car accident happen?'
          (Lit. 'The car suffering arrived for when?')

Aspect in general operates independently of the tense system of the language. For instance, *kíbíká* 'I broken' is in perfective aspect and it doesn't indicate that the action has taken place in the past. It could also indicate the action has happened in recent past or at the present moment. However, once the event is configured in time the whole narration may be viewed in temporal perspective. The following two examples (7.81) and (7.82) are taken from a story titled 'How the Mursi crossed the Omo River'.

(7.81) [mà dĭné-ó-ni ŋà=mà=á [Ø bè
water full-3.IRR-RS DEM=water=NEAR [Ø DIST.PAST
kó-hóɲ-čó tùnò=ŋà]_{SUBORD:CL} [jòg
1SU-come.IMPERV:PL-APPL.1PL.INC.SU up.hill/on.top=DEF 3PL
héj-Ø čúg-Ø káráné]
go.IMPERV.PL-3.IRR chase/run-3.IRR down.stream
'The river is full. The river that we (inc.) were coming along with, they go to the top and then run to downstward.' (MH 0:23:5)

(7.82) hírí bè k-èlì ké káwúlókɔ̀rɔ̀ á
person DIST.PAST PASS.call.PERV QUOT Kawulokoro COP.3.IMPERV
hírí bárárí [Ø kén wárr]_{RC}
person powerful+NRSTR [Ø 3.SBJV.break.PERV Omo.river]
'There was a man called Kuwulokro, Kawulokoro was a powerful man who can make the Omo River stop.' (MH 0:38:2)

As can be shown in (7.81), all verbs are in the imperfective aspect. Once the appropriate lexical time particle is set before all verbal arguments and put into temporal perspective, no time word will be stated again in any part of the narration until the time word is required in the next narration/text. The particle *bè* indicates the remote past time in which the events of the whole story is narrated. On the other hand, the verbs in (7.82) are in the perfective aspect—one in passive and the other in the relative clause.

The interaction of tense and aspect may be shown either on the verb itself or by the bound subject pronominal suffixes. Most importantly, the interaction of past tense-perfective aspect on the one hand and future tense-imperfective aspect on the other hand can be clearly seen in the declarative mood.

(7.83) a. àggè bè k-élíd-íɲ-ó ìɲè
1PL DIST.PAST 1SU-call.PERV-1SG.OBJ-1PL.SU.EXC.PERV 2SG
'We (exc.) had called you (sg.).'

b. àɲè wà kó-dőj gɔ̀r-ɔ̀
1SG REC.PAST 1.SBJV-tread.on.PERV road-OBL
'I was walking down the street.'

Both (7.83a) and (7.83b) are simple declarative sentences and as long as past tense markers exist, the requirement that the verbs in these sentences occur in the perfective aspect is obligatory. Interestingly, any verbal word that inflects for aspect or tense and precede the two primary tense markers must occur in the past tense form. *áná* [án-á] ⟨is.IMPERV-ANA/past⟩ is equivalent to the English 'was/were', but it refers to an event at a specific point in time. It is also used as anaphoric reference marker *áná* ⟨ANA:REF⟩.

(7.84) a. [ịnè án-á¹² bè dól-ép-ó [dórí-á
2SG is.IMPERV-PST DIST.PAST show-1SG.OBJ-MT house-RSTR
n=ùnù]_NP] [nà àṇè wà díṇákáṇó bá
SG.PSD=2SG.PSR CCN 1SG REC.PAST forgot place
íṣ-á òrì nòŋ?]
present.PERV-3SG.SU.PERV where 3SG
'You (sg.) had shown me your house, but I have forgotten where it is?'

b. án-á wà k-ók-á
is.IMPERV-PST REC.PAST 1SU-go.PERV-1SG.SU.PERV
'Behold, I'm just about to go.'

In both narrative and non-narrative text, the primary tense markers can be specified more than one time within texts containing coordinated clauses.

(7.85) í-∅ bè àggè be
to.be-3SG.SU.IMPERV DIST.PAST 1PL DIST.PAST
[ŋà=lòg=tùnù=ŋà]_NP ká jòg bè mès-ó
DEM=issue=FAR=DEF maybe 3pl DIST.PAST do-3.IRR
[dàdá-ú]_NP bè kíŋịŋ
father.PERT.SG.1.PSR-NOM DIST.PAST long.time.ago
'It is (said) to be the case that maybe our fathers used to do it in ancient time.'

... nà [hùllì bè kòná=ŋà]_SUBORD:CL [jòg
CCN when DIST.PAST grandfather.PERT.1.PSR=DEF 3PL
[konɛ n=èj]_NP] bì-o
grandfather.PERT.SG.3.PSR SG.PSD=3PL.PSR cow-pl
'... and when our grandfather, their grandfather, cows, ...'

---

12 This particle is composed of the first/second person copula verb root form in the imperfective aspect (equivalent to the third person eroded copula verb root form) in the imperfective aspect *án* ⟨COP.IMPERV⟩ and the third person singular subject of the perfective aspect *-a*.

... zùw-à   [Ø ké   hámár]_RC [dág-Ø   hózò-j
people-RSTR [Ø QUOT Hamar]   hit-3SG.SU.IMPERV hunger-NOM
hóɲ   íw-án-έ   [bì-ò-á   mùn-ùɲ]_NP]
come.IMPERV.PL take-MT-3PL.SU.IMPERV cow-PL-RSTR Mursi-GEN
[nà   [héj-ε   húŋ]
CCN go.IMPERV.PL-APPL simply
'... the people called 'Hamar hit by Hunger' came, they took the cows of the Mursi and went (away).' (MH 5:50:9)

7.3.1.4.1.2   /wà/ 'Recent Past'

The recent past and distant past time particles sometimes can be very confusing and ambiguous when denoting whether the real event actually happened in distant past or in recent past. But, the two can be disambiguated by combining the temporal shifter ŋàméá 'today' to a clause that contains the recent past particle wà to see if the whole clause can imply a perfective completive situation in recent past.

(7.86) wà   ŋàméá k-ódʒ-èsè-à   érmì-á
        REC.PAST today 1SU-put-BEN-1SG.SU.PERV child-RSTR
        n=ànù   dórí-á   tímírt-íɲ   tó-jé
        SG.PSD=1SG.PSR house-RSTR education-GEN in-OBL
        'I entered my son in school today.'

In contrast, the distant past time particle bè cannot be combined with any of the temporal shifters in a clause in an attempt to denote an event that has happened in the past or a little earlier. Maybe the two free tense marking types can co-occur in a clause in one condition, i.e. in a cause-result referring clause where the cause clause specifies the cause that might have been done in the past time. Whereas the result clause specifies the result that is obtained from the previous clause—as can be seen in the example below (ŋàméá).

(7.87) húllí   kù-gùɲ   lɔ̀g-á   [Ø bè   táá
        TEMP/COND PASS-see.PERV issue-RSTR [Ø DIST.PAST UNCERT
        mès-ó]_RC   bábò=jè   bá   ŋàméá dáfí
        do-NOMZ] foolish=SUBORD REAS/CAUSE now   work
        ímág-íné-ɔ̀
        not.know-AP-VFS
        'In light of his earlier behavior, it would be unwise to give him a job.'
        (Lit. 'When seen the foolish thing that perhaps he did in the past, placing (him) now at work would be not knowing.')

7.3.1.4.1.3   /bòrtɔ̀/ 'Middle Past'

This time word *bòrtɔ̀* does not specifically specify a short time duration, but if there is one fact known about this time word, it is that it does not indicate a distant past time. It may refer a time 'more than two to three days ago', 'in early days', 'many days ago' or even 'years ago'.

(7.88) a. ŋànìjè   íggé-à   [Ø bòrtɔ̀   mès-ɛ́-á
CONTR 3PL.PN.SP-RSTR [Ø days.ago do-3PL.SU.IMPERV-RSTR
gèrès-ìn]_RC   hàlì   bás-án-ɛ́   nà
bad-NOMZ]   later   live-MT-3PL.SU.IMPERV   CCN
kí-ʃíl-ɛ-ɔ̀
3.SBJV-accuse-RES-VFS
'... and they that have done evil, unto the resurrection of damnation.'
(Lit. 'However, those that were doing bad earlier, then later they live to be accused.')

b. [ŋà=sààn=á   ŋànì čàg=ŋà̀]_NP ídó-nɛ̀   kó
DEM=news=NEAR still   new=DEF   add-APPL.3 PNC
íggé-à   [Ø bòrtɔ̀   sábú-né   nà   hàlì
3PL.PN.SP-RSTR [Ø days.ago first-ORD CCN later
kí-ʃíl-ɛ́   nɔ̀ŋ
1SU-accuse-1PL.INC.SU.IMPERV-APPL   3SG
'Together with the evidence we already have, will be enough to convict him.'
(Lit. 'The evidence added together with those of the earliest the first, then we will accuse him/her.')

c. dórí-á   bortɔ̀   bù   čàll-à   ká-tál-á-ɛ̀
house-RSTR days.ago big   good.STV-ADJ 3.JUSS-buy-PL-VFS
'Buy that good house (polite)!'

In (7.88c), *bòrtɔ̀* functions as a distal demonstrative marker in a construction where the third person plural jussive mood expresses a polite command.

d. àɲè bòrtɔ̀   k-ár-á   ŋànìjè [bá-á
1SG days.ago 1SU-see.PERV-1SG.SU.PERV but   place-RSTR
[ɛ́né-á   [èrmì-á   tùmù-ɲ]_NP]_NP]_NP kó-jóg-èsè-ɔ̀
appeareance-RSTR child-RSTR God-GEN   1SU-tell-BEN-VFS
'And I saw, and bare record that this is the Son of God.'

The time word *bòrò* has an allomorph *bòrò*, as in (7.89a) and can also occur as an anaphoric referential demonstrative, as in (7.89b).

(7.89) a. [hùll-á   bòrò   ká-tál-čó   dórá=jè]
        when-NOMZ ANA:REF 1SU-buy-APPL.1PL.EXC.SU house=SUBORD
        ŋànì   ʃĭgt-è-ɔ̀?
        not.yet hear.PERV-IRR-VFS
        'Did you not hear that we have bought a house?'
        (Lit. 'When we (exc.) then buy a house, you (sg.) haven't yet heard?')

     b. rúm-á   bòrògà   góló̗ɲ-á
        cloth-RSTR REF:DEM   red-RTSR:ATTR
        hín-í-ɔ̀?   iɲɲ
        want.IMPERV-2SG.SU.IMPERV-VFS INTERJ
        kí-hín-í-ɔ̀
        1SU-want.IMPERV-2SG.SU.IMPERV-VFS
        'Do you want that red shirt?' 'Yes, I do.'
        (Lit. 'the earlier shirt (we know)')

7.3.1.4.1.4   /bè kíɲíɲ/ 'a Very Long Time Ago'

The distant past marker *be kíɲíɲ* is made of two words *bè* 'distant past' and *kíɲíɲ* 'long time ago, ancient'. The latter functions as an intensifier of the former.

(7.90) a. bè   kíɲíɲ   túrúmél níɲè
        DIST.PAST long.time.ago car   not.present
        'In olden times, cars were unknown.'

     b. àɲè bè   kíɲíɲ   táá
        1SG DIST.PAST long.time.ago ATTU/UNCERT
        kó-tód-í   kútúl
        1SU-climb-1SG.SU.IMPERV mountain
        'I used to go mountain climbing at one time.'

táá is equivalent to the English adverb 'already' and has various functions when used side by side with the tense system of the language. It can function as an instantaneous, momentaneous/punctual marker referring to the happening of an event at a specific point in time, it may refer to just a specific time part of an event in the past or present.

(7.91) nà   búná   nòŋ   á   gálá   kó   [zíbúná
        CCN   coffee 3SG   COP.3.IMPERV thing.PL CRD   medicine.PL
        kíŋíɲi   háŋ   bè   kíŋíɲ   mùn-ùɲ]_NP1
        long.time.ago   INTENS   DIST.PAST long.time.ago Mursi.PL-GEN
        mes-o-nè   [zùw-á   sábɔ-ne]_NP2
        do-MT-AP.3   people-RTSR   first-ORD
        '… and coffee, it is something like a medicine of the Mursi in ancient time; the first people have long been doing this …'

As it is shown in (7.91), the two separate temporal words are within the first NP in a way by intervening between the head *zíbúná* and the dependent *mùnùɲ*.

7.3.1.4.1.5   /bè sábɔ/ 'at the Beginning, a Long Time Ago'
be sábɔ is almost similar in function to *bè kíŋíɲ* except the former is in part derived from a body part noun *sábá* 'head' extended to refer to a space notion 'in front' and then a temporal notion 'beginning'. It can also function as an adverb 'first' like *bè kíŋíɲ*.

(7.92) àggè bè   sábɔ kíŋíɲ   mùnì
        1PL DIST.PAST first long.ago   Mursi.SG
        kú-súd-íné-ò,   nà   rés-è   níŋè
        1SU-shed-AP-1PL.EXC.SU.PERV CNN   die.IMPERV-NOMZ   not.present
        'A long time ago we (inc.) Mursi shed our skins, and there was no death.'
        (ND 3.1)

The example below is taken from a story which narrates how the Mursi men and women are punished when they violated the norms and values of the community in which they lived in. This corporal punishment is known as *kòmà kɔ́da* 'kneeling'.

(7.93) ŋɲ   čùànéŋ   ŋàméá lɔ̀g-iɲà   [Ø kòm-à
        INTERJ   again   now   issue-PL   [Ø knee-PL
        kɔ́d-áɲ]_RC   á   mèrì
        1SU-stab.IMPERV-1SG.OBJ]   COM.3.IMPERV   many
        '(Recalling) again now, the issues that we kneel for are many.'

        lɔ̀g-iɲà   bè   kíŋíɲ=è   bè
        issue-PL DIST.PAST   long.time.ago=SUBORD   DIST.PAST
        él-á   sábɔ   bè   kɔ́d-é-á
        exist:PL-3PL.SU.PERV   first dist.past   3.SBJV.kneel-RES-3PL.SU.PERV

THE VERB AND PREDICATE STRUCTURE

zùg-ú
people-NOM
'The issues that were there long time ago, in the beginning, for which people kneeled for (the issues) ...'

bè   sábɔ́ kó-jóg-ó-ɛ   ŋà=zùg=tá
DIST.PAST first 3.SBJV-tell.PERV-MT-IRR DEM=people=NEAR
'At the begining, they will tell to these people.' (KM 2:26:8)

As can be seen in (7.93), the phrasal form *be sábɔ́* can be used in reverse order without changing its meaning, i.e. indicating the time location of the situation in the distant past.

7.3.1.4.1.6   /dírr/ 'for a Long Time'

The durative *dírr* 'for a long time' (abbreviated below as DUR) has two functions. First, it just indicates an indefinite time of the durative situation in the past.

(7.94) nà   k-ów-ónó   ŋàŋà=ŋà   dírr   nà
        CCN   1SU-go-MT-1PL.INC.SU.IMPERV like.this=DEF DUR CCN
        [hùllì   té   [bá-á   éré-í=nè]ₙₚ]ₛᵤʙₒᵣᴅ:ᴄʟ
        when/if COP.3.PERV place-RSTR cross-NOMZ-SUBORD
        k-érés-ó   bòi   k-èlì
        1SU-cross.IMPERV-1PL.EXC.SU.IMPERV COMPLET PASS.call.PERV
        ké   dol
        QUOT Dol
        'As we (exc.) kept going like this for a long time and when we (exc.) came to the crossed place, we (exc.) crossed a place called Dòl.' (MH 0:31:2)

Second, it shows a durative time of an event which took place in the past and continuing up until the event is terminated. In this case, the function of *dírr* not only indicates the terminative time of an event but also indicates the beginning time of the event.

(7.95) a. kɔ́b-ú   dírr [ín-á   tòŋòkórí]ₙₚ
           follow-3SG.SU.PERV   DUR   3SG.PN.SP-RSTR Toŋokori
           [bánás-ɛ́   zùwò]ʀᴄ ír-ú   mà-ì-ni
           [stand.up-3PL.SU.PERV people] drink-3SG.SU.PERV water-LOC-RS
           'He followed it until it came to a place of Toŋokori [on the Omo River] where there were people. That's where he drank.'

The durative *dírr* may denotes various readings—'until' in (7.95a), 'all the way' in (7.95b), and 'until indefinitely' in (7.95c).

    b. *bék-ú*   *dírr nà húllí bì-ò*
        watch-3SG.SU.PERV DUR CCN COND cow-PL
        dóŋ-číŋ-áná   *ŋáà, òlí čúj*   *dóróg-ì, háʃ!*
        pick-APPL-3SG.SU.PERV here bull chase.away bush-LOC ideo
        'He watched his bull carefully and when the cows came to drink he crashed off into the bush.'

The clause containing the durative *dírr* and the conditional/subordinate clause with an instrumental-purposive marked verb are coordinated by the clausal coordinative particle *nà*. Both clauses express a prior action in the past before the controlling clause.

    c. [*húllí égí*   *dírr*] *mà*   *účúr-sɛ-nor*[*nɛn*]
        when/if BOIL.3PL.IRR DUR water finish-BEN-RECIP
        'If it boils for a long time, the water will be finished.'
        (Lit. 'finish for itself')

7.3.1.4.2 *Durative: Future*

Durative future indicates a future time of an event from now. Dixon (2012: 7) pointed out that future time is perceived only by looking forward from now. In fact, some lexical time adverbs can occur in two or more categories—for example, Mursi has a few of them that either can function as future time reference or as temporal shifters. Future lexical time adverbs often occur with imperfective aspect.

However, lexical time adverbs may occur with perfective aspect if the verb is in subjunctive mood, as shown in (7.96a).

(7.96) a. *nà*   *ŋà=zùg=tá*   [*húllí*   *sé*
        CCN DEM=people=NEAR COND/TEMP say.COMPL
        ké-té   *rònó*   *bíbí=jè*]$_{SUBORD:CL}$ *bárá*
        3.SBJV-be.PERV in.the.future big:REDUP.PL-SUBORD bárá
        '... and when these people become seniors (Bara) in the future.'
        (KM 2:26:8)

TABLE 7.38 Durative future time words

Durative: future tense

Particles	Meaning
ròn ɔ́ [a]	'in the future, tomorrow'
tíí	'always, all the time'
hàlì	'later'
ɗóg	'forever' ⟨for all future time⟩

a   Turton (1973:186) noted that *ròn ɔ́* can mean anything from a day to twenty years later.

7.3.1.4.2.1   /ròn ɔ́/ 'in the Future, Tomorrow'
The lexical time adverb *ròn ɔ́* is one of the few time words in the language which is able to indicate future time reference often implying some degree of remoteness of future tense and temporal shifter. The one we saw in (7.95a) clearly shows a non-modal form depicting degree of remoteness in the future. The non-specific future time use of *ròn ɔ́* does not require other specific time words to be combined with it, as can be shown in (7.96b).

    b. *ŋà=mád-á=á*   *támáríná* [Ø *ròn ɔ́*
       DEM=teach-NOMZ=NEAR student.PL [Ø tomorrow
       hóɲ-ɛ́-á]_RC
       come.IMPERV.PL-3PL.SU.IMPERV-RSTR
       k-ádʒ-ɛ-a
       1SU-give.IMPERV-APPL-RSTR?
       'I shall give the book to the students who are coming tomorrow.'

However, when *ròn ɔ́* functions as a temporal shifter, it often occurs with other specific time words (see §7.3.1.4.5).

7.3.1.4.2.2   /tíí/ 'Continuative, for a Long Time, All the Time'
The other lexical time adverb is *tíí*—has two functions: progressive/continuous marker (on its own) and habitual/frequency (when reduplicated). When it is used in an event that has taken place in the past, the continuity of the event can be made to denote a definite time reference by situating a time in which the event stops at some point. This is possible by adding another event that has an end-point on its own, as in (7.97).

(7.97) nà   k-ów[g]-ónó   mà   tán-ɔ̀   tíí
       CCN   1SU-go.IMPERV-MT.1PL.INC.SU.IMPERV   water   side-OBL CONT
       nà   kó-hóɲ-Ø   nà   [hùllì
       CCN   1SU-come.IMPERV.PL-1PL.INC.SU.IMPERV   CCN   when/if
       ké-héj-ó
       1SU-go.IMPERV.PL-1PL.EXC.SU.IMPERV
       kɔ́-dɔ́g-Ø-ɛ   bá   ké
       1SU-tread.on.IMPERV-1PL.INC.SU.IMPERV-COM   place   QUOT
       dòl=ŋà]_SUBORD:CL
       Dol=DEF

'And we (inc.) kept going o the other side of the river and we (inc.) came and we (inc.) tread on (walked on) the land then arrived at a place called the Dòl.' (MH 0:06:6–0:17:6)

(7.98) a. gáj-Ø   dákákán   tíí
           know-3SG.SU.IMPERV   all   all.the.time/DUR
           bá-á   ánčáɲɲá   bítómó   dóg
           place/CAUSE-RTSR   since:INCEPT   lie   forever

'He knew all along that it was a lie.'

In (7.98a), the word ánčáɲá 'since (the beginning), already' is an inceptive particle/marker is within ⟨resultative⟩ clause which may indicate a situation that began in the past and continued as the result of the past situation. For instance, see (7.98a1) below.

   a1. bá   ánčá   [bùràn-a   bú-sís-ó
       place/CAUSE   since:INCEPT   territory-RSTR big-AUG-RSTR.MOD
       kómóró-ɲ]_NP
       priest/leader-GEN

'For it is the city of the great King.'

   b. ŋà=hír=á   ŋàs=ŋà   tíí   kèŋì[13]-tí
       DEM=person=NEAR   female=DEF   all.the.time   belly.PL-NRSTR
       mèrì   bég-áɲ   àɲè
       many   watch-1SG.OBJ   1SG

'I waited for a long time for the woman.'

---

13 kɛŋi 'belly (pl.)' is a grammaticalized body part term used to derive a multiplicative number marking forms 'times'. As can be seen in (7.115b), it has a sense of 'many times' and it takes a non-restrictive suffix since its modifier mèrì 'many' is a quantifier.

THE VERB AND PREDICATE STRUCTURE

The continuative *tíí* may also denote a durative future tense as can be shown in the following example.

    c.   àɲè tíí   kí-ʃi   k-ɔ́g
          1SG always 1.SBJV-hear.PERV 1.SBJV-go.PERV
          'I am ready at any time.'
          (Lit. 'I am always to listen to go.')

The continuative *tíí* 'until' also introduces a temporal participant, as shown below.

    d.   àggè ké-ré-nèn-ó   tíí
          1PL 1SU-wait.IMPERV-RECIP-1PL.INC.SU.IMPERV CONT/DUR
          dàɲ
          evening
          'We waited until evening.'

When *tíí* occurs clause-finally, it denotes a situation that may happen for an indefinite or non-specific length of time—particularly, it acquires a sense of an 'everlasting', as in (7.98a–b).

(7.99) a. nɔ̀ŋ [ín-á   bág-Ø-á
             3SG [3SG.PN.SP-RSTR eat-3SG.SU.IMPERV-RSTR
             ŋà=tílá=á]$_{RC}$ nɔ̀ŋ háŋ=è   í-Ø
             DEM=food=NEAR] 3SG INTENS=SUBORD EXIST-3SG.SU.IMPERV
             bás-é-ò   tíí
             live-NOMZ-OBL CONT/DUR
             'He that eats of this bread shall live forever.'
             (Lit. 'exist in life forever')

      b. ŋànìje   ŋà=ìggè=à   héj
           GEN:ADVRS DEM=3PL.PN.SP=NEAR go.IMPERV.PL
           číb-ín-á   kó tíí   ŋànìjè íggé-á
           tie.IMPERV-N.S-NOMZ PNC CONT/DUR BUT 3PL.PN.SP-RSTR
           [Ø hɔ̀l-a]$_{RC}$ héj   bás-é-á]
           [Ø white.STV-RSTR go.IMPERV.PL live-NOMZ-RSTR
           íʃ-ó   tíí
           exist.PERV.PL-3PL.IRR CONT/DUR
           'And these shall go away into everlasting punishment, but the righteous into life eternal.'
           (Lit. 'but the righteous go for life to exist continuously.')

Note that the continuous marker both in (7.99a and b) tend to acquire a further vowel length when it occurs clause-finally. So, the form of *tíí* seems to be dependent on the phonetic environment in which it occurs and may alter its shape in various environments.

7.3.1.4.2.3   /hàlì/ 'Later'

Despite the fact that the temporal *hàlì* could indicate a relative-degree of remoteness of a future time, it also refers to a definite future time when combined with relator time word *wùréɔ́* 'after, behind, last'. Some examples are illustrated below.

(7.100) a. *čùànéŋ ŋà=lɔ̀g=tù   hàlì áj-t-έ*
again   DEM=issue=FAR later take-PERV.PL-APPL
tèrò-ú-ni   té   [lɔ̀g-tí   g=èj]ₙₚ   nà
Teri.PL-NOM-RS COP.3.PERV issue-NRSTR PL.PSD=3PL.PSR CCN
hàlì nès-έ   bì
later kill-3PL.SU.IMPERV   cow
'Then later the Teru take up this issue (Kili) and thus it becomes their issue. After that they will slaughter a cow.' (KW 1:28:8)

b. *àɲè hàlì kó-jóg-ón   nɔ̀ŋ čùànéŋ*
1SG   later 1SU-tell-MT.1PL.INC.SU.IMPERV 3SG   again
'I will tell him again.'
(Lit. 'I will tell to him later again.')

c. *àɲè hàlì k-ɔ́g-ó-í   ɓòì*
1SG   later 1SU-go.IMPERV-MT-1SG.SU.IMPERV   all
hín-í   ɲɔ́j=è   húŋ
want.IMPERV-2SG.SU.IMPERV   2SG.NOM=SUBORD simply
'I will go anywhere you like.'

d. *nɔ̀ŋ hàlì kɔ́ɔ́j-Ø   gáwá-ɲá   ràmànò   wùréɔ́*
3SG   later 3.SBJV.GO-3.IRR market-PL   two.MOD   after
'He will go after two weeks.'

As it is shown in (7.100a–d), the temporal marker *hàlì* renders a future time reference rather than a modal meaning.

7.3.1.4.3 Frequency-Habitual

Mursi has three durative adverbial time words to refer to frequency or habitual aspectual meanings—*ríb* 'all day', *tíítíí* 'often, always', and *kàlì kàlì* 'everyday' (Lit. 'day day').

7.3.1.4.3.1 /tíítíí/ 'Often, Always'

It is the continuous marker particle *tíí* which gives rise to a frequency-habitual marker *tíítíí*. It is the fact that *tíítíí* is a reduplicated form of the continuative form *tíí*. However, in some cases, it happens as a repeated form of *tíí* rather than as a reduplication. The difference between the two morphological manifestations of *tíítíí* lies in whether it is uttered in slow speech or in fast speech.

(7.101) a. nɔ̀ŋ   tíítíí   í-Ø   bàì
         3SG CONT/DUR:REDUP exist.IMPERV-3SG.SU.IMPERV sit
         'S/he always sits.'

The verb *bàì* may have been derived from the noun *bá* 'place' and from the locative marker *-i* ⟨place-LOC⟩ 'place-at'. The real verb that should have represented the semantics of 'sit' is the perfective copula *té* 'be.PERV' which can also functions as an existential verb 'exist, present'.

        b. àggè   zùw-á   [Ø kà-bàg-ó   kàrì]_{RC}
           1PL   people-RSTR [Ø 1SU-live-1PL.EXC.SU together]
           tíítíí   éjá-nè   [ŋà=múwáí=tùnù   jàgà=ŋà]_{NP}
           CONT/DUR:REDUP help-3.RECIP DEM=woman=FAR old=DEF
           'Our neighbours were always helping that old woman.'

Reduplication could be a justifiable morphological nature of particles such as *tíí* to reduplicate their partial or full form when functioning as frequency/habitual temporal markers. See the example given below.

        c. ŋà=hír=á   jàgá   [Ø óól-Ø   biró=ŋà]_{RC}
          DEM=man=NEAR old:RSTR [Ø beg-3SG.SU.IMPERV money=DEF]
          [úŋ-á   k-óól-čá   tùmù]_{NP} tíí   tíí
          [day-RSTR 3.SBJV-beg-APPL god   CONT CONT
          kún-Ø-ɔ̀
          come-3SG.SU.IMPERV-VFS
          'That old man who is begging for money comes every Sunday.'

(7.102) *jesusi sɛ́-á   ké dada   tíí   tíí*
jesus say-3SG.SU.PERV D.SP father.PERT.1SG.PSR CONT CONT
mès-íné-ɔ̀   kó   ạ̀ɲè kè-mèsí-nèn-ɔ̀   jàg-ɛ̀sɛ̀   ŋàŋà
work-AP.3-VFS PNC 1SG 1SU-work-AP.1-VFS answer-3.BEN like.this
'Jesus answered them, "My Father works hitherto, and I work."'
(Lit. 'Jesus said this, "my father always works and I work", answered like this.')

In (7.102), the continuative marker has both clauses as its scope. It refers a continued habitual past action that also covers the present and future habitual actions.

7.3.1.4.3.2   /ríb/ 'All the Day'
The particle *ríb* may be used as frequency as well as habitual marker. It always occurs clause-finally—either often preceded by the specific time span word *kàlì* 'day' (7.103a–c) or rarely followed by a temporal shifter *bàrì* 'yesterday' (7.103d).

(7.103) a. *hàlì sán-í   kátámá-í-jè?   ɪmm ɪmm! ạ̀ɲè hàlì*
later stay-2SG.SU.IMPERV town-LOC-OBL no no   1SG later
k-ó-í   ɔ́r-ɔ́   ríb
1SU-go.IMPERV-1SG.SU.IMPERV home-OBL all.the.day
'Will you (m) spend the day at the market? No, I shall stay all day at home.'

As it is shown in (7.103a), frequency/habitual marker *ríb* always occurs in a typical adverbial position in AVO order. In contrast, future time marker *hàlì* always occurs clause-initially if the clause in which it occurs is subordinate, otherwise often occurs immediately after the subject AVO order as it is illustrated in (7.103a–d; 7.103a).

   b. *ìggè bàrì   rúm-ịɲá čúr-ó   kàlì ríb*
2PL yesterday cloth-PL wash-2PL.SU.IMPERV day all.the.day
'Were you (pl.) washing clothes all day?'

   c. *nɔ̀ŋ kɔ́n-nèn-á   kàlì ríb*
3SG write-AP-3SG.SU.PERV day all.the.day
'He was writing (letters) all day.'

THE VERB AND PREDICATE STRUCTURE 351

The fact is that antipassive and progressive are marked in the same way by the derivational suffix -nèn. But as shown in (7.103c) above, it is a typical antipassive construction where the object of the clause is demoted. But, a progressive meaning can be rendered by adding a temporal shifter word clause-finally.

    d. àɲè ká-támárí-nèn-í   kàlì ríb   bàrì
        1SG 1SU-learn-AP-1SG.SU.IMPERV day all.the.day yesterday
        'I was studying the whole day.'

So, the temporal shifter bàrì refers to the fact that the entire event has happened from yesterday onwards. In fact, no definite time reference is made about the stopping time of the event.

7.3.1.4.4 Specific Time Spans

All specific time span references in Mursi have a span of a single day or twenty four hours or a single day-night cycle. For example, let us start with the first particle in Table 7.39 below. The generic time word úŋó 'night' may also refer to 'a day'. The specific time span sense is derived from (⟨a night; one sleep⟩) a cycle of a single time span. All particles operate within a single cyclic time span of úŋó.

Despite the fact that úŋó is a dedicated time word in referring to a twenty-four hour time span, kàlì may also be used as a generic term with this meaning. As a generic term, when kàlì is used for a specific time reference, a definite marker should be specified by grammatical means appropriate to this generic term, as in (7.104).

(7.104) ŋà=kàlì=tá   àhì-tí   ká-dáʃ-í   níɲè
        DEM=day=NEAR thing.SG-CS 1SU-do-1SG.SU.IMPERV not.present
        'I have nothing else to do today.'

In fact, in the absence of additional definite time reference markers, both dàiɲ(n) and kàlì may refer to different time span stages of the night time and of the day time, respectively. The examples given below illustrate the use of úŋó and kàlì as indefinite time spans.

(7.105) a. àggè ká-már-ó   bá   kàlì-ò   kó   dàìn-ò
        1PL 1SU-travel-1PL.EXC.SU.PERV place day-OBL PNC night-OBL
        kàrì
        together
        'We travelled day and night.'

TABLE 7.39 Specific time span words of Mursi

Special time span

Particles	Meaning	Remark
úŋó	'night'	'sleep (n.), a single day'
bàrɔ́	'at night'	
bàrkèŋɔ̀	'mid-night'	⟨night-center.obl⟩ compound
ɓèlè	'night around 4 am'	
ɓèlèʃàù[a]	'dawn (before sunrise)'	⟨early early⟩ ɓele
ɓùrèʃàù	'dawn (before sunrise)'	⟨morning early⟩
ɓùrè	'morning'	
kàlìkèŋɔ̀	'noon'	⟨day-center.obl⟩ compound
mírè	'afternoon'	
kàlì	'day'	⟨kàlì kàlì⟩ 'everyday'
dàìɲ⟨n⟩	'evening'	(a time before eight o'clock in the evening; late afternoon)
gáwá<j	'week'	Lit. ⟨market⟩
tágís	'month'	Lit. ⟨moon⟩
bérgú	'month'	Lit. ⟨moon-month period; lunation⟩
ójó	'year'	Lit. ⟨rainy season⟩

a ɓele 'bald spot' and ɓele ʃau can literally be translated as 'bald early' ~ is a metaphorical expression of time.

b. tílá   kàlì-nè   ɓón-á-Ø
   food   day-OBL   arrive.PERV-MT-3SG.SBJV
   'Lunch is about ready.'
   (Lit. 'Food from day is to arrive.')

c. séɲó=jè   ìláág-á   nà   úɲó ràmàn-nò wùréɔ́
   monday=SUBORD sick-3SG.SU.PERV CCN sleep two-MOD after
   ér-Ø=è
   die.PERV-3.IRR=SUBRD
   'He fell sick on Monday, and died two days after.'

d. nɔ̀ŋ kɔ́-í   ɔ́r-ɔ́   sátí sàkkàl-ò mírè
   3SG go.IMPERV-3.IRR home-OBL time   nine-MOD afternoon

>   *mírè*
>   afternoon
>   'He goes home every afternoon at nine o'clock.'

Except for the last four particles on Table 7.39, all particles denote different stages of a single full cycle time references of one day.

7.3.1.4.5 Temporal Shifters

Despite the fact that most of Mursi temporal shifters specify the precise time point in the present moment *méá* 'now', some others are even more specific when referring to a time today. Due to this, some appear to have phrasal-like forms, as illustrated in Table 7.40 below.

The temporal function of *méá* would make sense and be clear if a time reference is seen from the viewpoint of the present and momentary situation (right here-and-now). For instance, let us examine the examples given below.

> (7.106) *ín-á*   [Ø *bè*   *á*   *méá*]$_{RC}$
>   3SG.PN.SP-RSTR [Ø DIST.PAST COP.3.IMPERV now]
>   'at this time'
>   (Lit. 'It is that it was at this time')

Example (7.105) shows a past time reference and refers to a situation that already took place exactly on the same day, today. In fact, it is the tense marker *be* that made it possible for us to understand that the whole expression is about something that happened at some point in the past but has now become a reference to the present moment. Thus, as shown in (7.106), the past time reference has a distant past temporal marker *bè* as its main meaning, and the present time marker *méá* indicates that the temporal situation of past is seen in relation to the present moment.

> (7.107) a. *ójó-á*   *sábú-né*   (*nòŋ*) *gùjò dág wáŋ*   *méá*
>   year-RSTR first-ORD (3SG) rain hit INTENS now
>   *ŋà=ʔójó=á*   *nòŋ*   *dák-ú*   *ké*   *tíiní*
>   DEM=year=NEAR 3SG hit-3SG.SU.PERV 3.SBJV.be.PERV small
>   *sòŋ*
>   only
>   'Last year it rained much. But this year it has only rained a little.'

TABLE 7.40 Mursi temporal shifters

Temporal shifters

Particles	Meaning	Remark
méá	'now'	⟨present moment⟩ (Lit. 'right here-and-now')
ŋàméárè	'now'	⟨ŋà=méáre⟩ (DEM=immeadiately)
ŋàméá	'today, now'	⟨ŋà=méá=a⟩ (DEM=now=NEAR)
ŋakàlìkena	'at that time/moment (same day)'	⟨ŋà=kàlì-ken=a⟩ (DEM=day-center=NEAR)
ŋàhùllùnù	'time, at the time'	⟨ŋà=hùll=ùnù⟩ (DEM=TEMP/COND=FAR)
bàrì	'yesterday'	
kàlìkón	'the same day'	⟨kàlì-kón⟩ (Lit. 'day-one')
rònɔ́ ɓèlè	'tomorrow'	⟨future-OBL early morning⟩ (Lit. 'in the future early morning')
hàlì ɓèlè	'tomorrow'	⟨later early morning⟩ (Lit. 'later in early morning')
rònɔ́ ɓùrètùnù	'day after tomorrow'	⟨rònɔ́ ɓùrè=tùnù⟩ (future-OBL morning=FAR) (Lit. 'in the future morning')

b. méá kó-hóɲ-Ø   nà
  now 1SU-come.IMPERV.PL-1PL.INC.SU.IMPERV CCN
  k-èlè   ké mùn dóg=ŋà
  PASS-call.PERV QUOT mursi.PL forever=DEF
  'So now we (inc.) came and were able to be called Mursi (pl.) forever (permanently).' (MH 2:37:6)

c. méá ŋàméá ŋà=bérgú=á=ŋà [nɔ̀ŋ bíméj]_TOP nɔ̀ŋ
  now (today) DEM=M=NEAR=DEF 3SG Bime.SG 3SG
  [Ø [hír-á tánɨj-té]_NP]_RC té bíméj sɔ̀ŋ
  [Ø man-RSTR difficult.ADJ-NRSTR COP.3.PERV Bime.SG only
  'Nowaday more than ever, he the Bime is a person who became diffucult only Bime.' (MH 6:27:8)

Even if the meaning and the function of *méá* is mostly a momentary temporal deictic center, its meaning sometimes can be fluid and depends on other relative time contexts. On the other hand, *méá* can be changed into an absolute

THE VERB AND PREDICATE STRUCTURE

tense marker in order to express the time of utterance referring only to today. This is possible by attaching the deictic clitics to *meá*, resulting in two other temporal markers that would help in locating events that occurred on the same day as the speech events: *ŋàméárè* and *ŋàméá*.

(7.108) a. [*húllí   ìggè   dáʃída-o   ʃéé=jè*]_{SUBORD:CL} *àggè*
when/if 2PL work.PERV:PL-2PL.SU.PERV well-SUBORD 2pl
hàlì   déj-án-ó   dáʃí   ŋàméárè
later finish.IMPERV-MT-2PL.SU.IMPERV work now
'If you (pl.) do well, you (pl.) will finish your job today.'

Note that in conditional clauses, time words often occupy the final slot of the main clause.

b. *ŋàméárè* nɔ̀ŋ hàlì íw-ána   [*dàmùsí-á*
now   3SG later receive-MT.3SG.SU.IMPERV salary-RSTR
n=ènè]_{NP}
SG.PSD=3SG.PSR
'Today he will receive his salary.'

c. *ŋàméárè   ŋà=ká-dáʃí-è*
now   NEG=1.HORT-do.PERV-VFS
'Let me not do (it) now.'

d. *ŋàméá   ŋɔ́jɔ̀   úhán-Ø*   [*tán-á*
today wind blow-3SG.SU.IMPERV other.side-RSTR
ŋɔ́-čá   sús-ɔ̀]_{NP}
descend-APPL/INSTR.RSTR sun-OBL
'An easterly wind is blowing today.'
(Lit. 'other side where the sun descend')

e. [*tútú-á   [dórí-á   ákímí-ɲ*]_{NP}]_{NP} *hàlì ój-é   ŋàméá*
gate-RSTR house-RSTR doctor-GEN later open-APPL now
'The gate of the hospital will be opened now.'

Except for reported speech, one cannot use these two temporal words when speaking of a past and future time. The two are used as reference or deictic points of a present moment 'now' and 'today'. Attempting to establish a distinction between *ŋàméárè* and *ŋàméá* can be complex and irrelevant because there is no clear boundary where the two precisely denote location in time within 'today'. Imagine how nonsensical it would be to try to understand the meaning of the example below in a way other than 'now/today'.

(7.109) ŋànì nɔ̀ŋ ih-ìnɛ̀n-Ø-ɔ̀[14]   kó
       still 3SG exist.IMPERV-PROG/RECIP-3SG.SU.IMPERV COM.PREP
       ŋàméá?
       now
       'Is he still alive?'
       (Lit. 'Is he still existing with today?')

Like the above two temporal shifters, ŋàkàlìkènà and ŋàhùllùnù are temporal constructs from other time words and the deictic elements.

(7.110) a. nà   mà   díné-ó   ŋà=kàlkèn=ná
           CCN water full-3.IRR DEM=day.center=NEAR
           kód-ó-ɛ́   òrì
           1SU.take.out-1PL.EXC.SU.IMPERV-APPL:RES where?
           'And at that time the river is full, we (exc.) take out to where?'
           (Lit. 'Where side of the river?') (MH 0:23:5)

ŋàkàlkènnà can be substituted by similar temporal marker ŋàhùllùnù but with little change in meaning.

       b. jóg-óɲ   àɲè ŋàhùllùnù
          tell-1SG.OBJ 1SG at.the.time
          'Tell (sg.) me at once!'
          (Lit. 'Tell (sg.) me at a time (at the same time)!')

The addressee is second person thus it is not marked for person in Mursi. If the addressee is plural, then a plural number marker is added to the verb after the object marker. The verb 'to tell' is a ditransitive verb so it requires two object arguments.

       c. ŋàhùllùnù   ŋà=ɓ=ùnù   zùwò   hírkón kó tɔ̀mɔ̀n
          at.the.time DEM=place=FAR   people twenty PNC ten

---

14   íh is an transitive verb in singular form and requires a conjunction particle kó in order to show reciprocal/joint action.

él-έ
exist.IMPERV:PL-3PL.SU.IMPERV
'There were about thirty people present'.
(Lit. 'At the time thirty people were present.')

d. *bè   ŋàhùllùnù   nɔ̀ŋ   ŋànì   k-ìrì-čà=ó*
   DIST.PAST at.the.time 3SG not.yet PASS-born-PASS.3SU=NEG
   'At the time, he was not yet born.'

As illustrated on above examples (7.110a–d) *ŋakàlìkena* and *ŋàhùllùnù* have a comparable temporal functions in that both locate a situation with the same/exact moment of the situation.

All these temporal words operate based on the notion of time and deixis vis-à-vis an established present moment as a reference point. The deictic circumclitics in Mursi can be viewed in terms of temporal operators in addition to their function in denoting degree of distance of the speaker in reference to the hearer. They may also serve either to refer to a speech situation as the reference point as discussed in examples above (present location and time of speaking), or to refer to a reference point other than the location and time of speaking. The demonstrative proclitic *ŋà=* provides a definite sense to the reference point while the two enclitics (*=á* 'near') and (*=ùnù* 'far') serve to denote the degree of remoteness from the present moment. Some examples are given below.

(7.111) *hàlì [kàl-á   ŋà=kàlì]ₙₚ [dórí-á   tímírtí-ɲ]ₙₚ*
        later day-RSTR   DEM=day   house-RSTR   education-GEN
        ŋà=k-el-án-í=ó
        NEG=1SU-present.IMPERV-MT-1SG.SU.IMPERV=NEG
        'I shall not spend the day at school.'
        (Lit. 'Later the day of today I will not present at school.')

(7.112) *bá   bàrì   jóg-ó-Ø   hàlì ŋà=kàlì=tá   tímírtí*
        place yesterday tell-MT-3.IRR later DEM=day=NEAR   education
        níɲè
        not.present
        'As (I) said yesterday, there is no school today'

Being be able to speak about 'today' as yesterday is quite an interesting temporality notion. As shown in (7.112), it is possible to talk about 'today' while being 'in yesterday'. A reported speech construction may not be even necessary.

The interaction of aspect and tense is necessary within the main clause where both are expressed in a way appropriate to the temporal condition of the main clause. This is the case below in (7.113), where the aspect on the verb of the main clause is imperfective, but the entire temporal situation of the clause expresses something that happened in the distant past.

(7.113) bè   kàlìkón   jesusi bóns-áná
        DIST.PAST day.one jesus   leave/exit.IMPERV-MT.3SG.SU.IMPERV
        dórí   tó-jé
        house in-OBL
        'The same day Jesus went out of the house.'

In fact, temporal words of any sort can occur with clauses predicated by imperfective and perfective verbs as long as they are not in the main clause. The time word 'tomorrow' has a number of lexical forms: rònɔ́ (7.114), rònɔ́ ɓèlè and rònɔ́ ɓùrètùnù (7.115), and hàlì ɓèlè (7.116).

(7.114) [hùllì   rònɔ́   ká   án-á   ɓèlè
        when/if tomorrow UNCERT   COP.IMPERV-PST   early.morning
        áɨ́w-ò=jè]_SUBORD:CL   damosi hàlì
        come.PERV-MT.3SG.IRR=SUBORD   salari later
        k-ádʒ-Ø-í-ɔ̀
        1SU-give.IMPERV-3SG.OBJ-1SG.SU.IMPERV-VFS
        'In case he comes tomorrow, I shall give him his salary.'

(7.115) a. nà   hàlì   [rònɔ́   ɓèlè   [hùllì
           CCN later in.future morning when/if
           ká-báns-áná=jè]_SUBORD:CL   dàà   bàrì
           1SU-get.up-MT.1PL.INC.SU.IMPERV=SUBORD truly/MIRR   yestarday
           ísíkán-Ø-é   káráné ŋà=ɓ=ùnù
           approach-MT-3SG.SU.IMPERV-APPL   down   DEM=place=FAR
           '... and the morning, when we (inc.)) wake up, I has submerged down down there already! (from its position yesterday).' (MH 2:21:3)

       b. [rònɔ́   ɓùrè=tá   kó   kón=e]_SUBORD:CL   [húllí
          future morning=NEAR   PNC   one=SUBORD   when
          ká-báns-áná   dàà   wà   té-ì
          2/3.SBJV-get.up-MT   SURPRISE   REC.PAST   COP.PERV-3SG.IRR
          tùnò=ŋà]_SUBORD:CL   nà   nɔ̀ŋ í-Ø
          on.top=DEF   CCN   3SG   exist-3SG.SU.IMPERV

ŋà=ɓá=á   dóg
DEM=place=NEAR forever

'the next morning there is one, when we (inc.) wake, (that piece of wood) which was on the top, it is still down there!'

In relative clauses, time words always occur at the beginning of the clause following the gapping relative clause construction which is always indicated by zero marking. When the relative clause and main clause share the same common argument, which often precedes both clauses, time words may also appear at the beginning of the main clause. An example of such instance is given below.

(7.116) hòj-á-ú   [Ø bàrì   mád-á   ŋànì
        girl-RSTR-NOM   [Ø yesterday learn-NOMZ   not.yet
        kú-húč-á=ó]_RC   rònɔ́   ɓèlè
        3.SBJV-pay-3SG.SU.PERV=NEG]   future   early.morning
        húít-ò
        pay.PER-3SG.IRR
        'The girl who did not pay for the book yesterday will pay tomorrow.'

7.3.1.4.6   Expectation Temporals

Mursi utilizes a few time particles with respect to expectation—negative perfective form *ŋànì* 'not yet, still', *húŋ* 'already, just', *taa* 'already', and *húllí* 'when'.

7.3.1.4.6.1   *ŋànì* 'Not Yet, Still'

The form (*ŋànì*) often occurs in negative declarative mood preceding the perfective verb root (see Chapter 13). In the subjunctive mood which expresses the action that has not yet taken place but that could happen in the future, it occurs before the subjunctive verb form.

(7.117) háránčí-nèn   (ámbíbí)   gáj-Ø-ɔ̀?
        white.person- (read)   know.IMPERV-3SG.SU.IMPERV-VFS
        'Is he able to read English?'
        (Lit. 'He (read) knows English?')

        ŋà=gáj-Ø=ó   ŋànì
        NEG=know.IMPERV-3SG.SU.IMPERV=NEG   not.yet
        í-Ø   gɔ̀r-ɔ̀
        exist-3SG.SU.IMPERV   road-OBL
        'No, not yet.'
        (Lit. 'He doesn't know, not yet to that way (road).')

ŋànì   kó-bón-ó=tó=só
not.yet 3.SBJV-arrive.PERV-MT=NEG=EMPH
'Yet before the time arrive.'

(7.118) wà   tílá   wà   ŋànì   kákó   k-úʃá
       REC.PAST food REC.PAST not.yet UNCERT 3.SBJV-finsih.PERV
       'Isn't lunch ready?'
       (Lit. 'Food was not yet maybe ready?')

On further distribution of ŋànì other than the syntactic slots shown in (7.116) and (7.118), see also example (7.110d) and/or other examples in this grammar.

7.3.1.4.6.2   húŋ 'Already', 'Just, Simply'

As a temporal marker particle, húŋ bears the meanings 'already' and 'just'. By carrying these two meanings, it often takes the position available immediately after the nominals.

(7.119) [hùllì   k-ár   gímá   húŋ]_SUBORD:CL
       when/if 1.SBJV-see.PERV mead   already
       [kà-màt-í   kèŋɔ̀   hólóló húŋ]_MAIN:CL
       1SU-drink.IMPERV-1SG.SU.IMPERV stomach empty   already
       'If I had gotten some mead, I would have drunk (it) even on an empty stomach.'
       (Lit. 'If night mead already, I would drink it already.')

As it is shown in (7.119), húŋ is clearly in a temporal function, thus it follows nominals rather than verbal predicates. In fact, it would be really good if the two meanings are treated as one, with the difference between them being just contextual, as in (7.120a–c).

(7.120) a. nɔ̀ŋ hír-a   [Ø k-èlì   ké   bímé-ì=ŋà]_RC   nɔ̀ŋ
          3SG person-RTSR [Ø PASS-call.PERV QUOT Bime-SG=DEF]   3SG
          bák-ú   kíɲáŋ   húŋ-ni
          eat-3SG.SU.PERV crocodile just/simply-RS
          'He, the man who is called the Bime ate a crocodile!' (MH 4:24:5)

       b. ténèŋ hùllì kó   lɔg-ti   [Ø k-ɔ́gɔ́]_RC   dìb
          why   if   PNC word-NRSTR [Ø 3SBJV-go.PERV] straight

húŋ?
simply/just
'I wish he had told the truth.'
(Lit. 'I wish if he went simply straight with the word.')

c. *tílá   ŋànì   ká-ɓák=ó   nà   túŋ-ú]*
food   not.yet 3.SBJV-eat.PERV=NEG CCN PERV.sleep-3SG.SU.PERV
húŋ
simply/just
'He went to bed without eating his supper.'
(Lit. 'He didn't yet eat food and he just slept.')

Note that the combination of *ténèŋ+húllí* ⟨why+if⟩ in (7.120b) is a subordinate clause form which is used to denote 'wish'. In (7.120b), *húŋ* follows the predicate, thus it functions adverbially.

7.3.1.4.6.3   *táá* 'Already'

The polysemous particle *táá* has two functions. It can be used as an expectation temporal word 'already', and can also function as an uncertainty marker 'maybe'. The examples given below are those that deal only in its temporal function.

(7.121) a. [*kè-á   kà-ɓàì+ča*[15]   *írsásí-ŋá*]$_{NP}$ *táá*
thing-RSTR PASS-sharpen+APPL pencil-RSTR   already
ɓí-ča   ɓòì
break-APPL.3 completely
'The pencil sharpener is broken.'

b. [*érmì-á   íláás-á*]$_{NP}$ *ŋàméá táá   té*
child-RSTR sick.STV-RSTRT:ATTR today already COP.3.PERV
čàllì
good
'The sick child is better today.'
(Lit. 'The sick child today (now) already became good.')

---

15   Although *-ča* still functions as an instrumental marker suffix, in some cases, it still occurs with some lexicalized verbal words. Thus, it appears that *-ča* is on the way of losing its morphological productivity leaving some verbal words in unsegmentable forms.

c. kènɔ̀   táá   bàrì   dák-ú   ʃírɔ́
    tree.PL   already yesterday hit-3SG.SU.PERV   weed
    'The whole garden is full of weeds.'

7.3.1.5 The Completive Particle ɓòì

Completive aspect expresses the completion of an event (Payne 1997: 240). In Mursi, completive aspect can be indicated by the multifunctional particle ɓòì 'all, at all, completely' which usually occurs at the end of the clause following the predicate. In line with Bybee et al. (1994: 57), some of the semantics which could possibly be associated with ɓòì includes: an action done thoroughly and completely, and affectedness of the object of the action (consumed or destroyed).

(7.122) a. [érmì ɖɔ̀ɔ̀nὲ]ₙₚ ér-á   ɓòì
           child mother   die.PERV-3SG.SU.PERV   COMPLETIVE
           'The baby's mother died.'

       b. báwúrú bán-ú   [tán-á
          plane   fly.PERV-3SG.SU.PERV   other.side-RSTR
          ŋɔ́-čá   sús-ɔ̀]ₙₚ   nà   gár-á
          descend-INSTR:RSTR   sun-OBL   CCN   dissaper-3SG.SU.PERV
          ɓòì
          COMPLETIVE
          'The plane disappeared flying eastward.'

       c. hírí   ìr-ú   gésó ɓòì   bú-sís. (nà)
          man   drink.PERV-3SG.SU.PERV   beer COMPLETIVE big-AUG (CCN)
          sé-á   ké   ʃàj   ŋà=kí-hín=ó
          say-3SG.SU.PERV   QUOT   tea   NEG=1SU-want.IMPERV=NEG
          'The man drank much beer (local beer) then he said, "I don't want tea".'

In (7.122c), ɓòì denotes the sense of bringing the activity into a completion stage, or consuming the object exhaustively. In imperative construction, ɓòì has an emphatic function, as illustrated below in (7.123a–b).

(7.123) a. ŋà=hòì=tá   ŋà=rúm=ná   čúr-a
           DEM=girl=NEAR   DEM=cloth=NEAR   wash-1/2SG.IRR
           ɓòì
           all/COMPLETIVE
           'Girl, wash this shirt!'

b. *gár-á   ɓòì   ŋà=ɓá=á*
disappear-PERV.IMP all/COMPLETELY DEM=place=NEAR
'Go (sg.) away from here!'
(Lit. 'Disappear (sg.) completely from here!')

ɓòì can also indicate an aspectual completeness of an action as total affectedness of the object. This is related to intensity and can be achieved by repetition of the action. See the example below with the verb *bíg* 'break'.

(7.124) a. *bíg-ɛ*
break-3.IRR
'He may break (it).'

b. *bíg-á   ɓòì   bíg-á   ɓòì*
break-3SG.SU.PERV COMPLETELY break-3SG.SU.PERV COMPLETELY
'He shatters (it).'

7.3.1.6 Complex Predicate Constructions

In this section, I shall deal with two separate multiverbal constructions: subsecutive and coverb plus main verb which appear to be the result of language contact phenomenon. Given the existing diverse languages and language contact situations in the region[16] where Mursi is spoken, it would be difficult to provide a detailed analysis about these two morphosyntactic phenomena. At this stage, there is no information to point out whether they are common features of the Surmic languages or specific feature that exist only in Mursi. However, each are separately discussed below based on the limited data available.

Subsecutive is a multiverbal construction where one or more than one verb come together to express a subsequent event that might happen simultaneously. In Mursi, subsecutive construction is attested in imperative, hortative-jussive, and subjunctive moods. In his detailed description of Turkana (a Nilotic language spoken in Kenya), Dimmendaal (1983: 174) noted that subsecutive construction is a widespread feature of Nilotic languages. In addition to Turkana, it is attested in some Nilotic languages such as Nyangatom and Karimojong. However, unlike in these languages, in Mursi, subsecutive construction

---

16 Lower Omo Valley, the Southwest of Ethiopia is an area where the languages of the three major families were spoken side by side, Nilo-Saharan, Omotic and Cushitic.

TABLE 7.41 Subsecutive construction types

Types	Subsecutive form	Semantics
TYPE I	(V₁.PERV-SEQ +V₂.PERV-SEQ + V₃.PERV:IMP-VFS)	imperative
	(V₁.PERV-SEQ (NEG.PERV) V₂.PERV-SEQ + V₃.PERV-VFS)	hortative/jussive
TYPE II	(V₁.PERV-SEQ V₂.PERV:IMP 'X')	Imperative

is formed by marking a sequencializer suffix *-óna* (*-na*) on roots of the first and second verbs.

The fact is that the occurrence and function of the sequence marker *-óna* is limited. It is confined to only imperative and hortative/jussive constructions which normally utilize perfective aspect within the general irrealis mood.

(7.125) Type I—sequence of three verbs

a. *óg-óna   édʒ-óná   ér-ɛ̀*
   go.PERV-SEQ kill.PERV-SEQ die.PERV:IMP-VFS
   'Kill or die!'

b. *k-òw-ònà   ŋàni   k-àiw-óna*
   1.HORT-go.PERV-SEQ NEG.PERV 1.HORT-come.PERV-SEQ
   k-àgt-ò
   1.HORT-cook.PERV-VFS
   'Let me go back and cook!'

(7.126) Type II—sequence of two verbs

a. *óɣ-óná   góɲ   bì-ò*
   go.PERV-SEQ/MT? watch.PERV:IMP cow-PL
   'Go, see the catte!' 'Go and see the cattle!'

b. *áiw-ɛ̀-na   góɲ-á   bì-ò*
   come.PERV.SG-MA-SEQ watch.PERV:IMP-PL cow-PL
   'Go (pl.), see the cattle!'

By looking at these examples, Nilotists may argue that the suffix *-óna* is the same suffix which is used for marking motion towards (ventive). A plausible answer for this is that Mursi utilizes different morphs on imperfective and perfective verb roots to mark motion towards the deictic center: long or short forms (*-áná/-ónó*; *-án/-ón*) on imperfective verb roots and just *-a/-o* on perfective verb roots. In contrast, all verb roots in (7.125a–b) and (7.126a–b) are in perfective aspect. So *-óna* cannot be a marker of motion. In (7.126b), the suffix *-ɛ* is a valency increasing/applicative suffix regularly occurring with imperfective verbs such as 'come' and 'go'—*kúún-ɛ́* ⟨1SU.come.IMPERV-⟩ ('I bring') or *kɔ́-kɔ́-ɛ́* ⟨1SU-go.IMPERV-VT/TR⟩ ('I take'). The other interesting observation from the above subsecutive constructions is that the last verb can never be marked with *-óna* as it is the morphosyntactic canonicality designator of the imperative and hortative/jussive moods.

Moreover, the morphosyntactic canonicality of the imperative construction is expressed by the fact that imperatives take a different verb-final suffix (*-ɛ/-o*), as illustrated above in (7.126a–b). Quite a few coverb plus main verb predications are attested in Mursi. Verbs such as *hín* 'want', *mèsí* 'do', *úfá* 'finish' are found to be coverbs. Although coverbs, occurring before the main verb, often function as a single predicate in multiverbal constructions, it is hard to predict to what extent multiverbal constructions will be productive in filling the position of coverbs.

(7.127) a. *hín   ŋà=kéd-í*
          want.IMPERV NEG=cut.IMPERV-SG
          'Don't get discouraged!'

   b. *dɔ́nɛ́j kɔ́-tɔ́-ɛ̀=ó   ŋà=hín=nó*
       one   1.SBJV-lose.PERV-IRR=NEG NEG=want.IMPERV=NEG
      'I should lose nothing.'
      (Lit. 'I don't want to lose one.')

   c. *àɲè wà   [úfá ká-ɓák-á]*_{PRED}
       1SG REC.PAST finish 1SU-eat-1SG.SU.PERV
      'I have already eaten.'

   d. *iggè dǎkákán dáfí [mèsí-na déd-á]*_{PRED}
       2PL all   work do-SEQ   fulfill.PERV:IMP-PL
      'Finish your (pl.) work, all of you!'

In (7.127b), the coverb *hín* has moved to a clause-final slot. It is in a typical canonical order of negated verbs in negated clause constructions. Note that the morphosyntactic productivity of multiverbal sequences in Eastern Sudanic languages has not been investigated in detail yet. It is obvious that more research is needed to supplement and verify the data reported here.

CHAPTER 8

Adjectives

8.1 Introduction

Adjectives are one of the three open word classes of Mursi. Adjectives are an open class by derivation. They share a number of grammatical properties with nouns and verbs. Moreover, adjectives can be formed from compounds. Elements of a compound adjective can be both adjectives or from other word classes. There are also two loan adjectives from Amharic (an Ethio-Semitic language) often used by Mursi speakers in informal conversations (or code-switching and spontaneous translation): *áddísí*[1] ~ [ádǐsí] 'new' and *kánísí*[2] 'small'. Adjectives always bear the general adjectiviser suffix *-i*, regardless of the adjective's morphological property. Specifically, adjectives and verbs share one phonological property, i.e. like verb roots, most adjective roots end in consonants (for further discussion, see §8.2.2). Based on the morphological properties they display, Mursi adjectives can be divided into two major categories: underived (*tííní* 'small' and *búí* 'big')[3] and derived (Type I—mainly from stative verbs; Type II—derived from stative verbs and from other word classes through productive and unproductive morphological derivations). Syntactically, adjectives can modify the head of an NP, fill the head of an intransitive predicate slot, fill copula complement slots, and denote degree of the compared quality in comparative constructions. The adjective class of Mursi covers all semantic types that can be conveyed by adjectives.

---

1 The geminated alveolar stop /dd/ that triggers the implosive [ɗ] often occurs in loan words from Amharic (an Ethio-Semitic language of Ethiopia). Place names such as *addis ababa* (= *addis* 'new', *ababa* 'flower') and *Sudan* are sometimes pronounced as *aɗisawa* and *suɗan* respectively.
2 *kanisi* is a loan adjective from the Amharic second person singular imperative form of the verb *k'änis* 'You (sg.) subtract!', and whose non-imperative form is *känäsä* 'He subtracted'.
3 Gerrit Dimmendaal (p.c.) has pointed towards an alternative interpretation for these two adjectives, namely as forms derived from the quantifiers for 'little' and 'much', respectively.

8.2 Phonological Properties of Adjectives

Underived adjectives as one category (§ 8.2.1) and both Type I and II derived adjectives as a separate category (§ 8.2.2 and § 8.2.3) display distinct phonological properties.

8.2.1 *Underived Adjectives*

Underived adjectives differ phonologically from the derived ones in two ways. Firstly, the underived adjectives *tííní* 'small' ~ *tíín-í* ⟨small-ADJ⟩ and *búí* 'big' ~ *bú-í* ⟨big-ADJ⟩ have monosyllabic roots. The final segment (-*i*) attached to both roots is a general adjectivizer and occurs with adjectival roots of all type. Secondly, underived adjectives display sound iconicity. This phenomenon is an association between sound and meaning. Dixon (2010:69) pointed out that a high front vowel *i* is often naturally associated with a little/small object and a high back vowel *u* with a big/large one. The high-front vowel /i/ in *tííní* and the high-back vowel /u/ in *búí* appear to have strong correlation with the semantics of the two words—particularly in conveying the sense of smallness and largeness. The morpheme -*o* is a portmanteau suffix, and it can only be attached to singular and plural (reduplicated) forms of underived adjectives.

(8.1) a. [hòj-á   tíín-ó]ₙₚ   ók-ú   ɔ́r-ɔ́
       girl-RSTR small-MOD.RSTR go-3SG.SU.PERV village-OBL
       'The little girl went home.'

   b. nɔ̀ŋ eč-ú   zìní [túré-á   tíín-ó]ₙₚ
      3SG shoot.PERV-3SG.SU.PERV thief gun-RSTR small-MOD.RSTR
      'He shot the robber with a pistol.'

In (8.1a–b), the morpheme -*o* now carries two pieces of information—it is an adjectiviser and a restrictive suffix. The second coalescence of vowels appear to be between the vowel of the *búí* 'big' and again the construct suffix -*a*, thus the two coalesce into *bó* < *bú+a*, as in (8.2).

(8.2) [[gòdóná-á   n=ànù]ₙₚ   bó]ₙₚ
      brother.PERT.SG.1.PSR-RSTR SG.PSD=1SG.PSR big.MOD
      í-Ø   bá-á   itijobija-ì
      exist.IMPERV-3SG.SU place-RSTR Ethiopia-GEN
      'My elder brother is in Ethiopia.'

Here the new stem *bó* becomes one phonological and grammatical word, thus it is this stem that carries the two pieces of information.

8.2.2 *Derived Adjectives Type I*

Type I derived adjectives have certain similarities with verb roots in terms of segmental structure. Like verb roots, almost all adjective members of Type I end with consonants. Having a consonant-final word root is one of the most salient features of Mursi verbs. Type I derived adjectives, in particular, show a remarkable similarities of syllable shape with the stative verbs. Thus, it is plausible to claim that this phonological property of adjectives is what they share with stative verbs. Depending on the segmental features they display, they can be sub-divided into three types: (i) those that have disyllabic monomorphemic roots and whose first and second vowels are always one and the same $V_1=V_2$, (ii) those that have disyllabic monomorphemic roots and whose roots contain inherently reduplicated syllables, and (iii) those that are different syllabic shapes but are mainly monomorphemic.

8.2.2.1 Disyllabic Monomorphemic Roots ($V_1=V_2$)

Derived adjective that have the same first and second vowels within their disyllabic monomorphemic roots constitute the largest number of Mursi adjectives. As illustrated in the examples below, they all have monomorphemic roots composed of two syllables and each syllable has vowels that have the same phonetic value. The adjectivizer *–i* is a morphologically segmentable element. In (3a) below are disyllabic monomorphemic adjective roots that reduplicate their first syllable (CV).

(8.3) a. Adjective   Meaning
       /lílíbí/[4]   [lil.li.bi]   'sweet'
       /lúlúmí/   [lul.lu.mi]   'dark brown'
       /réréhí/   [rɛr.rɛ.hi]   'thin'
       /bárárí/[5]   [bar.ra.ri]   'powerful, hot (of food)'

---

4 /lilibi/ ~ [liliwi], i.e. intervocalically, the voiced bilabial plosive /b/ lenites to bilabial approximant [w].

5 The adjective *bárárí* can be used in very broad contexts. The common usage of this adjective is in relation to taste such as for spicy foods, coffee (Mursi coffee is often prepared from coffee leaf, pepper, ginger and salt), when referring to the strength of the taste of sour milk, and so on. It has even a deeper meaning than these, i.e. with respect to the attribution of hidden and dangerous situations, for example, certain plants, amulets, and dew are *bárárí*.

As can be seen in (8a), the re-syllabification has been made based on the occurrence of the alveolar lateral approximant /l/ and alveolar liquid /r/ at word-medial position. Thus in all adjectives of (8a), both /l/ and /r/ occur at the onset of cross-syllable consonant clusters. The lateral alveolar approximant /l/ can never be preceded by other consonants except by /l/ itself and by the liquid /r/. Similarly, /r/ often occurs as cluster (or sequence) at syllable onset position in words that have reduplicated syllables.

b. Adjective   Meaning
  d̪ɔ́rɔ́sí   'hard, dry, strong'
  múčúgí   'half, few'
  mɔ̀kɔ̀ɲì   'short'
  múɲúɲí   'cruel'
  mɔ̀d̪ɔ̀sí   'be tired, soft (human physical)'
  ràmàgì   'long'
  ɲàgàsì   'old'
  gɔ́lɔ́ɲí   'red'
  lɔ́tɔ́gì   'wet'
  rɔ̀ŋɔ̀d̪ì   'crooked, curved'

Unlike those in (8.3a), adjectives of (8.3b) can be transformed into nouns of states either by stative marker suffix -tin (lɔ́tɔ́gì ~ lotok-tin 'liquid') or by a copula verb té (tewa [té-a] d̪ɔ́rɔ́sí ⟨be.PERV-3SG.SU.PERV hard.STV-ADJ⟩ 'hardness'). Above all, between (8.3a) and (8.3b) two differences have been recorded. First, the adjectives in (8.3a) have non-stative verb origin and they may have originated from nouns. For example, múɲúɲí 'cruel' is highly likely derived from múɲúgí 'monster, one who eats a lot of meat'. Second, a slight difference between those in (8.3a) and (8.3b) is that root medial consonants in (8.3a) display a non-contrastive phonetic geminate intervocalically. However, when the adjectival roots of (8.3a) re-syllabified, they apparently acquire syllable shapes which resemble those of (§ 8.2.2.2). For example, /lilib/ will be [lil-lib] and so will /lul-lum/ ~ [lul-lum]. These are non-stative verb origin adjectives that contain a resemblance between σ_1 and σ_2 inherently reduplicating shapes. Thus to some extent they resemble those adjectives in (§ 8.2.2.2), that appear to have a unique symmetry of $\sigma_1 = \sigma_2$.

8.2.2.2   Disyllabic Monomorphemic Roots ($C_1V_1C_1 = C_2V_2C_2$)

Many of the derived adjectives within this phonological set have inherently reduplicated $C_1V_1C_1$ syllable shapes, a rare segmental property neither shown on regular verbs nor on nouns. Almost all are members of two semantic classes of adjectives—physical property and human propensity.

(8.4)	Adjective	Meaning
	gùrgùrì	'clever, wise, knowledgeable'
	gìlgìlì	'soft, smooth, slippery'
	ɗálɗálí[6]	'difficult, expensive'
	ɗíŋɗíŋí	'heavy'
	kárkárí	'rough, lazy'
	ɗúrɗúrí	'thick'
	hólhólí	'light (of weight)'
	dʒàmdʒàmì	'mistaken'
	ɓóŋɓóŋí	'blistered'
	mùrmùrì	'straight'

Note that reduplication is not productive in Mursi. It is totally nonexistent in nouns and only a handful of examples are present for verbs. Despite the adjectives in (8.4) having fully reduplicated disyllables in a $\sigma_1{=}\sigma_2$ symmetry, they are analyzed as monomorphemic roots. Even if the adjective in (8.4) have fully reduplicated syllables compared to those in (8.3a), they are analyzed as monomorphemic forms. Even if they are few, verb forms that have fully reduplicating $\sigma_1{=}\sigma_2$ can be morphologically segmentable into simpler and analyzable morpheme forms.

8.2.2.3   Monomorphemic but Different Syllable Shapes

Derived adjectives of this category have monomorphemic roots and they can be distinguished from other word classes but mainly from verbs in having roots consisting of several syllables and vowel-initial and final roots, as in (8.5). The first two appear to have inherently reduplicated final syllables before the adjectiviser suffix.

(8.5)	Adjective	Meaning
	déléléì	'rich'
	hólólóì⟨j⟩	'free, empty, naked'
	kètèŋèsì	'shallow'
	áɲákɔ́náì	'lame'
	íɗíbèní	'fat'

There are also a few members whose root medial positions is composed of C_1C_2 clusters (where C_1 is liquid), which is common in the root-internal structure of nouns, but not in verbs.

---

6   /ɗálɗálí/ can be pronounced as [ɗáɗálí] in fast speech.

(8.6) Adjective   Meaning
       sìrwàì   'blackish with cream undercoat; dark brown colour'
       gèrsì   'bad'
       tòlgòɲì⁷   'lazy'
       čàrgì   'wet'
       túrgúlì   'bent, deformed (of stick/tree)'

8.2.3 Derived Adjectives Type II

The majority of Type II derived adjectives are monosyllabic. However, there are a few disyllabic and multisyllabic adjectival roots that are derived from other classes mainly from adjectives and verbs by a number of morphological derivations. They can occur without the general adjectiviser suffix or with a nominalizer-attributive marker.

(8.7) Monosyllabic shapes
       Adjective   Meaning
       ʃòì   'delicious'
       ríí   'shady'
       gái⟨j⟩   'intelligent'
       lùì   'spotted, multi-colour'
       làì⟨j⟩   'silent'

(8.8) Disyllabic shapes
       Adjective   Meaning
       bútógí⁸   'lying'
       léságí   'greedy'
       mìrò   'colourful, multi-colour (pattern)'

---

7 A consonant cluster /lg/ does not occur in Mursi, thus *tolgoɲi* must be either a loan word or dimorphemic form of some kind. In fact, three nouns that contain /lg/ clusters have been identified in the language. All of them have inherently reduplicated-like syllables: *galgali* 'a person or animal with large ears', *gelgeɲai* 'bat', and *gelgan* 'veranda'. Besides, one loan word *alga* 'bed' (a loan word (Amharic)) and one adjective *gilgili* 'smooth' have been identified in the language.

8 In 1896 an Italian Geographical Society expedition led by Vittorio Bottego travelled southwards through Mursi territory, following the left bank of the Omo River as far as Lake Rudolf. According to Turton (1973: 416), Bòttego might be the first explorer who reached Mursi country. The adjectival word *bútógí* 'lying' is named after Captain Bòttego who crossed the Omo River sometime between 1895 and 1897. It was during my second trip to the Mursi village, that I was able to identify this word for the first time. Thus, I asked a number of elders in the village; from multiple sources, finally I confirmed that the word 'lying' in Mursi is derived from the name of this Italian Captain.

ɓɔ̌čá   'thin'
ɗárá   'shortsighted'

As can be seen in (8.7) and (8.8), except for the two colour patterns, which are often the result of similes of different names of animals or objects, the rest of the adjectives may be examined metaphorically based on semantics. As in (8.7), the Mursi attribute word *ríí* 'shade' as *lálíní* 'cool' which is also the term used to expresses a stable or settled quality of a person. Despite the fact that *lálíní* doesn't seem be to be in direct semantic opposition with the adjective *bárárí* 'powerful', it can yet denote a meaning of 'hot' through a non-linguistic sense that can be extended to a 'hot and spicy drink/food' Metaphorically. *bárárí* does not denote the word delicious, but *lálíní* does. In the same way, the semantic extension of *gáí* and *lai* match the adjective *lálíní*. All of them were derived from various word classes—*ríí* from the noun *ríí* 'shade', *gáí* from the verb 'know', and *làì* can modify a verb into a manner modifying adjective or into an adverb. On the other hand, the adjectives listed in (8.8) may infer abnormalities, and their word class source is not yet confirmed.

Mursi has also a dozen multisyllabic adjectives, which may be partly composed of lexicalized compounds plus metathesis or just simple compounds, as in (8.9).

(8.9)   Multisyllabic shapes
        Adjective   Meaning
        lùmìróì   'cheating'
        έɲérsíɲógí   'cowardly'
        lɔ̀gɔ́ʃéέ   'true'
        rèzáhí   'thin' (or *rɛsalizahi*)[9]
        kéɗánító   'interesting, attractive'

As shown in (8.9), *lùmùróì* and *kéɗánító* are multisyllabic whereas *έɲérsíɲógí* is a derived adjective from the stative verb marked with an agentivizer suffix *-ɲóg* ⟨be afraid-AGTV-ADJ⟩, and *lɔ̀gɔ́ʃéέ* from a noun-adverb compound from [lɔ̀gɔ́-ʃéέ] ⟨word-correct/right⟩.

Multisyllabic adjectives composed of bimorphemic roots by compounding undergo recurrent segment reduction.

---

9   *rɛsalizahi* seems to be a multiword adjective in some kind of metathesis form—[rɛ-ali-zahi] ⟨body-stool-??⟩ or *[rɛhi-sai-zal] ⟨body.PL-skin-stick⟩ or *[rɛga-zali(zel)] ⟨spine-stick⟩.

(8.10) a. /čàkɔ̀rɔ̀i/   [čàgì-kɔ̀rɔ̀i]   'dark-green'
       b. /čàhɔ́lí/   [čàgì-hɔ́lí]   'blue'
       c. /dʒààrhɔ́lí/ [dʒààrè-hɔ́lí]   'white-legged'

In the examples shown in (8.10a–b), the voice velar consonant /g/ is reduced from the first element of the compounds as is always the case for g-final roots. The adjectiviser suffix /-i/ cannot be marked twice thus it is omitted from the first element of the compound adjectival word. Mursi does not have an exact colour term dedicated to green or blue, instead the word čàgì 'green, unripe, raw' is used to represent both colours. Whenever the distinction between the two is necessary, then the compounds in (8.10) shall be referred to where (8.10a) [čàgì-kɔ̀rɔ̀i] ⟨green-black⟩ denotes 'green, deep green' while (8.10b) [čàgì-hɔ́lí] ⟨green-white⟩ denotes 'blue, white/light blue'. Both are adjective-adjective compounds with the same word class and semantic output. On the other hand, the last example (8.10c) is a noun-adjective compound that denotes a colour pattern on cattle.

With respect to phonological additional property of adjectives, tonal melody of adjectives should be taken into account in the attempt to distinguish adjectives from the other two open word classes. For example, like nouns, adjectives do not have inherent tone. In contrast, verbs have inherent tone and stable tonal melodies.

8.3 Morphological Properties of Adjectives

8.3.1 *Inflection*

Underived adjective can be inflected for number and case. Number on underived adjective is shown by reduplication, as in (8.11) below.

(8.11) a. búí   'big (sg.)'   bíbí   'big (pl.)'
          tííní 'small (sg.)' tíítí 'big (pl.)'

There is an exceptional suffix which only occurs with búí, i.e. the degree of magnitude marker -sís (or augmentative).

(8.12) ɔ́g-ú   ɔ̀g-tí   bú-sís-í-j
       cry-3SG.SU.PERV   voice.NOMZ-NRSTR   big-AUG-ADJ-OBL
       'He cried with a loud voice.'

(8.13) nà dɔ́ŋ-á   bè-tí   bú-sís-í   nà
CCN pick.up-3SG.SU.PERV stone-NRSTR big-AUG-ADJ CCN
ɲɔ́g-é   lòg tútúg nà nɔ̀ŋ ɔ́k-ú
open-APPL.3 hole door CCN 3SG go-3SG.SU.PERV
'And he rolled a great stone for the door of the sepulchre, and departed.'
(Lit. 'And he picked up a very big stone and opened the hole door, then he left.')

Note that the degree or augmentative marker always follow the adjectiviser as it is shown in (8.12) and (8.13). Only the two underived adjectives can take comparative markers, as in (8.14).

(8.14)   Bare form   Comparative form   Meaning
   a. tííní   číɲí-n   'smaller, younger, thinner'

   b. búí   bú-ɲ   'greater, bigger, elder'

   c. àɲè [[ŋà=tùg=tá   n=ɛ̀j]$_{NP}$ číɲ tíín=ŋà]$_{NP}$
      1SG DEM=mouth=NEAR SG.PSD=3SG.PSR thin small=DEF
      ŋà=kí-hín-í=ó
      NEG=1SU=want.IMPERV-1SG.SU.IMPERV=NEG
      'I don't like her sharp voice.'

The suffix –n which is attached to the root číɲí is a suffix often used to derive nouns of state from adjectives—such as 'young, small' (of boy or girl). The word 'búɲ' may also bear a derived noun of state 'largeness'. Both underived adjectives can be modified by the intensifier háŋ/wáŋ 'very'.

(8.15) a. ŋòná-á   n=ànù   á   tííní háŋ   nà
        siste-RSTR SG.PSD=1SG.PSR COP.3.IMPERV small INTENS CCN
        kéd-áɲ   àɲè
        cut-1SG.OBJ 1SG
        'My sister is much smaller than I am.'

     b. ŋà=dórí   kèŋ=ná   á   búí háŋ
        DEM=house center/belly=NEAR COP.3.IMPERV big INTENS
        'That room is very big.'

Example (8.15a) is a kind of comparative construction where the verb kéd 'cut, subtract' indicates that the comparee is lower than the compared or minus the standard. In the same way, the underived adjective *búí* may function as modifier of other adjectives or as an intensifier of other modifiers.

(8.16) a. [zùg-tí   bú mèrì]ₙₚ
  people-NRSTR big many
  'Very many people'

b. *mes-ú*   [bɔ̀g-ìɲà-i   bu mèrì čàll-ì]ₙₚ
  do-3SG.SU.PERV issue/thing-PL-NRSTR big many good.STV-ADJ
  háŋ
  INTENS
  'He did very many wonderful things.'
  (Lit. 'He did big many good things.')

In (8.16b), semantically both *bú* and *háŋ* are intensifiers but syntactically they have distinct functions—*bú* modifies or intensifies the quantifier *mèrì* (quantity) while *háŋ* intensifies the adjective *čàllì* (quality). The adjective *tííní* may be used as a specifier of the degree of an activity *ɓòitííní* [ɓòì-tííní] ⟨all-small/little⟩ 'a little bit', as in (8.16c).

c. *á*   *àggè k-ài-ò*   *ɔ́r-ɔ́*   *nà*
  COP.3.IMPERV 1PL 1.HORT-go.PERV:PL-1PL.INC home-OBL CCN
  k-àùs-ò   *ɓòitííní*
  1.HORT-rest.PERV.PL-1PL.INC little.bit
  'Let us go home and rest a little bit!'

Derived adjectives also inflect for nominal categories in the same way as nouns, namely number, case, bound demonstrative circumclitics, and definiteness. Note that only the following four dimension and colour adjectives bear an overt plural number marking.

(8.17) Adjective   Adjective
  Singular   Plural
  ràmàgì 'long (sg.)' ràmài-tá 'long (pl)'
  mɔ̀kɔ̀ɲì 'short (sg.)' mɔ̀kɔ̀j-ná 'short (pl.)'
  kɔ̀rɔ̀ì 'black (sg.)' kɔ̀rɔ̀-tá 'black (pl.)'
  gɔ́lɔ́ɲí 'red (sg.)' gɔ́lɔ́ɲ-á 'red (pl.)'

Despite the adjectivizer suffix *-i* of the singular forms, the adjectives in (8.17) utilize the 'suppletive' number marking system of nouns (where singular nouns are marked by *-i* and plural nouns by *-a*). As far as number marking on adjectives is concerned, there are two main reasons that could justify why the number marking system of the above plural forms wouldn't be treated as 'marked plural'. First, we have no plausible evidence whether the singular suffix *-i* and the adjectivizer suffix *-i* have coalesced into one or the function of singular number is covered by the adjectivizer. Second, all the adjectives in (8.17) were derived from stative verbs and they are exceptions. Besides, one adjective that has a replacive number marking has been found in the language—*bɔ́čá* (sg.) and *bɔ́čèn* (pl.) 'thin'

As it is the case in some languages, a modifying adjective within an NP may take some or all of the same morphological marking as nouns (Dixon 2004:11). In light of this fact, in Mursi, adjectives can be inflected for case, bound demonstrative circumclitic, and definiteness when modifying a noun within an NP.

(8.18) a. ŋà=hír=á]_NP [gèrs-i-ɲ=ŋà]_NP
DEM=man=NEAR bad.STV-ADJ-GEN=DEF
'Of the bad man'

b. nɔ̀ŋ jóg-èsè éró [sààn-á čùmùn-ùɲ]_NP
3SG tell-3.BEN/DAT children story-RSTR happy.STV-GEN
'He told the children a funny story.'
(Lit. 'He told for (to) children a happy story.')

(8.19) ŋà=čàll-ìn=á á ésèd-á
DEM=good.STV-NOMZ=NEAR COP.3.IMPERV think-RSTR.NOMZ
támárí-ɲ
student-GEN
'... of the handsome intelligent student'
(Lit. 'Of this smart/handsome is thinking student')

As can be seen in (8.18), the stative *gèrsì* is marked for genitive case by the suffix *-ɲ* and for definiteness by an enclitic *=ŋà*. Example (8.19) is a rare and exceptional NP type where the derived adjective are marked for bound demonstrative circumclitics. The fact that *čàlli* 'good (=smart)' in (8.19) is a stative verb—in this case it uses the stativizing suffix *-in* as a nominalizer. The *-in* is a derivational prefix, whose primary function is to derive nouns of state (abstract nouns) from stative verbs (see § 8.3.2.3). In Table 8.1 below is a summary of some of the categories that adjectives can share with nouns.

In Mursi, number on nouns refers to the quantity of objects, while on adjectives it is an agreement feature. In addition, adjectives derived from stative

TABLE 8.1   Categories adjectives share with nouns

Inflectional categories	Semantics associated	Marker	Adjective type
Number	dimension and colour	-ta (vowel-final roots) -a (consonant-final roots) -na (nasal-final roots)	derived from stative verbs
Case	dimension and value	nominative (-u)	both underived (see § 8.4.1, Ex. 38) and derived (see § 8.4.1, Ex. 39)
	dimension, value and colour	genitive -ɲ (vowel-final) -ùɲ (consonant-final)	derived (see § 8.3.1, Ex. 15a–b; § 8.4.4, Ex. 52)
	dimension	oblique -j (following vowel)	both underived and derived (see § 8.3.1, Ex. 12)
Demonstratives	value	ŋà= ... =á/=ùnù	derived (see § 8.3.1, Ex. 16)
Definite	dimension and value	=ŋà	derived (see § 8.3.1, Ex. 15a; § 8.4.1, Ex. 39 & 41)

verbs can inflect for some verbal categories such as for S and O arguments. They can also be negated and can take verb-final suffix when they function as intransitive predicate (see § 8.4).

8.3.2   *Derivation*
8.3.2.1   The Adjectiviser -*i*
About one-third of Mursi adjectives are derived from stative verb roots. The primary derivational marker in Mursi is the suffix -*i*. Thus, derived adjectives can be formed by attaching the general adjectivizer suffix -*i* to roots of stative verbs.

(8.20) Stative verb   Derived adjective
      íláágá   '(be) sick'   íláágái   '(be) sick'
      mɔ̀ɗɔ̀sà   '(be) tired'   mɔ̀ɗɔ̀sì   '(be) tired, soft'
      ʃɔ̀n   '(to) be sweet'   ʃɔ̀ì   '(be) sweet'

TABLE 8.2 Categories adjectives share with stative verbs

Verbal categories	Syntactic function	Semantics associated	Adjective type
S	intransitive predicate	state, inchoative, causative	underived and derived adjectives from stative verbs
passive-nominalizer	intransitive predicate	state	derived adjectives from stative verbs
benefactive-applicative	transitive predicate comparative marker	state	derived adjectives from stative verbs
Negation	intransitive predicate	opposite state/quality	derived adjectives from stative verbs
verb-final suffix	intransitive[a] predicate		derived adjectives from stative verbs

a The verb-final suffix indicates that adjectives have indeed a well-established syntactic function as an intransitive predicates.

The derived adjective *eŋersiɲogi* can only occur with the agentive singular nominalizer suffix *-ɲógi*. Even if the adjectiviser suffix *-i* is attached to the root of the stative verb, it doesn't function on its own without the agentive suffix, as shown in (8.21a).

(8.21) a. *éŋérs* 'be afraid' < *éŋérsí-ɲógí* 'coward (ADJ./N.)'

As far as adjectives are concerned, *éŋérsíɲógí* is an exception. In Mursi, one cannot derive adjectives from other word classes with an agentive nominalizer. It can also occur without the agentive suffix but in an opposite meaning. In addition, a nominalizer and restrictive markers are suffixed when the form functions as relative clause modifier.

b. *hír-á*   [Ø *ŋà=éŋérs-ínén-á=ó*]_RC
man-RSTR [Ø NEG.IMPERV=afraid-NOMZ-RSTR=NEG]
'One who is not afraid'

The function of the restrictive suffix *-a* in the relative clause is to indicate dependency relation between the head and its modifier.

8.3.2.2 The Stativising -tin

Despite the fact that both adjectives and nouns show significant similarities when they inflect for number, in terms of derivational suffixes they utilize, there is a remarkable difference between the two. Nouns of state can be formed by suffixing the stativising marker -mò to nouns, as in (8.22). On the other hand, nouns that denote state can be derived from adjectives by stative marker -tin, as in (8.23).

(8.22)
Nouns			Nouns of state
kómórú	'priest, leader'	< kómórú-mò	'priesthood'
hírí	'person, man'	< hírí-mò	'manhood'
zìní	'thief'	< zìní-mò	'stealing, theft'

(8.23)
Adjective			Nouns of state (abstract)
ràmàgì	'tall, long'	ràmàj-tìn[10]	'tallness'
gùrgùrì	'wise, skilled'	gùrgùr-tìn	'wisdom, knowledge'
lɔ̀tɔ̀gì	'(be) wet'	lɔ̀tɔ̀k-tìn	'liquid'
múčúgí	'few'	múčúk-tín	'fewness'
ɗáldálí	'hard'	ɗáldá-ín	'hardness'
ɗĩŋɗĩŋí	'heavy'	ɗĩŋɗĩŋ-ín	'weight'
ɓàsèní	'easy, cheap'	ɓàsén-ín	'easiness, cheapness'
kɔ̀rrɔ̀ɲ	'(be) dark'	kɔ̀rrɔ̀-ìn	'darkness'
kɔ̀rɔ̀i	'black'	kɔ̀rɔ̀j-tìn	'blackness'
hɔ̀lì	'white'	hɔ̀l-ìn	'righteous'
gèrsí	'bad'	gèrès-ìn	'sin'
babi	'fool'	bábí-tín	'foolishness'
sìɔ ɗɔ́rɔ́si	'greediness'	sìɔ̀ ɗɔ́sɔ́s-ín	'state of being stingy'
ɗɔ́rɔ́rsí	'dry'	ɗɔ́sɔ́s-ín	'drought'

Adjectives can also be derived from nouns. Adjectives derived from nouns retain some aspect of the semantics of the nouns from which they have been derived.

(8.24)
Adjective		Noun		Noun of state	
délélèi	'rich'	délélémá	'treasure'	délélémó	'treasure, richness'
bútógí	'lying'	bútómó	'false, lie'	bú(í)tógá	'state/condition of being a liar; a liar'

---

10 /g/ becomes [ɣ] intervocalically or even finally sometimes deleted.

TABLE 8.3 Different derivation markers to derive nouns of state

Derivation type	Semantics associated	Marker	Remark
nouns of state from nouns	state	-mò	state of being/condition
nouns of state from adjectives	state	-tin	noun/adjective (see e.g. 22)
nouns of state ↔ nouns	state/noun	-o/-a	suppletive-like
nouns of state ↔ adjectives	state/adjective	-a/-i	suppletive-like

As shown in (8.24) there is a tendency for adjectives derived from nouns to still denote the semantic state or character of nouns. We shall examine their syntactic distributions and functions in §8.3.

(8.25) nà   [bá-á   [Ø ŋà=zùg=tá
        CCN:SEQ place-RSTR/CAUSE [Ø DEM=people=NEAR
        hɔ̀l-ìn-a]_RC   [sárá-á   g=ɛ̀j=è]_NP]_SUBORD:CL
        white.STV-N.S-RSTR] [name.PL-RSTR PL.PSD=3PL.PSR=SUBORD
        [hɔ̀l-ìn   [sárá-á   g=ɛ̀j=e]_NP]_SUBORD:CL
        [white.STV-N.S [name.PL-RSTR PL.PSD=3PL.PSR=SUBORD
        [hɔ̀l-ìn-ɲ   ʤɔ-án-ɛ-ɔ̀[11]]_MAIN:CL
        white.STV-N.S-GEN get-MT-3PL.SU.IMPERV-VFS
        '... and he that receives a righteous man in the name of a righteous man shall receive a righteous man's reward.'

The meaning for hɔ̀lìn 'righteous' is a sematic extension, from hɔ̀lì 'white'.

8.3.2.3 Compound Adjectives

Compound adjectives are common in Mursi, and adjectival derivation by compounding is perhaps the second most productive derivational strategy after the adjectiviser –i. There are two real compound adjectives combinations: adjective-adjective (where both elements denote concurrent properties) and noun-adjective.

---

11   Note that the suffix –nɛn has various morphological and syntactic functions (i) can be used as a nominalizer.

(8.26) Adjective-Adjective   Meaning
       /čàkɔ̀rɔ̀i/   [čàgì-kɔ̀rɔ̀i¹²]   green-black   'dark green'
       /čàhɔ́lí/   [čàgì-hɔ́lí]   green-white   'blue'

(8.27) Noun-Adjective   Meaning
       a. /kààrèčàgì/   [kààrè-čàgì]   eye-new (green)   'blind'
       b. /sìɔ̀dɔ́rɔ́sí/ [sìɔ̀-dɔ́rɔ́sí] hand-dry   'greedy, stingy'
       c. /dʒààrhɔ́lí/ [dʒààr-hɔ́lí] leg-white   'white-legged
                                                         (colour pattern)'

As can be seen in (8.26–27), all are real compound adjectives because there is no relator marker -*a* between them that often indicates syntactic dependency. As Aikhenvald (2007: 26) puts it, 'compounds can be characterized by the absence of a marker of syntactic dependency'. As far as Mursi compounds are concerned, this is the only valid criterion to be used to distinguish compounds from modified NPs. With the exception of *kààričàgì*, compound adjectives occur only in copular clauses and can function as copula complements, while the compound *kààričàgì* can also modify a noun in an NP, as in (8.28).

(8.28) [zùw-á   kààrèčàg-á]ₙₚ hód-á   [bá-á
        people-RSTR   blind-RSTR   come.PERV.PL-MT:3PL.SU place-RSTR
        n=ènè]ₙₚ
        SG.PSD=3SG.PSR
        'The blind men came to him.'
        (Lit. 'The blind people came to his place.')

The compound adjectives in (27a–c) are also called *bahuvrīhi* compounds, a Sanskrit term to refer to a person, or an object, with a quality described by a compound (Aikhenvald 2007:31).

There are also two compound adjectives that have noun-verb and adverb-adverb elements. The first, as it shown in (8.29) below, bears the same semantics but by a different syntactic construction.

(8.29) NOUN-VERB kààrè [∅ díkt-é]ᴿᶜ
        /kààrèdíkté/ eye   [∅ close.up.PERV-NRSTR:REL]
        'Blind'
        (Lit. 'One who is eye closed up')

---

12 *kɔ̀rɔ̀i* as the second element may also be used to mark intensity of the quality expressed by the first, i.e. *čagi*.

Unlike the first two compound adjective types, noun-verb compound adjectives have different morphosyntactic properties. The general adjectivizer suffix *–i* is not attached to a compound form. Since the second element of the compound adjective is occupied by a verb, they do not directly modify head nouns but rather modify nouns in embedded relative clauses. Word boundary phenomena and phonological rules may apply to the two elements of the compound adjectives—reduction of the adjectiviser suffix *–i* and deletion of a segment from the first element. The second is the adverb-adverb compound adjective /ʃééʃéé/ [ʃéé-ʃéé] ⟨correct-correct⟩ 'true, real' which doesn't take the adjectiviser suffix.

8.3.2.4   Phrasal Adjectives

Phrasal adjectives have similar syntactic construction as noun phrases. They are often composed of a noun (in head position) which is followed by an adjective or a verb (in modifier position). Morphologically, elements of a phrasal adjective may be marked like an NP for the dependency relation they bear. Phrasal adjectives function predicatively and somehow require relative clause construction in order to modify nouns as one single element.

(8.30)   a. [lɔ̀g-á   čàg-á]$_{NP}$
            issue-RSTR new.STV-RSTR:MOD
            'Modern' (see also example 8.26c)

        b. [bá-á   ùtùrèi]$_{NP}$
            place/earth-RSTR end
            'Earthly'

        c. [mèsí nànì-ò]$_{NP}$
            work expert.SG-RSTR:MOD
            'Useful'

However, phrasal adjectives that have dynamic verbs in the modifier slot may occur with certain verbal derivational elements which puts the verbal modifier in a relative clause function, as in (8.31a–b).

(8.31)   a. [hír-á   kà-gà]
            man-RSTR   PASS-know.PERV:RSTR
            'Famous'
            (Lit. 'man known')

OR hír-á   [Ø ká-gá]₍RC₎
    man-RSTR [Ø 3.SBJV-know.PERV]
    'a man that is known'

b. hír-á   kí-hín-ò
   man-RSTR   3.SBJV-want-SG.IRR
   'Important, necessary'

OR hír-á   [Ø kí-hín-ò]₍RC₎
    man-RSTR   [Ø 3.SBJV-want-3.IRR]
    'that a man needs'
    (Lit. 'man that lets need')

8.3.2.5 Clausal Adjectives

Mursi has some clausal-like adjectives. Clausal adjectives may occur as full copular or relative clauses but all the elements within their clause are used to denote a single adjectival meaning. Certainly, they can never function as intransitive predicates or as copula complements.

(8.32) a. ʤààrí á   čàllì
         leg   COP.3.IMPERV good
         'Lucky'
         (Lit. 'leg (it) is good')

      b. è   á   čàllì
         appearance/beauty COP.3.IMPERV good
         'Beautiful/handsome'
         (Lit 'appearance (it) is good')

      c. kèŋɔ̀ á   bùrtàì
         belly COP.3.IMPERV hot
         'Corpulent, one who eats a lot'

      d. lɔ̀g-á   [Ø ŋànì čàg-à]₍RC₎
         word/issue-RTSR [Ø yet new.STV-RSTR:ATTR]
         'Modern'
         (Lit. 'word (issue) that is still/yet new')

e. rè   [Ø ŋà=hín-Ø-nè]_RC
   body [Ø NEG=want-3SG.SU.IMPERV-AP]
   'Boring'
   (Lit. 'body that doesn't want (something)')

f. éŋéré   kààrì
   afraid.APPL.3 eye
   'Shy'

g. ád-èsèn   rè   dùj-ì
   constrain-3.BEN/DAT body plant-ADJ
   'Stubborn'
   (Lit. 'one that body-planted')

Example (8.32h) is an exceptional case where the adjectivizer suffix –*i* can also be suffixed to a dynamic verb to produce a kind of relative clause (clausal adjective) that modify a noun.

8.3.2.6   Inchoative Derivation by Copula Verb

The perfective copula *tè* 'became (COP.3.PERV)' can be used along with derived adjectives to form intransitive stative-inchoative readings. The fact is that the majority of derived adjectives of Mursi are stative verbs. The syntactic subject may be overtly stated in one way or another by the copula verb; whereas the agent is neither overtly stated nor implied.

(8.33) tè kɔ̀rɔ̀i   'became dark'
        tè kɔ̀rɔ̀i kɔ̀rɔ̀i   'get (became) gradually darker'
        tè kɔ̀rɔ̀i ba   'past the evening'
        tè ràmàì   'became tall (long)'
        tè hólí   'became light'
        tè rɔ́ŋɔ́dǐ   'became crooked'

By repeating the adjective, it is possible to express the process that is denoted by stative-inchoative verbs (adjectives) as happening gradually. All the stative-inchoative readings in (8.33) are obtained by derivation as copula verbs and copula complements. However, stative-inchoative can also be obtained with S or O but without a semantic agent and the perfective copula *té* (see § 8.4).

Another inchoative reading of adjectives can be derived by substituting the copula *té* with the subjunctive copula form *ké*. Analyzing *ké* as a subjunctive form of the perfective copula *té* seems to require further investigation. The fact that some verbs of Mursi undergo either partial or full root suppletion to indicate aspect, in which case the desiderative *hín* 'want, desire' is a typical example. Thus the imperfective root *hín* should undergo a partial root suppletion before it is being marked by the perfective aspect marker prefix *t(V)-*, which is a dedicated perfective aspect marker prefix for desiderative, affection, stative and a few other verb types. *hɛn* is the perfective suppletive form of *hín*, so [té-hɛ́n] ⟨PERV-want⟩ is the perfective form. Similarly, *á* ⟨COP.3.IMPERV⟩ is the imperfective copula form while *té* ⟨COP.3.PERV⟩ is the perfective copula form. This means, *te* can be reanalyzed as [t-e] ⟨PERV-COP.3⟩ instead of a morphologically unsegmentable particle. When the subjunctive mood prefix *k(V)-* is added to the third person perfective copula form *e*, it results in *ké*, as can be shown in (8.34a–b) below.

(8.34) a. sú kɔ́ɔ́j-Ø ké kɔ̀rɔ̀-ì
sun 3.SBJV.go-3.IRR 3.SBJV.COP.PERV dark.STV-ADJ
'The sun be darkened.'

b. kɔ̀rɔ̀ɲ ké búí kɔ́ɔ́j-Ø ɛ̀nɛ̀ŋ?
dark 3.SBJV.be.PERV big 3.SBJV.go-3.IRR how
'How great is that darkness!?'

The *ké* often follows the verb in the subjunctive *kɔ́ɔ́j* 'go' but it always precedes the adjective. The adjective in (8.34a) in a typical canonical position of adjectives when they function as copula complements.

The other polysemous-like particle but with a different syntactic of its own is the preposition *ké/*.[13] The polysemous *ké* whose origin is a preposition, has an elaborative and extended functions: as coordinative conjunction (with its variant *kó*), as an instrumental marker prefix in instrumental-comitative construction (where comitative is shown by a suffix -ε [-čo][ča]), purposive (means), and reason (along with other particles). As is shown in (8.34c) below, the adjective *čàllì* appears in a prepositional phrase.

c. téj ké/kó čàll-ì
be.PERV:IMP with good.STV-ADJ
'Good bye!'
(Lit. 'Stay with peace!')

---

13 The particle *ke* has various functions in Mursi: preposition, purposive (subsequent reason marker along the cause marker particle *ɓa*), and coordinative conjunction (*ko* between nouns or numbers). The development of *ke* as a polysemous multifunctional particle has been discussed at different stages of this grammar.

However, in the context of the scope of irrealis which covers imperative, hortative/jussive, and subjunctive, (8.34c) can be viewed and interpreted as (8.34d).

> d. *kén   ké   tíítí*
> cut.PERV.IMP 3.SBJV.COP.PERV small.PL
> 'Cut (it) into pieces!'
> (Lit. 'Cut into being smalls! Make it become pieces!')

8.4 Syntactic Properties

Except for underived adjectives, all derived adjectives of Mursi occupy various syntactic slots within NPs and clauses depending on the syntactic and semantic properties of word classes from which they have been derived. Due to their morphological make up, some derived adjectives cannot modify a noun in an NP directly, for example compound adjectives of colour. Thus a number of sub-adjectival categories may exist in each semantic classes of adjectives since not all function equally as modifiers of nouns or hold possible adjectival slots reserved for them.

8.4.1 *Modifier of an NP Head*

Both underived and derived adjectives can modify nouns in a NP. When underived adjectives modify head nouns, they take the modification suffixes of both types (restrictive and non-restrictive). Underived adjectives agree in number with the head nouns they modify by reduplicating their roots partially or fully.

(8.35) a. [*hòj-á   tíín-ò*]$_{NP}$ *ók-ú*   *ór-ó*
girl-RSTR small-RSTR go-3SG.SU.PERV village-OBL
'The little girl went home.'

b. *k-ár-á*   [*hòi-tí   tííní-í*]$_{NP}$
1SU-see.PERV-1SG.SU.PERV girl-NRSTR small-NRSTR
'I saw the little girl.'

c. [*ùrgùsá-í   tíítí-j*]$_{NP}$
fish.PL-NRSTR small.REDUP:PL-NRTSR
'small/little (pl.) fishes'

d. [[zùw-á   bíbí-ò]ₙₚ   bá-ɲ-ɲ]ₙₚ
   people-RSTR big.PL-RSTR local-GEN-GEN
   'Village elders'
   (Lit. 'big (pl.) people of the local area')

Reduplication is the main and the only way of marking number on underived adjectives. Only the underived adjective can take degree of magnitude markers: free form *gòdě* (*gèdé*) (diminutive 'very small') and the suffix *-sís* (augmentative 'very big').

(8.36) a. *íggé-á*   [[Ø jéw-ìnèn-á   bá-á
         3PL.PN.SP-RSTR [Ø believe-NOMZ-RSTR place-RSTR
         n=ànù]_RC   tíítí-ò   gòdě]_NP
         SG.PSD=1SG.PSR small.PL-RSTR DIM
         'These little ones which believe in me.'

      b. *ʃúné   á   búí hán   kóó   [ʃúné-á*
         harvest COP.3.IMPERV big INTENS DIS.CRD harvest-RSTR
         zùw-á   mèsí-nèn-à]_NP   á   tííní gòdè sòŋ
         people-RSTR work-NOMZ-RSTR] COP.3.IMPERV small DIM only
         'The harvest truly is plentiful, but the labourers are few.'
         (Lit. 'the harvest working people')

In (8.36a), the embedded relative clause modifier is within the NP. As a secondary modifier, a relative clause intervenes between the head noun (in the 3rd person specific pronoun form) and the direct modifier *tíítí*. In (8.36b), *búí* is modified by the general intensifier *hán* 'very', and *tííní* by the diminutive *gòdě* which also bears a quantity reading 'very few'.

(8.37) nà   ŋɔ́-tí   [bú-sís-í]_NP   bán-á   jírísí tó-jé
       CCN wind-NSTR big-AUG-ADJ raise-3SG.SU.PERV sea in-OBL
       'Then (there) arose a great tempest in the sea.'

(8.38) ŋà=ŋɔ̀rɔ̀   [àhì-á   bú-sís-í-ó   gàf-ùŋ]_NP¹⁴
       DEM=elephant thing.SG-RSTR big-AUG-ADJ-RSTR forest-GEN
       'An elephant is a big animal.'
       (Lit. 'An elephant is a huge thing of the forest.')

---

14   *àhìá gàfùn* is 'Wild animal' (lit. 'thing of the forest').

(8.39) hírí ìr-ú gèsò ɓòì bú-sís (nà)
man drink.PERV-3SG.SU.PERV beer COMPLT big-AUG (CCN)
se-a ké ʃàj
say-3SG.SU.PERV QUOT tea
ŋà=hín-∅=ó
NEG=want.IMPERV-3SG.SU.IMPERV=NEG
'The man drank much beer. "I don't want tea", he said.'

With the augmentative marker -sís, the adjective búí sometimes denotes quantification as in (8.39). Similarly, the adjective tííní can also be used as a quantifier of 'a little'—(8.40).

(8.40) ójó-á sàbù-nè (nɔ̀ŋ) gùjò dʼág-∅ wáŋ méá
year-RSTR first-ORD (3SG) rain hit-3SG.SU.IMPERV INTENS now
ŋà=ʔójó=á nɔ̀ŋ dʼák-ú ké tííní sɔ̀ŋ
DEM=year=NEAR 3SG hit-3SG.SU.PERV 3.SBJV.BE.PERV small only
'Last year it rained much. But this year it has only rained a little.'

Before further description of the syntactic properties of derived adjectives, two major difference have been noted between underived and derived adjectives. The first difference is that underived adjectives take a separate modification marker suffix –o (as illustrated in §8.2.1) whereas the derived adjectives take the regular construct suffixes -a [-ta] (restrictive) and -i [-ti] (non-restrictive). The second difference is that only underived adjectives can be marked with a nominative case, as in (8.41a–b)

(8.41) a. [[zùw-á kàhèn[15]-á]$_{NP}$ bíbí-ú]$_{NP}$ kó [bárá dákákán]$_{NP}$
people-RSTR priest-RSTR big.PL-NOM PNC adult.PL all
'All the chief priests and elders'
(Lit. 'All the big (pl.) priests and adults.')

b. [[zùw-á kàhèn-á-j] bíbí-ú]$_{NP}$ kó [zùw-á
people-RSTR priest-RSTR-GEN big.PL-NOM PNC people-RSTR
ɔ́r-ùɲ]$_{NP}$ bíbí-ú]$_{NP}$
village-GEN big.PL-NOM
'the chief priests and elders'

---

15 kahen is a loan word from Amharic kahin 'priest'.

ADJECTIVES

In fact, both underived and derived adjectives may be marked with the genitive case if they occur as direct modifiers of the head within NPs. When the head is modified by bound deictic demonstrative circumclitics or is in bound demonstrative pronouns form, the modifier adjective may take the definite marker enclitic =ŋà. This means, adjectives agree with the head in definiteness but it doesn't mean they agree always. Some examples are below.

(8.42) a. [ŋà=támárí-ná=á   àggè-a   čàll-ú=ŋà]
              DEM=student-PL=NEAR 3PL.PN.SP-RSTR   good.STV-NOM=DEF
              'These the good students'

        b. [[ŋà=iggè=á]_NP   čàll-i=ŋà]_NP
              DEM=3PL.PN.SP=NEAR   good.STV-ADJ=DEF
              'These the good.'

As noted above, not all derived adjective can modify head nouns within NPs. For example, basic colour terms including the compound ones can modify heads nouns directly whereas colour pattern terms cannot modify the head directly rather they can be copula complements.

(8.43) a. rúm-ná   kɔ̀r-á   čàll-i
              cloth-RSTR   black.STV-RSTR   good.STV-ADJ
              ŋà=ʔán[16]=ó
              NEG=COP.3.IMPERV=NEG
              'The black dress is not nice.'

        b. rúm-á   čakɔ̀r-á   čàll-i
              cloth-RSTR   black.STV-RSTR   good.STV-ADJ
              ŋà=ʔán=ó
              NEG=COP.3.IMPERV=NEG
              'The blue dress is not nice.'
              (Lit. 'The blue dress good-it is not.')

There is an exceptional case where both the head noun and an adjectival modifier is left unmarked for the dependency relation they show within an NP.

---

16   The copula verb has a consonant final root [an] realisation underlyingly.

(8.44) ɔ́g   gɔ̀rɔ̀ 6ó   6ùnù ŋùčùg=ŋà
        go.PERV.IMP road out(side) there narrow=DEF
        'Go on the narrow road.'

The NP in (8.44) has the locative postposition 6ó and local adverbial demonstrative 6ùnù, thus there is no dependency marking between the head noun and the modifier adjective.

8.4.2 Intransitive Predicate

Derived adjectives from stative verbs can function as head of an intransitive predicate. As can be shown in (8.45a), adjectives that function as intransitive predicates can be negated, thus bound negation clitics can negate intransitive predicative adjectives in the same way as other regular verbs.

(8.45) a. [nɔ̀ŋ]_S [ŋà=ídíbèn-Ø=nó]_INTR.PRED
          3SG   NEG.IMPERV=fat-3SG.SU.IMPERV=NEG
          'He is not fat.'

       b. [àɲè]_S kù-čùmùn-ɛ̀-í]_INTR.PRED   [6á   nɔ̀ŋ
          1SG   1SU-happy-APPL-1SG.SU.IMPERV COMPL/CAUSE 3SG
          kún-Ø-ɛ́=jè]_SUBORD:CL
          come-3SG.SU.IMPERV-RES:APP=SUBORD
          'I was glad that he came.'
          (Lit. 'I rejoiced at his coming.')

       c. [k-íláás-í-ɔ̀]_S:INTR.PRED
          1SU-sick-1SG.SU.IMPERV-VFS
          'I am sick.'

       d. wà   [kɔ́-gɔ́lɔ́ɲ-á]_S:INTR.PRED   háŋ
          REC.PAST 1SU-black-1SG.SU.PERV   INTENS
          'I just became very black!'

       e. iɲè múɲ-ɛ̀sɛ̀   ɔ̀ŋ?
          2SG sad-BEN/DAT what
          'What are you angry about?'

(8.46) [ŋà=ɔ̀dàiɲà=á]_NP   [rɔ́ŋɔ́d-ùŋ=nè]_NP:INTR.PRED iggè
       DEM=generation=NEAR   bent-2PL.OBJ=SUBORD   2PL
       'You (pl.) the crooked generation.'

In (8.46), the second person pronoun is optional because the second person object pronominal suffix is attached to the adjective which can stand as elliptical NP on its own. In non-elliptical construction, the second person pronoun is its canonical order, as shown below in (8.47).

(8.47) [iggè]_S [mɔ̀dɔ̀s-á]_INTR.PRED dákákán hód-á
2pl   be.tired.STV-RSTR all   come.PERV:PL.IMP-MT
'All you (pl.) tired, come!'

Interestingly, when S and O pronominal arguments attach to adjectival roots, their main meaning of the inflected adjectival root is causative and inchoative. In fact, inchoative readings come in two ways: by bound pronominal in S function (8.48) and by the perfective copula *te* (8.49).

(8.48) [kɔ̀-kɔ̀rɔ̀-í-ɔ̀]_S:INTR:PRED
1SU-black-1SG.SU.IMPERV-VFS
'I become black.'
(Lit. 'I am blackening.')

(8.49) nɔ̀ŋ té   ʃèmèlì bá   nɔ̀ŋ úrɔ́
3SG COP.3.PERV very.thin CAUSE 3SG milk
ŋà=màt-Ø-ɛ̀=ó=jè
NEG=drink-3SG.SU.IMPERV-APPL:RES=NEG=SUBORD
'S/he became thin by her/him not drinking milk.'

In (8.48), the head noun which denotes a state of quality is a derived noun from the adjective *kɔ̀rɔ̀ì*. It is an NP on its own (in S function) followed by an intransitive predicate with an optional oblique argument. The multi-function particle *bá* 'place, in place, by' is a cause marker in reason clauses, and along with reason-applicative marker *-ɛ*, may denote a substantival deverbal nominalization reading 'for (by) not drinking'. In this case, the adjective is a copula complement.

Unlike the O argument in (8.46), *nɔ̀ŋ* in (8.49) indicates the object of a causative. Since grammatical relations in Mursi mostly depend on participant reference marking on the verb, independent arguments are not required as such. When independent arguments are present as in (8.46) above (*iggè*), then they give additional emphasis to the pronominal argument (be it focal or topical). In addition, the underived adjective in (8.50) may behave like a stative impersonal verb when being made causative by adding object marker.

(8.50) a. [bíbí-ùŋ-Ø]　　　　　　háŋ
　　　　big.PL-2PL.OBJ-3SG.SU.IMPERV INTENS
　　　　'It made you (pl.) very big.'
　　　　(Lit. 'It very big (pl.) you (pl.).')

When the subject is substituted with interrogative pronouns (which are mostly pro-phrasals), a causer can be separately stated by the content interrogative pronouns even if in the indefinite sense. In which case, the adjective can only be marked for object of a causative.

　　　　b. tíín-óɲ　　　bónnój?
　　　　　　small-1SG.OBJ where
　　　　　　'What made me small?'
　　　　　　(Lit. 'Where (from who) does my becoming small come from?')

To illustrate (8.50b), for instance, *bókónó* 'somewhere; anywhere' is derived from the indefinite place particle *bo* ⟨place.INDEF⟩ and indefinite number word (or indefinite pronoun) *kón-ɔ* ⟨one/another.INDEF-OBL⟩. Likewise, *bónnój* 'where' is pro-phrasal interrogative derived from the indefinite place particle *bó* ⟨place.INDEF⟩ and from the interrogative pronoun in nominative case *nój* 'who? (singular human subject)'. Therefore, when one uses *bónnój* for asking questions, one needs to take into account that one is asking something like 'where-who' type of questions, as in (8.50b) above. Besides, adjectives derived from stative verbs can be nominalized, and cannot occupy the predicate slot, as in (8.51).

(8.51) [kɔ̀rɔ̀-i-tín]ₛ　[kún-Ø]_INTR.PRED　　mìrò-jè
　　　　black-ADJ-N.S　come-3SG.SU.IMPERV earmark.PL-OBL
　　　　'The blackness comes from the earmarks.'

Whereas underived adjectives cannot be nominalized.

8.4.3 Copula Complement

Adjectives can also function as a copula complement in a copular clause. With no syntactic restriction, all the adjective classes of Mursi can be copula complements. Below are examples that illustrate the function of adjectives as copula complement (8.52).

(8.52) a. [àɲè]_CS [k-án-í]_C.PRED　　　　　　[kɔ̀rɔ̀-i]_CC
　　　　　　1SG　1SU-COP.IMPERV-1SG.SU.IMPERV black.STV-ADJ
　　　　　　'I am black.'

ADJECTIVES 393

    b. *ójó   tó-jé   wóčč-in   á   dáldál-í*
       year in-OBL walk-NOMZ COP.3.IMPERV difficult.STV-ADJ
       'Travel in winter is difficult.'

    c. [*jírísí ŋà=ɓá=á*]_{CS:S}   *á*   *dèŋì   háŋ*
       sea   DEM=place=NEAR COP.3.IMPERV shallow INTENS
       'The lake is very shallow at this point.'

    d. *írsásí tùg-ɔ̀   á   lèfi*
       pencil mouth-OBL COP.3.IMPERV sharp
       'The pencil point is sharp.'

    e. [*ɓá-á   k-ílób-ó   ŋà=hír=á*]_{COMPL:CL}
       place-RTSR/CAUSE 3.SBJV-try.PERV DEM=man=NEAR
       á   *hólólój*
       COP.3.IMPERV empty
       'It's useless to try to convince him.'
       (Lit. 'As far as trying of the man is concerned, is empty.')

The particle *ɓa* introduces reason or purpose in reason clauses. In (8. 52e), other than the copula verb and the copula complement 'empty', the whole construction is a complement clause particle, but not a copula subject.

8.4.4 *Parameter of Comparison*
Mursi makes use of adjectives as a parameter of comparison in comparative constructions.

(8.53)   COMPAREE   PARAMETER STANDARD
        a. [*írsásí-á   n=ànù*]   [*ràmàg-ɛ̀sèn*] [*ín-á*
           pencil-RSTR SG.PSD=1SG.PSR tall-BEN/DAT 3SG.PN.SP-RSTR

        n=ùnù]
        SG.SPD=2SG.PSR
        'My pencil is longer than yours.'
        (Lit. 'My pencil taller from that of yours.')

       b. *dáfí čàll-ɛ̀sèn   tìráŋ*
         work good-BEN/DAT play
        'Work is better than play.'

Two comparees can be conjoined by the coordinative conjunction particle *kó* 'with'. Morphologically, the adjective (the parameter) following the two comparees is not marked for adjectivizer suffix -*i*. Besides, in such case, copular verb is not required, as shown in (8.54).

(8.54) a. ŋɔ̀rɔ̀   kó   čár   [tìr]ₚₐᵣₐₘₑₜₑᵣ   čár-ɔ́
       elephant CCN leopard fast   leopard-NOM
       'The leopard is faster than the elephant.'
       (Lit. 'of the elephant and the leopard, the leopard is the fast one.')

However, as shown in (8.54b), in the phrasal plus mono-clausal comparative construction (see § 11.3), the same adjective can be marked by adjectivizer suffix -*i*, thus it can occur at CC syntactic slot.

   b. ŋɔ̀rɔ̀   kó   čár   [čár]_CS   á   [tìr-i]_CC
      elephant CCN leopard leopard COP.3.IMPERV fast-ADJ
      'The leopard is faster than the elephants.'
      (Lit. 'The elephants and the leopard, the leopard is fast.')

It is also possible to use two semantically opposing adjectives in two different copular clauses (bi-clausal), as in (8.54c).

   c. dórí-á   n=ànù   á   tííní dórí-á
      house-RSTR SG.SPD=1SG.PSR COP.3.IMPERV small house-RSTR
      n=ùnù   á   búí
      SG.SPD=2SG.PSR COP.3.IMPERV big
      'My house is small; your house is big'
      (Lit. 'My house is smaller than yours or Your house is bigger than mine.')

As shown below in (8.54d), within a mono-clausal construction, adjectives can function as both parameter of comparison and the mark when the benefactive/dative suffix is added to their roots as a mark of the standard.

   d. nɔ̀ŋ   mɔ̀kɔ̀ɲ-èsèn   támárí-ɲá
      3SG short-BEN/DAT student-PL
      'He is the shortest of the students.'

   e. ŋà=ìn=ù   án-á   tíín-èsèn-á
      DEM=3SG.PN.SP=FAR is.IMPERV-PERV:TEMP small-BEN-RSTR

dɔ́nénén
one:RECIP
'That is the thinnest one.'

8.4.5 Adjectives Functioning as Manner Modifiers

Adjectives and adverbs may have the same forms but they can only be distinguished by the syntactic slots they occupy in clauses. When adjectives function as modifiers, they often occur immediately after the verb they modify. When they occur in this position, they most likely are marked by the suffix –o [-no].

(8.55) a. *àɲè k-ígóm-á   čùmùn-ò*
   1SG 1SU-accept-1SG.SU.PERV happy-ADV
   'I gladly (Lit. being glad) agreed.'

   b. *nɔ̀ŋ bɔ̀rɔ́t-ú   čùmùn-ò*
   3SG jump-3SG.SU.PERV happy-ADV
   'He jumped cheerfully.'
   (Lit. 'happily')

   c. *ŋà=támárí=nù   ád-áɲ-Ø   àɲè čùmùn háŋ*
   DEM=student.PL=FAR give.PERV-1SG.OBJ 1SG happy INTENS
   'That pupil gives me much joy.'

   d. *nɔ̀ŋ jóg-èsè   éró   sààn-á   čùmùn-ùɲ*
   3SG tell-3.BEN/DAT children story-RSTR happy-GEN
   'He told children a funny story.'
   (Lit. 'He told for (to) children a happy story.')

As shown in (8.55), the adjective *čùmùni* 'happy' is functioning as verbal modifier in (8.55a–b), as a noun in (8.55c), and as an adjective in (8.55d). Some examples are illustrated below.

(8.56) a. *nɔ̀ŋ ɔ́k-ú   čàll-ì-nò*
   3SG go-3SG.SU.PERV good.STV-ADJ-ADV
   'He went well.'

   b. *múgáj   á   čàll-ì*
   woman.SG COP.3.IMPERV good.STV-ADJ
   'The woman is good.'

However, adjectives and verbal modifiers do not often necessarily coincide in form, rather the two have their own forms.

(8.57) Adjective   Adverb
       tìrì   ʃàù   'fast/quick'
       dìŋìlì   hàlè hàlè   'slow'
       téí lététéb làì   'silent'
       mùrmùrì   dìb   'straight'

    a. čár   á   tìr-ì
       leopard   COP.3.IMPERV   fast-ADJ
       'The leopard is fast.'

    b. àɲè kú-čúg-í   ʃàù
       1SG 1SU-chase-1SG.SU.IMPERV fast
       'I drive fast.'

    c. kɔ́-hɔ́l-í   ʃàù
       1SU-white-1SG.SU.IMPERV fast
       'I am becoming white fast.'
       (Lit. 'I am whitening fast.')

8.4.6 Ordering of Adjectives

Mursi is a free-constituent order language; the order among adjectives within NPs and in sentences is relatively free. As to the ordering of adjectives within NPs, as has been noted throughout this chapter, no more than two adjectival modifiers are available.

(i)   [N-ADJ$_1$(size)-ADJ$_2$(value)]$_{NP}$ ... (8.58a)
(ii) [N-ADJ$_1$(size)-ADJ$_2$(colour)]$_{NP}$ ... (8.58b)

(8.58) a. [[hòj-á   ràmàg-á   čàll-à]$_{NP}$ másábí]$_{NP}$
        woman-RSTR tall-RTSR good-RSTR book
        'the book of the tall pretty woman'

    b. [[hárté bú-sís-í]$_{NP}$ kɔ̀r-à]$_{NP}$
       donkey big-AUG-ADJ black-RSTR:ATTR
       'The big black donkey.'

8.5 Semantic Properties

The size of the set of adjectives in each semantic type may vary, but Mursi adjectives cover all semantic classes. All thirteen semantic classes of adjectives proposed by Dixon (2004:3) have been attested in Mursi.

A. DIMENSION—this set is comprised of about ten adjectives. It is a unique set where the two underived adjectives belong.

B. VALUE—a dozen adjectives referring to values, animate and inanimate objects comprise this set.

C. AGE—only the following four adjectives referring to age have been attested in Mursi: *čàgì* 'new',[17] *ǹàgàsi* 'old', *kíŋíní* 'ancient, antique', and *tèrì* 'young'.

D. COLOUR—The Mursi utilize a most complex colour and colour pattern systems. This is due to the complicated use of coat-colour of cattle for personal naming as well as for names of cattle herds (see Chapter 1 §1.8). Colour adjectives in Mursi occur in two different cognitive semantic categories: colours and patterns which can be used alone or in combinations of colours and patterns. As is shown in Table 8.4 below, those listed under colour category are basic colour terms in Mursi. The rest are patterns which denote non-basic colour terms. There are also two other colour categories that exist either in concrete terms or hetero-compound forms. The concrete terms are similes of animals, trees, objects, etc., thus they are hetero-compounds composed of colour terms and objects. The following examples illustrate how colours and patterns or colours and concrete terms are combined together; and how they are used in the Mursi person naming system (see §1.8).

E. PHYSICAL PROPERTY—Some physical-property-referring adjectives may have metaphoric meanings. For example, *lálíní* 'cold' can be used to express general quality of coolness—*ri a lálíní* 'the shade is cool'. Besides, some adjectives referring to abnormal properties of humans such as *bɔ̀čá* 'thin' and *dárá* 'shortsighted' do not take the adjectivizer suffix.

F. CORPOREAL PROPERTIES—*íláágáí* 'be sick', *mɔ̀dɔ̀sì* 'be tired, soft (of human condition)', and *rèsì* ⟨j⟩ 'dead'.

---

17 /addisi/ is a derived adjective from Amharic—*addis* 'new, name a city'.

TABLE 8.4 Dimension

Adjective	List
Dimenstion	búí 'big, large', tííní 'small', ɓòì 'wide', kètèŋèsì 'shallow', hòrí 'deep', ŋùčùgí 'narrow', mòkòɲì 'short', ràmàgì 'tall', tákáɲá 'stumpy', kùmùlì 'round, circular'

TABLE 8.5 Value

Adjective	List
Value	čàllì 'good, fine, nice', gèrsì 'bad', déléléì⟨j⟩ 'rich', dʒàmdʒàmì 'mistaken', táɲíl '(be) wrong', géréŋ 'terrible', dʒólí ífá 'amazing', fòì 'delicious', lilibi 'sweet', fééféé 'real, true, genuine', fééháì 'perfect', lògòféé 'true', kédánító 'interesting, attractive'

TABLE 8.6 Colour adjectives

Adjective	Meaning	Category	Remark
hólí	'white'	colour	pure white
kòròì	'black'	colour	black with blue-purple patches
gólòɲí	'red'	colour	red-purple in high saturation, reddish
gìdàɲì	'brown'	colour	red, orange and yellow in low saturation and gray
ɓìlèì	'yellow'	colour	yellow-orange
régéì⟨j⟩	'pink'	colour	⟨devil colour⟩
čàgì	'green, blue'	colour	yellow-green, green and blue
čàkòròì	'blue green'	colour	⟨čàgì-kòròì⟩ green-black
čàhólí	'blue, sky blue'	colour	⟨čàgì-hólí⟩ green-white
sórálí	'white-gray'	pattern	white with greyish areas
lúlúmí	'dark brown'	pattern	brownish colour
ɓìséní	'black and white colour'	pattern	sprinkled colour pattern
ɓáláí	'multi-colour'	pattern	black and white

ADJECTIVES

TABLE 8.6 Colour adjectives (cont.)

Adjective	Meaning	Category	Remark
lɔ́ɔ̀rì[a]	'blackish and greyish undercoat'	pattern	white with few red spots
tùlàì	'vertical striped'	pattern	patterns involving straight and wavy lines
lùì	'spotted, multi-colour'	pattern	black head and hindquarter (tail-tip)
mìrò	spotted	pattern	'colourful, multi-colour'
sírwàì	'dark brown'	pattern	blackish with cream undercoat
dʒààrhɔ́lí[b]	'black and white'	colour+ pattern	white-legged (of cattle leg)
kìwó	spotted	pattern	white-black
bólóì	spotted	pattern	multi-colour
kòrí	spotted	pattern	white with red spots

a The vowel length is due to the intervocalic deletion of /g/, which otherwise is interpreted as a trisyllabic monomorphemic word in Suri (a Southeast Surmic language and forms a single dialect cluster together with Mursi)—i.e., [lɔgɔri].
b gìdàɲ-dʒààr-hɔ́lí 'brown-leg-white' ~ it could be colour+pattern of cattle or òlí-gìdàɲ-dʒààr-hɔ́lí 'ox-brown-leg-white' name of a person.

TABLE 8.7 Physical property

Adjective	Meaning	Remark
ɓɔčá	'thin'	for appearance of humans and objects
bùrènì	'hot'	also 'warm'
lálíní	'cold'	also 'cool'
ídíbènì	'fat'	
kúmúlí	'fat'	See dimension 'round, roundish'
dárá	'shortsighted'	abnormality
dɔ́rɔ́sí	'dry, strong'	place, cloth (of objects in general)
lɔ́tɔ́gí	'wet'	lɔ́tɔ́ktín 'liquid'
čárgi	'wet'	cannot be stativized like lɔ́tɔ́gí
bájsí	'partly dried out'	also 'clever person'
kómàì	'strong'	physical strength of human
dúrdúrí	'thick'	(of porridge, gèsò 'traditional beer')
gódírí	'thick'	gìrgìrí 'slippery'

TABLE 8.7 Physical property (*cont.*)

Adjective	Meaning	Remark
gìlgìlì	'soft, smooth'	Its verbal use requires mèsí 'make'
zírwàì	'rubbish'	generic term for something useless
húgínèì ⟨j⟩	'clean'	
kààrèčàgì	'blind'	(kààrìɗíkté)
ʃàbàlì	'flat'	
rɔ̀ŋɔ̀ɗì	'bent, curved'	can also refers to human character
túrgúlí	'bent, deformed'	of wood/tree
ríí	'shady'	derived from noun ríí 'shade'
bèná	'rocky'	bè 'stone'+ -na (pl.)
rèsàlìzàlì	'thin'	a compound word (not clear)
rèrèhí	'thin'	of human/animal body
ʃèmèlì	'very thin'	maybe Amharic ʃɪmäl 'stick'
áɲákɔ́náì	'lame'	word class origin is not known
mùrmùrì	'straight'	has an adverbial form dìb 'straight'
káwàì	'ugly'	
lèʃì	'sharp'	tip of an object
mùʤùsì	'rotten'	stink, smell (bad)
bèlèì⟨ʔ⟩	'bald'	early morning before sunrise (dawn)
bìtìkáɲì	'(be) sour'	libiso 'become sour (of milk)'
mèčèkèrì	'bitter'	appears to be a compound word
ŋàhì	'female'	⟨hira ŋaha⟩ 'woman'
màì [màgì]	'male'	⟨hira maga⟩ 'man'

G. HUMAN PROPENSITY—Adjectives referring to physical properties are not only related to denoting a particular attribute of an object but also of having sensory meanings. For example, the adjective *bárárí* 'powerful' would refer to taste of a hot food or spicy coffee; even a milk, after early stages of the souring process is called *lálíní* 'cool; cold' then after it transforms into a stage that causes a burning sensation in the mouth it becomes *bárárí*. Dew is *bárárí* because if there is no rain or it is *dɔ̌rɔ́sí* 'dry'. *bá dɔ̌rɔ́sí* 'dry place, drought' is *bárárí* whereas *ri* 'shade' is *lálíní*. There are also plants that are considered *bárárí* because they can heal or kill humans when they are worn as amulets (cf. Turton 1973).

H. DIFFICULTY—this set is composed of few members—just five: *baseni* 'easy, cheap', *dáldálí* 'difficult, hard, expensive', *dĭŋdĭŋí* 'heavy', *hɔ́lhɔ́Ĭ* 'light', and *tání* 'difficult'.

SPEED—this set is the smallest of all adjectival types—*dıŋílín* 'slow' and *tìrì* 'fast'. Not only has it just two members but the functions of its members are also covered by adverbs.

SIMILARITY—*búbúí* 'different, separate', *gènà* 'other', and *hétɔ́* 'similar, the same'. *búbúí* is a seemingly underived adjective but whose real word class source is unknown. It doesn't take any morphological inflection but it does function as NP modifier and does occur as a copula complement. Tentatively, the status of *búbúí* lies somewhere between underived and derived adjectives.

I. QUANTIFICATION—some members of the quantification set may function adverbially. *dɔ́nénín* is a derived adjective from the numeral *dɔ́néj* 'one'; can also be used as an adverb 'alone'.

J. POSITION—position adjectives are also directional markers—*ʤá* 'near', *útúrei* '(at the) end', *rènì* 'far', *sìtèn* 'right', and *kèŋìtèn* 'left'.

K. CARDINAL NUMBERS—*sábɔ̀* 'first' and *wùréɔ́* 'second' can function as cardinal numerals. Both can function adverbially. *sábɔ̀* is a derived adjective from the grammaticalized body part noun *saba* 'head' whereas *wùréɔ́* is a time adverb 'after, next'. In addition to these two, the numerals *ràmàn* 'two' and *sízzì* 'three' can function as cardinal numerals; when an adverbializer suffix –*o* is added to *ràmàn* ⟨ràmàn-ò⟩ 'second', and when the ordinal number marker suffix –*ne* is added to *sízzì* ⟨sízzì-nè⟩ 'third'.

8.6 Summary

Like nouns and verbs, adjectives constitute an open word class. Two underived and about one hundred fifty derived adjectives have been attested in Mursi. The source for the majority of derived adjectives are stative verbs. Some derived adjectives may belong to more than one word class. Adjectives differ from nouns and adjectives in a number of ways (an illustrative summary is given below in Table 8.10).

Mursi adjectives can function as modifiers of head nouns in NPs and as heads of an intransitive predicate, can occupy copula complement slots, can serve as markers of parameter of comparison in comparative constructions, and can form adverbs. Below is a summary of the syntactic function of both underived and derived adjectives.

Below is a summary of the syntactic function of both underived and derived adjectives.

TABLE 8.8 Human propensity

Adjective	List
Human propensity	ádɛ̀sɛ̀n rè dùjì 'stubborn', áɲáné 'weak, frightened', bábí 'foolish', dálnéì 'foolish', bárárí 'powerful, strong taste', bàsí 'kind', kɔ̀màì 'kind', ɓírá '(be) impotent', bú(ì̀)tógí 'lying', ɓóŋɓóɲí 'blistery', čùmùnì 'happy, joyful', dárí 'sneaky', dòɲà 'honest', ɛ́ɲérsɨɲógí 'cowardly', gáí 'intelligent', gèrèsín 'sinful', gèrèsì/ʃólái 'troubled', gòɲàì 'mean', gùrgùrì 'clever, wise', írán 'proud', kárkárí 'rough', léságí 'greedy, stingy', lèsìnè 'jealous', líjá, 'shy', lójá 'lazy, cowardly', lùmùróì 'cheating', múɲí 'sad', múɲúɲí 'cruel', ŋɔ̀lí 'lame', ódénéí ⟨j⟩ 'brave', tòlgòɲì 'lazy'

TABLE 8.9 Quantification

Adjective	List
Quantifcation	dĭní(o)/dĭ 'full (filled to capacity of a something)', dákákán 'all (whole)', ɓòì 'all', dàài 'all (whole)', tój 'full', hólólój 'empty, free', dɔ̆nénín 'only', múčúgí 'few, half', and mèrì 'many, abundant'

TABLE 8.10 A comparative summary of adjectives vs verbs/nouns

Morphophonological properties	Adjectives	Verbs	Nouns
Diysllabic monomorphemic roots ($V_1=V_2$)	YES	SOME	SOME
Disylabic monomorphemic roots ($C_1V_1C_1=C_2V_2C_2$)	YES	SOME	SOME
inflect for number	YES (just one)	NO	YES (many patterns)

ADJECTIVES

TABLE 8.10 A comparative summary of adjectives vs verbs/nouns (cont.)

Morphophonological properties	Adjectives	Verbs	Nouns
inflect for S,O arguments	SOME	YES	NO
inflect for case	YES	NO	YES
inflect for aspect	SOME[a]	YES	NO
Take - èsèn as comparative marker	YES	NO[b]	NO
take a definite marker	YES	YES	YES
take stativising marker -tin	YES	NO	YES
can form compounds	YES	SOME	SOME

a Aspect on adjectives is within the bound pronominal suffixes in S function.
b On adjectives, the suffix -èsèn may function as comparative marker suffix, and it is a polyfunctional extension marker covering various functions such as benefactive, dative, transitiviser and so on.

TABLE 8.11 A comparative syntactic summary of adjectives vs stative verbs/nouns

Syntactic properties	Adjectives	Verbs	Nouns
modifier to noun	YES	NO	YES
head of intransitive predicate	YES	YES	NO
copula complement	YES	NO	RESTRICTED GRAMMATICAL CONTEXTS
modifier to verb	SOME	NO	NO

TABLE 8.12 A summary of the syntactic functions of adjectives

Syntactic function	Underived adjectives	Derived adjectives
Modifier within an NP	YES	YES
Modify NPs	YES	FEW
Head of NPs	NO	YES
Intransitive predicate	YES (only tííní 'small')	YES
Copula complement	YES	YES
Parameter of comparison	YES	YES
Form adverbs	NO	YES
Can modify as intensifier	YES (only búí 'big')	NO

TABLE 8.12 A summary of the syntactic functions of adjectives (*cont.*)

Syntactic function	Underived adjectives	Derived adjectives
Can be modified by intensifiers (general intensifiers *háŋ* and *wáŋ*)	YES	YES
Can be modified by specific intensifiers	YES *gòdé* (gèɗé) 'very small' *gòrí* 'powerfully'	NO
Agree in number with head nouns by reduplication	YES	NO
Agree in number with head nouns by plural number inflection	NO	FEW??
Can be negated	NO	YES

CHAPTER 9

Valency Changing Operations

9.1 Introduction

Valency constitutes the basis for how verbs are divided into distinct semantic and grammatical classes on the basis of the number of arguments (valents) they take. The term valency, according to Crystal (2008: 503), refers to the number and type of bonds which syntactic elements may form with each other, determined by the valency attributed to the verb. Valency relates to the number of core arguments (Dixon and Aikhenvald 2000: 3). Valency of verbs can be adjusted by valency changing operations (derivations) that certainly affect predicate arguments.

Four valency decreasing and four valency increasing derivations have been found in Mursi. The valency decreasing derivations are passive (§ 9.2.1), antipassive (§ 9.2.2), reciprocal (§ 9.2.3), and reflexive (§ 9.2.4). Benefactive-applicative (§ 9.3.1), applicative/comitative (§ 9.3.2), causative (§ 9.3.3), and directional/motion (§ 9.3.4) increase the number of core arguments. Each valency changing derivations may employ more than one strategy/possibility. For example, the reciprocal derivation has four different possibilities while reflexive derivation has at least two possibilities.

In the subsequent sections we will see how the three main components (morphological, syntactic and semantic) interact with each other in the language. Except for the reflexive, all other derivations are expressed by attaching valency changing morphological devices to verbs. In Mursi, despite the fact that it is a language which predominantly utilizes suffixes in most of its valency derivation operations, prefixes are also used in passive and causative derivations. Table 9.1 below illustrates the derivational markers being used by each type of valency changing operations.

TABLE 9.1 Valency-changing derivational affixes in Mursi

Derivation type	Prefix	Suffix	Person/number/aspect
Passive	k(V)-		– bound pronominal O argument marking suffixes
		-V	– for 3rd person
Antipassive	none	-nèn	1st and 2nd persons
		-nè	1st plural inclusive and 3rd person
Reciprocal	none	-nèn	1st and 2nd persons
		-nè	1st plural inclusive and 3rd person
Benefactive-applicative	none	-èsèn	for all persons
		-èsè	3rd person, positive imperative, hortative, and jussive
Applicative/ comitative	none	-ɛ	for all persons
		-čo	for 1st person plural exclusive, 2nd person plural
		-čV	{-ča, -či } rare and/or unpredictable
causative	í-	∅	– on verb with a root ending in a plosive
		-ísí	– on all other verb roots
directional/motion	none	-áná	motion towards (ventive), imperfective
		[-án]/	
		-ónó	
		[-ón]	
		-a/-o	motion towards (ventive), perfective
	none	-sèn	motion away from (itive), imperfective
		-ɛ/-sè	motion away from (itive), perfective

9.2 Valency Decreasing Derivations

In the subsequent subsections, the four valency decreasing derivations are discussed in detail.

9.2.1 *Passive*

The passive derivation in Mursi is of two types: the prototypical passive and the agentless passive. The core argument reassignment for both types remains the same but there is a difference in the assignment of the underlying A argument (the peripheral argument). Thus, a prototypical passive derivation shows the following major syntactic properties:

- Passive applies to an underlying transitive clause to derive an intransitive clause.
- The underlying O becomes S argument.
- The original A argument becomes a peripheral argument, being marked by the multi-functional grammaticalized nominal *bá* 'place' > 'in place of' > 'instead' 'because (of)' > 'therefore' (rarely) > 'by'; or by a preposition/comitative marker *ké* 'with'.
- There is an explicit formal marking of the passive construction in Mursi, as it shown in Table 9.1, which has both a prefix *k(V)-* (as a general passivizer prefix) and the suffix -*V*—following consonant-initial verb roots; identical with the vowel of the verb root due to vowel copying and following non-consonant-initial verb roots.

The criteria/properties listed above satisfy nearly all criteria for a prototypical passive construction in Dixon and Aikhenvald (2000: 7). In addition to these criteria, in a passive clause construction, the verb must occur in perfective aspect, and must always have a low tone. Let us see how they interact and work in a clause:

(9.1) a. [òlélù]_A àk⟨g⟩-ú   [tílá]_O
       Olelu   cook.PERV-3SG.SU.PERV food
       'Olelu cooked food.'

   b. [tílá]_S kà-àg-á   [bá-á   olelu-j]_{PERIPHERAL}
      food   PASS-cook.PERV-3.SU.PASS place-RSTR Olelu-GEN
      'The food was cooked by Olelu.'

(9.2) a. [múdăí]_A áŋít-ú   [ròsò]_O
       rat   bite-3SG.SU.PERV dog
       'The rat bit the dog.'

b. [rɔ̀sɔ̀]_S k-àŋìd-í   [ké múdáɾ]_PERIPHERAL
   dog   PASS-bite.PERV-3.SU.PASS PREP rat
   'The dog was bitten by the rat.'

In both (9.1a) and (9.2a), the O arguments in the active clauses (*tílá* and *rɔ̀sɔ*) are S arguments in the passive clauses (as in (9.1b and 9.2b)). The original A arguments become optional arguments thus they are pushed into a peripheral function—either by the grammaticalized nominal *bá* (as in (9.1b)) or by preposition/comitative particle *ké* (as in (9.2b)). When the grammaticalized nominal *bá* functions as preposition, it acts as head of an NP thus the original A argument following it, will be marked with genitive case, the same as regular head modifiers within an NP.

If the active clause contains A, O and peripheral arguments, the A argument may not be important at all. Therefore, in the passive version of such active clause will only contain the derived S (the original O) and the peripheral arguments, as in (9.3). The examples illustrated below were obtained by elicitation, and some questions were taken from Mütze (2014)

(9.3) a. [nɔ̀ŋ]_A ŋé-Ø   [kìɔ̀]_O [bé-ɔ̀]_PERIPHERAL
      3SG   cut-3SG.SU.IMPERV tree.SG axe-OBL
      'He cut the tree with an axe.'

   b. [kìɔ̀]_S kè-tèŋéd-è   [bé-ɔ̀]_PERIPHERAL
      tree.SG PASS-cut.PERV-3.SU.PASS axe-OBL
      'The tree was cut with an axe.'

In the passive clause shown in (9.3b), the agent (the original A) is downgraded but one knows that there was an agent involved to carry out the activity with the instrument shown by the peripheral argument. The peripheral argument in (9.2b) differs from (9.3b) in that the preposition/comitative particle *ke* in the former directly functions as agent (original A). On the other hand, the peripheral argument in (9.3b) only refers to the instrument used by the agent. When the peripheral argument is being made optional, verb-final suffix may be attached to the verb in passive form (9.3c).

   c. [kìɔ̀]_S kè-tèŋéd-é-è
      tree.SG PASS-cut.PERV-3.SU.PASS-VFS
      'The tree was cut.'

Note that the verb ŋɛ⟨t⟩ 'cut' indicates perfective aspect by adding a prefix *t(V)-* to its root.

On the other hand, agentless passive, which is the second type of passive clause construction in the language, is identical to the prototypical passive type in many respects, except: (i) the original A argument is not stated in any way, (ii) the form utilizes bound object pronominal suffixes marking the new S argument, and (iii) the form takes verb-final suffix. Even though both the A and the O arguments are cross-referenced on the verb in active transitive clauses, only O arguments will be cross-referenced on the verb (derived S arguments). Among Surmic languages, Tirmaga (Bryan, 1999: 94), and Tenet (Randall 1998: 244), also have agentless passive constructions. Syntactically, it is clear that it is impossible to express the original A argument in this construction either overtly or covertly.

(9.4) a. kù-tùs-áɲ-ɔ̀
       PASS-spit/bless.PERV-1SG.OBJ-VFS
       'I am blessed.'

   b. kù-tùs-ì-ɔ̀
      PASS-spit/bless.PERV-1PL.OBJ-VFS
      'We are blessed.'

   c. kù-tùs-úɲ-ɔ̀
      PASS-spit/bless.PERV-2PL.OBJ-VFS
      'You (pl.) are blessed.'

As can be shown in (9.4a–c), the bound pronominal suffixes marking O arguments in active clauses are the same as those in passive clause constructions. The third person has zero suffix realization for bound pronominal marking of the O argument, instead it takes the suffix *-V* as O argument marker in agentless passive constructions.

(9.5) a. kù-tùh-ó-ɛ̀
       PASS-spit/bless.PERV-3.SU.PASS-VFS
       'He was blessed.'

   b. kù-tùs-á
      PASS-split/bless.PERV-3.SU.PASS
      'They got blessed.'

We can see from the examples illustrated in (9.4) and (9.5) that the first and second persons utilize the verb-final suffix -ɔ whereas the third person utilizes a different verb-final suffix -ɛ. Rarely, the third person plural form of the agentless passive construction may not take a verb-final suffix at all (as in (9.5b)).

The agentless passive construction in Mursi and Chai (Southeast Surmic group language) is the same. Therefore, it is appropriate to cite here one major claim made by two linguists who studied the Chai language. The following quote is about the agentless passive construction type in Chai:

The logical object, which becomes the grammatical subject in passive constructions in other languages, remains the grammatical object in Chai, as the object agreement suffixes are similar to the object suffixes used in active forms. The verb agrees with the agent in number and person. The agent normally is not explicitly specified elsewhere in the sentence (Last and Lucassen 1998: 387).

In Mursi, what the verb-final suffixes could indirectly denote is that syntactic elements are not allowed to follow the agentless passive forms once the verb-final suffixes is attached to the verb. Even adverbs, which are not part of core or peripheral arguments, can follow the agentless passive verb form before the verb-final suffix is applied. See the example given below.

(9.6) [tílá]₍S₎ kà-ɓàg-á ʃàù
food PASS-eat.PERV-3.SU.PASS fast
'The food is eaten fast.'

9.2.2 *Patient-like Antipassives*

Antipassive is another valency-decreasing derivation in which a transitive clause is de-transitivized to an intransitive one by an antipassive derivation operation. Antipassive applies to an underlying transitive clause and forms a derived intransitive (Dixon and Aikhenvald, 2000:10). In particular in Mursi, a valency decreasing antipassive derivation is normally used to downplay the core argument of a transitive verb by omitting the underlying O argument. In this case, Mursi's antipassive construction adheres to the prototypical patient-like antipassive criteria set by Dixon and Aikhenvald (2000: 9). The criteria are:

– Antipassive applies to an underlying transitive clause and forms a derived intransitive.
– The underlying A becomes S of the antipassive.
– The underlying O argument is omitted.
– Antipassive construction is formally marked by two antipassive suffixes (see Table 9.2 below).

TABLE 9.2 Antipassive suffixes

Person	Suffix imperfective	Suffix perfective
1st and 2nd persons	-nèn[a]	-ɛ
1st pl.INC and 3rd person	-nè	-ɛ

[a] The epenthetic /i/ is inserted between consonant-final verb roots and antipassive/reciprocal suffixes.

It is not possible to place the O argument into a peripheral argument function,—therefore it must be omitted, as in (9.7a–b).

(9.7) a. [ìggè]_A màt-ó   [gèsò]_O
       2PL   drink-2PL.SU.IMPERV   beer
       'You (PL) are drinking beer.'

   b. [ìggè]_S màt-ínèn-ó-ó
      2PL   drink-1/2.AP-2PL.SU.IMPERV-VFS
      'You (PL) are drinking.'

The Mursi antipassive derivation type displays a patientless antipassive; in most cases the O can be implied but in no way can it occur after the derived intransitive verb. Following the absence of the O argument that can be placed after the derived intransitive verbs, antipassive clause constructions usually take the verb-final suffix -ɔ.

(9.8) a. [ànè]_A kóóh-í   [gùj]_O
       1SG   1SU.clear.IMPERV-1SG.SU.IMPERV   field
       'I clear a garden.'

   b. [ànè]_S kóóh-ínèn-ó
      1SG   1SU.clear.IMPERV-1/2.AP.IMPERV-VFS
      'I am clearing/weeding.'

   c. [rɔ̀sɔ̀]_S áŋíd-íné-ɔ̀
      dog.SG   bite-3.AP.IMPERV-VFS
      'The dog is biting.'
      (Lit. 'The dog will bite.')

As far the aspectual status of the verb in the antipassive clause construction is concerned, at this stage, I would say imperfective is a default aspect of the verb being used by the antipassive clauses. In order to receive a verb-final suffix, the verb usually has to be an intransitive and an imperfective verb. In light of this, the antipassive verb form satisfies both requirements. The passive verb forms are being marked with the verb-final marker because they all have an intransitive value. Referring to the antipassive derivation, in particular the suffix -nèn, Mütze (2014) wrote, 'it is impossible for intransitive verbs to occur with the –nɛn suffix, unless for the function of joint action'. When she says 'joint action', she is referring to a reciprocal[1] construction, which we see in the next section.

Semantically, the antipassive construction differs from the passive construction in that the former 'focuses on the activity itself (that is, on the agents performing the activity)' (Dixon and Aikhenvald 2000: 9).

9.2.3 *Reciprocals*

In Mursi, reciprocal actions are expressed by the same suffixes being used to derive antipassive constructions. The same antipassive suffixes are used to indicate reciprocal or joint actions. Hence the suffixes in Table 9.2 are being employed as verbal derivational suffixes to derive intransitive forms with reciprocal meaning. The S of this derived verb then indicates the set of participants involved in the reciprocal construction, in the case of Mursi, a plural form which shows plural S participants (cf. Dixon and Aikhenvald 2000: 11). Therefore, the most important point here that we should take into account is that plural S suffixes are obligatory parts in the reciprocal construction—since reciprocity involves more than one participant.

(9.9) [àggè]$_S$ kí-ʃĭg-ínèn-Ø-ɔ́
1PL 1SU-hear.IMPERV-RECIP-1PL.EXC.SU.IMPERV-VFS
'We (exc.) hear each other.'

(9.10) [tàmàrì-ɲà]$_S$ ɛ̀kɛ̀kɛ̀ɲ-à-nɛ̀-ɔ́
students-PL quarrel-EPEN-RECIP-VFS
'The students are arguing with each other.'

Number agreement between the subject of the reciprocal clause and the intransitive predicate is obligatory, as in (9.9) and (9.10). As we can see in the examples

---

1 According to Gerrit Dimmendaal (p.c.), the VFS is the actual antipassive marker in Mursi, whereas the reciprocal/antipassive is a middle voice marker.

shown above, number of subject is shown by a separate subject pronominal suffix—zero morpheme for first person plural exclusive subject (9.9), and a coalesced third person plural S marker -ε (9.10). Transitive verbs are detransitivized, thus no O argument follows the reciprocal form.

The newly derived intransitive verb always occurs in plural form and can convey reciprocal or joint action using the suffixes, as in (9.11) and (9.12).

(9.11) [lùkùr-á   g=ànù]_{NP.S}   dág-inè-ɔ́
friend.PL-RSTR PL.PSD=1SG.PSR beat.IMPERV-RECIP.3-VFS
'My friends are beating each other.'

(9.12) [nɔ̀ŋ]_S zámí-nèn-ɔ̀
3SG   swim.IMPERV-RECIP-VFS
'He swims together (with someone).'

However, when the intransitive subject is singular, the preposition *kó* is used to indicate the other participant involved in the reciprocal construction. Some examples are presented as follows.

(9.13) [àɲè]_S kí-číb-ínèn   [kó   lúsà]
1SG   1SU-tie.IMPERV-1/2.RECIP with boy.PL
'I am tying (it) together with the boys.'

(9.14) [bàrtùj kó   ŋàtùj] gá-nè-ɔ́
Bartuy and Ngatuy know.IMPERV-RECIP-VFS
'Bartuy and Ngatuy know each other.'

kó in (9.13) is a preposition whereas it is a conjunction in (9.14), in both cases its primary function is to conjoin singular participants.

What we have seen in the aforementioned examples is one out of the four reciprocal construction strategies in the language. There are three additional strategies for expressing reciprocity:
- A body part noun *kèɲɔ̀* 'stomach/belly' in a grammaticalized function 'each other, among'.
- The sociative marker *kàrì* 'together'—it also expresses joint actions or Collectivity.
- Reduplication.

As was attempted to demonstrate in the examples above, the verb derivation technique is a productive way to express reciprocal meanings in Mursi. One more common strategy in many languages but that Mursi lacks, is a reciprocal construction containing an inherently reciprocal verb.

The grammaticalized body part noun *kèŋɔ̀* 'stomach/belly' > 'each other, among' functions as a reciprocal marker grammatical word. Both transitive and intransitive verbs can occur with the reciprocal marker *kèŋɔ̀* within one reciprocal construction. In Chai, a closest relative to Mursi within the Southeast Surmic language group, *kèŋɔ̀* means 'occurrences, times'. In a clause, *kèŋɔ̀* usually takes a clause final slot (occurs at the end of a clause).

(9.15) [*éró*]_S *tìráɲ-á* **kèŋɔ̀**
children play-3PL.SU.PERV RECIP
'The children play with each other.'

(9.16) [*jɔ̀g*]_S *séd-á* **kèŋɔ̀** *ké*
3PL say.PERV:PL-3PL.SU.PERV RECIP QUOT
'They said to each other.'

(9.17) [*òlítùlà kó òlìkìwò*]_S *dágt-é* **kèŋɔ̀**
Òlítùlà PNC Òlíkibo hit.PERV.PL-RECIP RECIP
'Olitula and Olikibo hit each other.'

(9.18) *zùwò dágt-é* **kèŋɔ̀**
people hit.PERV.PL-RECIP RECIP
'The men hit each other.'

(9.19) [*bàrtùj kó ŋàrùgɔ̀*]_S *čɔ́bɔ́s-ó* **kèŋɔ̀**
Bartuy PNC Ngarugo kiss-3PL.IRR RECIP
'Bartuy and Ngarugo kissed each other.'

In (9.17) and (9.18), the co-occurrence of the verbal derivation suffixes together with the reciprocal marker *kèŋɔ̀* requires further investigation, but at this stage, seems to be related to transitivity of the verb, i.e. specifically a transitive verb. The rest of the reciprocal constructions (9.15, 9.16 and 9.19) have verbs that are not marked for the reciprocal derivation marker suffix. An additional transitive verb example is presented below.

(9.20) [*éró ràmàn*]_S *čúgt-è* **kèŋɔ̀** *gɔ̀r-ɔ́*
children two chase.PERV.PL-RECIP RECIP road-OBL
[*ín-á tíín-ó dʒìm-Ø sábɔ́*]
3SG.PN.SP-RSTR small-RSTR.MOD lead-3SG.SU.IMPERV in.front
'The two kids chased each other down the street, the younger one in front all the way.'

In (9.20), the structure in a closed bracket literally mean, 'the small one leads in/from front'.

The sociative marker *kàrì* 'together' can denote reciprocity in its own. It also expresses joint actions or participants being in a 'collectivity'. Similar to a reciprocal construction that involves a transitive verb and the reciprocal marker *kèŋɔ̀*, it occurs together with a transitive verb marked for a reciprocal derivational suffix. See the examples illustrated below.

(9.21) [ŋàtùj kó bàrtùj]_S óg-ìnè   **kàrì**
Ngatuy and Bartuy cook.IMPERV-RECIP.3.IMPERV **together**
'Ngatuy and Bartuy cook together for each other.'

(9.22) [kùčùbà-nèn kó habarawia]_S tùj-í ìw-íné
amhara-NOMZ and Hebrew mouth-PL attach-RECIP.3.IMPERV
kàrì kàrì
together together
'The Amharic and Hebrew languages are related to each other.'

(9.23) hír-á [Ø wà ɲàj-nèn-á]_{RC} kó hír-á
man-RSTR [Ø REC.PAST harverst-NOMZ-RSTR] PNC man-RSTR
[Ø bè dúg-ìnèn-á]_{RC} čùmùn-è̀
[Ø DIST.PAST plant-NOMZ-RSTR] be.happy.STV-RECIP.3.PERV
kàrì
together
'He that sows and he that reapeth may rejoice together.'
(Lit. 'The person who plants and the person who harvests can rejoice together.')

The apposed participants (subjects) within the reciprocal construction represented by relative clause modified NPs do not bring a change in the meaning.

The last strategy that could properly deliver a reciprocal meaning is reduplication. Intransitive verbs may require a reduplicated adverb or number word. Thus, a reduplicated adverb may show whether the action is performed simultaneously but not sequentially (as in (9.24–9.26)). In contrast, a reduplicated number word *dɔ́néj* 'one' > *dɔ́nédɔ́né* is an etymon for 'one another' (Lit. 'one-one'), and has an additional meaning to the reciprocity of the action, i.e. the action is performed sequentially (for example, the sequentiality of the act of talking in (9.26)).

(9.24) [éró]₍S₎ él   ʤáʤá   bɔ̀
       childen exist.IMPERV.PL near:REDUP outside+OBL
       'The children sit next to each other on a bench.'

(9.25) [éró]₍S₎ él   rɔ̀ɲá ʤáʤá   [bá-á
       childen exist.IMPERV.PL side near:REDUP place-rstr
       lúg-inèn-à]
       hole.in.the.ground-NOMZ-RSTR
       'The children sit next to each other in a circle.'

(9.26) [àstàmàrì-ɲà]₍S₎ áli-ɛ́   kèŋɔ̀ dɔ́nédɔ́né
       teacher-PL   talk-3PL.SU.IMPERV RECIP one:REDUP
       'The teachers are speaking one after the other.'

In fact, in (9.26) the grammaticalized reciprocal maker *kèŋɔ̀* appears to provide the real reciprocal meaning, but its real function is to provide a distributive meaning (see §6.11.4). Only one intransitive verb that I know of can be combined with reduplicated adverbial form—*tɛ́l-i ʤáʤá* ⟨exist.PERV.PL-3pl.IRR near-near⟩ 'approach each other' > *kɛ́-tɛ́l-i ʤáʤá* ⟨3.JUSS-exist.PERV.PL-3pl.IRR near-near⟩ 'cause to approach each other'. A transitive counterpart *ítíɲán-ú* ⟨CAUSE.meet-3sg.SU.PERV 'cause to approach each other' has a lexicalized form merged with the unproductive causative prefix *i*-forming.

9.2.4 Reflexive

Semantically, as suggested by Dixon (2012: 146), a prototypical reflexive construction shows reflexive situations happen when two arguments of a single verb have identical reference. Syntactically, in Mursi, a reflexive construction has two reflective elements in O slot—(i) a reflexive pronoun (it is normally an NP containing the grammaticalized body part nouns *sábá* 'head' and 'body' *rè* as its head nouns) and possessive pronouns as modifiers, and (ii) an autoreflexive-like particle *búí* 'self, own, alone' (an invariant form for all persons and number of the A=O arguments). With regard to cross-linguistic reflexive and reciprocal constructions, Dixon (2012: 151–156) suggested eight generalizations. Accordingly, Mursi complies with GENERALIZATION D, where reflexive and reciprocal pronouns may both be invariant or informative. However, as he suggests, 'if only one is informative, then this is reflexive'. This is the first truth. There is the second truth that perfectly reflects Mursi reflexive construction in general, 'there are languages with informative reflexive pronouns and an invariant reciprocal pronoun (not the reverse)' (p. 154).

In Mursi, a reflexive meaning is conveyed in two ways:

i. [*sábá* 'head'/*rè* 'body'+ POSSESSIVE PRONOUNS]REFLEXIVE.PRO:NP/
O—'informative'
ii. [*bii*] AUTOREFLEXIVE:NP/O—'invariant'

9.2.4.1   *sábá* 'Head'/*rè* 'Body'+ Possessive Pronouns

A prototypical reflexive construction in Mursi can be formed from an A argument (also known as 'controller'/'antecedent'), a transitive verb, and from an O argument (the two grammaticalized body part nouns plus possessive pronouns). The argument, which is placed in O function is a reflexive pronoun/an NP [*sábá-á/rè-a*—Possessive pronouns], sometimes referred to as 'informative'—because it copies information about the person and number of the controller (cf. Dixon 2012: 154). Examples are illustrated as follows.

(9.27) [*nɔ̀ŋ*]_A *hàlì   óɲ-Ø*   [*sabá-á*
       3SG   later wash.IMPERV-3SG.SU.IMPERV head-RSTR
       n=ènè]_REFLEXIVE.PRO:NP/O
       SG.PSD=3SG.PSR
       'He will wash himself.'

(9.28) [*ỵnè*]_A *mès-í*   *sábá-á*   [*n=ùnù*]_REFLEXIVE.PRO:NP/O
       2SG   do-2SG.SU.IMPERV   head-RSTR   SG.PSD=2SG.PSR
       'You (sg.) do (it) yourself.'

(9.29) (*ỵnè*)_A *ɛja*   [*sábá-a*   *n=ùnù*]_REFLEXIVE.PRO:NP/O
       (2SG) help.PERV.IMP   head-RSTR   SG.PSD=2SG.PSR
       'Help yourself!'
       (Lit. 'You (sg.) help yourself!')

(9.30) (*ỵnè*)_A *dól-èsè*   *rè-á*   *n=ùnù*]_REFLEXIVE.PRO:NP/O
       (2SG) show-BEN.PERV.IMP   body-RSTR   SG.PSD=2SG.PSR
       [*ŋà=bá=à*]_IO/E
       DEM=place/world=NEAR
       '(You (sg.)) show yourself to the world!'

As it is shown in these examples, the reflexive pronouns formed by the two human body nouns and possessive pronouns fill the O argument slot. All (9.27–9.30) are transitive clauses. The reflexive pronouns in Mursi are NPs in their own right—two human body nouns as NP heads marked with the restrictive dependency/relator marker *–a* and possessive pronouns as modifiers. Any change of the head will result in an anaphoric inequivalency with the subject.

For example, when *sábá* 'head' of the reflexive pronoun in (9.27) is changed into *sènɔ̀* 'hand.PL' (as in (9.31)), it will result in A≠O.

(9.31) [nɔ̀ŋ]_A tóɲ-à   [sèn-á   g=ɛ̀ɲɛ̀]_NP/O
       3SG   wash.PERV-3SG.SU.PERV hand.PL-RSTR PL.PSD=3SG.PSR
       'S/he washed her/his own hands.'

The anaphoric reference in O function (9.30) is part of the subject but does not fully specify the subject itself—because it cannot function as a reflexive pronoun. The anaphoric reference in (9.30) is a simple possessive O NP. There is one possibility where the pertensive form of *rè* ⟩ *rèɛ̀* (body.PERT.SG.3.PSR) functions as O without the possessive pronoun. Outside some close kinship nouns, this is the only noun that can be possessed inalienably. But *rèɛ̀* can be placed in O argument slot if it has a 3rd person singular controller—with a meaning 'his body' (possessive NP) > 'himself' (reflexive), as in (9.32).

(9.32) ɔ́k-ú   nà   íláák-ú   [rèɛ̀]_NP/O
       go-3SG.SU.PERV CCN hang-3SG.SU.PERV body+PERT.SG.3.PSR
       'S/he went and hanged herself/himself.'
       (Lit. 'his body')

An extended transitive (ditransitive) verb (as in (9.31)) can be re-adjusted and made a transitive verb. This can easily be achieved by attaching the coreference of the E argument to the ditransitive verb root. Thus the benefactive marker suffix -*ese* indicates the coreference of the E (*ŋàbà(à)* ~ 'this world'), not of the A. The coreference of the A argument (2nd person singular suffix) will be omitted. In this particular case, as also noted by Dixon (2012: 160), the O argument for the English verb 'give', is either 'gift' or 'recipient'. So, in the English reflexive construction, the preferred structure is to treat the 'Gift' as O. As it is illustrated in (9.30) above, *rèá nùnù* is the O argument. However, the reflexive construction in (9.30) is an exception. There are certain syntactic constraints which could be regarded as exceptions of a Mursi reflexive construction, for example, attaching the benefactive marker suffix in (9.30) to the transitive verb of (9.28) is not allowed. If the benefactive marker suffix -*ese* is attached to the verb root *mès*, the meaning would become that of a benefactive applicative or dative referring to 'recipient'/'gift', as in (9.33).

(9.33) [iɲà]_A mès-ésèn   [sábá-á   n=ùnù]_NP/O
       2SG   do-1/2.BEN.IMPERV head-RSTR SG.PSD=2SG.PSR
       'You (sg.) do it for/to yourself.'

Therefore, (9.33) is a benefactive construction which has an unspecified third person singular constituent in its O argument.

9.2.4.2 The Invariant Reflexive Particle *bíí* 'Self, Own, Alone'

The reflexive particle *bíí* has an invariant form for all persons. This lexicalized reflexive marker can function as genuine reflexive and emphatic reflexive marker/autoreflexive. An equivalent English form for *bíí* is 'self'. As Dixon (2012: 167) described, in the English, the reflexive form 'self' functions as the provider of an argument slot other than the subject. In Mursi, *bíí* functions the same way as in English. When it functions as a genuine reflexive marker, it takes the O argument slot following the predicate. In order to get the genuine reflexive reading, a transitive verb is always preferred over an intransitive one.

(9.34) [íggè-á   [Ø mà]_RC]_A   kɔ̀m-ɛ̀sɛ̀-n-ɛ̀
        3PL.PN.SP-RSTR [Ø male]   count-BEN.3-EPEN-3PL.SU.IMPERV
        [bíí]_O [íggè-á   [Ø ŋàhà]_RC]_A   kɔ̀m-ɛ̀   [bíí]_O
        REFL   3pl.PN.SP-RSTR [Ø female]   count-3PL.SU.IMPERV REFL
        'Those who are males counsel for themselves, those who are females counsel themselves.' (MCC, 3:03–3:16)

(9.35) a. [k-úlúg-í]_A   [bíí]_O
          1SU-hide-1SG.SU.IMPERV REFL
          'I settled myself.'

The second clause of (9.34) and (9.35a) are typical reflexive construction. But, in two instances, its meaning may be changed into an emphatic reflexive one. The first is due to a coreferential constraint where the invariant reflexive marker *bíí* is preceded by the informative reflexive pronoun (as in (9.35b)).

    b. [k-úlúg-í]   [sabá-á   n=ànù]_O   [bíí]
       1SU-hide-1SG.SU.IMPERV head-RSTR SG.PSD=1SG.PSR REFL
       'I settled myself.'

In (9.35b), the invariable reflexive form *bíí* relates to the informative reflexive pronoun in O slot (*sábáá nànù*) than to the subject, which is shown by bound pronominal A argument marker *k-* or *–i* on the verb. The second instance in which *bíí* changes into emphatic reflexive meaning is due to different factors such as: a valency increasing derivation (benefactive marker *-ɛ̀sɛ̀* in the first clause of 9.34) or when used with intransitive verbs (9.36a–c).

(9.36) a. [érmì]_S ŋàméá wòj-Ø   [bíí]_AUTOREFLEXIVE
       child.SG now move-3SG.SU.IMPERV REFL
       'The child now walks by himself.' (Mützе 2014)

   b. [bàg-ì]_S   [bíí]_AUTOREFLEXIVE
      live-3SG.IRR   REFL
      'He lived by himself'

   c. [kà-bàg-í]_S   [bíí]_AUTOREFLEXIVE
      1SU-live-1SG.SU.IMPERV REFL
      'I live by myself.'

A multi-functional grammaticalized word *bá* may be inserted between the S and the invariant reflexive form *bíí* (as in (9.37)). In this case, *bíí* will be pushed further to a peripheral slot.

(9.37) [kà-bàg-í]_S   bá   [bíí]_AUTOREFLEXIVE
       1SU-live-1SG.SU.IMPERV place/by   REFL
       'I'm living by myself'.

The subject of a reflexive construction could be an NP modified by a relative clause. The meaning is not altered, i.e. genuine reflexive (9.38).

(9.38) àggè kɔ̀m-á=ná   ŋà=kɔ́ɔ́d̚-ɛ̀sɛ̀n=ó]   [zùw-á
       1PL knee-PL=DEF NEG=1SU.stab-1/2.BEN=NEG people-RSTR
       [Ø k-èlè   ké   dòŋà]_RC]_S bíí
       [Ø PASS-call.PERV QUOT   dhonga   REFL
       'We (inc.) don't bow to the people who call themselves 'Dhonga'.'
       (Lit. 'We don't stab knees')

9.3   Valency-Increasing Derivations

In the subsequent sections, valency increasing derivations are discussed in detail.

9.3.1   *Benefactive-Applicative*
The benefactive-applicative (or one can call it 'dative-applicative') increases the valency of either an intransitive or a transitive verb. The benefactive-applicative derivation adds an O argument to an underlying intransitive clause and forms a derived transitive clause.

VALENCY CHANGING OPERATIONS 421

TABLE 9.3 Benefactive-applicative suffixes

Benefactive suffix	Person	Semantic role
-sèn [-èsèn]	For all persons	beneficiary or recipient
-sɛ [-ɛsɛ]	3rd persons, positive imperative, and rarely with hortative/jussive forms	

The examples below illustrate the way in which the benefactive-applicative derivation is applied. In transitive benefactive constructions, the beneficiary or recipient may be shown explicitly by the new incoming O argument (as in (9.39)) or shown by the bound benefactive-applicative suffixes (as in (9.40–9.41)).

(9.39) [dàdá-čo-a   g=àw]_{NP:A}   án-á
       father.PERT.1.PSR-PL-RSTR PL.PSD=1PL.EXC.PSR COP.IMPER-TEMP
       bè   kɔ́d-ésén-è-à   [ŋà=kútúl=á]_O
       DIST.PAST   stab-BEN.3-APPL-3PL.SU.PERV DEM=mountain=NEAR
       kɔ̀mà
       knee.PL
       'Our (exc.) fathers worshipped on this mountain.'

(9.40) [bá-á   [bùràn-á   isirael-i]_{NP}]_{NP} dǎkákán]_{NP:O}
       place-RSTR camp-RSTR Israel-GEN   all
       [ŋà=bóns-èsèn=ó]_A
       NEG.IMPERV=arrive-1/2.BEN=2PL.SU.IMPERV.NEG
       'You (sg.) will not reach for/to all the cities of Israel.'

(9.41) àŋè k-ár-á   dòŋuj   báns-áná
       1SG 1SU-see.PERV-1SG.SU.PERV vulture.SG rise-MT.3SG.SU.IMPERV
       bà-ì   nà   bán-ésé-á   [dórí-á
       place-LOC CCN fly-BEN/DAT.3-3SG.SU.PERV house-RTSR
       n=ènè]_{NP}
       SG.PSD=3SG.PSR
       'I saw a vulture rise from the ground and fly to its nest.'

In (9.39), in addition to the benefactive-applicative suffix -ɛsɛ, it takes the applicative/comitative marker -ɛ, which is another verb valency increasing derivational marker. The co-occurrence of the two valency increasing derivations on a single intransitive verb may result in the structural meaning of 'they worshipped on their own, on the mountain'.

(9.42) [k-òg]   ná   [kɔ́ɔ́d-ɛ̀sé]_A   kɔ̀mà
       1.HORT-go.PERV CCN   1.HORT.stab.PERV-BEN   knee.PL
       'I may come and worship him.'

(9.43) [rìɩ̀-a   rès-ɛ̀-ɲ]_NP   bón-ɛ̀sɛ̀-Ø
       shade-RSTR die.IMPERV-NOMZ-GEN]   get.up-BEN.3-3SG.IRR
       [hɔ́l-ín-ɔ]_A
       light-N.S-NOM
       'The shadow of death, a light arose upon them.'

Most frequently, independent personal pronouns are optional as subjects and are usually shown by the bound pronominal suffixes attached to the verb. In other words, subjects of the intransitive clauses can be recoverable from the person/subject markers expressed by bound pronominal suffixes on the verb. But when the A argument is an NP, it cannot be an optional constituent. But, when the A argument is an NP instead of a pronoun, it usually be specified fully.

(9.44) dóólá   kó   ràmàn   áw-ò-ni   jàg-t-ɛ̀sɛ̀
       girl.PL   CRD:PART   two   come.PERV-3PL.IRR-RS   return-PL-3.BEN
       zùw-á   [Ø wágá   ké   bú
       people-RSTR   [Ø ANA:REF   QUOT   be_big
       kí-bir-ɛ̀sɛ̀n-a   ólʃó]_RC   ké   bárá-ni
       1SU-collect-1/2.BEN-1PL.INC.SU.PERV   stalk.PL]   QUOT   Bara.PL-RS
       'Two among the girls will come and go back to those the elders to whom we collect the sorghum stalks called Bara.' (KW 1:38:5)

In (9.44), we see benefactive markers being applied on both intransitive (jàg 'return') and transitive (bír 'collect') verbs. Yet, as discussed below, we shall see how the benefaction derivation applies to transitive verbs.

A benefactive applicative derivation can also raise the number of arguments of a transitive verb by one more argument and can turn it into a ditransitive verb. In a ditransitive benefactive construction, the beneficiary or recipient is one for whom the action is being done. In other words, syntactically, in clauses containing benefactive-driven ditransitive verb forms, a new O argument is will be introduced in addition to the existing original O argument (Mütze 2014).

(9.45) a. [àɲè]_A k-ér-á   [mà]_O
       1SG   1SU-pour-1SG.SBJ.PERV water
       'I pour water.'

   b. [àɲè]_A k-ér-ésén   [hùlè]_O1 [mà]_O2
      1SG   1SU-pour-1/2.BEN flower   water
      'I am watering the flowers.'
      (Lit. I pour water for the (benefit of) flower.)

(9.46) a. [nɔ̀ŋ]_A číb-Ø   [búŋái]_O
       3SG   tie.IMPERV-3SG.SU.IMPERV bull.SG
       'He ties the bull.'

   b. [nɔ̀ŋ]_A číb-èsèn-Ø   [lúsì]_O1 [búŋái]_O2
      3SG   tie.IMPERV-BEN-3SG.SU.IMPERV (boy)   bull.SG
      'He ties the bull for the boy.' (~ He ties the bull for someone else.)

As it can be shown in (9.45–9.46), like in a prototypical applicative derivation that applies to an underlying transitive clause (Mursi's version 'comitative /applicative'), in Mursi the benefactive applicative derivation in a transitive clause seems to apply the same way because the underlying A argument stays as is (cf. Dixon and Aikhenvald 2000: 14). The underlying O argument will be moved out from its primacy slot and be placed in a secondary O (O_2) slot following the new O (O_1) argument. Thus, hùlè and lúsì can be called the new direct objects while mà and búŋái become the new indirect objects.

When the benefactive suffix is used in a dative function, the direct object remain as is, as in (9.48 and 9.49).

(9.47) [nɔ̀ŋ]_A kɔ́d-á   [wàrkátì]_O
       3SG   write-3SG.SU.PERV paper
       'He wrote a letter.'

(9.48) [nɔ̀ŋ]_A kɔ́d-èsèn [wàrkátì]_DO [nɔ̀ŋ]_IO
       3SG   write-BEN paper   3SG
       'He wrote a letter to him.'

(9.49) [nɔ̀ŋ]_A géɲ-èsèn [érʃá]_DO [nɔ̀ŋ]_IO
3SG repair/create-BEN traditional.bed 3SG
'He made a bed for him.'

Syntactically, in many instances, although it is not possible to increase the valency of the verb without showing the newly added argument, in Mursi, it is possible to increase valency in such a way as long as the benefactive marker suffix is attached to the verb. For example, from the clauses in (9.47–9.49), one can easily understand or imply that there are beneficiaries/recipients (the participants whom the actions are being done for) even if the indirect objects are absent.

9.3.2 Applicative/Comitative

Applicative is the second productive valency increasing derivation in Mursi. Intransitive and Transitive Mursi verbs can enter into applicative derivation. Thus, a typical applicative derivation in Mursi applies to an underlying intransitive clause or transitive clause by attaching the applicative marking suffixes shown in Table 9.4 to verbs.

The -čV appears to be a phonologically conditioned morphological shape where the V is the vowel of the consonant-initial verb root.

When an applicative derivation is applied to an underlying intransitive clause, the argument in underlying S function goes into A function; whereas when it is applied to an underlying transitive clause, the argument in A function stays as is (cf. Dixon 2012: 13–14). In underlying intransitive clauses, the peripheral argument which occurs with the oblique case remains as it is in its peripheral position. The peripheral argument will not be promoted to an AP-O argument, instead a new argument will be introduced as an AP-O argument in O function. In underlying intransitive clauses, peripheral arguments which always occur with oblique cases, remain in their position, and will not be promoted to an AP-O argument, as in (9.50–9.51).

(9.50) a. [kúún-í]_S [mákkò-jé]_PERIPHERAL
1SU.come.IMPERV-1SG.SU.IMPERV Mákkí-OBL
'I came from Mákkí.'

b. [kúún-é]_A [ʃíg-á]_O [mákkò-jé]
1SU.come.IMPERV-APPL:COM hear-NOMZ Mákkí-OBL
'I bring what I heard from Mákkí.'
(Lit. 'I come-with the hearing from Maki.')

TABLE 9.4 Applicative/comitative suffixes

Applicative suffix	Person	Semantic role/function
-ɛ	for all persons	comitative, reason
-čo	for 1st plural exclusive, 2nd person plural	comitative, reason
-čV ([-ča], [-či])	rarely and unpredictably	comitative, reason

(9.51) a. [àggè]_S kó-hóɲ-ó   [gàf-ɔ̀]_{PERIPHERAL}
          1PL   1SU-come.IMPERV-1PL.EXC.SU.IMPERV forest-OBL
          'We (excl) came from the forest.'

   b. [àggè]_A kó-hóɲ-čò   [kìɔ̀]_O
          1PL   1SU-come.1PL.IMPERV-APPL:COM.1PL.EXC.SU wood
          [gàf-ɔ̀]_{PERIPHERAL}
          forest-OBL
          'We (inc.) bring wood from the forest.'
          (Lit. 'We came-with wood from the forest.')

In (9.50b) and (9.50b), the nominal fígá 'hearing' and kìɔ̀ 'wood' are the new AP-O 'applicative arguments' but they were not stated in the underlying intransitive clauses (9.50a and 9.51a).

In other types of constructions, the sociative marker kàrì 'together' is a marker of accompaniment or joint action, as discussed in (§ 9.2.3). In (9.52) below, kàrì expresses the same function, a 'joint action'. The example below is given for clarification purpose to avoid a possible semantic ambiguity which may arise between the comitative applicative derivation and the sociative marker kàrì.

(9.52) ìggè ŋà=hóɲ-čo
        2PL NEG.IMPERV=COME.PL.IMPERV-APPL:COM.2PL.SU+NEG
        [màì=gù-á[2]   g=ùj]   kàrì   nà
        husband=PERT.PL.2.PSR-RSTR PL.PSD=2PL.PSR together CCN

---

2 Note that 'husband' cannot be possessed inalienably, but it can be marked by pertensive morphology since there is a separate possessive pronoun that follows it.

> *hóɲ-n-ó*   *búná (màt-ínèn)?*
> come.PL.IMPERV-EPEN-2PL.SU.IMPERV coffee (drink-NOMZ)
> 'Won't you (pl.) bring your husbands with you (pl.) and come for coffee?'
> (Lit. 'Won't you (pl.) come together with your husbands and come for coffee (drinking)?')

We recall that the syntactic position of negated verbs within negated clauses are clause final. But in (9.52), the predicate, which is marked by the applicative comitative derivational suffix *-čo*, has to occur in a canonical constituent order, i.e. preceding the applicative argument in O function (*màigùá gùj* 'your (pl.) husbands'). Likewise, question clauses containing derived applicative arguments will always follow the canonical constituent order, as in (9.52).

(9.53)   *àhì-tí*   [Ø *hín-í*   *sé*
        thing.SG-NRSTR [Ø want-2SG.SU.IMPERV say.COMPL
        óg-ɛ́=jè]_{SUBORD/RC:CL}   [*kóná*]_{CS} *á*   *ɔ̀ŋ*]_{CC}?
        go-APPL:COM-SUBORD another COP.3.IMPERV what?
        'What else do you (sg.) want to take along?'
        (Lit. 'A thing that you want to go-with—(another) is what?')

In (9.52), either the copula subject or the entire copular clause can be a syntactic slot for placing an applicative argument.

A prototypical derived applicative clause in Mursi involves a subject argument of a derived applicative clause (A), an object argument a derived applicative clause (AP-O), and the original object argument of the underlying transitive clause (O).

(9.54)   a.   [*nɔ̀ŋ*]_A *nìs-Ø*   [*bì*]_O
           3SG   kill-3SG.SU.IMPERV cow
           'He kills a cow.'

       b.   [*nɔ̀ŋ*]_A *nìs-Ø-ɛ́*   [*dòòlèj*]_{AP.O} [*bì*]_O
           3SG   kill-3sg.SU.IMPERV-APPL:RES girl   cow
           'He kills a cow because of the girl.' (~because he wants to marry her)

Once the applicative derivation has taken place, as Dixon (2012: 296) puts it, the derived applicative remains transitive; and the argument in the underlying A function (as in (9.54a)) stays as is in the applicative (as in (9.54b)). However, with regard to the new applicative argument (AP-O), Mursi follows what Dixon called 'quasi-applicative derivation'. That is, unlike in a canonical applicative derivation, the new applicative argument (AP-O) will not appear in the underlying transitive clause. In (9.54b), the new applicative argument dòòlèj 'girl' is introduced because the applicative marker -ɛ (has a semantic role of 'reason') attached to the transitive verb nìs. Therefore, the original O, bì 'cow', may be treated as secondary object. Additional examples were given as follows:

(9.55) [kɔ́-dɔ́g-Ø-ɛ́]_A   [bá]_AP-O   ké
       1SU-tread.on.IMPERV-1PL.INC.SU.IMPERV-APPL place/land QUOT
       [dol=ŋà]_O
       Dol=DEF
       'We (inc.) tread on (walked on) the land called the Dòl.' (MH 0:06:6–0:17:6)

The semantics of the underlying transitive clause in (9.55) could be 'We (inc.) arrived at Dòl'. It is the applicative derivation, which is attached to the verb in a transitive reading ('arrive') that caused the new AP-O argument to come into the original O argument slot. Since the quotative marker functions as a complementizer, the original O argument has the status of a complement clause, but it cannot be omitted. In (9.56), it is an instance in which two different valency changing derivations are taking place on a single transitive verb simultaneously: passive and applicative.

(9.56) [mádání-á   n=àj]_NP
       medicine-RSTR SG.PSD=1PL.INC.PSR
       kà-dàg-Ø-čà   ŋɔ̀dɔ̀rì á
       PASS-hit-PASS.1PL.INC.OBJ-APPL.COM wound COP.3.IMPERV
       lómáj   hékɔ́   ŋà=mádání=tá   ŋàméá ádʒ-á
       Loma.SG similar DEM=medicine=NEAR now   give-3SG.SU.IMPERV
       máŋísí-ó
       government-NOM
       'Our (inc.) medicine. (When) we (inc.) are struck (with) a wound, it is Lomay; similar with the medicine that the Government is giving now.' (MH 9:03:9)

As we can see in (9.56), the passive derivation decreases the valency of the verb dáǵ 'hit' from two to one whereas the applicative-comitative derivation increases from one to two. There is no agent involved in (9.56) because the construction is an agentless passive type in the first place. Thus, ŋɔ̀dɔ̀rì neither takes an instrumental marker (the verb is already markerd with comitative), nor shows the multi-functional grammaticalized agentive marker nominal *bá* 'place' > 'by' (it is an agentless construction). In other words, the valency of the verb remains as is, i.e. transitive.

9.3.3 *Causative*

Causative is another valency increasing derivation in Mursi. Causative derivation in Mursi as well as in other Surmic group languages is not productive, although it is not absent as Dimmendaal (1983: 302) claims. He claimed that the causative prefix **I/i* is found in Proto-Nilotic and in other Nilo-Saharan languages, but this seems to be absent in the closest relatives of the Nilotic group, i.e. the Surmic group. Contrary to this, Unseth (1997: 41) claimed that this causative prefix is still found in at least three languages (and probably more) Surmic languages namely: Me'en, Murle and Majang. Here, I would add Mursi as the fourth Surmic group language that has not only a causative prefix but also a causative suffix. Thus, the causative derivation in Mursi can be shown by morphological markers circumfixed directly to the verb, i.e. *í- ... ísi*. Rarely can it be shown by the prefix *í-* alone.

In addition, the causative suffix *-ísí* has three allomorphs: *-ísí* following consonant-final verb roots; *-sí* following vowel-final, fricative/liquid/nasal-final verb roots, and *-s* for some verb classes to be identified.

Syntactic function of the causative application in Mursi is to derive a transitive clause by applying morphological causative derivational markers to an underlying intransitive clause. As Dixon (2012: 240) described it, the argument in underlying S argument goes into O function in the causative. A new argument (also known as the causer) is introduced in A function.

(9.57) a. [*bón-á*]$_S$
leave/exit-3SG.SU.PERV
'S/he/it left.'

b. [*nɔ̀ŋ*]$_A$ *í-bón-sí-ú*   [*sátíní bú-sísí-ó*]$_{NP:O}$
3SG   CAUS-leave-CAUS-3sg.SU.PERV box   big-AUG-RSTR:MOD
[*tútúg-á   tííní-ó*]$_{NP}$
door-RSTR small-RSTR:MOD
'He eased the big box through the narrow door.'
(Lit. 'He caused the big box to leave through the narrow door.')

TABLE 9.5 Causative suffixes

Causative affix(es)	Morphophonemic rules
í- ... -ísí	verb roots carrying a and o as their first vowels
í- ... (-Ø)	prefixed on any non-vowel-initial verb roots; the suffixed -ísí is absent following stop-final verb roots
V- ... -ísí	complete vowel assimilation; following the first vowel of the verb root regardless of vowel-/consonant-initial status of the verb root—but only for verb roots carrying ɛ and u vowels.

    c. [hír-á   tímírtí-j]_{NP:A} í-ɓón-sí-ú
       man-RSTR teacher-GEN CAUS-leave.PERV-CAUS-3SG.SU.PERV
       [éró-á   sáɓ-í   gɛ̀rs-à]_{NP:O}
       children-RSTR head-PL bad.STV-RSTR
       'The teacher weeded out the students of bad character.'
       (Lit. 'caused leave')

(9.58) a. [bán-á]_S
       get.up-3SG.SU.PERV
       'S/he/it get up/wake up.'

    b. [ɔ̀g]_A í-bán-sí-ú   [érmì]_O
       noise CAUS-wake.up-CAUS-3SG.SU.PERV child.SG
       'The noise woke up the child.'

(9.59) a. [bás-Ø-ɔ̀]_S
       cure/heal-3sg.SU.IMPERV-VFS
       'S/he/it is cured/healed.'

    b. [jesusi]_A í-bá-ísí-ú   [hírí]_O
       Jesus CAUS-cure/heal-CAUS-3SG.SU.PERV man
       rɛ̀ɛ̀   sórálí
       body+PERT.SG.3.PSR reddish-brown_with_white_at_center
       'Jesus healed a man with leprosy.'
       (Lit. 'Jesus healed a man, his body reddish-brown with white.')

As it is shown in the examples above, arguments in the underlying S function are shown by bound pronominal arguments. They can only be known when they are being caused to go into O function in the causative constructions. Accordingly, the S of (9.57a) can be either *sátíní búsísíó* 'big box' (9.58b) or *éróá sábí gèrsà* 'students of bad character' (9.57c). The S of (9.58a) and (9.59a) are *èrmì* and *hírí* consecutively. One important point that I noticed from the causative derivation examples illustrated above is that it seems to be the case that the third person bound pronominal marker -*a* usually marks the S of an intransitive clause whereas the -*u* marks the A of a transitive clause.

In addition, both the causer (A) and the causee (O) arguments in the clause can be cross-referenced on the verb, as in (9.60).

(9.60) a. bàrì   [bón-á]_S
           yesterday leave.PERV-3SG.SU.PERV
           'He left yesterday.'

   b. bàrì   í-bón-sí-óɲ-Ø-ó
      yesterday CAUS-leave.PERV-CAUS-1SG.OBJ-3SG.SU.IMPERV-VFS
      'He made me leave yesterday.'

   c. ŋà=k-í-bón-sí-Ø-í=ó
      NEG.IMPERV=1SU-CAUS-leave-CAUS-3SG.OBJ-1SG.SU.IMPERV=NEG
      dóg
      never
      'I will in no wise cast him out.'
      (Lit. 'I will never cause him leave/exit out.')

In (9.60), following the absence of a morphological form for the third person object marker, the high front vowel of the causative suffix and the first person subject marker suffix -*i* have coalesced, which otherwise appear very similar to the structure ⟨ŋà=k-í-bon-sí=ó⟩.

The O argument of the causative clause may be semantically implied or can be retrievable from the context. Above all, the verb *táb* 'deceive/lie' has a 'labile' (A-S) nature on its own.

(9.61) a. [táb-á]_S
           deceive/lie-3SG.SU.PERV
           'He deceived/he told a lie.'

b. *í-táb-Ø*
CAUS-deceive/lie-3SG.SU.IMPERV
'He deceived (someone).'

In order to show both the causer and the causee, one has to move the causee to a peripheral argument slot, as in (9.61c).

c. [*hírí*] *í-táb-Ø* [*ménéɲí-ɔ̀*]
man CAUS-deceive/lie-3SG.SU.IMPERV spirit-OBL
'Man is tempted by Satan.'
(Lit. 'Devil deceived man.')

As mentioned earlier (see morphophonemic rule(s) in Table 9.5), the complete vowel assimilation rule often applies to verb roots whose first syllable carry /ɛ/ and /u/ vowels. In fact, the morphophonemic (the complete vowel assimilation) rule is similar to vowel height harmony. For example, the causative marker prefix *í-* assimilates to [ɛ] (9.62a) and to [u] (9.62b).

(9.62) a. *ɛ́dɛ̆mɩ́ɔ́* 'learn' *ɛ́dɛ̆mɛ́s-sí* 'teach; cause to learn'
b. *súr* 'burn (intr.)' *úsúr-sí* 'cause to burn (tr.)'

Following this particular morphophonemic-driven assimilation process that happens due to the formal morphological technique for deriving a causative construction, it is plausible to imagine that such morphophonological process/rule (e.g. vowel height harmony) could have contributed to the obsolete old causative prefix *ɪ-/í-. Furthermore, as far as other Surmic group languages is concerned and my understanding of the language I worked on for some years (Mursi), such morphophonological process not only contributed to obsolescence or archaism of this prefix but also to the emergence of many verbs whose underlying intransitive forms (non-causative) later became V-initial verbs (with causative meanings).

9.3.4 *Directional/Motion Markers*

Mursi has two morphological directional/motion markers: ventive (motion towards the deictic center/source) and itive (motion away from the deictic center/source). Consequently, ventive and itive markers can be attached to intransitive verb roots (often motion verbs) to derive transitive clauses. In many instances, the itive that specifies motion directed away from the speaker adds a new argument in O function (semantically, it refers to 'goal'). The ventive marker which offers the notion of movement towards the point of reference to the semantics of the verb occasionally also adds a new argument.

TABLE 9.6   Directional/motion suffixes

Suffix	Person/number	Aspect	Motion
-áná/ -ónó	1st person plural (inc.) and 3rd person singular	imperfective	ventive (motion towards speaker)
-án/ -ón	for all other persons other than 1st person plural (inc.) and 3rd person singular	imperfective	ventive (motion towards speaker)
-a/-o	for all persons	perfective	ventive (motion towards speaker)
-sèn	for all persons	imperfective	itive (motion away from speaker)
-sɛ	for all persons	perfective	itive (motion away from speaker)

Note that the itive marker is the same as the benefactive marker. The suffix *-sèn* can be called a 'multi-functional' suffix which is more often used as benefactive marker (as in (§ 9.3.1)), as index of comparison in comparative constructions (see Chapter 11; 'comparative-benefactive'), and as dative marker (as secondary semantics of benefactive).

Directional/motion suffixes often occur with intransitive motion verbs such as *gol* 'crawl', *ŋɔw* 'recede; go down; drop', *jag* 'return', and so on.

(9.63)   [érmì]_A   gól-èsén   [kìɔ̀]_O
         child   crawl-MA   tree
         'The child crawled away towards the tree.'

In (9.64), the child crawled from here to down there (to the tree). Thus, the itive is a derivational marker used to intoduce a new argument in O function. The tree is an O argument. In the absense of the itive marker, it could be a simple intransitive clause syntax and it could have the meaning of 'The child crawled'. Compare example (9.64a) with (9.64b–c):

(9.64)   a.   [kɔ́-ŋɔ́w-án-ɔ́]_S
              1SU-go.down.IMPERV-MT.1SG.SU.IMPERV-VFS
              'I will fall.'

         b.   kɔ́-ŋɔ́-sèn   [báhùn]
              1SU-go.down-MA.1SG.SU.IMPERV   cliff
              'I will fall (down there) off the cliff.' (someone standing on a cliff)

c. [bàlógì]   ŋɔ́-sèn   [bá]
   leaf.SG   go.down-MA.3SG.SU.IMPERV   ground
   'The leaf fell away towards the ground.'

The ventive marker attached to the verb in (9.64a) does not change the valency of the verb, but when the itive marker is attached to the same intransitive verb (as in (9.64b–c)), it derives a transitive clause. In (9.64a), the speaker is the deictic center, where, the action referred to by the verb terminates. In (9.64b), the speaker is doing a motion which requires changing his/her deictic center (source) to another deictic center (goal). The instance in (9.64a) doesn't mean that the ventive marker never changes the valency of the verb. For example, in the example shown below (repeated from 9.41), the ventive marker attached to the underlying intransitive verb of the first clause has an argument in O function, i.e. bà 'ground'.

(9.65) àɲè   k-ár-á   dòŋuj   báns-áná
        1SG   1SU-see.PERV-1SG.SU.PERV   vùlture.SG rise-MT.3SG.SU.IMPERV
        bà-ì   nà   bán-ésé-á   [dórí-á
        place-LOC   CCN fly-BEN/DAT.3-3SG.SU.PERV   house-RTSR
        n=ɛ̀nɛ̀]_NP
        SG.PSD=3SG.PSR
        'I saw a vulture rise from the ground and fly to its nest.'

The same applies to the second clause. In second clause, the itive (motion away) marker -sɛ (or -ɛsɛ on consonant-final verb roots) adds a new argument in O function ⟨dória nènè⟩ and the intransitive clause is changed to a transitive one. Some examples are given below illustrating the use of ventive marker in the valency increasing derivation. The examples in (9.66 and 9.68) were taken from Mütze (2014).

(9.66) [lúsì]_A   ɔ́g-áná   [bì]_O   [kìɔ̀]_IO
        boy   untie-MT.3SG.SU.IMPERV cow.SG   tree.SG
        'The boy unties the cow from the tree.'

(9.67) [nɔ̀ŋ]_A   jàg-áná   [ískírító-á n=ànù]_NP:O
        3SG   return-MT.3SG.SU.IMPERV   pen-RSTR   SG.PSD=1SG.PSR
        'He returned my pen.'

(9.68) [jàg-án]_A   [bè]_O
        return-MT.2SG.SU.IMPERV   axe.SG
        'You (sg.) return the axe.'

As it is shown in these examples, the ventive, even if it is not a productive valency changing mechanism in the language, it still used on intransitive verbs to increase their valents from one to two. It is also important to take into account that these directional/motion suffixes do not always co-occur with motion verbs. For example, motion verbs such as 'come' and 'go' are among those that rarely co-occur with directional/motion marking suffixes.

CHAPTER 10

Grammatical Relations

10.1 Introduction

Grammatical relations in Mursi are marked by constituent order and case. According to Dixon (1994: 63ff.) and König (2006: 657f.) Mursi is a multilayered language in that it utilizes a constituent order AVO/SV (neither the A nor the S arguments can be unmarked for nominative case) and the OVA/VS order in which post-verbal A and S arguments are for marked-nominative case. However, case-marking is often employed depending on the constituent order system of the language. Mursi is a nominative-accusative language. Although Mursi utilizes case-marking, it is also a head-marking language that has cross-referencing bound pronominal forms to indicate grammatical relations. As a head-marking language, it has participant reference markings on the verb which predominantly indicate grammatical relations. This operates by indexing bound pronominal A and O argument affixes on the verb. In clauses with ditransitive verbs, argument indexing on the verb often operates according to referential prominence scale hierarchy and verb-adjacency constraint principles.

There is no single rigid and imperative approach of analyzing the relations of constituents within individual languages from multiple but plausible morphological, syntactic and semantic approaches. This is often possible, however, if and only if the analysis make sense for a particular instance such as to indicate relation of constituents within a clause. And above all, if the analysis conforms to the basic grammatical properties of the language under description. While the treatment of case marking strategy in Mursi largely depends on syntax, the discourse prominence of arguments such as animacy and definiteness are indispensable tools that enable us to understand the way in which pronouns and nouns function in clauses.

For example, free pronouns in the S or A function of the canonical constituent order SV/AVO will in no way be marked for case, nor will it trigger any morphological markings which may indicate the relation of constituents in a clause, whereas in a non-canonical OVA/VS constituent order, pronouns in S/A are marked for nominative case, thus now encode further pragmatic function, i.e. focus/topic. For example, in a copular clause, the first person plural pronoun in CS function precedes the copula verb, as is always the case in the canonical order—*àggè kánó* 'We (exc.) are'. Or to turn this into a question clause, the copula verb should be moved to a clause initial position, i.e. *kánó àggè?* 'Are we?'. But, to put the focus on the CS, the same pronoun but in nominative case form will be inserted between the copular verb and the unmarked form pronoun, as in (10.1).

(10.1) k-án-ó   àggè-ò   àggè?
       1SU-COP.IMPERV-1PL.EXC.SU 1PL-NOM 1PL
       'Who are *we*?'

Since the copula verb is now at clause initial position, the marked-nominative pronoun is in line with the principle of "case after the verb", in contrast to "no case before the verb".

For what appear to be due to the morphosyntactic and pragmatic interaction of constituents in the non-canonical order, post-verbally Mursi nominals in marked-nominative case form can often function as either topical-S or topical-A.

In this chapter, among many, are two major topics which have been discussed in detail, each of them are typologically rare and could perhaps be typical features of Mursi. These are Noun Modification Construction and marked-nominative case. The noun modification construction system of Mursi is the bearer of genitive case, whereas the locus of marked-nominative case and other grammatical cases that mark both core and non-core constituents is in the canonical and non-canonical constituent orders. Thus this chapter of grammatical relations shall present various morphosyntactic topics which particularly deals with constituent order (§10.2), case marking (§10.3), postpositions (§10.4), and verb-final suffix (§10.5).

10.2 Constituent Order

Mursi has three types of constituent order: canonical AVO/SV, non-canonical OVA/VS where the A/S is marked with morphological marked-nominative case suffixes, and non-canonical OAV (a somewhat a strict constituent order of negation). With respect to grammatical relations, each is dealt with in subsequent sub-sections below.

10.2.1 *Canonical Order (AVO/SV)*
In a canonical constituent order AVO/SV, A precedes the verb and O follows it. AVO/SV is by far the most frequently found constituent order in Mursi clauses uttered in isolation. Thus, non-case involving grammatical relations of the A

and the O in transitive clauses are marked by this constituent order. In canonical order, both nominative and accusative cases are not marked morphologicaly and formally. The subject position may be filled by any NP in citation form.

(10.2) SV—intransitive clause
    a. [nɔ̀ŋ]_S dɔ́t-Ø-ɔ̀
        3SG   leave-3SG.SU.IMPERV-VFS
        'S/he is about to leave.'
        (Lit. 'S/he is leaving.')

    b. [nɔ̀ŋ]_S túŋ-ú
        3SG   sleep.PERV-3SG.SU.PERV
        'S/he slept.'

Interestingly, as can be shown in (10.2a), the verb-final suffix -ɔ̀ is the morphological marker that shows the canonicity of this constituent order and is often added to an intransitive verbs in the imperfective aspect. However, this suffix is absent when the verb is in the perfective aspect or when manner modifiers and oblique arguments follow the intransitive imperfective verb—compare the examples given below (10.2c–e).

    c. [lúsì]_S bɔ̀rɔ́t-Ø-ɔ̀
        boy   jump-3SG.SU.IMPERV-VFS
        'The boy jumps.'

    d. [nɔ̀ŋ]_S bɔ̀rɔ́t-ú   čùmùn-ò
        3SG   jump-PERV-3SG.SU.PERV happy.STV-MN
        'He jumped cheerfully.'

    e. [nɔ̀ŋ]_S bɔ̀rɔ́t-ú   tùm-ɔ̀
        3SG   jump-PERV-3SG.SU.PERV sky-OBL
        'S/he jumps up.'
        (Lit. 'He jumps towards the sky.')

Mursi marks both S and A in the same way on the verb. Like the S of an intransitive clause, any NP constituent can be in A position. The fact is that pronouns, proper nouns or common nouns in both A and O functions normally occur in citation form in the AVO constituent order. But, with regard to constituents that can fill the O position, there are at least certain distinctions between pronouns and proper/common nouns.

But before we go into these details, there are three crucial points that we should take into consideration when cross-referencing bound pronominal (A and O) arguments on verbs.

(i) The first person plural inclusive and third person singular bound pronominal A argument markers have zero suffix realizations on verbs in the imperfective aspect.

(ii) The third person singular and plural bound pronominal O argument markers have always zero suffix realizations on verbs in imperfective and perfective aspects,

(iii) When the bound pronominal of the A arguments from (i) and bound Pronominal of the O argument from (ii) co-occur on a verb, they are marked by no (two zero) suffixes.

By giving these clarifying notes of the bound pronominal (A, O) argument markers, we now shall see how arguments in the monotransitive clause of the AVO constituent order are marked. Thus, apart from those mentioned in (i–iii), all bound pronominal suffixes that cross-reference S/A and O arguments have a non-zero realizations.

In AVO constituent order, whenever the subject occurs before the verb (pre-verbal), both the subject and the object that follows the verb are treated as an unmarked nominative and unmarked accusative case. By an unmarked case, we mean morphologically and functionally unmarked, as shown below in (10.3a–d).

(10.3) AVO—monotransitive clause

a. [nɔ̀ŋ]_A čúg-ú   [zìnî]_O
   3SG   chase.away-3SG.SU.PERV thief
   'S/he chased (away) the thief.'

b. [hólísój]_A mák-ú   [zìnî]_O
   police   grab-3SG.SU.PERV thief
   'The policeman arrested the thief.'

c. [hólísój]_A ódʒ-Ø-é   [zìnî]_O [màlk-ɔ̀]_OBL
   police   shoot-3SG.SU.IMPERV-APPL thief   animal.snare-OBL
   'The police set a trap for the thief.'

d. [hírí]_A dɔ́t-ú   [zùw-á   ɔ́r-á
   man   leave-3SG.SU.PERV people-RSTR home-RSTR
   g=ɛ̀ɲɛ̀]_NP:O
   PL.PSD=3SG.PSR
   'The man abandoned his family.'

In (10.3c), since oblique case does not mark core argument, it is easy to know the direct object. The O NP in (10.3d) does not take any marking in relation to accusative case. As a head-marking language, syntactic function of core arguments can be shown by cross-referencing bound pronominal suffixes on the verb. As can be shown in (10.3a–d), a bound pronominal suffix of one core argument is being cross-referenced on the predicate, i.e. A. This is due to the fact that the referential status of the O NPs in (10.3a–d) are common nouns. So when compared to first/second or even to third person pronouns, it is natural to see common nouns in O function rather than in A (Dixon 1994: 85). Mursi is a language that has a strict rule of 'no case before the verb' (König 2008:247). Although core constituents occur in S, A or O syntactic function in SV/AVO order, no change will occur with respect to case marking.

(10.4) a. [zùwò]_S múkt-έ   nà   kὲ-mὲz-ì
       people gather.PERV-3.RECIP CCN PASS-discuss.PERV-3.IRR
       lɔ̀gɔ́
       word/issue
       'The people gathered and discussed the matter.'

   b. [kirtosi]_A í-bá-ísí   [zùwò]_O
      jesus   CAUS-cure/heal.IMPERV-CAUS people
      'Christ saves people.'

There is however a difference when first and second person free pronouns are used in O function. First and second person singular free pronouns are more definite than third person pronoun singular, which is also used as a dummy/impersonal pronoun. At the same time, first and second person free pronouns have bound pronominal suffixes which look like shortened forms of these free pronouns. Moreover, Dixon (1994: 95) noted that there is a tendency for cross-referencing systems to be normally pronominal, which have developed from free-form pronouns at some early stage of the language. This seems to be true for Mursi, for which the first and second person singular bound pronominal object suffixes -áɲ [-óɲ] ⟨1SG.OBJ⟩ and -iɲ ⟨2SG.OBJ⟩ appear to have evolved from àɲè 'I/me' and iɲè 'you (sg.)'. Note that both the third person free pronouns have no such bound pronominal morphological suffixes to cross-reference third person O arguments on the verb.

When first and second person pronouns are in O function in AVO order, as can be seen in the examples given below, bound pronominal O and A argument markers are attached to the verb. When both subject and object bound pronominal suffixes occur in a transitive clause, the object pronominal suffix always precedes the subject pronominal suffix.

(10.5) AVO—mono-transitive clause
    a. [nɔ̀ŋ]_A téhén-áɲ-ɲó   [ȧɲè]_O
       3SG   want.PERV-1SG.OBJ-3SG.SU.PERV 1SG:ACC
       'S/he wanted *me*.'

    b. [ȧggè]_A bè   k-élíd-íɲ-ɲo
       1PL   DIST.PAST 1SU-call.perv-2SG.OBJ-1PL.EXC.SU.PERV
       [ìɲè]_O
       2SG:ACC
       'We (exc.) had called *you* (sg.).'

    c. [nɔ̀ŋ]_A hín-ùŋ-Ø   [ìggè]_O
       3SG   want.IMPERV-2SG.OBJ-3SG.SU.IMPERV 2PL:ACC
       'S/he wanted *you* (pl.).'

Compare the above examples (10.5a–c) with those given below in (10.6a–b), where we see the third person pronoun in O function having no bound pronominal suffix attached to the verb.

(10.6) a. nɔ̀ŋ wà   dáʃí-á   nɔ̀ŋ
       3SG REC.PAST do-3SG.SU.PERV   3SG
       'S/he has done *it*.'

    b. nɔ̀ŋ wà   ɲànì   ká-dáʃí-á=ó   nɔ̀ŋ
       3SG REC.PAST NEG.PERV   3.SBJV-do-3SG.SU.PERV=NEG   3sg
       'He has not done it.'

In (10.6a), only the perfective bound pronominal suffix -*a* for the third person A argument is cross-referenced on the verb while no bound pronominal marking for the third person O argument is cross-referenced on the verb. Since there is no morphologically bound pronominal marking for the third arguments in O function, the constituent order we see in (10.6b) could be unusual with respect to O slots in negated clauses. Mursi has the non-canonical AOV/SV constituent order for negative clauses, as it is shown in (10.7).

(10.7) [nɔ̀ŋ]_A [sátí]_O ɲà=hín-Ø=ó
       3SG   watch   NEG.IMPERV=want.IMPERV-3SG.SU.IMPERV=NEG
       'He does not want the watch.'

But, due to the absence of a bound pronominal O argument marking morphological form on the verb, the negative clause in (10.6b) has no option but to behave the same way as a clause in the AVO constituent order.

Furthermore, the fact is that most interrogative words in Mursi are pronominal (10.8a) or pro-phrasal (10.8b). They often occur at clause final slot of the AVO canonical order—in O function.

(10.8) a. [i̯nè]_A hín-í   [nèŋ?]_O
       2SG   want.IMPERV-2SG.SU.IMPERV who.OBJ
       'Whom do you want?'
       (Lit. 'You (sg.) want who?')

   b. [jɔ̀g]_A édʒ-é   [ɲàtùɲ]_O [ɔ́nɔ̀ŋɔ́?]_OBL
      3PL   kill-3PL.SU.IMPERV lion   what.OBL
      'With what did they kill the lion?'
      (Lit. 'They killed the lion with what?') (=instrument)

Note that interrogatives in Mursi take all types of case markers that nouns can take (see Chapter 12). However, rhetorical questions could trigger unusual constituent order in the language. An instance of such is unusual constituent order is found in the rhetorical question constructions in which the canonical AVO order become VAO. See the examples given below.

(10.9) a. wà   ár-ú   [nɔ̀ŋ]_A [nɔ̀ŋ?]_O
       REC.PAST see.PERV-3SG.SU.PERV   3SG   3SG
       'Has he seen it?'

In (10.9a), the recent past time particle wá appears at clause-initial position only in rhetorical type questions that require a confirmatory answer 'yes/no'. This is a similar question construction to one used to make a question from a declarative copula construction—just by moving the copula verb into a clause initial position. In the end, the copula subject and copula complement tend to occur side by side, as in (10.9b).

   b. á   [lɔ̀gɔ́]_CS [nɔ̀ŋ]_CC?
      COP.3.IMPERV   word   3SG
      'Is it true?'
      (Lit. 'It this the word?')

Except for specific functions stated above (10.9b), most copula constructions will have a canonical constituent order. Emphasized copula subjects may follow the copula complement, (10.9c).

    c. k-án-í   [mùnì]$_{CC}$ [àɲè]$_{CS}$
       1SU-COP.IMPERV-1SG.SU.IMPERV Mursi.SG 1SG
       'I am Mursi.'

With regard to indicating syntactic relation by bound pronominal cross referencing on the verb, there are a number of exceptions to the generalization. The exceptions include:

A. When independent pronouns are in S/A and O function, verbs are inflected for person and number of the S/A and O arguments. In addition, verbs are inflected for person of the S/A arguments—this takes place in a k(V)- prefix for first person unlike the second and third person S/A arguments.

(10.10) (jɔ̀g)$_A$ dág-áɲ-é   (àɲè)$_O$
        3PL beat-1SG.OBJ-3PL.SU.IMPERV 1SG
        'They beat me.'

B. Independent pronouns in (10.10) are optional unless they are necessarily Required to indicate topicality or focus. Yet they may not be considered as fully optional independent arguments for the reasons stated in (C–F).

C. In the imperfective mono-transitive (rarely ditransitive) clause, when the first person O argument suffix is cross referenced on the verb, second person subject suffix is omitted (10.11a–b). In the perfective mono transitive clauses, both A and O argument suffixes shall be retained (10.11a c).

(10.11) a. (iɲè/iggè)$_A$ jóg-óɲ   [àɲè]$_O$
            2SG/2PL   tell-1SG.OBJ 1SG
            'You (sg./pl.) tell me.'

      b. húllí [jɔ̀g]$_A$ kéŋn-áɲ   [àɲè]$_O$
         if   1PL   deny-1SG.OBJ 1SG
         'If they prevent me.'

(10.12) a. [iɲè]$_A$ tákt-í-ó   [àggè]$_O$ [i+u] > o
            2SG know.PERV-1PL.OBJ-2SG.SU.PERV 1PL
            'You (sg.) knew us.'

b. [nɔ̀ŋ]_A wà   ár-í-ó   [àggè]_O
   3SG   REC.PAST see.PERV-1PL.OBJ-3SG.SU.PERV 1PL
   'S/he has seen us.'

An exception of the imperfective mono-transitive clause statement of (C) has been found, as can be shown below.

c. [jɔ̀g]_A hàlì ɛ́ján-áɲ-ɲɛ́   [ɑ̀ɲè]_O
   3PL   later help-1SG.OBJ-3PL.SU.IMPERV 1SG
   'They will help me.'

D. In the imperfective mono-transitive (rarely ditransitive) clause, when the second person O argument suffix is cross referenced on the verb, first and third person subject suffixes are omitted (10.13a–b).

(10.13) a. k-ór-íɲ   dórí tó-jé
          1SU-see.IMPERV-2SG.OBJ   house in-OBL
          'I see you (sg.) in the house.'

b. [ɑ̀ɲè]_A hàlì k-ɛ́ján-ùŋ-ɛ́   [ìggè]_O
   1SG   later 1SU-help-2PL.OBJ-APPL   2PL
   'I will help you (pl.).'

c. [ɑ̀ɲè]_A hàlì kó-jóg-ó-íɲ   [ìɲè]_O
   1SG   later 1SU-tell-MT-2SG.OBJ   2SG
   'I shall tell you.'

In the examples above, there are two options why the A argument is retained: (i) by the first person prefix kó-, and (ii) by the independent pronoun (a plausible reason why independent pronouns shouldn't be considered as optional constituents). Even if the verb jóg 'tell' in (10.13c) is a ditransitive verb, it does not require a secondary object.

E. In the imperfective mono-transitive clause, the bound pronominal suffixes of the third person singular A argument and both singular and plural bound pronominal suffixes of the O arguments are omitted (10.14a–b). However, the bound pronominal suffix of the A argument can be recovered if the verb is in the perfective aspect (10.15a–b).

(10.14) a. [nɔ̀ŋ]_A mé-Ø-Ø   [nɔ̀ŋ]_O
          3SG   do-3SG.OBJ-3SG.SU.IMPERV 3SG
          'S/he makes it.'

  b. [nɔ̀ŋ]_A hín-∅-∅   [jɔ̀g]_O
    3SG want.IMPERV-3PL.OBJ-3SG.SU.IMPERV 3PL
    'S/he wanted them.'

(10.15) a. [nɔ̀ŋ]_A ʃík-∅-á   [nɔ̀ŋ]_O
    3SG hear-3SG.OBJ-3SG.SU.PERV 3SG
    'S/he heard her/him.'

  b. [jɔ̀g] bè   tɔ́n-∅-á   [jɔ̀g]
    3PL DIST.PAST write.PERV-3PL.OBJ-3PL.SU.PERV 3PL
    'They had written them.'

F. Interestingly, in a ditransitive clause, both bound pronominal suffixes of the A and O arguments may not be even obligatory. This time the third person benefactive suffix -ɛsɛ may be used as dative marker.

(10.16) [jɔ̀g]_A hàlì jóg-ésé [jɔ̀g]_O [dib]_{IO}
   3PL later tell-BEN.3 3PL [truth]
   'They will tell them the truth.'

In addition to what we saw in simple mono-transitive clauses illustrated above, the canonical constituent order AVO may have also various syntactic manifestations in double object or ditransitive clause constructions and in other types of clauses. In order to explain how syntactic relations of the direct and indirect object of a double object or ditransitive clause constructions be recognized, there are certain key points to be taken into account. For instance, in a double object construction, the indirect object or secondary object may be placed at the first post-verbal slot and will have a semantic role of recipient/beneficiary, or it can be moved to a clause-final position in the same semantic role. This can be shown in two ways—(i) when the benefactive applicative suffix -èsèn is attached to the verb in its primary function (benefactive), and (ii) when it is attached to the verb in its secondary function (dative).

  The primacy of one object over another may be based upon person and non-person forms. For example, when the double object construction makes use of the benefactive suffix and if both the objects are non-person forms, the post-verbal adjacency priority is given to the beneficiary, or to the indirect object, as in (10.17).

GRAMMATICAL RELATIONS

(10.17) a. [ḁɲè]_A k-ér-èsèn   [hùlèj]_IO [mà]_O
         1SG   1SU-pour-BEN.IMPERV flower   water
         'I am watering the flowers.'
         (Lit. 'I pour water for the flowers.')

When both person (human) and non-person object forms occur in a clause, the person form O will be left-adjacent to the verb but it can also be optional as long as semantically implied.

   b. [nɔ̀ŋ]_A číb-èsèn   (hírí)_IO [mɔ̀r]_O
      3SG   tie-BEN.IMPERV   man   calf
      'S/he ties the calf for the man.'

   c. [nɔ̀ŋ]_A dól-èsèn   [lúsà]_IO [dórí]_O
      3SG   show-BEN.IMPERV   boy.PL   house
      'S/he shows the boys the house.'

In example below (10.17c), nɔ̀ŋ is an impersonal pronoun functioning as direct object. The benefactive function here looks more of a motion away (itive) marker than showing benefactive reading. The impersonal pronoun nɔ̀ŋ will not be regarded as a person form object, thus semantically it does not make any difference whether or not it appear in its position.

   d. ḁɲè hàlì k-ódʒ-èsèn   nɔ̀ŋ àlèj tùn
      1SG later 1SU-put-BEN/MA.IMPERV 3SG chair on
      'I shall put (it) on a chair.'

When one of the two objects is a free personal pronoun form, then the pronoun is treated as a human beneficiary/recipient and placed at the end of a clause as a secondary object.

(10.18) a. [nɔ̀ŋ]_A géɲ-èsèn   [érfá]_O [nɔ̀ŋ]_IO
         3SG   make/repair.IMPERV-BEN.IMPERV   bed   3SG
         'S/he made a bed for her/him.'

Note that first and second person singular subject suffixes are omitted whenever the benefactive suffix is attached to the verb.

   b. [nɔ̀ŋ] kód-èsèn   wàrkátì nɔ̀ŋ
      3SG write.IMPERV-BEN.IMPERV paper   3SG
      'S/he wrote a letter to her/him.'

However, the way syntactic Os can be coded in ditransitive clauses is different from the way two object arguments are coded in double-object clauses. The syntactic position of O arguments in ditransitive clauses may rely on the semantic roles and animacy status of the respective objects. Mütze (2014) noticed that the object of a mono-transitive verb is marked like a [+human] argument of the ditransitive verb for which human arguments have semantic recipient roles. On the other hand, object and recipient (R) behave in the same way as primary objects while the theme (T) is a secondary object. Recall the object of monotransitive clauses given in the examples above and compare with the following ditransitive clauses below.

(10.19) [jɔ̀g]_A ádʒ-án-έ [ànè]_O [còj]_IO
3PL give.IMPERV-1SG.OBJ-3PL.SU.IMPERV 1SG salt
'They give me salt/They give salt to me.'

However, there is clear evidence that Mursi shows grammatical splits when coding recipient and theme in ditransitive constructions. This is mainly observed in ditransitive constructions when both objects are personal pronouns and the coding of one is based on the referential prominence scales. Haspelmath (2015) pointed out that referential split object marking (differential object marking) is a situation where only objects that are definite and/or animate and/or personal pronouns have special accusative marking, while others follow a neutral pattern. In addition, Næss (2007, cited in Dimmendaal 2010: 39) claims that the marked participant in differential object marking is primarily the [-volitional], [-instigating] and [+affected] participant of a prototypical transitive situation. Accordingly, the accusative element differentially marks the affected participant. In Mursi, it is bound pronominal object suffixes which behave like accusative case markers and are even used to mark objects on the verb, because postverbal objects are never marked for accusative case.

(10.20) a. [nɔ̀ŋ]_A ádʒ-án [ànè]_O [iggè]_IO
3SG give.IMPERV-1SG.OBJ 1SG 2PL
'He gives me to you (pl.).'

b. [nɔ̀ŋ]_A ádʒ-ùŋ [iggè]_O [ànè]_IO
3SG give.IMPERV-2PL.OBJ 2PL 1SG
'He gives you (pl.) to me.'

Here, as shown in (10.20a–b), both recipient and theme are [+human] but the one cross-referenced on the verb is the theme ([+human, [+patient/affected] and [+1st or 2nd person]). The gift argument is often associated with lower referential prominence. In (10.20a–b), part of the referential prominence scales applied is the person scale where the first and second person pronouns are higher than the third person on the scale (1st/2nd > 3rd). In both ditransitive clauses, two further points need to be made clear: markedness and aspect of the verb. With respect to the marking of core arguments by cross-referencing bound pronominal suffixes on the verb, the third person singular of the A argument has zero realization in the imperfective aspect. Hence, as illustrated above in (10.20a–b), the third person singular of the A is being relatively unmarked in contrast to O. Not only unmarked with respect to the O, but also zero realization when cross-referenced on verbs that are in the imperfective aspect. Therefore, Mursi exhibits a split system, which is motivated by the referential prominence of gift and recipient.

The other interesting argument coding splits the one made depending on person of the A argument and person of O argument. As shown below in (10.21a–b), both arguments (A and O) are cross-referenced on the verb, where the first and second person pronouns appear to have the semantic role of gift and/or recipient.

(10.21) a. [jɔ̀g] hàlì jóg-óɲ-é   [àɲè] [dìb]
       3PL   later tell-1SG.OBJ-3PL.SU.IMPERV [1SG] [truth]
       'They will tell me the truth.'

    b. [jɔ̀g] hàlì jóg-íɲ-ɛ́   [ìɲè] [lɔ̀gɔ̀]
       3PL   later tell-2sg.OBJ-3pl.SU.IMPERV [2SG] [word]
       'They will tell you the truth.'

In contrast, in (10.21c–d), when both A and O have the same person-form status (3rd=3rd), they will never be coded by participant cross-referencing on the verb, instead the benefactive suffix -èsèn/-ɛsɛ would be attached to the verb.

    c. [jɔ̀g]_A hàlì jóg-ésén-é   [nɔ̀ŋ]_O [dìb]
       3PL   later tell-BEN.IMPERV-3PL.SU.IMPERV 3sg   truth
       'They will tell him the truth later.'

    d. [jɔ̀g]_A hàlì jóg-ésé   [jɔ̀g]_O [dìb]
       3PL   later tell-BEN.PERV 3PL   truth
       'They will tell them the truth later.'

Both nɔ̀ŋ and jɔ̀g are beneficiaries filling the syntactic function of object. For unclear reason, although the ditransitive verb ádʒ is in the imperfective aspect, as it is shown in (10.22a–b), it is marked with a perfective-value motion towards (dative) suffix -o. The function of -o in both clause is dative.

(10.22) a. [nɔ̀ŋ]_A ádʒ-ó   [hùlèj]_O [[nɔ̀ŋ [dʒɔɔnɛ]_{NP}]_{IO}
       3SG   give.IMPERV-3.IRR flower   3sg   mother.PERT.SG.3.PRS
       'S/he gave the flower to her/his mother.'
       (Lit. 'S/he gave the flower to (it) her/his mother.')

     b. [ànè]_A hàlì k-ádʒ-é-o   [nɔ̀ŋ]_O [màm-á
       1SG   later 1SU-give.IMPERV-APPL-IRR 3SG   mother-RTSR
       n=ànù]_{NP:IO}
       SG.PSD=1SG.PSR
       'I shall give it to my mother.'

Note that the semantics role of the post-verbal *nɔ̀ŋ* in (10.20a and b) are different, where the free pronoun *nɔ̀ŋ* in (10.22a) is due to speaker's occasional use when referring to kinship nouns without optional modifying possessive pronouns. Or otherwise there may be similar constructions with (b) *dʒɔ̀ɔ̀nè-á n=ènè* (mother-RSTR SG.PSD=3SG.PSR) 'his mother' or simply a pertensive form *dʒɔ̀ɔ̀nè*. Such occurrence of free pronouns in the expression of possession with kinship nouns seems to be common in languages that have no grammatical gender. So *nɔ̀ŋ* in (a) is part of the indirect object/dative construction, or it is within the role of the semantic recipient. On the other hand, *nɔ̀ŋ* in (10.22b) is a direct object or it is a semantic theme.

The other interesting point seems to be regarding the coding of core arguments on ditransitive verbs, in which ditransitive verbs themselves divide into two types. Mursi ditransitive verbs are: *ádʒ* 'give' *jóg* 'tell' and *dól* 'show, announce'. Despite the fact that languages employ different strategies for these verbs (cf. Dixon 1994: 120), all of them have three core roles in Mursi. The ditransitive *ádʒ* 'give'.—(i) The bound object pronominal form of the recipient (if human recipient) is cross-referenced on the verb and the gift as peripheral argument without being coded by postposition or case markers (e.g. 10.19). (ii) The bound object pronominal form of the gift/theme (human patient/affected) is cross-referenced on the verb following differential object marking while the recipient is placed as peripheral argument coded by no overt postposition or case marker (e.g. 10.20a–b). (iii) Only the subject in A function (the agent role) is cross-referenced on the verb while the gift is placed in O function and the recipient (if human) is placed as peripheral argument by suffixing a motion towards marker (dative) on the verb (e.g. 10.22a–b). The verb *ádʒ* does not take a benefactive suffix like the other two ditransitive verbs. Moreover, it undergoes a three-term root suppletion for aspect while *jóg* and *dól* do not alter their roots for aspectual distinction. When two semantic roles of the O arguments follow this verb, free ordering is possible as long as the recipient is human, as in (10.23a–b).

(10.23) a. àɲè k-ádʒ-έ   hírí   mà
          1SG 1SU-give.IMPERV-APPL man water
          'I give the man water.'

    b. àɲè k-ádʒ-έ   mà   hírí
          1SG 1SU-give.IMPERV-APPL water man
          'I give the man water.'

Both R and T can be cross-referenced on the verb when they are pronominal. The same free ordering applies in the imperative construction, as in (10.23c).

    c. áín-έ   bíró   ʃúúnú!
          give.PERV:IMP-APPL money father.PERT.SG.2.PRS
          'Give (sg.) the money to your father!'

On the other hand, the ditransitive verbs *jog* (with core roles 'message' and 'addressee') and *dol* (with core roles 'thing-shown' and 'person-to-whom-it-is-shown') take both motion towards and benefactive suffixes to encode either or both O arguments.

(10.24) a. ɨ̀ɲè jóg-óɲ-í   àɲè-jè
          2SG tell-1SG.OBJ-2SG.SU.IMPERV 1SG-OBL
          'You (sg.) were telling me.'

    b. ɨ̀ɲè bè   jóg-ésé-ú   nɔ̀ŋ
          2SG DIST.PAST tell-BEN.PERV-2SG.SU.PERV 3SG
          'You (sg.) had told him.'

    c. wà   kó-dól-ó-óɲ-ò   sábɔ̀
          REC.PAST 1SU-show-MT-2PL.OBJ-IRR? before
          'I have showed you before.'

d. ŋànì   kó-dǒl-ésé=ó   nòŋ [ŋòná-à
   NEG.PERV 1SU-show-BEN.PERV=NEG   3SG sister-RTSR
   n=ànù]_NP
   SG.PSD=1SG.PSR
   'I did not show (it) to my sister.'

Whenever the addresses (R-role) is known, the message (T/P-role) may not be necessarily expressed overtly (especially if it is expressed in an earlier stage of the story/narration), as in (10.24e–f).

e. lòg-á   [Ø kó-jóg-ó-úŋ-ù]_RC
   word-RSTR   [Ø 1SU-tell-MT-2PL.OBJ-IRR]
   'The words that I tell to you (pl.) …'

f. ŋà=kó-jóg-ón-óŋ-Ø=ó-ò
   NEG.IMPERV=1SU-tell-MT-2PL:OBJ-1PL:INC:SU:IMPERV=NEG-VFS
   'We (inc.) will not tell (it) to you (pl.).'

With respect to the stability of mono-transitive and ditransitive clauses in the canonical constituent order AVO, both appear to have a rather clear boundary and remain stable when combined with other type of clauses such as subjunctive/purpose/adjunct, relative and subordinate clauses. Some examples are given below.

(10.25) a. [àŋè]_A k-áín-ɛ́-ò   [hír-á   óól-nèn-á]_NP:O
           1SG   1SU-give.PERV-MT-IRR   man-RSTR   beg-NOMZ-RSTR
           [sántímíó háánán]_NP:IO [ká-tál-á   [tílá kàlì-nè]_NP]_ADJUNCT
           cent   five   3.SBJV-buy-3SG.SU food day-OBL
           'I gave the beggar fifty cents to buy his dinner.'

       b. k-áín-ɛ́-ò   érmì-á   [Ø wà   k-óg-á]_RC
          1SU-give.PERV-MT-IRR   child-RSTR [Ø REC.PAST 3.SBJV-go-3SG.SU
          'I gave it to the boy who went (away).'

10.2.2 Non-canonical OVA/VS

The non-canonical constituent order OVA/VS is the sole order that brings an overt case marking scenario to the language, i.e. the marked-nominative. Crosslinguistically, marked-nominative is a rare case system mainly found in African languages. König (2008: 138) reported that marked-nominative case system are an almost unique African phenomenon, which is only attested in few languages outside Africa. A commonly known scenario in a marked-nominative system is to treat/mark S and A the same way and treating the O differently. Whatsoever is the constituent order it occurs in, the O is in no way morphologically marked. The O always has the same form (citation/basic form). Straightwardly, the marked-nominative case system of Mursi operates based on an OVA/VS constituent order. Thus post-verbal subjects in this constituent order are morphologically and formally marked by marked-nominative case suffixes.

Since this section is about the case system of the language, I prefer to mention two terms from de Hoop and Malchukov (2008: 567) who also outlined two basic functions of case marking—identifying function and distinguishing function. Accordingly, the identifying function of case encodes internal properties of the arguments, whereas the distinguishing function of case encodes and depends on the relation between the arguments. The former is used more in case morphology to encode specific semantic/pragmatic information about the nominal argument in question (p. 567 ff.). For example, the noun with nominative case in (10.26) is an agent [+control, +volitional, etc.].

(10.26) àɲè dág-áɲ-Ø   hírí-ó
       1SG beat-1SG.OBJ-3SG.SU.IMPERV man-NOM
       'The man beat me.'

As de Hoop and Malchukov (2008: 568) put it: "the distinguishing strategy is a more specific strategy that is used for distinguishing between the two core arguments of a transitive clause, that is, the subject and the object". Example (10.26) above is a transitive clause thus it has two core arguments. Therefore, case has marked one of the arguments, the post-verbal subject is case-marked to avoid argument ambiguity. If the two arguments are already cross-referenced on the verb, one may of course ask why is the case marking in (10.26) important. The simplest answer is; what if the object argument in (10.26) is a noun or third person pronoun? This is due to the fact that when the object equals the subject in animacy and definiteness (as in (10.27)), then the nominative case becomes the only way to distinguish the actual subject.

(10.27) [lúsì]_O dág-Ø   [hírí-ó]_A
       boy   hit-3SG.SU.IMPERV man-NOM
       'The man beats the boy.'

Such types of cases and other similar issues are discussed in the subsequent sections (§10.2.2.1 and §10.2.2.2).

TABLE 10.1 Free and nominative pronoun forms of Mursi

	Preverbal subject and post-verbal object pronouns (AVO)	Postverbal subject pronouns (OVA)	Remark on forms of marked nominative pronouns
1SG	àɲè	áɲój	⟨aɲ+oj⟩
2SG	ìɲè	íɲój	⟨iɲ+oj⟩
3SG	nɔ̀ŋ	nɛ̀àj	⟨nɛ+aj⟩
1PL.INC	àggè	ággéò	⟨àggè-o⟩ also ⟨àggèù⟩
1PL.EXC	àggè	ággéò	⟨àggè-o⟩ also ⟨àggèù⟩
2PL	ìggè	íggéò	⟨ìggè-o⟩ also ⟨ìggèù⟩
3PL	jɔ̀g	jɔ̀kù/jɔ̀kíù	⟨jɔ̀k-u⟩ or ⟨jɔ̀kì-ù⟩

10.2.2.1 Nominative Case Marking on Pronouns

Mursi personal pronouns exist in two forms: (i) in neutral forms when occurring as pre-verbal subject and post-verbal object, and (ii) in nominative forms when occurring as post-verbal subjects. In the non-canonical constituent order VS/OVA, the verb agrees in number with the post-verbal nominative form pronouns. The first person plural nominative form pronouns do not distinguish inclusive and exclusive subjects. Even though nominative form pronouns have similar positions within clauses with nouns in marked-nominative case, one basic difference can be noticed between the two. See the two examples given below.

(10.28) a. kí-ʃíl-Ø   jɔ̀kì=jè   tùn-ɔ̀
            1SU-stand-1PL.INC.SU.IMPERV 3PL.NOM=SUBORD on-OBL
            'We stood on them.'

     b. kɔ́ɔ́d-í   nɛ̀àj-è
         1SU.write.IMPERV-1SG.SU.IMPERV 3SG.NOM-OBL
         'I wrote with it.'

As shown in (10.28a–b), only the S argument is cross-referenced on the verb.

Form-based similarities of nominative suffixes and their attestations in different word categories:
- Both *aɲ* and *iɲ* forms of the first and second person post-verbal subjects are attested as first and second person bound pronominal object suffixes.
- The bound form ⟨oj⟩ in the first and second person post-verbal subjects is attested in the interrogative pronominal *nój* ⟨n+oj⟩ 'who.NOM'.

- The nominative marker suffix -*j* has unclear distribution but seems to occur mostly following nouns which end in a vowel.
- The nominative marker suffix -*o* is the primary nominative marker and often occurs following singular nouns.
- The nominative marker suffix -*u* often occurs following plural nouns (see Table 10.1).

(10.29) a. kátámá kúún-í   [áɲój]$_S$ [ádísábá]
city   1SU.come.IMPERV-1SG.SU.IMPERV 1sg.NOM adisaba
'The city I come (from) is Addis Ababa.'

b. [ìggè]$_O$ kó-jóg-í   [áɲój]$_A$ jéb-ó
2PL 1SU-tell-1SG.SU.IMPERV 1sg.NOM believe-2PL.SU.IMPERV
ènèŋ?
how
'How shall you (pl.) believe my words?'
(Lit. 'I told you (pl.), you (pl.) shall believe how?')

In the absence of a question clause, in the AVO order, the position of the second person plural pronoun *ìggè* would be after *kójógí* and while in the current order, it tends to be at a position between the first person nominative pronoun *áɲój* and the verb *jébó*.

c. ŋànìjè nɔ̀ŋ [ín-á   màt-∅-á]$_{RC}$
but 3SG [3SG.PN.SP-RSTR drink.IMPERV-3SG.SU.IMPERV-RSTR
[mà]$_{IO}$ k-ádʑ-á-í   [áɲój]$_A$ [nɔ̀ŋ]$_O$
water 1SU-give.IMPERV-MT-1SG.SU.IMPERV 1SG.NOM 3SG
'... but whosoever drinks of the water that I shall give him ...'
(Lit. 'but he that drinks the water I shall give him')

As can be shown in the examples stated above, post-verbal pronouns in the intransitive clause (10.29a) and in the transitive clauses (10.29b–c) are marked-nominative forms. In ditransitive clauses such as (10.29c), the recipient/beneficiary is always placed next to the A in O function.

(10.30) bá   bàrì   [rè-ʃa[1]   òlíkɔ̀rɔ̀-j]$_{NP}$ hùllì
place/CAUSE yesterday die-RSTR:IDEO Olikoro-GEN if

---

1 The suffix -ʃa appears to function as a nominalizer and may have been derived from the

k-èr [*ąnój*]$_S$ *í-Ø* *ènèŋ?*
1.SBJV-die.PERV 1SG.NOM to.be-3SG.SU.IMPERV how?
'I wish I had died instead of Olikoro.'
(Lit. 'In place of the Olikoro death, if I died is who/how')

Following the verb *ker* the nominative pronoun form is in the S function, and following the copula verb there is an interrogative word *ènèŋ*, a form often used for the expression of 'will or wish'. Note that the occurrence of the conditional/temporal word *húllí* 'if/when' does not show that the clause is a conditional/subordinate clause. Conditional clauses have their own specific formula—always begin with *húllí* and always end with a word marked by a subordinate marker suffix =*jè* (*húllí* (x) (y) ... (z)=*jè*). In addition, clauses that refer to speakers 'will/wish' have *húllí* at their clause-initial positions in the same way as conditional clauses.

In passive construction, S is treated like O thus object pronominal suffixes of active clauses are used to indicate the S. The underlying A argument (semantic agent) can in no way be expressed after the passive verb has been omitted. Since Mursi has zero realization of the third person O suffix, the third passive form attaches a vowel suffix -V (usually by copying the vowel of a consonant-initial verb root).

(10.31) a. *nòŋ gáwái-jè* *k-èg-ò* *àggèù*
3SG market-OBL PASS-send-PASS.3 1PL.NOM
'S/he was sent to the market by us.'

Here, the canonical constituent order is SV-Obl (may reflects an underlying A) passive construction, even though it is impossible to add an A argument after the passive verb (unless as a peripheral argument with an oblique case), as is shown in (10.31a). Due to the post-verbal marked-nominative principle in non-canonical OVA, the nominative pronoun *àggèù* may reflect a semantic agent. As König (2008: 178) pointed out, nominative can have function encoding agents in a passive-like clause. König listed Maa and Dinka languages as having a system where agents are encoded by the nominative in passive construction. As the example (10.31a) clearly shows, Mursi has a similar encoding strategy where it uses post-verbal nominative pronoun forms as agents in passive-like constructions. A plausible explanation may be the

---

ideophones such as *luʃ* (describes a situation or the way of dying suddenly), *ɓeʃ* (describes something happening abruptly, all of a sudden) and so on. It may be analyzed as a sound-maker marker.

one provided by König referring to Gerrit Dimmendaal's personal communication. Whether for the possibility of Mursi's passive constructions be sources for ergative constructions, or for such related enquiries, I suggest the most recent article of Cassaretto, Dimmendaal, Hellwig, Reinöhl, Schneider-Blum (2020).

Accordingly, marked-nominative may have come into existence first as a marker of peripheral A/S arguments in passive-like constructions (König 2008: 179). Morphological devices such as instrumental and locative that are used to encode peripheral participants can also be used to encode agents of passive-like clauses in some languages. Although this is not the exact scenario for Mursi, there seems to be the case where the markers of the post-verbal nominative subjects and markers of the agent-like peripheral arguments that follow the passive verb are alike. Compare the nominative case suffix -ɔ of (10.26) with the oblique (instrumental) -ɔ on the peripheral argument of (10.28a). Compare the nominative marker suffix -ɔ [o] in (10.26) with the instrumental marker suffix -ɔ on the peripheral argument below in (10.31b).

 b. *kìɔ*   *kè-tèŋèd-è*   *bé-ɔ̀*
   tree PASS-cut.PERV-PASS.3 axe-OBL
   'The tree was cut with/by an axe.'

Compare (10.31a–b) with the one below in (10.31c–d).

 c. *nɔ̀ŋ bè*   *ŋà=bá*   *nà*   [*nɔ̀ŋ bá*]ₒ *bè*
   3SG DIST.PAST DEM=place+NEAR CCN 3SG place DIST.PAST
   gèn-ónó   [*nèàj*]ₐ
   create.IMPERV-MT.3SG.SU 3SG.NOM
   'He was in the world, and the world was made by him.'

 d. *áw-ó*   *nà*   *bég-é*   *dàmì-tí*
   go.PERV:IMP-PL CCN guard.PERV.IMP-PL custum-NRSTR
   bég-čó   *iggèù=jè*
   guard-COM.2PL.SU 2PL.NOM=SUBORD
   'Go and guard it as the way you guarded it (tomb)!'
   (Lit. 'You (pl.) go guard it in a way it is guarded by you!')

The comitative marker can also be used as reason applicative marker. In (10.31c), the O argument is not overtly stated but we know from the source text where it is adopted from (cf. the Bible, Matthew 27:65), i.e. 'tomb'.

TABLE 10.2 A list of Mursi case markers

Case suffixes	Case type	Function	Conditions
-ɔ	oblique (instrumental, locative, allative and ablative)	non-core argument/constituent	-ɔ (+consonant final nouns) -je (+vowel final nouns) -e/-ne (+alveolar nasal plural nouns) -i (+vowel final plural nouns)
-o [-ɔ]	nominative	core argument (S/A) in VS/AVO order	-o/-ɔ (+vowel final plural pronouns) -u (+third plural pronoun)
-o	nominative	core argument (S/A) in VS/AVO order	-o (+singular nouns) -u (+plural nouns) -j (unclear distribution)
Ø	nominative	core argument (S/A) in VS/AVO order	final vowel reduction (unclear distribution)
-ɲ [-i/-j/ iɲ] ... etc.	genitive	NP modifier	(see Chapter 4)

(10.32) ŋànìjè ʤáláwáɲá [Ø kó bítóg-á]_NP mès-é-á]_RC
thus   prophet.PL [Ø PNC false-RSTR do-3PL.SU.IMPERV-RSTR
jɔ̀kù   gáj-ó-ɔ̀
3PL.NOM know-2PL.SU.IMPERV-VFS
'Thus, you (pl.) will know the false prophets by what they do.'

(10.33) ŋànìjè lɔ̀g-á   [Ø mès-é-á]_NP]_RC/COMPL:CL   jɔ̀kíù
but   word-RTSR [Ø do-3PL.SU.IMPERV-NOMZ:RSTR] 3PL.NOM
ŋà=mésí-ó
NEG.IMPERV=do.IMPERV.IMP-PL
'But don't do what they do!'

As can be seen in (10.32 and 10.33), the distinction between the two third person plural nominative form pronouns is not clear.

We see a striking similarity between case markers of the post-verbal nominative pronouns/nouns and case markers of peripheral arguments in the language. Case suffixes may have one common origin, but we do not know that origin at this stage.

Another relevant deduction that can be made for sure from the discussions we saw in the aforementioned sections is that the syntactic position of independent pronouns in both AVO and OVA constituent orders can also be viewed from a pragmatically driven point of view. In most cases, as long as the bound pronominal S, A and O argument markers are cross-referenced on the verb, independent pronouns can be optional. However, pragmatically, S/A referring independent pronouns in the SV/AVO order are often topical constituents while in the VS/OVA order they can be seen as focused constituents. Indeed, this requires further investigation.

10.2.2.2   Nominative Case Marking on Nouns

From the syntactic point of view, nouns that take various nominative case suffixes operate in the same way as nominative form pronouns (i.e. post-verbally). The semantic motivation behind nouns that take nominative case markers is more important than in personal pronouns. Almost all nouns that take post-verbal nominative case morphology are animate, definite, and culturally important items (see Mütze 2014).

Mursi nouns can be grouped into three types based on how they mark the nominative case. The three types stated below are based on the way singular nouns behave in relation to the nominative case. Nouns in the plural form take the invariable nominative *suffix -u*.

- Type I—nouns that take the nominative case suffix *-o* (singular) and *-u* (plural),
- Type II—nouns that take the nominative suffix *-j* (singular) and *-u* (plural), and
- Type III—nouns that mark/indicate nominative case by final segment reduction.

For instance, *mèdèrè/mèdér* 'sheep/sheep.NOM', *rɔ̀sɔ̀/rɔ̀s* 'dog/dog.NOM', *tɔ̀ŋɔ̀/tɔŋ* 'goat/goat.NOM', *gùfùrɔ́/gùfùr* 'hyena/hyena.NOM' and so on. The segment which is often reduced from noun roots is the vowel *-ɔ*, in most cases from nouns that end in this vowel. The case of *-ɛ* reduction from the animate noun *mèdèrè* may be taken as an exceptional case, if this is the only instance, but we can't be sure at this stage. See the examples given below:

(10.34) a. [lúsì]₀   dág-Ø   [hírí-ó]ₐ
           boy   hit-3SG.SU.IMPERV   man-NOM
           'The man beats the boy.'

       b. [hírí]₀   dág-Ø   [lúsì-ó]ₐ
           man   hit-3SG.SU.IMPERV   boy-NOM
           'The boy beats the man.'

TABLE 10.3 Nouns that take nominative case (a selection)

Singular	Singular nominative	Plural	Plural nominative	Meaning
lúsì	lúsìó	éró	éróu	'boy'
hírí	híríó ⟨híréɔ́⟩	zùwò	zùwù	'man'
kònù	kɔ̀nɔ̀ɔ̀/kɔ̀nùj	kòná	kònáù	'snake'
mèdèrè	mèdér mèdèréj mèdèrɔ̀	mèdèrní	mèdèrnù	'sheep'
òlí	òléɔ̀ ⟨io⟩ òléj ⟨ij⟩	òlíɲá	òlíɲáù	'bull'
rɔ̀sɔ̀	rɔ̀s/rɔ̀sɔ̀j	rɔ̀sì	rɔ̀sìù	'dog'
tɔ̀ŋɔ̀	tɔ̀ŋ	tènò		'goat'
hárté	hártéj	hárčá		'horse/mule'
gùʃùrɔ́	gùʃùr	gùʃùréná		'Hyena'
bɛ̀	bɛ̀ɔ̀/béj	bèná	bènù	'stone'
kìɔ̀	kí/kíj	kènɔ̀	kènù	'tree'
ɗékɛ̀	ɗékéɔ́/ɗɛkɛj	ɗèkén	ɗèkènù	'leather dress'
hózò	hózòj			'hunger'

As we see in (10.34a–b), both nominative marked nouns are topical constituents in subject function. In addition, both are human agents, thus they are always marked by a non-zero nominative case forms.

c. [rɔ̀sɔ̀]_A áɲít-ú   [tɔ̀ŋɔ̀]_O
   dog   bite-3SG.SU.PERV goat
   'The dog bit the goat.'

d. ʃàù ŋè-Ø   [rɔ́s-Ø]_S
   fast run-3SG.SU.IMPERV dog-NOM
   'The *dog* runs fast.'

e. [múdáí]_O áɲít-ú   [rɔ̀s-Ø]_A
   rat   bite-3SG.SU.PERV dog-NOM
   'The *dog* bit the rat.'

GRAMMATICAL RELATIONS   459

    f. [áčúgéná]_O bág-é   [rɔ̀sí-u]_A
       meat.PL   eat.imperv-3PL.SU.IMPERV   dog.PL-NOM
       'The dogs eat all the meat.'

In (10.34c), rɔ̀sɔ̀ is in A function in the canonical constituent order AVO so only the A argument is cross-referenced on the verb. Had it been the NP in O function as a pronoun, its argument would also being cross-referenced on the verb. In the non-canonical constituent order (VS/OVA), also an order which enables both intransitive and transitive subjects be topical/focal, constituents are marked by nominative case. However, unlike human subjects, non-human post-verbal subjects are subject to segment reduction, usually for nouns that end in -ɔ. Previous knowledge of the language's constituent ordering system might help, otherwise it would be difficult to distinguish the subject from the object in clauses such as (10.35a).

(10.35) a. tɔ̀ŋɔ̀]_A [bág-Ø   [lúsì]_O
        goat   bite-3SG.SU.IMPERV   boy
        'The goat bites the boy.'

       b. [lúsì]_O bág-Ø   [tɔ́ŋ-Ø]_A
        boy   bite-3SG.SU.IMPERV   goat-NOM
        'The goat bites the boy.'

In (10.35a), it is the constituent word order that identifies the two arguments which otherwise are almost identical and both arguments can equally share the same bound pronominal suffix which is cross-referenced on the verb. In (10.35b), it is the nominative case that identifies both arguments that come with strict ordering of the post-verbal S/A argument.

   Nouns that take nominative case morphology may also occur independent of the strict ordering of post-verbal S/A. In this case, they may occur in NPs that are topical as well as focal within a clause, as in (10.36).

(10.36) iggè [ŋà=éró=á   kòná-ù=ŋà]_{NP}   [číb-ín-á
        2PL   DEM=children=NEAR snake.PL-NOM=DEF punish-NOMZ-RTSR
        gó-ɲ]_{NP}   hàlì   dʒór-ó   bónnój?
        fire-GEN later run.IMPERV-2PL.SU.IMPERV where
        'You (pl.) serpents, you (pl.) generation of vipers, how can you (pl.) escape the damnation of hell?'
        (Lit. 'You (pl.), the children of serpents, where will you (pl.) escape from the fire punishment?')

Both pronouns and nouns can occur at one position as topical plus focused constituents.

(10.37) àggè [kènà-á   g=àw]_NP   ká-ɓág-ó
      1PL tree.PL-RSTR PL.PSD=1PL.EXC.PSR 1SU-eat-1PL.EXC.SU.PERV
      àggè-ù   mùn-ù
      1PL-NOM Mursi.PL-NOM
      'Our (exc.) trees that we (exc.) the Mursi eat ...'

Even non-animate nouns can behave like subjects as long as they are taking the nominative case. As can be shown in (10.38), *hózò* 'hunger' is the agent while the first person object pronominal suffix attached to the verb is the object. It can literally mean 'I am hit by hunger'.

(10.38) kó   ɓásáj   ɓák-ú   kè ɔ̀ŋ dág-áɲ   hózò-j
      PNC monitor.lizard eat-3SG.SU.PERV why? hit-1SG.OBJ hanger-NOM
      aj!
      INTERJ.oh.no
      '... also you (sg.) ate a monitor lizard why? Don't say, "Hunger hit me?!" Aj!' (MH 4:30:6)

10.2.3 *The Non-canonical Order (AOV)*

The third and the strictest constituent order in the language is AOV. In an AOV order, due to strict orders of constituents, where negated verbs need to be moved to a clause final positions, arguments in A function are often forced to appear at clause-initial position. Unless in few exceptional constructions, this applies to all negated verbs regardless of the type of clauses or moods in which they belong.

(10.39) [àɲè]_CS k-án-í   [támárí]_CC [àɲè]_CS
      1SG   1SU-COP.IMPERV-1SG.SU.IMPERV student   1SG
      [ástámárí]_CC ŋà=k-án-í=ó
      teacher   NEG=1SU-COP.IMPERV-1SG.SU.IMPERV=NEG
      'I am a student, I am not a teacher.'

(10.40) a. òlíɓisɛ́ní ádísáwá-jè   ŋànì   k-ók-Ø=ó
         Oliɓisɛni addis.ababa-OBL NEG.PERV 3.SBJV-GO-3SG.IRR=NEG
         'Oliɓisɛni did not go to Addis Ababa.'

b. *zùwò túrúmél ŋànì   k-úgún-ù=tó*
   people car   NEG.PERV 3.SBJV-push-3PL.IRR=PL.NEG
   'The men did not push the car.'

c. *támárí-ɲá rúm-íɲá ŋànì   kú-čúr-ù=tó*
   student-PL cloth-PL NEG.PERV 3.SBJV-wash-3PL.IRR=PL.NEG
   'The students were not washing their clothes.'

As shown in above negative declarative clauses, both A and O arguments precede the verbal predicate. Note that in the negative perfective aspect, the third person S/A argument is marked on the verb as subjunctive marker in the same way as first person subjects, i.e. *k(V)-*. The second persons are marked differently from first and third person subjects, so they do not make use of the *k(V)*-prefix (as in (10.41)).

(10.41) *ìggè wà   ŋànì   dáfí-d-ó=ó   nɔ̀ŋ*
        2PL REC.PAST NEG.PERV do-PERV.PL-2PL.SU=NEG 3SG
        'You (pl.) have not done it.'

Furthermore, the position the O argument in AOV ordered clauses may vary when it is a pronoun and when it is a simple or common noun. When the O argument is a pronoun, it has been observed that there is a tendency for the O argument to follow the verb regardless of the aspect and transitivity (transitive and ditransitive) value of the verb. Compare the above examples given (10.38) with the following examples.

(10.42) a. *àɲè wà   ŋànì*
           1SG REC.PAST NEG.PERV
           k-ár-Ø-á=ó   jɔ̀g
           1SU-see.PERV-3PL.OBJ-1SG.SU.PERV=NEG 3PL
           'I have not seen them.'

       b. *jɔ̀g hàlì ŋà=kɔ́d-Ø-á=ó*
          3PL later NEG.IMPERV=kill.IMPERV-3P.OBJ-3PL.SU.PERV=NEG
          jɔ̀g
          3PL
          'They will not kill them.'

       c1. *nɔ̀ŋ ŋànì   k-áín-áɲ-Ø=nó   àɲè*
           3SG NEG.PERV 3.SBJV-give.PERV:SG-1SG.OBJ-3SG.IRR=NEG 1sg

OR c2. *nɔ̀ŋ ŋànì àɲè k-áín-áɲ-Ø=nó*
3SG NEG.PERV 1SG 3.SBJV-give.PERV:SG-1SG.OBJ-3SG.IRR=NEG
'He did not give me (something).'

As it is shown in (10.42a–c), all arguments in O function are pronouns, for which at first glance it appears to be the case that this applies when the O argument is a pronoun. But, the second option in (10.42c1) shows that the O argument can also be between the perfective negative particle *ŋànì* and the negated verb. In other word, the O argument now comes in its typical AOV order. From argument structuring point of view, the O arguments can be optional constituents as long as they are indexed as pronominal forms on the verb. Otherwise in clauses such as (10.42c2), they can be very ambiguous especially when the A equals O both in person and number. In (10.43) below one assumes that the slots of A and O arguments in (10.42c2) are occupied by the A and O.

(10.43) a. *nɔ̀ŋ wà   ŋànì   ká-dáfí-Ø-á=ó*
3SG REC.PAST NEG.PERV 3.SBJV-do-3SG.OBJ-3SG.SU.PERV=NEG
nɔ̀ŋ
3SG
'He has not done it.'

b. **[nɔ̀ŋ]_{A/O} wa ŋànì [nɔ̀ŋ]_{A/O} ká-dáfí-Ø-a=ó*

(10.43b) is ungrammatical because we cannot identify the A or the O argument. It is customary for peripheral arguments to be placed in the last position of a clause. The adposition phrase in (10.44a) and possessive phrase in (10.44b) are peripheral arguments thus follow the negated verb.

(10.44) a. *àɲè [àhì   kóná]_{INDEF.PRO} húŋ*
1SG thing.SG one.INDEF just
ŋà=ká-dáfí-í=ó   [*ŋà=lɔg=tá   tó-jé*]_{ADPO:P}
NEG=1SU-do-1SG.SU.IMPERV=NEG DEM=issue=NEAR in-OBL
'I can't do anything in this case.'

b. *àɲè ŋà=hín-í=ó   ɛ̀kɛ̀kɛ̀ɲ-à*
1SG NEG.IMPERV=want.IMPERV-1SG.SU=NEG argue-NOMZ
[*bá-á   n=ùnù*]_{NP}
place-RSTR SG.PSD=3SG.PSR
'I don't want any argument from you.'

10.3 Case Markers

In addition to marked-nominative case, Mursi make use of two other case markings: oblique (§ 10.3.1) and genitive (§ 10.3.2) cases. Genitive case was also discussed extensively in chapter 4 and 5.

10.3.1 *The Oblique*

The oblique case is used as a general case label for many specific oblique functions: instrumental, locative, allative, and ablative. So, in Mursi, oblique as a general label includes all ranges of versatile case marking suffixes by these four case types. The oblique which is invariably used throughout the chapters of this grammar, marks non-core constituents. Each of the four case types labeled as oblique cases will be elaborated on in the subsequent sections. We should also take into account that sometimes verbs may become the sole providers of the basic meaning. This means, these case markers on their own may not necessarily provide a full-fledged meaning even if they occur on nouns as well as on some noun modifying categories.

10.3.1.1 Instrumental Meaning

The instrumental case is marked on non-core NPs occurring in the peripheral functions. It functions as marker of the instrument or agency by which an action has been carried out. Note that if a noun ends with the vowel -ɔ, it often merges with one of the allomorphs of the instrumental case markers, i.e. -ɔ. See the examples given below—instrument (10.45a–c) and means ('by means of') (10.45d).

(10.45) a. [nɔ̀ŋ]$_S$ kɔ́n-Ø   [ísíkírìbí   tóí-jè]$_{OBL}$
        3SG   write-3SG.SU.IMPERV pen-INSTR in-OBL
        'He wrote with a pen.'

   b. [gìgèj]$_O$ wà   [kéd-á]$_A$ [wàrà-jè]$_{OBL}$
      bone   REC.PAST 1SU.cut.PERV-1SG.SU.PERV knife-OBL/INST
      'I cut bone with a knife.'

   c. [ŋà=hòì=tá]$_S$ bág-nèn-Ø
      DEM=female=NEAR eat.IMPERV-HAB-3SG.SU.IMPERV
      [kólóʃ-ɔ]$_{OBL}$
      spoon-OBL/INSTR
      'She eats with a spoon.'

d. [zùw-á   bì-ò-ɲ]_NP:S   [jɔ̀g]_S:TOP gáj-ɛ́
   people-RTSR COW-PL-GEN 3PL   know-3PL.SU.IMPERV
   [bì-á   g=èj]_NP::O   mít͡ʃíró-a   [έl
   COW-RSTR PL.PSD=3PL.PSR mark-RSTR exist.IMPERV:PL
   [ɲàwà-jè]_OBL]_RC
   ear.PL-OBL/INSTR
   'The owners recognize their cattle by means of earmarks.'

The structure *mít͡ʃíróá él ɲàwàje* in (10.45d) can be analyzed as a relative clause having a meaning 'by mark that exist (with/on) ears'. Instrumental applicative is discussed in Chapter 9.

10.3.1.2   Locative Case

A locative case in Mursi is used to mark location or direction, but certainly does not have any connection with ventive and rarely itive markers that are found on verbs.

(10.46) [íggé-á   [àgg=ìnù   dɔ̌t-ìnὲ]_RC kúrúm-ò=ŋà]_SUBORD:CL
        3PL.PN.SP-RSTR [3PL.PN.SP=FAR leave-AP.3 Kurum-LOC=DEF
        'Those others remained at the Kurum ...' (MH 4:00:6)

According to some Mursi elders, *Kurum* is a place at the South where their ancestors used to live in before they moved towards the Lower Omo Valley. Some examples are provided below.

(10.47) a. nɔ̀ŋ   kún-Ø   bà-ì   í-Ø   rὲnà
           3SG come-3SG.SU.IMPERV place-LOC to.be-3SG.SU.IMPERV far
           'He came from a faraway country.'

       b. wà   múgáj   kɔ́-ì   gàʃ-ɔ̀   nà
          REC.PAST womean.SG go.IMPERV-3.IRR forest-LOC CCN
          bíg-ú   kὲnɔ̀
          break-3SG.SU.PERV wood.PL
          'The woman goes to the forest and breaks wood.'

As illustrated in (10.47a–b), locative case marking suffixes are attached to nouns referring to both non-specified and specified/specific static places. The other rare as well as controversial locative marker is morpheme *-ni*. At this stage I was unable to make any assertion about its grammatical status—whether it is a locative case or some sort of locative suffix. Last and Lucassen (1998) have claimed that the suffix -*ni* in Chai (a dialect of Tirmaga, a Southeast Surmic group language) is a locative particle.

However, Bryant (2007: 42) rejected the claim made by Last and Lucassen. Bryant has noted that -*ni* is not a locative particle in Tirmaga rather it has a discourse function on its own. As evidence for this, he presented -*ni* which can occur where there is no anaphoric reference to a previously mentioned location. In addition to this, he also added that anaphoric references to a previously mentioned locations are found in Tirmaga without the locative suffix -*ni*.

Mursi and the two languages mentioned above together constitute a single dialect continuum, and these languages in fact display almost identical grammatical structure with Mursi. The evidence stated by Bryant about the suffix -*ni* as having a discourse function is plausible, but it cannot prevent the suffix -*ni* from being a locative marker. However, what I have observed in my corpus is that the locative suffix -*ni* often occurs on postpositions but it does not occur on simple nouns. See the examples below:

(10.48) a. *kóísí á   hír-á   [Ø mág-èsèn-à   hírí*
koysi COP.3.IMPERV man-RSTR [Ø hold-BEN.3-NOMZ man
kédém]ʀᴄ nɔ̀ŋ lɔ̀m-Ø
calabash] 3SG have-3SG.SU.IMPERV
ŋór-Ø   ɓùj-ɔ̀-ni
carry.IMPERV-3SG.SU.IMPERV back-OBL-LOC
'Koysi, a man who is the supporter (of the priest) or man of calabash, he keeps it by carrying it (the goat) on his back.'

ŋór-Ø   ɓùj-ɔ̀=je
carry.IMPERV-3SG.SU.IMPERV back-OBL=SUBORD
márág-é   bì-ò
round-3PL.SU.IMPERV cow-PL
'Carrying it (the goat) on his back, they round up the cattle.'
(MR 6:01)

b. *àggè kó-hód-á   tó-jé-ni*
1PL 1SU-come.PERV:PL-1PL.INC.SU.PERV in-OBL-LOC
kó-hóɲ-Ø   tó-jé   té
1SU-come.IMPERV:PL-1PL.INC.SU.IMPERV in-OBL COP.3.PERV
úrɔ́ ŋà=kà-màt-Ø=ó
milk NEG.IMPERV=1SU-drink.IMPERV-1PL.INC.SU.IMPERV=NEG
'We (inc.) come and enter inside (home). But when we (inc.) come inside (home), we should not drink milk.' (MR 7:45:8)

10.3.1.3 Allative and Ablative Cases

Even though the same versatile case marking suffixes that also mark allative (motion towards) and ablative (motion away from) cases, it is the verb which renders part of the meaning.

(10.49) a. àɲì kɔ́ɔ́-í ɔ́r-ɔ́
    1SG 1SU.go-1SG.SU.IMPERV homestead-ALL
    'I going toward the homestead.'

  b. áɲí kɔ́ɔ́-í gàɟ-ɔ̀
    1SG 1SU.go-1SG.SU.IMPERV forest-ALL
    'I am going toward the forest.'

  c. dóólèj ɔ́k-ú hólóg-ɔ̀
    girl go.PERV-3SG.SU.PERV dance-ALL
    'The girl went to the dance.'

  d. bàrì kúún-í mákó-jé
    yesterday 1SU.come.IMPERV-1SG.SU.IMPERV Mákkí-ABL
    'Yesterday I came from Mákkí.'

  e. àɲì kúún-í ɔ́r-ɔ́
    1SG 1SU.come.IMPERV-1SG.SU.IMPERV homestead-ABL
    'I came from the homestead.'

10.3.1.4 Genitive Case

The genitive case in Mursi is a case which is marked on nouns or on any other categories that modify heads of NPs. In particular, common nouns can be modified by other nouns with a genitive case form. All the modifying nouns must occur in genitive case form while the head noun must be marked with a modification form (see Chapter 4; § 4.2.3). The morpheme -ɲ is a general genitive case marker suffix and has a number of other allomorphs.

(10.50) a. [bá-á [óɟ-ó bèrá-ɲ]ₙₚ]ₙₚ
    place-RSTR stalk-PL sorghum.type-GEN
    'place of the sorghum stalks.'

  b. [àlè-á gùɟúr-ùɲ]ₙₚ
    stool-RSTR hyena-GEN
    'Hyena's stool' (i.e. 'inedible mushroom')

c. òlítùlà á   [érmì-á   ŋàkútúl-ì]_NP
   Òlítùlà cop.3.imperv child-RTSR Ngakutul-GEN
   'Olitula is Ngakutul's child.'

The genitive case can follow the oblique case, for which both cases form an instance of double case marking scenario in the language. Both case suffixes often occur on modifier relator nouns. See the examples given below—where the relator noun in (10.51a) is a grammaticalized body part noun carrying two different morphological case forms.

(10.51) a. [mà-à   mùm-ɔ̀-ɲ]_NP
           water-RSTR face-OBL-GEN
           'Water at the front'
           (Lit. 'water-from the face of')

       b. jɔ̀g á   sú á   [sú-á   tán-ɔ̀-j]_NP
          3PL COP.3.IMPERV Aari COP.3.IMPERV Aari-RSTR side-OBL-GEN
          'They are the Aari of that side of the river.' (MH 4: 10:7)

10.4 Adpositions

Mursi postpositions are monomorphemic particles suffixed with case markers. Phonologically, they can be made of two types: simple monomorphemic monosyllabic roots (as shown in Table 10.4 below; from *tójé* to *rɔɲɔ*) and monomorphemic roots in disyllabic CV_1CV_1C shapes. Note that the syllable shapes of both types were presented without their respective case suffixes. Some members of Mursi postpositions are relator nouns and often occur with an oblique case extensions. Postpositions normally occur in two forms—as particles and as particle plus suffixes.

Mursi, as it is dominantly a postpositional language (except *sábɔ̀* 'front' both postposition and preposition; *wùréɔ́* 'behind' prepositions), it does not correlate with Greenberg's Universal principle II. Both *sábɔ̀* and *wùréɔ́* are multifunctional words such as postpositions (following nouns), as adverb or ordinal number (following some selected verbs), and as preposition (when used as time words). Thus, in relation to noun and verb modifier, they may occur in different syntactic positions in a clause. Greenberg's universal principle II states that in languages with postpositions, the genitive always precedes the governing noun (Greenberg 1966: 45). The fact is that Mursi is a typical postpositional language, but the genitive always follows the noun. However, Greenberg's principle 27

TABLE 10.4 Adpositions

Postposition	Meaning	Remark
tójé	'in, inside, through'	tó-jé ⟨in-OBL⟩
tùnɔ̀	'on, top, above'	tùn-ɔ ⟨on-OBL⟩
ɓàì	'under'	ɓà-i ⟨place/ground-OBL/LOC⟩
ɓó	'top'	
ɓɔ́(ɔ́)	'outside'	ɓɔ́-ɔ́ ⟨out-OBL⟩
sábɔ̀	'front, first, in front of'	sáb-ɔ ⟨head-OBL⟩
mùmɔ̀	'in front of'	mùn-ɔ ⟨forehead-OBL⟩
kɛ̀ŋɔ̀	'center, middle'	kɛ̀ŋ-ɔ ⟨belly-OBL⟩
rɔ̀ɲɔ̀	'beside, next to'	rɔ̀ɲ-ɔ ⟨rib-OBL⟩
tùtùɔ̀	'top, tip'	tùtù-ɔ ⟨mouth-OBL⟩ ≈ ⟨tútúg⟩
ɓùgùjɔ̀	'behind, beyond'	ɓùgùj-ɔ ⟨back-OBL⟩
sùgùmɔ̀	'bottom, foot'	sùgùm-ɔ ⟨rump-OBL⟩
kàrànè	'bottom, below, down'	'down there, lower'
márágɔ̀	'around'	≈ (from the verb *marag* 'round')
kɛ̀rgɛ̀nɔ̀	'middle, between'	also 'through, among'
wùréɔ́	'behind, last, after'	preposition
níŋɛ̀	'without'	negation of possession

highly correlates with Mursi, it says, 'if a language is exclusively suffixing, it is postpositional (p. 57)'.

With regard to their morphological status, it is not easy to state whether these postpositions (other than the grammaticalized body part nouns in the form of relator nouns) were all once independent forms or bound to nouns as the genitive case markers on dependents.

(10.52) a. mà   tó-jé
water in-OBL
'Water on (the) inside'

b. *lúsì bɔ̀rɔ́t-ú   sárí tùn-ɔ̀ nà ŋè-ú*
boy jump-3SG.SU.PERV fence on-OBL CCN run-3SG.SU.PERV
ɓɔ́-ɔ́
out-OBL
'The boy jumped over the fence and ran away.'

c. nɔ̀ŋ ʃíl-Ø   [àlèj tùn-ɔ̀]
   3SG stand-3SG.SU.IMPERV chair on-OBL
   'S/he stood upon the chair.'

d. bótó   í-Ø   [térébéízá tùn-ɔ̀]
   photo to.be-3SG.SU.IMPERV table   on-OBL
   'The picture is above the table.'

e. jɔ̀g bàg-é   [kɔ́náj tùn]
   3PL live-3PL.SU.IMPERV grain.store above
   'They live above the store.'

f. mà   hód-á   kɔ̀mà   wà
   water come.PERV:PL-3PL.SU knee.PL REC.PAST
   g=àj   tùn
   PL.PSD=1PL.INC.PSR above/on.top
   'The water came above our knees.'

Furthermore, as shown in (10.52), postpositions may occur with oblique markers (as in (10.52a–d)) or without them (as in (10.52e–f)). The co-occurrence of postpositions and case markers is not always clear. In (10.53a) below, at first glance, the postpositional particle *bàì* looks like a verbal word. The fact is that it is not a verbal word, but it may be used as a lexicalized verb form 'to sit'. Even if this is the case, in some previous linguistic works on Southeast Surmic languages, this particle is mentioned as an independent verbal word. The verb 'to sit' in Mursi can be referred to by the existential verb *íh* 'to exist/(be) present' with three term root suppletions /changes depending on person and number. Postpositions can be moved to a clause-initial position when they occur with negated verbs, as in (10.53a).

(10.53) a. bà-ì   ŋà=íʃ-ón-í
           place-LOC NEG.IMPERV=exsit.IMPERV-MT-SG
           'Do not (sg.) sit down!'
           (Lit. 'Don't (sg.) exist/be down')

       b. kìɔ̀ bà-ì   bà-ì
          tree ground-LOC ground-LOC
          'Under the tree'

Even if the repetition of *bai* is not clear as in (10.53b), the relational concept of 'under (something), down, below' can be shown by repeating it. More interestingly, the literal expression of the possessive NP ('your seats') presents additional evidence to what was already noted above that *bai* can serve as the verb (secondary) only when there is no verb dedicated to the meaning 'sit/stay/exist' in the clause. Therefore, the literal meaning of *báá kèlčàɲà* is ≈ ('a place for (the purpose of) sitting')—(10.53c).

    c. [*hír-á   éján-á   zùwò*]_{NP}
       man-RSTR help-NOMZ:RSTR people
       ídǎn-úŋ-Ø   [*bá-á*
       lead-2PL.OBJ-3SG.SU.IMPERV place-RSTR
       k-èl-čàɲ-à]_{NP}   *bà-ì*
       PASS-exist.PERV:PL-INSTR-RSTR:MOD ground-LOC
       'The usher will show you to your seats.'
       (Lit. 'The people-helping-man will lead you (pl.) (to) a place of the seat on the ground.')

Here, the verb *él* ('exist.IMPERV.PL') is prefixed with a passive marker *k(V)*- and suffixed with an instrumental nominalizer marker *čaɲ*. Tentatively, I regard the passive prefix form *k(V)*- to be the domain of the emergence of the multifunctional particle *ké/kó* (preposition, instrumental, coordinative conjunction, etc.). Note that -*ča* is a comitative marker with additional meaning of reason-applicative or purpose. Thus then, in (10.53c), *bài* has a unique postposition function. See further elaborations of the postpositions given below.

(10.54) a. [*mà   bà   tò-nì*]
       water place in-LOC
       'water from below the ground/place'

    b. [*dórí-a   bó-ì-ɲ*]
       house-RSTR top-LOC-GEN
       'house on the top'
       (Lit. 'house of the upper place')

    c. [*bá   káráné*]
       place down
       'the land below'

d. [dórí bùgùj]
   house back
   'back of the house (the house's back)'

e. [mà kèrgèn]
   water middle
   'water in the middle'

f. ʃíl térébéízá rɔ̀ɲ-ɔ̀
   stand.PERV table side-OBL
   'stand (sg.) beside the table!'

With regard to the different morphological forms and syntactic position possibilities of postpositions such that additional spatial relation specification and respective meaning variation of them appear to be of not much significance. In spite of this solid fact, minor semantic variations may exist when oblique case marking suffixes are directly attached to oblique arguments and when oblique case markers attach to normal postposition particles. For example,

(10.55) a. [wàrkátì-á n=ànù] í-Ø sátíní tó-jé
   paper-RTSR SG.PSD=1SG.PSR to.be-3SG.SU.IMPERV box in-OBL
   'My book is inside the box.'

b. ŋà=hòì=tá ʃúúnú í-Ø
   DEM=female=NEAR father.PERT.SG.3.PSR to.be-3SG.SU.IMPERV
   òrì? í-Ø órí-jè
   where to.be-3SG.SU.IMPERV house-OBL
   'Where is your (f) father? He is at home.'

c. dàìn-ò kú-dúl-ó tó-jé
   night-OBL 1SU-enter-1PL.EXC.SU.IMPERV in-OBL
   'We (exc.) got in at night.'

In (10.55a), the independent postposition particle follows the oblique argument and both constitute a single unit, call it a postpositional phrase. An extra spatial relation meaning in (a) is, that it tells the specific place of the item. In (10.55b), the oblique case is attached to the noun and appears in its general function. In this case, the oblique case marker does not supply specific spatial relation information in relation to the exactness. (10.56) has no oblique argument so the postposition follows the predicate as complement. The postposition *tójé* can also mean 'through/by' (as in (10.56a–c)).

(10.56) a. *zìní dúl-Ø   máskótí tó-jé*
   thief enter-3SG.SU.IMPERV window in-OBL
   'The thief entered through (by) the window.'

   b. *jɔ̀g gól-ɛ́   làɲɔ̀j tó-jé*
   3PL crawl-3PL.SU.IMPERV grass in-OBL
   'They crawl through the grass.'

   c. *gùjò dér-ò   tárár tó-jé*
   rain leak-3.IRR roof in-OBL
   'The rain comes through the roof (=the roof leaks)'

The syntactic position of postpositions may change depending on the type of clauses in which they occur. The examples given below show some instances—negative imperative (10.57a), question (10.57b), and negation (10.57c).

(10.57) a. *jɔ̀g tó-jé   ŋà=hóɲ-í*
   3PL in-OBL NEG.IMPERV-come.IMPERV:PL-PL
   'Let them not come in!'

   b. *tó-jé   jɔ̀g ŋà=hóɲ-í?*
   in-OBL 3PL NEG.IMPERV-come.IMPERV:PL-PL
   'Shall they not come in?'

   c. *lúsì dórí tó-jé   níŋè*
   boy house in-OBL not.present
   'The boy is not in the house.'

10.5   Verb-Final Suffix

In the attempt to understand how different grammatical constituents interact within sentences or clauses, we shouldn't forget that some minor but important morphological forms such as verb-final suffixes that might contribute certain pragmatic and semantic roles in various types structures in which they occur. The verb-final suffix, an obligatory syntactic requirement for affirmative declarative, imperative, hortative/jussive, and negative clauses, is a morphological element that occurs often on clause-final intransitive verbs.

   The verb-final suffixes do not occur on the verb if there is another constituent that follows the verb. They basically allow the verb to be a focalized

TABLE 10.5 Verb-final suffixes

Verb-final suffix	Clause type	Constituent type	Remark
-ɔ	affirmative declarative	SV	on intransitive imperfective verb following bound pronominal S suffixes
-ɔ	negative intransitive clause	SV	can also occur following the negative enclitic =ó
-ɔ/-ɛ	passive	(S)V	-ɔ (1st/2nd persons), -ɛ (3rd person)
-a/-ɛ/-o	hortative/jussive	(S)V	unpredictable
-a/-ɛ/-o	imperative	(S)V	-a (singular), -ɛ (plural), -o (unpredictable)

constituent. The verb which contains verb-final suffixes may be the only clausal constituent. At least in relation to some other constituents in a clause, for obvious reasons, there will be no constituent other than the verb which is to be made a focal element.

(10.58) a. *kí-bíg-í-ɔ̀*
1SU-break.IMPERV-1SG.SU.IMPERV-VFS
'I will break.'

b. *ʃíg-í-ɔ̀*
hear.IMPERV-2SG.SU.IMPERV-VFS
'You (sg.) will hear.'

c. *úrɔ́   màt-Ø-ɔ̀*
milk drink.IMPERV-3SG.SU.IMPERV-VFS
'S/he drinks milk.'

In (10.58c), the verb precedes the object—which also shows that sentential/clausal focus always occurs on the element that will take the last position of the clause. The preverbal object in (10.58c) is an optional element for the topic under discussion, thus it is only the verb-final suffix (focus marker) which is always obligatory especially if the verb is the sole constituent in a clause.

(10.59) a. *ŋà=ká-báns-Ø=ó-ɔ̀*
NEG.IMPERV=1SU-wake.up.IMPERV-1PL.INC.SU.IMPERV=NEG-VFS
'We (inc.) will not wake up.'

b. *nɔ̀ŋ ŋànì úŋús-Ø-ɔ̀*
3SG NEG.PERV sleep.IMPERV-3SG.SU.IMPERV-VFS
'S/he is still sleeping.'

c. *ŋà=hír-á ŋàtùɲ*
DEM=man=NEAR lion
ŋà=éŋérés-Ø=ó-ɔ̀
NEG=afraid.IMPERV-3SG.SU.IMPERV=NEG-VFS
'This is a man who does not fear lions.'

In non-content/constituent question, as can be shown below in (10.59d), the verb-final suffix resides on the verb that substitutes the focused-constituent question positions.

d. *mà ŋànì k-údús-à=ó màt-ó-ɔ̀?*
water NEG.PERV 3.SBJV-boil-3.IRR=NEG drink-2pl.SU.IMPERV-VFS
'Do you (pl) drink unboiled water?'

As shown below, the verb-final suffixes in the imperative clauses have predictable morphological manifestations, except the *-o* (as in (10.60b)). Even for the suffix *–o*, a tentative suggestion can be made, i.e. following verb roots that end in vowels.

(10.60) a. *čúr-à*
wash.PERV:IMP-VFS
'Wash (sg.)!'

b. *lámí-ò*
find.PERV:IMP-VFS
'Seek (sg.)!'

c. *čúr-ú-è*
wash.PERV:IMP-PL-VFS
'Wash (pl.)!'

However, as illustrated in hortative-jussive constructions (as in (10.61a–c)), the verb-final suffixes are not predictable.

(10.61) a. *kì-ɓìk-á*
 1.HORT-break.PERV-VFS
 'Let me break (it)'

 b. *kà-làmì-ó*
 1.HORT-find.PERV-VFS
 'Let me seek (it)'

 c. *kí-ɓíg-í-ɛ̀*
 3.JUSS-break.PERV-PL-VFS
 'Let them break (it)'

CHAPTER 11

Comparative Constructions

11.1 Introduction

Comparative construction is a grammatical means of showing two or more items in order to note similarities and differences between them (Dixon 2012: 343). In order to make a comparison between two items, there must be at least one quality (essence) which could be used as a parameter, and that the two items share in common. In other words, comparing of two or more items involves quality association, an indispensable approach which would help us to understand where the difference between the items lies or to what extent/degree the difference between the items in comparison is viable. One cannot compare two items unless there is at least a single difference in quality between them, thus the difference comes by means of associating the two items.

As suggested by Dixon (2012: 344), a prototypical comparative construction has three elements—the comparison of participants (COMPAREE and STANDARD OF COMPARISON), the property (PARAMETER of comparison), and the INDEX of comparison. Although Mursi does not adhere to all types of comparative constructions that different languages employ, it can indicate an elaborative and distinct comparative construction techniques by using various grammatical means. Of the three prototypical comparative construction elements mentioned above, Mursi explicitly indicate participants being compared and parameter of comparison (often adjectives). Index of comparison may be indicated by attaching a benefactive/dative marker suffix to the element of the parameter of comparison. Therefore, by combining these elements and other grammatical elements in distinct syntactic environments, Mursi presents five types of comparative constructions: mono-clausal (§11.2), phrasal plus mono-clausal (§11.3), bi-clausal Type I (§11.4), and bi-clausal Type II (§11.5), and a comparative construction which involves the connector *ba* (§11.6).

11.2 Mono-clausal Comparative Construction

A mono-clausal comparative construction is a single clause construction which consists of a comparee, a parameter and a standard. Elements of the parameter of comparison are often derived adjectives from stative verbs. The two

COMPARATIVE CONSTRUCTIONS 477

derived adjectives *búí* and *tíiní* can also function as parameters. In addition to the presence of its mono-clausality, a distinct feature that may distinguish the mono-clausal comparative construction type from a non-mono-clausal comparative construction types, there is the fact that the mono-clausal type utilizes the derivational benefactive suffix *-èsèn* as index of comparison. I call it 'comparative-benefactive'. From now on throughout the chapter the benefactive suffix *-èsèn* is glossed as COMPAR ('comparative'). See the following mono-clausal comparative construction:

(11.1) COMPAREE   PARAMETER-INDEX   STANDARD
   a. [òlítùlà]   ràmàg-èsèn   [òlélùì]
      Òlítùlà   tall.STV-COMPAR   Olelu
      'Olitula is taller than Olelu.'

     COMPAREE   PARAMETER-INDEX
   b. [írsásí-a   n=ànù]$_{NP}$ [ràmàg-èsèn]
      pencil-RSTR   SG.PSD=1SG.PSR   tall.STV-COMPAR
     STANDARD
     [ín-á   n=ùnù]$_{NP}$
     3SG.PN.SP-RSTR   SG.SPD=2SG.PSR
     'My pencil is longer than yours.'
     (Lit. 'My pencil taller from that of yours.')

     COMPAREE   PARAMETER-INDEX   STANDARD
   c. [dáʃíØ]   čàll-èsèn   tìráŋØ
      work.NOMZ   good.STV-COMPAR   play.NOMZ
      'Work is better than playing.'

In (11.1c), there is one only way which would help distinguish between comparee and the standard which is the constituent order, even then it is not totally convincing. Recall that the index of comparison *-èsèn* has its own original function as a benefactive marker 'for, to'. It can be realized as *-sèn* when it occurs following vowel-final adjectives, as in (11.1d).

     COMPAREE   PARAMETER-INDEX   STANDARD
   c. jɛnas   bú-sèn   [gòdìnè-á
      yonas   big-COMPAR   brother.PERT.3SG.PSR-RSTR
     n=ɛ̀nɛ̀]$_{NP}$
     SG.PSD=3SG.PSR
     'Yonas is taller/bigger than his brother.'

A single instance where the mark of standard is indicated by the postpositional particle *bó* 'upon, above, over' has been found. This happens when the typical element that functions as parameter of comparison (adjective) is being replaced by the verb.

(11.2)   INDEX   COMPAREE   MARK   STANDARD
        nòŋ   jél-èsèn   dáfí   bó   úŋó
        3SG   like-COMPAR   work   above   sleep
        'S/he likes work better than sleeping.'
        (Lit. 'S/he likes work more above sleeping.')

In (11.2), the index is added to the parameter *jel* 'like, love'. Thus, syntactically speaking, the standard is in peripheral function marked by the postposition *bó*. The fact is that in Mursi both verbs and adjectives can function as predicate head. The scenario in (11.2) can be further justified by the fact that in comparative constructions, only adjectives can function as parameter of comparison. The other interesting comparative construction of a mono-clausal type comes when comparing two items that are almost equivalent in the parameter of comparison. In this case, two adjectives will be utilized,—one to be used as a parameter of comparison and the other as a modifier of the standard within an NP, as in (11.3).

(11.3)   COMPAREE   PARAMETER-INDEX
        [ŋà=dórí=á]_NP   í-Ø=ŋà   ràmàg-èsèn
        DEM=house=NEAR   to.be-3SG.SU.IMPERV=DEF   tall.STV-COMPAR
        STANDARD
        [[ŋà=kì=tá]_NP   bó]_NP]
        DEM=tree=NEAR   high.RSTR
        'This house is about as high as that tree.'
        (Lit. 'This house is taller like that tall tree.')

Thus in (11.3) *bó* is a modifier of the standard, which is an NP in its own. The most interesting of all mono-clausal comparative constructions is the acquisition of a superlative reading when the standard is plural. Unlike other languages, for instance English where the superlative adjective modifies the head noun within an NP plus the definite article *the*, Mursi never changes the syntax of comparative construction in order to form a superlative construction.

(11.4) a. nòŋ bú-sèn   [gòdìngè-á   g=èɲè]ₙₚ
        3SG big-COMPAR brother.PERT.3PL.PSR-RSTR PL.PSD=3SG.PSR
        'He is the eldest of his brothers.'

    b. nòŋ mòkòɲ-èsèn   támárí-ɲá
        3SG short.STV-COMPAR student-PL
        'He is the shortest of the students.'

    c. nòŋ čàll-èsèn   dóólé
        3SG good.STV-COMPAR girl.PL
        'She is the prettiest of the girls.'

Regarding superlative constructions, Dixon (2012: 364) noted that many languages express the superlative by using a comparative construction where the standard may be specified by quantifies such as 'all'. Mursi adheres to this according to Dixon's statement, which means that syntactically both comparative and superlative constructions remain the same except for minor adjustments on the standard (as in (11.4a–c)). The sole difference between the two types of constructions is that the standard in the superlative is being made plural instead of other forms. In (11.4d) below it is a relative clause which consists of the parameter of comparison *busɛn* 'bigger/est' and the standard *ŋaiggɛa* 'these'. It appears that the relative clause is a modifier of the comparee *ina*. The copula complement *jela* 'love' refers to the compare *ina* 'one, that'.

    d. [ín-á]_CS   [bú-sèn-á   ŋà=ìggè=à]_RC
        3SG.PN.SP-RSTR big-COMPAR-RSTR DEM=3PL.PN.SP=NEAR
        á   [jél-à]_CC
        COP.3.IMPERV love-NOMZ
        'The greatest of these is love.'
        (Lit. 'It that the greatest of these is love.')

    e. ŋà=ìn=ù   án-á   [tíín-èsèn-á
        DEM=3SG.PN.SP=FAR COP.3.IMPERV-TEMP small-COMPAR-RTSR
        dónénén]
        one+NOMZ
        'That is the thinnest one.'

In (11.4e), the comparee is explicitly mentioned while the standard is not. But we know for sure that the comparee referred to in (11.4d) is one of its type from among many of the standards.

11.3 Phrasal plus Mono-clausal Construction

The main reason for the term 'phrasal' used here instead of just bi-clausal is that both the COMPAREE and the STANDARD OF COMPARISION can be conjoined by the phrasal coordinative conjunction particle *kó*, for they often form a phrase. Here, one important point that we must take into account is that the conjoined elements labeled as comparee and standard only refer to the participants, otherwise there is no means to distinguish between the two participants, at least at this stage, unless one of them is re-mentioned in the clause. There are two types of phrasal plus mono-clausal comparative construction strategies: (i) one that contains no copula verb and which looks like a single clause, and (ii) one that has a phrase and a copular clause. Both strategies do not make use of the benefactive suffix -*èsèn* as a comparative degree marker. Illustrations of both types are presented as follows (Mütze 2014):

(11.5)   PARTICIPANTS   PARAMETER   COMPAREE
   a. [ŋɔ̀rɔ̀   kó   čár],   [tìr]   čár-ɔ́
       elephant PCN leopard fast   leopard-NOM/FOC
   'The leopard is faster than the elephant.'
   (Lit. 'of the elephant and the leopard, the leopard is the fast one.')

       PARTICIPANTS   COMPAREE
   b. [ŋɔ̀rɔ̀   kó   čár]   [čár]$_{CS}$ á
       elephant PCN leopard leopard   COP.3.IMPERV
   PARAMETER
   [tìr-ì]$_{CC}$
   fast-ADJ
   'The leopard is faster than the elephant.'
   (Lit. 'from the elephant and the leopard, the leopard is fast.')

As seen in (11.5a), the comparee and the standard of comparison are conjoined by the phrasal conjunction *kó* 'with', and both are topicalized elements. The parameter that follows the phrase has lost its adjectivizer suffix -*i* because it is neither in a copula complement position nor is it a full-fledged parameter. Since almost all Mursi adjectives are derived from stative verbs, it is not uncommon for adjectives to behave like verbs. Two proofs for this assertion are, (i) the deletion of its adjectiviser suffix, and (ii) the post-verbal marked-nominative case suffix on the comparee.

However, the suffix can also function as a focus marker. In (11.5a), the crucial point seems to be the way the comparee is distinguished from the object. The

COMPARATIVE CONSTRUCTIONS 481

first and foremost answer to this will be a language-specific strategy. Individual languages may have their own information structuring strategies and one of which is the strategy they employ for comparative constructions. Besides, two genuine answers are presented,—one hypothetical but depending on the way the language tend to arrange constituents in a clause, and the other depending on the structure in (11.5b). With regard to the first, the participants are already mentioned first. Thus, due to this discourse context in place, repeating the standard seems irrelevant and therefore it has been omitted. In addition to this, had ŋɔ̀rɔ̀ been the comparee, it wouldn't be marked for nominative case. This is due to the fact that nouns that have ɔ-final roots can be marked for nominative case by reduction of the same vowel (/ɔ/). The second explanation is based on the principle of 'more adjacent' to the mono-clausal construction where the participants and other constituents are syntactically placed (as in (11.5b)). Accordingly, from the two conjoined participants in the NP, čár is adjacent to the copular clause, so it is the one being picked for copula subject position. Additional examples of the first type is given below (Mütze 2014):

(11.6) PARTICIPANTS PARAMETER COMPAREE
[múwáj kó hírí], [bú] hírí-ɔ́
woman PCN man big man-NOM/FOC
'The man is bigger than the woman.'
(Lit. '(from) the woman and the man, the man is the big one.')

This is a more similar comparative construction to (11.5b) but containing a different index hétɔ́ 'same as, similar'. This applies if both comparee and the standard are equivalent in value. Indeed the example in (11.7) is one that shows comparison of equality.

(11.7) PARTICIPANTS PARAMETER   INDEX
nɔ̀ŋ kó àɲè ój-íɲá á hétɔ́
3SG PNC 1SG year.PL COP.3.IMPERV same
'S/he is about my age.'
(Lit. 'S/he and me, (our) years are the same.')

As can be seen in (11.7), a statement of equivalence can be achieved in the same way as a comparative construction with phrasal plus copula clause technique, i.e. by conjoining comparee and standard participants as a single NP, and by incorporating the parameter and the index in a copula clause.

11.4 Bi-clausal Construction Type I

Bi-clausal comparative construction Type I can be expressed by using two copular clauses for comparative constructions and three copular clauses for superlative constructions. The fact is that the parameter of comparison remains the same in all clauses but can be modified by one or more degree intensifiers. Type I bi-clausal comparative constructions have the following templates:

(i) {[STANDARD$_1$]$_{CS}$ [PARAMETER$_1$]$_{CC}$}CLAUSE$_1$
{[COMPAREE$_1$]$_{CS}$ [PARAMETER$_1$]$_{CC}$ INDEX$_1$} CLAUSE$_2$ ... comparative construction

(ii) {[STANDARD$_1$]$_{CS}$ [PARAMETER$_1$]$_{CC}$}CLAUSE$_1$
{[STANDARD$_2$]$_{CS}$ [PARAMETER$_1$]$_{CC}$ INDEX$_1$} CLAUSE$_2$
{[COMPAREE$_1$]$_{CS}$ [PARAMETER$_1$]$_{CC}$ INDEX$_1$ INDEX$_2$} CLAUSE$_3$ ... superlative construction

(11.8) STANDARD   PARAMETER   COMPAREE
        [bàrìhúɲ]$_{CS}$ á   [tíín-í]$_{CC}$ òlélùì
        barihuny COP.3.IMPERV small-ADJ   olelu
                             PARAMETER   INDEX
        á   tíín-í   háɲ
        COP.3.IMPERV   small-ADJ   very
        'Barihuny is small. Olelu is very small.'
        (Lit. 'Olelu is smaller than Barihuny.')

(11.9) STANDARD   PARAMETER   STANDARD
        [bàrìhúɲ]$_{CS}$ á   [tíín-í]$_{CC}$ [òlélùì]$_{CS}$
        barihuny COP.3.IMPERV small-ADJ   olelu
                   PARAMETER   INDEX   COMPAREE
        á   [tíín-í]$_{CC}$ háɲ   [òlítùlà]$_{CS}$ á
        COP.3.IMPERV small-ADJ very   Òlítùlà   COP.3.IMPERV
        PARAMETER   INDEX   INDEX
        [tíín-í]$_{CC}$ háɲ   háɲ
        small-ADJ   very   very
        'Barihuny is small. Olelu is very small. Olitula is very very small.'
        (Lit. 'Olitula is the smallest one.')

As it is shown in (11.7), the bi-copular clauses can indicate a comparative construction; where the first clause only contains the standard and the parameter while the second clause often contains the comparee, parameter and the index of comparison. The same syntactic construction applies to a superlative construction, as we saw in (11.8). Two major differences have been noted between the comparative in (11.7) and the superlative (11.8),—the superlative construction requires three copular clauses and two index markers.

There is also another form of comparative construction that involves two copula clauses but requires the use of two semantically opposing parameters (adjectives), as in (11.9).

(11.10) STANDARD   PARAMETER
  [dórí-á   n=ànù]_NP:CS   á   [tíín-í]_CC
  house-RSTR SG.SPD=1SG.PSR   COP.3.IMPERV small-ADJ
  [dórí-á   n=ùnù]_NP:CS   á   [bú-í]_CC
  house-RSTR SG.SPD=2SG.PSR   COP.3.IMPERV big-ADJ
  'My house is small; your house is big'
  (Lit. ~ 'My house is smaller than yours' or 'Your house is bigger than mine.')

As Dixon (2012: 359) states, this type of comparative construction can be called a 'comparative strategy'. A language called Alamblak (a Sepik Hill family, Papua New Guinea) has similar comparative construction to the one illustrated in (11.9) (p. 359).

11.5 Bi-clausal Construction Type II

Type II bi-clausal comparative construction is similar to Type I in a way it syntactically arranges its copular clause constituents. The difference lies in the use of a third clause which is a typical subordinate clause that contains all sorts of elements necessary for subordinate clause construction. Thus, Type II bi-clausal comparative construction can have the following four main syntactic constituents:

(i) Two copular clauses having the same parameter of comparison.
(ii) A subordinate clause that contains the verb èlèhèn 'compare, measure, make same, mark'.
(iii) A clausal coordinator nà 'and' which shows narrative progression. A clausal coordinator nà 'and' shows narrative progression. In this case, it shows the continuity of the first copular clause. When nà alone occurs at clause initial position, it denotes narrative/discourse progression but when nà is used together with the conditional/temporal marker particle húllí 'if/when' it can denote a disjunctive meaning (nà húllí 'but when' (lit. ~ 'and if/when')).

(iv) The comparee must be mentioned in both subordinate clause as well as in the second copula clause.

(11.11) STANDARD   PARAMETER
       [òlígìdànɪ́]_CS   á   [tíín-í]_CC
       Oligidhanyi COP.3.IMPERV small-ADJ
       COMPAREE
       nà   [húllí   k-èlèhèn-Ø   kó
       CCN   if/when   1SU-compare-1PL.INC.SU.IMPERV   PNC
       márítà=jè]_SUBORD:CL
       Marita=SUBORD
       COMPAREE   PARAMETER   INDEX
       [márítà]_CS   á   [tíín-í]_CC hán
       Marita   COP.3.IMPERV small-ADJ   very

'Oligidhanyi is small. But when we (inc.) compare (STANDARD) with Marita, Marita is very small.' (Mütze 2014).
(Lit. 'Marita is smaller when compared with Oligidhanyi.')

The subordinate clause in (11.10), can fill the gap seen in comparative constructions that are expressed by simply juxtaposing two copula clauses, for instance (11.8).

11.6   ɓá Construction

Comparative constructions that make use of the multifunction word *ɓá* are of two types: (i) copula clause + *ɓá*+ STANDARD, and (ii) *ɓá* in various syntactic slots. The word *ɓa* 'place, ground' may be used in the first type of construction the same way as in reason clauses and passive clauses (as agent marker). Thus, when *ɓá* is linked to the standard of comparison by the restrictive modification marker *-a*, both forms an NP, whose semantics is more similar to a reason clause.

(11.12)   COMPAREE   PARAMETER   MARK
      a.   [ŋɔ̀rɔ̀]_CS   á   [bú-í]_CC   [ɓá-á
           elephant COP.3.IMPERV big-ADJ   cause/place-RSTR
           STANDARD
           bì-ɲ]_NP
           cow-GEN
           'The elephant is bigger than the cow.'
           (Lit. 'In place of the cow, the elephant is bigger.')

	COMPAREE		PARAMETER	MARK
b.	[bì]$_{CS}$	á	[bú-í]$_{CC}$	[bá-á
	cow	COP.3.IMPERV	big-ADJ	cause/place-RSTR

STANDARD
ròs-ùɲ]$_{NP}$
dog-GEN

'The cow is bigger than the dog.'
(Lit. 'In place of the dog, the cow is bigger.')

The examples in (11.12a–b) were taken from Mütze (2014). Even though both are syntactically well-formed comparative constructions, the literal meanings that were provided by Mütze do not fully reflect their structure. For instance, Mütze glossed the NP within a frame of reason clause ('because of the cow' (11.12a) and 'because of the dog' (11.12b)). Mütze's literal interpretation (reason clause) comes from the fact that she considered the genitive case marked nouns as the standards of the comparative constructions, which is true. Yet, as can be seen from the examples given above, bá has little to do with reason clauses. The second function of bá 'in place of' is as marker of standard. In fact, in examples above (11.12a–b) bá seems to have the same function. However, unlike the above examples, the phrase that bá forms with the standard does not follow copula clauses, rather it follows simple intransitive or transitive clauses. Some examples are given below:

(11.13) PARAMETER   COMPAREE   MARK
a. nɔ̀ŋ   jél-Ø   [nɔ̀ŋ   [ʤɔ̀ɔ̀nɛ̀]$_{NP}$]$_{NP}$
   3SG   like-3SG.SU.IMPERV 3SG   mother.PERT.3.PSR
             STANDARD   INDEX
[bá-á   nɔ̀ŋ [ʃúúnɛ́]$_{NP}$]$_{NP}$ bó-ɔ́
place-RTSR 3SG father.PERT.3.PSR   above/high-OBL

'He loves his mother more than his father.'
(Lit. 'In place of his father, he likes his mother more.')

Here, the mark and the standard will comprise a single NP. Independent personal pronouns can occasionally be used by speakers in what appears to be an idiolect scenario and optional NP elements.

b. àggè wà   kúrt-ó   bá
   1pl   REC.PAST 1SU.dig.PERV-1pl.EXC.SU.PERV   place

	INDEX	COMPAREE	MARK	STANDARD
	ɓó	ŋàméá	[ɓá-á	bàrì
	above/high	today	place-RSTR	yesterday

bàrì-ne]_{NP}
yesterday-OBL/RS

'We have dug more ground today than yesterday.'
(Lit. 'In place of from yesterday, we (exc.) have dug more ground today.')

	PARAMETER	INDEX	COMPAREE	
b. [nòŋ]_S	ŋè-ú	wáŋ	[ŋàméá]	ɓó
3SG	run-3SG.SU.PERV	very	now	above/high
MARK	STANDARD			
[ɓá-á	bàrì	bàrì-ne]_{NP}
place-RSTR	yesterday	yesterday-OBL

'It is running more today than yesterday.'
(Lit. 'In yesterday's place, it is running very much (high) today.')

The index *wáŋ* in (11.13c) is modifier of the intransitive predicate while *ɓó* is a modifier of *ŋàméá*. Furthermore, (11.14c) shows that in Mursi, actions can be compared (see also e.g. 11.14). Further illustrations were provided below.

(11.14)

	COMPAREE	PARAMETER-INDEX	STANDARD
a.	nòŋ tìráŋ-Ø	jél-èsèn	dáfǐ
	3SG play-3SG.SU.IMPERV	like-COMPAR	work
	MARK		
	ɓó		
	above/high		

'He likes playing more than working.'

	COMPAREE		PARAMETER-INDEX	MARK
b.	[ɓá-á	ɓó-á]_{NP}	čàll-èsèn	[ɓá-á
	place-RTSR	wide-RSTR	good.STV-COMPAR	place-RTSR
	STANDARD			
	ŋùčù-à]_{NP}			
	narrow-RSTR			

'The wide one is better than the narrow one.'
(Lit. 'In place of the narrow, the wider one is better.')

11.7 Other Types of Comparative Constructions

In addition to the comparative constructions we saw in the aforementioned sections, Mursi employs two additional comparative strategies—one by employing a grammatical degree marker suffix -*sís* on the underived adjective *búí* 'big' and the other by employing a separative-like strategy. The degree marker suffix -*sís* only occurs on the adjective *búí* and can either be used to indicate degree of magnitude (see further in chapter 8) or augmentative.

(11.15) COMPAREE　　　　　　　　　　PARAMETER-INDEX
　　　 ŋà=ŋɔ̀rɔ̀　　[àhì-á　　bú-sísí-ó　　　　　gàʃ-ùɲ]_NP
　　　 DEM=elephant　thing.SG-RTSR big-AUG-RSTR　forest-GEN
　　　 'An elephant is a big animal (beast).'
　　　 (Lit. 'An elephant is the biggest thing of the forest.')

(11.15) is a verbless construction where both the parameter and index are in the NP. Due to the absence of the copula verb, the PARAMETER-INDEX is intervened between the head and the modifier of the NP. Had it been a copula clause, *búsísíó* would be placed in copula complement position while NP (just *àhìá gàʃùɲ*) would take the next position. The index is the augmentative suffix -*sísí* [-*sís*].

The other type of comparative construction is the one which employs a separative-like strategy (or subtractive "X's Y is small(er), and subtracted/cut-from X"). Cross-linguistically, the separative-like comparative construction is a very rare strategy. I have found one such example for which the verb *kéd* 'subtract, cut' denotes a separative-like reading.

(11.16) COMPAREE　　　　　　　　　　　　　　　　PARAMETER　INDEX
　　　 [ŋòná-á　　n=ànù]_NP:CS　　á　　　　　　　 [tíín-í]_CC　háɲnà
　　　 sister-RSTR SG.PSD=1SG.PSR COP.3.IMPERV　small-ADJ　very_CCN
　　　 　　　　　　　　　　　　STANDARD
　　　 kéd-áɲ　　　　àɲè
　　　 subtract/cut-1SG.OBJ 1SG
　　　 'My sister is much smaller than I am.'
　　　 (Lit. 'My sister is very small, (and/then/when) subtract/cut from me.')

This being an absolutely rare type of comparative construction strategy, it thus needs further research in the future.

11.8   Equality Construction

Equality construction in Mursi can be shown by either *hékó ... téb* '(the) same ... as' (*hékó* stands for 'same, similar') or by combining *hétɔ́* 'be same, look like' with the particle *téb* 'as/just'.

(11.17)

	COMPAREE		PARAMETER	INDEX	STANDARD
a.	[*túrúmél-á*	*ràmàg-à*]_{NP}	*tìr-tìn-ó*	*hékɔ́*	*báwùrù*
	car-RSTR	long.STV-RTSR	fast-N.S-MOD	same/like	plane

MARK
téb
as/just!
'A train is as fast as a plane'
(Lit. 'The long car is fast, the same as the plane.')

	COMPAREE	INDEX		STANDARD	PARAMETER
b.	*čár*	*hét-éné*	*kó*	*ŋàtùɲ*	*бág-ò*
	leopard.SG	be.same-AP.3	PNC	lion.SG	eat-3SG.IRR

INDEX
téb
as/just
'Leopard is as dangerous as lion.'
(Lit. 'Leopard be (the) same with/as lion, as/just dangerous.')

	COMPAREE	PARAMETER	STANDARD	INDEX	MARK
c.	*dórí*	*ràmà-tìn-ó*	*túrúmél*	*hékɔ́*	*téb*
	house.SG	long.STV-N.S-MOD	car.SG	same	as/just

'The house is as tall as the car.'

In (11.17a,c), the parameters are nominalized stative verbs denoting 'state'. Dixon (2012: 363) noted that the majority of languages of the world have a grammatical construction for 'the same as', a separate form from that for 'more than'.

CHAPTER 12

Questions

12.1 Introduction

A question is one of the three speech act types whose grammatical mood value is expressed by interrogative (cf. Dixon 2012). The two best known question types are content questions and polar questions. Mursi has both types. Mursi employs content question words (mostly pronominals) which usually take clause-final argument slots. Mursi question words occur immediately following the verb at syntactic positions where grammatical objects naturally belong. Moreover, sentence-final positions, syntactic slots for core and non-core arguments may typically function as focus-bearing positions when filled by question words. By using Mursi content questions words, one can question the referents of clause final argument slots (NPs), location, time, quantity, and so on. On the other hand, a polar question in Mursi can be formed either by raising the intonation of the lexical constituents that occur at end of a clause or by placing non-interrogative particles at the end of a declarative statement.

Besides, Mursi does not adhere to Greenberg's Universal Hypothesis 12. Greenberg predicted that VSO languages always have interrogative words sentence-initially. In Mursi and in other Southeastern Surmic group languages (AVO), interrogative words always occur sentence-finally. Syntactically, as long as the O argument a is sentence-final constituent, the difference between VSO [VAO] and AVO is not significant in interrogative constructions. Of all interrogative words, *ténèŋ* 'why' deviates from the sentence-final pattern. The interrogative word 'why' has two varieties, one of which, *ténèŋ*, can be placed at sentence-initial position when used in some rhetorical questions. In the light of the two straightforward question construction formation types and other less common strategies of interrogatives, this chapters presents a detailed discussion of the structure of questions of the language. Thus, in the subsequent sections, content questions (§12.2), non-interrogative particles (§12.3), polar questions (§12.4), and other questioning strategies (§12.5) in the language are discussed in detail.

TABLE 12.1 Question (interrogative) words

Question words	Meaning	Core/non-core functions	Section
ɔ̀ŋ	'what?'	O (-human objects)	§12.2.1
ɔ́nɔ́ŋ	'what?'	A/S (-human)	§12.2.1
ɔ́nɔ́ŋɔ́	'with what?'	~ 'by what means' non-core (instrumental)	§12.2.1
ɛ̀nɛ̀ŋ	'how?'	method	§12.2.2
kɛ̀ ɔ̀ŋ	'why?'	~ 'for what' reason, rhetorical, incredulity	§12.2.2
ténèŋ	'why?'	reason, rhetorical	§12.2.2
mìnáŋ	'when?'	temporal (point of time)	§12.2.3
òrì	'where?'	location (place)	§12.2.4
ɓónnój	'where?'	~ 'place/out.where' definite, indefinite	§12.2.4
ísɔ̀ŋ	'how many?'	quantity (number)	§12.2.5
nèŋ	'who?'	O (±human objects), CC, peripheral argument	§12.2.6
nój	'who?'	O (+human)	§12.2.6
nì	'whose?'	modification form, singular possession	§12.2.7
gì	'whose?'	modification form, plural possession	§12.2.7
nì+nì	'whose?'	pronoun form, singular possession,	§12.2.8
gì+gì	'whose?'	pronoun form, plural possession	§12.2.8

12.2 Content Questions

Content question words normally fill both core and non-core argument slots. Since question words occur at clause-final argument slot within strict constituent order, the original constituents at the clause-final slot can be placed at clause-initial position. Moreover, content question words are 'pro-phrasals' therefore they may come with marked case and modification forms (cf. Mütze 2014). Content question words are of two types: question words and interrogative pronouns. This distinction is based on the properties that question words often display whenever they fill the non-question words' syntactic slots, because both types of question words can fill whatever position is natural for the non-question words corresponding to the same slot.

One basic observation that can be made from the forms of question words in Table 12.1 is the reoccurrence of /n/ and /g/ to distinguish between singular and plural numbers. Typologically, the *n/g*(k) singular versus plural alternation is one of the most common areal features, not only in Surmic languages but also in most languages of Eastern Sudanic. Besides, except the interrogative *ténèŋ*

QUESTIONS 491

that can occur only sentence-initially, all the rest of the interrogative words always occur at sentence-final positions.

Regarding the morphological status of interrogatives, some appear to have originated from one common form ɔ̀ŋ even if it is not easy at this stage to trace back how they fused in such way. Especially, many of the question (interrogative) words appear to have the formative ɔ̀ŋ or -ɔŋ, may be at some point in early stages of the language. Yet it is possible to analyze some of them as separate forms or morphemes, for which each segmentable unit will carry its own independent grammatical meaning. For example, the interrogative word ɔ́nɔ́ŋɔ́ 'with what?' is derived from the non-human A nominative form ɔ́nɔ́ŋ 'what?' and the oblique case marker suffix -ɔ. The interrogative ɔ́nɔ́ŋ itself appears to be a derived form possibly from nɔ̀ŋ '3sg' (or third person impersonal pronoun) (see Table 12.1) and the nominative case marker -ɔ (as prefix). As the forms themselves hint, a number of such plausible explanations could be presented in order to trace back the origins of Mursi interrogative forms—but they may not consist of more than three formative.

Last and Lucassen (1998: 415) noted that the form */a-ŋa/ 'what' (with a copula) have been attested in Proto-Nilotic. They also suggested that this could be one of the oldest question word formation within the Eastern Sudanic language family. For instance, present-day languages such as Luo (*a-ŋɔ* 'what') and Päri (*a-ŋo* 'what', *a-ŋa* 'who') have maintained the proto-forms.

12.2.1 ɔ̀ŋ, ɔ́nɔ́ŋ and ɔ́nɔ́ŋɔ́

A common similarity of these question words is that they all occur sentence-finally. They can question core and non-core arguments. In referring to non-human participants, both ɔ̀ŋ 'what.OBJ' and ɔ́nɔ́ŋ 'what.NOM' also share certain syntactic properties, for instance, both occur in O function and can be copula complements immediately following regular or copula verbs. The question word ɔ̀ŋ normally refers to non-human object participants while ɔ́nɔ́ŋ refers to non-human subject participants.

(12.1) a. [iɲɛ]ₐ múɲ-ɛ̀sɛ̀   [ɔ̀ŋ]ₒ
          2SG   annoy-BEN.3   what
          'What are you angry about?'

      b. [gáwá-jè]₀ᵦₗ [sábá-á   n=ùnù]ᵣₑₗғ   tál-ésé-ó
          market-OBL head-RSTR SG.SPD=2SG.PSR buy-BEN-2SG.SU.PERV
          ɔ̀ŋ
          what
          'What did you buy for yourself in the market?'

In both (12.1a–b), ɔ̀ŋ is in O function following the transitive predicates. In (12.1b), since the interrogative word has taken over the sentence-final position, the oblique argument is put in sentence-initial position. In addition, the verb root tál 'buy, sell' does not distinguish between imperfective and perfective aspects. So, the second person bound pronominal suffix -o performs the temporal duty of the verb. Following a copula verb, the interrogative ɔ̀ŋ can fill a copula complement slot as predicate nominal, as in (12.2). Since post-verbal position is associated with focus, and content questions typically also have similarities with focus constructions.

(12.2) [ìggè]_{CS} án-ó   [ɔ̀ŋ]_{CC}
       2PL   COP.IMPERV-2PL.SU.IMPERV what
       'What are you (pl.)?'

       [àggè]_{CS} k-án-ó   [támárí-ɲá]_{CC}
       1PL   1SU-COP.IMPERV-1PL.EXC.SU.IMPERV student-PL
       'We are students.'

A copula clause consisting of the associative (accompaniment and instrument) word kàrì 'together', and ɔ̀ŋ can be combined into a single function, i.e. to question an instrument/object used to perform a certain the action. Even if the object used is already stated in the question statement, the main function of kàrì plus ɔ̀ŋ is to denote an incredulous situation. Thus the whole copula structure may be moved to a sentence-initial position, as in (12.3).

(12.3) [kàrì]_{CS} á   [ɔ̀ŋ]_{CC} bíró-a   wà   ìɲè
       together COP.3.IMPERV what.OBJ money-RSTR REC.PAST 2SG
       tál-a-nè   nɔ̀ŋ=ŋà
       buy-MT-RECIP 3SG=DEF
       'With what money did you buy it with?'

It is used to question a non-human subject expressing doubt. The question word ɔ́nɔ́ŋ occurs in nominative form and it occasionally denotes 'by who; by what means', as in (12.4a–b).

(12.4) a. kámá ám-Ø   ɔ́nɔ́ŋ
         bag   eat-3.IRR what.NOM
         'What ate the bag?' (~How did it tear?)

b. *hírí bág-Ø ɔ́nɔ́ŋ bág-Ø*
man bite-3SG.SU.IMPERV what.NOM bite-3SG.SU.IMPERV
gùfúr-Ø
hyena-NOM
'What bit the man? (It is) the hyena (that) bit.'

The occurrence of *ɔ́nɔ́ŋ* in my corpus is very rare hence it requires further in-depth research. On the other hand, *ɔ́nɔ̀ŋɔ́* 'with.what' as pointed out above is a question word that may be used to ask about an instrument used. The instrument function is indicated in two ways: (i) by an oblique case marker suffix *-ɔ*, which is added to the form *ɔ́nɔ̀ŋ* and yelds the instrumental form *ɔ́nɔ̀ŋ-ɔ́*, and (ii) by a multifunctional free from particle *kó* (has an instrumental or a comitative linker function in the examples below).

(12.5) *zùkt=ùnù k-èlì ké mùnì búná mèsí kó*
people=FAR PASS-call.PERV QUOT Mursi coffee do.NOMZ PNC
ɔ̀ŋ dáfí ɔ́nɔ̀ŋ-ɔ́
what.OBJ work what-OBL⟨with.what⟩
'The Mursi coffee will be made from what and (by) *with what?*'
(Lit. 'The people called the Mursi, coffee will be made from what and (prepared) with what?')

Since *ɔ́nɔ̀ŋɔ́* occurs with an oblique case marker, it fills the peripheral argument slot that immediately occurs following the direct object, as in (12.6).

(12.6) *jɔ̀g édʒ-ɛ́ ŋàtùɲ ɔ́nɔ̀ŋ-ɔ́*
3PL kill.IMPERV-3PL.SU.IMPERV lion what-OBL⟨with.what⟩
'With what did they kill the lion?'

If the O argument of the clause is mentioned in the previous section of the discourse or if it is something known from the context, *ɔ́nɔ̀ŋɔ́* may then takes the O slot and simply follows the verbal predicate.

(12.7) *ŋànìje [éró-á g=ùj]*_{NP} *čúg-ɛ́*
thus children-RSTR PL.PSD=2PL.PSR chase.away-3PL.SU.IMPERV
ɔ́nɔ̀ŋ-ɔ́
what-OBL⟨with.what⟩
'Thus, by whom (how) do your children cast them out?'

The coordinator particle *kó* is used to relate the cause marker particle *bá* with the instrument that caused the cause. Even in the absence of it one can ask about the instrument/the means by which the cause happened, thus *kó* has a secondary function. See the examples illustrated below:

(12.8) a. *bá   kó   ɔ́nɔ̀ŋ-ɔ́*
place/CAUSE CRD what-OBL⟨with.what⟩
'What is the matter?'

b. *wà   bá   kó   ɔ́nɔ̀ŋ-ɔ́*
REC.PAST place/CAUSE CRD what-OBL⟨with.what⟩
'What has happened?'

12.2.2 *ènèŋ, kè ɔ̀ŋ and ténèŋ*

The question word *ènèŋ* 'how?' is used to question the method in which an action is carried out. In addition, it may be used for asking about the name of a person or location; and occasionally to refer to the amount (quantity) of referents.

(12.9) a. *dógtér ìɲè ké   mɔ̀kɔ̀ɲ-ì   kɔ́d-í*
doctor 2SG 3.SBJV.COP.PERV short.STV-ADJ write-2SG.SU.IMPERV
ènèŋ
how
'How do you (sg.) abbreviate doctor?'

b. *nɔ̀ŋ úŋó ènèŋ*
3SG night how
'How did you spend/pass the night/evening?'
(Lit. 'It the night is how?')

OR c. *wà   túŋ-nò   ènèŋ*
REC.PAST sleep.PERV-2.IRR how
'How did you (sg.) spend the evening?'

Depending on the discourse context in which they occur, both expressions are appropriate even if (12.9c) is more appropriate than (12.9b), because it is expressed by a predicate rather than by deverbal noun/NP. (12.9b) explicitly shows person and number of human participant of the discourse who is being questioned. Thus, obviously the second person singular is the addressee questioned. One can also ask for the name of a person or location, as is shown below (as in (12.10a–b)).

(12.10) a. sárá   k-èlì-íɲ   ènèŋ
            name   PASS-call.PERV-2SG.OBJ how
            'What is your (sg.) name?'
            (Lit. 'Your (sg.) name is called/said how?')

     b. sárá   ŋà=bà-ì=nù   k-èlì   ènèŋ
         name   DEM=place-LOC=FAR   PASS-call.PERV how
         'What is the name of the country?'
         (Lit. 'The name that place called how?')

Another means to ask, the name of a person is by using a possessive pronoun as NP, a copula verb, and the human participant interrogative pronoun nèŋ (12.10a1).

     a1. [sárá-á   g=ùɲù]ₙₚ:cs   á   [nèŋ]cc
         name-RSTR   PL.PSD=2SG.PSR COP.3.IMPERV   who.OBJ
         'What is your name?'
         (Lit. 'Your name is who?')

Note that 'name' in Mursi is inherently plural, thus the plural number proclitic g= is used to indicate a plural possessed item. Despite there being a correct interrogative word for questioning number/quantity, ènèŋ may also be used under certain circumstances but whose distribution is not clear. The examples below in (12.11) and (12.12) will illustrate this assertion.

(12.11) [bì-ò   kó   tènè]ₙₚ   kàrì   bá-á   án-á
        cow-PL   PNC   goat.PL   together   place-RSTR   COP.IMPERV-TEMP
        [mèr-tìn-ó   kèt-á]ₙₚ   él   ènèŋ
        many-N.S-RSTR   thing-RSTR exist.PL.IMPERV   how
        'How many cattle and goats do you have?'
        (Lit. 'Cows and goats together the whole thing in place exist how (many)?')

(12.12) hín   ídɔ́-nèj   á   ènèŋ
        want.IMPERV   add-NOMZ   COP.3.IMPERV   how
        'What is the amount?'
        (Lit. 'Amount you want is how?')

Mursi speakers frequently use the interrogative word kè ɔ̀ŋ 'why?' to question the reason why a certain incredible situation happened. kè ɔ̀ŋ has stylistic dominance over *ténèŋ* 'why?', which is the only sentence-initial interrogative word. See example 12.13 below (repeated from 7.24).

(12.13) *híh!   ná   ɲè   kɨ́ɲáŋ   húŋ   ɓák-ú   kè ɔ̀ŋ   kó*
       INTERJ CCN   2SG   crocodile simply eat-3SG.SU.PERV   why   PNC
       ɓásáj   ɓák-ú   kè ɔ̀ŋ   dág-áɲ-Ø
       monitor.lizard eat-3SG.SU.PERV   why   hit-1SG.OBJ-3SG.SU
       hózò-j   aj!
       hanger-NOM   INTERJ
       '"Hih!" why did you (sg.) eat a crocodile? Also you (sg.) ate a monitor lizard, why? Don't say, "Hunger hit me?!" Aj!' (MH 4:30:6)

As the form points out, *kè ɔ̀ŋ* is composed of purpose-like preposition particle *kɛ* and the formative *ɔ̀ŋ* 'what', the combination of the two obviously did produce a meaning: 'for what'. For instance in (12.14), the question sentence seeks an answer for the reason why the human participant stayed long. However, (12.14) can also be used to question by which method the participant being questioned used to stay.

(12.14) *ŋáà   tíí   kó   ŋàméá   ŋáà   té-ú   ké ɔ̀ŋ*
       here DUR CRD   now   here be.PERV-2SG.SU.PERV   why
       'How did you (sg.) stay here until now?'
       (Lit. 'Why did you (sg.) stay here until now?')

An interesting scenario is found in (12.15) where *kè ɔ̀ŋ* is used with *ténèŋ* in the same interrogative sentence.

(12.15) *ténèŋ   ʃíl-Ø-è-o   kè ɔ̀ŋ*
       why   stand-3SG.IRR-COM-MT   why
       'Why did he bring an accusation against him?'

The fact is that both occur in their designated syntactic slots. The enquiry here should be regarding the function of each reason interrogative words. *ténèŋ* always occurs before a verb sentence-initially and has a semantic scope over the entire sentence. So *ténèŋ* in (12.15) has the function of questioning the whole motive of the sentence in a single explanation. On the other hand, since *kè ɔ̀ŋ* is a bimorphemic form with one of its component being *ɔ̀ŋ* 'what', it makes sense for its meaning to express inquiry of the purpose 'for what'. As Aikhenvald (2015: 278) states, 'interrogatives in many languages do not form one word class in terms of their morphological categories and syntactic functions'. Mursi adheres to this assertion, for the reason that membership of interrogative words to one particular word class seems always to be problematic as they are made up of more than one component. Besides, interrogative words such as *kè ɔ̀ŋ* and *ténèŋ* can belong separate syntactic categories despite sharing the same semantics. The fact is that this view does not include the interrogative pronouns of the language. Of the syntactic deviation of *ténèŋ* from the other question word members, not much is known at this stage. However, a piece of information has been stated from (Dixon 2012, Li and Thompson 1981) may indicate the syntactic nature of *ténèŋ* in relation to other languages. A good example is Mandarin Chinese where a single question word can mean 'how' and 'why'. In Mandarin, 'why' is a sentential adverbial requesting the respondent to provide a semantic frame for the entire sentence (Dixon 2012: 414). In addition, it can be moved to the beginning of the sentence if the interpretation intended to be delivered is 'why'.

In light of this, *ténèŋ* in Mursi behaves the same way as in Mandarin. The real semantics of 'why' can only be delivered by *ténèŋ* and certainly not by *kè ɔ̀ŋ*. The verb, mostly, occurs in the irrealis mood. As can be shown in the following sentences, the interrogative word *ténèŋ* is fronted for emphasis, when it enquires about the reason why certain actions took place and expressing a strong rebuke.

(12.16) a. *ténèŋ ɪ̀nè kéŋá-Ø-ò   jɔ̀g tìráŋ=ŋà*
  why   2SG deny-3PL.OBJ-2SG.IRR 3PL play=DEF
  'Why do you forbid them to play?'

 b. *ténèŋ ɪ̀nè kéŋá-Ø-ú   nɔ̀ŋ čól=ŋà*
  why   2SG deny-3SG.OBJ-2SG.IRR 3SG sing=DEF
  'Why do you forbid him to sing?'

 c. *ténèŋ ɪ̀nè kéŋá-áɲ-ò   àɲè woč-in-no*
  why   2SG deny-1SG.OBJ-2SG.IRR 1SG go.IMPERV-NOMZ-COMPL
  ŋà=b=ùnù=ŋà
  DEM=place=FAR=DEF
  'Why do you forbid me to go there?'

In addition, as shown in all of (12.16a–c), sentence-final NPs are marked by a definite marker enclitic =*ŋà*. Note that definiteness in Mursi is phrasal-marked at the end NPs or on constituents that occur at the end of a sentence. *ténèŋ* can rarely occur sentence-finally, but only in special circumstances, as in (12.17).

(12.17) [dórí-á   tímírtí-ɲ]_NP   wóč-ín-nó
       house-RTSR education-GEN go.IMPERV-NOMZ-COMPL
       dɔ̃t-έ-ù   [sabá-á   n=ùnù]_NP   húŋ-ne   ténèŋ
       leave-APPL-IRR head-RTSR SG.PSD=2SG.PSR simply-RS why
       'Why did you absent yourself *from school*?'
       (Lit. 'Why did you absented yourself from walking to school?')

Following the second person reflex form, the temporal-like adverb *húŋ* 'simply, just' is sentence-final followed by *ténèŋ* in focal function. It doesn't seem part of the clause. When there is a topic or a pre-posed thematically prominent participant marker at the beginning of a sentence, *ténèŋ* becomes a sentence second constituent (as in (12.18)).

(12.18) kómórú ténèŋ hólóiɲa dɔ̃t-á   kɔ́ɔg-ò
       learder why   empty   leave-3SG.SU.PERV   3.SBJV-go-3PL.IRR
       'Why did *the king* abdicate?'
       (Lit. 'The leader (pol.), why did he (pol.) empty leave and went? Or Why did the leader (pol.) empty leave and went?')

12.2.3 mìnáŋ 'When'

The temporal interrogative word *mìnáŋ* is used to question a point in time. Like other members of its class, it takes a sentence-final slot.

(12.19) a. *bongoso   ké-héj-Ø   mìnáŋ*
          Bongoso.OBJ 1SU-go.IMPERV:PL-1PL.INC.SU.IMPERV   when
          'When do we (inc.) go to Bongoso?'

       b. *bè   túrúmél ʃólá-j   bóns-èsèn   mìnáŋ*
          DIST.PAST car   suffer-NOMZ arrive.IMPERV-BEN.3   when
          'When did the automobile accident happen?'

Unlike other interrogative words (not interrogative pronouns), the interrogative *mìnáŋ* can occur in subordinate clauses in direct or indirect speech, as in (12.19c).

       c. *nɔ̀ŋ ʤɔ̀ɔ̀nè   sésé   nɔ̀ŋ ké   ŋŋ*
          3SG mother.PERT.3SG.PSR   say.BEN.3.PERV   3SG QUOT INTERJ
          [*bóns-í   ɔ́r-ɔ́   mìnáŋ=nè*]_SUBORD:CL
          arrive.IMPERV-2SG.SU.IMPERV home-OBL when=SUBORD

hàlì ɓág-è
later eat-2SG.IRR
'His mother said to him, "when you (sg.) get (reach) home, you (sg.) will eat".'

In (12.19d), *mìnáŋ* occurs in a relative clause as the modifier the noun *uŋ[o]* 'day'. But the relative clause itself is embedded within the subordinate clause.

    d. àggè k-ímág-ó-ɔ́   [úŋ-ní
        1PL 1SU-not.know-1PL.SU.IMPERV=NEG day-NRSTR
        [Ø mìnáŋ=e]_{RC/SUBORD:CL} kirtos hàlì mírčíŋá-nè=jè=jè]_{SUBORD:CL}
        [Ø when=SUBORD]   christ later return-AP.3=SUBORD=EMPH
        'We (inc.) do not know the day when Christ will return.'

12.2.4 òrì *'Where'* and ɓónnój *'Where'*

The interrogative words *òrì* and *ɓónnój* have one meaning 'where'. Both are used to ask questions eliciting answers which would fill the local adverbial slots of a clause. No locative or oblique case marker is possible to attach to these two location question forms. The choice of the local interrogative word may depend on the point of reference of a known location within the speaker's view, or a location which is not known by the speaker. The examples given below illustrate this further: *òrì* (12.20a–c) and *ɓónnój* (12.21a–d).

(12.20) a. díŋíʃéní k-ój-Ø   òrì
          potato 1SU-put-1SG.IRR where
          'Where shall I store the potatoes?'

         b. [hír-á   kɔ́h-ìnèn-á]_{NP}   ɔ́k-ú   òrì
            man-RSTR farm-NOMZ-RSTR go-3SG.SU.PERV where
            'Where did the farmer go?'

         c. dóólej í-Ø   òrì
            girl exist.IMPERV-3SG.SU.IMPERV where
            'Where is the girl?'

In (12.20a), the verb is *ódʒ* but the palatal the affricative stop /dʒ/ becomes approximant /j/ word-finally (see §2.5.3).

(12.21) a. [kè-á kód-á-ɲ]_NP wà kón-nèn-ì
thing-RSTR write-NOMZ-GEN REC.PAST 1SU.write.PERV-AP-SG
ók-ú bónnój
go-3SG.SU.PERV where
'Where is the pen I wrote with (yesterday)?'
(Lit. 'by which I wrote')

b. ìggè [ŋà=éró=á kòná-ú=ŋà]_NP
2PL DEM=children=NEAR snake.PL-NOM=DEF
[čib-in-a go-ɲ]_NP hàlì ʤur-o
punish-NOMZ-RTSR fire-GEN later run.IMPERV-2PL.SU.IMPERV
bónnój
where
'You (pl.) *serpents, you (pl.) generation of vipers*, how can you (pl.) escape the damnation of hell?'
(Lit. 'You (pl.), *the children of serpents*, where will you (pl.) escape from the fire punishment?')

c. báʔsígá tílá dàìnè hàlì k-ám-Ø bónnój
passover food evening later 2.SBJV-eat-SG.IRR where
"Where do you want to eat the Passover?"

d. [čúr-á-á johanisi-j]_NP kún-Ø bónnój
baptize-NOMZ-RSTR john-GEN come-3SG.SU.IMPERV where
kún-Ø tùmù tùn-ò kóó
come-3SG.SU.IMPERV sky above-OBL CRD.DISJ
kún-Ø [bá-á hírí-ɲ]_NP
come-3SG.SU.IMPERV place-RSTR man-GEN
'The baptism of John, from where was it? from heaven, or of men?'

Syntactically, Mursi adverbs may split between sentence-initial and sentence-final positions. Most manner adverbs occur sentence-finally, even if few of them can occur at initial positions. The same syntax applies to locative adverbs. Nevertheless, the clause-final slots occupied by the local interrogative words *òrì* and *bónnój* in the examples illustrated above are slots which could be filled by demonstrative formative type locative adverbs.

For example, *bónnój* in (12.22) does not refer a particular place or location so it may mean also 'what'. Compare the following examples: the answer to question (12.22) a question of its answer could generate a particular location, and (12.23) may not necessarily have such interpretation.

(12.22) [ŋà=hòi=tá]_NP:TOP   [ʃúúnú]_NP   í-Ø
DEM=female=NEAR   father.PERT.3SG.PSR   to.be-3SG.SU.IMPERV
òrì   í-Ø   dórí-jè
where   to.be-3SG.SU.IMPERV   house-OBL
'Where is your (f) father? He is at home.'
(Lit. 'Girl, where is your (sg) father?')

(12.23) tíín-óɲ   bónnój
small-1SG.OBJ   where
'What made me small?'
(Lit. 'Where (from who) does my becoming small come from?') (Mütze 2014)

12.2.5 ísɔ̀ŋ 'How Many/Much'

Any sentence containing the quantitative interrogative word *ísɔ̀ŋ* 'how many, how much' is one that questions a quantifiable, countable/non-countable, number of referents.

(12.24) a. àlèj   ɲè   hín-í   ísɔ̀ŋ
chair   2SG   want.IMPERV-3SG.SU.IMPERV   how.many
'How many chairs do you want?'

When *ísɔ̀ŋ* occurs following a copula verb, it functions by filling a copula complement slot. A Mursi copula complement slot mostly involves predicate nominal/lexical number words. In this case, *ísɔ̀ŋ* can be interpreted as 'what', as in (12.24b).

b. írsásí   gáwá   á   ísɔ̀ŋ
pencil   market   COP.3.IMPERV   how.many
'What is the price of a pencil?'

In fact, the noun *gáwá* 'price' (lit. 'market ≈ week') has contributed to the meaning of 'what'. In the absence of *gáwá*, this sentence would be 'how many pencil'—just referring to the quantity instead of the price. The difference between these two meanings of the question word *ísɔ̀ŋ* 'how many'/'how much' requires further study. If the question is presented as in (12.24b), the possible replies would involve a lexical number word either as copula complement or as modifier of a head noun within NP, as in:

(12.25) a. támáríɲá-ì   él-έ
            student.PL-LOC exist.IMPERV:PL-3PL.SU.IMPERV
            á   ísɔ̀ŋ
            COP.3.IMPERV   how.many
            'How many students are present/there?'

   a1. támáríɲá-ì   él-έ
        student.PL-LOC exist.IMPERV:PL-3PL.SU.IMPERV
        á   háánán
        COP.3.IMPERV   five
        'There are five students.'

   a2. ŋà=ɓ=ùnù   támáríɲá   háánán
        DEM=place=FAR   student.PL   five
        él-έ
        exist.IMPERV:PL-3PL.SU.IMPERV
        'Five students are present.'

During my long corpus collection in the Mursi community, one important point that I learned from Mursi speakers is that their preference for specific types of grammatical constructions out of many other types mostly depends on stylistic and ideolectal differences. For instance, (12.25a1) is more preferred than (12.25a2). In addition to 'how many', using *ísɔ̀ŋ*, one can ask questions such as 'how much' and 'how old'.

(12.26) a. ìɲè [gáwá-j   dɔ̌néj]ₙₚ tó-jé   ór-í
            2SG week-NRSTR   one   in-OBL see.IMPERV-2SG.SU.IMPERV
            ísɔ̀ŋ
            how.many
            'How much do you earn a week?'
            (Lit. 'How much do you see in one week?')

   b. [érmì-á   n=ànù]ₙₚ   òìɲá   án-íɲ
       child-RSTR   SG.PSD=1SG.PSR   year.PL   COP.IMPERV-1SG.OBJ
       ísɔ̀ŋ
       how.may
       'How old are you, my child?'

12.2.6 nèŋ and nój 'Who'

The interrogative pronouns *nèŋ* and *nój* refer to the identity of human referents. The interrogative pronoun *nèŋ* can occur in O function either following a main verb or a copula verb. There are two main syntactic slots in which *nèŋ* occurs: direct object of a transitive verb and extended argument of a ditransitive verb. *nèŋ* may not be marked for object case by an overt morphological form because it is inherently an object form in its own right.

(12.27) a. mà   gočč-a-sèn   nèŋ
water draw-MT-BEN who.OBJ
'You fetch water for who?'

    b. ɨɲè hín-í   nèŋ
2SG want.IMPERV-2SG.SU.IMPERV who.OBJ
'Whom do you want?'

    c. [ŋɔ̀ŋ [érmì [ʤɔ̀ɔ̀nè]_NP]_NP·CS   á   [nèŋ]_CC
3SG child mother.PERT.3SG.PSR COP.3.IMPERV who.OBJ
'Who is the baby's Mother?'

Interrogative sentences that involve some degree of force do not cross-reference second person singular A argument on the verb. In this respect, certain interrogative verb forms are similar with person singular imperative forms.

(12.28) a. bíró áʤ-έ   nèŋ
money give.IMPERV-APPL who.OBJ
k-áʤ-Ø-έ   érmì
1SU-give.IMPERV-1PL.INC.SU.IMPERV-APPL child
'To whom did you (pl.) give the money? We gave (it) to the boy.'

    b. kún-έ   bá á   nèŋ
come.IMPERV-APPL place COP.3.IMPERV who.OBJ
sé-ù   wà   áín-έ   nèŋ
COMPZR/say-IRR REC.PAST give.PERV:SG-APPL who.OBJ
'From whom do you take and to whom do you give?'
'From whom do you take and to whom do you want to give?'

As shown in the interrogative examples above, bound pronominal A argument suffixes are not cross-referenced on the main verbs. As in the interrogative examples below, bound pronominal A argument suffixes are not cross-referenced on the main verbs.

(12.29) tèréfè édʒ-é ŋàtùɲ kó nèŋ
Terefe kill-COM lion with who.OBJ
'With whom did Terefe kill the lion.' (Mütze 2014)

In (12.29), *nèŋ* is in peripheral function and represents a human referent participant in the joint action carried out with the A. When a joint state/action involves an intransitive verb, inherently plural verb form may be used, as in:

(12.30) él-ú kó nèŋ
exist:PL-2SG.SU.PERV with who.OBJ
'With who are you?'

On the other hand, the interrogative pronoun *nój* may occur at the same syntactic position of the *nèŋ*, but in a different function. *nój* mainly has a human reference when it occurs in nominative form.

(12.31) a. wà áɨw-ó-Ø nój
REC.PAST come.PERV-MT-3SG.SU.PERV who.NOM
'Who came?'

b. wà jów-ò í-Ø nój
REC.PAST speak-3PL.IRR to.be-3SG.SU.IMPERV who.NOM
'Who they say to you?'
(Lit. 'Who, did they tell you?')

c. nà àlèj kɔ́-é nój
CCN chair 3.SBJV.go-APPL who.NOM
'Who took the chair away?'

Mursi does not have an interrogative word dedicated for 'which'. However, *nój* may also be used to enquire 'which' type of questions. Dixon (2012: 411) noted that 'who' can only be used as head of an NP. It could replace 'which' as in '*which X*' if 'X' is a noun with human reference (as in (12.32)).

(12.32) a. á   í-Ø   nój
        COP.3.IMPERV to.be-3SG.SU.IMPERV who.NOM
        'Which one?'
        (Lit. 'It is be who?')

    b. á   ígg-í   nój
        COP.3.IMPERV 3PL.PN.SP-NRSTR who.NOM
        'Which ones?'

As it is shown in (12.32a), the number of the referents has been indicated by the verb *to be* (also singular existential verb form). Besides, *nój* is not a modifier since there is no noun to be modified. However, in (12.32b), the plural specific/relative pronoun is in a modified form and the modifier could be any noun since the modification/relator marker attached to it is non-restrictive. Further study is needed to see whether *nój* is used to refer to non-human reference. The singular counterpart of (12.32b) is as follows.

    c. ìnè hàlì kɔ́-í   ín-í   nój
        2SG later go-2SG.SU.IMPERV 3SG.PN.SP-NRSTR who.NOM
        'Which of you will go?'

One could ask about the place of origin of a person. It is not the place which is asked for but the identity of a person. See the example given below.

(12.33) a. á   nèŋ   hírí bà-ì   nój-é
        COP.3.IMPERV who.OBJ man place-LOC who.NOM
        'What country (or what district of the country) do you come from?'
        (Lit. 'of which country a person are you?')

Obviously, the example below can be rephrased as: 'It is the house of whom, which one of your brothers?'

    b. dórí   á   nèŋ   gòdónù   nój-é
        house COP.3.IMPERV who.OBJ brother.PERT.SG.2.PSR who.NOM
        'To which one of your brothers does the house belong?'

Both interrogative pronouns with human referents were used in the above examples. The function of the interrogative pronoun *nèŋ* in both constructions is simply part of the language's question construction strategy. Finally, *nój* may be used to ask about a non-human referent, as in the example given below.

(12.34) wà	tál-án	túrmél nój-é
REC.PAST buy-MT.2SG.SU.IMPERV car who-NOM
'Which car did you buy?'

The suffix -e attached to the interrogative pronoun is unusual and/or has unclear function. In most cases, second person singular subject suffix is omitted if a motion suffix is attached to the verb.

Note—I mentioned earlier that Mursi lacks an interrogative word for 'which'. Although my position is still the same, two unusual forms that appear to have a 'which' reading have been attested in my data. They are *inój* 'which.SG' and *gioj* 'which.PL'. As shown in the examples given below, both interrogative forms can refer either to a human referent or a non-human referent.

(12.35) a. ìggè hín-ó	k-ɔ̀g-á-ùŋ
2PL want.IMPERV-2PL.SU.IMPERV 1SU-untie.SG-MT-2SG.OBJ
inój
which.SG
'Which of the two (human) do you want me to release to you?'

b. màmà	á	nèŋ	kó
mother:PERT.SG.1.PSR COP.3.IMPERV who.OBJ PNC
[gòdóngà	g=ànù]ₙₚ	á
brother:PERT.PL.1SG.PSR PL.PSD=1SG.PSR COP.3.IMPERV
gìój
who.PL+NOM
'Who are my mother and my brothers?'
(Lit. 'Who is my mother and who are my brothers?')

In Turton and Bender (1976: 540), the two have been mentioned as *ainoi* (singular) and *agyoi* (plural). They are alike with the forms in (12.35a–c) despite a slight difference from Turton and Bender's suggestion. The segment *a* of the *ainoi* and *agyoi* is a copula verb—and the final segment is approximant rather than a high vowel. Despite the fact that in Mursi there are some fused grammatical forms which require further investigation, in fused form *gìój* in (12.35b), the form *-ój* is a nominative case marker; since it follows the copula verb.

12.2.7 nì *and* gì *'Whose'*

The interrogative pronouns *nì* and *gi* are singular and plural possessive forms of 'who'. Both *nì* 'who.GEN.SG' and *gì* 'who.GEN.PL' occur in modifier position within an NP. Consequently, any noun that may replace these two possessive interrogative pronouns is required to occur either in genitive case form or in possessive form. The head noun form remains unchanged,—it always occurs in modified/modification form.

(12.36) a. nà [érmì-á   nì-j]ɴᴘ   jɔ̀g séd-á   ké
          ᴄᴄɴ child-ʀsᴛʀ who.sɢ-ɢᴇɴ   3ᴘʟ say.ᴘᴇʀᴠ-3ᴘʟ.sᴜ.ᴘᴇʀᴠ   ǫᴏᴜᴛ
          á   [érmì-á   dawiti-j=so]ɴᴘ
          ᴄᴏᴘ.3.ɪᴍᴘᴇʀᴠ child-ʀsᴛʀ david-ɢᴇɴ=ᴇᴍᴘʜ
          'Whose son is he? They say to (him), "The son of David".'

    b. ŋà=ìn=à   á   [mád-á-á]ɴᴘ
       ᴅᴇᴍ=3sɢ.ᴘɴ.sᴘ=ɴᴇᴀʀ ᴄᴏᴘ.3.ɪᴍᴘᴇʀᴠ learn-ɴᴏᴍᴢ-ʀsᴛʀ
       nì
       who.ɢᴇɴ.sɢ
       'Whose book is this?'

       á   [mád-á-á   n=ànù]ɴᴘ
       ᴄᴏᴘ.3.ɪᴍᴘᴇʀᴠ learn-ɴᴏᴍᴢ-ʀsᴛʀ sɢ.ᴘsᴅ=1sɢ.ᴘsʀ
       'It is mine.'

    c. ŋà=dórí=á   á   [dórí-á   nì]ɴᴘ
       ᴅᴇᴍ=house=ɴᴇᴀʀ ᴄᴏᴘ.3.ɪᴍᴘᴇʀᴠ house-ʀsᴛʀ who.ɢᴇɴ.sɢ
       'Whose house is this?'

       án-á   ŋà=zùg=tùnù
       ᴄᴏᴘ.ɪᴍᴘᴇʀᴠ-ᴛᴇᴍᴘ ᴅᴇᴍ=people=ꜰᴀʀ
       'It is theirs.'

In (12.35a–c), we can see that the possessors are human referents so the modifiers may come in various forms such as proper nouns, possessive pronouns, and so on.

(12.37) ŋà=ìggὲ=à   á   [gáwát-íná-á   gì]ɴᴘ
        ᴅᴇᴍ=3ᴘʟ.ᴘɴ.sᴘ=ɴᴇᴀʀ ᴄᴏᴘ.3.ɪᴍᴘᴇʀᴠ plate-ᴘʟ-ʀsᴛʀ who.ɢᴇɴ.ᴘʟ
        'Whose plates are these?'

12.2.8 nìnì and gìgì 'Whose'

The possessive interrogative pronouns *nìnì* 'who.ᴘʀᴏ.sɢ' and *gìgì* 'who.ᴘʀᴏ.ᴘʟ' appear to have CV duplicates of the genitive forms—*nì* and *gì*. The major difference the genitive forms is that both *nìnì* and *gìgì* can occur in full pronoun forms. This means they may occur as modifiers of NP heads, but in order to stand on their own as predicate nominals or as copula complements, they do not necessarily require to occur in genitive form or in any other forms.

(12.38) a. [ŋà=dórí=á]   á   nì+nì
         DEM=HOUSE=NEAR COP.3.IMPERV who+PRO.SG
         'Whose house is this?'

   b. sírà   á   nìnì
      skirt COP.3.IMPERV who.PRO.SG
      'Whose skirt is this?'

      sírà án-á   hòjà ké   gúɲákèŋì
      skirt COP.IMPERV-TEMP girl QUOT Gunyakengi
      'It is the skirt of a girl known as Gunyakengi.'

   c. ŋà=ìn=à   á   [ísíkíríbító-á
      DEM=3SG.PN.SP=NEAR COP.3.IMPERV pen-RTSR
      nì+nì-j]_NP   án-á   n=ànù
      who+PRO.SG-GEN COP.IMPERV-TEMP SG.PSD=1SG.PSR
      'Whose pen is this? It is mine.'

   d. ŋà=ìggè=à   á   àggè-á
      DEM=3PL.PN.SP=NEAR COP.3.IMPERV 3PL.PN.SP-RSTR
      gì+gì
      who+PRO.PL
      'Whose are these?'

In the examples above, each possessive interrogative pronouns contain two bound number clitics (as proclitic as well as enclitic)—in which they indicate only the grammatical number of referents (possessors) and the possessed items. They can be segmented into separate pieces of morphemes. They can even be glossed in almost equivalent way as possessive pronouns.

12.3 Non-interrogative Particles

Non-interrogative particles have different grammatical functions in the language. In interrogative sentences having non-interrogative particles, the particles (see below in Table 12.2) can be in a particular discourse context, for

TABLE 12.2 Non-interrogative particles

Particle	Meaning	Remark
dá	'was it, really'	mirativity ~'surprisingly' discourse marker
ká	'perhaps/maybe'	uncertainty/dubitative marker
tá	'maybe'	uncertainty/dubitative marker
čírr	'really'	mirativity, discourse marker

instance if the information was known and in circulation for some time in the past, and/or if the information is believed to contain hidden facts in a way that creates an exclamative or a dubious situation.

In many instances, *dá* is used in information questions that require verification. Thus they can contain discourse particles such as *kó* 'so, then' at the beginning of the question (as in (12.39b)).

(12.39) a. *ín-í   elijas   dá*
          3SG.PN.SP-NRSTR Elijah really
          'Are you Elijah?'

   b. *kó   ịnè   ín-í   [hírí galila-i]*_{RC} *dá*
       PNC 2SG 3sg.PN.SP-NRSTR [man Galilee-NRTSR] really
       'Are you also of Galilee?'
       (Lit. 'so you (sg.) is that of Galilee man (really)?')

The relative clause in (12.39b) lacks a main verb and it appears to be the only instance where interrogative sentence construction is possible without a verb overtly stated. In addition, the uncertainty particles *ká* 'perhaps' and *tá* 'maybe', which are not interrogative words on their own, but they may denote interrogative sense in the sentence in which they occur, as in (12.40a–c).

(12.40) a. *ká   á   kiritosi ká*
           perhaps COP.3.IMPERV   Christ   perhaps

OR   *ŋà=hír=á   á   kirstosi ká*
       DEM=man=NEAR   COP.3.IMPERV   Christ   perhaps
       'Is not this the Christ?'

b. *tá   wà   hírkón-a   ádʒ-έ   tílá nà*
   maybe REC.PAST man-RSTR give.IMPERV-COM food CCN
   ɓák-ú   ká
   eat-3SG.SU.PERV perhaps
   'Has any man brought him something to eat?'

c. *tá   ŋà=hír=á   sé   kɔ́ɔ́n*
   maybe DEM=people=NEAR say/COMPL 3.SBJV.KILL.PERV
   rὲὲ   ká
   body.PERT.SG.3.PSR perhaps
   'Will he kill himself?'
   (Lit. 'Maybe the man wants to kill himself perhaps?')

As is shown above, the particle *ká* can occur simultaneously at the beginning of a sentence or at the end, or just at the end. Whereas the syntactic slot of *tá* appears to be confined to a sentence initial position. The mirativity marker particle *čírr* 'really' may expresses the doubtful sense of the speaker to information that has been circulated previously.

(12.41) a. *ŋà=gɔ̀r=á   á   gɔ̀r-á   [Ø kɔ́w-á]$_{RC}$*
          DEM=road=NEAR COP.3.IMPERV road-RSTR [Ø follow-RSTR]
          nazretɛ-ɔ   čírr
          Nazareth-OBL really
          'Is that the road which goes (takes) to Nazareth?'

   b. *lɔ̀g-á   bàrì   íf-o   ŋàŋà*
      issue-RSTR yesterday present.PERV-IRR like.this
      gá-ó   čírr
      know-2PL.SU.IMPERV really
      'Do you (pl.) know what happened the day before yesterday?'

12.4 Tag Questions

Tag questions may carry the expectation of confirmation (cf. Dixon 2012: 396). Tag questions in Mursi are formed by initial declarative clause (the anchor) followed by adjoined interrogative clause (the tag). Tag questions are normally different from polar questions in that the tag clause is absent in polar questions. Moreover, the truth value of the propositions that the answers of polar questions may contain can be fully stated. It doesn't matter whether the answers are positive or negative.

(12.42) a. ìɲè [ʃúúnú-á   n=ùnù]ₙₚ   á
         2SG father.PERT.2SG.PSR-RSTR SG.PSD=2SG.PSR COP.3.IMPERV
         ákímí,   ŋà=ʔán=ó
         doctor, NEG=COP.IMPERV=NEG
         'Your (sg.) father is a doctor, isn't he?'

   b. ìggè án-ó   [zùw-á   kɔ́h-inèn-ó]ₙₚ,
      2SG COP.IMPERV-2PL.SU.IMPERV people-RSTR farm-NOMZ-RTSR
      ŋà=ʔán-ó=ó
      NEG=COP.IMPERV=2PL.SU.IMPERV=NEG
      'You (pl.) are farmers, aren't you (pl.)?'

   c. àɲè k-án-í   támárí,
      1SG 1SU-COP.IMPERV-1SG.SU.IMPERV student
      ŋà=k-án-í=ó
      NEG=1SU-COP.IMPERV-1SG.SU.IMPERV=NEG
      'Am I not a student?'

The operator verb in both declarative and in the tag clause is a copula verb in imperfective aspect. The bound negation system on the copula verb of the tag clause and the raised intonation onto the entire tag clause are main operators which help to achieve the question.

12.5 Polar Questions

The term polar question is a more appropriate label than 'yes' and 'no' question (Dixon 2012: 377). As Dixon argues, some languages may lack words 'yes' and 'no' in their lexicon and Mursi is one of them. Instead Mursi utilizes default interjections, negative particle word/particle or copula verbs—see the examples given in (12.43a–c).

(12.43) a. [kídó tó-jé]ₚₚ ár-ú   kíɲáŋ   mmm! mmm! àɲè
         river in-OBL see.PERV-2SG.SU.PERV crocodile no   no   1SG
         ŋànì   k-ár=ó
         NEG.PERV 1SU-see.PERV=NEG
         'Did you see any crocodiles in the river?' 'No I didn't.'

b. *hàlì sán-í   kátámá-ì-jè   ɩmm ɩmm! ànè hàlì*
later stay-2SG.SU.IMPERV town-LOC-OBL no   no   1SG later
k-ó-í   ɔ́r-ɔ́   rɩ́b
1SU-go.IMPERV-1SG.SU.IMPERV home-OBL all.the.day
'Will you (m) spend the day at the town? No, I shall stay all day at home.'

Like in interrogative words, in polar questions, a constituent which is the focus takes sentence-final position. In other words, it is the constituent with a raised intonation that is expected to take the focus position and this could be by moving the constituent to the right most slot of the clause—for example *kíɲáŋ* in (12.43a). In polar questions, if the sentence involves copula verb, obviously the copula complement will be a constituent upon which a high pitch rests, as in (12.43c).

c. *ìɲè án-í   támárí ŋɲ! àɲè*
2SG COP.IMPERV-2SG.SU.IMPERV student yes!   1SG
k-án-í   támárí
1SU-COP.IMPERV-1SG.SU.IMPERV student
'Are you (sg.) a student?' 'Yes, I am a student.'

In almost all cases, the syntactic order of constituents of declarative sentence and polar questions are exactly the same. The English equivalents to the Mursi interjections in above examples will be *ɩmm* 'no' and *ŋɲ* 'yes'. It is quite common for interjections to have a different phonology. For instance, both of these interjections contain a short central vowel which is not part of the sound system of the language and may have a monosyllabic VCG shape (where G stands for geminates).

When a intransitive clause is set to indicate a polar questions, it is on the intransitive verb that the high pitch level can be shown,—otherwise the verb remains high-toned in most cases.

(12.44) a. [*zíwúɲá   dákákán*]ₙₚ *kò-gòd-à   ŋànì,*
medicine.PL all   PASS-swallow.PERV-PASS.3.SU NEG.PERV
jɔ̀g ŋànì   dákákán
3PL NEG.PERV all
'Should all the medicine be swallowed? No, not all.'

b. ŋà=ɓá=á   [àhà-á   gàʃ-ùɲ]_NP
   DEM=place=NEAR thing.PL-RSTR forest-GEN
   él-ɛ́
   exist.IMPERV:PL-3pl.SU.IMPERV
   'Are there any wild animals about?'
   (Lit. 'things of the forest are present there?')

Positive declarative sentences are not the only syntactic structures that have identical order of constituents with polar questions, negative declarative sentences have also identical order. Thus, in negative polar interrogative and negative declarative sentences, the verb is placed in focus position at the end of the sentence, as in (12.45a–b).

(12.45) a. *iggè hàlì dìb   àɲè ŋà=jóg-óɲ-ó=ó*
           2PL later truth 1SG NEG=tell-1SG.OBJ-2PL.SU.IMPERV=NEG
           'Will you (pl.) not tell me the truth?'

       b. *iggè hàlì dìb   nɔ̀ŋ ŋà=jóg-ésén-ó=ó*
           2PL later truth 3SG NEG=tell-BEN.3-2PL.SU.IMPERV=NEG
           'Will you (pl.) not tell him the truth?'

The fact that both positive and negative polar interrogatives are equivalent in a way they cause their propositions to generate answers. Both positive polar interrogatives (12.43–12.44) and negative polar interrogatives can have either *yes* or *no* answers.

12.6   Other Question Strategies

In addition to the major ways to ask questions elaborated on in the sections above, Mursi also employs two questioning strategies: disjunctive questions (§ 12.6.1) and a clause with lowered intonation on its entire structure (§ 12.6.2).

12.6.1 *Disjunctive Questions*

Disjunctive questions in Mursi are formed with two copular clauses conjoined by the disjunctive particle *wo* [oo]. The first copular clause will have a full copular clause constituent: copula subject, copula verb and copula complement while the second consists only of the latter two constituents. Both clauses share a single subject, which is the subject of the first copula clause.

(12.46) a. [mèdèrè]_CS á [búí]_CC óó á [tííní]_CC
sheep COP.3.IMPERV big.SG DISJ COP.3.IMPERV small.SG
'Is the sheep big or small?'
(Lit. 'The sheep is big or small?')

b. mìrèn á bíbí óó á
courfull.bull.PL COP.3.IMPERV big.REDUP.PL DISJ COP.3.IMPERV
tíítí
small.PL
'Are the bulls big or small?'

The interrogative statements above seek confirmation whether their references should be referred by one of the semantically opposing attributes or not. Therefore, the answers to the propositions in (12.46) can be selected from their copula complements—as *big/small* rather than as *yes/no*.

The disjunctive particle *óó* can be also used to show speculation or uncertainty. Especially, obviously used when someone is not sure of one's own choices. In this regard, the disjunctive interrogatives in (12.47a–b) are different from the copular clauses above. As shown below, the first clause is a subordinate followed by the main clause connected by the disjunctive *óó*.

(12.47) a. [hùllì té-í kó ɔ́r-ɔ́ á
if exist-2SG.SU.IMPERV with home-OBL COP.3.IMPERV
čàll=è]_SUBORD:Cl óó kɔ́-í tìráŋ-ɔ
good.STV=SUBORD DISJ go.IMPERV-2SG.SU.IMPERV play-OBL
'Would you rather stay home or go to the game?'
(Lit. 'Would you (sg.) stay at home is better or go to the play?')

b. ké-héj-Ø dʒààrí-ɔ óó
1SU-go.IMPERV:PL-1PL.INC.SU.IMPERV foot-OBL DISJ
ké-hé-Ø túrúmél-ɔ̀
1SU-go.IMPERV:PL-1PL.INC.SU.IMPERV car-OBL
'Shall we walk or take the bus?'
(Lit. 'Shall we go by (with) foot or go by (with) car?')

Here, one can pick an answer from the two choices of staying or playing (12.47a). For (12.47b) the answers will be one of the two choices—*walking by foot* or *taking the bus*.

QUESTIONS   515

12.6.2 *A Clause with Lowered Intonation*

The interrogative clauses below are all marked by lowered intonation of all their constituents They behave like those interrogative sentences with proper interrogative words. They are completely different from tag and polar interrogatives despite all three lacking independent interrogative words. For instance, the interrogative clauses below have a lowered pitch level—quite the opposite from what we saw in tag and polar interrogatives.

(12.48) a. wà   érmì=tùnù   áíw-ó
           REC.PAST child=INDEF come.PERV:SG-MT.3SG.SU.PERV
           'Which child came?'

       b. wà   lámí-ɔ̀
           REC.PAST find.2SG.SU.IMPERV-VFS
           'What do you (sg.) want?'

       c. hírí бá   á   nɔ̀ŋ
           man place/CAUSE   COP.3.IMPERV 3SG
           rès-Ø-ɛ̀
           die.IMPERV-3SG.SU.IMPERV-COM
           'Due to what (causes) did the man die?'
           (Lit. 'The man because of what he died?')

In (12.48a), number agreement on the verb is shown by the form of the verb root itself—*aiw* ⟨perfective singular form⟩. Besides, person agreement is shown by the absence of any overt marker for the third person. However, if it is only in relation to the first and second person singular perfective forms—*kaiwo* ⟨1st person⟩ and *aiwou* ⟨2nd person⟩. To see a possible interaction between intonation and narration or other discourse contexts, further study is required.

CHAPTER 13

Negation

13.1 Introduction

Typologically, negation constructions in Mursi show various striking features. In Mursi, a number of different negation strategies may be employed to negate verbal constituents. The strategies vary depending on grammatical systems or categories such as aspect, mood, and person-subject. For instance, a verb in the imperfective aspect can be negated by bound circumclitics while a verb in the perfective aspect is negated by independent perfective negative particle *ŋànì* ⟨NEG.PERV⟩ 'not, not yet, still' plus by the negative enclitic *=ó* attached to the perfective verb root. For instance, a verb in the imperfective aspect can be negated by bound circumclitics [ŋà= ... =ó] ~ ⟨ŋà=ROOT.IMPERV=ó⟩, while a perfective verb can be negated by independent perfective negative form particle *ŋànì* ⟨NEG.PERV⟩ 'not, not yet' and by the negative enclitic attached to the root ~ ⟨ŋànì k(V)-ROOT.PERV=ó⟩. So, when the negative is a perfective verb, only the negator enclitic *=ó* will be utilized. A further interesting point here is that in a negative imperative, only the negator proclitic *ŋà=* will be used thus the enclitic *=ó* can be replaced by markers of other grammatical categories appropriate to that slot such as number and verb-final suffix.

The grammatical function of the *k(V)-* prefix when negating a perfective verb is to refer to first person subject. Besides, the subjunctive which often times applies to the third person irrealis mood can be indicated by the same prefix. This prefix cannot occur if the negated verb involves second person subject.

Furthermore, negative declarative clauses have an obligatory SV/AOV constituent order, in which negated verbs always occur clause-finally. This is confined to the negative clause constituent order, which is different from the affirmative canonical constituent SV/AVO order. The negation system that operates in the imperfective aspect will have AO[Neg=V=Neg] while the perfective aspect have AO Neg.PART [V=Neg].

Therefore, this chapter provides a detailed account of negators which occur in bound as well as independent forms. Accordingly, bound negators are discussed in §13.2 followed by various independent negator words or particles in §13.3.

13.2 Bound Negators

Bound negators in Mursi are circumclitics in which the imperfective verb root is nested within the ŋà=VERB.ROOT=ó circumclitic negation marker. They are realized as the proclitic ŋà= (on verbs in imperfective aspect) and as the enclitic =ó (on verbs in the imperfective and perfective aspect). Thus all bound negators are discussed in separate subsections below—circumclitics as negators of verbs of the imperfective aspect §13.2.1 and an enclitic negator of verbs in the perfective aspect §13.2.2.

13.2.1 *Imperfective Verb Negators*

Verbs in the imperfective aspect can be negated by using two negator clitics ŋà= and =ó. Due to the fact that they are applied to a single constituent simultaneously on the verb, they can be called double negation (markers). For the interpretation of the proclitic ŋà= two paths were followed depending on the aspect of the verb being utilized: (i) negative imperfective ⟨NEG.IMPERV=⟩ when procliticized to the host (an imperfective verb), and (ii) negative perfective or just negative when procliticized to a perfective imperative verb form host. The latter has been elaborated on in the section dealing with interaction of negation and imperative.

There is always a coalescence at the right edge of a negated constituent. That is, the first person plural exclusive and the second plural subject suffixes on one hand and the negator enclitic =ó on the other may coalesce as a single unit.

(13.1) íggé-á [[ŋà=gótó-ɲá=ìnù]_NP g=àw=ŋà]_NP
3PL.PN.SP-RSTR DEM=culture-PL=FAR PL.PSD=1PL.EXC.PSR=DEF
ŋà=gárs-ɛ́=ó
NEG.IMPERV=disappear.IMPERV-3PL.SU.IMPERV=NEG
'Those of our (exc.) cultures were not lost (disappeared).' (MH 1:48:7)

(13.2) nɔ̀ŋ mà ŋà=ám-Ø=ó-ni
3SG water NEG.IMPERV=eat-3SG.SU.IMPERV=NEG-RS
'... (the) water does not eat it!' (MH 2:47:0)

As it is shown in (13.1 and 13.2), the negators (circumclitics) occur on both sides of the verbal predicate, which is a clause final constituent. The negative clitics in Mursi attach only to the verb, and certainly do not attach to other constituents other than the verb. For negated predicate, aspect can be shown in multiple ways—by the negator proclitic, by verb root, and by bound pronominal S/A argument suffixes.

TABLE 13.1 Imperfective verb negators

Person	Singular	Plural
1	ŋà=k(V)-ROOT.IMPERV-i=ó	(INC.) ŋà=k(V)-ROOT.IMPERV-Ø=ó
		(EXC.) ŋà=k(V)-ROOT.IMPERV-o=ó
2	ŋà=ROOT.IMPERV-i=ó	ŋà=ROOT.IMPERV-o=ó
3	ŋà=ROOT.IMPERV-Ø=ó	ŋà=ROOT.IMPERV-ɛ=ó

(13.3) a. *ŋà=kí-hín-í=ó*
NEG.IMPERV=1SU-want.IMPERV-1SG.SU.IMPERV=NEG
'I don't want'

b. *ŋà=hín-í=ó*
NEG.IMPERV=want.IMPERV-2SG.SU.IMPERV=NEG
'You (sg.) don't want'

c. *ŋà=hín-Ø=ó*
NEG.IMPERV=want.IMPERV-2SG.SU.IMPERV=NEG
'S/he doesn't want'

As elaborated in (13.3a–c), Mursi may arguably employ an obligatory double negation in the imperfective aspect, where two negator clitics simultaneously code predicate/clausal negation. If a bound pronominal for the S/A argument is marked by zero morpheme, a few verb roots that end in the alveolar nasal [n] may undergo a compensatory lengthening process, as in (13.3c). In (13.3c), *ŋàhínó* may be realized as [ŋahinno] in surface form. When the S/A argument is first person plural inclusive, eventually there will be a tendency for a sequence of vowels to co-occur, as in (13.4). In this case, *t* is epenthesised to avoid sequence of vowels as well as to mark plural number.

(13.4) a. *whɔ̀i   ŋà=k-éj-Ø=tó*
warthog NEG.IMPERV=1SU-kill/shoot-1PL.INC.SU.IMPERV=NEG
'We (inc.) will not kill the pig.'

When the verb acquires identical root form in both imperfective and perfective aspect, the negator proclitic becomes the sole grammatical morpheme which shows aspect of the verb. The first person plural exclusive bound pronominal S/A suffix -*o* often fuses/coalesces with the negative enclitic =*ó* as in (13.4b).

b. ŋà=kó-jóg=ó
   NEG.IMPERV=1SU-speak=1PL.INC.SU.IMPERV.NEG
   'We (exc.) will not speak; we (exc.) don't speak.'

Underlyingly, (13.4b) will be realized as ⟨ŋà=kó-jóg-o=ó⟩. Despite these rare and specific morphophonemic changes, in other forms of the negation of declarative clauses, the interaction of verbs and negator clitics show consistency regardless of the form of verb roots. Examples strengthening this fact are given below.

(13.5) a. ŋà=dáʃí-Ø=ó
        NEG.IMPERV=work-3SG.SU.IMPERV=NEG
        'S/he, it doesn't work.'

   b. ŋà=k-ítóón-í=ó
      NEG.IMPERV=1SU-send-1SG.SU.IMPERV=NEG
      'I don't send.'

   c. ŋà=k-ór-né=ó?
      NEG.IMPERV=1SU-see.IMPERV-RECIP:1PL.INC.SU.IMPERV=NEG
      'We (inc.) don't meet.'
      (Lit. 'We (inc.) don't not see each other.')

Thus, all, vowel-final verb root (13.5a), vowel-initial verb root (13.5b), and derivational morpheme suffixed verb (13.5c) operate freely without morphophonemic processes.

The obligatory double negation system that is used for the imperfective aspect can be transformed into an optional triple negation system. The optional triple negation system can be achieved by combining the imperfective verb root with the preverbal perfective negation word *ŋànì*. Thus, the optional preverbial negative word *ŋànì* together with the negator circumclitics on imperfective verbs forms the triple negation system.

(13.6) a. nɔ̀ŋ ŋànì   ŋà=ór-Ø=ó
        3SG NEG.PERV NEG.IMPERV=see.IMPERV-3SG.SU.IMPERV=NEG
        'S/he still could not see.'

   b. nɔ̀ŋ té   hírí ódénéí   ŋà=bà=nù   kó   túmúrá
      3SG COP.3.PERV man   strong.ADJ DEM=place=FAR PCN Tumura

ŋànì   ŋà=gán-ɛ́=ó   á
NEG.PERV NEG=know-3PL.SU.IMPERV=NEG COP.3.IMPERV
ŋàŋà
like.this
'... on the other side of Sudan, and he is a strong man there.' 'They don't agree with Tumura. It is like this.' (MH 6:53:2)

Therefore, both examples, the optional preverbial perfective negative word *ŋànì* has a meaning of 'still'. *ŋànì* also has a 'persistive marker' function in other grammatical constructions. The occurrence of the perfective negative *ŋànì* and the imperfective aspect verb in the same clause may indicate an ongoing process/state.

(13.7) [húllí nɔ̀ŋ ŋànì   gùjò ŋà=dák-Ø=ó
        if   3SG NEG.PERV rain NEG.IMPERV=hit-3SG.SU.IMPERV=NEG
        ŋàméá=jè]_SUBORD:CL
        today=SUBORD
        'If it does not rain today, ...'

A combination of persistive and modal meaning can be rendered by the same negation structure, as in (13.8).

(13.8) múɲús-é   úlúgúɲ-ú   nà   ŋànì
        angry-NOMZ hide-3SG.SU.PERV CCN NEG.PERV
        ŋà=ɔ́wáná=ó
        NEG.IMPERV=manage.3SG.SU.IMPERV=NEG
        'He couldn't hide his emotion.'

Another occasion where the two co-occur in a clause is in the 'consequence clause' for which *ŋànì* becomes in the subordinate clause while the verb, which is negated by imperfective negative circumclitics itself becomes the main clause.

(13.9) a. [hùllì ŋà=zùwɔ̀ɲá=á   ŋànì
           if   DEM=medicine.PL=NEAR NEG.PERV
           ìr=ó=jè]_SUBORD:CL
           drink.PERV=NEG=SUBORD
           [ŋà=bás-e=ó]_MAIN:CL
           NEG.IMPERV=heal.IMPERV-2SG.SU.IMPERV=NEG
           'Unless you (sg.) drink this medicine, you (sg.) will not get well.'

(Lit. 'If this medicine—you (sg.) haven't yet drank, you (sg.) don't be healed.')

b. hùllì ŋànì   tóíj=ó   béténá
   if   NEG.PERV read/count=NEG exam
ŋà=ʔálb-í=ó
NEG.IMPERV=pass-2SG.SU.IMPERV=NEG
'You (sg.) will not pass the examination unless you study.'

In (13.9a), the second person singular bound pronoun suffix is -*i* and it undergoes a vowel height harmony change. So *i* has became *e* following the negator enclitic =*ó*. In negative conditional clauses, the verb of the subordinate clause cannot be negated, rather the perfective negative particle *ŋànì* always occurs preceding it. As can be seen in the examples above, it makes sense for conditional clauses to operate depending on imperfective aspect because the propositions they contain are often hypothetical. It is also highly likely the case that the negation in imperfective aspect indicates a given action is not going to happen. Considering this we may assume that subordinate conditional clause verbs therefore, will obviously occur in the imperfective aspect.

However, this is not the case in Mursi. In Mursi, the subordinate conditional clause can contain the negative word *ŋànì* followed by a verb in subjunctive form. Like in the imperative constructions, person cannot be marked on the subjunctive form when the subject is second person. Person on the subjunctive form may be shown by various forms of the verb root itself. Regarding this, Randal (1998: 248) pointed out that there may be a possibility that historically the negative marker was a verb. This is due to the fact that, when the main verb is negated it appears in the subjunctive form, which usually cannot mark the main verb of the subordinate clause. At this point, it is appropriate to mention that proclitics in Mursi can form a grammatical word while enclitics cannot. I hypothesize that the negative perfective particle *ŋànì* 'not yet' may be a derived grammatical word that got its modal dependent form from the negative marker proclitic *ŋà*=—plus a copula verb **an* and singular imperative suffix **i*. But this has to be proven, which I guess is a matter of time. In the meantime, the following structural similarities have been found in negative jussive and negative interrogative constructions using a copula verb, as in (13.10a–b).

(13.10) a. nòŋ ŋà=án-í
         3SG NEG.IMPERV=COP.IMPERV-SG
         'Let him not become/be (!)'

b. ŋà=án-í   nòŋ?
   NEG.IMPERV=COP.IMPERV-SG 3SG
   'Shall he not become/be?'

In Mursi, the negative word ŋànì whether imperfective or perfective, always occurs before the main verb. Arguably, Dixon (2012: 95) puts it, 'Cross-linguistically, there is a strong tendency for negative particles to occur early in the clause'.

Therefore, in (13.9a–b), the negative particle ŋànì comes in the subordinate clause following the object or immediately following conditional/temporal marker húllí and is followed by the main clause which contains a negative imperfective main verb. Note that, however, a perfective verb root can never be combined with the imperfective negation proclitic ŋà=.

In addition, negation in the imperfective aspect can be used to ask rhetorical questions in a way that also indicates the sarcastic attitude/characters that people may show or possess.

(13.11) àŋè k-án-í   támárí
       1SG 1SU-COP.IMPERV-1SG.SU.IMPERV student
       ŋà=k-án-í=ó?
       NEG.IMPERV=1SU-COP.IMPERV-1SG.SU.IMPERV=NEG
       'Am I not a student?'

The speaker does know that he is indeed a student, so everybody knows this fact. But he is talking as if his studentship as well as the education he got is a joke.

The other interesting but unusual behavior of the bound imperfective negator is in the imperative clause. Imperative clause in Mursi is formed by attaching the negator proclitic ŋà= to an imperfective verb. The negator enclitic =ó cannot be used in the negative imperative clause construction. The template of a negative imperative construction is as follows:

$$\begin{bmatrix} \text{ŋà=ROOT.IMPERV-i ... singular} \\ \text{ŋà=ROOT.IMPERV-o ... plural} \end{bmatrix}$$

(13.12) a. ŋà=ɓág-í
          NEG.IMPERV=EAT.IMPERV-SG
          'Don't (sg.) eat!'

b. ŋà=čóll-i
NEG.IMPERV=sing.IMPERV-SG
'Don't (sg.) sing!'

c. ŋà=bág-ó
NEG.IMPERV=eat.IMPERV-PL
'You (pl.) don't eat!'

d. ŋà=čóll-ó
NEG.IMPERV=sing.IMPERV-PL
'You (pl) don't sing!'

On the other hand, positive imperative is formed by using a perfective verb root. Besides, singular cannot be on the verb, while plural is usually marked on the verb by copying the vowel of the verb root. This means that there are distinct number markers being utilized by negative and positive imperative clauses— negative imperative -i (singular) and -o (plural); positive imperative *unmarked* (singular) and -V (plural). Once again, vowel coalescence may happen between the first person plural bound pronominal O argument suffix -i and singular negative imperative –i, as in (13.13b–c).

(13.13) a. ŋà=éʤ-óɲ-í
NEG.IMPERV=kill.IMPERV-1SG.OBJ-SG
'Don't (sg.) kill me!'

b. ŋà=éʤ-í-í
NEG.IMPERV=kill.IMPERV-1PL.OBJ-SG ~ I < I+I
'Don't (sg.) kill us!'

c. ŋà=áʤ-í-í
NEG.IMPERV=give.IMPERV-1PL.OBJ-SG
'Don't give (to) us!'

In (13.13b–c), the vowels coalesce into a single high front vowel. There are other multiple morphophonological processes that take place while forming negative hortative clauses. The first person plural inclusive negative hortative has a template of ŋà=k(V)-ROOT.IMPERV-Ø while first person plural exclusive negative hortative has a template ŋà=k(V)-ROOT.IMPERV-(t/n)o.

(13.14) a. *ŋà=k-èj-tò*
NEG.IMPERV-1.HORT-kill-1PL.EXC.SU.IMPERV
'Let us (exc.) not kill!'

b. *ŋà=kò-hòɲ-nò*
NEG.IMPERV-1.HORT-come.IMPERV:PL-1PL.EXC.SU.IMPERV
'Let us (exc.) not come!'

The change arises with the formation of first person plural inclusive negative hortative form when being used as indirect negative imperative. In this case, the hortative form may convey a negative obligation meaning. The following examples demonstrate this fact:

(13.15) a. *ŋà=kì-fì*
NEG.IMPERV=1.HORT-listen+PL.INC
'Let us (inc.) don't listen!'
(Lit. 'We (inc.) will not listen!')

b. *ŋà=kè-rè-ì*
NEG.IMPERV=1.HORT-wait-PL.INC
'Let us (inc.) not wait!'

c. *ŋà=kò-hòɲ*
NEG.IMPERV=1.HORT-come.IMPERV:PL
'Let us (inc.) not come!'

As can be shown in (13.15a–c), the hortative forms are not marked for plural number even if all are types of imperatives, i.e. non-canonical negative imperatives. (13.15a) has a consonant-final verb root—*fíg*, then /g/ becomes [ʔ], and finally it will be deleted as it gets less audible word-finally. It appears that the more harsh the imperative is, the shorter the forms tend to appear. Outside this, plural number marking on non-canonical negative mild imperatives is straightforward; (i) by copying the vowel of the verb root, or (ii) by inherently plural form of the verb. Some examples are given below:

(13.16) a. *àggè ŋà=kì-fìl-ì*
1PL NEG.IMPERV=1.HORT-stand-PL.INC
'Let us (inc.) not stand!'

b. ŋà=kè-hèj-ò
NEG.IMPERV=go.IMPERV:PL-VFS
'Let us (sg.) not go!'

Singular forms are indicated by the suffix -i, which is identical to first person singular bound pronominal S/A argument marker.

(13.17) a. ŋà=k-èdʒ-ì
NEG.IMPERV=1.HORT-kill.IMPERV-SG
'Let me not kill!'

b. ŋà=kùùn-ì
NEG.IMPERV=1.HORT.come.IMPERV-SG
'Let me not come!'

Note that singular and plural number marker of suffixes may come to be identical; especially, whenever the verb root contains the high front vowel where plural number marker is derived.

13.2.2 Perfective Verb Negators

Verbs that have perfective aspect can be negated by the independent perfective negator particle ŋànì 'not yet' and by the negator enclitic =ó attaching to a perfective verb root. Negated perfective verbs in first and third persons take a prefix $k(V)$-. This prefix is used as person marker for first person S/A argument while as subjunctive marker for third person. (13.18) below illustrates a 'typical' example of negation of the perfective aspect verb and literal meaning of the negator particle ŋànì.

(13.18) bè   ŋà=hùl=ùnù   nɔ̀ŋ   ŋànì   k-íríčá=ó
DIST.PAST DEM=time=FAR 3SG not.yet 3.SBJV-born.PERV=NEG
'At the time, he was not yet born.'

The structure of a clause in negative perfective aspect is shown in Table 13.2 below.

As can be shown in the examples given below, the $k(V)$- is prefixed to refer to first person subjects. Plural number can be indicated by inserting either [t/d] between the verb root and the bound pronominal S/A argument markers or by inherently plural verb roots.

TABLE 13.2 Perfective verb negators

Person	Singular	Plural
1	ŋ̀ànì k(V)-ROOT.PERV=ó	ŋ̀ànì k(V)-ROOT.PERV=t/ɗ/no
2	ŋ̀ànì ROOT.PERV=ó	ŋ̀ànì ROOT.PERV=t//ɗ/no
3	ŋ̀ànì k(V)-ROOT.PERV=ó	ŋ̀ànì k(V)-ROOT.PERV=t/ɗ/no

(13.19) a. àɲè   ŋ̀ànì   kí-ɓíkt=ó
         1SG NEG.PERV 1SU-break=NEG
         'I did not break (it).'

    b. àɲè wà   ŋ̀ànì   kí-ɓík-á=ó
       1SG REC.PAST NEG.PERV 1SU-break-1SG.SU.PERV=NEG
       'I have not broken (it).'

    c. àɲè bè   ŋ̀ànì   kí-ɓík-á=ó
       1SG DIST.PAST NEG.PERV 1SU-break-1SG.SU.PERV=NEG
       'I had not broken (it).'

However, some verb roots that have the same root shapes/forms both in imperfective and perfective aspects may also insert [t] (as in (13.19a)), but not [ɗ]. Nasal ending verb roots may epenthesize [n] in the same way as [t/ɗ]. The negative particle ŋ̀ànì always precedes the perfective aspect verb root, and provides a full account of an action that has not yet happened/taken place but may happen at some point of time in the future.

(13.20) a. [ŋà=mé-á=á   dórí]_NP áčúg ŋ̀ànì   k-ɔ́s=ó
         DEM=do-NOMZ=NEAR douse meat NEG.PERV 3.SBJV-roast=NEG
         'The worker did not fry meat.'

    b. dóóléj làsàj [hír-á   óól-nèn-á]_NP ŋ̀ànì
       girl   bread man-RTSR beg-NOMZ-RSTR NEG.PERV
       k-áín-ɛ́=ó
       3SBJV-give.PERV.SG-MA=NEG
       'The girl will not give the beggar bread.'

    c. ìɲè ŋ̀ànì   kè-bèrtà-íɲ=nó
       2SG NEG.PERV PASS-choose.PERV-2SG.OBJ=NEG
       'You (sg.) were not chosen.'

d. ìggè wà   ŋànì   dáʃíd-ó=ó   (nɔ̀ŋ)
   2PL REC.PAST NEG.PERV work.PERV-2PL.SU.PERV=NEG (3SG)
   'You (pl.) were not working.'

e. lɔ̀g-ɪ́ɲá mèsí-nèn   ŋànì   ódá=ó
   issue-PL work-NOMZ NEG.PERV finish.PERV:PL=NEG
   'You (pl) did not finish your work.'

f. [nɔ̀ŋ hùll-á   bè   tál-á   túrúmél]_COMPL:CL
   3SG when-NOMZ DIST.PAST buy-3SG.SU.PERV car
   [ɪ̀ɲè ŋànì   ár=ó?]_MAIN:CL
   2SG NEG.PERV see.PERV=NEG
   'Didn't you (sg.) know that he has bought a car?'

As it is shown in (13.20a–b), negative perfective construction in the third person requires subjunctive mood, which is always indicated by attaching a *k(V)*- prefix to the negated perfective verb root. In terms of taking a *k(V)*-, the subjunctive of the negative perfective is almost identical with first person subjects, hortative-jussive, and passive constructions.

Negative perfective verbs in the second person do not require this subjunctive prefix, as illustrated in (13.20d–f). In addition, in (Turton et al. 2008: 81), *hula* was glossed as 'when', but not as a temporal interrogative word. It is identical with the temporal/conditional *húllí* 'when/if', and only differs in having a geminated lateral due to the high vowel. Above all, in (13.20f), the aspect of the main clause and the subordinate clause is identical, which is not always the case in conditional clauses where aspect of the main and the subordinate clauses differ sometimes. Note that complement strategies in Mursi do not always show clear indicators of complementizers. The absence of any such indicator (as in (13.20f)) can be regarded as one type of complementization strategy.

However, since most of the time complement clauses utilize a perfective verb in the subjunctive mood plus an eroded verb from *sé* 'say'. Reason and/or purpose clauses may sometimes use purpose clause marker particle *bá* 'place, cause' which occurs following *sé*. Apart from this, in most cases both affirmative and negative complement clauses will have similar syntactic structures plus utilize identical subjunctive verb forms. See also the examples given below:

(13.21) a. nɔ̀ŋ ɲànì   ŋà=hín-Ø=ó
        3SG NEG.PERV NEG.IMPERV=want.IMPERV-3SG.SU.IMPERV=NEG
        ɓá   kú-húč-έ   bíró
        COMPL/place 3.SBJV-pay.PERV-MA money
        'She did not want to pay the money.'

   b. àɲè ɲànì   ká-ták=ó   ɓá   [nɔ̀ŋ
      1SG NEG.PERV 1SU-know.PERV=NEG COMPL/place 3SG
      wà   kúč-á-á]_COMP:CL
      REC.PAST come.PERV-MT-3SG.SU.PERV
      'I did not know that he has come.'
      (Lit. 'at his coming; reason for his coming')

In (13.21a), both perfective negative particle and negated imperfective aspect are within the main clause which have a function of denoting that the situation will likely never happen. On the other hand, (13.21b) is a statement of fact although the verb in the complement clause hasn't been set in subjunctive form. In the imperfective aspect, a complement clause does not occur with the perfective aspect negator ɲànì, as in (13.22a–b).

(13.22) a. ŋà=ɓùrè=tá   ɓá
        DEM=morning=NEAR COMPL/place
        [ŋà=hóɲ-čá=ó
        NEG.IMPERV=come.IMPERV.PL-APPL=NEG
        ká-gáj-Ø-ɔ̀]_COMPL:CL
        1SU-know.IMPERV-1SG.SU.IMPERV-VFS
        'I know that they will not come today.'

   b. àɲè ká-gáj-ɔ̀   ɓá
      1SG 1SU-know.IMPERV-1SG.SU.IMPERV-VFS COMPL/place
      [éró   ŋà=lɔ̀m-čá=ó]_COMPL:CL
      children NEG.IMPERV=have.IMPERV-RES-MT=NEG
      'I know that he has no children.'

The approximant of the verb root-final and the bound pronominal first person subject prefix have been merged/fused—/gáj/ > [gáj+i].

(13.23) [ɓá-á   nɔ̀ŋ ɲànì   kɔ́-ɲɔ́g-í=ó
        place-RSTR/CAUSE 3SG NEG.PERV 3.SBJV-cloth.PERV-SG=NEG

tútúg=tè]_SUBORD:CL *zìní dúl-ú*
door=SUBORD thief emerge-3SG.SU.PERV
'By his not shutting the door a thief entered.'

An exceptional negation construction is found in (13.24), in which a direct speech is being used in the subordinate clause.

(13.24) *bá ké ŋà=kúún-i* [*hùllì ŋànì*
CUASE QOUT NEG.IMPERV=come.IMPERV-SG when/if NEG.PERV
tód-a=jè]_SUBORD:CL *maksaɲɔ*[1]
write.PERV-IRR=SUBORD tuesday
kúún-é[*ì*]
1SU.come.IMPERV-1SG.SU.IMPERV
'I will come Tuesday unless you write (to me) not to come.'
(Lit. 'Unless you are writing saying "don't come!", I will come Tuesday.')

Now the negated verb is within a direct speech report and has been negated in the same way as a negative imperative, which is formed using imperfective verb root preceded by negative imperfective proclitic *ŋà=* followed by singular imperative suffix *-i*. The direct speech introduced by the quotative marker *ké* is a negative imperative given to second person singular addressee.

Negative relative clauses in Mursi follow the same syntactic pattern of affirmative relative clauses. It is very plausible to assume that almost all negative relative clauses come out of noun modification forms structured by a gapping strategy.

(13.25) a. *hír-á* [Ø *ŋànì kè-ŋè-à=ó*]_RC
person-RSTR [Ø NEG.PERV 3.SBJV-run.PERV-NOMZ:RSTR=NEG]
'He who did not run'

b. *hòj-á* [Ø *ŋànì kè-ŋè-à=ó*]_RC
female-RSTR [Ø NEG.PERV 3.SBJV-run.PERV-NOMZ:RSTR=NEG]
'She who did not run'

c. *ŋà=zùg=tùnù* [Ø *ŋànì kè-ŋèt=ó*]_RC
DEM=people=FAR [Ø NEG.PERV 3.SBJV-run.PERV:PL=NEG]
'They/those who did not run'

---

1 A loan word from Amharic *maksäɲo*.

With regard to these negative relative clause formations and the semantics which can be associated with them, the following points need to be taken into account:

(i) Since Mursi is a language that has no grammatical gender, gender related constructions can be substituted by appropriate nouns or natural gender displaying words. Thus *hírí* 'man' in (13.25a) may refer to both genders but it usually refers to a masculine ~⟨3SG.M⟩. The noun *hòja* 'female' in (13.25b) displays feminine ~ ⟨3SG.F⟩. In fact, *hírí* alone may be used to refer to a male referent. It can refer to a female referent when some natural gender referring nouns are attached to it. The other justification may be the fact that personal pronouns cannot be modified (maybe only if they are in relative pronoun forms).

(ii) In order to be modified, the head noun must occur in noun modification form by carrying appropriate restrictive marker which signals that the modifier should also have the same form. Thus, both the head and the modifier relative clause must carry a restrictive modification marker suffix *-a*. In a modifier relative clause, the restrictive marker suffix *-a* not only functions as restrictive modification marker but also functions as verbal nominalizer. As can be shown in the above examples, it always attaches to the right edge position of the verb root.

(iii) The restrictive modification plus nominalizer marker *-a* will always changes the verb into participle form and the entire construction into nominal phrase.

(iv) Subjunctive forms in Mursi always can come in the irrealis mood, therefore, the verbs always have a perfective aspect. Besides, first and third persons in the subjunctive forms are shown by *k(V)-* prefix. As usual singular number is being shown on the verb itself, whereas plural number is marked by [t/d].

(v) NP heads in demonstrative constructions can be modified but they do not take a noun modification marker suffix *-a*, they are already in modification form. Due to this, the restrictive modification/nominalizer cannot be attached to the perfective negative verb root (as in (13.25c)).

Note that when an imperfective aspect verb is used in negative relative clause, the subjunctive will not be marked, however subject suffix is marked (see example 13.26).

(13.26) ŋà=hír=á   [Ø ŋàtùɲ
DEM=man=NEAR [Ø lion
ŋà=éɲérés-Ø=ó]_{RC}
NEG.IMPERV=afraid.IMPERV-3SG.SU.IMPERV=NEG]
'This is a man who does not fear lions.'

13.3 Negating a Copula Clause

Mursi copula verbs can be negated in the same way as regular verbs. Thus, copula clauses are also negated in the same way as verbal clauses. In copula clauses, the copula complement indicates either identity or attribution, as in (13.27a–c).

(13.27) a. [nɔ̀ŋ]_CS á   [támárí]_CC
           3SG   COP.3.IMPERV   student
           'S/he is a student.'

           [nɔ̀ŋ]_CS [ástámárí]_CC   [ŋà=ʔán=ó]
           3SG   teacher   NEG.IMPERV=COP.3.IMPERV=NEG
           'S/he is not a teacher.'

      b. [nɔ̀ŋ]_CS [čàll-i]_CC   ŋà=ʔáj=ó
           3SG   good.STV-ADJ   NEG.IMPERV=COP.3.IMPERV=NEG
           'It is not good.'

           [nɔ̀ŋ]_CS á   [gèrs-i]_CC
           3SG   COP.3.IMPERV   bad.STV-ADJ
           'It is bad.'

Since all negated constituents in Mursi take clause final positions, copula complements in negative copula clauses will move to clause second position and thus take the syntactic slots next to the copula subjects. The third person copula verb form has the invariable form *a*.

It has two negative varieties: (i) *ŋaano* ([ŋaʔano] ~ ⟨ŋà=án=ó⟩) (13.27a) which indicates that it has been a consonant-final root at an early stage of the language, and (ii) *ŋajo* ([ŋajo] ~ ⟨ŋà=á=ó⟩) which shows it is indeed an uninflected form of *a*.

The second and third person singular and plural have identical forms even if the second person subject suffixes are overtly marked on the copula verb. But this match occurs when negated copula forms are being used in tag question constructions. In addition, the instance in which the tag forms occur with independent pronouns can be substantiated by the fact that the sentences (but not the tags) involve non-copula verbs.

TABLE 13.3 Negative imperfective copula forms

Person	Form	Underlying forms	Meaning
1sg.	/ŋàkáníó/	[ŋà=k-án-i=ó]	'I am not'
2sg.	/ŋàànó/	[ŋà=án-i=ó]	'You (sg.) are not'
3sg.	/ŋàànó/	[ŋà=án-ó]/[ŋajo]	'S/he, it, is not'
1pl.INC	/ŋàkánó/	[ŋà=k-án-Ø=ó]	'We (inc.) are not'
1pl.EXC	/ŋákánó/	[ŋà=k-án-o=ó]	'We (exc.) are not'
2pl	/ŋààno/	[ŋà=án-o=ó]	'You (pl.) are not'
3pl	/ŋààno/	[ŋà=án-ó]/[ŋajo]	'They are not'

(13.28) a. jòg àggì=nù   éŋér-é=ŋà,   jòg
         3PL 3PL.PN.SP=FAR afraid-3PL.SU.IMPERV=DEF 3PL
         ŋà=ʔán=ó?
         NEG.IMPERV=COP.3.IMPERV=NEG
         'They were afraid, weren't they?'

     b. ịnè án-á   kún-í
        2SG COP.IMPERV-TEMP come.IMPERV-2SG.SU.IMPERV
        wúr-ú=ŋà²   ịnè
        return.back-2SG.SU.PERV=DEF 2SG
        ŋà=án-í=ó?
        NEG.IMPERV=COP.IMPERV-2SG.SU.IMPERV=NEG
        'You (sg.) are coming back, aren't you?'

The tags in (13.28a–b) repeat the subjects—pronouns. As opposed to (13.28c) where the tag is just negated copula verb.

     c. jòg   á   págádíó,
        3PL COP.3.IMPERV merchant.PL
        ŋà=ʔán=ó?
        NEG.IMPERV=COP.3.IMPERV=NEG
        'They are traders, aren't they?'

---

2 It is not clear but there seems to be a connection between the verbal form *wur* 'return back' and preposition/relator/adverbial form *wùréɔ́* 'after, afterwards, later, behind, last, etc'.

With regard to scope, it is worth mentioning the distinction between the negative clitics and negative copula forms in sentences. The negator clitics ŋà= and =ó have scope over the predicate of a clause while the negative copula forms in Table 13.3 above have sentential/clausal scopes. The third person negative copula form ŋààńó {ŋàʔánó or ŋàjó ~ [ŋà=á=ó]} can negate almost any sentence/clause and therefore has a scope that extends beyond negating a single constituent of a sentence/clause. So ŋààńó/ŋàjó can be called sentential/clausal negator.

13.4 Negative Existential Verb níɲɛ 'Not Present'

The negative verbal lexeme níɲɛ 'not present, without' is used to negate existential or locational clauses. níɲè is an impersonal form that functions as a general negator of existential or locational clauses regardless of person or number of the subject.

(13.29) a. nɔ̀ŋ dórí tó-jé níɲè
       3SG house in-OBL not.present/exist.3.IMPERV
       'S/he (it) is not in the house.'

     b. bè kíɲíɲ túrúmél níɲè
       DIST.PAST long.time.ago car not.present/exist.3.IMPERV
       'In olden times, cars were unknown.'
       (Lit. 'cars were not present')

The negative lexeme níɲè has also a sense of 'without/absence of X', which normally infers the absence of an object or entity/property, as in (13.30).

(13.30) àɲè kí-hín-í búná ʃúkárí
       1SG 1SU-want.IMPERV-1SG.SU.IMPERV coffee sugar
       níɲè
       not.present/exist.3.IMPERV
       'I want coffee without sugar.'

Furthermore, the same negative lexeme níɲè can also function as negated possessive predicate. In examples given below, níɲè occurs in both forms: uninflected (13.31a) and inflected (13.31b).

TABLE 13.4 Negative existential verb—imperfective aspect

Person	Form	Meaning
1sg.	níŋ-n-áɲ-ɔ̀	'I am not present'
2sg.	níŋ-n-íɲ-ɔ̀	'You (sg.) are not present'
3sg.	níŋè	'S/he, it is not present, there is not'
1pl.INC/ EXC	níŋ-n-í-ɔ̀	'We (inc/exc.) are not present'
2pl	níŋ-n-ùŋ-ɔ̀	'You (pl.) are not present'
3pl	níŋè	'They are not present, there are not'

TABLE 13.5 Negative existential verb—perfective aspect

Person	Form	Meaning
1sg.	níŋ-n-áɲ-i	'I didn't exist'
2sg.	níŋ-n-íɲ-i	'You (sg.) didn't exist'
3sg.	níŋ-n-Ø-a	'S/he, it didn't exist'
1pl.INC/ EXC	níŋ-n-i	'We (inc/exc.) didn't exist'
2pl	níŋ-n-ùŋ-u	'You (pl.) didn't exist'
3pl	níŋ-n-Ø-a	'They didn't exist'

(13.31) a. àɲè làsàj   níŋè
    1SG bread not.present
    'I don't have bread.'

b. àɲè làsàj   níŋ-n-áɲ-ɔ̀
    1SG bread not.present-EPH-1SG.OBJ-VFS
    'I don't have any bread.'
    (Lit. 'There is no bread to me.')

It can inflect for person of the S argument but in a rather unique way. Only bound pronominal O argument markers can be marked on it. The alveolar nasal *n* is inserted between the root-like form of the negative existential verb and participants that occur as direct objects.

As illustrated in Table 13.4 and Table 13.5, negative existential verb form in the imperfective and the perfective aspects are almost identical in a number of ways. There are however two exceptional differences,—(i) the forms in the third person display inflected and uninflected forms, and (ii) those in Table 13.4 take verb-final suffixes because they are intransitive verbs in the imperfective aspect whereas those in Table 13.5 take portmanteau suffixes. At a first glance, these portmanteau suffixes look like those that are copied from the vowel of the verb root, for instance, the suffix *-i*. But they are not applicable to all and do not show any consistency throughout the paradigm.

Therefore, regarding the nature of these portmanteau suffixes, further study is needed. Note that the negative existential verb *nŋè* has a positive counterpart which exhibits inherently singular and plural forms in its roots. Most importantly, this negative existential verb does occur anywhere in the clause where it is deemed necessary. Some examples are given below:

(13.32) a. [ɓa   ké   ká-dáʃĩ=jè]$_{SUBORD:CL}$
CAUSE QUOT 1SU-do.1SG.SU.IMPERV=SUBORD
ké-jél-í   háŋ   ŋànije   sátí
1SU-like-1SG.SU.IMPERV INTENS however time
nŋ-n-áɲ-ɔ̀
not.present-EPH-1SG.OBJ-VFS
'I would like to do it (Lit. 'If only I did, I would like'); however, I have no time.'

b. [hír-á   [Ø lùkùr-á
person-RSTR [Ø friend-RSTR
nŋ-n-Ø-á]$_{RC}$]$_{CS}$ á   [dáhá³]$_{CC}$
not.present-EPH-3SG.OBJ-NOMZ:RSTR] COP.3.IMPERV poor
'A man who has no friend is poor.'

In (13.32a), *ŋànijè* itself may sometimes function as a contrastive negative marker and has been discussed in one of the subsequent sections. In (13.32b), the relative clause construction functions as a copula subject. Like any other regular verbs, the negative existential verb *nŋè* can also be restrictively nominalized when it occurs in relative clauses (as in (13.32b)).

---

3 A loan word from Amharic *däha* 'poor'.

13.5 Inherently Negative Verb ímág

The inherently negative lexeme *ímág* '(I) don't know, be ignorant of' can function as negative predicate and occur with or without first person prefix. But it always takes bound pronominal subject suffixes.

(13.33) a. *ɓá   sé   k-áít-ɛ*
place/CAUSE say.COMPZR 3.SBJV-go.PERV.PL-MA
ímág-í-ɔ̀
don't know-SG.SU.IMPERV-VFS
'I did not know of their going.'

b. *ɓá   án-á   [hír-á   mád-ínén-á]*$_{NP}$
place/CAUSE COP.IMPERV-TEMP man-RSTR teach-NOMZ-RSTR
k-ímág-í-ɔ̀
1SU-don't.know-1SG.SU.IMPERV-VFS
'I did not know that he is a teacher.'

c. *kó   hàlì kún-Ø   kó mìnáŋ*
PNC later come.IMPERV-3SG.SU.IMPERV CRD when
k-ímág-í-ɔ̀
1SU-don't.know-1SG.SU.IMPERV-VFS
'I don't know when he will come.'

d. *àɲè [húllí   k-ɨ́w-án   mád-á-ɲá*
1SG if/when 1SU-take-MT.1SG.SU.IMPERV teach-NOMZ-PL
sízzì=jè]$_{SUBORD:CL}$ *jɔ̀g ímág-έ-ɔ̀*
three=SUBORD   3PL don't know-3PL.SU.IMPERV-VFS
'They do not know that I took three books.'

A *k(V)*- prefix for first persons and independent personal pronouns for all other non-first persons may be employed in S function. Yet the morphology of this negative lexeme is very odd and does not have consistency; it even resembles verbs which have irregular inflectional nature. Despite its morphology, the inherently negative verb *imag* behaves the same way as negated verbs; it usually takes clause-final position. When it is being passivized, it will have a meaning 'unknown, not known', as in (13.34).

NEGATION 537

(13.34) hírí [rè-á n=ènè]_{NP} k-ìmàgt-ò
man body-RSTR SG.PSD=2SG.PSR PASS-not.know.PERV-3.PASS
'A person whose identity is unknown.'

It may also denote the meaning 'be ignorant of, forgot' when followed by the adverbial intensifier ɓòì 'all, at all, completely'.

(13.35) [sárá-á g=ùɲù]_{NP} bè
name-RTSR PL.PSD=2SG.PSR DIST.PAST
kí-tímág-á ɓòì
1SU-not.know.PERV-1SG.SU.PERV at all
'I have forgotten your name.'

13.6 Indefinite-Like Words

Mursi lacks independent negative indefinite words in its negation constructions. Not only in Mursi but also across world's languages, negative indefinite words are rare (cf. Dixon 2012: 121). However, this doesn't mean that they don't exist along other negator particles. For instance, Mursi has two indefinite-like words: àhìtí ~ [àhì-ti] ⟨thing.SG-INDEF:NRSTR⟩ 'thing' and hírkóna ~ [hír-kón-a] ⟨person-one-INDEF:RSTR⟩ 'someone, a certain person, anybody'. When they are being used with the negative existential lexeme níŋè, they may convey negative indefinite meanings 'nothing' and 'nobody' respectively. The negative existential níŋè can potentially occur anywhere, but usually in its typical clause-final position.

(13.36) a. ŋà=kàlì=tá àhì-tí ká-dáʃi
DEM=day=NEAR thing.SG-INDEF:NRSTR 1SU-do+1SG.SU.IMPERV
níŋè
not.present/exist.3.IMPERV
'I have nothing else to do today.'

b. nɔ̀ŋ jàg-á ké [ɓòì àhì-tí
3SG answer-3SG.SU.PERV COMPL all thing.SG-INDEF:NRSTR
gáj-Ø nɔ̀ŋ níŋè]_{COMPL.CL}
know.IMPERV-3SG.SU.IMPERV 3SG not.present/exist.3.IMPERV
'He answered that he knows nothing.'

In (13.36b), the third person pronoun in the complement clause can be an optional element as long as the argument is cross-referenced on the verb. Thus, it doesn't cause a difference in meaning if deleted.

(13.37) a. ŋà=bʉ́=ùnù   dórí   tó-jé   hírkóná[4]
DEM=place=FAR house in-OBL one.INDEF
núŋɛ̀
not.present/exist.3.IMPERV
'There is nobody in the house.'

In contrast, the indefinite pronoun *hírkóná* in (13.37b) can appear without the negative existential *núŋɛ̀* whose meaning would mean 'anybody'.

b. hirkón-a   ŋà=bá=á   íʃé?
one-INDEF DEM=place=NEAR present/exist.IMPERV
'Is anybody else here?'

One without the negative existential word has been found—*hírí dɔ̌néj* ~ ⟨person.SG INDEF one⟩ 'no one' (Lit. a certain person). Literally, both *hírkóná* and *hírí dɔ̌néj* would mean 'one / (a certain) person.' However, there is one major distinction between the two, i.e. *hírkóná* is a compound word indefinite pronoun derived from the indefinite generic noun *hírí* 'man' and from indefinite pronoun *kóna* 'another/certain' (a grammaticalized number word *kón* 'one'). Whereas *hírí dɔ̌néj* is derived from the same generic noun *hírí* plus a non-grammaticalized number word *dɔ̌néj* 'one' (cf. Jesperson 1917). Compare the indefinite pronoun *hírí dɔ̌néj* of the following examples with one *hírkóná* shown above in (13.38a):

(13.38) a. jɔ̀g   géná   hín-ɛ́
3PL others want.IMPERV-3PL.SU.IMPERV
kí-ʃíl-ɛ   nɔ̀ŋ ŋànìjè hírí   dɔ̌néj
3.SBJV-stand/accuse-IRR 3SG but   person one
tád-á   nɔ̀ŋ sìɔ̀   gár-ú
put.on-3SG.SU.PERV 3SG hand.SG lost-3SG.SU.PERV
'And some of them would have taken him; but no man laid hands on him.' (John 7:44)

---

4 The suffix *-a* is a restrictive/indefinite nominalizer at phrase level. Without *-a hirkon* means 'twenty' (Lit. 'one man/person, referring to 10 fingers and 10 toes.').

b. ŋà=ɓ=ùnù   kó   hírí   dɔ́néj   jàg-èsèn   lɔ̀gɔ́
   DEM=place=FAR CRD man one answer-BEN.3 word
   '(there) and no man was able to answer him a word.' (Matthew 22:46)

13.7 Interjection ɪmm ɪmm 'No'

The negative interjection *ɪmm ɪmm* 'no' can be used for answering a yes/no question. But an important point that we may have to notice here is that the non-repeated form *ɪmm* does not provide the intended negative meaning. Instead the *ɪmm* form alone is used to answering a yes/no question positively or it would mean ~ 'yes', as in (13.39c–d).

(13.39) a. hàlì sán-í   kátámá-í-jè?   ɪmm! ɪmm! àɲè hàlì
   later stay-2SG.SU.IMPERV town-LOC-OBL no no 1SG later
   k-ó-í   ɔ́r-ɔ́   ríɓ
   1SU-go.IMPERV-1SG.SU.IMPERV home-OBL all.the.day
   'Will you (m) spend the day at the market? No!, I shall stay all the day at home.'

b. ɓèlè hàlì mír-čí-ɲ-án-ò   ìɲè?
   night later return-APPL-EPENT-MT-IRR 2SG
   'Will you return tomorrow?'

   ɪmm! ɪmm! ŋà=kí-mir-čí-ɲ-án=ó
   no no NEG.IMPERV=return-APPL-EPENT-MT=NEG
   'No!, I won't return'

c. ŋà=ŋɔ̀r=ùnù   gúɲ-ɛ́-ɔ̀?
   DEM=elephant=FAR see.IMPERV-2SG.SU.IMPERV-VFS
   'Do you (sg.) see that elephant?'

   ɪmm! kú-gúɲ-ɛ́[í]-ɔ̀
   yes 1SU-see.IMPERV-1SG.SU.IMPERV-VFS
   'Yes!, I saw.'

d. ŋà=ója=á   tímírtí   tɔ́n-čá-ò?
   DEM=year=NEAR education begin.PERV-APPL-IRR
   'Did you start school this year?'

> *ɪmm! kɔ́ɔ́n-čá-ó*
> yes 1SU.begin.PERV-APPL-1PL.INC.SU.PERV
> 'Yes!, we (inc.) have begun'

As can be clearly shown in (13.39a–b), *ɪmm ɪmm* can be used to negate a full question sentence because oftentimes part of the question or at least the predicate will be repeated as part of the answer. It is common and natural to get such repeated forms from the class of interjection and being used as negators.

13.8 Tracing and Linking Negators

While different types of negators constitute the negation system of the language, it is yet possible to trace the origin of the form which recurs in some of the negative particles. Some of the negator forms are attested in a number of Surmic group languages while few forms were also attested outside the group. In view of Mursi negators, there is relatively compelling evidence in the negator proclitic *ŋà=* which in one way or another is the origin for the rise of the following independent negative forms:

- /ŋàánó/ ~ [ŋà=ʔán=ó] (see §13.9). The same morphological process, cliticization, should have applied to Chai verbs because Chai has almost identical morphological verbal negation process to Mursi. However, Last and Lucassen (1998) didn't adequately describing the exact morphological process that has to be employed in the negation system of the Southeasten Surmic languages. Due to this, in their grammatical sketch of Chai language, the negator enclitic =*ó* has been presented as being a final suffix -*o*.
- /ŋànì/ may well be reconstructed from the negator proclitic *ŋà=* and the imperfective copula verb *an* ⟨COP.IMPERV⟩. The morpheme *i* which occurs following the copula could possibly be a singular number marker—~ [ŋà=án-i]. The existence of *i* possibly as a sole singular number marker suggests that the particle has no self-standing form and cannot be inflected for further grammatical categories including for plural number.
- The negative existential-locative imperfective verb /nɪ́ŋè/ has the same forms for third person singular and plural. It perhaps developed from the locative suffix *ni* added to the negator proclitic *ŋà=* and the singular positive existential verb /íh/ ⟨exist.SG.IMPERV⟩ which always has [i] realization due to recurrent deletion of glottal fricative /h/ word-finally—/h/ ~ ∅. Finally we will get a form *nɪ́ŋai* [ni-ŋà=i] ⟨LOC-NEG=exist.IMPERV:SG⟩ which I believe developed into a fully fledged verb form *nɪ́ŋè*—'x' at/in is not present/exist or 'x' not at/in 'y' or 'x' without 'y'. But what we cannot be certain of is that

it can inflect for person like any other regular verb. Contrary to the claim made above, this suggest that *níŋ* could be a root form rather than a derived form from different grammatical categories. An in-depth study is required in order to identify its actual form. Last and Lucassen (1998: 420) claimed that *níŋè* would perhaps be a negative copula. It is a hypothesis that makes sense until disproved by new evidence.

- The contrastive clause marker particle *ŋànijè* looks like a derived form because the form in itself gives a hint it may be from *ŋàni* and from the subordinate marker enclitic *=jè*. Also, in most cases, the element that follows this contrastive marker is the main clause.

Therefore, in all negator forms listed above, there is one constant form recurring, i.e. /ŋa/ ~ [*ŋa/*ŋà=/*ŋ/. In fact negators have not been given proper place and attention by some Surmic language investigators. Due to this, a number of inconsistent and incoherent negator markers have been reported in different literatures.

For instance, the Mursi main negators *ŋà=* and *=ó* undoubtedly have clitic status while in Chai (another Southeastern Surmic group language), *ŋa* has been reported as an independent particle (Last and Lucassen 1998: 418). Last and Lucassen also reported another independent negative particle *ŋásò*. However, such form has not been found in my corpus so far, despite it being an acceptable morphological form in Mursi. If any such form exist in Mursi, it is undoubtedly reconstructed from two clitics—the negator proclitic *ŋà=* and from floating emphatic enclitic *=so*.

CHAPTER 14

Clause Types, Clause Combining and Coordination

14.1 Introduction

Clause types can be classified by internal structure, transitive, distransitive and extended intransitive. These were discussed in the previous sections. This chapter presents a selection of clause types not specifically discussed in the previous chapters (see the list in §14.2). Mursi deals in ways in which different clause types can be combined together to form complex clauses. Of the three major clause combing strategies, the relativization strategy was discussed in Chapter 4. Thus in this chapter, the focus is on the point of intersection between relativization and complementization clause combining strategies.

In Mursi, clauses can be combined or linked by the following four major clause combining techniques—subordination, complementization, relativization (rarely), and coordination. In a rather few instances and contexts, a given clause construction type may involve complementation as well as relativization strategies. Therefore, in general, this chapter explores various clause types of the language, and most importantly the strategies/ways in which they are being combined/linked.

14.2 Clause Types

Mursi has the following clause types, each are discussed in subsequent subsections: conditional (§14.2.1), temporal (§14.2.2), speech report clause (§14.2.3), complement clause (§14.2.4), copular clause (§14.2.5), and obligation/deontic clause (§14.2.6). It is important to note that each clause type utilizes one or more varieties of clause combining/linking strategies.

14.2.1 *Conditional Clause*
A conditional clause mainly presents hypothetical proposition which may or may not happen in the main clause (apodosis) depending on the condition in the subordinate clause (protasis). The subordinate clause of a Mursi conditional construction must contain the conditional particle *húllí* 'if, when', which almost always occurs at the beginning of the subordinate clause. The following template shows the actual syntactic structure of the subordinate clause of the conditional construction:

$$\left[húllí \begin{bmatrix} \textit{if} \text{ (CONDITIONAL)} \\ \\ \textit{when} \text{ (TEMPORAL)} \end{bmatrix} \text{... 'X'}\textit{=jè/=è}_{\text{SUBORD:CL}} \right]$$

Accordingly, 'X' represents any constituent that appears at the end of a dependent/subordinate clause. Therefore a constituent that occurs at the subordinate clause-final position is marked by the subordinate clause marker enclitic =jè (following vowel-final) and =è (following consonant-final constituent).

(14.1)   [húllí nɔ̀ŋ ŋàni   gùjò ŋà=dák-∅=ó
         if   3SG NEG.PERV rain NEG.IMPERV=hit-3SG.SU.IMPERV=NEG
         ŋàméá=jè]_SUBORD:CL
         today=SUBORD
         'If it does not rain today, ...'

(14.2)   [hùllì kɔ́-gɔ-i   adisawa=jè]_SUBORD:CL
         if   1SU-go.IMPERV-1SG.SU.IMPERV addis.ababa=OBL+SUBORD
         [kɔ́-tóí   kùčùmbà-nèn]_MAIN:CL
         1SU-count.1SG.SU.IMPERV amhara-NOMZ
         'If I go to Addis Ababa, I will study Amharic.'

Note that in Mursi, an allomorph of the oblique case marker suffix =jè and the subordinate marker enclitic =jè are identical, as is shown in (14.2). When the two co-occur at the same position as in (14.2), it is really difficult to know whether or not they undergo fusion. I would say it is highly likely that the fusion process is occurring. In most cases, both the subordinate and the main clauses will have the same aspect, as in (14.2). This does not mean necessarily that is always the case. The verb of the subordinate clause may be in perfective aspect and an imperfective aspect verb may predicate the main clause, as in (14.3a).

(14.3) a. [hùllì ɔ́k-ú=jè]_SUBORD:CL   [ànè
          if   go-3SG.SU.PERV=SUBORD   1SG
          k-í=ŋà]_MAIN:CL
          1SU-exist.IMPERV:SG.1SG.SU=DEF
          'If s/he goes, I will stay here.'

In fact, the change in aspect of the verb in the subordinate clause will have an effect on the semantics, which is different from the formal semantics of a subordinate conditional clause. The subordinate clause in (14.3a) may be expressed in an equivalent but less formal way—'as long as'. So, it may also mean 'As long as he is gone, I shall stay here'. The subordinate verbs of conditional clauses usually utilize perfective aspect. Even the copula predicate has to occur in perfective aspect when used in the subordinate clause in the stative intransitive sense 'be good', as in (14.3b).

  b. [hùllì [rònó ɓèlè] ŋɔ́jɔ̀ té čàll=è]_{SUBORD:CL}
    if   [in.future morning] wind COP.3.PERV good.STV=SUBORD
    [kɔ́-gɔ́-í   kútúl-ɔ̀]_{MAIN:CL}
    1SU-go.IMPERV-1SG.SU.IMPERV mountain-OBL
    'If the weather is good tomorrow, I will go to the mountains.'

The subject of the subordinate clause can be left unspecified if the same subject has to be employed in both clauses on the basis of context and is recoverable from the main clause.

(14.4) [hùllì bíró él-ɛ́=jè]_{SUBORD:CL}
    if   money exist.IMPERV:PL-3PL.SU.IMPERV=SUBORD
    [k-ádʒ-ɨ́n   húŋ]_{MAIN:CL}
    1SU-give.IMPERV-2SG.OBJ simply
    'If I have money, I will give you (some).'

In addition to declarative, the main clause could also be an imperative or an interrogative clause.

(14.5) a. [hùllì hín-í=è]_{SUBORD:CL}   [ɔ́g-ó]_{MAIN:CL}
     if   want.IMPERV-2SG.SU.IMPERV=SUBORD go.PERV:IMP-VFS
     'If you (sg.) want, go (sg.)!'

    b. [hùllì gùjò dák-ò=jè]_{SUBORD:CL} [máskótí ɲɔ́g-à]_{MAIN:CL}
     if   rain hit-3.IRR=SUBORD window close.PERV:IMP-VFS
     'If it should rain, close (sg.) the window!'

As always, the verb has to be in the perfective aspect when being used in the imperative mood. The imperative verb form can also be accompanied by different verb-final suffix markers. Negative imperative in the main clause can be expressed in the same way as regular negative constructions, as in (14.5c).

c. *hùllì ɛ́ɲɛ́rs=è*]¹ₛᵤʙₒʀᴅ:cʟ   [*érmì-á*
   if   afraid.IMPERV-2SG.SU.IMPERV.SUBORD child-RSTR
   ŋà=ɓ=ùnù   *ŋà=ítóón-í*]ₘₐɪɴ:cʟ
   DEM=place=FAR NEG.IMPERV=send.IMPERV-SG
   'If you are worried, you shouldn't send your child to that place.'
   (Lit. 'If you (sg.) afraid, don't send your child there!')

(14.6) a. [*hùllì ìɲè ŋà=kí-ʃíg-í=jè*]ₛᵤʙₒʀᴅ:cʟ
        if   2SG NEG.IMPERV=1SU-listen.IMPERV-SG=SUBORD
        [*ʃíg-án[ɲ]-ɛ*   *á*   *nèŋ?*]ₘₐɪɴ:cʟ
        listen-1SG.OBJ-APPL COP.3.IMPERV who.OBJ
        'If you don't listen to me, who is going to listen to me?'

    b. [*húllí ìɲè jél-í*   *jɔ̀g ŋà=dàmì=tùnù*
       if   2SG like-2SG.SU.IMPERV 3PL DEM=manner=FAR
       jél-číɲ-é   *ìɲè=jè*]ₛᵤʙₒʀᴅ:cʟ [*ìɲè hàlì*
       like-APPL-3PL.SU.IMPERV 2SG=SUBORD   2SG later
       lɔ̀m-í   *ʃílímátí² Í-Ø*   *ɔ̀ŋ?*]ₘₐɪɴ:cʟ
       have-2SG.SU.IMPERV prize to.be-3SG.SU.IMPERV what
       'If you love them that love you, what wages will you have?'

In (14.6b), *dàmì* 'custom, rule' can be interpreted as 'according to' or 'in (the same) manner'. This also aligns with some of Ethiopian languages which use accord phrases and clauses in accordance with the information presented earlier or agreement with rules, traditions, etc. (Kuteva et al., 2019: 397–398).

14.2.2 *Temporal Clause*

The second function of *húllí* 'when, while' is coding temporal relation between two events. The temporal relation of clauses may be simultaneous or sequential. The two can be grouped under overlap and succession respectively (Longacre 2007: 379). Like conditional clauses, a temporal coding element (temporal linker) *húllí* always occurs at the beginning of a subordinate clause, in this case at the beginning of a temporal subordinate clause. However, in temporal

---

1 The second person subject suffix and the subordinator suffix might have been fused but I found it difficult to point out the complex phonological process involved. It should have been ⟨i+je⟩. It is also not clear why the second person possessive pronoun is left unspecified (14.5c).
2 A loan word from Amharic *filmat* 'prize'.

clause constructions, clauses may be juxtaposed. In such instance, the temporal linker *húllí* takes a modification marker suffix *-a*, possibility as a relativizer.

The examples given below depict the temporal relation of two events, that is, the event in the main clause is the durative result of the event that is initiated in the subordinate clause. So, the relation between the temporal subordinate clause and main clause may be characterized as a 'beginning-postspan' relation.

(14.7) a. [*hùlli kɔ́d́-á-nɛ-Ø*
when/if begin.IMPERV-HAB-EPENT.APPL-3SG.SU.IMPERV
tímírtí=jè]_{SUBORD:CL} [*tóíØ ká-gáj-ò*]_{MAIN:CL}
education=SUBORD count.NOMZ 3.SBJV-know.PERV-3.IRR
'Since s/he started school, s/he knows how to read.'

The verb *kɔ́d́* 'begin' often comes with the habitual/progressive marker suffix *-nè* (third person), of the otherwise polysemous verb 'write, kill/stab/spear, build'. The verb of the main clause is in subjunctive mood. With respect to the subjunctive mood, even if it expresses something not totally true, Mursi displays the characteristic of Semitic languages. This adheres to the statement made about Semitic languages (maybe the result of language contact), 'the subjunctive indicates an act dependent upon the statement of the previous clause, and future to it in terms of time' (Gray 1934, as cited in Dixon 2012: 8).

When the two clauses are apposed, *húllí* will have a meaning of '(ever) since, from the time (that)', as in (14.7b).

b. [*nɔ̀ŋ wà óól-á tùmù*]_{MAIN:CL} [*hùll-á nɔ̀ŋ*
3SG REC.PAST pray-3SG.SU.PERV god when-RSTR 3SG
ʃíg-ɛ-Ø woŋgilau-i=tè]_{SUBORD:CL}
hear-APPL-3sg.IRR gospel-SG=SUBORD
'S/he has prayed (ever) since s/he heard the Gospel.'
(Lit. 'from the time s/he heard the Gospel')

The subordinate clause also contain a relative clause because *húllí* is marked by a restrictive marker *-a*. So the whole structure (*nɔ̀ŋ ʃígɛ woŋgilauite*) may be a modifier of *hulla* ⟨from the time that⟩. The noun gospel is a loan word from the Amharic *wängel*. Surprisingly, as it is shown in (14.7b), the definite marker of the source language was also adopted with the form, i.e. *wängel-u* ⟨gospel-(3MASC.):DEF⟩.

14.2.2.1 Simultaneous Clause

A simultaneous clause encodes temporally coterminous events/actions expressed by temporal subordinate clause and by the main clause. The temporal word *húllí* 'when, while' will be employed as temporal coordinator, but cannot entirely be considered a sole subordinator marker. In a simultaneous clause, the sole function of *húllí* is coordinating two temporally parallel clauses. This can easily be shown by the absence of the subordinator marker enclitic *=jè* from the subordinate clause margin. In simultaneous situations, two clauses can possibly be arranged according to the temporal continuity of the activities they indicate. This includes: punctiliar-continuous, continuous-punctiliar and punctiliar-punctiliar (Longacre 2007: 379–380).

i. Punctiliar-continuous

The punctiliar-continuous temporal relation indicates an activity that has already taken place and was completed but during which another activity is taking place simultaneously. *húllí* 'when' and *ŋàhùllùnù* 'at the same time' are temporal words that typically encode punctiliar-continuous relations.

(14.8) a. [húllí ŋà=lɔ̀g=tùnù ké-séd-á]
when DEM=issue/matter=FAR 1SU-think.PERV-1SG.SU.PERV
[kí-číg-í háŋ]
1SU-laugh.IMPERV-1SG.SU.IMPERV very
'When I think of that I laugh very much.'

b. (nà) [ŋà=hùll=ùnù tó-jé [lùkùr-à jesusi]$_{NP}$
CCN DEM=when.NOMZ=FAR in-OBL friend-RTSR jesus.GEN
hód-á [bá-á n=ɛ̀nɛ̀]$_{NP}$ nà
come.PERV:PL-3SG.SU.PERV place-RSTR SG.PSD=3SG.PSR CCN
gín-ɛ́=jè]
ask-3PL.SU.IMPERV=SUBORD
'At the same time came the disciples unto Jesus, saying,...'
(Lit. 'At the same time, disciples of Jesus came to his place, asking...')

But, if *húllí* is nominalized and changed into a *húllà* 'at a (the) time' reading, the subordinate clause can be placed after the main clause. This means, a punctiliar event/action possibly with one or more additional optional co-ranking medial structures may precede the continuous event/action. Also, the temporal continuous structure will have the nature of subordinate and relative clauses, as in (14.9).

(14.9) *jesusi íw-á   tílén   (nà dóŋ-ú)   (nà*
       jesus take-3SG.SU.PERV food.PL CCN pick.up-3SG.SU.PERV CCN
       óól-ésé   tùmù) (nà bík-ú)   [húll-á
       pray-BEN:PERV.3 god   CCN break-3SG.SU.PERV when-NOMZ:RSTR
       ám-íné-nè-á=jè]_SUBORD/RC
       eat.imperv-AP-3PL.SU.IMPERV-RSTR=SUBORD
       'Jesus took bread, (and blessed it), (and broke it) as they were eating,...'
       (Lit. 'At the time that they are eating,...')

ii. Continuous-punctiliar

The other simultaneous temporal relation of clauses is continuous-punctiliar, in which an action which is taking place terminates at some point in time.

(14.10) a. [*húllí sé   kɔ́n   wàrkàtì=ŋà*]
           when say.3SG.AUX 3.SBJV.write.PERV paper=DEF
           [*élí-ú   ŋɔ̀nè-j*]
           call-3SG.SU.PERV sister.PERT.3.PSR-NOM/FOC
           'When he was writing the letter, his sister called him.'

        b. [*húllí ké   kɔ́n   dádáb=ŋà*] [[*kɔ́mɔ́n sízzì*]_NP
           when say.1SG.AUX 1.SBJV.write.PERV letter=DEF   guest.PL three
           hód-á]
           come.PERV:PL-3PL.SU.PERV
           'While I was writing a letter, three visitors came.'

The auxiliary verb *se* 'say' in (14.8a–b) covers a range of meanings such as 'intend, want, think, and have in mind'. It is also a modal marker commonly used to refer to future time. In (14.8-ab), the auxiliaries may express subject's or speaker's intention/attitude towards the predicate of the subordinate clause. Note that this auxiliary verb also has a grammaticalized form, a quotative marker (*ké* ⟨QUOT⟩) which we see anywhere in speech clauses.

Apposing of clauses may lead the subordinate clause to behave like a relative clause, it even may change its meaning. Therefore, in simultaneous clauses whose subordinate clauses are made up of a temporal coordinator *húllí* clause, apposition is not possible as far as my corpus is concerned. Therefore, in the simultaneous clauses whose subordinator or temporal coordinator is *húllí*, apposing clauses are simply not possible. Besides, the continuity of activity in the subordinate clause has to be maintained until another activity in the main clause takes place.

c. [húllí ŋɔ̀n-à=ŋà]   [dák-ú   bá]
   when step.down-MT.3SG.SU.PERV=DEF fall-3SG.SU.PERV ground
   'He fell while walking down the stairs.'

d. *[dak-u baa] [húll-á ŋon-a=ŋà]

As can be shown in (14.9c), the temporal transition from continuous to punctiliar can be achieved by maintaining the sequential flow of the narration. In place of the subordinate marker enclitic =jè/=è, the definite marker enclitic =ŋà is used. An interesting phenomenon to notice in (14.9c) is that this definite marker is attached to the verb. This is mainly due to the use of aspectual neutral verbs in narrative texts which are characterized by simultaneous bounded events. In this case, the function of the definite marker is to adjust the intended aspectual meaning,—the perfective reading 'while he was stepped down' may be closer to the intended reading of the text ('while he stepping down'). The perfective aspect information was obtained from the short form motion suffix -a which would otherwise be the long form -áná on the third person imperfective aspect verb.

iii. Punctiliar-punctiliar

Two punctiliar activities/events that are taking place simultaneously may overlap. Nevertheless, the subordinate clause verb does not necessary have to be in a perfective aspect. But the verb of the main clause must be in perfective aspect unless the activity/event timed is in present tense (as in (14.11c)).

And in the following examples imperfective aspect verbs do almost always appear in the subordinate clause.

(14.11) a. [à̀ɲè húllí k-ó-í   tútú=ŋà]$_{SUBORD:CL}$
         1SG when 1SU-open.IMPERV-1SG.SU.IMPERV door=DEF
         [ŋà̀ɲùr ŋè-ú   gàʃ-ɔ̀   háŋ]$_{MAIN:CL}$
         cat   run-3SG.SU.PERV forest-OBL simply/just
         'As he opened the door, out went the cat.'

b. [ʤɔ̀ɔ̀nɛ̀   húllí kún-Ø=ŋà]$_{SUBORD:CL}$
   mother.PERT:3.PRS when come.IMPERV-3SG.SU.IMPERV=DEF
   éró   ŋè-sé   wárán-ɔ̀
   children run-BEN/MA.3.PERV gate-OBL
   'When their mother came, the children ran towards the gate.'

c. [bì-ò   húllí   héj   ʃaura-je]   [òlí-ɲá   héj
   cow-PL when go.IMPERV:PL shaura-OBL bull-PL go.IMPERV:PL
   wárr-ɔ̀]
   Omo.river-OBL
   'When the cows went to drink at Shaura, the bulls went to the Omo.'

The definite marker on the imperfective aspect subordinate verb is the one which gives the punctiliar sense to the verb. In other words, it is highly likely that the definite marker =ŋà may have developed as marker of simultaneous clause subordinator on imperfective verbs in the subordinate clause. In simultaneous clause types which normally deal with temporal overlapping, temporal progression marker words cannot be used unless as coordinators or repeaters of two or more temporally equivalent clauses. For example, we don't see the temporal progression marker (coordinator) nà in the text below.

(14.12) ké-héj-Ø   kí-bír-Ø
        1SU-go.IMPERV-1PL.INC.SU.IMPERV 1SU-pick.up-1PL.INC.SU.IMPERV
        ólʃ-ó   dàài   ŋànìjè   [tó-jé ŋà=b=ùnù
        sorghum-PL all/COMPLET However in-OBLDEM=place=FAR
        kí-bír-ó   ólʃ-ó=ŋà]_SUBORD:CL
        1SU-pick.up-1PL.EXC.SU.IMPERV sorghum-PL=DEF
        'We (exc.) go and pick up sorghum stalks.' However, while we (exc.) are collecting the sorghum stalks ...

        tó-jé   lò   zùg-tí   [gɛ
        in-OBL have/exist people-NRSTR [PL.PN+NRSTR
        k-éŋérs-ó]_RC
        1SU-fear.IMPERV-1PL.EXC.SU.IMPERV]
        '... there are those people out there whom we are afraid of.'
        (Lit. 'inside it (the sorghum stalks' place) has people of whom we (exc.) are afraid') (KW 0:32:0)

14.2.2.2   Succession Clause

In narrative texts, two or more clauses can be arranged based on temporal succession of actions or events. Succession clause is identical with consequence clause in that the time or the cause in the subordinate clause almost always precedes the main clause. That is, the main clause is a temporal causality or successor of the subordinate clause. nà 'and', nà húllí 'and then', wurɛa 'after' are used as coordinators of clauses in temporal succession. Events/actions involved in temporal succession can be span-span, span-event, event-span, and event-event.

i.   Span-span

Span-span is a temporal succession of two or more prolonged activities. The state/activity which will be reported in the subordinate clause is one span while the same or different state/activity in the following clause will indicate another span. The state/activity which will be described in the subordinate clause is one span while the same state/activity that continues from the subordinate clause will indicate another span.

(14.13) [húll-á   kɔ́n-čán-a   sátí-á   [Ø wà
        when-RSTR begin-APPL-RSTR time-RSTR [Ø REC.PAST
        kɔ̀-dɔ̀m-čà=jè]_RC]_SUBORD:CL/SPAN [tíí   sàkkàl [bá-á   dákákán]_NP
        PASS-trespass-APPL=SUBORD   DUR   nine   place-RTSR   all
        té   kɔ̀rɔ̀-í]_SPAN
        COP.3.PERV dark.STV-ADJ
        'From the (sixth hour) there was darkness over all the land up to the ninth hour.'
        (Lit. 'From the time that was being trespassed up to nine all the land became dark.')

An embedded relative clause marked by gap strategy is embedded within the subordinate clause.

ii. Span-event

We may also find temporal succession indicating clauses containing a prolonged activity and an event, as can be shown below.

(14.14) nà   [k-ów-ónó   ŋàŋà=ŋà   dírr]_SUBORD:CL nà
        CCN   1SU-go-MT.1PL.INC.SU.IMPERV   like.this=DEF long.time   CCN
        [hùllì té   bá-á   éré-í=nè]_SUBORD:CL:SPAN
        when   COP.3.PERV   place-RSTR   cross-NOMZ=SUBORD
        [k-érés-ó   bòì   k-èlì
        1SU-cross.IMPERV-1PL.EXC.SU.IMPERV   COMPLET   PASS-call.PERV
        ké   dòl]_MAIN:CL:EVENT
        QUOT   Dol
        'As we (inc.) keep going like this for a long time and when we are at the crossing-place, we (exc.) crossed at a place called Dòl.' (MH 0:31:2)

The clausal coordinator *nà* that occurs clause-initially has a function of depicting the logical progression point of an argument. (14.14) is a piece of narration from a story titled 'Mursi history'—about how the Mursi occupied their present territory and then expanded it by crossing the Omo River. So, we can see that *nà* wouldn't exist if the event-line does not show forward movement can be shown from the story's lines *nà* exists because there is temporal succession as well as progression. Otherwise, it wouldn't occur if the activity described by the event-line were not moving forward.

iii. Event-span

An event/activity at a specific point in time can be followed by another prolonged activity.

(14.15) [*kó-hód-á   k-ói-tó   ólʃó*
        1SU-come.perv.pl-1PL.INC.SU 1SU-put.PERV-1PL.EXC.SU stalk.PL
        bà-i-ni]   [*ká-dág-á   hóló-ni tíí nà húllí*
        ground-LOC-RS 1SU-hit-1PL.INC.SU.PERV dance-RS DUR CCN when
        dóólá   kó   ràmàn   áw-ò-ni]
        girl.PL CRD:PART two come-3PL.IRR-RS
        'We come and put stalks on the ground, *then* we will start dancing *and then* two girls will come.' (KW 1:38:5)

In (14.15), on the last element of the event (or marginal element), i.e. *ba* 'ground', the suffix *-ni* is a resolution marker and is an equivalent of English 'then' and has a narrative function, i.e. shows a state of equilibrium that has been reached at the conclusion of an episode. The first bracket shows the event while the second bracket shows the span. Thus as it is shown in the span, the durative particle *tíí* clearly shows that the activity will take place for an unspecified or prolonged period of time.

Note that in temporal overlapping conditions—continuous-punctiliar can be a permutation of punctiliar-continuous. But in temporal succession, span-event cannot simply be a permutation of event-span.

iv. Event-event

Event-event type is another temporal succession of events where an event 'Y' merely follows event 'X'.

(14.16) *mɔ̀r bág-Ø   čáláì   nà ók-ú*
        calf eat-3SG.SU.IMPERV necklace CCN go.IMPERV-3SG.SU.PERV
        kèŋɔ̀   tùi   nà gár-á
        stomach inside CCN disappear-3SG.SU.PERV
        'The calf swallowed the necklace, and it went into their stomachs and was lost.'

The event-event temporal succession in (14.16) outlines a connection, the actual chronology of the three event of the narration. In this case, *nà* may be considered as a chronological sequencer of the events taking place in the narration.

14.2.2.3   Causal

Events can also be related to each other through causality by temporal antecedence marker words with their consequents. In terms of clausal and of maybe subordination strategies, the causal-consequent clauses are structured almost in the same way as clause types above. The major difference between causal and other types of clauses is that causal-consequent circumstances or relations are overtly shown by causal-consequent connectors. These causal-consequent connectors are *wùréɔ́* 'after, later', *ŋàhùllùnù* '(and) then, after that', *ŋànije* 'therefore, thus, because of this', and *nà* 'therefore'.

(14.17) [wùréɔ́ jɔ̀g ʃúúné   bè   ér-á]
       after 3PL father.PERT.SG.3.PSR DIST.PAST die.PERV-3SG.SU.PERV
       ɓòì=tè]_{SUBORD:CL}   [jɔ̀g tálí-ɛ   dórí]
       COMPLET=SUBORD 3PL sell/buy-3PL.SU.IMPERV house
       'After their father had died (pol), they sold the house.'

Note that not all the connectors listed above necessarily indicate causal relationships. But since most of them are temporal adverbs, the temporal order (= the chronological order of the events in the antecedent and the consequent) would likely suggest the intended clausal relationship. Likewise, in (14.17), *wùréɔ́* merely shows a temporal sequence, not a causal relationship. In causal-consequent clause relations, the aspect of the verb in the cause/subordinate and the one in the consequent/main clause may vary. The latter frequently contains imperfective aspect verbs.

(14.18) nà   bè   ŋà=hùll=ùnù   bá-á
       CCN DIST.PAST DEM=when/time=FAR place/CAUSE
       lɔm-Ø   ŋɔ̀jɔ̀ nà   jírísí mà
       have-3SG.SU.IMPERV wind CCN sea   water
       ʃiŋɔ-nè-ɔ̀
       tremble-EPENT.APPL-VFS
       'And the sea arose by reason of a great wind that blew.'
       (Lit. 'And then (and at that time) by of having wind, the sea water trembled.')

The real causal meaning in (14.18) that tells us the cause of the sea arousal is the trembling of the water caused by wind, shown by causal marker *ba* 'place/cause'. However, it is possible to indicate this causal-consequent relation without the causal phrase *ba (lɔm)* 'by having', that is, as long as *ŋàhùllùnù* is in the causal clause along with the causal object *ŋɔ́jɔ́* and occurring prior to the consequent clause. Then two clauses can optionally be coordinated by the clausal coordinative conjunction *nà*.

The other cause-consequent marker is *ŋànìjè*, as we remember from negation Chapter, is a derivation,—from the negative perfective *ŋànì* (or one can call it contrastive marker particle 'not yet' or persistive 'still') and the subordinator enclitic *=jè*.

(14.19) ká-tál-ɛ̀   bà-ì-nù   kè-mèsí   ʤù-ɲá   kó₁
       3.SBJV-buy/sell-COM place-LOC=FAR 3.SBJV-do clay.pot-SG PNC
       kúr-ɛ́   kɔ́mɔ́n-nè
       bury-RES   guest.PL-OBL
       '(they) bought with them the potter's field, to bury strangers in.'

       ŋànìjè   kó₂ ŋàméá tó-jé   ŋà=b=ùnù   k-èlì   kó₃
       therefore PNC today in-OBL   DEM=place=FAR   PASS-call.PERV   PNC
       bá-á   kó₄   ɲàwà
       place-RTSR PNC   blood
       'Wherefore that field was called, the field of blood, unto this day.'

As it is clearly illustrated here, when *ŋànìjè* occurs between the two clauses,—the first one is the general causal clause while the second is the consequent clause. Mursi has a complex and unclear distribution of participant nominalization markers some of which appear to have an agent nominalizers (referring to the actor) and yet others have the causer agent nominalizers (see Chapter 3). The preposition *kó* has various functions,—the one in causal clause *kó₁* shows purpose, *kó₂* preposition, *kó₃* instrumental, and *kó₄* could refer to source.

The clause coordinative conjunction *nà* may also be used to expresses relation of causality as in (14.20a–b).

(14.20) a. ŋà=gáwátí=tá   á   bàséní nìs-á   nà
          DEM=plate=NEAR COP.3.IMPERV easy   crack-3SG.SU.PERV   CCN
          ìɲè   hín   íw-í   ʃɛ́ɛ́
          2SG want.DEO   look.after-2SG.SU.IMPERV   well
          'This cup is easily (cracked) broken therefore you have to take care.'

b. [ànè ŋà=kɔ́-lɔ́m=è̀]   bíró   tíríbí   nà   [ànè
   1SG NEG.IMPERV=1SU-have=SUBORD money enough CCN 1SG
   ŋà=ká-tál-í=ó   nɔ̀ŋ]
   NEG.IMPERV=1SU-buy/sell-1SG.SU.IMPERV=NEG 3SG
   'I have not enough money, therefore I can't buy it.'

tíríbí is a loan word from the Amharic ~*tirf* 'enough/additional', and now has a determiner role in the NP. The absence of the labiodental fricative /f/ in the language has caused the changed into a bilabial stop /b/. Despite the fact that the coordinator is being used as causal marker, it is the first clause that is treated as the cause for the latter action.

The temporal/conditional marker *húllí* itself can also be used as reason marker if it occurs at its typical syntactic position within the subordinate clause. However, this time its original temporal/conditional meaning 'when/if' may be modified to a reason-centered one, 'since', and it could semantically be extended into 'because'. The example given below tells us this fact.

(14.21) [húllí kí-hín-Ø   dórí
       since 1SU-want.IMPERV-1PL.INC.SU.IMPERV house
       tál-á=jè]_{SUBORD:CL} [hín   bíró-j   mèrì]
       buy/sell-=SUBORD want money-NOM man
       'Because we (inc.) are going to buy a house, much money is needed.'

(14.22) [húllí ʃúúnɛ ér-ò=jè]   [érmì-á   bó]_{NP}   kó
       when father die.PERV-IRR=SUBORD child-RSTR big.MOD CRD
       áú   kɔ́ɔ́j-Ø   ké   [[hír-á   bó]
       eldest.child 3.SBJV.go-3.IRR 3.SBJV.be.PERV man-RSTR big.MOD
       ɔ́r-ùɲ]_{NP}]_{NP}
       home-GEN
       'The eldest son becomes the head of the family when the father dies.'

An exceptional relation of the consequence-cause clause has been found where the cause is encoded by reason applicative marker suffix -ɛ on irrealis verb form.

(14.23) [zùw-á   óól-nènè-á]_{NP}   tó-jé   ŋáà=jè]_{SUBORD:CL}
       people-RSRT beg-NOMZ-RTSR] in-OBL here=SUBORD
       kó-hód-á   wárán tútúg ɲóg-ɔ̀-ɛ̀
       3.SBJV-come.PERV:PL-3PL.SU gate door close-3PL.IRR-APPL
       'They shut the gate so that beggars would not come in.'
       (Lit. 'They closed the gate door from beggars coming inside.')

14.2.2.4   Reason Clause

Reason and purpose clauses are almost identical structurally, but the purpose clause may be indicated alone without needing a grammaticalized cause marker particle *ba ~ ɓa* 'place'. As Heine and Kuteva (2002: 239–240) suggested, a nominal word for 'place' can be grammaticalized into cause marker in certain languages. The original locative meaning will be transformed into causal marker through a gradual process—which supposedly denotes the following meanings:

['place' > 'in place of' > 'instead' > 'because (of)' > 'therefore' (rarely)]

The following five remarks can best manifest the characteristics of reason clauses as well as their syntactic temple:

i. *ɓá/ɓá* always occurs preceding the causer (sometimes tense marking particles may intervene between the two).
ii. A purpose clause can have an optional (ii) template but requires the reason applicative/commitative marker suffix *-ɛ* for all persons except for first person plural exclusive and second person plural which are indicated by *čo*.
iii. The subordinate clause which contains the reason clause may precede or follow the main clause.
iv. The preposition particle *ké* may occur in a reason clause, where it Precedes the causal *ɓá/ɓá* and shows purpose when reason and purpose are expressed in a single clause.
v. A reason clause has an obligatory template:
[*ɓá/ɓá* ... CAUSER ... VERB-REASON(=SUBORD)], or along with purpose marker *ké* [*ké ɓá/ɓá* ... CAUSER ... VERB-(REASON) (=SUBORD)].

(14.24) [*lúsì túrú*]_{MAIN:CL}   [*ɓá*   [*nɔ̀ŋ gòdínɛ̀*]_{NP}
   boy   cry.3SG.SU.PERV   CAUSE   3SG   brother.PERT:3.PSR
   íw-án-ɛ̀   *kowasi=jè*]_{SUBORD:CL}
   take/receive-MT-APPL:RES   ball=SUBORD
   'The boy cried because his brother took the ball.'

Since the causal marker *ɓá/ɓá* has a movable nature (no fixed position in a clause), it can appear anywhere in the subordinate clause along with the causer. As is illustrated in (14.24), *ɓá* preceding the possessive NP, shows the cause which is brought on by the causer specified in the subordinate clause (*nɔ̀ŋ*) *gòdínɛ̀*, (lit. 'he his brother'). The third person singular pronoun is optional since the bound pertensive suffix *-ɛ* fully provides information about the possessor person and number. Note that the verb 'cry' shows aspect by adding a *t(V)*- prefix verb in which the imperfective form *rui* drops the final vowel and becomes *ru* which with a perfective aspect marker *t-* and by copying the vowel of the root ~ *turu*, ends in a consonant like most consonant-final verb roots *tur*. However, if it is decomposed into further pieces **tu-r-u* *⟨PERV-cry-3SG.SU⟩, it does not make sense, so it is better to keep it as it is, i.e. *tu-ru*. See further examples below, where in the majority of subordinated clauses, the subordinate clause precedes the main clause.

(14.25) a. [*bá   ká-tálí-čó   dórí=jè*]_{SUBORD:CL}
CAUSE 1SU-buy-APPL:RES.1PL.EXC.SU house=SUBORD
[*kà-bày-ó   ŋà=b=á*]
1SU-live-1PL.EXC.SU.IMPERV DEM=place=NEAR
'We live in this country because we (exc.) have bought a house.'

b. [*bá   zìní   íb-čaɲ-áɲ-ò   [bíró-á*
CAUSE thief take-APPL-1SG.OBJ-3.IRR money-RTSR
g=àɲù]_{NP}   *dákákán=ne*]_{SUBORD:CL} [*àɲè*
PL.PSD=1SG.PRS all=SUBORD   1SG
kɔ̀-lɔ̀m-á   dolar dɔ̃néj sɔ̀ŋ]
1SU-have-1SG.SU.PERV dollar one only
'Because the thief has taken all my money, I have one dollar left.'

In all reason clauses shown above, in addition to the grammaticalized cause marker *bá/ɓá*, reason and mostly purpose indicating suffixes -*ɛ*, -*čo*, and -*čaɲ* have been attached to verbs,—either as RES/COM (reason/comitative) or APPL (applicative). It is quite difficult to make a distinction between reason and purpose clauses merely on the basis of semantics.

Nevertheless, there are two possibilities by which the two can be distinguished: (i) both purpose and reason can be indicated in the subordinate clause by *ké bá* where *ké* functions as purpose marker (as in (14.26–27)), and (ii) the purpose clause may be introduced by applicative/comitative markers -*ɛ*, -*čo*, and instrumental-applicative -*čaɲ*.

The examples given below present the *ké bá* clauses, and both were obtained from a short narration entitled '*kòmà kódá*' about a cultural ceremony that emphasises the distinct identity of grades and the rights and obligations of seniority and juniority. (cf. Appendices, Text I). The following is to give readers a brief introduction to the narrative in (14.26 and 14.27). According to the age grades stages and systems of Mursi, the *Bara* ('Elders') who are placed at the top of the age grade hierarchy are seen as being responsible for the socialization of the *Tèrò* ('Young men') and the unmarried girls. Those who are called the *Rórá* ('Adult men') are responsible for *Dhonga* [ɗɔ̀ŋà] (cf. §1.6). So, according to the Mursi tradition the *Tèrò* and the unmarried girls take sorghum stalks to the *Bárá* at the time of harvest. The *Dhonga* do the same for the *Rórá*.

The speaker in this narration is a young but married woman talking about the usual conflict with *Dhonga* while they are collecting sorghum stalks occurring every each year at the harvesting season. The purpose-reason markers in examples below are shown in bold face.

(14.26) *ké òrì?* [*ké ɓá jɔ̀g*
PURP/RES where PURP/RES CAUS 3PL
búr-èsèn-é-a rórá]_SUBORD:CL [*àggè*
collect-BEN-RES-3PL.SU.IMPERV Rora.PL 1PL
kí-búr-èsèn-ó bárá]
1SU-collect-BEN-1PL.EXC.SU.IMPERV Bara.PL
k-án-ó ɓííɓíí
1SU-COP.IMPERV-1PL.EXC.SU.IMPERV different
'At (on) what ground? Because for that they collect for the Rora, we (exc.) collect for the Bara; thus we (exc.) are different.' (KW 1:02:8)

The subordinate clause has is consistent independent sentence embedded within it. Besides, there is no subordination or coordination markers shown but rather the *ké ɓa* is used as bridging construction. One has to remember that clauses of the above types may have full-fledged internal structure of sentences.

In (14.27), the purpose-reason clause follows a rhetorical question which as is shown clearly seeks information.

(14.27) [*nà hàli nìs-é bì*] [*ŋà=zùgt=ùnù wà*
CCN later kill-3PL.SU.IMPERV COW DEM=people=FAR REC.PAST
gíná ŋáà kèɔ̀ŋ?] [*ké ɓá*
ANA:REF here why PURP/RES CAUSE
wàkén-čí-í-á]_SUBORD:CL *lɔ̀g-á*
REC.PAST3.SBJV.touch-APPL-1PL.OBJ-3PL.SU.IMPERV issue-RSTR
[Ø *wágá gɔ̀r-ɔ̀*]_RC
[Ø ANA:REF road-OBL]
'After that they will slaughter a cow. Why are those people are here? For the reason they have touched us on the road.' (KW 1:28:8)

This construction is ambiguous in that it can have two interpretations—(i) the one shown in the actual translation, and (ii) just a single clause ('Because they touched us then on the road.')

As mentioned earlier, the purpose clause can be expressed without the cause marker particle *bá/ɓá* just by attaching the comitative or reason applicative marker suffixes to verbs. Comitative and reason applicative markers in Mursi are identical. Thus the semantics of comitative, reason (reason-applicative), and purpose clauses may be shown by invariably identical morphological markers. Despite the fact that there is a considerable difference between Nilo-Saharan and Bantu linguistics, at the semantic level, applicative derivation seems to cover a number of other functions in both families. It has been noted by Dixon and Aikhenvald (2011: 53) that the term 'applicative' has different sub-types such as comitative, dative, and instrumental.

Likewise, the Mursi applicative derivation is a fairly productive means in which purpose clauses are being expressed, as in the examples given below.

(14.28) a. *nɔ̀ŋ [sábá-á   n=ɛ̀nɛ̀]ₙₚ   táli-Ø-ɛ*
        3SG head-RSTR SG.PSD=3SG.PSR sell-3SG.SU.IMPERV-COM/APPL
        bì
        cow
        'S/he sold a cow to her(him)self.'

   b. *nɔ̀ŋ [bì-á   n=ɛ̀nɛ̀]ₙₚ₂   [sabá-á   n=ɛ̀nɛ̀]ₙₚ₂*
      3SG cow-RTSR SG.PSD=3SG.PSR head-RSTR SG.PSD=3SG.PSR
      táli-Ø-ɛ́
      sell-3SG.SU.IMPERV-APPL:RES
      'S/he sold his own cow (for her(him)self).'

   c. *ŋès-Ø-ɛ   dóóléj*
      run-3SG.SU.IMPERV-COM girl
      'He runs away with the girl.'

Purpose clauses which are introduced by applicative/comitative marking devices, may depend on other higher level discourse organization to clarify their meaning. Broadly speaking, the semantics of the above clauses may seem largely determined by the context in which they are being used. In addition to the above expressions, purpose clause can also be shown without any subordination or linking particle at all but by using the imperfective aspect form of the desiderative verb *hin* 'want'. *hin* expresses desire or intent of speaker and often has identical aspect with the verb of the main clause (as in (14.29a)).

(14.29) a. [kí-hín-í   rúm-ı̧ná čúr-áná]
         1SU-want.IMPERV-1sg.SU.IMPERV cloth-PL wash-MT
         kɔ́-gɔ́-í   kú-čúr-í   rúm-ı̧ná
         1SU-go.IMPERV-1sg.SU.IMPERV   1SU-wash-1sg.SU.IMPERV   cloth-PL
         'I went to the river in order to wash my clothes.'
         (Lit. 'Wanting to wash clothes, I went to wash clothes; or I want to wash clothes so I went to wash clothes.')

In the example shown above, the first clause is a positive purpose clause, which also functions as complement of the main clause even if the main clause itself has another complementizer, i.e. *kúčúrí* ('to wash'). The fact that *kúčúrí* along with *rúmı̧ná* forms a nominalized possessive phrase O ('my washing of clothes'). Note that 'to wash cloth' and 'wash one's own body' are separate verbs in Mursi, the latter *oɲ* is more often used in intransitive sense. The other complementizer is the motion towards (ventive) suffix *-áná* (a full form, i.e. the form attached to an imperfective verb in the third person singular root form). When used in non-main clauses, *hín* may often seems to have the nature of nonfinite verbs (an uninflected form). It, however, as seen above is a fully inflected verb containing person and number markers for the sake of showing same-subject clauses.

The auxiliary *sé* 'say' in (14.30) occurs in uninflected form and cannot be marked for person but just be used as a complementizer of the negative purpose clause (intention) 'in order not to forget'.

(14.30) dádáb ɓá   hàlì sé   kí-dı̧́nák-áɲ-ò   [k-ódʒ-ésé-ò
         letter CAUSE later COMPL 1SU-forget-1sg.OBJ-IRR 1SU-put-BEN-IRR
         [úkúrá-j   tó-jé]_PP]_MAIN:CL
         pocket-GEN in-OBL
         'I put the letter into my pocket so that I should not forget it.'

14.2.2.5   Concessive Clauses
A concessive clause is a clause which makes a concession, against which the proposition in the main clause is contrasted (Thompson 2007: 262). Concessive clauses in Mursi can be shown by concessive clause subordinators: *ɲànìjè* 'however, but', *ɲànì* 'not (yet)', and *kó húllí* 'even though, even if' (Lit. 'and if').

(14.31) [ɓá   ké   ká-dáfí-ò   ké-jél-á-ò]
         place/CAUSE COMPL/3.SBJV.be.PERV 1SU-do-IRR 1SU-like-HAB-IRR

ŋànìjè   [sati ràmà-í   níŋὲ]
however time long.STV-ADJ not.present
'I would like to do it (Lit. 'If I do it, I would like'); however, I have no time.'
(Lit. 'If it becomes the case that I do, I would like; however, there is no long time.')

In most cases, the verb of the subordinate and the main clause occur in subjunctive mood. The verb *daſi* has an invariable verb root form in both aspects. But subjunctive mood normally applies only to verbs that are in the perfective aspects. Thus, as can be seen from the example above, the verbs in both clauses are in perfective aspect, in an ideal state to attach subjunctive/irrealis markers. Semantically, (14.31) is also more of a conditional-like concessive clause.

(14.32) a. [nɔ̀ŋ gúŋ-ó   [túrúmél-á ràmàn]_{NP}] [ŋànìjè   dɔ́néj
         3SG look-3SG.IRR car-RTSR two   but/however one
         ŋànì   ká-tál=ó]
         NEG.PERV 3.SBJV-buy.PERV=NEG
         'He looked at two cars, but did not buy either.'

As shown above, *ŋànìjè* may attract a contrastive coordinative reading particle (as in (14.32)) when used along with a numeral word or a quantifier—or just concessive reading as can be seen with *dɔ́néj* 'he didn't buy even one'.

     b. [ŋòná-à   n=ànù]   ók-ú   gáwá=jè]   nà
        sister-RTSR SG.PSD=1SG.PSR go-3SG.SU.PERV marker-OBL CCN
        ŋànì [àŋè kɔ́-dɔ́t-ìnɛ̀n   dórí-je-j]
        yet   1SG   1SU-leave-AP   house-OBL-LOC
        'My sister went to the market, but I stayed at home.'
        (Lit. 'My sister went to the market (and) yet I am staying inside at home.')

In previous sections, I have tried to show that it may never have been a genuine negative perfective particle. Both *ŋànì* (14.32b) and *ŋànìjè* (14.32a) are contrastive markers. The following changes may help us to understand how its present form *ŋànìjè* came to exist: concessive *ŋànìjè* (however, but) < *ŋànì=jè* ⟨not.yet=SUBORD⟩, 'still', negative perfective < 'not yet' (⟨NEG.PERV⟩).

(14.33) [nɔ̀ŋ ʃíg-í-Ø   àggè] nà   [àggè nɔ̀ŋ ɲànì
       3SG hear-1PL.OBJ-3SG.SU.IMPERV 1PL   CCN 1PL   3SG NEG.PERV
       kí-ʃígt-Ø-ó=ó]
       1SU-listen.PERV:PL-3SG.OBJ-1PL.EXC.SU.PERV=NEG
       'She heard us, but we did not hear her.'

The other concessive marker is *kó húllí* that may show a plausible semi-grammaticalization scenario when a temporal preposition develops into concessive marker. *hulla* 'at the time (that)' may first develop into *húllí* (temporal marker 'when') then adopted as conditional 'if' and then finally settle as marker of concessive.

Concessive *kó +húllí*, < conditional/temporal *húllí* 'if/when', < temporal *hulla* 'at the time' < *hàlì (later/future tense/modal). In the concessive clauses given below, by following the preposition *kó* the concessive marker *húllí* occupies its original subordinate clause position.

(14.34) a. [kó   hùllì dáʃí ké-te   bú háŋ]   [bá   kún-nèj
          PNC if   do   3.SBJV-be.PERV big INTENS CAUSE come-NOMZ
          ŋà=dɔ́t-íné=ó
          NEG.IMPERV-absent-APPL=NEG
          'Even though he has a lot of work to do, he will certainly come.'
          (Lit. 'It isn't the case that he will absent from coming.')

       b. [kó   hùllì kɔ́-dɔ́m-áɲ-ò]
          PNC if   1SU-insult-1SG.OBJ.1SG.IRR
          [ŋà=ké-lésí=ó]
          NEG.IMPERV-3.SBJV-pout=NEG
          'Even if I insulted him, he wouldn't be offended.'

14.2.2.6   Substitutive Clauses

A substitutive clause is another means of clausal subordination in which the notion of 'rather than, instead of' being expressed by one of the most recurring particles in the language—*bá/bá* 'place' ⟨in place of⟩.

(14.35) zùgò   [ŋà=b=á   tíí]   [bért-á
       people DEM=place=NEAR DUR   choose.PERV:PL-3PL.SU.PERV
       rès-è̀]
       die.IMPERV-NOMZ
       'The people chose death rather than (instead of) denying (betraying) their faith).'

(14.36) [ɓá   sé   [sátí-tí   búí]_NP té   ŋàŋà   húŋ]
place say.3.AUX time-NRSTR big   COP.PERV like.this simply
[tóŋ́-í́   másábí́]
read-2SG.SU.IMPERV book
'Read a book rather than (instead of) wasting your time.'

(14.37) [àɲè ɓá   sé   ké-té-é́   hínéno] [hín
ISG place say.3.AUX 1.SBJV-COP.PERV-APPL alive   want.IMPERV
ɓòì   k-ér   húŋ   á
completeley:DEO 1.SBJV-die.PERV simply COM.3.IMPERV
čàll-ì]
good.STV-ADJ
'Being dead is better for me than being alive.'
(Lit. 'I instead of being alive, it is better if I should rather die.')
(Lit. 'I rather than alive, it is better for me if should die.')

In all the examples shown above, the substitutive marker ɓá usually occurs at subordinate clause initial position,—and if the subordinate clause contains subject NP, it may then immediately be preceded by this NP. The combination of the desiderative or intent verb hín 'want' and the completive marker particle ɓòì 'completely, at all' is used mainly to express deontic or optative mood.

The example shown below is an expression of wish—which in Mursi is typically expressed by a combination of the conditional marker húllí and the interrogative words ènèŋ 'how'/ténèŋ 'why' ~ 'how if/why if'.

(14.38) ɓá   bàrì   [rè-ʃa   òlíkɔ̀rɔ̀-j]_NP hùllì
place/CAUSE yesterday die-RSTR:IDEO Olikoro-GEN if
k-èr   [áɲój]_S   í-Ø   ènèŋ?
1.SBJV-die.PERV 1SG.NOM to.be-3SG.SU.IMPERV how?
'I wish I had died instead of Olikoro.'
(Lit. 'In place of the Olikoro death, if I died is who/how')

The interrogative word used in (14.38) is ènèŋ 'how', which seems more of a rhetorical question in that the speaker is expressing his/her wish or intent; but at the same time it does looks like he/she asking for an opinion 'how would it be if ... or what others might say if he/she is willing to die instead of (on behalf of someone, and so on'). In fact, the notion of wish or a wish/intent clause in Mursi is mainly expressed by the rhetorical/reason interrogative word ténèŋ 'why' followed by the conditional marker húllí 'if' > ~ ténèŋ hùllì 'why if'. If, however, it is the case of a typical wish expressions, *tɛnɛŋ hùllì* becomes a complement of the main clause, as in (14.39).

(14.39) [*ténèŋ hùllì*]_{COMPL:CL} [*lómíɲá k-íɡí húŋ?*]
why if lemon.PL 3.SBJV-ripe.PERV simply/just
'I wish the oranges were ripe.'

The main verb always is in a subjunctive mood thus it is a perfective aspect verb.

14.2.2.7 Future Time Clause

Future time clause is a subordinate clause which unlike other clause types follows the independent clause. Future time clauses are mainly shown by *kó bòì* 'until', which is derived from two particles: preposition/coordinative conjunction *kó* and completive marker adverbial particle *bòì* ~ 'every, all'. These two particles come together to express a temporal concept, and is believed to be a more generalized grammaticalized forms. For example, *kó+bòì* seems to have originated from goal plus spatial source *kó* ⟨at/with/to⟩ and *bo+i* ⟨outside+loc⟩ ~ (perhaps to unspecified goal). See the examples below.

(14.40) [*ŋà=lòg=tá ór-ón-ó kààrè=ŋà*
DEM=word=NEAR see.IMPERV-MT-2PL.SU.IMPERV eye=DEF
ŋà=jóg=ó tíí] [*kó+bòì* [*èrmì-á*
NEG.IMPERV=tell.IMPERV:IMP DUR/CONT until child-RSTR
k-ùhùd-ò hír-íɲ]_{NP} *húllí hàlì rèè*
PASS-clean.PERV-PASS.3 man-GEN when later body+PERT.SG.3.PSR
hàlì báns-áná=jè]_{SUBORD:CL}
later raise.IMPERV-MT.3SG=SUBORD
'Don't (pl.) tell anyone what you have seen, until (after) the Son of Man has been raised from the dead.'
(Lit. 'Until the Son of Man when his body will raise up.')

The activity in the independent clause may or may not take place until the activity in the subordinate clause takes place. What is so special with this type of clause combination is that the future time clause is a subordinate controlling clause.

(14.41) *áín-έ zùw-á* [Ø *íláág-ɛ-á*
give.PERV:SG-MA people-RTSR [Ø hang-3PL.SU.IMPERV-RTSR

zùwò]   nà   sé-sé   ké   "tɔ̀lɔ̀m-Ø-ɔ
people CCN say-BEN.PERV.3 QUOT   have.PERV-3SG.OBJ-2pl.SU
tíí"   [kó+bòi   hàlì   húč-áɲ-Ø=nè]_SUBORD:CL
DUR/CONT   unitl   later pay-MT-3SG.SU.IMPERV=SUBORD
'... delivered him to the tormentors, said, "keep him" until he should pay all that was due unto him.'

(14.42) [ɨ́w-á   érmì   kó   ʤɔ̀ɔ̀nè   nà   gibsɛ-ɔ
take-3SG.SU.PERV child PNC   mother.PERT.SG.3.PSR CCN   Egypt-OBL
nà   tél-í   ŋà=bà-ì-nù]   tíí]   [kó+bòi
CCN   exist.PERV-3PL.IRR DEM=place-LOC=FAR   DUR/CONT   until
hàlì   [rès-ɛ̀   herediwosi-j]_NP]_SUBORD:CL
later die.IMPERV-NOMZ Herod-GEN
'He took the young child and his mother by night, and departed into Egypt and was there until the death of Herod.'

As it is shown above, the independent clauses often end with the durative/continuative marker *tíí*. The durative/continuative *tíí* provides temporal information about the continuity of the activity in the main clause until it is interrupted by another activity in the controlling clause.

If the activity in the main clause is a one-time activity, it becomes optional and does not appear in the independent clause, as shown in (14.44).

(14.43) [[míróg-á   bá-á   [ʤààr-á   g=àɲù]_NP]_NP   bà-ì
enemy-RTSR place-RSTR leg-RSTR PL.PSD=2SG.PSR   ground-LOC
bà-ì-jè   kó+bòi   hàlì   mès-ón=è]_SUBORD:CL   [ìɲè
ground-LOC-OBL until   later do-MT=SUBORD   2SG
té-áɲ   sìɔ̀   sìtèn]
be.PERV-1SG.OBL hand right
"Sit at my right hand, until I put your enemies under your feet."

Mursi future time clause has also another variety which I called 'repetitive-terminative'. A repetitive-terminative clause type normally refers to a sequence of repeated clauses (which refer to the continuation of identical states or activities) followed by a terminative clause which refer to the termination of activity. However, the way in which clauses are repeated is different from the way commonly known, i.e. repeating of two or more clauses. Instead, a single clause will be counted as a repeated clause, where the repeater may be either the durative marker *dírr* (14.44) or by lengthening the final segment of the verb of the independent clause (14.45). The durative marker particle *dírr* also has identical meaning with *tíí*, at least functionally.

(14.44) [kɔ́b-ú   dírr] [ín-á   tɔ̀ŋɔ̀kúrí]
follow-3SG.SU.PERV DUR 3SG.PN.SP-RTSR person.name
[bón-á-sɛ   zùwò]   [ìr-ú
arrive.PERV-MT-BEN.3 people drink.PERV-3SG.SU.PERV
mà-ì-ni]
water-LOC-RS
'He followed it and followed it until it came to a place (on the Omo River) where there were people. That's where it drank.'

(14.45) [dàinò   zùwò   mèzìd-ò-ni]   [mèzìɛɛɛ ...]_REPETITION
evening people discuss.PERV-3PL.IRR-RS discuss-3PL.SU.IMPERV
nà   sén-é   ké   'hàlì ɓèlè
CCN said-3PL.SU.IMPERV QUOT later morning
kè-tè-é   zigi-ni'
1.HORT-COP.PERV-1PL.INC.SU move-RS
'In the evening the people debated. They debated and debated until eventually they say "Let's leave tomorrow morning."'

The verb in the speech report appears in non-finite verb form,—it has no information about person-number information about the subject. Unless, for the sake of the terminology, the above cases are straightforward subordination of sequential clauses with temporal subordinate morphemes introducing temporal sequential clauses. On many occasions, the future time clause marker *kó ɓòì* may appear with an allomorph of the preposition *kó*, i.e. *ké*, as in (14.46).

(14.46) [ré]   [ké+ɓòì wà   ké-déd-á-o
wait.PERV:IMP until   REC.PAST 1SU-finish.PERV-1PL.INC.SU-IRR
àggè dáfí]
1PL   work
'Wait (sg.), until we (inc.) have finished our work!'

14.2.3 Speech Report Clauses

A speech report clause in Mursi is introduced by the quotative marker *ké* 'that', which seems to have developed out of the generic noun *ké* 'thing'. It always precedes the speech verbs such as *élí* 'call' and *sé* 'say'; but it may precede or follow the speech report. Subject of the addressees may intervene between the speech verb and the quotative marker. *ké* also functions as complementizer, so the term 'quotative-complementizer' would best explain it. The other justification for this term is that even though it introduces both direct and indirect speech reports, it is primarily in charge of indirect speech reports. A direct speech report content can be introduced by the verb *sé* 'say', without the need for *ké*. In this case, the function of *ké* as an indirect speech report marker could secondarily be regarded as complementizer.

(14.47) a. [*áɨw-ó*   *dór+tó-jé*]   *fúúné*
        come.PERV.SG-IMP.MT house+in-OBL father.PERT.SG.3.PSR
        se-á
        say.PERV-3SG.SU.PERV
        '"Come (sg.) home!", the father said.'

   b. *áɨw-ó*   *dór+tó-jé*
      come.PERV.SG-IMP.MT house+in-OBL
      ké-sén-áɲ-ò-ɔ̀
      1SU-say.IMPERV-1SG.OBJ-IRR-VFS
      '"Come (sg) home!", I said.'

   c. *nɔ̀ŋ sé-sé*   *jírísí ké*   *té-i*   *làì*   *tíí*
      3SG say.PERV-BEN.3 sea   QUOT COP.PERV-SG silent CONT
      'He said to the sea. "Be silent, (be still)."'

As it is shown in (14.47a–b), the quotative marker is absent because the speech report option has been shown by an obligatory verb of speech *sé*. The suffix *-o* of *késénáɲòɔ̀* in (14.47b) is an irrealis marker. In (14.47c), the quotation marker *ké* is being used in addition to the verb of speech. Besides, there is one more optional element which usually comes at the end of the direct speech clause, i.e. *ŋàŋà*[3] 'like this; this way'. *ŋàŋà* is a verbatim quotative, as can be seen in the following example.

(14.48) [*zùw-á*   [*ɔ́r-á*   *n=àj*]ₙₚ]ₙₚ
        people-RTSR village-RTSR SG.PSD=1PL.INC.PSR
        sén-έ   *ké*   *ká-tál-á*
        say.IMPERV-3PL.SU.IMPERV QUOT 1SU-sell-1PL.INC.SU.PERV

---

3 There is evidence that *ŋaŋa* fucntions as adverb of manner and may have developed from another manner adverb *ŋáà* 'here' and the definate marker enclitic =*ŋà*. The manner adverb *ŋáà* is also developed from another source, i.e., a combination of the demonstative proclitic *ŋà*= and the near distance marker =*a*. A nonverbatim quotative marker can also be formed by adding one more demonstrative proclitic—*ŋaŋaŋa* 'so and so forth' (Lit. 'like.this like.this; this this this').

[dórén-á   g=àj]_NP   sén-έ
house.PL-RSTR PL.PSD=1PL.INC.PSR say.IMPERV-3PL.SU.IMPERV
ŋàŋà
like.this
'"We shall sell our houses", say our neighbors.'
(Lit. 'Our neighbors said "We shall sell our houses", say like this.')

Interestingly, in (14.49), it is the reporter who chooses the verbatim quotative marker in order to put the original speech said by the author as it is. A verbatim quotative has the function of bringing extra effects such as imitation of the intonation, expression, and so on, of what had originally been said (Aikhenvald 2011: 291).

(14.49) ŋàméá [číg-ín-á   n=èj]_NP   [hùlli
        now   laugh-N.S-RSTR SG.PSD=3PL.PSR when/if
číg-έ=jè]_SUBORD:CL   [jòg sén-έ
laugh.IMPERV-3PL.SU.IMPERV=SUBORD 3PL say-3PL.SU.IMPERV
ké   hee!   hee!   [číg-ín   jòg]_NP:CS á   [dɔ́néj]_CC
QUOT INTERJ INTERJ laugh-N.S 3PL   COP.3.IMPERV one
'Now for their laugh, when they laugh, they say, "Hee! Hee!". (Their) laugh is one (the same)' (MH 5:19:0)

We may consider that the subordinate clause in (14.49) would be optional, but it has an important function as this speech report itself is different from speech report types. As Aikhenvald (2011: 291) points out, expressions such as *hùlli čígéjè* may add certain vocative effects to direct speech reports, be it 'mimetic' or 'theatrical effect'. Nevertheless, the reporter will not use *hùlli čígéjè* alone, but rather he/she may also add other paralinguistic features such as facial expressions or gestures.

14.2.3.1 Speech Verbs

In addition to the primary speech verb 'say', Mursi has also other speech verbs (reporting verbs), but many of them do not have a direct speech framing function as the primary speech verb. Table 14.1 below contains a list of both direct and indirect speech verbs.

The template below shows the general internal structure of speech reports of both types:

$$\begin{cases} [sén\ (\text{PRONOUNS, NAMES} ...)\ ké ...]\ \text{DIRECT SPEECH REPORT} \\ [\text{Other speech verbs} ...\ ké ...]\ \text{INDIRECT SPEECH REPORT} \end{cases}$$

TABLE 14.1 Speech (reporting) verbs

Reporting verb	Meaning	Function	Remark
sén	'say'	direct speech verb	often follows the quotative marker ké
élí	'call'	indirect speech verb	very rarely may be used in direct speech report and always requires the quotative marker ké
jàg	'answer; reply'	indirect speech verb	may also occur preceding the speech verb sén in direct speech report clause
jóg	'tell'	indirect speech verb	may introduce direct speech report following a pause plus context and may not require the quotative marker ké
gín	'ask'	indirect speech verb	does not take quotative marker ké

In §14.2.3, we have seen that the speech verb *sén* 'say' is a primary speech verb with the function of introducing direct speech. Nevertheless, there are two conditions in which *sén* is being used to introduce direct speech without the quotative marker *ké*: (i) when *sén* is preceded by one of the above secondary speech verbs (as in (14.50)), and (ii) when the manner adverb *ŋàŋà* 'like this; this way' is being used as speech report introducer (14.50).

(14.50) [nɔ̀ŋ [ʤɔ̀ɔ̀nɛ̀]_NP]_NP   élé-ú   sé-sé
       3SG mother.PERT.SG.3.PSR call-3SG.SU.PERV say-BEN.3.PERV
       [áɨw-ó   nà   bág   [tílá-á   dàine
       come.PERV.SG-IMP.MT CCN eat.PERV:IMP food-RTSR evening
       n=ùnù]_NP]
       SG.PSD=2SG.PSR]
       'His mother called saying, "come and eat your dinner".'

Note that the third person perfective aspect and the positive imperative forms of the verb utilize identical benefactive suffix -(ɛ)sɛ.

(14.51) [húllí úʃĩn-áná=jè]_SUBORD:CL
       when finish.MT.3SG.SU.IMPERV=SUBORD

ád-í-ì lɔ̀gɔ́ jógt-o-i
give.PERV-1PL.OBJ-3PL.IRR word tell.PERV-MT-1SG.OBJ+3PL.IRR
lɔ̀gɔ́ màt-í-ó dàài nà [húllí
word drink-??-2PL.SU.IMPERV all CCN when
uʃɨŋ-áná=jè]_SUBORD:CL [àggè
finish-MT.3SG.SU.IMPERV=SUBORD 1PL
k-áw-ó [hóló dág-á-ni]_NP]_MAIN:CL [húllí
1SU-go.IMPERV-1PL.EXC.SU.IMPERV dance hit-NOMZ-RS when
séd-á-í ŋàŋà=jè]_SUBORD:CL
say.PERV-MT-1PL.OBJ+3PL.IRR like.this-SUBORD

'When it is over, they give us a word, they tell us a word, "you (sg.) drink!."'

'And when it is finished, then we (exc.) go dance hitting. When they talk to us like that,...' (KW 2:48:0)

The combination of the above two conditions ((i) and (ii)) are rarely applied at the same time, as in (14.52).

(14.52) nà johanisi jàg-èsè nà sé-se ŋàŋà àŋè
CCN john answer-BEN.3.PERV CCN say-BEN.3 like.this 1SG
kú-čúr-ùŋ mà-i
1SU-baptize-2PL.OBJ water-OBL
'John answered and said to them (like this), "I baptize you (pl.) with water".'

Other than the primary speech verb, the rest of the verbs do not guarantee where to draw the distinction between direct and indirect speech report clauses,—unless there are other additional ways to do so, such as pause or the context in which speech reports are told. While this is the case, secondary speech verbs in general may function as complementizers in indirect speech complement clauses. In particular, the secondary speech verb élí can be used in both direct and indirect speech reports, but in indicative form. In the example given below, élí in the impersonal passive form has an indicative function rather than as direct speech introducer.

(14.53) [k-èlì ké maŋu=ŋà]_CS á [kómórú]_CC
PASS-call.PERV QUOT Mangu.PL=DEF COP.3.IMPERV kómórú
á [kómórtéséní]_CC á ŋà=hír=á-ni
COP.3.IMPERV priestly.clan.PL COP.3.IMPERV DEM=man=NEAR-RS

> ŋàméá tó-jé ké-sé-Ø ké káwúlókòrò
> now in-OBL 1SU-say-1PL.INC.SU.IMPERV QUOT Kawulokoro
> káwúlókòrò kén-Ø wárr
> Kawulokoro cut-3SG.SU.IMPERV omo.river
> 'When called the Mangu, they are priests, they are priestly clans. It is this man today, we (inc.) are saying, "Kawulokoro, Kawulokoro cut Omo River".' (MH 2:53:9–2:58:6)

When the speech verb *élí* is being used as in indicative mood, things to be indicated or introduced by it are most likely personal names, place names or nominals from any other type. The first copular clause seems copula subject to the second copular clause, but it is just a type of disjunctive coordination strategy. In the presence of two copular clauses that share one and the same subject, notion of 'or' is indicated by dropping one of the copular subject. The case in the example (14.54) below, however, depicts that place or other types of names (concrete and abstract) can be introduced without the speech verb *élí*. Features in discussion are shown in bold.

(14.54) kód-ónó [bà-ì ké dirka nà
1SU.take.out-MT.1PL.INC.SU.IMPERV **place-LOC QUOT Dirka** CCN
k-ów-ónó ŋàŋàŋà dírr nà [hùllì
1SU-go-MT.1PL.INC.SU.IMPERV like.this+like.this DUR CCN when
té [bá-á éré-í=nè]$_{NP}$]$_{SUBORD:CL}$
COP.3.PERV place-RSTR cross-NOMZ=SUBORD
k-érés-ó bòi k-èlì
1SU-cross.IMPERV-1PL.EXC.SU.IMPERV COMPLET PASS.call.PERV
ké dol nà [hùllì k-érés-án-ó
QUOT Dol CCN when 1SU-cross.IMPERV-MT-1PL.EXC.SU.IMPERV
bá ké dòl=ŋà]$_{SUBORD:CL}$ mà dǐné-ó-ni
place QUOT dol=DEF water full.STV-3.IRR-RS
''At that time the place where we (inc.) were heading for was called Dirka.' As we (exc.) kept going like this for long time and when became at the crossing place, we (exc.) crossed a place called Dòl. When we (exc.) cross the place called the Dòl, the river was full.' (MH 0:31:2)

As it can be understood from the illustrated example above, there is a clear difference when the impersonal passive verb *élí* is present in the second line and when it is absent in the first and third lines. In the first and third of underlined structures, *élí* is replaced by the general place word *bá*. The occurrence of *bá* will give these two structures a second sense that would become more or less indirect speech complement (Lit. '(a) place that becomes').

In fact, the primary speech verb *sén* itself may loose its direct speech introducer status when preceded by *bá* especially when being used to indicate one's intention, thought, reason, and purpose, and so on. (Recall that in Mursi, clauses designed to express the listed aspects will often employ *bá/bá*.) The reason clause in particular is shown by the discontinuous morpheme [*bá* ... -ɛ]. Thus, the cause marker *bá* takes the initial position of the subordinate clause while the reason marker suffix -ɛ will be shown on the main verb of the subordinate clause. See the example given below.

(14.55) [*bá   sé-á   ké*
         CAUSE/INTENT say-3SG.SU.PERV QUOT
         ká-báns-è-ɔ̀   *dák-ú   bá*
         1SU-get.up.IMPERV-APPL-VFS fall-3SG.SU.PERV ground
         'He tripped while he was trying to get up.'
         (Lit. '"I will get up"—while he says, he tripped/it tripped him.')

The *k(V)*- prefix may be used to mark either first persons or third person subjunctive forms. So when used in instances such as (14.55), it could be very ambiguous. We don't know whether the prefix *k(V)*- is a personal deixis shifter or a complementizer. The verb which appears to be in the direct speech report changes its root form for aspect by segment reduction/subtraction,—imperfective *báns* 'get up' and perfective *bán*. Despite this verb having identical root form for all persons which belong in each of these two aspectual categories, very surprisingly, it shows distinict root shapes for first and third persons in the imperfective aspect.

Therefore in (14.55), the *báns* of first person imperfective form changes into third person form *bánás* within the same aspect. Unless otherwise indicated by the insertion of the vowel /a/ which overtly makes personal dexis shift from first person to third person subject, the speech report remains open for both type of interpretations.

All other secondary speech verbs can be used in the main clause or preceding the indirect speech complement clause. But they must be accompanied by the quotative marker *ké* in complement function. The following example is repeated from (13.36b).

(14.56) *nɔ̀ŋ jàg-á   ké   бòi*
         3SG answer-3SG.SU.PERV QUOT/COMPL COMPLETELY
         àhìtí   gáj-Ø   nɔ̀ŋ
         thing.SG.INDEF know.IMPERV-3SG.SU.IMPERV 3SG

níŋè
not.present.3.IMPERV
'He answered that he knows nothing.'

For obvious reasons, speech verbs other than *sén* are unproductive in direct speech reports, but the speech verb *jàg* may be used as direct speech introducer when it is placed after the speech report. When it does so, it does not require the quotative marker *ké*—see below:

(14.57) [nòŋ àlèj   ŋà=ʔán=ó]   nòŋ
3SG table/chair NEG.IMPERV=COP.3.IMPERV=NEG 3SG
jàg-á
answer-3SG.SU.PERV
'"It is not the table", S/he answered.'

An exceptional example is given below in which a direct speech was reported in a narration without the speech verb *sén*. The only way we would know the direct speech report from the narrative given below is by the secondary speech verb *jóg* 'tell' which comes after the speech report.

(14.58) *nà   húllí   dóólá kó   ràmàn áw-ò-ni*
CCN when/if girl.PL CRD:PART two come-3PL.IRR-RS
jàg-t-èsè   zùw-á   [Ø wágá   ké   bú
return-PL-BEN/DAT.3. [people-RTSR [Ø ANA:REF QUOT/COMPL big
kí-bír-èsèn-á   ólʃó]ᴿᶜ   ké
1SU-collect-BEN.1PL.INC.SU.IMPERV-RSTR stalk.PL] QOUT/COMPL
bárá-ni]COMPL:CL *bèlè*   *hód-án-ì*   *hàlì*
Bara.PL-RS early.morning come.PERV.PL-MT-3PL.IRR **later**
k-ìtìŋ-aŋ-èsè[4]   *ŋà=b=ùnù*
1.HORT-meet-MT.EPENT-BEN DEM=place=FAR
'(and) then, two among the girls will come and go back to those elders to whom we collect the sorghum stalks called Bara. They come (in the) early morning. "Let us meet later for our own (meeting) there."'

jógt-ó-i   *bár-ú*   *bá*   *bàrì*   *gá*
tell.PERV.PL-MT-1SG.OBJ Bara-NOM **place** **yesterday** ANA/ATTU

---

[4] The benefactive suffix -ɛsɛ is used mostly on perfective verb roots as well as on positive imperative forms.

```
       k-áw-ò                  ór-ó
       3.SBJV-come.PERV-3PL.IRR village-OBL
```
'It is the Baras who tell us this. "At that place and time", they (the two girls) come back to the village.' (KW 1:38:5–1:54:4)

14.2.3.2   The Syntactic Role of Direct and Indirect Speech Verbs

It is always important to distinguish the syntactic role of the secondary speech verbs whenever they occur within direct speech reports. Speech verbs introducing both direct and indirect speech reports may occur in direct speech report clauses. In such a scenario, indirect speech report introducer verbs always become part of the clause that introduces the direct speech. Both direct and indirect speech reporting verbs coordinated by clausal coordinative conjunction *nà* and share the same current speaker. See the following examples:

```
(14.59) a. nà    jesusi jàg-èsè              nà   sé-sé              ké
           CCN   jesus  answer-BEN.3.PERV    CCN  say-BEN.3.PERV     QUOT
           [óg           nà    élí          [hír-á      n=ùnù]_NP
           go.PERV:IMP   CCN   call.PERV:IMP man-RSTR   SG.PSD=2SG.PSR
           nà    hód-á
           CCN   come.PERV.PL:IMP-VFS
```
'Jesus answered (and) said to her, "Go (sg.)!, call (sg.) your husband and come (pl.) here!".'

```
       b. nà    gín-Ø-ó-ni,              nà    sé-Ø                ké    heee!!
          CCN   ask-3SG.OBJ-3.IRR-RS     CCN   say-3SG.SU.IMPERV   QUOT  Heee!!
          sén-í                 k-ér                  nój
          say-2SG.SU.IMPERV     3.SBJV-die.PERV       who.NOM?
```
'He asked him, saying: "Heee! who are you saying will die?"' (ND: 3.6)

In (14.59a), following the outcome of the commands made in the first and second imperative clauses, there is a change in the number of addressees in the third imperative clause. Note that the coordinative conjunction which often appears at clause-initial position has a role of conjoining independents marking a logical, sequential, temporal progression in narration.

14.2.3.3   Indirect Speech Report Markers

Indirect speech reports can be introduced in three major ways: (i) by the quotative *ké* (ii) by the subjunctive prefix *k(V)-*, and (iii) by the speech verb *sén* 'say' being used as auxiliary verb. This is regardless of optional secondary speech verbs for indirect speech reports that can be shown by the quotative (also complementizer) marker *ké* (see examples 14.53–14.56). On the other hand, subjunctive mood marker suffix *k(V)-* is a default complementizer which is always attached to a perfective aspect verbs, as in (14.60b).

(14.60) a. [*dàdá-á   n=ànù*]_{NP}   *mád-áɲ-Ø*   *ȧɲè*
father.RTSR SG.PSD=1SG.PSR teach-1SG.OBJ-3SG.SU.IMPERV 1SG
sén-áɲ   *ké*   [*dóŋ-á*
say.IMPERV-1SG.OBJ QUOT put.down.PERV:IMP
kèì=tùnù   *nà*   *kò-hòd-á*
thing=FAR/INDEF CCN 1.HORT-come.PERV:PL.INC-MT.PERV
kàrì   *kó*   *ȧɲè*]_{DIR:SPEECH}
together PNC 1SG
'My father ordered me saying, "Leave (sg.) that thing and come with me!"'

b. [*dàdá-á   n=ànù*]_{NP}   *mád-áɲ-ɲo*
father.RTSR SG.PSD=1SG.PSR teach/instruct-1SG.OBJ-3SG.SU.PERV
ȧɲè kɔ́-dɔ́   *ŋàdàmìtù*   *nà*
1SG 1.SBJV-leave.PERV DEM=manner=FAR CCN
kó-hód-á-ù   *kó*   *nɔ̀ŋ*
1.SBJV-come.PERV:PL-MT-IRR PNC 3SG
'My father ordered me to leave that and to come with him.'

The verb *dóŋá* 'put down' of the direct speech has been adjusted to *dɔ́t* 'leave' in the indirect speech. Consequently, as the deletion rule of the language it is only being applied to some word-final obstruents, the alveolar plosive /t/ is deleted. Note that the demonstrative *that* is not a complementizer (or complement clause) marker. The last indirect speech report marker is the speech verb 'say' in which it turns into an auxiliary verb for the purpose of secondary role as complementizer. Even if unproductive. Example presented as follows:

(14.61) a. *í-Ø*   *òrì*   [*kùrì-á   n=ànù*]_{NP}
exist.IMPERV-3SG.SU.IMPERV where hat-RTSR SG.PSD=1SG.PSR
nɔ̀ŋ gín-ú
3SG ask-3SG.SU.PERV
'"Where is my hat?", he asked.'

b. nòŋ gín-Ø   bòi   sé   [kùrì-á
   3SG ask-3SG.SU.IMPERV all/COMPLETELY say.3.AUX hat-RTSR
   n=ὲnὲ]_NP   òrì
   SG.PSD=1SG.PSR where
   'He asked where his hat was.'
   (Lit. 'He asked to know where his hat was.')

The verb 'say' in the imperfective aspect can also be used to expresses intention, perception or curiosity but it may not fully express the state or activity of the clause as a whole. As can be seen in (14.61b), it can be combined with the adverbial particle *bòi* 'all, at all, completely', which is also a marker of completed actions in most cases. The indirect speech report shown by the auxiliary verb complementizer *se* is the same as direct speech complement clause. Therefore, the auxiliary verb in the indirect speech above was used by the reporter to show the perception or intention of the author (original speaker), (Lit. 'want(ed) to know').

14.2.4 *Complement Clauses*

A complement clause is a type of clause which fills an argument slot in the structure of another clause (Dixon 2012: 370). A typical complement clause is one that functions as an argument of another clause—mostly embedded within the matrix clause. Complement clauses in Mursi can be shown in the following ways:

i.   Complementizer *ké* §14.2.4.1 (also indirect speech marker, as illustrated in §14.2.3.3)
ii. *bá* (reason/purposive) marker §14.2.4.2
iii. Apposition §14.2.4.3
iv. Complement-taking verbs §14.2.4.4

14.2.4.1 Complement Marker *ké*

The particle *ké* is by far the most productive complement marker in the language. As we have seen in the speech report section, the particle *ké* is also an indirect speech report marker.

(14.62) jòg έŋérs-έ   nà   òg-έ
        3PL afraid.IMPERV-3PL.SU.IMPERV CCN shout-3PL.SU.IMPERV
        [ké bòi   [rú-έ   bó-ó]_S]_COMPL:CL
        REASON/COMPL cry.IMPERV-3PL.SU.IMPERV wide-MN
        'They were so afraid that they cried out.'

ké ɓòì is a temporal or adverbial subordinator marker 'until', and it can also indicate reason 'since'. Thus, I have interpreted it as reason clause complementizer, as in (14.62). Accordingly, the consequence clause may come first and be linked to the causal clause by the causal subordinator 'since': 'They cried out since they were (so) afraid.' However, a complement clause construction which involves the complementizer *ké* could result in a complex construction since it shares certain syntactic similarities with a relative clause. Compare the complement clause, in (14.63a), and the relative clause construction, in (14.63b).

(14.63) a. *hír-á   wà   sé-Ø   [ké*
        man-RSTR REC.PAST say-3SG.SU.IMPERV QUOT:COMPL
        ká-bádár-ı́ɲ   bíró]$_{COMPL:CL}$ á   nèŋ?
        3.SBJV-lend.PERV-2SG.OBJ money]   COP.3.IMPERV who
        'Who told you that he would lend you money?'
        (Lit. '"money he-will-lend-you" he-saying who-told-you?')

    b. *hír-á   [Ø wà   sé-Ø   ké*
        man-RSTR [Ø REC.PAST say-3SG.SU.IMPERV QUOT:COMPL
        [ká-bádár-ı́ɲ   bíró]$_{RC}$ á   nèŋ?
        3.SBJV-lend.PERV-2SG.OBJ money]   COP.3.IMPERV who
        'The man that told you (that) he would lend you money is who?'

In (14.63a), the prefix ká which is attached to the verb *badar-* (a loan verb from Amharic) carries a high-tone because it is a subjunctive marker. Note that the subjunctive marker is a complementizer on its own even if it is not productive (14.2.3.3). Had it been a low-toned prefix, it would then indicate first person subject and it would result in another meaning ('Who told you that I would lend you money?'). In the relative clause construction shown in (14.63b), all constituents other than the subject and interrogative word (copula complement) are within the relative clause that operated by the gapping-strategy. In the absence of the relative clause, the construction in (14.63b) would mean *hírá á nèŋ?* (Lit. 'The man is who?'). The complement clause embedded within the relative clause may still be accessible whenever it is needed for further purposes.

(14.64) *hírí   [ɓá   sén-o   ké   á   zinı́]$_{COMPL:CL}$*
        man CAUSE say.IMPERV-IRR QUOT COP.3.IMPERV thief
        nà   kɔ́w-á   kɛsɛsɛ[5]-o   [lɔ̀g-á   g=èɲè]$_{NP}$
        CCN follow-3SG.SU.PERV accuse-NOM issue-RSTR PL.PSD=3SG.PSR

---

5 A loan word from Amharic *kəssəsə* (v.) ~ *kəss* (n.) accusation.

dɔ́t-ɛ́
abandon-APPL:RES.3
'The man denied the accusation that he was a thief.'
(Lit. 'The man rejected to follow his accusation because he is said that he is a thief.'; OR 'because the man said to be that he is a thief, he rejected to follow the case, which he is accused for.')

As it is shown in (14.64), the predicate of the main clause comes last in the matrix clause. The above structure as a whole is two coordinated clauses linked by the clausal coordinative conjunction nà,—the reason clause containing the complement clause in one hand and the rest of the structure on the other hand. However, since nà not only links syntactic structures but also links propositions, I say, the clausal coordinator nà is just a proposition linker that occurs in wider discourse context. However, the first clause that contained the reason plus the complement clause as a whole, can be called reason-complement clause, otherwise the entire structure may also be called reason-consequent clause (the reason marker suffix -ɛ also marks a consequence clause).

14.2.4.2 Cause/Reason Marker as Complementizer

Introducing a complement clause by using cause/reason clause is in fact a complementization strategy. A causal/reason clause can also be used as the complement clause, which is a subordinate clause on its own. The main clause then follows the complement clause. There will be no overt complement marker when cause/reason clause is being used as complement clause. Besides, as in the previous complement clause type (§14.2.4.1), there will be no additional overt markers on verbs which would indicate when the subject of the complement clause is identical or different from the subject of the main or the matrix clause.

(14.65) a. [bá ŋànì bíró ŋànì íw-á-í=ó]$_{COMPL:CL}$
REASON NEG.PERV money NEG.PERV take-MT-3.IRR=NEG
[ŋà=k-ígóm-ésén=ó]$_{MAIN:CL}$
NEG.IMPERV=1SU-accept-BEN=NEG
'I don't accept his denial that he took the money.'
(Lit. 'The reason (denial) [that he didn't take the money], I don't accept it.') (Lit. '"the-money I didn't take" he-saying his denial I don't accept it.')

It is clear that the subject of the complement clause in (14.65a) is different from that of the main clause. But the subject markers used appear to be the regular way of cross-referencing S/A like any other clauses rather than by different subject markers specific to complement clauses. The reason marker particle bá links the complement clause with that of the main clause. The complement clause only seems to be embedded within the subordinate clause.

    b. [bá   k-óg-é[í]
       CAUSE/REASON 1SU-shout-1SG.SU.IMPERV
       tíí=ŋà]_{SUBORD:CL/COMPL:CL} [k-éŋérs-í
       DUR/CONT=DEF   1SU-afraid.IMPERV-1SG.SU.IMPERV
       kòná]
       snake.PL
       'I am so afraid of snakes that I scream.'
       (Lit. 'I shouted because I am afraid of snakes.')

When bá is combined with the auxiliary sé (expresses intent/desire) it will have a meaning 'instead of; in place of'.

(14.66) iggè [bá   sé   lámíd-ɛ́]_{COMPL:CL}
       2PL CAUSE/REASON say.3.AUX find.PERV:PL-APPL:RES
       [[ʃúúnú]_{NP}   nɔ̀ŋ]_{NP} gáj-∅-ɔ̀]
       father.PERT.SG.2.PSR 3SG know.IMPERV-3SG.SU.IMPERV-VFS
       'Because your Father knows what (the things) you (pl.) need.'
       (Lit. 'You, instead of what you need (ed), your father knows.')

The second person plural pronoun iggè is ellipted, and provides subject information to the complement verb which lacks subject specification. Note that the pertensive marker on the kinship term above is the last vowel with ʃúúnú ⟨u⟩, and provides grammatical information about the person or possessor. Thus, the independent personal pronoun has been added to the pertensive form to provide specification about number of the possessed.

Unlike what we saw in the aforementioned complement clauses, ba may stand on its own as a true complementizer when the complement and the main clauses are apposed. Below are examples of a complement clause construction where the causal marker ba be interpreted either as a complementizer or a relativizer. The semantics contained in the example below are a statement of fact (14.67a).

(14.67) a. à̰ɲè ɲànì ká-ták=ó [ɓá nɔ̀ŋ
1SG NEG.PERV 1SU-know.PERV=NEG COMPL/REASON 3SG
wà kɔ́-čá-á]_{COMPL:CL}
REC.PAST 3.SBJV-come.PERV-APPL-3SG.SU.PERV
'I did not know that he has come.'
(Lit. 'of his coming')

b. [à̰ɲè kù-čùmùn-ɛ̀-í] [ɓá
1SG 1SU-happy.STV-APPL:RES-1SG.SU.IMPERV COMPL/REASON
nɔ̀ŋ kún-Ø-ɛ=jè]_{SUBORD/COMPL:CL}
3SG come-3SG.SU.IMPERV-APPL=SUBORD
'I was glad that (because) he came.'
(Lit. 'I rejoiced at (by) his coming.')

The change of *bá/ɓá* from referring a concrete object ('dirt/land') to a complementizer is not a sudden one but rather a gradual process, and it still accommodates both semantics. In other words, it neither completely lost its lexical source meaning nor it fully attained grammatical meaning. Below is a summary of the stages or grammaticalization processes that have taken place in the transition of *bá/ɓá* into a compliment marker.

*bá bá/ɓá *b/ɓ (clitic)[6]
dirt/land > { 'Place'
'Country' } > {ŋà=ɓ=ùnù} 'there'
'Earth'
'World' }
stage I

postposition > (VERB) *cause/reason/purpose* > *replacive/substitutive* > *relativizer* > *complementizer*

{bai bai} 'under; below' > { 'in place of' } > {'that'}
place+LOC (REPETETION) 'instead'
'because of'
'therefore' }
stage II

---

6 Note that a prototypical case of grammaticalization involves boundary loss and morphological/phonological fusion or "bonding"—mostly manifested by the loss of phonological segments or coalescensce (cf. Brinton and Traugott 2005: 27).

The fact is that there are no written sources exist to count on the early stages of the language thus it is almost impossible to provide a diachronic analysis at this stage. The grammaticalization stages illustrated above, however, are based on synchronically driven lexical and contextual evidences obtained from the current actual use of the language. Thus, this may be a helpful analysis at some point to understand early stages of the language, and is believed to be significant by being an initial stage source for such further reconstructions.

14.2.4.3   Complementation by Apposition

Complementization by apposition is an independent complementization strategy where two clauses are simply apposed. There will be no overt marking that intervenes between them or that may provide a complement sense.

(14.68) (ŋà=dàmì=tá⁷)   [kɔ́-ŋɔ́-čó
      DEM=manner/way=NEAR 1SU-decline-APPL-1PL.EXC.SU
      gérés-in-á   [Ø zùw-á   mès-o-í-á]_RC
      trouble.STV-NOMZ:NST-RSTR [Ø people-RTSR do-MT-3PL.IRR-RSTR
      àggè] [[gèrès-ìn-á   n=áu]_NP
      1PL   sin.STV-N.S-RSTR SG.PSD=1PL.EXC.PSR]
      tɔ́ŋ-á]
      thow.away.PERV:IMP-VFS
      'and forgive us our sins, *as* we (exc.) have forgiven those who have sinned against us.'

ŋadàmìta which is translated as 'so that, accordingly, in accordance, based on the manner' and so on—it might point out that the two clauses are linked by cause-consequence (effect) relations. But, even in its absence, the meaning remains the same and the complementation lies in the fact that two independent clauses are apposed. The applicative/comitative suffix attached to the verb of the first clause has a semantic role of reason,—so it may have had triggered the counter-expectation sense, i.e. 'as'. In (14.69) below, a similar example of a complementization construction is given. The only difference from that of the strategy in (14.69) is that the first clause is a subordinate clause. In addition, we see the coordinative conjunction particle *kó* whose function is not only conjoining nouns or noun phrases but also in this case to distinguish the two

---

7   It is a logical as well as and cause-consequence sequencer of two intedependent events/activities. It has also an assertive role as a means of generalizing what is being made about an event that happened in previously tend to contribute to another event that will happen later.

nouns that unusually occur side by side. As can be seen below, the coordinated NPs occur at the two clause boundaries, but each noun belongs to its respective clause.

(14.69) ŋà=dàmì=tá   [lɔ̀g-á   hín-í
         DEM=manner/way=NEAR word-RSTR want.IMPERV-2SG.SU.IMPERV
         ɨ́nój   mèsí-nὲ[8] tùmù tùn-ò=jè]_SUBORD:CL [kó] [bà-ì   ŋáà
         2SG.NOM do-AP   god on-OBL=SUBORD   PNC   place-LOC here
         àj   ké-més-ὲ]
         JUSS.PART 3.JUSS-do.PERV-VFS
         'May your will be done on earth *as* it is in heaven.'

The subject of the first clause is second person singular while the subject of second clause is the third person singular in jussive mood (Lit. 'Let it be). done on earth'

14.2.4.4   Complement-Clause-Taking Verbs

A complement-taking verb is a verb which may have a complement clause as one of its arguments (Aikhenvald 2015: 467). Mursi has few complement-taking verbs. They are not different from other verbs except that they usually take a complement clause as its O argument. The complement-taking verbs can, however, be small in number, and only a few of them have been discussed in this section. Based on Dixon's (2006: 9) verb type division, the majority of Mursi complement-taking verbs are of Primary -B type. This includes: VERBS OF THINKING *gáj* 'know' (including the inherently negative verb *ímág* 'don't know'), *ését* 'think', VERB OF ATTENTION *gón* 'see, visit', VERB OF LIKING *jél* 'like', and VERB OF SPEAKING *élí* 'call'. Apart from primary-B type, two other verbs have been found,—one secondary -A type of beginning type *tɔ́d* 'begin' and the other secondary -B type (WANTING VERB) *hín* 'want (decide)'.

All the semantic based verb types listed above roughly carry one of the following manifestation:
i.   Take subjunctive marker *k(V)*- (the verb has to always be in perfective aspect)
ii. Purpose/intention/perception indicating auxiliary verb *se* 'say'
iii. Nominalization

---

8 Second person singular subject and other two subject suffixes (1sg and 3pl) may be omitted when antipassive derivation is applied on a verb.

The first manifestation is that the complement-taking verb of the main clause may be in imperfective or perfective aspect but the verb in the complement clause must occur in perfective aspect if being marked for subjunctive prefix (also known as infinitive form) *k(V)-*. Some examples are given below:

(14.70) a. àɲè kí-hín-í   [k-ókt-ò]
1SG 1SU-want.IMPERV-1SG.SU.IMPERV 1SBJV-go.PERV-IRR
'I want to go.'

b. àɲè kí-hín-í   k-áíw-ò
1SG 1SU-want.IMPERV-1SG.SU.IMPERV 1.SBJV-come.PERV.SG-IRR
'I want to come.'

(14.71) k-án-i   k-óg-Ø
1SU-COP.IMPERV-1SG.SU.IMPERV 1SU-go.PERV-1SG.IRR
[kí-gín   [bɛ̀nɛ̀nɛ̀-á   n=ànù]_NP]_COMPL:CL
1SBJV-ask.PERV relative-RTSR SG.PSD=1SG.PRS
'I went to visit my relative.'

One unusual suffix that I mentioned in some earlier examples is -*o*. I am not yet sure about its exact function but you might see it glossed as complement marker in some examples or as same subject marker in others (as in (14.70a–b)). In the above examples, the subjunctive marker is on the complement verb, but in the following example, it is on the complement-taking verb.

(14.72) nɔ̀ŋ (wà)   wà   hín-ó   ʤɔ̀ɔ̀nɛ̀
3SG (REC.PAST) REC.PAST want.IMPERV-COMPL mother.PER:3.PSR
góɲ-á
see-3SG.SU.PERV
'S/he was longing (wanting) to see her/his mother.'

One among the two tense marker particle *wa* may generate an idiomatic (adverbial like) meaning 'rather, especially, moreover'. For instance, it can be interpreted as either as ('S/he was longing (wanting) rather (especially) to see her/his mother.') or with a particular emphasis on 'her/his mother' ('S/he was longing (wanting) that of seeing her/his mother.')

The second manifestation of the complement-taking verbs is that they may be preceded by a purpose/intention/perception indicating auxiliary verb *se* 'say'. *se* always occurs between the complement-taking verb and the subjunctive form of the complement verb. The function of *se* is like the 'intention marker' modality suffix as in some languages, for example in Jarawara (a small Arawá family language spoken in the Amazon, Brazil) (cf. Dixon 2006: 12).

(14.73) a. *nɔ̀ŋ hín-∅*   [*sé*   *k-éjá*
        3SG want.IMPERV-3SG.SU.IMPERV say.3.AUX 3.SBJV-help-3PL.SU
        támárí-ɲá]_{COMPL:CL}
        student-PL
        'She wants to help the students.'

     b. *nɔ̀ŋ hín-í-∅*   *àggè* [*sé*
        3SG want.IMPERV-1PL.OBJ-3SG.SU.IMPERV 1PL say.3.AUX
        k-édá   *támárí-ɲá*]_{COMPL:CL}
        3.SBJV-help.PERV:PL student-PL
        'She wants us to help the student.'

When the complement-taking verb is negated, the negated verb alone goes to sentence-final position. Following this, the auxiliary *se* aligns with the subjunctive form of the complement verb, and finally the two form a reason/purpose complement clause. The newly formed reason/purpose complement clause is almost identical with that of a purpose clause complementizer in §14.2.4.2, except it becomes a complement clause of the complement-taking verb, as illustrated in the following examples.

(14.74) a. *ŋà=hòì=tá*   [*bá*   *sé*
        DEM=girl=NEAR REASON/PURPOSE say.3.AUX
        k-áíw-ò-ɛ̀]_{COMPL:CL}
        3.SBJV-come.PERV.SG-3.IRR-APPL
        ŋà=hín-∅=ó
        NEG=want.IMPERV-3SG.SU.IMPERV=NEG
        'The girl does not want to come.'

     b. *bá*   *sé*   *k-áít-ɛ*]_{COMPL:CL}
        REASON/PURPOSE say.3.AUX 3.SBJV-go.PERV:PL-APPL:RES
        ímágɛ́-ɔ̀
        don't_know-VFS
        'I did not know of their going.'

CLAUSE TYPES, CLAUSE COMBINING AND COORDINATION 585

    c. *aŋè* [*bá*   *sé*   *kí-dǐd-ò*
        1SG REASON/PURPOSE say.3.AUX 1.SBJV-go.with.PERV:PL-IRR
        kó   [*ŋà=zùg=tùnù*]_{NP}]_{COMPL:CL} *ŋànì*   *k-ését=ó*
        PNC DEM=people=FAR   NEG.PERV 1SU-think=NEG
        'I did not think of going with them.'

When a negated main clause verb follows the complement clause that has no auxiliary *se*, the complement clause tends to resemble a relative clause. Yet it can have either interpretation, as in (14.75a–b).

(14.75) a. [*lɔ̀g-á*   *wà*   *kó-jóg-ǐ*]_{COMPL:CL}   *ŋànì*
        word-RTSR REC.PAST 1SU-tell-1SG.SU.IMPERV NEG.PERV
        ʃǐk=ó
        hear=NEG
        'S/he did not hear what I said.'

     b. *lɔ̀g-á*   [Ø *wà*   *kó-jóg-ǐ*]_{RC}   *ŋànì*
        word-RTSR [Ø REC.PAST 1SU-tell-1SG.SU.IMPERV NEG.PERV
        ʃǐk=ó
        hear=3.IRR:NEG
        'S/he did not hear the word that I said.'
        (Lit. 'The word that I tell (said), she did not hear.')

The object slot of Mursi complement-taking verbs can also be filled by nominalized verbs. In the following examples, the nominalized verb *wočin* functions as O argument of the complement-taking verb 'want'.

(14.76) a. *lúsì téhén-ú*   [*wóč-ín*]_{COMPL:CL/O}
        boy want.PERV-3SG.SU.PERV walk.IMPERV-NOMZ
        'The boy wants to go.'

     b. *kí-hín-ó*   [*wóč-ín*
        1SU-want.IMPERV-1PL.EXC.SU.IMPERV walk.IMPERV-NOMZ
        [*ɔri-á*   *g=àw*]_{NP}]_{COMPL:CL/O}
        home-RSTR PL.PSD=1PL.EXC.PSR
        'We (exc.) want to go to our home.'

The subject of the nominalized verb must be identical with the subject of the main clause. Evidence for this is that the first person plural exclusive subject of the main clause (as in (14.76b)) is also shown in the possessive NP of the complement clause. For reasons not yet clear, in the examples given above, the nominalizer being used is the one that commonly is used in the language to nominalize stative verbs, and also with intransitive verb roots. Maybe the latter can be a sufficient reason. The original verb 'go' is *óg*, and it cannot be nominalized,—instead the verb *wóč* ([*wój*] word-finaly) 'to walk' is being used.

In addition to the major complementation types we saw under each section, there is one more complementation strategy in which two clauses can be coordinated, i.e. the main clause can be linked to the second clause by a clausal coordinator *nà* 'and'. Clause coordination as complemetization strategy is not productive, but it seems to be achieved under two particular conditions: when the matrix clause is a purposive type and when both the complement clause and matrix clause have the same subject. See example (14.77).

(14.77) *jesusi kún-Ø*   [*nà k-éjá*
jesus come.IMPERV-3SG.SU.IMPERV CCN 3.SBJV-help
k-í-bá-ísí   [*zùwò dákákán*]_{NP}]_{COMPL:CL}
3.SBJV-CAUS-heal/cure-CAUS people all
'Jesus came to save all people.'

Here, it is important to note that the clausal coordinator *nà* does not indicate temporal progression or succession, or a logical marker. Such function of the coordinative conjunction is found widely in narrative structures, as in (14.78).

(14.78) *nà áíw-ó*   *nà téhén-ú*
CCN come.PERV:SG-MT.3SG.SU.PERV CCN want.PERV-3SG.SBJ.PERV
[*básá-í   bág-ò*]_{COMPL:CL}
monitor.lizard-SG eat-3SG.IRR
'So he came and decided to eat the monitor lizard.' (ND: 3.5)

The *nà* at clause-initial position can be narration or temporal progression marker, or logical continuity marker while the second *nà* is a clausal coordination (sequential clause or even other types). An exceptional type of complementation strategy is presented below, where a very peculiar NP type coordinator is functioning as complementizer.

(14.79) [*nòŋ gáj-Ø*   (*dákákán tíí*)]
3SG know.IMPERV-3SG.SU.IMPERV all   CONT/DUR
[*bá-á   ánčáŋ-ɲá*]   [*bító-mó dóg*]_{COMPL:CL}
place-RTSR beginning-NOMZ:STR lie.STV-N.S forever
'He knew all along that it was a lie.'
(Lit. 'He knew all the way from the beginning that it was a lie.')

In the main clause, *dákákán tíí* can be interpreted as 'all the way' and has an optional adverbial function. Remember that this time *bá* in *baa áncáṇṇá* 'in the first place, from the beginning' is not a complementizer but it is a kind of logical-temporal subordinate linker. Yet *báá áncáṇṇá* as a whole tends to act as a complementizer.

14.2.5 Copula Clause

A copular clause in Mursi consists of a predicate (semi inflected copula verb), and two core arguments,—copula subject (CS) and copula complement (CC) (see Table 7.28 for a full list of copula verbs). Semi inflected means copula verbs do not inflect for all inflectional categories available for regular verbs. Dixon (2012: 159) identified five major semantic relations that can be shown in copula constructions: (i) identity, (ii) attribution, (iii) possession, (iv) benefaction, and (v) location. Of these, only the last one will be shown using an existential verb while the rest can be shown by copula verbs.

(I) IDENTITY

(14.80) a. [àṇè]_CS k-án-í [támárí]_CC
         1SG   1SU-COP.IMPERV-1SG.SU.IMPERV student
         'I am a student.'

     b. [àṇè]_CS bè   k-án-í   [nígídí]_CC
        1SG   DIST.PAST 1SU-COP.IMPERV-1SG.SU.IMPERV merchant
        'I was a merchant.'

     c. nà áná   bè   ké-téw-á   [kɔ̀mɔ̀nì]_CC
        CCN REF:DEM REC.PAST 1SU-COP.PERV-1SG.SU.PERV   guest
        'I was a guest.'
        (Lit. '(and) that I was a guest; (and) it was that I was a guest.')

As it is shown in (14.80a–b), the notion of past time on copula verbs can be applied in two ways—by using the appropriate tense marker particle before the copula verb (as in (14.82b)) and by perfective form of the copula verb itself (as in (14.81c)). The distant past marker particle *be* in (14.81c) can be optional, and it is the recent past referential demonstrative particle *ana* ('the one (that)') that triggers it.

(II) ATTRIBUTION

(14.81) [múgáj]$_{CS}$ á   [čàll-i]$_{CC}$
woman   COP.3.IMPERV good.STV-ADJ
'The woman is good.'

(III) POSSESSION

(14.82) [ŋà=ìn=à]$_{CS}$ á   [dàdá-á
DEM=3SG.PN.SP=NEAR COP.3.IMPERV father-RSTR
n=àw]$_{NP:CC}$
SG.PSD=1PL.EXC.PSR]
'This is our father.'

(IV) BENEFACTION

(14.83) nà   kɔ́ɔ́d-à   [dúká-čín   sízzì]$_{NP}$ [dónéj]$_{CS}$
CCN 1SU.build.IMPERV-1/2SG.IRR umbrella-PL three   one
ké-té   [muse]$_{CC}$ [dónej]$_{CS}$ ké-té   [elijas]$_{CC}$
3.SBJV-COP.3.PERV muse   one   3.SBJV-COP.3.PERV Elijah
[dónéj]$_{CS}$ ké-té   [ìnè]$_{CC}$
one   3.SBJV-COP.3.PERV 2SG
'... I will put up three shelters—one for Moses one for Elijah and one for you.'
(Lit. 'one be for Muse, one be for Elijah, one for You (sg.)')

The subjunctive marker prefix *ké-* attached to the perfective form of the copula verb is a complementizer which has a meaning ~ 'that it should become.'

14.2.6 *Obligation/Deontic Clauses*

An obligation clause construction in Mursi can be shown by combining the desiderative verb *hín* 'want, need' and the completive adverbial-like particle *бòì* 'completely, at all'. The verb *hín* does not take any sort of inflection when used in what are also known as optative or deontic type clauses. Thus, *hín бòì* 'must, should, ought' may follow optional subject arguments but always precedes the subjunctive form main verb of the clause (see also Chapter 7, §7.3.1.3.4).

(14.84) nà   nòŋ [hín   ɓòì]_DEO   bè
       CCN   3sg [want.IMPERV completely] DIST.PAST
       k-áɗá-ì   samaria
       3.SBJV-pass.through-3.IRR Samaria
       'And he must need to go through Samaria.'

(14.85) zùw-á   [Ø wój-έ-á   gòr-ɔ̀]_RC
       people-RSTR [Ø walk.IMPERV-3PL.SU.IMPERV-RSTR   road-OBL]
       [hín   ɓòì]_DEO   kó-ɗól-o   [wàrkátì-á
       want.IMPERV completely 3.SBJV-show.PERV-3PL.IRR paper-RTSR
       kɔ́ɔ́y-ò-čà
       3.SBJV.go-3PL.IRR-APPL
       'Travelers must show their paper at the border.'
       (Lit. 'People who are going to road must show a paper for going.')

(14.86) áná   [hín   ɓòì]_DEO   ké-té
       REF:DEM [want.IMPERV completely] 3.SBJV-COP.3.PERV
       ʤáláwá-á   [Ø bè   ké-ɓέg-á]_RC   nà
       prophet-RTSR [Ø DIST.PAST 3.SBJV-keep-RSTR] CCN
       k-áɨ̀w-ó   ŋà=bá=á
       3.SBJV-come.PERV-MT.3SG.SU.PERV DEM=place=NEAR
       'This must be the Prophet who is to come into the world!'

Note that subjunctive irrealis mood in Mursi is usually used to express obligation, desire, wish, perception, uncertainty, possibility, and so on.

14.3   Clause Coordination

Mursi utilizes various clause coordinating particles to link two independent clauses. Yet the commonest ones are: the coordinative conjunction particle *nà* 'and', the disjunctive particle *wó/óó* 'or', and the contrastive particle *ŋànìjè* 'but, however'. It is worth noting, however, that clause coordinating particles such as the coordinative conjunction *nà* 'and' functions differently when being used to combine/conjoin or coordinate two or more clauses in non-narrative texts and when being used for higher level discourse purpose in narrative texts.

14.3.1 Coordinative Conjunction

Mursi has a clausal coordinative conjunctive *nà* 'and' distinct from phrasal coordinative conjunction *ké/kó* 'with/and'. As we remember from the discussion of temporal clause (§ 14.2.2), the coordinative conjunction *nà* can also play a role in conjoining two clauses which are temporally simultaneous (§ 14.2.1.1) or successive (§ 14.2.1.2) to one another. In this respect, i.e. just as a clausal coordinating/linker particle, a justifiable instance is its occurrence in succession clauses as temporal linker of successive events either alone or with other temporal marker particles such as *húllí* 'when' as in *nà húllí* 'and then'.

The existence of a single linker/conjoining particle which operates both at clausal and at a higher level in narratives shows that Mursi clauses are indeed independent units on their own in relation to a higher level structure,—yet they are concatenations of events that form larger discourse units.

(14.87) [nɔ̀ŋ gín-Ø-ú-n   nɔ̀ŋ
         3SG ask-3SG.OBJ-3SG.SU.PERV-? 3SG
         ká-gám-né-á]   nà   [nɔ̀ŋ ígóm-ú]
         3.SBJV-marry-AP/RECIP-3PL.SU and 3SG accept-3SG.SU.PERV
'He asked her to marry him, and she accepted.'
(Lit. 'He asked her (that) they marrying and she accepted.')

As I mentioned earlier, Mursi utilizes different coordinative conjunctions for conjoining clauses and phrases. As can be seen in the example given below, the NPs can be conjoined by a phrasal conjunction (PNC) particle *kó*.

(14.88) ànè ká-tál-á-ni   [čòj] kó [bárbárí] gáwá-jè
         1SG 1SU-buy-1SG.SU.PERV-RS salt PNC pepper   market-OBL
'I bought salt and pepper from the market.'

The fact, however, that there is a clear functional distinction where we could clearly draw a boundary between conjoined clauses on one hand and story/event-lines of narratives on the other hand. To illustrate the distinction between the two functions of this coordinative conjunction *nà*, an example is given below. It is a story that tells that there was no death in the Mursiland, and then tells how death was introduced into the Mursi society by a monitor lizard.

(14.89) àggè bè   sábɔ̀ kíɲín   mùnì
         1PL DIST.PAST first long.ago Mursi.SG

L1 kú-súd-íné-ó   nà   rès-è
    1SU-shed-AP-1PL.EXC.SU.PERV   CCN/and   die.IMPERV-NOMZ
    níŋè
    not.present
    'A long time ago we (inc.) Mursi shed our skins, and there was no death.'
    (ND: 3.1)

L2 nà   rès-è   àggè b[ɓ]ásá-j   nà
    CCN/and   die.IMPERV-NOMZ   1PL monitor.lizard-SG   CCN/and
    ŋàméá àggè ɓúh-á-j   b[ɓ]ásá-Ø
    now   1PL curse-NOMZ-GEN   monitor.lizard.SG-NOM
    ɓòì
    COMPLETIVE
    '(And) death was brought to us by the monitor lizard, so now we have been cursed by the monitor lizard.'

The function of the first coordinative conjunction (L1) is clausal while the second one is within a narrative (L2) that shows an event-line clause continued from L1. Then the third *nà*, which is second in the story-line (L2) shows the consequence as the result of the narrative in the first line of the story (the death brought by the monitor lizard). Thus it holds the two story lines together and presents them as one event-line. However, at the peak of a story, especially when the information is backgrounded or highlighted, it may be absent from the second-line of the story, but it is retained in first and third lines.

L3 nà   súd-é-á   [Ø]_RC   áín-Ø-é
    CCN/and   shed-NOMZ-RSTR   [Ø]   give.PERV.SG-3.IRR-APPL:RES
    kònù
    snake.SG
    'And the shedding (of skin that was ours), he gave to the snake.'
    (Lit. 'And the shedding, he gave to the snake.')

L4 ŋàméá súd-Ø-é   kònù
    now   shed-3SG.SU.IMPERV-APPL   snake
    'So now the snake sheds its skin, ...'

L5 nà   àggè gér-í-à
    CCN/and   1PL terrible-ADJ-NOMZ
    'and we die!'
    (Lit. 'we dead!')

TABLE 14.2 The coordinative conjunction *nà*

Coordinator	Clausal linker	Narration operator
nà	predication, relation of causality, succession of events, reason,	continuity, logical/temporal progression, temporal sucession of events, specific-generic relationship, head-tail linker (Example 14.90, L1–L2)
nà+húllí	–	logical/temporal progression of events, pivotal result
nà+ŋànì(jè)	counter-expectative contrast /propositions	counter-expectative contrast /propositions

L6   *nà*   [*húllí   kònù   súd-íné=ŋà*]ₛᵤʙₒᵣᴅ:ᴄʟ
      ᴄᴄɴ/and   when/if   snake   shed-ᴀᴘ.3.ꜱᴜ=ᴅᴇꜰ
      ʃíg-Ø   [*hóló-á*
      hear.ɪᴍᴘᴇʀᴠ-3ꜱɢ.ꜱᴜ.ɪᴍᴘᴇʀᴠ   song-ɴᴏᴍᴢ
      b[ɓ]ásá-í-nè]
      monitor.lizard-ꜱɢ-ᴇᴘᴇɴᴛ+ᴏʙʟ
      '(And) now when the snake sheds its skin it was because it heard the singing of the monitor lizard.'

L7   *b[ɓ]ásá-í*   *érók-Ø*   *kìɔ*   *tùn-ɔ̀*   *nà*
      monitor.lizard-ɢᴇɴ   climb-3ꜱɢ.ꜱᴜ.ɪᴍᴘᴇʀᴠ   tree.ꜱɢ   on-ᴏʙʟ   ᴄᴄɴ/and
      čɔ́ll-ú   *hóló? nà*   *sé-á*   *ké*   "*mùnì*
      sing-3ꜱɢ.ꜱᴜ.ᴘᴇʀᴠ   dance ᴄᴄɴ/and   say-3ꜱɢ.ꜱᴜ.ᴘᴇʀᴠ   ǫᴜᴏᴛ   Mursi.ꜱɢ
      súd-Ø-έ,   *kònù*   *èr-Ø-έ*   *mùnì*
      shed-3.ɪʀʀ-ᴀᴘᴘʟ   snake.ꜱɢ   die.ᴘᴇʀᴠ-3.ɪʀʀ-ᴀᴘᴘʟ:ʀᴇꜱ   Mursi.ꜱɢ
      súd-Ø-έ,   *kònù*   *èr-Ø-ε*"
      shed-3.ɪʀʀ-ᴀᴘᴘʟ:ʀᴇꜱ   snake.ꜱɢ   die.ᴘᴇʀᴠ-3.ɪʀʀ-ᴀᴘᴘʟ:ʀᴇꜱ
      'The monitor lizard climbed a tree and sang a song and said this, "The snake died, the Mursi sheds his skin. The snake dies, the Mursi sheds his skin".' (ND 3.1–3.4)

As can be seen in the story-lines illustrated above, the distribution and function of the coordinative conjunction nà is clear—from L3 to L6 being a narration operator for which it always occurs at clause initial positions, and in L7 being a clausal linker between two clauses temporally, causally, logically, and so on. Table 14.2 above is a summary of nà both as clausal linker as well as operator of a higher level discourse in narratives.

As shown in Table 14.2, *na* also occurs in combination with other temporal particles such as *húllí* 'when/if' ~ 'then'. In addition, it can be combined with the negative perfective word *ŋàni* so as to indicate a counter-factual linker of propositions. The first operates at the level of narration while *nà* + *ŋàni(je)* 'but if; and yet (however)' operates both at clausal and narrative levels.

(14.90) [nà húllí] dóólá kó ràmàn áw-ò-ni
CCN when girl.PL CRD:PART two come.PERV-3PL.IRR-RS
'(and) then, two among the girls will come and go ...' (KW 1:38:5)

However, if a conditional subordinate clause immediately follows *nà*, the meaning fades away because *húllí* itself is conditional clause introducer, as in (14.91).

(14.91) ... nà [húllí hód-á nà
CCN when come.PERV:PL-MT.3PL.SU.PERV and
íbt-á-ì [ólf-á g=àj=è]_NP]_SUBORD:CL
take.PERV-MT-3PL.IRR stalk-RSTR PL.PSD=1PL.INC.PSR=SUBORD
[ká-dág-íné-Ø háŋ háŋ]
1SU-hit-RECIP-1PL.INC.SU INTENS INTENS
'And when they come and take our (inc.) sorghums, we (inc.) fight each other very very much.' (KW 0:55:6)

In narratives, the word *čùànéŋ* 'again' is used to indicate enumerations and some sort of recapitulative linkages of clauses. Below is a narration, which is a story taken from an age-grade ceremony called *koma kodha* 'kneeling'. It is a ceremony in which members of a senior grade discharge their seniority duties by beating the juniors. And in (14.92) below, *čùànéŋ* acts as an introducer of a clause being repeated in the narration.

(14.92) ... [jɔ̀g bír-ésén-é-a rórá] [àggè
3PL collect-BEN-APPL-3PL.SU.IMPERV-DS Rora.PL 1PL
kí-bír-ésén-ó bárá]
1SU-collect-BEN-1PL.EXC.SU.IMPERV Bara.PL
[k-án-ó búbúí]_COP:CL
1SU-COP.IMPERV-1PL.EXC.SU.IMPERV different
'Because of that they collect for the Rora, we (exc.) collect for the Bara; thus we (exc.) are different.' (KW: 1:02:8)

Even if *čùànéŋ* has a great deal of functions in narratives, it still can occur in clause medial position being a linker/coordinator,—but at clause level, its occurrence is very limited, as can be seen in the story lines below. The story below is a continuation of the above.

>
> *čùànéŋ gɔ̀rɔ̀ čó   čùànéŋ tèrì gɔ̀rɔ́ ŋànì*
> again   road even *again*   Teri road NEG.PERV
> *k-íj-í=t=ó*   [*húllí   nè*
> 3.SBJV-touch-1PL.OBJ-PERV.PL=NEG when/if 3SG
> *k-íj-ó=jè*]_SUBORD:CL   *té   kili-ni*
> 3.SBJV-touch-1PL.OBJ-3.IRR=SUBORD COP.3.PERV 'Kili-RS'
> *té   gèrs-ì*
> COP.3.PERV bad.STV-ADJ
> 'Again even (on) the road, again those Teri do not touch us. If he (Teri (sg.)) touch us, it becomes "Kili!". It gets bad.' (KW: 1:17:8)

>
> *čùànéŋ ŋà=lɔ̀g=tù   hàlì áj-t-é   tèrò-ú-ni*
> again DEM=issue=FAR later take-PERV.PL-APPL teri.PL-NOM-RS
> *té   [lɔ̀g-tí   g=èj*]_NP
> COP.3.PERV issue-NRSTR PL.PSD=3PL.PSR
> 'Again (~then later), the Teru takes up this issue (Kili) thus it becomes their issue. After that they will slaughter a cow.' (KW: 1:28:8)

14.3.2 *Contrastive Coordination*

In Mursi, clauses can be coordinated by the contrastive coordinative marker *ŋànìjè* 'but, however'. The contrastive coordinator *ŋànìjè* always occurs at clause medial position, and its primary role will be introducing a contrastive proposition. The examples illustrated below are repeated from (14.32) and (14.12).

(14.93) [*nɔ̀ŋ gúɲ-ó*   [*túrúmél-á ràmàn*]_NP] [*ŋànìjè   dɔ́néj*
         3SG look-3SG.IRR car-RSTR   two   but/however one
         ŋànì   ká-tál=ó]
         NEG.PERV 3.SBJV-buy.PERV=NEG
         'He looked at two cars, but did not buy either.'

(14.94) *ké-héj-Ø   kí-bír-Ø*
         1SU-go.IMPERV-1PL.INC.SU.IMPERV 1SU-pick.up-1PL.INC.SU.IMPERV
         óļf-ó   dààì   ŋànìjè [tó-jé ŋà=b=ùnù
         sorghum-PL all/COMPLET however in-OBL DEM=place=FAR
         kí-bír-ó   óļf-ó=ŋà]_SUBORD:CL
         1SU-pick.up-1PL.EXC.SU.IMPERV sorghum-PL=DEF
         'We (exc.) go and pick up sorghum stalks.' However, while we (exc.) are collecting the sorghum stalks ...

tó-jé   lò   zùg-tí   [gɛ
in-OBL have/exist people-NRSTR [PL.PN+NRSTR
k-ɛ́ŋɛ́rs-ó]_RC
1SU-fear.IMPERV-1PL.EXC.SU.IMPERV]
'… there are those people out there whom we are afraid of.'
(Lit. 'inside it (the sorghum stalks' place) has people whom we (exc.) are afraid of') (KW 0:32:0)

As is shown in (14.93–14.94), the contrastive coordinator is a clause medial constituent, and usually introduces a counter-proposition or counter-presuppositional proposition that is contrary to the first clause. Since negative and contrastive clauses tend to often be similar in Mursi, whenever the first clause is negative, ŋànìjè whose function is marker of a contrastive in the second clause may indicate a counter-expectation of the first clause,—or add a contrastive emphasis by focusing on the second clause.

(14.95) [ìggè]_TOP/FOC lògó   [Ø bè   kód-a]_RC
        2PL   word   [Ø DIST.PAST 3.SBJV-write-3SG.SU.PERV]
        ŋànì   jébt=ó   ŋànìjè   [ìggè]_TOP/FOC
        NEG.PERV   believe.PERV:PL=NEG   but   2PL
        kó-jóg-i   ápój   jéb-ó   ènèŋ?
        1SU-tell-1SG.SU.IMPERV 1SG.NOM believe-2PL.SU.IMPERV how
'But since you do not believe what he wrote, how are you going to believe what I say?'
(Lit. 'You (pl.), the word that he wrote—you (pl.) didn't believe, but you (pl.), you (pl.) believe me what I say—how?')

However, ŋànìjè does not always convey a contrastive meaning, but rather it may be used as causal-result linker 'therefore, thus', as in (14.96).

(14.96) lúsì ín-ú   [ré-á   [ʤɔ̀ɔ̀nɛ̀]_NP]_NP
        boy break-3SG.SU.PERV cooking.pan-RSTR   mother.PERT.SG.3.PSR
        ŋànìjè   bák-ú   líjá wáŋ
        but/however eat-3SG.SU.PERV   shy INTENS
'The boy broke his mother's (injera)[9] pan, he is therefore very much ashamed.'

---

9 Injera [əŋǧära] is a sourdough risen flatbread with a slightly spongy texture, originating from Ethiopia-Eritrea. Traditionally made with teff flour (Eragrostis teff), and is the national dish of Ethiopia as well as Eritrea.

Logically, it makes sense because it has been used in a counterexpectative contrast sense,—the boy is ashamed because he broke the pan. Note that *bákú líjá* '(he) ashamed' is an idiomatic verb—literally meaning 'to eat (feel) shame/shy'. The above example is not the only instance where this contrastive coordinative marker semantically behaves like as cause-result (adversative) linker, but it often denotes the same semantics especially when it is placed at clause initial position.

(14.97) *nà   ŋànìjè   nɔ̀ŋ   ŋàméá sé-Ø   ké*
CCN however 3SG now   say-3SG.SU.IMPERV QUOT
kɔ́-nɔ́w-án   tùm-ɔ̀   ɛ̀nɛ̀ŋ?
1SU-come.down-MT sky/god-OBL how
'How then (therefore/thus) he say, "I came down from heaven"?'

The fact that *nà ŋànìjè* literally means 'and yet', which is partly due to a grammaticalization process where it got its original adversative semantics from *ŋànì* 'not yet, still' and the subordinate enclitic *=jè*. Therefore, what can be said at this stage is that the contrastive coordinative marker *ŋànìjè* may no longer have an adversative function when being used at the left most periphery of a given discourse but rather functions as a coordinative particle (see the example given below).

(14.98) *ŋànìjè   [íggé-á   hɔ̀l-á]ₙₚ*
however 3PL.PN.SP-RSTR white.STV-RSTR:NOMZ
ʃíl-έ   sìtèn ŋànìjè   [íggé-á   gèrs-à]ₙₚ
stand-3PL.SU.IMPERV right however 3PL.PN.SP-RSTR bad.STV-RSTR
ʃíl-έ   kàŋìtèn
stand-3PL.SU.IMPERV left
'And those that are righteous stand at the right, but those that are bad stand at the left.'

The mirativity marker *čírr* 'actually/really' can occasionaly be used for a contrastive purpose by creating a sudden or counter-expectational interpretation. It has no fixed position within clauses. As a result of this, the semantics of it is more contextual than structural. See the following example:

(14.99) *nɔ̀ŋ   sé-sé   ké   ŋà=ʃɔ́l-ínɛ̀n=ó*
3SG say-BEN.PERV.3 QUOT NEG.IMPERV=afraid-AP=2PL.SU:NEG
k-án-í   àŋè čírr
1SU-COP.IMPERV-1SG.SU.IMPERV 1SG actually/really
'But s/he said to them, "It is me, you (pl.) don't be afraid."'

One exceptional contrastive clause coordination has been identified in my corpus which doesn't involve the contrastive coordinative ŋànìjè (see 14.100).

(14.100) [nɔ̀ŋ úgún-óɲ-ò àɲè] nà [àɲè nɔ̀ŋ ŋànì
3SG push-1SG.OBJ-3SG.IRR 1SG CCN 1SG 3SG NEG.PERV
k-úgún=nó]
1SBJV-push.PERV=NEG
'He pushed me, but I did not push him.'

In (14.100), the relation between two clauses is that of counter-expectation type, thus may be achieved by negating the proposition in the second clause.

14.3.3 Disjunctive Coordination

Disjunctive clauses can be indicated by various ways but primarily by disjunctive coordination (conjunction) markers *wo* [óó] 'or' and rarely by *kóó* 'or'. Both disjunction markers can also be combined with other epistemic modality marking particles such as dubitative *ká* 'perhaps/maybe' and *kákó* 'perhaps'.

The disjunctive coordinators óó and kóó can be used in coordinated clauses each of which containing either question type or affirmative type component propositions, as in (14.101–14.104a).

(14.101) [hùllì té-í ɔ́r-ɔ́ á čàll-ì] óó
if be.PERV-SG home-OBL COP.3.IMPERV good.STV-ADJ or
[kɔ́-í tìráŋ-ɔ̀]
1SU.go-1SG.SU.IMPERV play-OBL
'Would I rather stay home or go to the game?'

(14.102) [ràmàmàn] óó [čàll-ì kàrì]
two.PART.INDEF or good.STV-ADJ together
'Either (one) is correct; Either one or both are good.'
(Lit. 'both are correct/good.')

(14.103) hàlì húll-á kún-Ø-έ túrúmél-ɔ̀ kóó
later when-NOMZ come-3SG.SU.IMPERV-APPL car-OBL or
bábúr-ɔ̀
train-OBL
'S/he will come by car or by train.'

TABLE 14.3 Disjunctive coordinative particles

Disjunctive particles	Meaning	Remark
wó [óó]	'or'	a primary disjunctive coordinator
kóó	'or'	In Suri language, kóó is translated as 'then, following' (cf. Bryant 1998: 94)
ká ... óó	'either ... or'	Lit. 'perhaps/maybe ... or'
ka ... kóó	'either ... or'	Lit. 'perhaps/maybe ... or'
kóó ... kóó	'whether (it is) ... or'	Lit. 'or ... or'; the first coordinand or both of coordinands may be introduced by the conditional húllí 'if'
kóó ...NEG	'whether its is ... or'	only the first coordinand can be introduced by the conditional húllí 'if'
NEG kóó NEG	'neither ... nor'	kóó may be omitted
kákó ... kóó ... kóó	'or'	Lit. 'perhaps ... or'
kákó ... kóó ... kákó		Lit. 'perhaps ... perhaps'

(14.104) a. [ŋà=ìggὲ=á]$_{CS}$ á   [čàll-i]$_{CC}$ kóó
     DEM=3PL.PN.SP=NEAR COP.3.IMPERV good.STV-ADJ or
     [gèrs-i]$_{CC}$
     bad.STV-ADJ
     'Is that good or bad?'
     (Lit. 'Is that good or is that bad?')

   b. [ŋà=ìggὲ=á]$_{CS}$ á   [čàll-i]$_{CC}$
     DEM=3PL.PN.SP=NEAR COP.3.IMPERV good.STV-ADJ
     á   [gèrs-i]$_{CC}$
     COP.3.IMPERV bad.STV-ADJ
     'Is that good or bad?'
     (Lit. 'Is that good—is that bad?')

In (14.104a), the copula subject stands for both copula complements conjoined by the disjunctive marker. As can be seen in (14.105b), normally it is possible to convey the same meaning without the disjunctive marker, i.e. by adding a copula verb to second copular clause. It logically makes sense since the propositions in both do not normally hold true or false—as they are question types that seek confirmation and whose answer can be either a 'yes-no' type or repeat the whole clause, or just repeat the subjectless copular clause form (á čàllì/á gèrsì).

As listed in Table 14.3, the primary disjunctive marker óó and that of kóó can be combined with the dubitative marker ka to indicate clauses coordinated in alternative conjunction ways. The dubitative marker is always a peripheral constituent,—it may either occupy the position available before a clause or appear at the right edge of a clause (see also Chapter 12, §12.3). Their combination enables us to form a none-question type alternative conjunction construction between two clauses and NPs, i.e. *either ... or* type coordination. This type of coordination is often called correlative coordination. On the basis of the current observation, the following templates have been proposed:

i. [ká CLAUSE1 óó CLAUSE2]
ii. [(NP) ká ALTERNATE1 kóó ALTERNATE2 (CLAUSE)]

And structurally we might not see a significant difference between CLAUSE1 and CLAUSE 2, as the two can be identical in many respects, as in (14.105).

(14.105) ká   [hàlì kún-Ø   túrmél-ɔ̀] óó [hàlì
          perhaps/maybe later come-3SG.SU.IMPERV car-OBL   or later
          kún-Ø   bábúr[10]-ɔ̀]
          come-3SG.SU.IMPERV train-OBL
          'S/he will come (either) by car or by train.'

(14.106) a. ká   [ʃáj] kóó [búná]
            perhaps/maybe tea   or coffee
            kí-hín-ɛ́   (hékɔ́-ni)[11]
            1SU-want.IMPERV-1SG.SU.IMPERV look.like-RS
            'I want either tea or coffee.'

         b. sátí ká   ràmàn kóó sátí sízzì
            time perhaps/maybe two   or time three
            áíw-ó
            come.PERV.IMP-MT.3SG.SU.PERV
            'Come (sg.) (either) at two or three o'clock!'

---

10 *babur* [ba.bur/bʷur] 'train' is a loan word from Amharic.
11 *hékɔ́* 'look like (this/that), same as (this/that)' can be used in singular and has a plural counterpart that is only used with plural, i.e. *hétɔ́* 'similar, same as, resemble, look like.' But in some instances both may be used interchangeably. The example given below illustrates the context in which *hékɔ́* is being used:
    [kù-gùŋ-ónó   jírísí ɓó=ŋà   hékɔ́   [kè-á   téríŋ-ùŋ][NP]
    PASS-look-MT.3SU sea   above=DEF *look.like* thing-RSTR mirror-GEN
    'Seen from above, the lake looks like a mirror.'

The other clause coordination is the one being established by *kóó ... kóó*, literally meaning 'or ... or', which is an equivalent to the typical English correlative type construction 'whether (it is) ... or'. The only structural difference from the type mentioned above is that the coordinator *kóó* is repeated,—one appearing before first clause and the other in its usual position. Examples are presented below:

(14.107) a. *kóó hùllì kɔ́-dɔ́t-ɛ*   *kóó hùllì kɔ́ɔ́g-ò*
or if 3.SBJV-leave.PERV-APPL or if 3.SBJV.go-IRR
ɓòì   (kóó) ʃóláj   níŋè
at.all/completely or problem not.present
'I don't care whether he goes or stays here.'

b. *kóó [hùllì á   tíítíi   kóó*
or if COP.3.IMPERV small.PL:REDUP or
èlèhèŋ=nè]ₛᵤBORD:CL dɔ́ŋ-á   nà
compare=SUBORD abide.PERV:IMP-VFS CCN
íw-á
take.PERV:IMP-VFS
'Small or big (Lit. 'whether it is little or much') accept (sg.) with gratitude.'
(Lit. 'or if it is small (pl.) or comparable, abide (2sg.) and accept (sg.)!')

As we can see in (14.107b), the coordinand to be referred to by the second coordinator is not mentioned, thus the second coordinand can either be recoverable from the context (small or ...?) or has been substituted with the expression—'small or *comparable*'.

A similar meaning may be expressed with the correlative type disjunctive coordination, by placing the disjunctive coordinator *kóó* before the first coordinand and by negating the second coordinand. I called this one a *kóó ...NEG* type.

(14.108) a. *kóó [hùllì búí] ŋànì   [ín-á   tíín-ò]ₙₚ*
or if big NEG.PERV 3SG.PN.SP-RSTR small-RSTR:MOD]
ŋà=ká-gá-í=ó
NEG.IMPERV=1SU-know.IMPERV-1SG.SU.IMPERV=NEG
'I didn't know whether it is big or small.'
(Lit. 'or if big—not yet of a small one, I don't know.')

The perfective negator ŋànì may be omitted, and at the same time a copula verb in subjunctive mood may be added between the conditional húllí 'if' ('whether') and the first coordinand (14.108b).

> b. kóó [hùllì ké-té   búí̱] [ín-á
> or if   3.SBJV-be.PERV big 3SG.PN.SP-RSTR
> tíín-ò]ₙₚ
> small-RSTR:MOD
> ŋà=ká-gáj-Ø=ó
> NEG.IMPERV=1SU-know.IMPERV-1PL.INC.SU.IMPERV=NEG
> 'We (inc.) don't know whether it is big or small.'

In addition to the correlative coordinator 'either ... or', Mursi has a system to express 'neither ... nor'. This type of correlative coordinator is often used in contrastive negative coordination. In this type of coordination, two negated coordinands will be coordinated by kóó (['X' NEG+verb or NEG+verb]).

(14.109) a. bàrkáɗé [ŋànì   kú-čùmùn=ó]   kóó [ŋànì
          Bàrkaɗe NEG.PERV 3.SBJV-happy.STV=NEG or   NEG.PERV
          kú-múɲí=ó]
          3.SBJV-sad.STV=NEG
          'Barkaɗe was neither happy, nor was he sad.'
          (Lit. 'Barkadhe didn't be happy and/or didn't be sad.')

Or without the disjunctive marker kóó (['X' NEG+verb NEG+verb]), as in (14.109b).

> b. bàrkáɗé [ŋànì   kú-čùmùn=ó]   [ŋànì
> Barkaɗe NEG.PERV 3.SBJV-happy.STV=NEG NEG.PERV
> kú-múɲí=ó]
> 3.SBJV-sad.STV=NEG
> 'Barkaɗe was neither happy, nor (was he) sad.'

The last type of disjunctive coordination utilizes the disjunctive marker kóó and the epistemic modality marker kákó 'perhaps'. Interestingly, it is very logical to assume that the reason/cause marker particle bá is triggered by the epistemic marker kákó.

TABLE 14.4 A summary of major clause types, clause combining and coordination strategies

Clause type	Markers	Possible template
Conditional clause	*húllí* 'if/when' and subordinate marker enclitics (when the main clause follows the subordinate clause)	[*húllí* ... 'X'=*jè*/=*è*/=*tè*]_{SUBORD:CL}
Temporal clause (simultaneous, succession)	i. *húllí* 'if/when' and subordinate marker enclitics ii. *hulla* 'since' (when the subordinate clause follows the main clause) iii. *húllí* and the definite marker enclitic =*ŋà* iv. other markers such as *ŋàhùllùnù* 'at the same time', *nà* 'and', and *nà húllí* 'and when', *wùréɔ́* 'after'	i. [*húllí* ... 'X'=*jè*/=*è*/=*tè*]_{SUBORD:CL} ii. [*hulla* ... 'X'=*jè*/=*è*/=*tè*]_{SUBORD:CL} iii. [*húllí* ... 'X'=*ŋà*]_{SUBORD:CL}
Causation clause	*ŋàhùllùnù* '(and) then, after that', *ŋànìjè* 'therefore, thus, because of this', and *nà* 'therefore', *wùréɔ́* 'after, later'	no fixed template
Reason clause	(*ké*) *ɓa* 'because'	i. [*bá*/*ɓá* ... CAUSER ... VERB-REASON(=SUBORD)] ii. [*ké bá*/*ɓá* ... CAUSER ... VERB-(REASON) (=SUBORD)]
Concessive clause	*ŋànìjè* 'however, but', *ŋànì* 'not (yet)', and *kó húllí* 'even though, even if' (Lit. 'and if').	no fixed template
Substitutive clause	*bá*/*ɓá* 'place' (in place of)	no fixed template
Future clause	*kó ɓòì* 'until', durative/continuative markers *tíí* and the durative *dírr*	no fixed template
Speech report clause	quotative marker *ké*, verbatim quotative marker *ŋàŋà* 'like this', the verb to 'say' *sé*	[*sén* (PRONOUNS, NAMES ...) *ké* ...] DIRECT SPEECH REPORT [Other speech verbs ... *ké* ...] INDIRECT SPEECH REPORT
Complement clause	complementizer *ké*, reason/purposive marker *ɓa*	no fixed template
Coordinated clauses	clausal coordinative conjunction marker *nà* 'and', contrastive coordination marker *ŋànìjè* 'but, however' and *čírr* 'actually/really', primary disjunctive coordination markers *óó* and *kóó* 'or', and so on	For a detailed information, see Table 14.2 & 14.3 of this chapter

(14.110) a. [*kako á   ba   kóó dìb kóó*
         perhaps COP.3.IMPERV CAUSE/REASON or correct or
         ŋà=án=ó=jè]_SUBORD:CL
         NEG.IMPERV=COP.3.IMPERV=NEG=SUBORD
         'Right or wrong ...'
         (Lit. 'perhaps is the reason or correct or not')

   b. [*kako húllí á   bá   kóó dìb*
      perhaps if   COP.3.IMPERV CAUSE/REASON or correct
      kákó   ŋà=án=ó=jè]_SUBORD:CL
      perhaps NEG.IMPERV=COP.3.IMPERV=NEG=SUBORD
      'Right or wrong ...'
      (Lit. 'perhaps whether it is (the reason) or correct perhaps not.')

APPENDIX

Transcribed Texts

Text I: Koma Kóɗa (Age Grade Related Cultural Practices)

Description—In the Mursi society, in relation to age grade, there is a type of social identity construction that all Mursi men should abide by certain rights and obligations, for they are being 'seniors' or 'juniors'. This social identity construction comes with a cultural ceremony called *kɔ̀mà kɔ́ɗa* 'Kneeling' (Lit. 'stubbing/piercing [the ground] with the knees'). In addition, Turton (1973: 153) describes it as 'the kneeling of the boys'. This ceremony refers to a process of the giving of gifts by the occupants of a junior to the occupants of a senior grade. In this ceremony, men who are at the *bárá* age grade level are the 'fathers' of the *tèrù*; in the same way, men who are at the *rórá* age grade level are the 'fathers' of the *ɗɔ̃́ŋà*.

The *kɔ̀mà kɔ́ɗa* ceremony takes place at least twice a year; the first is immediately following the harvest, in December–January, and the second takes place following the second harvest in June–July. Following these two harvest seasons, the *ɗɔ̃́ŋà* go in large groups into the cultivation areas and collect the decapitated sorghaum stalks, which are called *ólfó*. Turton (1973: 156–157) wrote, 'Just as the *ɗɔ̃́ŋà* intake sorghum stalks to the *rórá* following the harvest, so the unmarried girls take them to the *bárá*, and are similarly harangued and beaten with withies'. The *bárá* are also 'fathers' of unmarried girls. During the *ólfó* collection days, if unmarried girls bring accusations (especially if girls are beaten or touched by the *ɗɔ̃́ŋà*) against the *ɗɔ̃́ŋà*, later the *ɗɔ̃́ŋà* are made to kneel facing the *rórá*, who accuse them for not showing them proper respect. On the other hand, the occupants of the *bárá* age grade will therefore be charged with responsibility for the satisfactory behaviour of those members of the society, both male and female.

Narrator (informant):   Ngarori Kashai (Age 19, Female)
Place of recording: South Omo Research Center, Jinka Town, Ethiopia
Year of recording: 28 July 2017
Length of the record: 2min.58sec.
Text code: KW (Women Koma Kodha)

(1.1)   (KW 0:11:4–0:21:6)
        kɔ̀m-à   kɔ́ɗ-á   sábɔ̀ [dɛl-á   tíítí-o]_NP
        knee-PL KNEEL-NOMZ first girl-RSTR SMALL.REDUP.PL-RSTR.MOD
        múg-íné-ɔ̀
        gather-RECIP.3-VFS
        'Koma kóɗa, first, little girls gather together.'

nà   kú-múg   làlàŋ-à   dằài   nà
CCN   3.SBJV-collect.PERV bracelet-PL all/COMPLETELY CCN
[úʃɲ-áná=jè]_SUBORD:CL   kú-múg-íné-Ø
finish-MT.3SG.SU.IMPERV=SUBORD 1SU-gather-RECIP-1PL.INC.SU.IMPERV
ɓòì   dɔ̆néj
COMPLETIVE   one
'and collect bracelets. After it is finished, then we (inc.) gather as one

ké-héj-Ø   [bá-á   óIf-ó   bérá-ɲ]_NP
1SU-go.IMPERV-PL.INC.SU.IMPERV place-RSTR stalk-PL sorghum.type-GEN
and we (inc.) go to a place where sorghum stalks exist.'

(1.2) -(KW 0:32:0)
[húllí   ké-héj-Ø   [bá-á   óIf-ó
when/if 1SU-go.IMPERV-1PL.INC.SU.IMPERV place-RSTR stalk-PL
bérá-ɲ=nè]_NP]SUBORD:CL
sorghum-GEN=SUBORD
'When we (inc.) go up to the sorghum stalks' place.'

ké-héj-Ø   kí-bír-Ø
1SU-go.IMPERV-1PL.INCL.SU.IMPERV 1SU-cut.up-1PL.INC.SU.IMPERV
óIf-ó   dằài   ŋànìjè   [tó-jé   ŋà=ɓ=ùnù
sorghum-PL all/COMPLETELY   however   in-OBL   DEM=place=FAR
kí-bír-ó   óIf-ó=ŋà]_SUBORD:CL
1SU-cut.up-1PL.EXC.SU.IMPERV   sorghum-PL=DEF
'we (exc.) go and pick up sorghum stalks. However, while we (exc.) are collecting the sorghum stalks,...'

tó-jé   lò   [zùg-tí   [ké
in-OBL   have/exist-3SG.SU.IMPERV   people-NRSTR   [PL.PN+NRSTR
k-éŋérs-ó]_COMPL:CL
1SU-fear.IMPERV-1PL.EXC.SU.IMPERV
'There are those people out there whom we are afraid of.'
(Lit. 'inside it (the sorghum stalks' place) has people whom we (exc.) are afraid of')

(1.3) (KW 0:41:9)
čùànéŋ   zùg-tí   [Ø ké   "dɔŋà"]_RC
again   people-RSTR   [Ø QUOT   Donga]

kɔ́j-ɛ́=jè]_SUBORD:CL   bír-ésén-ɛ́
go-PERV-3PL.SU.IMPERV=SUBORD pick.up-BEN-3PL.SU.IMPERV
zùw-á   ké   "rórá"
people-RSTR QUOT Rora
'and again, They who for people called "Donga", they were are also collecting. They collect-up for people called the "Rora".'

nà   kí-bír-nè-Ø   ŋànì ŋáà àggè zùw-á
CCN 1SU-collect-AP-PL.INCL.SU.IMPERV yet here 1PL people-RSTR
[Ø k-èlè-ò   ké   "ɗoolɛ"]_RC
[Ø PASS-call.PERV-2/3.IRR QUOT girl.PL]
kí-bír-ésén-ó   bárá
1SU-pick.up-BEN-1PL.EXC.SU.IMPERV Bara
'whereas we (inc.) here the people called "girls" collect for the Bara.'

(1.4) (KW 0:48:2–0:55:6)
jòŋ[1] dɔ́ŋà bír-ésén-ɛ́   zùw-á   [Ø ké   rórá]_RC
3PL Donga collect-BEN-3PL.SU.IMPERV people-RSTR [Ø QUOT Rora
ŋànìjè kí-bír-nén-á
but   1SU-collect-RECIP-1PL.INC.SU.PERV
'They (the Donga) collect for the people called the Rora. But, when we (inc.) are collecting, and

[húllí   hóɗ-á   nà   hóɗ-á
when/if come.PERV.PL-3sg.SU.PERV CCN come.PERV.PL-3PL.SU.PERV
ib-t-a   ólf-ó   gál-a   gi
take-PERV.PL-3PL.SU.PERV stalk-PL thing.PL-RSTR who.GEN.PL
n=àj-ò=jè]_SUBORD:CL
SG.PSD=1PL.INC.PSD-RSTR:MOD=SUBORD
if they come, and come to take the stalks' things whose are ours (inc.),

àggè 6á   k-ɛ́l-Ø   kók háŋ nà
1PL place 1SU-exist.IMPERV-1PL.INC.SU.IMPERV ready INTENS CCN
kɔ̀-lɔ̀m-Ø   kállí   nà
1SU-have.IMPERV-1PL.INC.SU.IMPERV stick(switch) CCN
we (inc.) will be present here well prepared, and (we (inc.)) having a stick,

---

1 See also jɔ̀g or jɔk (may be an ideolectal difference).

[húllí hód-á nà
when/if come.PERV.PL-3PL.SU.PERV CCN
íb-t-á-ì ólf-á
take.PERV-PERV.PL-MT-3PL.IRR stalk-RSTR
g=àj=è]_{NP}]_{SUBORD:CL} ká-dág-íné-Ø
PL.PSD=1P.INC.PSR=SUBORD 1SU-hit-RECIP-1PL.INC.SU.IMPERV
háŋ háŋ
INTENS INTENS
'when they come and take our (inc.) sorghums, we (inc.) fight each other very very much.'

(1.5) -(KW 1:02:8)
ké òrì [ké bá jòg bír-ésén-ɛ́-a
PRE which.part PREP place/CAUSE 3PL collect-BEN-3PL.SU.IMPERV-DS
rórá àggè kí-bír-ésén-ó bárá
Rora] 1PL 1SU-collect-BEN-1PL.EXC.SU.IMPERV Bara
k-án-ó bííbíí
1SU-COP.IMPERV-1PL.EXC.SU.IMPERV different
'At (on) what ground? Because for that they collect for the Rora, we (exc.) collect for the Bara; thus we (exc.) are different.'

(1.6) -(KW 1:07:6)
àggè kí-bír-ésén-ó bárá jòg
1PL 1SU-collect-BEN-1PL.EXC.SU.IMPERV Bara 3PL
bír-ésén-ɛ́ rórá nà ŋànìjè [húllí
collect-BEN-3PL.SU.IMPERV Rora CCN but when/if
hód-á nà íb-t-á
come.PERV.PL-3PL.SU.PERV CCN take-PERV.PL-3PL.SU.PERV
[ólf-á g=àj=è]NP]SUBORD:CL àggè
stalk-RSTR PL.PSD=1PL.INC.PSR=SUBORD 1PL
ká-dág-íné-Ø háŋ-ne
1SU-hit-RECIP-1PL.INC.SU.IMPERV INTENS-RS
'We (inc.) women collect for the Bara. They collect for the Rora, but when they come and take our (inc.) sorghums, we (inc.) then fight each other very much.'

(1.7) -(KW 1:17:8)
čùànéŋ gòrò čó čùànéŋ tèrì gòrò ŋànì
again road even again Teri road NEG.PERV
k-íj-í-t=ó [húllí nè
3.SBJV-touch-1PL.OBJ-PERV.PL=NEG when/if 3SG

TRANSCRIBED TEXTS 609

    k-íj-ó=jè]_SUBORD:CL_   *té*   *kili-ni*
    3.SBJV-touch-1PL.OBJ-3PL.IRR=SUBORD COP.3.PERV Kili-RS
    té   *gèrs-ì*
    COP.3.PERV bad.STV-ADJ
    'Again even (on) the road, again those Teri do not touch us. If he (Teri (sg.))
    touch us, it becomes "Kili!". It gets bad.'

(1.8) -(KW 1:28:8)
    čùànéŋ   *ŋà=lɔ̀g=tù*   *hàlì* *áj-t-ɛ*   *tèrò-ú-ni*
    again   DEM=issue=FAR later take-PERV.PL-APPL Teri.PL-NOM-RS
    té   [*lɔ̀g-tí*   *g=èj*]_NP   *nà*   *hàlì*
    COP.3.PERV issue-NRSTR PL.PSD=3PL.PSR CCN later
    nìs-ɛ́   *bì*
    kill-3PL.SU.IMPERV cow
    'Then later the Teru take up this issue (Kili) and thus it becomes their issue.
    After that they will slaughter a cow.'

    ŋà=zùgt=ùnù   *wà*   *gíná*   *ŋáà* *kè ɔ̀ŋ*   *ké*   *ɓá*
    DEM=people=FAR REC.PAST ANA:REF here why.RHET PRE place/CAUSE
    wà   *k-én-čí-ɛ́-á*   *lɔ̀g-á*   *wágá*
    REC.PAST 3.SBJV-touch-APPL.1PL.OBJ-RES-RSTR issue-RSTR ANA:REF
    gɔ̀r-ɔ̀
    road-OBL
    'Why are those people are here? For the reason they have touched us on the
    road.'

(1.9) -(KW 1:38:5)
    ké-té-ú   *ʃéé*   *nà*
    1SU-COP.PERV-1PL.EXC.SU.PERV well CCN
    [*kó-hód-á*   *húŋ=nè*]_SUBORD:CL_
    1SU-come.PERV.PL-1PL.INC.SU.IMPERV simply=SUBORD
    'It would be good if we (inc.) come simply,...'

    kó-hód-á   *k-óí-tó*
    1SU-come.PERV.PL-1PL.INC.SU.PERV 1SU-put.PERV-1PL.EXC.SU.PERV
    ólʃó   *bà-ì-ni*   *ká-dǎg-á*   *hóló-ni* *tíí*
    stalk.PL place-LOC-RS 1SU-hit-1PL.INC.SU.PERV dance-RS DUR/CONT
    '... then we (inc.) come and we (exc.) put sorghum stalks on the ground. Then
    we (inc.) continue dancing.'

nà húllí dóólá kó ràmàn áw-ò-ni
CCN when girl.PL CRD:PART two come-3PL.IRR-RS
jàg-t-èsè zùw-á [Ø wágá [ké bú
return-PL-BEN/DAT.3 people-RSTR [Ø ANA.REF COMPL big
kí-bír-ésén-Ø-á óĺfó]_COMPL:CL]_RC ké
1SU-collect-BEN-1PL.INC.SU.IMPERV-RSTR stalk.PL QUOT
bárá-ni
Bara.PL-RS
'(and) then, two among the girls will come and go back to those elders to whom we collect the sorghum stalks called Bara.'

(1.10) -(KW 1:54:4)
ɓèlè hód-án-ì hàlì
early.morning come.PERV.PL.PERV-MT-3PL.IRR later
k-ítíɲá-ɲ-ɛsɛ ŋà=ɓ=ùnù
1.HORT-meet-PL-BEN DEM=place=FAR/(there)
jógt-ó-í bár-ú
tell.PERV-MT-3PL.IRR+1SG.OBJ Bara-NOM
'They come (in the) early morning. "Let us meet later for our own (meeting) there". It is the Baras who tell us this.'

ɓá bàrì gá k-áw-ò ɔ́r-ɔ̀
place yesterday ATTU 3.SBJV-come.PERV-3PL.IRR village-OBL
'"At that place and time", they (the two girls) come back to the village.'

nà sábɔ̀ [dódŏl-á [gèrs-á
CCN first hard.STV-RSTR bad.STV-RSTR
hét-é-á]_NP]_NP kó hádá
resemble-3PL.SU.IMPERV-RSTR CRD:PART sleeping_mat(of cow skin)
rúm ŋà=kí-bírí-Ø=ó
cloth.SG NEG.IMPERV=1SU-wear-1PL.INC.SU.IMPERV=NEG
'Then, first, from a skin that is dry and almost useless; we (inc.) don't wear clothes.'

[húllí kí-bírí-Ø rúm=nè]_SUBORD:CL kállí
if 1SU-wear-1PL.INC.SU.IMPERV cloth=SUBORD stick
k-ój-Ø tó-jé
1SU-inter-1PL.INC.SU.IMPERV in-OBL
'If we (inc.) wear clothes, the stick will get into (our body).'

TRANSCRIBED TEXTS

(1.11) -(KW 1:59:4)
nà   k-ɨw-áná   ró[úm]   [kèj-á   bú
CCN 1SU-take.IMPERV-MT.1PL.INC.SU cloth   thing-RSTR big
dőldől-á]_NP   kó   [sái   bú-sís-í   [dɔ́rɔ́s-á
hard.STV-RSTR PNC leather_dress big-AUG-ADJ   hard/dry.STV-RSTR
múgá-ɲ]_NP
woman.PL-GEN
'So, we (inc.) take cloth, a very solid thing and a much dried women's leather dress'.

(1.12) -(KW 2:06:6)
[kó-hód-á-έ-ni   kó
1SU-come.PERV.PL-1PL.INC.SU.PERV-APPL-RS   PNC
dɔ́ŋài=jὲ]SUBORD:CL   kó-hód-á
duelling.stick.SG=SUBORD   1SU-come.PERV.PL-1PL.INC.SU.PERV
'We (inc.) come, we (inc.) bring a duelling.stick.'

kí-ɲím-nὲ-Ø   kállí-ó-ni   [húllí
1SU-cringe-RECIP-1PL.INC.SU.IMPERV   stick-PL-RS   when/if
dág-í-έ=jὲ]
hit-1PL.OBJ-3PL.SU.IMPERV=SUBORD
'When they beat us, we protect ourselves from the sticks.'

(1.13) -(KW 2:11:0)
k-εj-áná-ni   g=àw
1SU-protect/support-MT.1PL.INC.SU.IMPERV-RS   PL.PSD=1PL.EXC.PSR
ŋà=kállí-ó=ìnù   ŋà=kèi-tá   sái=nù   wà
DEM=stick-PL=FAR   DEM=thing=NEAR   leather.dress=INDEF   REC.PAST
bú-sísí=ŋà   új-áná-ni   ɓóóù!   rεg
big-AUG=DEF   shout-MT.3SG.SU.IMPERV-RS!   IDEOPH   spine
n=àj-ni
SG.PSD=1PL.INC.PSR-RS!
'We (inc.) protect our (selves) from those sticks; the leather dress shouts very much, "BOOU!", (not) our (inc.) back.'

(1.14) -(KW 2:17:0)
ŋànìjὲ tó-jé   ŋà=ɓ=ùnù   čùànéŋ   ɓá   [hír-á   hír-íɲ]_NP
but   in-OBL DEM=place=FAR   again   CAUSE   man-RTSR   man-GEN
bás-áná   nà   dág-új[ɲ]-Ø   ŋàŋà
get.up-MT.3SG.SU.IMPERV   CCN   hit-2SG.OBJ-3SG.SU.IMPERV   like.this

húŋ   ŋà=dǎg-í-Ø=tó
simply NEG.IMPERV=hit-2SG-OBJ-3SG.SU.IMPERV=NEG
'However, in there, again, a human man gets up beats you (sg.) just like this (for no reason), he doesn't beat you (sg.).'

(1.15) -(KW 2:26:4)
lò-Ø   lò-Ø   [gótó-á   n=ènè]_NP   nè
has-3SG.SU.IMPERV has-3SG.SU.IMPERV rule-RSTR SG.PSD=3SG.PSR   3SG
[zèré-á   n=ènè]_NP   ká-dǎg-éné-Ø   zèrí-mò²
race-RSTR SG.PSD=3SG.PSR 1SU-hit-RECIP-1PL.INC.SU.IMPERV race-N.S
zèrí-mò-j
race-N.S-GEN
'It has its own rule (inside of it). In it, his race, we (inc.) beat each other, race by race, ...'

"jànù=gè-mò   jànù=gè-mò-j"
cousin.SG=PERT.PL.3.PSR-N.S   cousin=PERT.PL.3.PSR-N.S-GEN
[jànù=gè-mò]   á   бá   ké   ké
cousin=PERT.PL.3.PSR-N.S   COP.3.IMPERV place/CAUSE PREP QUOT
'"by cousinhood by cousinhood", instead, cousinhood is what it is called.'

(1.16) -(KW 2:34:4)
[màmà   kónó]_NP   kó   [ʤɔɔ̀nè]_NP
mother.PERT.SG.1.PSR+RSTR one.INDEF PNC mother.PERT.SG.3.PSR
á   dónéj ŋònigèn
COP.3.IMPERV   one   sister.PL
'My mother and his mother are one (the same), sisters (to each other).'

ŋànìjè ŋà=ìggì=nù   k-án-Ø
but   DEM=3PL.PN.SP=FAR   1SU-COP.IMPERV-1pl.INC.SU.IMPERV
[zùw-á   dónén-á]_NP   ká-dǎg-nén-á
people-RSTR one/same-RTSR 1SU-hit-RECIP-1PL.INC.SU.PERV
kállí-ó-í-ni
stick-PL-OBL-RS
'However those people, we (inc.) are the same people who beat/fight each other by (with) sticks.'

---

2 For example, -hood can acquire the meanings: 'state' (boyhood) and 'time' (childhood).

TRANSCRIBED TEXTS 613

[ŋɔ̀sɔ̀nì³-á   zùw-á]ₙₚ   kákó   dɔ́nén-á   ŋà=dàmì=tá
Ngosoni-RSTR people-RSTR perhaps one/same-RSTR DEM=rule=NEAR
lɔ̀m-á   ɓa   kɔ́d-á   ká-dág-t-é-ni
have-3PL.SU.PERV place/CAUSE write-NOMZ 1SU-hit-PL.PERV-RECIP-RS
dàài
COMPLETIVE
'Perhaps, if the people of Ngosoni are the same people having this rule recorded, we are people who beat each other.'

(1.17)   -(KW 2:48:0)
[húllí   úʃɲ-áná=jè]_SUBORD:CL
when/if finish-MT.3SG.SU.IMPERV=SUBORD
ád-í-ì   lɔ̀gɔ̀ jógt-ó-í+ì
give.PERV-1PL.OBJ+3PL.IRR word tell.PERV-MT-1PL.OBJ+3PL.IRR
lɔ̀g-á   "màt-í-ò"   dàài
word-RTSR drink-2SG.SU.IMPERV-VFS all/COMPLETELY
'When it is over, they give us a word, they tell us a word, 'you (sg.) drink'.'

nà   [húllí   úʃɲ-áná=jè]_SUBORD:CL   àggè
CCN when/if finish-MT.3SG.SU.IMPERV=SUBORD 1PL
k-áw-ó   hóló   dág-a-ni
1SU-go.IMPERV-1PL.EXC.SU.IMPERV dance hit-NOMZ-RS
'and when it is finished, then we (exc.) go dance hitting.'

[húllí   sed-a-i+i   ŋaŋà=jè]_SUBORD:CL àggè
when/if say.PERV-MT-1PL.OBJ+3PL.IRR like.this=SUBORD 1PL
k-ai-to   hóló-té   tíí
1SU-go.PERV-1PL.EXC.SU.PERV dance-OBL DUR/CONT
'When they talk to us like that, we go to the dancing and continue'

(1.18)   -(KW 2:52:4)
[jɔ̀g ɓá-á   làlàŋ-ŋà]ₙₚ kó jɔ̀g lò-Ø   làlàŋ-ŋà   bárí
3PL place-RTSR bracelet-PL PNC 3PL have-3PL.IRR bracelet-PL Bari.SG
bú kú-múg-ó-Ø
big 1SU-collect.IMPERV-MT-1PL.EXC.SU.IMPERV
k-ád-á-ni   kó   ólʃ-ó-á   [ga
1SU-give.PERV-1PL.INC.SU.PERV-RS PNC stalk-PL-RSTR PL.PN.RSTR

---

3 ZS, ZD, FZS, FZD, FBDS, FBDD (for kinship classification of the Mursi, see Chapter 1).

uʃa-Ø
finish-3SG.SU.IMPERV!
'Those bracelets and the bracelets there that we (inc.) collected at the big Bara, we (inc.) give them (the Bara) with those sorghum stalks. Finished!'

(1.19) -(KW 2:57:6)
[ŋà=ìn=nù]_{CS}   á   [gótó-á   zùw-á]_{NP:CC}   ké
DEM=3SG.PN.SP=FAR COP.3.IMPERV rule-RTSR people-RSTR QUOT
dóólɛ́   kɔ́n-ča   kɔ́n-ča   kɔ̀mà
girl.PL kneel-APP.3PL.SU.PERV kneel-APP.3PL.SU.PERV knee.PL
'That is a custom/culture of people called, "girls" for which they kneel.'

Text II: Naming

Description: To get more on the Mursi's naming system, see § 1.8. Aside from what is discussed in §1.8, there is some additional information that Text II below explains. One is that we will find an enumerated of peculiar Mursi female and male names. The other is that we see a discourse method in which Mursi speakers structure information by repetition.

Narrator (informant): Arsiregge Gomonyokawulo (40+, Male)
Place of recording: South Omo Research Center, Jinka Town, Ethiopia
Year of recording: 12 August 2017
Length of the record: 2min.31sec.
Text code: NM (Naming)

(2.1)   (0:04:2–0:17:2)
érmì   [húllí   íríčiɲan-áná   á
child.SG when/if born.APPL-MT.3SG.SU.IMPERV COP.3.IMPERV
ŋàhì=jè]_{SUBORD:CL}   [sárá-á   g=ɛ̀ɲɛ̀]_{NP}
female.ADJ=SUBORD name-RSTR PL.PSD=3SG.PSR
'Child, if it (s/he) is born and if it is female, her/his name,…'

[húllí   kɔ́n-Ø   dʒɔ̀ɔ̀nè   íríd-ónó   nà
when/if write.PERV-3SG.IRR mother born-MT.3SG.SU.IMPERV CCN
á   ŋàhì=ŋà]_{SUBORD:CL} nɔ̀ŋ [sárá-á   g=ɛ̀ɲɛ̀]_{NP}
COP.3.IMPERV female.ADJ=DEF 3SG name-RSTR PL.PSD=3SG.PSR
á   ŋà …ŋà …ŋà   sɔ̀ŋ
COP.3.IMPERV nga … nga … nga only
'when name is named (Literally means 'written'), and if the mother gives birth, her name is Nga, Nga, Nga (also mean 'wife') only.'

(2.2) -(0:28:4)
 kón-á   [Ø *k-èlì*   *ké*   *ŋàn-ó-j*]_RC   *á*
 one-RTSR   [Ø PASS-CALL.PERV   QUOT   Ngan-OBL-GEN]   COP.3.IMPERV
 sárá   kɔ̀ɔ̀d-èsèn-à   múgái-ni
 name   PASS.write-BEN-PASS.3.SU   woman.SG-RS
 'One who is called by Ngan, then is named for woman.'

 ŋàn-ò-j   *á*   [*sárá-á*   [*hír-á*   *ŋàh-á-ni*]_NP]_NP
 Ngan-OBL-GEN   COP.3.IMPERV   name-RSTR   person-RTSR   female-RSTR-RS
 ŋàtùj
 Ngatuy
 'Of by Ngan, a name of a woman (female person) Ngatun;

(2.3) -(0:35:6)
 á   [*sárá-á*   [*hír-á*   *ŋàh-á*]_NP]_NP   *ŋàbìò*
 COP.3.IMPERV   name-RSTR   person-RTSR   female-RTSR   Ngabìò
 a name of a woman Ngabio;

 á   [*sárá-á*   *hír-á*]_NP   *ŋàgèrì*   *á*
 COP.3.IMPERV   name-RSTR   person-RTSR   Ngageri   COP.3.IMPERV
 [*sárá-á*   [*hír-á*   [*ŋàh-á*]_NP]_NP   *ŋaŋatuj*
 name RSTR   person-RTSR   female-RTSR   Ngangatuy
 a name of a person Ngageri; a name of a woman Ngangatuy;

 án-á   *kó-jóg-á*   *dààì*   *ɪŋ!*
 COP.3-PAST   1SU-tell-1SG.SU.PERV   all   yes/ok!
 I having spoken all. Yes/Okay!'

 [*sárá-á*   [*zùw-á*   *ŋàh-á*]_NP]_NP   *jɔ̀g*   *k-ɔ́ɣ-ó-ì*
 name-RSTR   people-RSTR female-RSTR   3PL   3.SBJV-go-MT.PERV-3PL.IRR
 ŋà=bá=á
 DEM=place=NEAR
 'Name of women, they go through this (way/system):'

 ŋàméá [*ŋà=ìn=á*]_CS   *á*   [*ŋàbìò*]_CC
 now   DEM=3SG.PN.SP=NEAR   COP.3.IMPERV   Ngabìò
 [*ŋà=ìn=á*]_CS   *á*   [*ŋàgèrì*]_CC   [*ŋà=ìn=á*]_CS
 DEM=3SG.PN.SP=NEAR   COP.3.IMPERV   Ngageri   DEM=3SG.PN.SP=NEAR
 á   [*ŋàŋóì*]_CC
 COP.3.IMPERV   Ngangoy
 'Now, this is Ngabio; this is Ngageri; this is Ngangoy

(2.4) -(0:47:8)
[ŋà=ìn=à]_CS   á   [ŋàkáká]_CC [ŋà-ìn=à]_CS
DEM=3SG.PN.SP=NEAR COP.3.IMPERV Ngakaka   DEM=3SG.PN.SP=NEAR
á   [ŋàlúsì]_CC [ŋa=in=á]_CS   á   [ŋàtúrí]_CC
COP.3.IMPERV Ngalúsì DEM=3SG.PN.SP=NEAR COP.3.IMPERV Ngaturi
[ŋà=ìn=à]_CS   á   [ŋàrórí]_CC ìssàbàj
DEM=3SG.PN.SP=NEAR COP.3.IMPERV Ngarori   seven
'this is Ngakaka; this is Ngalusi; this is Ngaturi; this is Ngarori, seven.'

(2.5) -(0:59:0)
[sárá-á   [zùw-á   ŋàh-á]_NP]_NP   íggé-á   [Ø ké
name-RSTR people-RSTR female-RSTR 3PL.PN.SP-RTSR [Ø QUOT
ìssàbàì=ŋà]_RC á   ŋàŋà=ŋà   sòŋ
seven=DEF   COP.3IMPERV like.this=DEF only
'These are the seven names of women are just like this only.'

(2.6) -(1:40:9)
jòg [zùw-á   ŋàh-á]   [bá-á   n=èj]_NP
3PL people-RSTR female-RSTR place-RTSR SG.PSD=3PL.PSR
[gótó-á   n=èj]
culture/custom-RSTR SG.PSD=3PL.PSR
'They, women, their own (way) (Literally, 'their place'); their (own) culture.'

[zúw-á   ŋàh-á]_NP   jòg á   ŋà, ŋà, ŋà   sòŋ
people-RSTR female-RSTR 3PL COP.3.IMPERV Nga, Nga, Nga only
á   [lòg-á   ŋàh-á]_NP
COP.3.IMPERV issue-RSTR female-RSTR
'the women's, they are Nga, Nga, Nga only. They are of women.'

[zùw-á   màg-á]_NP]_NP ŋà=ìn=à   k-èlì   ké
people-RSTR male-RSTR DEM=3SG.PN.SP=NEAR PASS-call.PERV QUOT
òlíkòrò
òlíkoro
'Of men: one that is called Òlíkoro;

ŋà=ìn=á   k-èlì   ké   òlítùlà
DEM=3SG.PN.SP=NEAR PASS-call.PERV QUOT òlítùlà
ŋà=ìn=á   k-èlì   ké   òlíčàgìj
DEM=3SG.PN.SP=NEAR PASS-call.PERV QUOT Olichagiy

ŋà=ìn=á	k-èlì	ké	òlígidaŋi
DEM=3SG.PN.SP=NEAR	PASS-call.PERV	QUOT	Oligidhangi

ŋà=ìn=á	k-èlì	ké	òlísorali
DEM=3SG.PN.SP=NEAR	PASS-call.PERV	QUOT	Olisorali

ŋà=ìn=á	k-èlì	ké	òlíregge
DEM=3SG.PN.SP=NEAR	PASS-call.PERV	QUOT	Olirege

ŋà=ìn=á	k-èlì	ké	òlíkori
DEM=3SG.PN.SP=NEAR	PASS-call.PERV	QUOT	Olikori

one that is called Òlítùlà; one that is called Olichagiy; one that is called Oligidhangi; one that is called Olisorali; one that is called Olirege; one that is called Olikori;

(2.7) -(1:55:2)

ŋà=ìn=á	k-èlì	ké	òlídʒarhɔ̀lì
DEM=3SG.PN.SP=NEAR	PASS-call.PERV	QUOT	Olijarholi

ŋà=ìn=á	k-èlì	ké	òlíkibo
DEM=3SG.PN.SP=NEAR	PASS-call.PERV	QUOT	Olikibo

ŋà=ìn=á	k-èlì	ké	òlíɓiseni	tɔ̀mɔ̀n
DEM=3SG.PN.SP=NEAR	PASS-call.PERV	QUOT	Olibhiseni	ten

one that is called Olijarholi; one that is called Olikibo; one that is called Olibhiseni, ten.'

(2.8) -(2:02:4)

á	[ɓá-á	[zùw-á	màg-á]$_{NP}$]$_{NP}$
COP.3.IMPERV	place-RSTR	people-RSTR	male-RSTR

ké-sé-Ø	ké	òlé⟨í⟩	òlé⟨í⟩	sɔ̀ŋ
1SU-say-1PL.INC.SU.IMPERV	QUOT	Oli	Oli	only

'That of men's we (inc.) call are "Oli" "Oli" only.'

tɔ̀mɔ̀n	á	[sárá-á	[zùw-á	màg-á-ni]$_{NP}$]$_{NP}$
ten	COP.3.IMPERV	name-RSTR	people-RSTR	MALE-RSTR-RS

'These ten are names of men.'

héj	[tán-á	màg-á]$_{NP}$	á	ŋàŋà
go.IMPERV.PL.3.SU	side-RSTR	male-RTSR	COP.3.IMPERV	like.this

'They go on the men's side like this.'

[tán-á	[zùw-á	ŋàhà]$_{NP}$]$_{NP}$	[hír-á	ŋàh-á]$_{NP}$
side-RSTR	people-RSTR	female-RSTR	person-RSTR	female-RSTR

   ín-í   [Ø *k-èlì*   *ké*   *òlé*
   3SG.PN.SP-NRSTR [Ø PASS-call.PERV QUOT Òlé
   'On the women's side, a woman that is called "Oli";...'

(2.9)   -(2:18:0)
   ín-í   [Ø *k-èlì*   *ké*   *òlíkɔ̀rɔ̀ òlé*
   3SG.PN.SP-NRSTR [Ø PASS-call.PERV QUOT Olikoro Ole
   '...that which is called "Olikoro"...'

   í-Ø=ŋà   *òlé í-Ø=ŋà*   *òlé òlé*
   to.be-3SG.SU.IMPERV=DEF òlé to.be-3SG.SU.IMPERV=DEF òlé òlé
   níŋè
   not.present
   'There is not this (Literally, 'it is') here Oli, this here Oli Oli.'

   òlé òlé héj   [*tán-á*   *mà+á*]_NP   *sɔ̀ŋ*
   Ole Ole go.IMPERV.PL.3.SU side-RSTR male.RTSR only
   'Oli, Oli will go on the side of males only.'

   ŋà ... ŋà ... ŋà ...   *ín-í*   [Ø *ké*   *ŋàŋà*   *nà*
   Nga ... Nga ... Nga 3SG.PN.SP-NRSTR [Ø QUOT like.this CCN
   ké-sén-ì   *ín-á*   [Ø *màg-á*]_NP   *k-èlì*   *ké*
   1SBJV-say-PL.IRR 3SG.PN.SP-NRSTR [Ø male-RSTR PASS-call.PERV QUOT
   ŋà, ŋà]_RC   *níŋè*
   Nga, Nga] not.present
   'Nga, Nga, Nga which is called like this, "Nga" and of a male that we call like
   this (this way) does not exist;

(2.10)   (2:27:2–2:31:2)
   ín-á   [Ø *ŋàh-á*]_RC   *sɔ̀ŋ*
   3SG.PN.SP-NRSTR [Ø male-RSTR] only
   that is of a female only.'

   á   *ŋàŋà*   *ín-á*   [Ø *màg-á*]_RC   *á*   *òlé*
   COP.3.IMPERV like.this 3SG.PN.SP-NRSTR [Ø male-RSTR cop.3.imperv òlé
   tɔ̀mɔ̀n
   ten
   'Just like this, that of a male are ten Oli.'

Text III: 'There Was No Death'

Brief description—In order to keep the high quality of texts included in this grammar from various text genres, the texts referring to oral stories, cultural and ritual practices have been recorded by anthropologists who researched the Mursi society for many years. Thus the text glossed and translated below is adopted from David Turton's (mursi.org), a web source run by Oxford University within the Oxford Department of International Development.

(3.1) àggè bè   sábɔ kíɲíɲ   mùnì   kú-súd-íné-ò,
      1PL DIST.PAST first long.ago Mursi.SG 1SU-shed-AP-1PL.EXC.SU.PERV
      nà   rès-ɛ   níɲè
      and die.IMPERV-NOMZ not.present
      'A long time ago we (inc.) Mursi shed our skins, and there was no death.'

(3.2) nà   rès-ɛ̀   àggè b[ɓ]ásá-j,   nà   ɲàméá àggè
      CCN die.IMPERV-NOMZ 1PL monitor.lizard-SG CCN now   1PL
      ɓúh-à-j   b[ɓ]ásá-Ø   ɓòì
      curse-NOMZ-GEN monitor.lizard-NOM COMPLETIVE
      'Death was brought to us by the monitor lizard, so now we have been cursed by the monitor lizard.'

(3.3) nà   súd-é-á   [Ø]_RC áín-Ø-ɛ́   kònù
      CCN shed-NOMZ-RSTR [Ø]   give.PERV.SG-3.IRR-APPL:RES snake.SG
      'And the shedding of skin (that was ours), he gave to the snake.'

      ɲàméá súd-Ø-ɛ́   kònù, nà   àggè
      now   shed-3SG.SU.IMPERV-APPL snake.SG CCN 1pl
      gér-í-á
      terrible.STV-ADJ-NOMZ
      'So now the snake sheds its skin, and we die!'

(3.4) nà   [húllí kònù   súd-íné=ɲà]_SUBORD:CL ʃìg-Ø
      CCN when/if snake.SG shed-APPL.3.SU=DEF hear.IMPERV-3SG.SU.IMPERV
      hóló-à   b[ɓ]ásá-í-nè
      dance-NOMZ monitor.lizard-SG-EPENT+OBL
      'Now when the snake shed its skin it was because it heard the singing of the monitor lizard.'
      (Lit. 'singing from the monitor lizard')

básá-ì   érók-Ø   kìɔ̀ tùn-ɔ̀ nà
monitor.lizard-SG climb-3SG.SU.IMPERV tree.SG top-OBL CCN
čɔ́ll-ú   hóló,   nà   sé-á   ké
sing-3SG.SU.PERV dance CCN say-3SG.SU.PERV QUOT
'The monitor lizard climbed a tree and sang a song and said this,...'

"mùnì   súd-Ø-έ   kònù   èr-Ø-έ   mùnì
Mursi.SG shed-3.IRR-APPL snake.SG die.PERV-3.IRR-APPL:RES Mursi.SG
súd-Ø-έ   kònù   èr-Ø-έ"
shed-3.IRR-APPL snake.SG die.PERV-3.IRR-APPL:RES
'"The snake died, the Mursi sheds his skin. The snake dies, the Mursi sheds his skin."'

(3.5)   [ŋáá ʃíg-Ø   ŋàà] nà [kònú táw-á
        here hear.IMPERV-3SG.SBJ.IMPERV here CCN snake deceive-3SG.SU.PERV
        édʒ-à]   nɔ̀ŋ ʃíg-Ø   kònù nà
        kill-NOMZ 3SG hear.IMPERV-3SG.SU.IMPERV snake CCN
        támár-á   rès-e   бòì
        refuse.PERV-3SG.SU.PERV die.IMPERV-? COMPLETIVE (at.all)
        '[The snake was close by] and [he heard this (his deceiving of killing) and he didn't want to die,

        nà   áíw-ò   nà   téhén-ú
        CCN come.PERV.SG-MT.IRR CCN want.PERV-3SG.SU.PERV
        básá-í   [бág-ò]_COMPL:CL
        monitor.lizard-SG eat.IMPERV-3SG.IRR
        so he came and decided to eat the monitor lizard.'

(3.6)   nà   gín-ón-Ø-ì   nà   sé-Ø   ké   heee!!
        CCN ask-MT-3SG.OBJ-3SG.IRR CCN say-3SG.SU.IMPERV QUOT heee!!!
        sén-í   k-èr   nój   básá-ì
        say-2SG.SU.IMPERV 3.SBJV-die.PERV who.NOM? monitor.lizard-SG
        'He asked him saying, "Who are you saying will die?" The Monitor lizard ...'

        téŋér-á   бág-á-ɛ   nà
        afraid.PERV-3SG.SU.PERV eat.PERV-3SG.SU.PERV-APPL:RES CCN
        sén-á   ké   ah, ah, ah
        say-3SG.SBJ.PERV QUOT no no no
        'Was afraid of being eaten and said this, "No! No! No!".'
        (Implied: And the monitor lizard was afraid of being eaten and said this)

(3.7)   *"k-èr   mùnì-ó,   k-èr   mùnì-o"*
3.SBJV-die.PERV Mursi-NOM 3.SBJV-die.PERV Mursi-NOM
'"The Mursi will die, the Mursi will die."'

"eeeh! čɔl-o-ni!"   nà   méá basa-j   čóll-ón-i
yes sing-2/3.IRR-RS CCN now monitor.lizard-SG sing-MT-2/3.IRR
sé-á   ké
say-3SG.SU.PERV QUOT
"Okay then, sing!" So then when the monitor lizard sang, he said this,

"Mùnì èr-Ø-έ   kònù súd-Ø-έ   Mùnì
Mursi die.PERV-3SG.IRR-APPL:RES snake shed-3.IRR-APPL Mursi
èr-Ø-έ   kònù súd-Ø-έ"
die.PERV-3SG.IRR-APPL:RES snake shed-3.IRR-APPL
'"The Mursi dies, the snake sheds its skin. The Mursi dies, the snake sheds its skin."'

(3.8)   *nà   méá kònù súd-Ø-έ,   nà   àggè mùnì*
CCN now snake shed-3.IRR-APPL:RES CCN 1PL   Mursi
k-èr-έ-á
1SU-die.PERV-MA-1PL.INC.SU.PERV
'So now the snake sheds its skin, and we (inc.) Mursi die.'

nà   méá rès-έ   áìw-ò-sè   bá   dóg!
CCN now die.IMPERV-NOMZ come.PERV.SG-2/3.IRR-BEN.3 earth forever
'And this is how death came to earth forever!'

Text IV: About the Mursi—How the Mursi Crossed to Omo River

Brief description: As described in the introduction section of this grammar, there is not much known about their present day's territory, yet they still claim that their territory was vast and used to start from *Mákkí* (the Mursi's main village, until now) and stretches right across the Maji plateau in the west to the Bako range in the east (See Map 1). Likewise, the territorial claim of the Mursi is a historical narration of migration that comes from the Mursi's ancestors and apparently is a story to be told for generations to come, a story very similar to 'Crossing the Red Sea' or 'the Exodus', led by Moses. At the center of all their stories, there was a strong man called *Kuwulokoro*, who enabled them (the Mursi people) to cross the Omo River and settle at their present land. Therefore, the story below is about this brave man. In addition, in this story, we will find a complete list of Mursi number words plus names of some edible fruits that grow in Mursiland.

Narrator (informant):	Arsiregge Gomonyokawulo (40+, Male)
Place of recording:	South Omo Research Center, Jinka Town, Ethiopia
Year of recording:	12 August 2017
Length of the record:	9min.33sec.
Text code:	MH (Mursi History)

(4.1)   (MH 0:06:6–0:17:6)
àggè mùn   bá-á   [Ø bè   n=àw]_{RC}   [hùllì
1PL   mursi.PL place [Ø DIST.PAST SG.PSD=1PL.EXC.PSR when/if
kó-hóɲ-ó=jè]_{SUBORD:CL}
1SU-come.IMPERV-1PL.EXC.SU=SUBORD
kó-hóɲ-ó   mà   tùnò   nà
1SU-come.IMPERV-1PL.EXC.SU.IMPERV water on.top.of CCN
k-án-ó   zùg-tí   [Ø k-èlì   ké
1SU-COP.IMPERV-1PL.EXC.SU people-NRSTR [Ø PASS-CALL.PERV QUOT
bóʃú]_{RC}
Boshu]
'We (exc.) the Mursi, (from the very beginning), when we (exc.) came from our place, we came on the upper part of a river and we are the people from the place called Boshu.'

nà   k-ów[g]-ónó   mà   tán-ɔ̀   tíí   nà
CCN 1SU-go.IMPERV-MT.1PL.INC.SU.IMPERV water side-OBL DUR CCN
kó-hóɲ-Ø   nà   [hùllì
1SU-come.IMPERV-1PL.INC.SU.IMPERV CCN when/if
ké-hé-ó   kɔ́-dɔ́g-Ø-ɛ́
1SU-go.IMPERV-1PL.EXC.SU 1SU-tread.on.IMPERV-1PL.INC.SU.IMPERV-COM
bá   ké   dòl=ŋà̀]_{SUBORD:CL}
place QUOT Dòl=DEF
'And we (inc.) kept going on the other side of the river and we (inc.) tread on (walked on) the land called the Dòl. when we (inc.) come we will then arrive at a place called Dòl.'

(4.2)   (MH 0:23:5)
mà   dìné-ó-ni   [ŋà=mà=á   [Ø bè
water full-3.IRR-RS DEM=water=NEAR [Ø DIST.PAST
kó-hóɲ-čó   tùnò=ŋà̀]_{RC}]_{SUBORD:CL} jòg
1SU-come.IMPERV.PL-COM.1PL.INC.SU.IMPERV up.hill=DEF   3PL

héj-Ø čúg-Ø káráné nà mà díné-ó
go.IMPERV.PL-3.IRR chase-3.IRR down stream CCN water full-3.IRR
ŋà=kàlkèn=ná kód-ó-é òrì
DEM=day.center=NEAR 1SU.take.out-1PL.EXC.SU.IMPERV-APPL:RES where?
'The river is full. The river that we (inc.) were coming along with, they go to the top and then run to downward. And at that time the river is full, we (exc.) go to where?'

(4.3) (MH 0:31:2)
kód-ónó [bà-ì ké dírká nà
1SU.take.out-MT.1PL.INC.SU.IMPERV place-LOC QUOT Dirka CCN
[k-ów-ónó ŋàŋà=ŋà]_{SUBORD:CL} dírr nà
1SU-go-MT.1PL.INC.SU.IMPERV like.this=DEF DUR/LONG.TIME CCN
[hùllì té [bá-á éré-í=nè]_{NP}]_{SUBORD:CL}
when/if COP.3.PERV place-RSTR cross-NOMZ=SUBORD
k-érés-ó ɓòì k-èlì ké
1SU-cross.IMPERV-1PL.EXC.SU.IMPERV COMPLET PASS-call.PERV QUOT
dòl
Dòl
'At that time the place where we (inc.) were heading was for a place called Dirka. As we (exc.) kept going like this for a long time and when we (exc.) came to the crossing place, we (exc.) crossed a place called Dòl.'

nà [hùllì k-érés-án-ó bá ké
CCN when 1SU-cross.IMPERV-MT-1PL.EXC.SU.IMPERV place QUOT
dòl=ŋà]_{SUBORD:CL} mà díné-ó-ni
dòl=DEF water full-3.IRR-RS
'When we (exc.) crossed the place called Dòl, the river was full.'

(4.4) (MH 0:38:2)
hírí bè k-èlì ké káwúlókɔ̀rɔ̀ á
person DIST.PAST PASS-call.PERV QUOT Kawulokoro COP.3.IMPERV
hírí bárárí kén-Ø wárr káwúlókɔ̀rɔ̀ káwúlókɔ̀rɔ̀
person powerful break.PERV-3SG.IRR Omo.river Kawulokoro Kawulokoro
kéd-ú wárr-nì ór-Ø bèr
cut.3SG.SU.IMPERV Omo.river-LOC see/aim.IMPERV-3SG.SU.IMPERV spear
'There was a man called Kuwulokro. Kawulokoro was a powerful man who can make the Omo River stop. Kawulokoro, Kawulokoro cut the Omo River, he threw a spear.'

(4.5)   (MH 0:44:4)
      nà   [hùllì   ór-Ø   bèr   ŋàŋà]$_{SUBORD:CL}$ mà
      CCN when/if throw-3SG.SU.IMPERV spear like.this/this.way water
      kén-né-Ø   tásá! mà   gè-á   hój
      cut.PERV-RECIP-3SG.IRR apart water PL.PN-RSTR go.IMPERV.PL
      káráné   iggè-á   [Ø héj   tùnò]$_{RC}$ [bì-ò-á
      down.stream 3PL.PN.SP-RSTR [Ø go.IMPERV.PL on.top.of] cow-PL-RSTR
      g=àw]$_{NP}$ mùn-ùɲ]$_{NP}$
      PL.PSD=1PL.EXC.PSR Mursi.PL-GEN
      'And when he threw (Literally, 'when he sees/aim') the spear this way, the water (river) is cut apart, those go down and the others go on the top. The cattle of the Mursi,...'

(4.6)   (MH 0:50:5)
      sárá   ké   mùnì   kí-čít-ésé-ó   mà-nì
      name PNC mursi.SG 1SU-overfill-BEN/DAT-1PL.EXC.SU.IMPERV water-LOC
      k-éréd-á-ó   kìdò ŋà=táná=á   [hùllì
      1SU-cross.PERV-MT-1PL.EXC.SU.PERV river DEM=river.side=NEAR when/if
      k-érés-án-ó=ŋà]$_{SUBORD:CL}$ kó tèn-è]   kó
      1SU-cross.IMPERV-MT-1PL.EXC.SU.IMPERV=DEF CCN goat.PL-OBL PNC
      bì-ò-ì   kó   mèdèrní
      cow-PL-OBL PNC sheep.PL
      'With the Mursi name, we (exc.) overfilled into the water and we (exc.) crossed to the other side of the river. We (exc.) cross with goats, cattle, and sheep.'

(4.7)   (MH 0:56:0)
      kó-hóɲ-ó   zùw-á   [Ø bè
      1SU-come.IMPERV.PL-1PL.EXC.SU.IMPERV people-RSTR [Ø DIST.PAST
      g=àw   kɔ́-dɔ̌t-ó   tán-ɔ̀]$_{RC}$ ŋàméá
      PL.SPD=1PL.EXC.PSR 1SU-leave-1PL.EXC.SU.IMPERV river side-OBL] now
      k-èlì   ké   bófú
      PASS-call.PERV QUOT Boshu
      'We (exc.) came. The people who were ours (exc.) and abandoned (them) on the other side are now called Boshu ('eldest son').' (MH 0:56:0)

(4.8)   (MH 1:03:0)
      iggè-á   [Ø bè   kó-hóɲ-ó
      3PL.PN.SP-RSTR [Ø DIST.PAST 1SU-come.IMPERV.PL-1PL.EXC.SU.IMPERV
      ŋà=táná=á]$_{RC}$ ŋàméá k-èlì+ì   ké   mùn-ni
      DEM=river.side=NEAR now PASS-call.PERV-1PL.OBJ PNC Mursi-RS

TRANSCRIBED TEXTS 625

  [hùllì ŋàméá [zùw-á g=àw]_NP bóʃú bùnù]_SUBORD:CL
  [when/if now people-RSTR PL.PSD=1PL.EXC.PSR Boshu there
  [hùllì číg-έ=jè]_SUBORD:CL
  when/if laugh.IMPERV-3PL.SU.IMPERV=SUBORD
  sén-έ   ké "hee hee ... woinanoje ... bóʃójè"
  say.IMPERV-3PL.SU.IMPERV QUOT hee! hee! ... woynanoye ... boshoye
  sén-έ   ŋàŋà
  say.IMPERV-3PL.SU.IMPERV like.this
  'Those who we (exc.) (have) come from this side of the river are now called (with/by the name of) Mursi. When now our (exc.) people, the Boshu there, when they laugh, they say "Hee hee! woynanoye boshoye", they say it like this.'

(4.9) (MH 1:10:7)
  [zùw-á g=àw]_NP [Ø bè gén bè
  people-RSTR PL.PSD=1PL.EXC.PSR [Ø DIST.PAST other DIST.PAST
  kɔ́-dɔ̌t-ó   mà tùnò ìggè-á
  1SU-leave-1PL.EXC.SU.IMPERV water on.top 3PL.PN.SP-RSTR
  [Ø bè kó-hóɲ-ó
  [Ø DISTANT.PAST 1SU-come.IMPERV.PL-1PL.EXC.SU.IMPERV
  ŋà=táná=á kɔ́-dɔ̌-Ø   dòl nà
  DEM=river.side=NEAR 1SU-leave-1PL.INC.SU.IMPERV Dòl CCN
  kó-hóɲ-ó   ŋà=táná=á]_RC ŋàméá
  1SU-come.IMPERV.PL-1PL.EXC.SU.IMPERV DEM=river.side=NEAR now
  k-èlè   ké mùn-ni
  PASS-call.PERV QUOT Mursi.PL-RS
  'Our (exc.) other people (who) we (exc.) left at the top of the water (river); those who we (inc.) crossed Dòl and came to the other side of the river, we are now called "Mursi (pl.)!".'

(4.10) (MH 1:18:0)
  nà [hùllì k-èlì   ké mùn=ŋà]_SUBORD:CL hírí
  CCN when/if PASS-call.PERV QUOT mursi=DEF man
  n=àw   bárárí k-èlè   ké káwúlókɔ̀rɔ̀
  SG.PSD=1PL.EXC.PSR powerful PASS-call.PERV QUOT Kawulokoro
  éʃ-é   ín-á   [Ø bè kén-Ø
  exist.PERV-3.IRR 3SG.PN.SP-RSTR [Ø DIST.PAST cut.PERV-3SG.IRR
  wárr= ŋà] k-án-ó   [zùg-tí
  River.omo=DEF 1SU-COP.IMPERV-1PL.EXC.SU.IMPERV people-NRSTR

bárárí]_NP àggè háŋ!
powerful 1PL INTENS

'And when we (exc.) are called the Mursi, there was our (exc.) man who can make the Omo river stop called Kawulokoro. We (exc.) are very powerful people.'

[hùllì hírí ór-Ø bèr=nà]_SUBORD:CL kén-Ø mà
when/if man spear-3SG.IRR spear=DEF cut.PERV-3SG.IRR water
héj-Ø tásá nà mà iggè-á káráné
go.IMPERV.PL-3.IRR apart CCN water 3PL.PN.SP-RSTR down
iggè-á héj-Ø tùnò á
3PL.PN.SP-RSTR go.IMPERV.PL-3PL.IRR on.top COP.3.IMPERV
[zùg-tì bárárí]_NP
people-NRSTR powerful+NRSTR

'When the man threw the spear, he cut the water, and it separates. And some water goes down and some water goes to the upper part. They are powerful people.'

(4.11) (MH 1:23:2)
méá [áná bè kó-hóɲ-ó nà
now ANA:REF DIST.PAST 1SU-come.IMPERV.PL-1PL.EXC.SU.IMPERV CCN
ŋàméá k-èlè ké mùn nà méá
now PASS-call.PERV QUOT Mursi.PL CCN now
k-él-ó bà-ì=ŋà
1SU-exist.IMPERV.PL-1PL.EXC.SU.IMPERV place-LOC=DEF

'It was this way that we came and are now are able to be called the Mursi. And now we (exc.) live at this place.'

(4.12) (MH 1:29:0)
[hùllì kó-hóɲ-ó=ŋà]_SUBORD:CL [gótó-ɲá
when/if 1SU-come.IMPERV.PL-1PL.EXC.SU.IMPERV=DEF culture-PL
g=àw]_NP kó-hó-čá-ó
PL.PSD=1PL.EXC.PSR 1SU-come-APPL-1PL.EXC.SU.IMPERV
ŋà=gótó=á-ni
DEM=culture=NEAR-RS

'When we (exc.) came, we (exc.) brought (came with) our cultures too.'

(4.13) (MH 1:41:5)
k-èlè ké čáŋá čáŋ čáŋ úɲúl-Ø
PASS-call.PERV QUOT Changa Chang Chany fart-3SG.SU.IMPERV

```
              kè-sè-ŋè              čáŋálá-j,    dɔ̀ŋà-j,    tèrì,    rórí,    bàrì,
              PASS-say.PERV-PASS.3  Changalay-SG Dhonga-SG Teri-SG Rori.SG Bari.SG
              kárú-j    ŋàméá té         [gótó-ɲá   g=àw]_NP              bè
              Karu-SG   now    COP.3.IMPERV culture-PL PL.PSD=1PL.EXC.PSR  DIST.PAST
              kó-hóɲ-čó
              1SU-come.IMPERV.PL-APPL.1PL.EXC.SU.IMPERV
```
'(there is one) called Changa (also 'Rúmúɲój'), Chang Chang he farts, Changalay, Dhongay, Teriy, Rori, Bari, Karuy. Now these became our (exc.) cultures after we (exc.) brought (them).'

(4.14) (MH 1:48:7)
```
              čúg-Ø        bá      ké     bófú   nà     k-éréʃ-áɲ-o
              chase-3.IRR  place   QUOT   Boshu  CCN    1SU-cross-MT-1PL.EXC.SU.IMPERV
              kídó         ŋà=táná=á              [gótó-ɲá    g=àw]_NP
              river        DEM=river.side=NEAR    culture-PL  PL.PSD=1PL.EXC.PSR
```
'It is chased to a place known as Boshu, and we (exc.) crossed to the other side of the river with our (exc.) cultures.'

```
              [ìggè-á           ŋà=góto-ɲá=inù]_NP         g=àw=ŋà]_NP
              3PL.PN.SP-RSTR    DEM=culture-PL=FAR         PL.PSD=1PL.EXC.PSR=DEF
              ŋà=gárs-ɛ́=ó                                háŋ         [hùllì
              NEG.IMPERV=lost/dissapear-3PL.SU.IMPERV=NEG  INTENS      when/if
              ódʒ-ésé-ò      wárkátí  tò-jè=ŋà]_SUBORD:CL    él-Ø
              put-BEN-3.IRR  paper    in-OBL=DEF             exist-3SG.SU.IMPERV
              kókó]_SUBORD:CL
              ready/perhaps
```
'Those of our cultures were not lost, if they are put onto paper, they exist readily.'

(4.15) (MH 2:03:0)
```
              kó      hàlì   kíɲíɲ    [lɔ̀g-á     n=àw]_NP                mùn-ùɲ]_NP
              PNC     later  long.ago  word-RSTR  SG.PSD=1PL.EXC.PSR      mursi-GEN
              á                ŋàŋà      ŋà=kì=tùnù        [kí-ʃíl-à              mà
              COP.3.IMPERV  like.this  DEM=wood=FAR     3.SBJV-stand-3.IRR   water
              kèrgèn-ɔ̀=jè]_SUBORD:CL
              middle-OBL=SUBORD
```
'and later in the future, our (exc.) ways of Mursi (pl.) will be like this. That wood was standing in the middle of the water (river).'

ŋà=kì=à   á   dùrùmè sé   á
DEM=tree.SG=NEAR COP.3.IMPERV stump say.3.AUX COP.3.IMPERV
dùrùmè-tí   [Ø kó   ŋàŋà]ᵣᴄ ká   sé   á
stump-NRSTR [Ø PNC   like.this] maybe say.3.AUX COP.3.IMPERV
ʃɔ́l   bíí   bè   á   ɔ̀ŋ?
wood.sharp AUT.REF DIST.PAST COP.3.IMPERV what
'Whether that wood is a stump like this, or maybe was it was sharp wood by itself or what was it?'

(4.16)   (MH 2:12:09)
á   kì-tí   [Ø nɔ̀ŋ dáldál-í   hékɔ́   bɛ̀]ᵣᴄ   nà   nɔ̀ŋ
COP.3.IMPERV wood-NRSTR [Ø 3SG hard.stv-adj similar stone CCN 3SG
káráné ŋà=kɔ́ɔ́j-Ø=ó   tùnò   ŋà=kɔ́ɔj-Ø=ó
down   NEG=3.SBJV.go-3.IRR=NEG on.top NEG=3.SBJV-go-3.IRR=NEG
'It is wood, which is strong like stone. And it does not go down; it does not go upside down.'

bá   sé   kì   wà   mà-ìn-á   [Ø kègè   káráné]
place say.3.AUX tree REC.PAST water-LOC-RSTR [Ø thing/object down
ŋà=kɔ́ɔ́j=ó   nɔ̀ŋ ʃíl-Ø   ŋáà
NEG-3.SVJV.go=NEG   3SG stand-3SG.SU.IMPERV here
'The water at the bottom wasn't able to take the wood down (there). It stands here.'

(4.17)   (MH 2:21:3)
ʃíl-Ø   ŋáà dóg   nà   nɔ̀ŋ ʃíl-Ø=ŋà
stand-3sg.SU.IMPERV here forever CCN 3SG stand-3SG.SU.IMPERV=DEF
nà   hàlì [rònɔ́   bèlè]   [hùllì   ká-báns-áná=jè]ₛᵤʙᴏʀᴅ:ᴄʟ
CCN later in.future morning when/if 1SU-get.up-MT.1PL.INC.SU=SUBORD
dáà   bàrì   ísíkán-Ø-é   káráné
truly/MIRR   yesterday approach-3SG.SU.IMPERV-APPL   down
ŋà=b=ùnù
DEM=place=FAR
'It stands here forever, and it stands and the next morning, when we (inc.) wake up, it has submerged down there already! (from its position yesterday).'

(4.18)   (MH 2:26:3)
[hùllì   káwúlókɔ̀rɔ̀ ór-Ø   bɛ̀r=ŋà]ₛᵤʙᴏʀᴅ:ᴄʟ nɔ̀ŋ
when/if Kawulokoro see.IMPERV-3SG.SU.IMPERV spear=SUBORD   3SG

ŋè-Ø-έ káráné-ni
run-3SG.SU.IMPERV-APPL down-RS
'When Kawulok Oro throws the spear, so it is able to go down there.'

(4.19) (MH 2:31:2)
[hùllì ŋè-Ø káráné=ŋà]_SUBORD:CL mà
when/if run-3SG.SU.IMPERV down=DEF] water
kén-Ø-έ tásá ŋáà-jè jɔ̀g mà ìggèà
cut/separate-3SG.SU.IMPERV-APPL apart here-OBL 3PL water 3PL.PN.SP
hój káráné mà àggèà hój tùnò
go.IMPERV.PL down water 3PL.PN.SP go.IMPERV.PL on.top
'When it goes down, the water separates here; this water goes down
   whereas the other water goes up.'

(4.20) (2:37:6)
méá kó-hóɲ-Ø-ná k-èlè ké
now 1SU-come.IMPERV.PL-1PL.INC.SU.IMPERV-SEQ PASS-call.PERV QUOT
mùn dóg=ŋà [zùw-à g=àj]_NP [Ø bè
Mursi.PL forever=DEF people-RSTR PL.PSD=1PL.INC.PSR [Ø DIST.PAST
dɔ́t-ínén-á]_RC ŋàméá k-èlè ké bófú
leave-AP-3PL.SU.PERV] now PASS-call.PERV QUOT Boshu
àggì=nù él tùn-ɔ̀=ŋà
3PL.PN.SP=FAR exist.IMPER.PL up.hill-OBL=DEF
'So now we (inc.) came and are able to be called 'Mursi (pl.)' forever. Our (inc.)
people who remain now are called 'Boshu'. They live on the upper part.'

(4.21) (MH 2:43:0)
á [zùg-tí bárárí]_NP àggè ŋàméá
COP.3.IMPERV people-NRSTR powerful.STV.ADJ 1PL now
mùn=ŋà k-án-Ø bárárí ŋà=kì=tà
Mursi.PL=DEF 1SU-COP-1PL.INC.IMPERV powerful DEM=thing=NEAR
bè nɔ̀ŋ hékɔ́ dùrùmèj ŋàŋà nɔ̀ŋ kɔ́j-Ø
DIST.PAST 3SG similar stump like.this 3SG go.IMPERV-3SG.SU.IMPERV
ké kìɔ̀=ŋà
PNC wood.SG=DEF
'They are powerful (context: spiritually) people. We now are the Mursi. Since
we are powerful (people), that wood just resembles a stump, and it goes to be
'the wood' (Lit. 'it has spirit on it').'

(4.22) (MH 2:47:7)
nɔ̀ŋ mà   ŋà=ám=ó-ni   nɔ̀ŋ á
3SG water NEG.IMPERV=eat-3SG.SU.IMPERV=NEG-RS 3SG COP.3.IMPERV
bɛ̀   nà nɔ̀ŋ á   bɛ̀-tí   [Ø bɛ̀
stone CCN 3SG COP.3.IMPERV stone-NRSTR [Ø DIST.PAST
ŋó-sɛ̀n
fall-MA.3SG.SU.IMPERV
'Water does not eat it. It is stone. And it is a stone which couldn't fall away.'

(4.23) (MH 2:53:9)
[ŋà=hír=ùnù   ké   káwúlókɔ̀rɔ̀=ŋà á   hírí
DEM=man=FAR QUOT Kaulokoro=DEF COP.3.IMPERV man
n=àj]   á   máŋú-i-ni   [á
SG.PSD=1PL.INC.PSR COP.3.IMPERV Mangu-SG-RS COP.3.IMPERV
máŋú-i=ŋa   k-èlì   ke   máŋú=ŋà]_SUBORD:CL á
Mangu-SG=DEF PASS-call.PERV QUOT Mangu=DEF   COP.3.IMPERV
kómórú á   kómórtéséní   á
Komoru COP.3.IMPERV priestly.clan.PL COP.3.IMPERV
ŋà=hír=á-ni   ŋàméá tò-jè   ké-sé-Ø   ké
DEM=man=NEAR-RS now in-OBL 1SU-say-1PL.INC.IMPERV QUOT
'The man called 'the Kawulokoro' is a man of ours is a Mangu! When called the Mangu, they are priests, they are priestly clans. It is this man today, we (inc.) are saying.'

(4.24) (MH 2:58:6)
Káwúlókɔ̀rɔ̀ káwúlókɔ̀rɔ̀ kén-Ø   wárr   kén-Ø
Kaulokoro Kaulokoro cut.3SG.SU.IMPERV Omo.river cut.3SG.SU.IMPERV
wárr   kén-Ø   wárr=ŋa   á
omo.river separate-3SG.SU.PERV omo.river=DEF COP.3.IMPERV
ŋà=hír=á-ni   ŋàméá ká   ŋà=zùg=tà
DEM=man=NEAR-RS now UNCERT DEM=people=NEAR
k-án-Ø   ŋà=zug=tà   ké   mùn=ŋà
1SU-COP-1PL.INC.IMPERV DEM=man=NEAR-RS QUOT mursi.PL=DEF
'"Kawulokoro, Kawulokoro cut Omo River; he cut the Omo River; he cut the Omo River". This man now is from these people. We (inc.) are the Mursi people.'

(4.25) (MH 3:07:6)
á   hírí bárárí   bè   ló[r]ná-ni-Ø
COP.3.IMPERV man powerful DIST.PAST carry.on.shoulder-1PL.OBJ-3.IRR

bófó-jè   ŋà=tán=à   méá bè   á   bè
Bosho-OBL DEM=river.side=NEAR now DIST.PAST COP.3.IMPERV STONE
á   kìɔ́   [hùllì   ké-té   kìɔ́   nɔ̀ŋ
COP.3.IMPERV wood.SG when/if 3.SBJV-be.PERV tree 3SG
*gárá=sò   nɔ̀ŋ   ŋàméá   ŋà=ɓ=ùnù=ŋà]*_{SUBORD:CL}
disappear.3SG.SU.PERV=EMPH 3SG now DEM=place=FAR=DEF

'He was a powerful man; he carried us all (on his shoulders) from Bosho and made us cross now to this side of the river. It is a stone; it is a piece of wood. If it was wood, it would then disappear or it would have been down there now.'

(4.26) (MH 3:14:4)

ŋàméá   ŋà=ɓ=ùnù=ŋà   [hùllì
now   DEM=place=FAR=DEF when/if
*ké-hé-Ø=jè]*_{SUBORD:CL}   *kípáŋ-á*
1SU-go.IMPERV.PL-1PL.INC.SU.IMPERV=SUBORD crocodile-RSTR
*[Ø n=ɛ̀nɛ̀]*_{RC}   *úŋús-Ø-ɔ́*   *ŋà=ɓ=ùnù*
[Ø SG.PSD=3SG.PSR sleep-3SG.SU.IMPERV-VFS DEM=place=FAR
k-ɛ̀lɛ̀   ké   dòl   dòl   bè   dɔ́néj   mùn-ùŋà
PASS-call.PERV QUOT Dòl Dòl DIST.PAST one Mursi.PL-GEN+DEF

'Now when we (inc.) go to that place, a crocodile that sleeps (context: at the wood's place). That place is called Dòl Dòl; it was the same as that of the Mursi (context: the same direction the Mursi once transited through it to occupy their current territory.)'

(4.27) (MH 3:18:6)

*kípáŋí   [hùllì   ké-hé-Ø=jè]*_{SUBORD:CL}   *nɔ̀ŋ*
crocodile when/if 1SU-go.IMPERV.PL-1PL.INC.SU.IMPERV=SUBORD 3SG
í-Ø   ŋàŋà-ni   nà   àggè   [hùllì
exist.IMPERV-3SG.SU.IMPERV like.this-RS CCN 1PL when/if
ké-héj-Ø   nà
1SU-go.IMPERV.PL-1PL.INC.SU.IMPERV CCN
*kɔ́-dɔ́g-Ø   mà=ŋà]*_{SUBORD:CL} *nɔ̀ŋ*
1SU-tread.on-1PL.INC.SU.IMPERV water=DEF   3SG
í-Ø   bì-ò
exist.IMPERV-3SG.SU.IMPERV cow-PL
ŋà=ám-Ø=ó
NEG.IMPERV=eat-3SG.SU.IMPERV=NEG

'The crocodile, when we (inc.) go, he lives (there) that way! And when we (inc.) go and tread on the water, it is there. It does not eat cows.'

(4.28) (MH 3:24:1)
mùnì ŋà=bág-Ø=tó ŋà=kíɲáŋ=nùnù=ŋà
Mursi.SG NEG.IMPERV=eat-3SG.SU=NEG DEM=crocodile=FAR=DEF
ŋà=bè=tùnù [bè gíná] kúúj
DEM=stone=FAR IST.PAST ANA:REF PASS.bring.PERV.PASS.3.SU
k-ójk=è]_SUBORD:CL dùrùmè=ŋà bè bód-ó
PASS-open.PERV.PASS.3.SU=SUBORD stump=DEF DIST.PAST turn.into-3.IRR
ké kíɲáŋá
3.SBJV.be.PERV crocodile
'It does not eat Mursi. The crocodile, when that stone issue is brought and opened, the stump (that stood in the middle of the river) turned into a crocodile.'

(4.29) (MH 3:30:3)
ŋàméá í-Ø ŋà=b=ùnù ké dòl=ŋà dóg ná
now exist-3SG.SU.IMPERV DEM=place=FAR PNC Dòl=DE forever CCN
[hùllì zùwò ké-hé-Ø=jè]_SUBORD:CL ŋàméá
whe/if people 1SU-go.IMPERV.PL-1PL.INC.SU.IMPERV=SUBORD now
[hùllì sé k-áú-t=è]_SUBORD:CL zùw-á [Ø kó
when/if say.3.AUX 1.SBJV-rest.PERV-PL=SUBORD people-RSTR [Ø PNC
kómórté]_RC
Komorte
'Now it lives at that place called the Dòl, forever. And when the people we (inc.) go, now if we (inc.) want to rest—people who were from the Komorte (clan)...'

(4.30) (MH 3:37:6)
kɔ̀ɔ̀d-à kómórté bè kɔ̀ɔ̀d-à máɲú
PASS.write-PASS.3.SU Komorte DIST.PAST PASS.write-PASS.3.SU Mangu
[hùllì ké-hé-Ø=jè]
when/if 1SU-go.IMPERV.PL-1PL.INC.SU.IMPERV=SUBORD
'(or) named as Komorte, were named the Mangu. When we (inc.) come,'

k-íní-Ø bì kú-čúr-ó
1SU-kill-1PL.INC.SU.IMPERV cow 1SU-wash-1PL.EXC.SU.IMPERV
k-íní-Ø bì k-íní-Ø mèdèrè
1SU-kill-1PL.INC.SU.IMPERV cow 1SU-kill-1PL.INC.SU.IMPERV sheep
'we (inc.) slaughter cows, we (inc.) wash, we (inc.) slaughter sheep,...'

TRANSCRIBED TEXTS 633

ké-mé-Ø　　　　　　　　ŋàŋà　　á　　　[bá-á
1SU-do-1PL.INC.SU.IMPERV like.this COP.3.IMPERV place-RSTR
n=àj-ni　　　　　　　　nà　àggè ɓòì
SG.PSD=1PL.INC.PSR-RS CCN 1PL simply/COMPLETIVE
kó-hóɲ-Ø=è]_{SUBORD:CL}　　　　　　　　ɓókónó
1SU-COME.IMPERV.PL-1PL.EXC.SU.IMPERV=SUBORD somewhere
níŋè
not.present
'We (inc.) do like this. It is our (inc.) place/country. We (exc.) all came not from somewhere (else).'

(4.31)　(MH 3:47:0)
ŋà=bà=à　　　　　á　　　[bá-á　　n=àj]_{NP}　　　háŋ
DEM=place=NEAR COP.3.IMPERV place-RSTR SG.PSD=1PL.INC.PSR INTENS
dăkákán nà　áná　kó-hóɲ-Ø　　　　　　　　tii
all　　CCN ANA:REF 1SU-come.IMPERV.PL-1PL.INC.SU.IMPERV DUR
na　ŋàméá kó-hóɲ-Ø
CCN now　1SU-come.IMPERV.PL-1PL.INC.SU.IMPERV
kó-hóɲ+á
1SU-come.IMPERV.PL-MT.1PL.INC.SU.PERV
kó-ɓóns-áná　　　　　　　... ná
1SU-arrive-MT.1PL.INC.SU.IMPERV ... CCN
kó-hóɲ-čá　　　　　　　　　　　　　á　　　dòl ... ná
1SU-come.IMPERV.PL-APPL.1PL.EXC.SU.IMPERV COP.3.IMPERV Dòl ... CCN
kó-hóɲ-Ø　　　　　　　　ŋàŋà
1SU-come.IMPERV.PL-1PL.EXC.SU.IMPERV this.way
'This place is our (inc.) place and we (inc.) kept coming, and now we (inc.) came ... and we (inc) arrived at here. It is Dòl ... so we (inc.) came this way.'

(4.32)　(MH 4:00:6)
ìggè-á　　　[àgg=ìnù　　dɔ̌t-ìnè　　kúrúm-ò=ŋà]_{RC}
3PL.PN.SP-RSTR [3PL.PN.SP=FAR leave-AP.3 Kurum-LOC=DEF
ìggè-á　　　[Ø k-án-Ø
3PL.PN.SP-RSTR [Ø 1SU-COP.IMPERV-1PL.INC.IMPER
ŋà=ìggè=à]_{RC}　　kó-ɓóns-áná=ŋà
DEM=3PL.PN.SP=NEAR] 1SU-arrive-MT.1PL.INC.SU.IMPERV=DEF
á　　　　　ŋàŋà
COP.3.IMPERV this.way
'Those of the others remained at Kurum (place name, see Map 3) whereas those of us arrived at here. It is this way.'

zùg=tùnù   k-èlè   ké   túmúrá=ŋà   jòg   ké
people=FAR PASS-call.PERV QUOT   Tumura=DEF   3PL   3.SBJV.be.PERV
zùg-tí   [Ø bè   sé   á   sú]_RC[4]
people-NRSTR [Ø DIST.PAST say.3.AUX COP.3.IMPERV Aari]

'Those people are called the Tumura (Bodi/Tishena); they are people who were said to be the Aari.'

(4.33) (MH 4:6:8)

zùg-tá   [Ø k-èlè   ké   túmúrá=ŋà]_RC [ɓá-á
people-RSTR [Ø PASS-call.PERV QUOT   Tumura=DEF]   country-RSTR
n=èj]_NP   jòg   á   [sú-á   ɓá-á]   k-èlè
SG.PSD=3PL.PSR 3PL   COP.3.IMPERV   Aari-RSTR place-RSTR PASS.call.PERV
ké   ólkú nà   ŋàméá [hùllì   bú k-èlì-Ø   ké
QUOT   Olku CCN   now   when/if big 1SU-call-1PL.INC.SU.IMPERV QUOT
túmúr   túmúrá   kómórú á   nèŋ
Tumur   Tumur.PL leader COP.3.IMPERV   who?

'The people who are called Tumura, their place, they are Aari from a place called Olku, and now when we (inc.) all call Tumur, Tumura (pl.), who is their leader/priest?'

kómórú   á   gérɓálá   kómórú   á   nèŋ   kómórú
leader   COP.3.IMPERV   Garbhala leader   COP.3.IMPERV   who?   leader
á   gúnálému=ŋà   jòg   á   sú   á
COP.3.IMPERV   Gunalemu=DEF   3PL   COP.3.IMPERV   Aari COP.3.IMPERV
[sú-á   tán-ò-j]_NP
Aari-RSTR side-OBL-GEN

'The leader is Gerbhala. Another leader is who? The leader is Gunulemu. They are the Aari of that side of the river.'

(4.34) (MH 4:10:7)

nà   [hùllì   àggè   mùn   ké-héj-Ø
CCN   when/if   1PL   Mursi.PL   1SU-go.IMPERV.PL-1PL.INC.SU.IMPERV
ŋàŋà   nà   ŋàméá   ké-héj-Ø   nà
like.this   CCN   now   1SU-go.IMPERV.PL-1PL.INC.SU.IMPERV   CCN
k-ódʒ-ónó   ŋàŋà   ŋà=hír=á   ké
1SU-put-MT.1PL.EXC.SU.IMPERV   like.this   DEM=person=NEAR   QUOT

---

[4] Because the Aari are Mursi's eastern neighbour; in the direction where the sun rises.

bímé-j=ŋà
Bime-GEN=DEF
'and when we (inc.) the Mursi (pl.) travelled like this, and now we (inc.) travelled and we (inc.) put out toward this way. The man called the Bime (Nyangatom)'

(4.35) (MH 4:15:4)
kó   ŋà=hírí=nù   k-èlè   ké   túmúrí=ŋà   á
PNC   DEM=person=FAR   PASS.call.PERV   QUOT   Tumuri=DEF   COP.3.IMPERV
*dɔ́néj   [bè   ɓòi   n=ɛ̀j=è]*_{SUBORD:CL}   *sé   á*
one   DIST.PAST all   SG.PSD=3PL.PSR=SUBORD   say.3.AUX   COP.3.IMPERV
sú-ɔ̀-j
hand-OBL-GEN
'and that man called the Tumuri are one. In old times, they are from of the Aari.'

(4.36) (MH 4:24:5)
*nà   [hùllì   kén-ɛ́=ŋà]*_{SUBORD:CL}   *[hùllì   hóɲ-ná*
CCN   when/if   break-3PL.SU.IMPERV=DEF   when   come.IMPERV.PL-SEQ
*dɔ́g-ɛ́   bá   wárr-ò=ŋà]*_{SUBORD:CL}   *nɔ̀ŋ   hír-á*
tread.on-3PL.SU.IMPERV   place   Omo.River-OBL=DEF   3SG   person-RSTR
*[Ø k-èlì   ké   bímé-ì=ŋà]*_{RC}   *nɔ̀ŋ   ɓák-ú   kíɲáŋ*
[Ø PASS-call.PERV   QUOT   Bime-SG=DEF]   3SG   eat-3SG.SU.PERV   crocodile
húŋ-ni
simply-RS
'and when they crossed (context: crossing the Omo River), when they came and tread on a place at the Omo River, he, the man who is called the Bime ate a crocodile!'

(4.37) (MH 4:30:6)
hih!   nà   ìɲè   kíɲáŋ   húŋ   ɓák-ú   kè ɔ̀ŋ   kó
INTERJ!   CCN   2SG   crocodile   simply   eat-3SG.SU.PERV   why?   PNC
ɓásáj   ɓák-ú   kè ɔ̀ŋ   dág-áɲ-Ø
monitor.lizard   eat-3SG.SU.PERV   why?   hit-1SG.OBJ-3SG.SU.IMPERV
hózò-j   aj!   ìɲè   óg   ŋà=tán=ùn-ì
hanger-NOM   INTERJ/oh.no   2SG   go.PERV.IMP   DEM=side=FAR-LOC
'"Hih!" why did you (sg.) eat a crocodile? Also you (sg.) ate a monitor lizard why? Don't say, 'Hunger hit me?! Aj! you (sg.) go to the other side!"'

nà ɲè kɔ́h   wárr=nà   ɲè bág
CCN 2SG farm.PERV.IMP Omo.River=DEF 2SG eat.PERV.IMP
ŋà=gál=ùnù   gèrèŋ-à
DEM=thing.PL=FAR bad-NOMZ
'and farm at the Omo River! Eat (sg.) those bad things!'

ín-á   [Ø kó túmúrí=ŋà̀   nɔ̀ŋ áíw-ón-á
3SG.PN.SP-RSTR   [Ø PNC Tumuri=DEF   3SG come-MT-3SG.SU.PERV
kɔ́b-ú   márà
follow-3SG.SU.PERV   Mara (river.name)
'He who is with the Tumuri, he came and and settled ar Mara.'

(4.38) (MH 4:36:8)
ók-ú   tún-ó-ni   á   súí-á
go-3SG.SU.PERV   river.bed-OBL-RS   COP.3.IMPERV   Aari.SG-RSTR
ólkúí-ní   ŋàméá sé   ké   k-án-í
Olku.SG-LOC   now say.3.AUX QUOT 1SU-COP.IMPERV-1SG.SU.IMPERV
[hír-á   gínbír=ì=ŋà]_NP
person-RSTR   Gimbir-GEN=DEF
'He (the Bime) went to the top of the riverbed; he is Aari of the Olku, now when he says, "I am the Gimbir person".'

(4.39) (MH 4:47:4)
gínbír k-èlì   álí-Ø   nɔ̀ŋ áná   kún-Ø
Genbir PASS.called.PERV say-3SG.IRR   3SG ANA:REF come-3SG.SU.IMPERV
nà kɔ́ɔ́j-Ø   ké   túmúrí=ŋà
CCN 3.SBJV.go-3.IRR 3.SBJV.BE.PERV Tumuri=DEF
'When it is said Gimbir, he says ("Gimbir"), he (the same) came and went to become the Tumuri.'

nɔ̀ŋ [hùllì   kɔ́ɔ́j-Ø   ké   túmúrí=ŋà̀]_SUBORD:CL àhì-á
3SG when/if   3.SBJV.GO-3.IRR QUOT Tumuri=DEF   thing.SG-RSTR
[Ø wà   dóm-à   làléŋ   ké   gèrs-á   bák-é-á]
[Ø REC.PAST insult-NOMZ   emotion   COMPL bad.STV-RSTR   eat-3.IRR-RSTR]
nɔ̀ŋ wóó mà tò-jè   k-èlì-ò   ké   kíɲáŋ   kó
3SG or river in-OBL   PASS.call.PERV-PL? QUOT   crocodile   PNC
básáj   kó   [àhà-í   títí]_NP
monitor.lizard PNC   thing.PL-NRSTR   small:REDUP.PL
'He, whon it is said be Turmuri, the thing who slammed him saying he (Bime) ate bad things from the river, called a crocodile, monitor lizard, and small things.'

(4.40) (MH 4:53:7)
nòŋ [ín-á   hùll-á   kún-o   nà
3SG 3SG.PN.SP-RSTR when-NOMZ come.IMPERV-VSF CCN
kɔ́w-á   táná   tún=è=ŋà]RC   nòŋ bák-ú
follow-3SG.SU.PERV river.side on.top=SUBORD=DEF 3SG eat-3SG.SU.PERV
hírí   húŋ
man simply
'He, the one who while at that time came following the upper part of the river, he also ate a man!'

ɨ̀ɲè hír-á   [Ø [bòrtɔ̀   gíná]   dɔ́m-áɲ-í
2SG person-RTSR [Ø days.ago ANA:REF insult-1SG.OBJ-2SG.SU.PERV
ké   gèrs-ì]RC   ɨ̀ɲè bák-ú   hírí [hùllì
COMPL/QUOT bad.STV-ADJ] 2SG eat-2/3SG.SU.PERV man when
rès-è]SUBORD:CL   ɨ̀ɲè bák-ú   áčúg kè ɔ̀ŋ
die-NOMZ+SUBORD 2SG eat-2/3SG.SU.PERV flesh why?
ŋɔ́kt-é-Ø-ni
fight.PERV-RECIP-3.IRR-RS
'You (sg.) are the person who in the past used to insult me saying, 'bad'; you (sg.) ate dead humans; you (sg.) ate flesh; why? Then they fought each other.'

(4.41) (MH 5:03:0)
aj!   ɨ̀ɲè bák-ú   hírí áčúg=ŋà   ɨ̀ɲè
INTERJ 2SG eat-2/3SG.SU.PERV man flesh=DEF 2SG
tésé=ŋà   dɔ́g-ni   ìnù   kó bímé=ŋà   nòŋ
separate.PERV.IMP=DEF forever-RS 3SG.PN.SP PNC Bime=DEF 3SG
tésé-Ø
separate-3SG.SU.IMPERV
'Since you (sg.) ate human flesh, you (sg.) will be separate forever! He and the Bime, he separated.'

ŋà=6=ùnù   dɔ́g   ŋàméá 6á-á   [Ø kó-tóɲ-á
DEM=place=FAR never now   place-RTSR [Ø 1SU-sleep.PERV-1SG.SU.PERV
bè   gàj]RC ŋàméá bíméj bág-Ø   kíɲáŋ=ŋà
dist.past bush now   Bime eat-3SG.SU.IMPERV crocodile=DEF
'Never ever (came) to the place (there) that I used to sleep in the bush. Now Bime eats crocodile.'

(4.42) (MH 5:10:0)
eej   káŋáj   ɓát-ò   eej   gùʄɛ̀nì   ám-nò   ɓásáj
INTERJ monkey   eat-3.IRR INTERJ Guereza eat-3SG.IRR monitor.lizard
ám-nò   kén-Ø-ni   ŋért-έ
eat-3.IRR cut.down-3.IRR-RS separate.PERV.PL-APPL:RES
'Oh he eats monkey, Oh Guereza, he eats monitor lizard; due to this they broke up.'

(4.43) (MH 5:19:0)
[hùll-á   ŋérn-íné-á=ŋà]_SUBORD:CL   zùw-á   [Ø ɓè
when-RSTR separate-RECIP-3PL.SU.PERV=DEF   people-RSTR   [Ø DIST.PAST
dɔ̃nén-á]_RC jòg tón-nè   húŋ   té   míró
one-RSTR]   3PL break.up.PERV-RECIP.3   simply COP.3.PERV enemy
kón   té   ɓàlágárá-ɲá
one.INDEF   COP.3.PERV enemy/foe-PL
'While they were they were separate, they were one people. They separated from one another, and became enemies of their own (people); they became foes.'

ŋàméá [číg-ín-á   n=èj]_NP   [hùllì
now   laugh-N.S-RTSR   SG.PSD=3PL.PSR   when/if
číg-έ=jè]_SUBORD:CL   jòg sén-έ   ké
laugh.IMPERV-3PL.SU.IMPERV=SUBORD 3PL say-3PL.SU.IMPERV QUOT
hee   hee   číg-ín   jòg á   dɔ̃néj
INTERJ INTERJ laugh-N.S   3PL COP.3.IMPERV one
'Now for their laugh, when they laugh, they say, "Hee! Hee! (laugh)". (Their) laugh is one.'

(4.44) (MH 5:32:4)
ŋàméá [kómórú-á bímé-j]_NP té   [kómórú-á   túmúr-uɲ|_NP
now   leader-RSTR Bime-GEN   COP.3.PERV   leader-RSTR Tumur-GEN
[hùllì ɓè   hóɲ   ɓòì-nɛ=je]   á
when/if DIST.PAST come.IMPERV.PL all-??=SURBORD   COP.3.IMPERV
dɔ̃néj í-Ø   ŋàŋà
one   to.be-3SG.SU.IMPERV like.that
'Now there is a leader of Bime, and there is a leader of Tumuri. While they came, they were one. It is like this.'

(4.45) (MH 5:50:9)
í-Ø   bè   àggè bè   ŋà=lɔ̀g=tùnù=ŋà
to.be-3SG.SU.IMPERV DIST.PAST 1PL DIST.PAST DEM=issue=FAR=DEF
ká   jòg bè   mès-ò   dàdá-ù   bè
maybe 3PL DIST.PAST do-3PL.IRR father.PERT.1.PSR-NOM DIST.PAST
kíŋíɲ   bè
long.ago DIST.PAST
'It is (said) to be the case that maybe our fathers used to do it in ancient times.'

nà   hùllì   kòná=ŋà   [jòg [kònè
CCN when/if grandfather.PERT.1.PSR=DEF 3PL grandfather.PERT.SG.3.PSR
n=èj]ₙₚ   bì-ò   zùw-á   [Ø ké   hámár]ᵣᴄ   dág-Ø
SG.PSD=3PL.PSR cow-PL people-RSTR [Ø QUOT Hamar] hit-3PL.IRR
hózò-j   hóɲ   íw-án-é   [bì-ò-á
hunger-NOM come.IMPERV.PL take-MT-3PL.SU.IMPERV COW-PL-RSTR
mùn-ùɲ]ₙₚ   nà   héj-é   húŋ
Mursi-GEN CCN go.IMPERV.PL-3PL.SU.IMPERV simply
'And when our grandfather, their grandfather, cows, the people called 'Hamar were hit by hunger' came, they took the cows of the Mursi and went (away).'

(4.46) (MH 6:00:2)
[hùllì   íw-áná   [bì-ò-á   g=àɲù]ₙₚ
when/if take-MT.3SG.SU.IMPERV COW-PL-RSTR PL.PSD=1SG.PSR
hámárí-ó   kɔ́ɔ́-ɛ́=ŋà]ₛᵤʙᴏʀᴅ:ᴄʟ   àɲè [éró-á   g=àɲù]ₙₚ
Hamar.SG-NOM 3.SBJV.go-APPL=DEF 1SG childen-RSTR PL.PSD=1PL.PSR
ám-ɛ́   ɔ̀ŋ   áná-ni   nɔ̀ŋ [túrè rók-ú   húŋ]
eat-3PL.SU.IMPERV what? ANA:REF-RS 3SG rifle fire-3SG.SU.PERV simply
[túrɛ́ rók-ú   húŋ] [túrè rók-ú   húŋ]
rifle fire-3SG.SU.PERV simply rifle make.noise-3SG.SU.PERV simply
'If he takes my cattle, if Hamar takes then, what will my children eat? Due to this he started firing a gun ... he fired and fired ...'

(4.47) (MH 6:09:5)
hír-á   [Ø ké   ké   bímé-j   nɔ̀ŋ dàà   ɓá
man-RSTR [Ø 3.SBJV.be.PERV QUOT Bime-NOM 3SG truly/MIRR place
húŋ-ni   nɔ̀ŋ áíw-ó   nà   íw-á   [bì-ò-á
simply-RS 3SG come.PERV.SG-MT CCN take-3SG.SU.PERV COW-PL-RSTR
mùn-ùɲ]ₙₚ   húŋ
Mursi-GEN simply
'A man that became Bime in his place, came and just took the cattle of Mursi.'

nɔ̀ŋ bímé-j   kó   túmúrí   jòg   á   dṍnéj   háŋ
3SG Bime-SG PNC Tumuri 3PL COP.3.IMPERV one   INTENS
'He who is Bime and Tumuri, they are one.'

(4.48) (MH 6:14:9)
[nɔ̀ŋ kén-Ø-ɛ́=jè]_SUBORD:CL   túmúrí dàà   ɓá
3SG stub-3SG.SU.IMPERV-APPL=SUBORD Tumuri truly/MIRR place
húŋ   ʃùànéŋ   íw-á   bì-ò   àg-á
simply again   take-3SG.SU.PERV   cow-PL   cook-3SG.SU.PERV
ɓág-á   ɓòì   juuu!
eat-3SG.SU.PERV all INTERJ
'He stubbed the Tumuri in turn! Again he just took cattle, cooked and ate them all. Juuu!'

(4.49) (MH 6:22:2)
ŋà=zùg=tà   á   dṍnéj=è   á   hózò-ni
DEM=people=NEAR COP.3.IMPERV one=EMPH COP.3.IMPERV hunger-RS
[hùlì   méá hóp-ná   íw-án-ɛ́   [àh-á
when/if now come.IMPERV.PL-SEQ   take-MT-3PL.SU.IMPERV   thing-RSTR
zùw-òɲ]_NP   mát-áná   àhà-ná   g=àj]_NP
people-GEN drink-MT.3SG.SU.PERV thing.PL-RSTR PL.PSD=1PL.INC.PSR
zùw-á   [Ø bè   ká-tál-á]_RC
people-RSTR [Ø DIST.PAST 3.SBJV-buy-3PL.SU.PERV]
'They are one people in the first place. It is (because of) hunger when they now come and take away the things of our (inc.) people; drink our (inc.) things; the things people had bought …'

(4.50) (MH 6:27:8)
[méá ŋàméá ŋà=bérgú=à=ŋà]   [nɔ̀ŋ bíméj]   nɔ̀ŋ hír-á
now (today) DEM=year=NEAR=DEF 3SG Bime.SG 3SG man-RSTR
[Ø tánij-té]_RC   té   bíméj sòŋ nɔ̀ŋ túmúrí ŋàméá
[Ø difficult.STV.ADJ-NRSTR] COP.3.PERV Bime.SG only 3SG Tururi now
nɔ̀ŋ tésé   [ɓá-á   n=ɛ̀nɛ̀]_NP   lài   húŋ
3SG sit.PERV.APPL place-RSTR SG.PSD=3SG.PSR silent simply
'Nowaday more than ever, he the Bime is a person who became difficult (is) only Bime. Tumuri has now sat down in his place, just silently.'

(4.51) (MH 6:38:1)
bíméj   kó   túmúrí   jòg ʃìg-ìnè   tùg-í   ŋànìjè áná
Bime PNC Tumuri 3PL listen-RECIP.3 mouth-PL however ANA:REF

ʃígt-é-á   tùg-í-ná   ké-té
listen.PERV-RECIP-3PL.SU.PERV mouth-PL- 3.SBJV-COP.3.PERV
[zùw-á   dõnén-á]_NP   nà   jòg   ká-ták-t-é
people-RSTR one-RSTR CCN 3PL 3.SBJV-know-PL.PERV-APPL:RES
'Bime and Tumuri, they understand one another's language. However, since they understand each other's language they became one people and know each other.'

(4.52) (MH 6:53:2)
ŋànìjè   nòŋ   bímé   ók-ú   ké   tóŋ-Ø-é
however 3SG Bime go-3SG.SU.PERV COMPL/PNC stab.PERV-3.IRR-APPL
bà-ì-ni   mùnì   tód-ú   húŋ]   [túmúrí
place-LOC-RS Mursi.SG stab.PERV-3SG.SU.PERV simply tumuri
tód-ú   húŋ]   [hámárí bá   tód-ú
stab.PERV-3SG.SU.PERV simply Hamar place stab.PERV-3SG.SU.PERV
húŋ]   [kéràj tód-ú   húŋ]   [ŋídíní
simply Keray stab.PERV-3SG.SU.PERV simply Ngidi
tód-ú   húŋ]
stab.PERV-3SG.SU.PERV simply
'However, he, Bime was stabbing the Mursi; he stabs the Tumuri; he stabs the Hamar; he stabs Keray; he stabs Ngidi.'

bíméj nòŋ ók-ú   ké   toŋkaj⁵ méá nòŋ ók-ú
Bime 3SG go-3SG.SU.PERV COMPL sorcerer now 3SG go-3SG.SU.PERV
ké   hírí ódénéí-ni   nòŋ té-í   [bá-á   [tán-á
COMPL man strong.ADJ-RS 3SG COP.3.PERV-SG place-RSTR side-RSTR
sú'dán-ùŋ]_NP]_NP ná   nòŋ té   hírí ódénéí   ŋà=bà=nù
Sudan-GEN CCN 3SG COP.3.PERV man strong.ADJ DEM=place=FAR
'Bime went to become a sorcerer. Now, he went to be a strong man, and on the other side of Sudan, he is a strong man there.'

(4.53) (MH 6:55:9)
kó   túmúrá ŋànì   ŋà=gán-é=ó   á
PNC Tumura PERG.PERV NEG=know-3PL.SU.IMPERV=NEG COP.3.IMPERV
ŋàŋà
like.this
'They don't agree with Tumura. It is like this.'

---

5 A loan word from Amharic, tənkʰʷay.

(4.54) (MH 7:09:9)
àggè [kèn-á   g=àw]   ká-ɓág-ó   àggè-ù
1PL tree.PL-RSTR PL.PSD=1PL.EXC.PSR 1SU-eat-1PL.EXC.SU.PERV 1PL-NOM
mùn-ù   [bá-á   n=àw]ₙₚ   mùn-ùɲ]ₙₚ [kì-á
Mursi-NOM place-RSTR SG.PSD=1PL.EXC.PSR Mursi-GEN tree.SG-RTSR
n=àw]ₙₚ   ká-ɓág-ó   kì-á
SG.PSD=1PL.EXC.PSR 1SU-eat-1PL.EXC.SU.PERV tree-RSTR
[Ø k-èlè   ké   gúmúɲój]ᴿᶜ [ké   lúrú=jè]⁶
[Ø PASS-CALL.PERV QUOT Gumunyoy] [PNC/PREP second.harvest-OBL
ígís-ò   ɓùrá   á   gòlòɲ-ì
ripe-3.IRR fruit.PL COP.3.IMPERV red.STV-ADJ

'Our (exc.) trees that we (exc.) the Mursi eat in our (exc.) country of Mursi. Our (exc.) tree which we (exc.) eat is a tree called the Gumunyoy. At second harvest time, it ripens/gives red fruits.'

(4.55) (MH 7:17:2)
nà   [hùllì   gúmúɲój   sé   ká-gár-Ø=ŋà]ˢᵁᴮᴼᴿᴰ:ᶜᴸ
CCN when/if Gumunyoy say.3.AUX 3.SBJV-disappear.PERV-3.IRR=DEF
móìzój   ígís-ò   ɓùrá   á   gòlòɲ-ì   čùànéŋ
Moyzoy ripe-3.IRR fruit.PL COP.3.IMPERV red.STV-ADJ   again
té   ɓóɲ-à   ràmàn kì-tí   [Ø ké   gàwì]ᴿᶜ
COP.3.PERV reach-NOMZ two   tree-NRSTR [Ø QUOT Gawi]
íhé-ni
exist.IMPERV.SG-RS

'And when Gumunyoy is about to dissapear, Moyzo starts ripening red fruits. Again, it became ripe a second time. There is a tree which is called Gawi.'

(4.56) (MH 7:28:2)
ígís-ò   k-ám-nó   ɓóɲ-à   á
ripe-3.IRR 1SU-eat.IMPERV-1PL.EXC.SU.IMPERV reach-NOMZ COP.3.IMPERV
sízzí kì-tí   [Ø k-èlè   ké   àɲùj]ᴿᶜ⁷ íhé-ni
three tree-NRTSR [Ø PASS-CALL.PERV QUOT Anyuy   exist.IMPERV.SG-RS
ígís-ò   k-ám-nó   ɓóɲ-à   á
ripe-3.IRR 1SU-eat.IMPERV-1PL.EXC.SU.IMPERV reach-NOMZ COP.3.IMPERV
wùʃ   kì-tí   [Ø k-èlè   ké   dómógí]ᴿᶜ íhé
four tree-NRSTR [Ø PASS-call.PERV QUOT Domogi   exist.IMPERV.SG

---

6 Period of the second sorghum harvest (it is *luguru* in Chai).

7 *Doum palm* (Hyphaene thebaica).

TRANSCRIBED TEXTS

'It ripens; we (exc.) eat. It is a third reaching. There is a tree which is called Anyuy. It ripens; we (exc.) eat. It is a fourth reaching/time. There is a tree which is called Domogi.'

(4.57) (MH 7:35:6)
égís-ò ká-ɓát-ó ɓón-à á háánán
ripe-3.IRR 1SU-eat-1PL.EXC.SU.IMPERV reach-NOMZ COP.3.IMPERV five
kì-tí [Ø k-èlì ké ràgàj]ₙₚ⁸ thé égís-ò
tree-NRSTR [Ø PASS-call.PERV QUOT Ragay] exist.IMPERV.SG ripe-3.IRR
ká-ɓát-ó ɓón-à á íllé
1SU-eat-1PL.EXC.SU.IMPERV reach-NOMZ COP.3.IMPERV six
'It ripens; we (exc.) eat. It is a fifth time. There is a tree which is called Ragay. It ripens; we (exc.) eat. It is a sixth time.'

(4.58) (MH 7:44:7)
kèn-á [Ø ká-ɓág-á mùn-ù háŋ
tree.PL-RSTR [Ø 1SU-eat-1PL.INC.SU.IMPERV Mursi.PL-NOM INTENS
bímé-j ɓát-ò, túmúrí ɓát-ò, káʃáj ɓát-ò,
Bime-SG eat-3SG.IRR Tumuri.SG eat-3SG.IRR Kasha.SG eat-3SG.IRR
mùnì ɓát-ò jòg ŋà=kèn=ùnù ŋàméá kó íllé=ŋà
Mursi.SG eat-3SG.IRR 3PL DEM=tree.PL=FAR now PNC six=DEF
'All the trees that the Mursi (pl.) eat; Bime eats, Tumuri eats, Kashay eats, Mursi eats; these are the six trees I mentioned earlier.'

(4.59) (MH 7:50:0)
jòg [zùwò ɓág-έ dákákán kó ìggè=jè]ₛᵤʙₒᵣᴅ:ᴄʟ
3PL [people eat-3PL.SU.IMPERV all PNC 3pl.PN.SP=SUBORD
kùčùmbà⁹ [hùllì ár-í=jè]ₛᵤʙₒᵣᴅ:ᴄʟ ám-ò-ɔ̀ á
Amhara.PL if see.PERV-3PL.IRR=SUBORD eat-3.IRR-VFS COP.3.IMPERV
kèn-í čàll-ì ɓòì
tree.PL-NRSTR good.STV-ADJ all
'They, all people eat including those, the Amhara. If they see (them), they eat. These are very sweet trees.'

---

8 Tamarindus indica L. It is used to treat stomachaches, a concentrated preparation of fruit of the *ragaj* fruit mixed with water and drunk.
9 The term may also be used to refer to people who are believed to be from highland areas of the country.

(4.60) (MH 7:59:8)
á   kèn-í   [Ø ŋàméá ká-ɓág-Ø]
COP.3.IMPERV tree.PL-RTSR [Ø now 1SU-eat-1PL.INC.SU.IMPERV
àggè-ù=jè]_SUBORD:CL/RC á   ŋáà íllé kèn-á
1PL-NOM=SUBORD   COP.3.IMPERV here six tree.PL-RSTR
[Ø k-ám-á   háŋ]_RC á   íllé
[Ø 1SU-eat-1PL.INC.SU.PERV INTENS] COP.3.IMPERV six

'These are trees that we (inc.) now eat. There are six here. The trees that we (inc.) all eat. There are six.'

ŋànìjè   kì-tí   [Ø k-èlè   ké   gègý̀j]_RC íhé-ni
however tree-NRSTR [Ø PASS-call.PERV QUOT Gegiy] exist.IMPERV.SG-RS
[hùllì égís-Ø=è]_SUBORD:CL   ɓùrá   á
whe/if be.ripe-3SG.SU.IMPERV=SUBORD fruit.PL COP.3.IMPERV
régéj   ká-ɓág-Ø   ʃó   wáŋ   kú-čú
pink.STV.ADJ 1SU-eat-1PL.INC.SU.IMPERV sweet INTENS 3.SBJV-suck.PERV
nà   ká-mát-o
CCN 3.SBJV-drink-3.IRR

'There is also a tree, which is called Gegiy. When its ripens fruits, it is pink. We (inc.) eat; it is very sweet. It can be juiced and drank.'

(4.61) (MH 8:07:9)
á   ìssàbàj kèn-á   [Ø ká-ɓág-á
COP.3.IMPERV seven tree.PL-RSTR [Ø 1SU-eat-1PL.INC.SU.PERV
mùn-ù]_RC   kì-tí   [Ø k-èlì   ké   dèrèj]
Mursi.PL-NOM] tree-NRSTR [Ø PASS-call.PERV quot Dherey]
íhé
exist.IMPERV.SG

'These are seven trees that we (inc.) the Mursi eat. There is a tree called Dhegey.'

(4.62) (MH 8:16:2)
[hùllì   k-ídó́-Ø=jè]_SUBORD:CL   á   ísòŋ
when/if 1SU-add-1PL.INC.SUIMPERV=SUBORD COP.3.IMPERV how.many
íssé kèn-á   [Ø ká-ɓág-á   mùn-ù
eight tree.PL-RSTR [Ø 1SU-eat-1PL.INC.SU.PERV Mursi.PL-NOM
àggì=nù   kì-tí   [Ø ké   górsàj]_RC íhé   ɓùrá
3P.PN.SP=FAR tree-NRSTR [Ø QUOT Gorsay] exist.IMPERV.SG fruit.PL
á   ɓìlèì   [ígís-Ø=e]_SUBORD:CL
COP.3.IMPERV yellow be.ripe-3SG.SU.IMPERV=SUBORD

'When we (inc.) add, how many? Eight. Those are trees that we (inc.) the Mursi eat. There is a tree which is called Gorsay. Its fruit is yellow when it ripens.'

(4.63) (MH 8:24:6)
hùll-à ŋàméá ŋà=kì=tà kó máŋgói=ŋà]_SUBORD:CL
when-NOMZ now DEM=tree=NEAR PNC Mango=DEF
k-ám ŋàŋà-ni
PASS-eat.PERV like.this-RS
'There is now a Mango-like tree. It is eaten like this.'

(4.64) (MH 8:34:4)
kènɔ́ á ísɔ̀ŋ? sàkkàl kèn-á
tree.PL COP.3.IMPERV how.many nine tree.PL-RSTR
[Ø ká-bág-á mùn-ù]_RC á sàkkàl kóná
[Ø 1SU-eat-1PL.INC.SU.PERV Mursi.PL-NOM] COP.3.IMPERV nine another
kì-tí [Ø k-èlè ké kébúrkói]_RC
tree.SG-NRSTR [Ø PASS-call.PERV QUOT Keburkoy]
'How many trees? Nine. Trees that we (inc.) the Mursi eat are nine. Another One is a tree which is called Keburkoy.'

[hùllì égís-Ø=è]_SUBORD:CL bùrá á
when/if be.ripe-3SG.SU.IMPERV=SUBORD fruit.PL COP.3.IMPERV
gìdàŋ-ì kà-bàt-ò-ni
brown.STV-ADJ PASS-eat-PASS.3SU-RS
'When it ripens, it has a brown colour. It is eaten.'

(4.65) (MH 8:39:6)
ká-bá-Ø dàài [kó dàdá=jè]_SUBORD:CL [kó
1SU-eat-1PL.INC.SU.IMPERV all PNC father.PERT.SG.1.PSR=SUBORD PNC
màmà=jè]_SUBORD:CL [kó éro=jè]_SUBORD:CL jòg
mother.PERT.SG.1.PSR=SUBORD PNC children=SUBORD 3PL
ká-bá-Ø dákákán hírí márí nèŋ [hùllì
3.SBJV-eat-3.IRR all person refuse-3SG.SU.IMPERV who? when/if
k-ídó-Ø=jè]_SUBORD:CL kènɔ́ á ísɔ̀ŋ?
1SU-add-1PL.INC.SU.IMPERV=SUBORD tree.PL COP.3.IMPERV how.many?
'We (inc.) all eat it, my father, my mother, the children, they all eat it. What man could refuse it? When we (inc.), add them (up), how many trees are there?'

(4.66)　(MH 8:49:9)

tómón kóná　á　　　　kì-tí　　　　[Ø ké　lòmáj]_RC^10
ten　another COP.3.IMPERV tree.SG-NRSTR [Ø QUOT Lomay
ká-ɓág-áná　　　　　　　　ɓòì　　　kɔ̀-čɔ̀ɓɔ̀s-áná　　　　　nɔ̀ŋ
1SU-eat-MT.1PL.INC.SU.IMPERV COMPLETIVE PASS-suck-MT.PASS.3.SU 3SG
káŋáj　ɓát-ò　àggè mùnì　k-ám-nó　　　　　　　hírí
monkey eat-3.IRR 1PL Mursi.SG 1SU-eat-1PL.EXC.SU.IMPERV person
márí-Ø　　　　　níŋè　　ká-ɓá-Ø　　　　　　dákákán
refuse-3SG.SU.IMPERV not.present 1SU-eat-1PL.INC.SU.IMPERV all

'Ten. Another one is a tree, which is called Lomay. We (inc.) eat it or it is sucked. Monkeys eat it. We Mursi (exc.) eat it. There is no person who refuses it. We (inc.) all eat it.'

(4.67)　(MH 8:55:0)

ŋànìjè　ɓá　kó　ɓùràj　[hùllì　ʤààrì=ŋà ló-Ø
however place PNC fruit.SG when/if leg=DEF has-3SG.SU.IMPERV
ŋɔ̀dɔ̀rì=jè]_SUBORD:CL　ɓá　kó　ɓùràj　k-ós-ó
wound=SUBORD　place PNC fruit.SG 1SU-roast-1PL.EXC.SU.IMPERV
gó-jè　nà　ká-dág-é　　　　　　　　kó　ŋɔ̀dɔ̀rì　ŋàŋà
fire-OBL CCN 1SU-strike-1PL.INC.SU.IMPERV-COM PNC wound like.this
ŋànì　nɔ̀ŋ　ŋɔ̀dɔ̀rì　ígís-ò-ni
still 3SG wound ripe-3.IRR-RS

'However, with the fruit, when there is wound, we (ex.) roast it on the fire and strike the wound with it like this.'

(4.68)　(MH 9:03:9)

á　　　　　[zùw-á　　[mádání-á　　n=àj]_NP]_NP
COP.3.IMPERV people-RSTR medicine-RSTR SG.PSD=1PL.INC.PSR
[mádání-á　　n=àj]_NP　　kà-dâg-čà　　　　　　　　ŋɔ̀dɔ̀rì
medicine-RSTR SG.PSD=1PL.INC.PSR PASS-hit-1PL.INC.SU.APPL:COM wound
á　　　　　lòmáj hékɔ́　ŋà=mádání=tá　　[Ø ŋàméá
COP.3.IMPERV Lomay similar DEM=medicine=NEAR [Ø now
áʤ-Ø-á　　　　　　　　　　máŋísí-ó]_RC
give.IMPERV-3SG.SU.IMPERV-RSTR Government-NOM

'Our (inc.) medicine. (When) we (inc.) are struck (with) a wound, it is Lomay; similar with the medicine that the Government is giving now.'

10　Ximenia americana—The small, yellow-orange succulent fruits are edible. The oil from the fruit kernel is applied to flesh wounds to prevent infections, and it is also used by girls

nà   ŋàméá ká-dáfi-Ø-é   bá   kón
CCN now   1SU-do-1PL.INC.SU.IMPERV-APPL:COM   place   one.INDEF
hékɔ́
similar
'And now we (inc.) do similar if one has it (a wound).'

(4.69) (MH 9:11:4)
ŋà=kì=tà   á   [mádání-á   n=àɲ]_NP
DEM=thing=NEAR   COP.3.IMPERV medicine-RSTR   SG.PSD=1PL.INC.PSR
mùn-ùɲ]_NP á   lòmáj   sɔ̀ŋ
Mursi-GEN   COP.3.IMPERV   Lomay   only
'This tree is our (inc.) medicine of the Mursi. It is Lomay only.'

(4.70) (MH 9:17:6)
kó   kì-tí   [Ø k-èlì   ké   bólúíté]_RC[11] [hùllì
PNC   tree-NRSTR [Ø PASS-call.PERV   QUOT   Boluyte   when/if
kù-dùdùg   gó-ì=jè=ŋà]_SUBORD:CL   kɔ́ɔ́j-Ø   ké
PASS-look.up.PERV   fire-LOC=SUBORD=DEF   3.SBJV.go-3.IRR 3.SBJV.be.PERV
kɔ̀rɔ̀-ì-ni   ká-dág-Ø   ŋɔ̀dɔ̀rì
black.STV-ADJ-RS   1SU-hit-1PL.INC.SU.IMPERV   wound
'With a tree, that is called Boluyte, it will be inserted into the fire and when it becomes black, we (inc.) hit the wound.'

[hùllì   k-ídó-Ø=jè]_SUBORD:CL   té   ísɔ̀ŋ
when/if   1SU-add-1PL.INC.SU.IMPERV=SUBORD   COP.3.PERV   how.many?
tɔ̀mɔ̀n.   kó   tɔ̀mɔ̀n kó   dɔ́néj?
ten.   PNC   ten   PNC   one?
'When we (inc.) added (them up), it became how many? Ten or eleven?'

(4.71) (MH 9:32:8)
bórí   nɔ̀ŋ kì-tí   [Ø bórí]_RC nɔ̀ŋ   á   kì-á
Bori   3SG tree.SG-NRSTR [Ø Bori]   3SG   COP.3.IMPERV   tree-RSTR
[Ø k-àm-à   ɲɲ   [hùllì
[Ø PASS-eat.PASS.3.SU   INTERJ   when/if

---

who have their ears or lips pierced, for preparing cattle and goatskins for clothing, and in women's medicine (as a contraceptive).

11   Datura stramonium L.—when bitten and kept in the mouth, the root of Boluyte alleviates molar toothache.

k-ídő-Ø=jè]_{SUBORD:CL}   *á*   *tòmòn kó ràmàn*
1SU-add-1PL.INC.SU.IMPERV=SUBORD COP.3.IMPERV ten   PNC two

'Bori, it is a tree known as Bori. It is a tree, which is eaten/edible. Okay! When we (inc.) add them, there are twelve.'

kóná   á   bórí tòmòn kó ràmàn kóná   sèrtój tòmòn
another COP.3.IMPERV Bori ten PNC two another Sertoy ten
kó   sízzí
PNC three

'Another is Bori. Twelve. Another is Sertoy. Thirteen.'

Bibliography

Abbink, J. (1991). the deconstruction of "tribe": ethnicity and politics in Southwestern Ethiopia. *Journal of Ethiopian Studies* 24: 1–21.

Abbink, J. (1992). comments on "disentangling the two languages called 'Suri'". *Occasional Papers in the Study of Sudanese Languages* 7: 49–69.

Abbink, J., Bryant, M. and Bambu, D. (2013). *Suri orature*. Köln: Rüdiger Köppe Verlag

Aikhenvald, Alexandra Y. (2003). *typological parameters for the study of clitics*. In Dixon, R.M.W. and Aikhenvald, Alexandra Y. (eds.). *Word: a cross-linguistic typology*. Cambridge: Cambridge University Press. Pp. 42–78.

Aikhenvald, Alexandra Y. (2007a). "typological distinctions in word-formation", pages 1–65 of *Language Typology and Syntactic Description, Second Edition, vol. III*. Cambridge: Cambridge University Press

Aikhenvald, Alexandra. Y. (2010). *Imperatives and Commands*. Oxford: Oxford University Press.

Aikhenvald, Alexandra. Y. (2011). speech reports: a cross-linguistic perspective. In A.Y. Aikhenvald & R.M.W. Dixon (eds.), *Language at large. Essays on Syntax and Semantics* (pp. 290–326). Leiden: Brill.

Aikhenvald, Alexandra Y. (2015). *The art of grammar*. Oxford: Oxford University Press.

Aikhenvald, Alexandra. Y. (2019). *expressing 'possession': motivations, meanings, and forms*. In Lars Johanson, Lidia Federica Mazzitelli and Irina Nevskaya (eds.). *Possession in Languages of Europe and North and Central Asia*. John Benjamins. 7–25. https://doi.org/10.1075/slcs.206.02aik

Arensen, Jonathan E. (1988). names in the life cycles of the Murle. *Journal of the Anthropological Society of the Oxford* 19: 125–130.

Bender, M. Lionel (1971). the languages of Ethiopia: A new lexicostatistic classification and some diffusion. *Anthropological Linguistics* 13(5): 165–288.

Bender M. Lionel. (1997). *The Nilo-Saharan languages: A comparative essay*. Munich: Lincom Europa.

Bourg de Bozas, R. de (1903). d'Addis Abbaba au Nil Par le Lac Rodolphe. *La Geographie* Vol. 7:91–112.

Brinton, L.J. and Traugott, E.C. (2005). *Lexicalization and Language Change*. Cambridge: Cambridge University Press.

Bryan, M. (1945). a linguistic no-man's land: the Sudan-Ethiopian border. *Africa* 15(4): 188–205.

Bryan, M. (1968). the *N/*K languages of Africa. *Journal of African Languages*: 169–217.

Bryant, M. (1999). *Aspect of Tirmaga Grammar*. Unpublished MA Thesis. University of Texas at Arlington.

Bryant, M. (2007). *-Ni* as a marker of discourse resolution in Tirmaga. In: Doris Payne &

Mechthild Reh (eds) *Advances in Nilo-Saharan Linguistics*. Cologne: Rüdiger Köppe Verlag, pp. 41–58.

Bryant, M. (2013). suri language. In Jon Abbink, Michael Bryant & Daniel Bambu (eds.), *Suri orature: Introduction to the society, language and oral culture of the Suri people (Southwest Ethiopia)*, 23–99. Köln: Rüdiger Köppe Verlag.

Bybee, Joan, R. Perkins and W. Pagliuca (1994). *The Evolution of Grammar. Tense, Aspect and Modality in the Languages of the World*. Chicago: University of Chicago Press.

Cavendish, H.S. (1898). through Somaliland and around the South of Lake Rudolf, *Geographical Journal* 11: 372–396.

Comrie, B. (1976). *Aspect*. Cambridge, UK: Cambridge University Press.

Creissels, D. (2009). the construct form of nouns in African Languages, In Austin, P.K., Bond, O., Charette, M., Nathan, D., & Sells, P. (eds.) *Proceedings of Conference on Language Documentation and Linguistic Theory 2*. SOAS, London, pp. 73–82.

Crystal, David (2008). *A Dictionary of Linguistics and Phonetics*, 6th ed. Blackwell

Dimmendaal, Gerrit J. (1983). *The Turkana language*. Dordrecht, The Netherlands: Foris.

Dimmendaal, G.J. (1998). a syntactic typology of Surmic from an areal and historical-comparative point of view, in Dimmendaal, G.J. & Last, M. (eds.) *Surmic Languages and Cultures. Nilo-Saharan Linguistic Analyses and Documentation*, Köln: Rüdiger Köppe Verlag, pp. 35–81. Dimmendaal, G.J. (2000). 'number marking and noun categorization in Nilo-Saharan Languages'. *Anthropological Linguistics* 42(2): 214–261.

Dimmendaal, G.J. (2001). 'language shift and morphological convergence in the Nilotic area', *Sprache und Geschichte in Afrika* 16/17:83–124.

Dimmendaal, G.J. (2010). differential object marking in Nilo-Saharan. *Journal of African Languages and Linguistics*, 31(1): 13–46.

Dimmendaal, Gerrit J. (2011). some ecological properties of language development. In: Dimmendaal, Gerrit J. (ed.) *Historical Linguistics and the Comparative Study of African Languages*. Amsterdam: John Benjamins Publishing Company, pp. 347–372.

Dimmendaal, Gerrit J. 2018. on stable and unstable features in Nilo-Saharan. In Helga Schröder and Prisca Jerono (eds.), *Nilo-Saharan Issues and Perspectives*, pp. 9–23. Cologne: Rüdiger Köppe.

Diessel, Holger (1999). *Demonstratives: Form, Function and Grammaticalization*. Amsterdam: John Benjamins.

Dixon, R.M.W. (1994). *Ergativity*. Cambridge: Cambridge University Press.

Dixon, R.M.W. and Aikhenvald. Alexandra Y. (2000). 'introduction', pp. 1–29 of *Changing valency: Case studies in transitivity*, edited by R.M.W. Dixon and Alexandra Y. Aikhenvald. Cambridge: Cambridge University Press.

Dixon, R.M.W. and Aikhenvald, Alexandra Y. (2003). *word: a typological framework*. In Dixon, R.M.W. and Aikhenvald, Alexandra Y. (eds.). *Word: a cross-linguistic typology*. Cambridge: Cambridge University Press. Pp. 1–41.

Dixon, R.M.W. (2004). "adjective classes in typological perspective", pp. 1–49 of *Adjective Classes: A Cross-linguistic Typology*, edited by R.M.W. Dixon and A.Y. Aikhenvald. Oxford: Oxford University Press.

Dixon, R.M.W. (2006). "complement clauses and complementation strategies in typological perspective", pp. 1–48 of *Complementation*, edited by R.M.W. Dixon and A.Y. Aikhenvald. Cambridge: Cambridge University Press

Dixon, R.M.W. (2010a). *Basic Linguistic Theory Volume 1: Methodology*. Oxford University Press.

Dixon, R.M.W. (2010b). *Basic Linguistic Theory Volume 2: Grammatical Topics*. Oxford University Press.

Dixon, R.M.W. (2012). *Basic Linguistic Theory Volume 3: Further grammatical topics*. Oxford University Press.

Federal Democratic Republic of Ethiopia, Population Census Commission. (2007). *Summary and Statistical Report of the 2007 Population and Housing Census*. Addis Ababa. Available at: https://www.scribd.com/doc/28289334/Summary-and-Statistical-Report-of-the-2007 (Accessed: 30 January 2018)

Fleming, Harold C. (1983). surma etymologies. In Nilotic studies, eds. Rainer Voßen & Marianne Bechhaus-Gerst, 523–555. [Kölner Beiträge zur Afrikanistik, 10.] Berlin: Dietrich Reimer.

Givon, T. (1981). on the development of the Numeral 'One' as an Indefinite Marker. *Folia Linguistica Historica* II/1: 35–53.

Greenberg, Joseph H. (1955). Studies in African linguistics classification. New Haven, CT: Compass.

Gwynn, Charles W. (1911). a journey through southern Abyssinia. *Geographical Journal* 38(2): 113–139.

Haberland, Eike (1966). zur Sprache der Bodi, Muri, und Yidenich in Südwest Äthiopien. In *Neue Afrikanistische Studien*, ed. Johannes Lukas, 87–99. [Hamburger Beiträge zur Afrika-Kunde, 5.] Hamburg: Deutsches Institut für Afrika Forschung.

Haspelmath, Martin. (2015). ditransitive constructions. *Annual Review of Linguistics* 1. 19–41.

Heine, Bernd and Tania Kuteva (2002). *World Lexicon of Grammaticalization*. Cambridge: Cambridge University Press.

de Hoop and Malchukov (2008). case-marking strategies: in H. de Hoop, A.L. Malchukov. *Linguistic Inquiry* 39: 565–587.

Jørgesen, S.L. (2011). *ethnographic reflections on marriage in Mursi: a group of transhumant agro-pastoralists in Southwestern Ethiopia*. MA thesis, Norwegian University of Science and Technology.

König, C. (2006). marked nominative in Africa. *Studies in Language* 30(4): 655–732.

König, Christa (2008). *Case in Africa*. Oxford: Oxford University Press.

Last, M. and Lucassen, D. (1998). 'a grammatical sketch of Chai', In Dimmendaal, G.J. &

Last, M. (eds.) *Surmic Languages and Cultures. Nilo-Saharan.* pp. 3–33., Köln: Rüdiger Köppe Verlag.

Longacre, Robert E. (2007). sentences as combinations of clauses. In Timothy Shopen (ed.), *Language typology and syntactic description*, 372–420. Cambridge: Cambridge University Press. doi: 10.1017/CBO9780511619434.007

Li, Charles N. and Thompson, Sandra A. (1981). *Mandarin Chinese: A functional reference grammar*. Berkeley and Los Angeles: University of California Press.

Lüpke, Friederike (2010). rare and endangered—languages or features? *Journal of African Languages* XXXVII. 1: 1–21.

Marantz, Alec (1982). re reduplication. *LI* 13: 483–545

Matthews, P.H. (1997). *The concise Oxford dictionary of linguistics*. Oxford: Oxford University Press.

McCarthy, John & Prince, Alan (1995). faithfulness and reduplicative identity. *University of Massachusetts Occasional Papers in Linguistics* 18: 249–384.

Mütze, Betina (2014). *a sketch of the Mursi Language*. Unpublished MA Thesis. University of Gloustershire.

Payne, T., E. (1997). *escribing Morphosyntax*. Cambridge, UK: Cambridge University Press.

Randall, Scott (1998). a grammatical sketch of Tennet. In: Dimmendaal, Gerrit J. & Marco Last, eds, *Surmic Languages and Cultures*. Cologne: Rüdiger Köppe Verlag, pp. 219–272.

Reh, M. (1996). *Anywa Language: Description and Internal Reconstructions*. Köln: Rüdiger Köppe Verlag.

Smith, A.D. (1900). an expedition between Lake Rudolf and the Nile. *Geographical Journey*, 16: 600–625.

Tucker, A.N. and Bryan, M.A. (1956). *The non-Bantu languages of north eastern Africa*. [Handbook of African Languages, 3.] London: Oxford University Press for International African Institute.

Tucker, A.N. and Bryan, M.A. (1966). *Linguistic Analyses: the Non-Bantu Languages of North-Eastern Africa*. London: Oxford University Press.

Turton, D. and Bender, M.L. (1976). 'Mursi'. In Bender, M.L. (ed.) *The Non-Semitic Languages of Ethiopia*. Monograph, East Lansing, Michigan, U.S.A.: African Studies Center, Michigan State University, pp. 533–561.

Turton, David. (1973). *'the social organization of the Mursi'*. Unpublished PhD Thesis. University of Oxford.

Turton, David. (1988). 'looking for a cool place: the Mursi, 1890s–1990s'. *Ecology of Survival. Lester Crook Academic Publishing*, London, pp. 261–282.

Turton, D., Yigezu, M. and Olibùì, O. (2008). *Mursi-English-Amharic Dictionary*. Ermias Advertising, Addis Ababa, Ethiopia.

Unseth, P. (1991). 'possessive markers in Surmic Languages', In Bender, M.L. (ed.) Proceedings of the fourth Nilo-Saharan Linguistic Colloquium. Linguistic Analysis and Documentation, Hamburg: Helmut Buske Verlag, pp. 91–103.

Unseth, Peter (1997). an archaic Surmic causative prefix. *Occasional Papers in the Study of Sudanese Languages* 7: 49–69.

Vannutelli, L. and Citerni, C. (1899). l'Omo: Viaggi di esplorazione nell' Africa Orientale, (Milan).

Von Höhnel, Ludwig (1894). *discovery of Lakes Rudolf and Stefanie: a narration of Count Samuel Teleki's exploring and hunting expedition in Eastern Equatorial Africa in 1889 and 1888 by his companion Lodwig von Höhnel; translated [from the German] by Nancy Bell (N. d'Anvers)*. London: Longman, Green & Co.

Welmers, W.E. (1973). *African Language Structures*. Los Angeles: University of California Press.

Yigezu, M. & Dimmendaal, G.J. (1998). *notes on Baale*, In Dimmendaal, G.J. & Last, M. (eds.) *Surmic Languages and Cultures. Nilo-Saharan*. pp. 3–33., Köln: Rüdiger Köppe Verlag.

Yigezu, M. (2001). articulatory and acoustic effects of lip-plate speech in Chai and its implications for phonological theory. *Journal of the International Phonetic Association*. 31(2): 203–221.

Yigezu, M. (2001). *A comparative Study of Phonetics and Phonology of Surmic*. Brussels: Université Libre de Bruxelles (unpublished PhD thesis).

Yigezu, Moges (2005). latin based Mursi orthography. In: *ELRC Working Papers* 1 (2), pp. 242–257 (Addis Ababa: Ethiopian Language Research Center).

Subject Index

Ablative   456, 463, 466
    See also Oblique case   463
Accusative case   437, 446
Adjectival intensifier   190
Adjectives   7, 14–16, 50n2, 74, 101, 102, 104, 116, 119, 124, 129–131, 134, 143, 145, 147, 159, 160, 174, 177, 179–181, 186, 190, 207, 232, 235, 236, 260, 261, 263, 272, 366–390, 392–399, 401–404, 476–478, 480, 483
Administrative system   22
Adposition phrase   462
Adpositions   7, 101, 132, 151, 172, 467, 468
    Postpositions   101
    Prepositions   101
Adverbial intensifier   537
Adverbs   7, 101, 132, 143–149, 159, 164, 167, 171, 172, 318, 335, 344, 395, 401–403, 410, 500, 553
    Emphatic/Intensifier adverbs   143, 148
    Frequency and degree adverbs   143, 146–147
    Locative adverbs   143, 149, 318, 320
    Manner adverbs   143–144, 171, 500
    Time adverbs   143, 145–146, 335, 344
Affinity   27, 28
Affirmative clauses   17
Affirmative declarative   472, 473
Affixes   7, 16, 47–49, 51–54, 61, 78, 97, 98, 175, 283, 310, 406, 435
Affricates   45, 51, 53, 73, 91, 92, 280
Age set formation   29
Age set initiation   29
Age sets   24, 29, 189, 244
Agent nouns   124, 125
Agentive   378
Agentivizer suffix   372
Agentless passive   47, 84, 407, 409, 410, 427, 428
Agglutinating   7, 42, 94, 287
Agglutinating language   7, 287
Allative   456, 463, 466
    See also Oblique case   463
Allomorph   60, 108, 118, 123, 200, 293, 304, 341, 543
Allophones   60, 72

Alveolar liquid   58, 369
Ambitransitive   129
    See also Labile   129
Amharic-based orthography   38
Analytic structure   209, 218, 221
Anaphoric pronouns   132
Anaphoric reference   338, 418, 465
Anaphoric reference marker   338
Anaphoric referential demonstrative   341
Animacy   435, 446, 451
Animate   11, 33, 116, 237, 282, 397, 446, 457, 460
Antecedent   417, 553
    See Controller   417
Anticipatory request-reply marker   322
Antigenitive   194, 223n2
Antipassive   15, 124, 288, 304–306, 351, 405, 410–412
Aphorism   253
Apico-alveolar   46
Apico-dental   46
Apocope   66
Apodosis   542
Applicative   15, 288, 304, 334, 335, 365, 378, 391, 405, 406, 418, 420–427, 444, 455, 555–557, 559
Apposed NP   191
Apposition   576
Arguments   7, 9, 16, 117, 121, 125, 128–132, 139, 141, 151, 155, 198, 205n9, 235, 258, 259, 289, 294, 308, 318, 337, 356, 377, 391, 403, 405, 408–410, 416, 422, 424–426, 430, 435, 437–440, 442–444, 446–449, 451, 455, 456, 459–462, 471, 489, 491, 582, 587, 588
Aspect   7–9, 12–14, 16, 17, 40, 49, 63, 65, 71, 80, 84, 94, 95, 128, 129, 145, 153, 171, 226, 228, 236, 255, 258–262, 274–276, 279–281, 284, 287, 289, 290, 292, 295–300, 302–305, 307, 308, 310, 316, 317, 323, 324, 326, 329–331, 335–337, 338n12, 344, 358, 362, 364, 365, 379, 385, 403, 406, 407, 409, 412, 437, 438, 443, 447–449, 461, 511, 516–522, 525–528, 530, 534, 535, 543, 544, 549, 550, 553, 557, 559, 575, 582, 583

SUBJECT INDEX

Associative Construction   223n2
   See also Connective construction   223n2
Astronomy   21
Attenuative marker   321
   See also Attenuative particle   321
Attributive phrases   177n2
Augmentative   181, 373, 374, 387, 388, 487
   See also Diminutive   15
Autoreflexive   416, 417, 419
Auxiliary verbs   129, 130, 300, 309

Bahuvrīhi compounds   381
Basic Linguistic Theory   41
Benefactive   15, 16, 122n5, 288, 299, 316, 378, 394, 403, 405, 406, 418–424, 432, 444, 445, 447, 449, 476, 477, 480
Benefactive-applicative derivation   420, 421
Bi-clausal construction   482, 483
   See also Bi-copular clauses   482
Bi-copular clauses   482
Bicategorical markers   297
Bilabial   6, 45, 48, 49, 51, 53, 56, 71, 72, 91–93, 99, 100, 136n7, 280, 368n4, 555
Bilingual   38
Body decoration   29
Body part nouns   115, 151, 153, 182, 239, 243, 247, 248, 251, 416, 417, 468
Bonding   49
Borrowed words   59, 65, 75
Bound deictic circumclitics   61, 145, 175–178, 389
Bound demonstratives   120, 177, 184, 271
Bound negation clitics   390
   See also Circumclitics   390
Bound negators   517
Bound pronominal   8, 16, 88, 120, 128, 130, 131, 198, 258–260, 289, 291–294, 296, 308, 391, 403, 406, 409, 419, 422, 430, 435, 438–444, 446, 447, 452, 457, 459, 473, 492, 503, 504, 517, 518, 523, 525, 528, 534, 536
Bound pronoun systems   132
Boundary loss and morphological/phonological fusion or Bonding   580n6
Bridewealth   20, 27–31, 263
Bridging construction   558

Canonical constituent order   435
Cardinal number words   156, 267, 268, 270, 271, 401
   See also Number words   267
Cardinal number
   See Ordinal number   156
Cattle herding   6, 20, 21, 24, 33, 249
Cattle names and their coat-colors   112
   See also Personal names and Naming   112
   See also Personal names, Naming and Proper names   112
Causal-consequent relation   554
Causative   7, 8, 15, 60, 82, 128, 274, 282, 285–287, 299, 378, 391, 392, 405, 406, 416, 428, 430, 431
Celestial bodies   36
Central vowels   76
Chronological sequencer   163, 553
Circumclitics   8, 17, 61, 94, 95, 97, 103, 125, 128, 135, 136, 145, 149, 150, 175, 176, 179, 357, 375, 376, 389, 516, 517, 519, 520
Circumfixes   128
   See also Circumclitics   128
Clans   22, 24, 26, 251
Clausal coordinative conjunction   554
   See also Coordinative conjunction   590
Clausal coordinative particle   344
Clause combining strategies
   See Clause linking strategies   17
Clause combining techniques   17, 542
   Subordination   17, 542
   Complementization   17, 542
   Relativisation   17, 542
   Coordination   17, 542
Clause linking strategies
   See Clause combining strategies   17, 542
Clitics   7, 47–49, 51–54, 60, 61, 94, 95, 97, 98, 103, 104, 178, 192, 236, 255, 257, 298, 355, 508, 517–519, 533, 541
Close-mid vowels   58, 61
Cluster reduction   74
Coalesce   70, 260, 367, 517, 523
Coda   52, 57, 65, 74, 80, 92, 96, 138
Code-switching   366
Cognitive semantic association   35
Cohesiveness   93, 94
Collective nouns   26, 114n3, 216, 233, 236, 248, 252, 253

Collectiveness   252
    See also Mass nouns, Uncountable nouns: Collective nouns   252
Colour intensifier ideophone   170
Comitative   15, 162, 171, 226, 304, 385, 405–408, 422, 423, 425–428, 455, 470, 557, 559
Command strategy   308
Command
    See Imperative   12
Common argument   142, 194, 195, 359
Comparative-benefactive   16, 131, 432, 477
Comparative construction   16, 145, 162, 192n8, 374, 394, 476–483, 487
Comparative degree marker   181, 480
    See also Augmentative marker   181
Comparative strategy   483
Comparison of participants   476
    Comparee   476
    Standard of comparison   476
Compensatory lengthening   67, 275–277, 304, 518
Compensatory vowel lengthening   83, 84
Complement clause   17, 105, 140, 331, 393, 427, 528, 538, 542, 576, 578, 582, 583
Complement strategies   527
Complementizer   17, 162, 331, 334, 427, 566, 567, 575, 578, 580, 602
Complete deletion   34, 60, 69, 128, 154, 233, 236, 254, 331, 429, 431, 622
Compound adjectives   381
Compound word   34, 35, 59, 94, 95, 263, 400, 538
Compounding   70, 92, 372, 380
Concessive clause   560
Conditional clause   17, 162, 205, 344, 454, 483, 521, 522, 527, 542–545, 555, 598
Connective construction   223n2
Connectors   7, 101, 132, 161, 162, 553
    Clausal conjunction   162
    Clausal connector   162, 163
    Coordinative conjunction   161–162, 385, 385n13, 394, 470, 480, 554, 564, 574, 578, 581, 586, 589–593, 602
    Phrasal conjunction   161–162, 480, 590
    Simultaneous and successive marker   162–163
    Narration or temporal progression marker   162–163, 586

Conditional marker   162, 205, 555, 563
Concessive marker   162, 562
Cause or Reason   162
Complementizer   162, 578–580, 587, 602
Mark (in comparative construction)   162, 181, 478, 480, 484–488
Substitutive clause   162, 562, 602
Disjunctive coordination   162, 594, 602
Contrastive coordination   162, 594, 602
Future time clause   162, 564–565
Consequence clause   520, 550, 577–578
Consonant clusters   58, 60, 80, 83, 93, 303, 305, 369
Consonant length   56, 99
    See also Gemination   56, 57, 99, 304
Consonant lenition   72, 92, 95, 100
    See also Consonant weakening   72
    See also Consonant weakening   72
Consonant sequences
    See Consonant clusters   59
Constituent order   9, 15–17, 104, 206, 306, 396, 426, 435–438, 440–442, 444, 450, 451, 454, 459, 460, 477, 490, 516
Construct-Form   10–11, 176–177, 179–180, 181, 185, 190, 192, 194, 206
    See also Modified noun form   10, 194
    See also Status construction   223n2
Construct state   10, 194
Content questions   16, 489, 492
Continuous-punctiliar   547, 548, 552
Contrastive   6, 7, 42, 56, 62, 89, 132, 162, 369, 535, 541, 594, 602
Contrastive coordinative marker   594
    See also Counter-proposition   594
    See also Counter-proposition: Counter-presuppositional proposition   594
Contrastive marker particle   554
    See also Persistive   554
Contrastive particle   589
Controller   417, 418
Coordinand   598
Coordinative conjunction   161, 162, 385, 385n13, 394, 470, 554, 564, 589, 590, 592, 602
Coordinative partitive   207, 265
Copula complement   15, 102, 117, 120, 121, 123, 130, 131, 133, 157, 177, 198, 199, 228, 265, 266, 272, 273, 366, 391–393, 401,

SUBJECT INDEX

403, 441, 442, 479, 480, 487, 492, 501, 512, 513, 531, 587
Copula subject   102, 105, 117, 120, 121, 130, 176, 198, 199, 228, 266, 272, 393, 426, 441, 481, 513, 535, 587, 598
Copular clause   17, 130, 272, 306, 392, 426, 435, 480, 481, 483, 513, 542, 587, 598, 599
Core constituents   16, 104, 105, 121, 125, 130, 151, 174, 198, 210, 215, 235, 266, 295, 405, 407, 410, 436, 439, 447–449, 451, 456, 463, 489–491, 587
Corelative (left-adjoined) relative clause   196
Counter-expectative contrast   592
Counter-factual linker of propositions   593
Coverb   363, 365
Cross-height vowel harmony   248n3

Dative marker   16, 295, 394, 403, 418, 420, 423, 432, 444, 448, 449, 476, 559
De-verbal nouns   103, 117–120, 122n4, 128, 174
Definite time reference   345, 351
Definiteness   7, 103, 375, 376, 389, 435, 451, 497
Degree of magnitude   15, 373, 387, 487
Degree of remoteness   345, 348, 357
Deictic categories   7
Deictic center/source   431
Deictic demonstratives   177
Deletion   6, 8, 42, 46, 53, 63–71, 83, 91, 92, 95, 96, 108, 113, 116, 117, 238, 277, 282, 300–303, 307, 382, 399, 480, 540
Demonstrative   8, 94, 95, 97, 101, 103, 125, 127, 132, 133, 135–137, 145, 149, 174–176, 177n2, 178, 179, 206, 207, 236, 255, 257, 258, 271, 318, 320, 340, 357, 375, 376, 389, 390, 500, 530
Demonstrative manner adverb   316n4
   See also Referential demonstrative   316n4
Demonstrative pronouns   135
Dependency relation   133, 155, 157, 206, 209, 378, 382, 389
   See also Construct form   9
Dependent form   9
Derivational   7, 58, 119, 123, 124, 127, 129, 268, 286, 287, 304, 351, 376, 377, 379, 380,

382, 405, 406, 412, 415, 422, 426, 428, 432, 477, 519
Desiderative   385, 559, 588
Devoicing   66, 71
Diachronic   82, 257, 581
Dialect continuum   465
Dialectal continuum   37
Differential object marking   446, 448
Diminutive   166, 387
   See also Augmentative   15
Diphthongs   63
Direct speech verb   569
Discourse   7, 58, 65, 97, 101, 132, 161, 163–165, 167, 235, 435, 465, 481, 483, 493, 494, 508, 509, 559, 589, 590, 592, 614
Discourse particles   7, 65, 101, 132, 161, 163, 164, 167, 509
Disjunctive coordination   597, 602
Disjunctive questions   513
   See also Question strategies   513
Distal marker   60, 95, 133, 136
Distributive meaning   158, 189, 265, 270, 416
   See also Multiplicative meaning   158
Distributive quantifier property   189
   See also Floating quantifier   189
Disyllabic   46, 51, 57, 63, 69, 74, 82, 88, 89, 92, 129, 151, 169, 248, 274, 277, 278, 281, 285, 287, 368, 371, 467
Ditransitive   16, 128, 129, 262, 311n1, 313, 318, 356, 418, 422, 423, 435, 442–444, 446–450, 453, 461, 503
Dorso-velar   46
Double marking   8
Double negation   517
   See also Triple negation   517
Dubitative   509, 597, 599
Duelling   31
Dummy/impersonal pronoun   439
Durative adverbial time words   349
Durative particle   552
   See also Stative verb   384
Dynamic verbs   121, 382

Ear-plugs   32
Ego   27
Ejectives   45
Elicitation   408
Elliptical construction   221n1, 391

Embedded relative clauses   382
Emphatic reflexive marker   419
   See also Autoreflexive   419
Enclitic   7, 17, 49, 52–54, 60, 61, 95, 98, 103, 125, 136, 150, 164, 165, 184, 255, 288, 320, 376, 389, 473, 497, 508, 516–518, 521, 522, 525, 540, 541, 543, 547, 549, 554, 602
Epenthetic vowel   60, 122n5, 237
Epistemic adverbs   147
Epistemic modality marker particles   597
   See also Dubitative   597
Equality construction   488
Eroded verb from   527
Ethiopian calendar   21
Ethiopian languages   42, 545
Ethiopic-based orthography   44, 45
Ethiopic scripts/alphabets   38
Ethnographic   38
Ethnonym   19, 39, 48, 105n1
Existential possessive predication construction   227
Expressives   7, 58, 93, 99, 101, 132, 171

Fast speech   47, 71, 95, 270, 308, 349, 370n6
Female register
   See Body beautification: Body scarification: Body ornamentation   100
Fixed order   93, 94
   See also Conventionalized coherence and meaning   93
Floating clitic   95, 320
Floating emphatic enclitic   61
Floating emphatic marker   51
Floating enclitic   105
   See also Emphatic marker   105
Flood retreat cultivation   20, 22
Formally marked   9, 330, 410, 451
Free possessive pronouns   184
   See also Free possessive pronouns   184
Free pronoun systems   13, 15, 49, 51, 68, 74, 90, 105, 117, 132, 133, 137, 152, 157, 161, 183, 184, 249, 307, 308, 310, 313–316, 323, 327n10, 339, 370, 387, 396, 402, 435, 439, 445, 448, 449, 493
   See also Bound pronoun systems   132
Free variation   49, 51, 68, 74, 247n2
Frequency-habitual marker   349
Fricative simplification   74

Fricatives   45, 50, 53, 56, 66, 67, 74, 91, 92, 100, 118
Full reduplication   52, 298
Full suppletion   8, 129, 254
Functionally-unmarked   9
Fusion   7, 287, 543
Future time clause   564
   See also Repetitive terminative   564

Gap strategy   193, 196–198, 225, 551
Gapping strategy   529
   See also Gap strategy   529
Ge'ez   42, 43, 43n1, 44, 45
Geminate   49, 50, 56, 57, 59, 289, 302, 369
Genealogical   28
General intensifier   190, 387
General negator   533
General pronouns   192n7
Generic noun   538, 566
Generic place term   109
Genitive case   8, 11, 12, 109, 111, 113, 117, 126, 154, 181, 182, 194, 203, 205, 207, 210, 213, 214, 222, 224, 267, 376, 389, 408, 436, 466–468, 485, 507
Glides   45, 53
Glottal   6, 45–48, 51, 68, 70, 71, 73, 91, 92, 95, 298, 307, 327n10, 540
Grammatical categories   7, 89, 107, 109, 115, 128, 131, 205, 286, 287, 297, 516, 540, 541
Grammatical gender   102, 116, 204, 448, 530
   See also Natural gendered nouns   102
Grammatical mood   489
Grammatical morphemes   93
Grammatical number   90, 106
Grammatical relations   16, 435
Grammatical subject   410
   See also Logical object   410
Grammatical tone   7, 13, 89, 90, 255, 335
   See also Lexical tone   89
Grammatical word   6, 42, 91–96, 161, 368, 414, 521
Grammaticalization   49, 106, 135, 136, 140, 141, 268, 580n6, 581
Grammaticalized body part noun   158, 269, 401, 414, 467
Grammaticalized number word   538
Graphemes   43, 53

SUBJECT INDEX

Habitual actions   304, 350
Haplology   67, 69, 70, 275
Harmonic features   61
    Fronting   61
    Height   61
Head-marking   16, 174, 435, 439
Head-tail linker   592
Headless modifiers   187
Hetero-compound forms   35, 397
Heterogeneous vowel sequences   63, 68
High (close) vowels   58
High back vowel   15, 60, 96, 301, 367
Historical intervocalic consonant deletion
    1, 3, 6, 63, 69, 83, 91, 281, 621
Hoe-cultivation system   20
Homogenous   18
Homorganic sequences   52, 63, 70
Hortative   12–14, 47, 68, 73n4, 84, 90, 130,
    275, 279, 287, 292, 295, 310, 315, 316,
    322–328, 330, 363–365, 386, 406, 421,
    472, 473, 475, 523, 524, 527
Hortatory   66
Human referent participant   504

Iconicity   15
Ideolectal   502
Ideophones   7, 48, 51, 58, 60, 63, 65, 71, 93,
    99, 101, 132, 169–171, 285, 454n1
Idiolect   325, 485
Imperative   12, 13, 63, 68, 100, 122n5, 149,
    162, 185n4, 260, 261, 295, 308, 310–314,
    314n3, 315–318, 320–328, 330, 362–
    365, 366n2, 386, 406, 421, 435, 449,
    472–474, 503, 516, 517, 521–524, 529,
    544
Imperfective aspect   296
Impersonal pronoun   445, 491
Implosive   6, 48–50, 59, 66, 91, 92, 366n1
Inalienable possession   184
    See also Alienable possession   184
Inanimate   11, 397
Indefinite article   140, 187
    See also Determiner   140
Indefinite pronouns   138
Indefinite time marker   336
Independent possessive pronoun   183
Index of comparison   16, 476
Indirect speech verb   569
Individuative   252

Inflectional   7, 12, 106, 127–129, 274, 286, 287,
    304, 310, 323, 329, 330, 335, 536, 587
Informal conversations   366
Informal literacy   42
Information structuring strategies   481
Informative reflexive pronoun   419
Inherently gendered nouns   112, 116
Inherently reduplicated   48, 49, 51, 52, 58–
    60, 74, 92, 97, 169, 285, 368–370, 371n7
Innovation   50
Instantaneous, momentaneous/punctual
    marker   341
Instrumental applicative   464
Instrumental case   202, 463
Instrumental-comitative   385
Instrumental interrogative word   70
Instrumental nominalizer   470
Interjections   7, 58, 65, 71, 93, 99, 101, 132,
    168, 511, 512
Interlinearizing   40
Intermediate possessors   12, 222, 223
    See also Associative construction   12
Interrogative pronouns   490
Intervocalic   6, 46, 53, 63, 64, 66, 68, 72, 83,
    91, 100, 113, 116, 238, 257, 277, 282, 399
Intervocalic consonant deletion   99
Intonation   16, 489, 511–513, 515
Intransitive   9, 15, 17, 102, 118, 122, 126, 129–
    131, 226, 262, 274, 278, 284, 287, 289,
    295, 299, 304, 305, 315, 318, 366, 377,
    378, 383, 384, 390, 391, 401, 403, 407,
    410–414, 416, 419, 420, 422, 424, 425,
    428, 430–434, 437, 453, 459, 472, 473,
    485, 486, 504, 512, 535, 542, 544
Invariant reciprocal pronoun   416
Invariant reflexive particle   419
    See also Lexicalized reflexive marker   419
Irrealis   14, 72, 151n8, 275, 279, 289, 292, 293,
    317, 323, 330, 331, 335, 364, 386, 497, 516,
    530, 555
Iterative actions   171
Itive   288, 406, 431–433, 445, 464

Jussive   12–14, 47, 66, 73n4, 76, 84, 90, 130,
    275, 279, 287, 292, 295, 308, 310, 315, 316,
    322, 323, 325, 328–330, 340, 363–365,
    386, 406, 421, 472, 473, 475, 521, 527
Juxtaposed   11, 209, 210, 212, 546
Juxtaposed system   211

660　SUBJECT INDEX

Kinship-based plural marker   111
Kinship nouns
    See Kin terms   8
Kinship relationship   210, 218
Kinship system   24, 26–28, 112
Kinship terminologies   28

Labile   129, 279–281, 430
Labio-labial   46
Lamino-palatal   46
Lateral   45, 52, 369, 527
Latin-based orthography   38, 42, 43
Leadership hierarchy   23
Levirate   29, 111
Lexeme   533, 536, 537
Lexical deontic markers   332
Lexical time words   145
    See also Lexical time words   145
Lexical tonal contrast   89
Lexical tone   88
Lexical tone melodies   91, 93
Lexicalized reflexive marker   419
Lexicalized verb form   469
Linguistic groups   18
Lip-plate   32, 33, 100
Liquids   45, 58, 64, 106, 109, 232
Loan adaptation   75
    See also Phonetic mapping or Vowel decentralization   75
Loan word   156, 371n7, 388n15, 529n1, 535n3, 546, 555
Local adverbial demonstrative   175
Local adverbial word   320
Local groups   24
Local interrogative words   500
Locative adverbs   318
Locative case/marker   57, 107–109, 143, 145, 150, 152, 175, 205, 205n9, 206, 318, 319, 390, 455, 456, 463–465, 499, 500, 540, 556
Logical object   410

Marked-nominative case   9, 435, 436, 450–452, 463, 480
Marked plural   7, 232, 233, 235–237, 242, 244, 252, 262, 376
Masculine   50n2, 530
Mass nouns   106, 232, 233, 236, 252
Mass opposition   252

Matrix clause   576, 578
Melodic copying   83
    See also copy-vowel epenthesis or echo epenthesis   83
Melody   14, 87, 88, 91, 98, 279, 328, 373
Metaphoric transfer   248
    See also Semantic extension   248
Metaphorical expression of time   352
Metathesis   156, 303, 372, 372n9
Middle voice marker   412n1
Mild command   13, 316, 323
    See also Polite marker   316
Minimal pairs   54, 62
Mirative marker   58
Mirativity   164, 509, 510
Modal dependent form   521
Modification marker   10–12, 114, 116, 124, 133, 134, 152, 155, 182, 188, 194, 195, 264–266, 271, 388, 484, 530, 546
Modified noun form   10, 194
Mono-clausal   16, 394, 476–478, 480, 481
Monolingual   37, 75
Monomorphemic   275, 278, 368–370, 399, 402, 467
Monomorphemic particles   467
Monosyllabic   6, 48, 63, 64, 88, 89, 91, 96, 99, 117, 120–122, 129, 151, 171, 274, 285, 287, 298, 367, 371, 467, 512
Monotransitive clause   438
Mood   7, 12–14, 16, 40, 66, 73n4, 101, 128, 130, 274, 276, 279, 289, 292, 293, 295, 310, 316, 317, 322, 323, 327–335, 337, 340, 344, 359, 364, 385, 497, 516, 527, 530, 544, 546, 575
Morpheme boundaries   42, 46, 53, 57, 60, 61, 69, 73, 76, 91, 92
Morphemes   7, 42, 57, 58, 61, 91, 93, 122n4, 161, 169, 215, 232, 236, 257, 287, 491, 508
Morphophonological   6, 42, 71, 83, 85, 431, 523
Morphophonological processes   6, 431, 523
    Deletion   6, 66
    Devoicing   71
    Lenition   72
    Fricative simplification   74
    Cluster reduction   74
    Assimilation   75
    Coalescence   6, 523
    Copying   6, 83

SUBJECT INDEX 661

Harmony 6, 77
Subtraction 6
Morphosyntactic functions 83, 97, 201
Morphosyntax 82
Motion 7, 16, 78, 81, 108, 128, 130, 235, 260, 262, 279, 286, 288, 289, 304, 312, 316, 320, 330, 331, 335, 364, 365, 405, 406, 431–434, 445, 448, 449, 466, 506, 549
Motion towards 78, 81, 108, 260, 279, 364, 406, 431, 432, 448, 449, 466
    See also Ventive 78
Multi-functional grammaticalized nominal 407
Multifunctional particle 362, 385n13, 470
Multilingual 38
Multiple alternations 302
Multiple root alternations 129, 302, 303
Multiplicative meaning 158, 268–270
Multiverbal constructions 274, 365
Mutual intelligibility 37

Naming 33, 36, 113, 397, 614
Nasals 45
Natural classes 53, 58
Natural gender 115, 530
    See also Grammatical gender 530
Near minimal pairs 54
Negation 7, 8, 16, 17, 94, 95, 97, 101, 128, 130, 131, 141, 152, 286, 287, 289, 330, 335, 436, 468, 472, 511, 516–522, 525, 537, 540, 554
Nominal morphology 119, 123, 213
Nominalization 117–120, 122–124, 126, 210, 287, 554
Nominalizer 50n2, 57, 103, 117, 118, 120, 121n4, 122, 122n5, 123–127, 131, 145, 196, 201, 304, 305, 371, 376, 378, 380n11, 453n1, 530, 538n4
Nominative-accusative 9, 16, 435
Nominative personal pronouns 132
    See also Post-verbal pronoun 132
Non-agent nouns 125
    See also Agent nouns and Non-subject nouns 125
    See also Agent nouns 125
Non-canonical constituent order 452
    See also Canonical constituent order 452

Non-canonical
    See Canonical 13
Non-core constituents 104, 436, 463
    See also Core constituents 104
Non-human participants 491
    Non-human object participants 491
    Non-human subject participants 491
Non-interrogative 16, 489, 508
Non-interrogative particles 508
Non-restrictive relators
    See Dependency markers 94
Non-spatial settings 286
    See also Spatial settings 286
Non-subject nouns 125
Noun modification construction 105, 116, 117, 126, 135, 152, 176, 186, 190, 193, 194, 203, 205, 206, 214, 222–224, 228, 229, 271, 436
Nouns of state 118, 119, 127, 145, 226, 374, 376, 379, 380
Nouns
    Compound nouns 102, 106, 113–115, 127–128, 184, 211, 214
    Kinship nouns 8, 29, 102, 104, 106, 109–112
    Place names 102, 106–109, 112, 128, 366n1, 571
    Proper names 102, 106, 112–113, 128, 166, 210, 214, 230
    Relator nouns 102–103, 106–107, 128, 181–182, 243, 467–468
    Simple nouns 7, 102, 106, 109, 117, 175, 207, 208, 214, 246, 247, 252, 402, 403, 457–459
Number-determined suppletive verb forms 262
Number marking by Tone 254
Number marking system 7, 104, 114, 232, 233, 237, 244, 248, 252, 254, 375, 376
    Replacive 7, 114, 232–237, 242, 244, 246, 248, 250, 262, 376
    Marked plural 7, 232–233, 235–237, 242, 244, 252, 262, 376
    Singulative 7, 26, 104, 232–237, 248, 252–254
    Suppletive 7, 232–233, 235–236
    See also Tripartite number system 7, 104, 232–237
Number words 57, 155–157, 173, 236, 264

Obligation/deontic clause   17, 542
Oblique argument   85, 102, 105, 195, 391, 471, 492
Oblique case   106–109, 120, 151, 153, 205n9, 210, 213, 214, 223, 226, 243, 424, 439, 454, 463, 467, 471, 491, 493, 499, 543
Obsolescence or archaism   431
Obsolete   431
Obstruents   123
Onomatopoeic words   169
Onset   52, 57, 275, 369
Open (low) vowel   58
Open-mid front vowel   60, 61, 76
Open-mid vowels   58
Open word classes   102
Ordinal number words   153, 267
Orthographic transcription
   See Phonetic transcription   42
Ownership   11, 209–213, 215, 224, 230, 231

Palatal   6, 43, 46, 51, 53, 56, 57, 66, 68, 73, 75, 77, 92, 95, 113, 156, 210, 214, 257, 270, 275, 280, 307, 314n2, 499
Parameter of comparison   16, 393, 394, 401, 476, 478, 479, 482, 483
Partial reduplication   52, 88, 100, 135, 235, 386
Partial suppletion   8, 254
Participant reference   288, 289
Participle form   530
Particles   7, 16, 161, 163, 164, 168, 325, 335, 339, 349, 351, 353, 359, 385, 467, 471, 489, 508, 509, 516, 522, 537, 540, 556, 562, 564, 589, 590, 593, 597, 598
Partitive conjunction particle   177
Passive   15, 47, 84, 85, 130, 131, 197, 225, 275, 279, 295, 337, 378, 405, 407–410, 412, 427, 454, 455, 470, 473, 484, 527
Passivizer prefix   407
Pastoral nomads   20
Pastoralism   20
Pastoralist life   20
Patient-like antipassives   410
Patrilineal   26, 29
Patriliny   27
Perfective aspect   300
Peripheral arguments   120, 462
Persistive marker   333n11, 520
Personal names   34–36, 49, 113

Personal pronouns   132
Pertensive   11, 29, 103, 104, 109, 110, 183–185, 191, 204, 209, 210, 217–219, 221, 222, 228, 230, 231, 250, 255, 256, 418, 425n2, 448, 556
Pertensive morphology   104
Phonemes   6, 42, 43, 45, 46, 50–54, 58–62
Phonetic gemination   57
Phonetic mapping   75, 76
Phonological conditioned allomorphs   180n3
Phonological environment   54
Phonological properties   91, 97–99, 115, 274, 367
   Prosodic features   91
   Segmental features or internal syllabic structure   91
Phonological rules   51, 83, 92, 95, 214, 303, 382
   See also Phonological processes   83
Phonological word   6, 42, 46, 86, 91–96, 149, 150, 161
Phonosemantic   275
Phonotactic constraint rule   303
Phonotactic restriction   51, 52
Phrasal adjectives   382
Phrasal coordinative conjunction   480
Phrasal nouns   114, 115
Phrasal plus mono-clausal   476
Physiological effects in speech production   100
   See also Physiological organs   100
Pitch   512, 515
Pluralia tantúm   188, 232, 233
   See also Inherently plural mass noun   188
Polar questions   16, 489, 510, 512, 513
Polar tone   89
   See also Opposite tone   89
Pole fighting   31
Polite command   340
Polite marker   130, 163, 164, 316, 319
Politeness   130
Polyfunctional   47, 403
Polysemous   49, 305, 361, 385, 385n13, 546
Polysyllabic   48, 49, 51, 52, 88, 129, 285, 287
Portmanteau   8, 104, 236, 237, 240, 244, 304, 367, 535
Portmanteau suffixes   232, 237, 240, 535

SUBJECT INDEX 663

Possession
   Ownership   11, 112, 130, 138, 192, 204, 205, 209, 212, 217–219, 221, 225, 255, 258, 448, 468, 490, 587
Possessive interrogative pronouns   507
Possessive pronoun   11, 53, 70, 111, 176, 183, 184, 196, 197, 205, 209, 216, 223, 229, 231, 256, 314, 418, 425n2, 495
Possessive pronouns   137
Possessive relationships   210, 211, 229
   Association   209–210, 212, 214–215, 224, 230–231
   Attribution of a person/animal/thing   28, 210, 218
   Kinship relationship   210
   Ownership   11, 209–213, 215, 224, 230–231
   Statement of orientation or location   210
   Whole-part relationship   210–211
Possessum   105, 209
   See also Possessor   105
Post-alveolar   46, 48, 51, 52, 59, 66, 92, 113
Post-verbal nominative form pronouns   452
Post-verbal subject   9, 64, 451
Postpositional phrase   471
Posture verbs   130
Power structure   22, 23
Pragmatic   9, 435, 436, 451
Pragmatic roles   472
Prepositional phrase   385
Pro-phrasal interrogative   392
Proclitic   7, 13, 46, 49, 52, 54, 61, 95, 103, 135, 136, 215, 255, 256, 288, 307, 310, 317, 320, 330, 357, 495, 508, 516–518, 521, 522, 529, 540, 541
Progression marker   162, 163, 550
Progressive actions   83, 304–306, 345, 351, 546
   See also Habitual actions   304
Progressive harmony   83
Pronominal demonstratives   135
Pronouns   7, 57, 63, 69, 70, 101, 104, 123, 132–143, 145, 172, 174, 175, 178, 179, 183–188, 192, 193, 195, 197, 200, 206, 207, 210, 215–217, 219, 221, 230, 231, 233, 235, 236, 255–257, 257n4, 258, 265, 266, 316, 389, 392, 416, 417, 422, 435, 437, 439, 442, 443, 446–448, 452, 453, 456, 457, 460, 462, 485, 497, 498, 503, 505–508, 530–532, 536, 568, 602

Proper name   112, 178, 212, 214
   See also Personal name   112
Prosodic   6
Protasis   542
Prototype-based categorization approach   237
   See also Prototype theory   237
Prototype theory   237
   See also Prototype-approach   237
Proximal   103, 133, 135n7, 136n7, 175, 320
Punctiliar-continuous   547, 552
Punctiliar-punctiliar   547
Purposive   344, 385, 385n13, 576, 602

Quantifiers   7, 9, 101, 132, 134, 155, 159, 174, 188, 190, 207, 235
Quasi-applicative derivation   427
Question strategies   513
Question words   7, 16, 101, 132, 154, 155, 172, 489–491
Quinary form   156, 263
Quotative marker   17, 163, 164, 221n1, 427, 529, 548, 566, 569, 574, 575, 602

Realis mood   289, 290, 292, 293, 317
Reality   12, 289, 310, 317, 331
   Realis   289–290, 292–293, 296, 317
   Irrealis   14, 72, 151, 275, 279, 289, 292–293, 296, 317, 323, 330–331, 335, 365, 386, 449, 516, 530, 555, 561, 567, 589
Reason-applicative   470
Recipient/beneficiary   444, 453
Reciprocal   15, 16, 124, 171, 304–306, 405, 411–416
Reciprocals   57
Reduplication   15, 94, 96, 144, 236, 263, 266, 270, 272, 349, 370, 373, 387, 404, 413, 415
Referential demonstrative   316n4
Referential prominence scale   16, 435
Referential prominence scales   446, 447
Reflexive   15, 16, 128, 138, 286, 314, 315, 321, 405, 416–420
Register tones   6, 86
Relative (general) pronouns   192
   See also General pronouns: Specific pronouns   192
Relative clause   133, 142, 193–196, 199, 200, 203, 204, 206, 208, 225, 337,

Relative clause (*cont.*) 359, 378, 382, 384, 387, 415, 420, 464, 479, 499, 509, 530, 535, 546, 548, 551
Relative pronouns 142, 192n7
Relative spatial location 175
Relativization 196, 287, 542
Relativization strategy 196, 542
Removal of lower incisors 74
Replacive 7, 104, 232–236, 242, 244, 246, 248, 250, 262, 376, 580
Replacive number marking system 114, 246, 248, 250, 262
Reported speech 355, 357
Resolution marker 57, 164, 165, 552
Restrictive modification
    See Non-restrictive modification 9
Restrictive relative clause 196
Restrictive relators 9–12, 94, 104, 116, 121n4, 125, 133, 134, 139, 142, 152, 155–157, 159, 160, 176, 177, 180, 182, 186, 190, 193–196, 199–201, 203, 204, 206, 207, 209, 222, 223, 235, 257, 264–266, 271, 367, 378, 386, 388, 417, 484, 505, 530, 538n4, 546
    See also Non-restrictive relators or dependency markers 94
Rhetorical question 155, 441, 558
Ritual system 23

Sarcastic attitude/characters 522
Seasonal calendar system 21
Second language 38
Segmental spreading 83
Semantic agent 384, 454
Semantic ambiguity 425
Semantic category 57, 97, 244, 275, 305
Semantic extension 241, 248, 372
Semantic opposition 244, 372
Semantic roles 446, 449, 472
Sentential or clausal negator 533
Sentential/clausal focus 473
Separative-like strategy 487
    See also Subtractive 487
Sequencializer suffix 364
Shifting cultivation 21
Similes 35, 36, 372, 397
Simultaneous clause 547, 550
Singleton 252

Singulative 7, 26, 104, 186, 232–237, 248, 252, 253
    See also Singleton, Individuative, Mass opposition, Collectiveness 252
    See also Singular 7
Slow speech 349
    See also Fast speech 349
Sociative marker 413, 415, 425
Socio-spatial oriented reference 36
Sociolinguistic situation 37
Sound iconicity 367
Sound symbolic adverbs 171
Spatial 24, 36, 58, 107, 128, 178, 179, 182, 204, 205, 471, 564
Spatial relations 106
Spatial settings 286
Special phonology 58
Special possessive reflexive marker 149
Specific indefinite pronouns 174
Specific pronouns 132, 192n7
    See also Anaphoric pronouns 132
Speech (reporting) verbs 569
    Direct speech verb 569
Speech communities 18, 19
Speech register 33, 74
Speech registers 100
    See also Female register: Male register 100
Speech report clause 17, 542, 566, 569
Spirantization 72, 100
    See also Lenition 72
Spiritual leader 22
Split system 447
Stable tonal melodies 373
Standard marker 192n8
State of equilibrium 165, 552
State of quality 391
Stative-inchoative verbs 384
Stative locations 107
Stative verbs 15, 117–119, 121, 129, 130, 174, 217, 274, 287, 366, 368, 376–378, 384, 390, 392, 401, 403, 476, 480, 488
    See also Underived adjectives 15
Stativising marker 379, 403
Status Construction 223n2
Status constructs 10
Stems 57
Stops 6, 30, 45–48, 50, 57, 59, 63, 66, 69–73,

SUBJECT INDEX

91–93, 95, 99, 100, 113, 116, 117, 298, 307, 337, 366n1, 429, 499, 555
Stress   50, 50n2
Stylistic   325, 495, 502
Stylistic dominance   496
Stylistic preference of speakers   325
Subjunctive   12, 47, 84, 130, 292, 295, 310, 316, 316n5, 320, 327, 330–335, 344, 359, 363, 384–386, 450, 461, 516, 521, 525, 527, 528, 530, 546, 574, 575, 582, 583, 588
Subjunctive copula form   384
Subjunctive
   See Irrealis   14
Subordinate clause   17, 176n1, 331, 333, 344, 361, 454, 483, 484, 499, 520–522, 527, 529, 542–551, 555–558, 564, 578, 602
Subsecutive   363, 365
   See also Coverb   363
Subsequent reason marker   385n13
Subsequent time   176n1
Subsistence activities   21
Substantival deverbal nominalization   391
Substitutive clause   162, 562
Substrata or areal feature   255
Subtractive   487
Succession clause   550
   Span-span   550
   Span-event   550
   Event-span   550
   Event-event   550
Suffixation   236
   See also Tripartite number system   236
Suffixing language   7, 76, 287
Superlative   478, 479, 482, 483
Suppletive   7, 232, 233, 235, 236, 262, 298, 303, 312, 329, 330, 375, 380, 385
Surface tone   87
Syllabary system   43n1
Syllabic script   43
Syllable boundaries
   Intervocallic   6, 52, 56
Symmetry   51, 278, 279, 369, 370
Synchronic   68, 69, 124, 257
Syncretic   292
Syntactic canonicity   286
   See also Verb-final suffix   286
Syntactic dependency   114, 381

Synthetic   7, 42, 209, 218, 219, 222
Synthetic language   287

Tag clause   510, 511
Tag questions   510
Taxonomy   244
Temporal clause   17, 145, 146, 162, 163, 205, 289–291, 333, 335–337, 339, 342, 344, 345, 347, 348, 350, 351, 353, 355–358, 360, 361, 454, 483, 490, 492, 498, 522, 527, 542, 545–553, 555, 564, 590, 592, 593
Temporal deictic center   354
Temporal particle   58
Temporal shifters   335, 339, 344, 353, 354, 356
Temporally coterminous events/actions   547
   See also Simultaneous clause   547
Theoretical framework   41
Time words   7, 112, 153, 287, 335, 345, 355, 356, 359, 467
Tonal melodies   86, 88, 93
   See also Tonal patterns   86
Tone   42, 43, 84, 86–91, 93, 95, 236, 254, 255, 258, 259, 275, 276, 279, 300, 315, 335, 373, 407
Tone-bearing unit   86, 91, 93
Tongue height   61
   Vowel height harmony   6, 61, 78–82, 91–92, 237, 293–294, 313, 431, 521
Topical adjunct   120
Topical constituents   457, 458
Topicality or focus   442
Topicalized and fronted NP   196
Transcription   43
Transitive   9, 17, 102, 123, 126, 129, 225, 281, 289, 295, 313, 315, 318, 378, 407, 409, 410, 414–424, 426–428, 430, 431, 433, 437, 439, 440, 442–444, 446, 450, 451, 453, 459, 461, 485, 492, 503, 542
Transliteration   42
Trilingual   38
Trill   45, 52
Tripartite   7, 104, 232–234, 236, 237
Tripartite number system   232
   Replacive   7, 104, 114, 232–237, 242, 244, 246, 248, 250, 262, 376

Marked plural   7, 232–233, 235–237, 242, 244, 252, 262, 376
Singulative   7, 26, 104, 186, 232–237, 248, 252–254
Trisyllabic   63, 129, 274, 277, 282, 285, 287, 399
Truth value   510
Typological   6, 100

Uncertainty or Dubitative marker   309, 331, 361, 509, 514
Uncountable nouns   252
Unilineal groups   27
Universal Hypothesis 12   489
Unmarked accusative case   438

Valency   7, 15, 16, 40, 101, 128, 304, 305, 331, 335, 365, 405, 407, 410, 419, 420, 422, 424, 427, 428, 433, 434
Valents   405, 434
Velar   6, 46–52, 57, 63, 66, 69, 70, 72, 73, 75, 92, 113, 116, 117, 210, 298, 303, 373
Velarization   75
  See also Velar strengthening   75
Ventive   78, 260, 279–281, 288, 295, 304, 312, 320, 364, 406, 431–434, 464
  See also Motion towards   78
Verb-final suffix   61, 68, 85, 131, 281, 286, 287, 298, 312, 324, 328, 329, 334, 365, 377, 378, 408–412, 436, 437, 472–474, 516, 544
Verb-final suffixes   12, 310, 323, 473
Verbless clause complement   117
Voice changing devices   7

Voiceless stops   45
Volitional   129, 446, 451
Vowel assimilation   61, 76, 429, 431
Vowel coalescence   6, 42, 91, 116, 523
Vowel copying   6, 82–85, 261, 300, 407
  See also Melodic copying   83
Vowel fronting harmony   6, 61, 83, 281, 301
  See also Vowel rounding harmony   83
Vowel harmony restrictions   77
Vowel height assimilation   76, 77
  See also Vowel height harmony   76
Vowel height harmony   61, 78–82, 91, 237, 293, 294, 313, 431, 521
Vowel height harmony neutralization   313
Vowel inventories   42
Vowel length   46, 63, 65, 67, 69, 91, 99, 168, 348, 399
Vowel lowering   61
Vowel quality   83
Vowel rounding harmony   83, 97, 98
Vowel sequences   63, 65

Whole-part relationship   210, 211
Word-class crossing words   159
Word classes   7, 14, 15, 65, 77, 86, 94, 99, 101, 102, 129, 132, 142, 143, 168, 170, 172, 173, 201, 232, 366, 370, 372, 373, 378, 386
Wordhood   91

Zero-marked nominalization   126
  See also Zero derivation   126
Zero morpheme   89, 94, 113, 280, 413, 518
  See also Zero suffix   89
Zero suffix   88, 297, 409, 438